Major Problems in
Asian American History

MAJOR PROBLEMS IN AMERICAN HISTORY SERIES

GENERAL EDITOR
THOMAS G. PATERSON

Major Problems in Asian American History

Documents and Essays

SECOND EDITION

EDITED BY

LON KURASHIGE
UNIVERSITY OF SOUTHERN CALIFORNIA

ALICE YANG
UNIVERSITY OF CALIFORNIA, SANTA CRUZ

CENGAGE
Learning·

Australia • Brazil • Mexico • Singapore • United Kingdom • United States

CENGAGE
Learning®

Major Problems in Asian American History,
Second Edition
Lon Kurashige and Alice Yang

Product Director: Paul Banks

Product Manager: Joseph Potvin

Senior Managing Content Developer: Joanne Dauksewicz

Content Developer: Terri Wise

Product Assistant: Andrew Newton

IP Analyst: Alexandra Ricciardi

IP Project Manager: Betsy Hathaway

Manufacturing Planner: Fola Orekoya

Art and Design Direction, Production Management, and Composition: Lumina Datamatics, Inc.

Cover Image: Zuma Press, Inc./ Alamy Limited

For product information and technology assistance, contact us at **Cengage Learning Customer & Sales Support, 1-800-354-9706**.

For permission to use material from this text or product, submit all requests online at **www.cengage.com/permissions**. Further permissions questions can be emailed to **permissionrequest@cengage.com**.

Library of Congress Control Number: 2016937265

ISBN: 978-1-285-43343-1

Cengage Learning
20 Channel Center Street
Boston, MA 02210
USA

Cengage Learning is a leading provider of customized learning solutions with employees residing in nearly 40 different countries and sales in more than 125 countries around the world. Find your local representative at **www.cengage.com**.

Cengage Learning products are represented in Canada by Nelson Education, Ltd.

To learn more about Cengage Learning Solutions, visit **www.cengage.com**.

Purchase any of our products at your local college store or at our preferred online store **www.cengagebrain.com**.

Printed in the United States of America
1 2 3 4 5   23 22 21 20 19

MAJOR PROBLEMS IN AMERICAN HISTORY SERIES
TITLES CURRENTLY AVAILABLE

Jabour, *Major Problems in the History of American Families and Children*, 2005 (ISBN 978-0-618-21475-4)

Kupperman, *Major Problems in American Colonial History*, 3rd ed., 2013 (ISBN 978-0-495-91299-6)

Kurashige/Yang, *Major Problems in Asian American History*, 2003 (ISBN 978-0-618-07734-2)

McMahon, *Major Problems in the History of the Vietnam War*, 4th ed., 2008 (ISBN 978-0-618-74937-9)

McMillen/Turner/Escott/Goldfield, *Major Problems in the History of the American South*, 3rd ed., 2012
   Volume I: *The Old South* (ISBN 978-0-547-22831-0)
   Volume II: *The New South* (ISBN 978-0-547-22833-4)

Merchant, *Major Problems in American Environmental History*, 3rd ed., 2012 (ISBN 978-0-495-91242-2)

Merrill/Paterson, *Major Problems in American Foreign Relations*, 7th ed., 2010
   Volume I: *To 1920* (ISBN 978-0-547-21824-3)
   Volume II: *Since 1914* (ISBN 978-0-547-21823-6)

Merrill/Paterson, *Major Problems in American Foreign Relations*, Concise Edition, 2006 (ISBN: 978-0-618-37639-1)

Milner/Butler/Lewis, *Major Problems in the History of the American West*, 2nd ed., 1997 (ISBN 978-0-669-41580-3)

Ngai/Gjerde, *Major Problems in American Immigration History*, 2nd ed., 2012 (ISBN 978-0-547-14907-3)

Peiss, *Major Problems in the History of American Sexuality*, 2002 (ISBN 978-0-395-90384-1)

Perman/Taylor, *Major Problems in the Civil War and Reconstruction*, 3rd ed., 2011 (ISBN 978-0-618-87520-7)

Riess, *Major Problems in American Sport History*, 2nd ed., 2015 (ISBN 978-1-133-31108-9)

Smith/Clancey, *Major Problems in the History of American Technology*, 1998 (ISBN 978-0-669-35472-0)

Stoler/Gustafson, *Major Problems in the History of World War II*, 2003 (ISBN 978-0-618-06132-7)

Vargas, *Major Problems in Mexican American History*, 1999 (ISBN 978-0-395-84555-4)

Valerio-Jiménez/Whalen, *Major Problems in Latina/o History*, 2014 (ISBN 978-1-111-35377-3)

Warner/Tighe, *Major Problems in the History of American Medicine and Public Health*, 2001 (ISBN 978-0-395-95435-5)

Wilentz/Earle, *Major Problems in the Early Republic, 1787–1848,* 2nd ed., 2008 (ISBN 978-0-618-52258-3)

Zaretsky/Lawrence/Griffith/Baker, *Major Problems in American History Since 1945*, 4th ed., 2014 (ISBN 978-1-133-94414-0)

Contents

Preface

The 2010 U.S. Census identified Asian Americans as the fastest growing racial population within the United States. Between 2000 and 2010, the number of individuals who identified as Asian, either alone or in combination with one or more races, grew almost 50% to reach 17.3 million (nearly 6% of the total U.S. population). Although concentrated in California, New York, Washington, and Hawai'i, the Asian American population grew in all states, especially in Nevada, Arizona, North Carolina, North Dakota, Georgia, and other places where few had settled before. The largest self-identified Asian ethnic group was Chinese Americans (4.0 million), followed by Filipino Americans (3.4 million), Asian Indian Americans (3.2 million), and Vietnamese Americans and Korean Americans (1.7 million each). Japanese Americans (1.3 million) were notable because almost one third were of mixed race heritage. Other major Asian American ethnic groups included Pakistanis, Cambodians, Laotians, Hmong, Thais, Indonesians, and Malaysians. Pacific Islander groups included native Hawaiians, Samoans, and Guamanians.

Before the 1960s the classification "Asian American" did not exist. During the social movements of that decade, students, activists, and scholars began using the term to promote solidarity among people of Asian ancestry. Programs in Asian American studies, the first of which was founded in 1969, as well as early scholarship, often emphasized a common history of struggle by primarily Chinese and Japanese immigrants and their descendants. Since the 1980s, research has uncovered the histories of Korean Americans, Filipino Americans, Southeast Asian Americans, South Asian Americans, native Hawaiians, and mixed race individuals. What is striking about research on Asian American history today is the increased diversity of groups, topics, and issues examined. This burgeoning field includes studies on all major Asian ethnic groups in terms of their ethnicity, migration, politics, work, self-employment, class, legal issues, community, family, education, religion, gender, sexuality, and culture. Attention to transnational flows of people, goods, and ideas—as well as their boundaries—has been a particularly exciting development since we published the first edition of this reader in 2003.

Major Problems in Asian American History invites readers to explore the dramatic growth in scholarship through primary and secondary sources on the rich history of Asian Americans. Our main goal in this volume is to present outstanding research that portrays the variety and complexity of Asian American experiences from the eighteenth to the twenty-first centuries while paying attention to core narratives and historical trends. Most of our contributors are historians, but we also include journalists, sociologists, anthropologists, and interdisciplinary scholars who provide thoughtful analyses of historical and contemporary issues. Essential documents, such as General John L. DeWitt's rationale for Japanese American internment (1942), are placed alongside less conventional primary sources, such as ethnic press articles and unpublished oral histories that offer intimate views of Asian American agency and showcase individuals with diverse backgrounds.

Expanding the boundaries of what is considered Asian American history, we take great pains to encourage the comparative analysis of ethnic groups and individual experiences, paying particular attention to the significance of gender, sexuality, geographical region, and economic, political, and cultural conditions. In each chapter, we include documents and essays that focus on a wide variety of Asian American experiences, while at the same time making sure that the leading groups and issues in the designated period remain central. We perform this same balancing act to ensure that the voices and experiences of women and Asian Americans outside the West Coast are validated and included in the historical analysis. The book also facilitates comparison across different time periods. For example, the post-1965 migrations highlighted in Chapter 12 can be compared with the nineteenth-century labor migrations addressed in Chapter 2, while the national security fears after Pearl Harbor in Chapter 8 can be compared with the national security fears after 9/11 in Chapter 15.

The book's first chapter provides an introduction to historiographical issues and allows readers to make a personal connection to the material through three essays recounting biographical and autobiographical experiences. Chapters 2 through 7 cover the period from the seventeenth century to the mid-twentieth century, beginning with the Pacific dimension to early China trade in which ships sailed between the Spanish colonies of Mexico and the Philippines. Over two centuries later, American commercial relations bought the kingdom of Hawai'i into the U.S. orbit and created an avenue for Chinese immigration to the United States and Hawai'i. Subsequent chapters address the causes and consequences of the exclusion of Chinese immigrants, as well as that of Asian Indians, Japanese, and Filipinos. They also address the agency of Asian American actors opposing exclusion and other forms of discrimination and responding to new Pacific empires by the United States and Japan. The first half of the book ends at the precipice of the Pearl Harbor attack with a discussion of the Americanization of immigrants and the U.S.-born generations within the context of shifting international relations in the face of growing instability between the United States, Japan, and China.

The second half of the book examines the period during and after America's participation in World War II. Selections address debates about Japanese American cooperation or resistance to World War II internment policies and the impact of the Cold War on Asian American labor activism, suburbanization, interracial marriages, and adoption policies. These chapters look at how Asian American communities have been transformed by the influx of new immigrants following the Immigration Act of 1965, the arrival of refugees from Southeast Asia, and changing relations with other racial groups, including conflict between African Americans and Korean Americans during the Los Angeles civil disturbance of 1992. They challenge depictions of Asian Americans as "model minorities" and include a celebration of the 1960s "yellow power," a critique of heterosexism and patriarchy by an lesbian, gay, bisexual, and transgender (LGBT) activist, an account of transnational alliances against the trafficking of women and children in the Philippines, and a 2012 denunciation of the Pew Research Center's failure to acknowledge Asian American socioeconomic diversity. They also explore Asian American and Pacific Islander experiences outside the West Coast and Hawai'i with research on Arizona, Texas, Louisiana, Minnesota, Wisconsin, and Guam. A chapter on memory politics includes redress campaigns by Japanese Latin Americans, Filipino veterans, Hawaiian sovereignty advocates, and Guamanian independence activists. The book ends with a discussion of how Asian Americans have been policymakers, victims of racial profiling, and protesters during the War on Terror.

This book follows the same general format as other volumes in the Major Problems in American History series. Each chapter includes a short introduction that provides a general historical context, a selection of primary documents, and two essays. Headnotes to the document and essay sections explain the historical themes and interpretive issues in the selections. We provide a "Further Reading" list at the end of each chapter for students interested in additional research.

Many people have helped in the preparation of this second edition. We are grateful to the colleagues who reviewed drafts of our manuscript and gave us thematic and bibliographic suggestions: Madeline Y. Hsu, University of Texas-Austin; Gordon H. Chang, Stanford University; Christen T. Sasaki, San Francisco State University; Richard S. Kim, UC Davis; Nayan Shah, University of Southern California; Maile Renee Arvin, UC Riverside; Michael Jin, University of Illinois at Chicago; Yen Le Espiritu, UC San Diego; and Cindy I-Fen Cheng, University of Wisconsin at Madison.

We could never have completed this second edition without the editorial support of Terri Wise, Clint Attebery, and the staff at Cengage. Finally, we express our deep gratitude to our families for their encouragement and understanding as we completed this book. Lon Kurashige thanks Anne, Cole, and Reid Kurashige. Alice Yang thanks her parents, Kisuk and Sharon Yang, her husband Doug Bragdon, and her sons David and Michael Yang-Murray for sustaining her throughout this project.

We welcome comments, suggestions, and criticisms from students and instructors so that we can improve this book.

L.K.

A.Y.

About the Authors

LON KURASHIGE is associate professor of history at the University of Southern California. He is the author of *Two Faces of Exclusion: The Untold History of Anti-Asian Racism in the United States* (Chapel Hill: University of North Carolina Press, 2016) and *Japanese American Celebration and Conflict: A History of Ethnic Identity and Festival, 1934–1990* (University of California Press, 2002) which won the History Book Award from the Association for Asian American Studies in 2004. He is the coeditor of "Conversations in Transpacific History," a special edition of *Pacific Historical Review* (2014). His article "Rethinking Anti-Immigrant Racism: Lessons from the Los Angeles Vote on the 1920 Alien Land Law" won the Carl I. Wheat prize for best publication to appear in the *Southern California Quarterly* between 2012 and 2014. His writings have appeared in *Journal of American History, Pacific Historical Review, Reviews in American History*, and other academic journals. Kurashige also is the coauthor of the college-level textbook *Global Americans: A History of the United States* (2017).

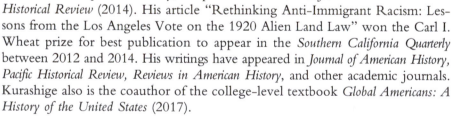

ALICE YANG is provost of Stevenson College and associate professor of history at the University of California, Santa Cruz. She serves as the codirector of the Center for the Study of Pacific War Memories and received a UCSC Excellence in Teaching Award in 2009. Her areas of expertise include Asian American history, historical memory, race, gender, oral history, World War II, and twentieth-century America. She is the author of *Historical Memories of the Japanese American Internment and the Struggle for Redress* (2007) and the editor of *What Did the Internment of Japanese Americans Mean?* (2000). Her articles have appeared in *Unequal Sisters: A Multicultural Reader in U.S. Women's History*

(2000), *The Human Tradition in California* (2002), and *Amerasia Journal*. She is currently researching transnational memories of World War II in the Pacific and has received funding from the National Endowment for the Humanities, the University of California Humanities Research Institute, the Pacific Rim Research Program, and the Center for Information Technology Research in the Interest of Society.

CHAPTER 1

Asian American History
by the Generation

Studying Asians in U.S. history is both an old and new endeavor. Early in the twentieth century, social scientists began to document the experiences of Asian immigrants to explain their impact on American society. Sociologists, who by profession were concerned with the negative effects of rapid industrialization, were especially interested in figuring out how a relatively small number of these newcomers provoked intense and widespread fears fueling anti-Asian stereotypes, practices, legislation, and violence. Scholarly studies came in two types. One type of study focused on the differences that set off Asian nations and their immigrants from Western peoples, civilizations, and standards of living. These studies emphasized the inability of Asian immigrants, due to race, culture, and civilization, to fit into American society. The other type of study, which was more racially liberal, documented ways in which the immigrants and their children were adapting to the host society and culture. This scholarship saw racial conflict not as a sign of permanent incompatibility, but, rather, as a stage in the long-term process of cultural adaptation through which Asians and whites eventually would reconcile their differences to reach a state of racial understanding and miscegenation.

A later generation of scholars emerging after World War II dismissed both types of earlier studies. The first type was seen as justifying popular and scientific theories of racism and racial hierarchy that had informed the Holocaust in Nazi Germany and thus had been soundly discredited. The second, liberal type was seen as an overly optimistic view of U.S. race relations that ignored the persistence of anti-Asian racism, as well as the efforts made by Asian Americans to retain their ethnic identities, cultures, and affinities. This was an understandable critique from a generation that during the 1960s and 1970s experienced the explosive atmosphere of racial unrest and animosity across the nation, in urban neighborhoods, in agricultural fields, and on college and university campuses. While earlier in the century the idea that Asian Americans were assimilating to white society was a liberal stance, it became conservative when the concept of white society became viewed as a site of "Anglo conformity" or "cultural genocide."

The study of Asian American history took off during this time when a critical mass of political activists reimagined the position and representation of Asian Americans in U.S. society. They catalyzed a social movement that revolutionized the conception of Asian Americans as silent, "model minorities" by casting them as vocal opponents to "white society" who stood in solidarity with black, Latino, Native American, and other radicals, as well as with overseas anticolonial revolutionaries, especially those fighting against U.S. forces in Southeast Asia. This explains the self-consciously political nature of much research on Asian American history, which has continued to the present.

By the 1980s, much, but not all, of the new scholarship began to orbit around the new scholarly field of Asian American Studies, within which a specialty on history emerged. By this time, many of the activists had become professors, and their PhD dissertations, books, journal articles, and teaching would produce the most robust scholarly attention that Asian Americans had ever received. By the 1990s, Asian American Studies had all the features of an academic discipline: its researchers could publish findings in two academic journals dedicated to their field, join a professional association, attend an annual conference, and teach in a sizable number of degree-granting academic programs and departments. Another sign of professionalization was the emergence of new and competing perspectives. These perspectives stem in part from a focus on different Asian American groups and time periods, but, in a more fundamental sense, they are rooted in different ways of approaching the past based on changing conditions in the present. Ever since the early twentieth century, pressing issues in a given historical period have influenced the approaches scholars have taken in studying the history of Asian Americans.

☀ ESSAYS

The first essay, by journalist Helen Zia, reveals the rise of a new consciousness in the 1960s and 1970s in which she transformed from knowing "nothing" about being Asian American to becoming a political activist fighting for the group's empowerment. Zia discusses her lack of a political consciousness as a girl and racial minority growing up in suburban New Jersey in the 1950s, attributing this to the invisibility of Asians in her hometown and to the male-centric cultural traditions of her Chinese parents. The second essay, by Trinity College historian Vijay Prashad, discusses the ways in which the efforts of Indian immigrants to achieve the American Dream and become white have costs both for those immigrants and for the larger U.S. society. As an immigrant coming to the United States in the 1980s, Prashad became aware that pursuing such a dream reinforced white supremacy by requiring that Asian Americans not just embrace whiteness but also stigmatize African Americans. In the third essay, writer Wesley Yang offers a more recent view of Asian American identity dilemmas that sees desires for academic success and cultural assimilation as sheepish conformity. Whereas Zia and Prashad emphasize the importance of developing a political consciousness, Yang celebrates critical individuality that seeks to escape from obligation to politics, family, tradition, or ethnic group. What can explain the different responses to Asian American identity by Zia, Prashad, and Yang?

The final two essays turn to the scholarly field of Asian American history. The first, by U.C. Santa Barbara historian Paul Spickard, discusses limits to the political coalition among Asian Americans by asking what it would mean to include peoples who were not originally considered "Asian American." In the last essay, University of Minnesota historian Erika Lee and Brown University historian Naoko Shibusawa explore the need to broaden the vision of Asian American history beyond the borders of the United States. They question the predominantly national focus of research in this field. Yet theirs is not simply a global vision, but a "transnational" one that follows circulatory flows of people, goods, and ideas within the Asia-Pacific region.

From Nothing, a Consciousness

HELEN ZIA

"Little China doll, what's your name?"

This question always made me feel awkward. I knew there was something unwholesome in being seen as a doll, and a fragile china one at that. But, taught to respect my elders at all times, I would answer dutifully, mumbling my name.

"Zia," they would cluck and nod. "It means 'aunt' in Italian, you know?"

To me, growing up in New Jersey, along the New York–Philadelphia axis, it seemed almost everyone was a little Italian, or at least had an Italian aunt.

One day in the early 1980s, the routine changed unexpectedly. I was introduced to a colleague, a newspaper editor. Making small talk, he said, "Your name is very interesting..." I noted his Euro-Anglo heritage and braced myself for yet another Italian lesson.

"Zia, hmm," he said. "Are you Pakistani?"

I nearly choked. For many people, Pakistan is not familiar geography. In those days it was inconceivable that a stranger might connect this South Asian, Pakistani name with my East Asian, Chinese face.

Through the unscientific process of converting Asian names into an alphabetic form, my romanized Chinese last name became identical to a common romanized Pakistani name. In fact, it was homonymous with a much despised ruler of Pakistan. Newspaper headlines about him read: "President Zia Hated by Masses" and "Pakistanis Cry, Zia Must Go." I'd clip out the headlines and send them to my siblings in jest. When President Zia's plane mysteriously crashed, I grew wary. After years of being mistaken for Japanese and nearly every other East Asian ethnicity, I added Pakistani to my list.

I soon discovered this would be the first of many such incidents. Zia Maria began to give way to Mohammad Zia ul-Haq. A new awareness of Asian Americans was emerging.

★ ★ ★

The abrupt change in my name ritual signaled my personal awakening to a modern-day American revolution in progress. In 1965, an immigration policy that had given racial preferences to Europeans for nearly two hundred years officially came to an end. Millions of new immigrants to America were no longer the standard vanilla but Hispanic, African, Caribbean, and—most dramatically for me—Asian. Though I was intellectually aware of the explosive growth in my community, I hadn't yet adjusted my own sense of self, or the way I imagined other Americans viewed me.

Up until then, I was someone living in the shadows of American society, struggling to find some way into a portrait that was firmly etched in white and, occasionally, black. And there were plenty of reminders that I wasn't relevant. Like the voices of my 1960s high school friends Rose and Julie. Rose was black, and Julie was white. One day we stood in the school yard, talking about the civil rights movement swirling around us, about cities engulfed in flames and the dreams for justice and equality that burned in each of us.

As I offered my thoughts, Rose abruptly turned to me and said, "Helen, you've got to decide if you're black or white." Stunned, I was unable to say that I was neither, that I had an identity of my own. I didn't know the words "Asian American." It was a concept yet to be articulated.

Somewhere between my school yard conversation and the confrontation with my Pakistani namesake, Asian Americans began to break through the shadows. By then we had already named ourselves "Asian American" and we were having raging debates and fantastic visions of an America *we* fit into. But few outside of Asian America cared about our shadow dreams.

Gradually we began to be visible, although not necessarily seen the way we wished. Then we had to discover what it meant to be in the light.

When I was growing up in the 1950s and 1960s, there were barely a half-million Asian Americans in the nation. Of those, only 150,000 were Chinese Americans—not enough to populate a small midwestern city. We made up less than 0.1 percent of the population. Most of us lived on the islands of Hawaii or in a few scattered Chinatown ghettoes....

On a clear day the Manhattan skyline is visible from Newark, but the insular familiarity of Chinatown was worlds away. Outside of Chinatown it was rare to encounter another person of Chinese or other Asian descent. In Newark and the various New Jersey communities where we later moved, the only way to meet Asians was to stop complete strangers on the street, while shopping, or at the bus stop—anywhere that we happened to see the occasional person who looked like us. At an A&P supermarket checkout counter, my mother met her friend Sue, who came to the United States as a war bride, having married a GI during the postwar occupation of Japan. The animosity between China and Japan that brought both women to New Jersey was never an issue. Each was so thrilled to find someone like herself.

Auntie Sue and her son Kim, who was of mixed race, white and Japanese, were regular visitors to our home. Though our mothers bonded readily, it was harder for their Asian American kids to connect simply because we looked alike. Mom and Auntie Sue had the shared experience of leaving their war-ravaged

Asian homes for a new culture, but Kim and I shared little except for our Asian features; we stuck out like yellow streaks on a white-and-black canvas. Outside of Chinatown, looking Asian meant looking foreign, alien, un-American. The pressure on us was to fit in with the "American" kids we looked so unlike, to conform and assimilate. Why would we want to be around other Asian kids who reminded us of our poor fit? At the tender age of six, I already felt different from the "real" Americans. I didn't feel comfortable with Kim and sensed his ambivalence to me. But the joke was on us, because no matter how hard we might try to blend in with the scenery, our faces gave us away.

Still, I was proud to be Chinese. Mom and Dad filled us with stories about their childhoods in China. Dad was born in 1912, one year after the founding of the Chinese Republic, and was imbued with a deep love for his native country. He was the second son of a widow who was spurned by her in-laws. His mother sold her own clothes to pay for his schooling. She beat my father every day so that he would study harder—this he told us proudly whenever we slacked off. Dad modeled his life after the ideal of the Confucian scholar-official: by studying assiduously he won academic honors and scholarships and achieved recognition as a poet and writer. China's system of open examinations was the foundation of the civil service—a Chinese creation, Dad pointedly reminded us as he turned the TV off. Studying hard, he said, was a time-honored route to advancement for even the poorest Chinese.

Mom grew up in Shanghai under the Japanese occupation. From the time she was a small child she lived with a fear and dislike of Japanese soldiers. Because of the war, her education was disrupted and she never went beyond the fourth grade—a source of regret that made her value education for her children. Mom's childhood memories were of wartime hardships and days spent picking out grains of rice from the dirt that had been mixed in as a way to tip the scales. Her stories taught me to be proud of the strength and endurance of the Chinese people.

Dad told us about our heritage. When other children made fun of us, or if news reports demeaned China, he reminded us that our ancestors wore luxurious silks and invented gunpowder while Europeans still huddled naked in caves. Of course, I knew that Europeans had discovered clothing, too, but the image was a reassuring one for a kid who didn't fit. My father wanted us to speak flaw-less English to spare us from ridicule and the language discrimination he faced. He forbade my mother to speak to us in Chinese, which was hard, since Mom spoke little English then. We grew up monolingual, learning only simple Chinese expressions—*che ve le*, "Come and eat"—and various Shanghainese epithets, like the popular phrase for a naughty child—*fei si le*, or "devilish to death." Dad also expected us to excel in school, since, he said, our Asian cranial capacities were larger than those of any other race. Pulling out the *Encyclopaedia Britannica* to prove his point, he'd make us study the entry, then test us to make sure we got the message. He told us about the Bering Strait and the land bridge from Asia to America, saying that we had a right to be in this country because we were cousins to the Native Americans.

These tidbits were critical to my self-esteem. In New Jersey, it was so unusual to see a person of Asian descent that people would stop what they were doing to gawk rudely at my family wherever we went. When we walked into a store or a diner, we were like the freak show at Barnum & Bailey's circus, where Chinese were displayed as exotic creatures in the late 1800s, along with the two-headed dog. A sense of our own heritage and worth gave us the courage and cockiness to challenge their rudeness and stare down the gawkers.

What Mom and Dad couldn't tell us was what it meant to be Chinese in America. They didn't know—they were just learning about America themselves. We found little help in the world around us. Asians were referred to most often as Orientals, Mongols, Asiatics, heathens, the yellow hordes, and an assortment of even less endearing terms. Whatever the terminology, the message was clear: we were definitely not Americans.

There is a drill that nearly all Asians in America have experienced more times than they can count. Total strangers will interrupt with the absurdly existential question "What are you?" Or the equally common inquiry "Where are you from?" The queries are generally well intentioned, made in the same detached manner that you might use to inquire about a pooch's breed.

My standard reply to "What are you?" is "American," and to "Where are you from?" "New Jersey." These, in my experience, cause great displeasure. Eyebrows arch as the questioner tries again. "No, where are you really from?" I patiently explain that, really, I am from New Jersey. Inevitably this will lead to something like "Well then, what country are your people from?" Sooner or later I relent and tell them that my "people" are from China. But when I turn the tables and ask, "And what country are your people from?" the reply is invariably an indignant "I'm from America, of course."

The sad truth was that I didn't know much about my own history. I knew that Chinese had built the railroads, and then were persecuted. That was about it. I didn't know that in the 1700s a group of Filipinos settled in Louisiana, or that in 1825 the first Chinese was born in New York City. I didn't know that Asian laborers were brought to the Americas as a replacement for African slaves—by slave traders whose ships had been rerouted from Africa to Asia. I didn't even know that Japanese Americans had been imprisoned only a decade before my birth. Had I known more about my Asian American history I might have felt less foreign. Instead, I grew up thinking that perhaps China, a place I had never seen, was my true home, since so many people didn't think I belonged here.

I did figure out, however, that relations between America and any Asian nation had a direct impact on me. Whenever a movie about Japan and World War II played at the local theater, my brothers and I became the enemy. It didn't matter that we weren't Japanese—we looked Japanese. What's worse, by now my family had moved to a new housing development, one of the mass-produced Levittowns close to Fort Dix, the huge army base. Most of our neighbors had some connection to the military.

At the Saturday matinee, my brothers and I would sit with all the other kids in town watching the sinister Zero pilots prepare to ambush their unsuspecting prey, only to be thwarted by the all-American heroes—who were, of course, always white. These movies would have their defining moment, that crescendo of emotion when the entire theater would rise up, screaming, "Kill them, kill them, kill them!"—them being the Japanese. When the movie was over and the lights came on, I wanted to be invisible so that my neighbors wouldn't direct their patriotic fervor toward me.

As China became the evil Communist menace behind the Bamboo Curtain, and the United States was forced to deal with its stalemate in the Korean War, the Asian countries seemed interchangeable. Back when Japan was the enemy, China was the good ally—after all, that's how my mom and dad got to come to America. But now, quixotically, Japan was good and China was evil.

Chinese in America were suspected to be the fifth column of Chinese Communists, as J. Edgar Hoover frequently said before Congress and throughout the McCarthy era witch-hunts. In the 1950s, while Japanese American families attempted to return to normalcy after their release from American concentration camps during the war, the FBI switched its surveillance eye onto hundreds of Chinese Americans. My father was one.

Our mail routinely arrived opened and damaged, and our phone reception was erratic. I thought everyone's mail service and phone lines were bad. Polite FBI agents interviewed our neighbors, asking if my father was up to anything suspicious. What attracted the attention of the FBI was Dad's tendency to write letters to newspapers and politicians when he disagreed with their views on China or anything else. Nothing ever came of the FBI investigations of my father, nor was a ring of Chinese American spies ever found—but I later learned that the probes succeeded in intimidating the Chinese American communities of the 1950s, creating a distrust of and inhibiting their participation in politics.

The FBI queries hardly bolstered our acceptance in our working-class housing tract. Neighbor kids would nose around and ask, "So what *does* your father do?" It didn't help that my father had instructed us to say, "He's self-employed." This only added to our sense of foreignness.

Like so many Asian immigrants unable to break into the mainstream American labor market, my father had to rely on his own resourcefulness and his family's labor. In the back room of our house we made "baby novelties" with little trinkets and baby toys and pink or blue vases that my father then sold to flower shops. Every day, in addition to doing our schoolwork, we helped out in the family business.

Our home was our workplace, the means to our livelihood, and therefore the center of everything. This conveniently matched the Confucian notion of family, whereby the father, as patriarch, is the master of the universe. In our household it was understood that no one should ever disobey, contradict, or argue with the patriarch, who, in the Confucian hierarchy, is a stand-in for God. My mother, and of course the children, were expected to obey God absolutely.

This system occasionally broke down when my mother and father quarreled, usually about my father's rigid expectations of us. But in the end, God always seemed to win. Growing up female, I [could see the Confucian order of the Three Obediences] in action: the daughter obeys the father, the wife obeys the husband, and, eventually, the widow obeys the son. The Confucian tradition was obviously stacked against me, as a girl.

I found similar lessons in the world beyond our walls. Mom's best friend from the Chinatown Shanghainese clique had followed us to New Jersey, attracted by the low home costs and the fact that we already lived there. Auntie Ching and her husband opened a Chinese restaurant at a major intersection of the highway. In those days, there were few places outside Chinatown to get real Chinese food. After they had spent their own money to upgrade the kitchen and remodel the restaurant, business was booming. But Auntie Ching had no lease for the restaurant—and the German American owner, sensing an opportunity for himself, evicted the Chings and set up his own shop.

Our tiny Chinese American community was horrified that the Chings would be treated so unjustly. My cantankerous dad urged them to fight it out in court. But they chose not to, believing that it would be better not to make waves. Chinese cannot win, they said, so why make trouble for ourselves? Such defeatism disturbed my father, who would often say in disgust, "In America, a 'Chinaman's chance' means no chance." He felt that the Chinese way of dealing with obstacles—to either accept or go around them, but not to confront them directly—would never get us very far in the United States.

As a child, I didn't see Chinese or other Asian Americans speaking up to challenge such indignities. When my parents were denied the right to rent or buy a home in various Philadelphia neighborhoods, they had to walk away despite my father's outrage. We could only internalize our shame when my mother and her troop of small children were thrown out of supermarkets because we were wrongly accused of opening packages and stealing. Or when Henry was singled out of a group of noisy third graders for talking and he alone was expelled from the lunchroom for the rest of the year. Or when my younger brother Hoyt and the few other Asian boys in school were rounded up because another kid said he thought he saw an "Oriental" boy go into his locker.

Other times the discomfort was less tangible. Why did my fifth-grade teacher, a Korean War veteran, become so agitated when topics of China and Asian culture came up? Was there a reason for his apparent dislike of me and my brothers, who also had him as a teacher? After my Girl Scout troop leader asked all the girls to state their religions, what caused her to scowl in disgust at me when I answered Buddhist? My family didn't practice an organized religion, so I didn't know what else to say.

Absorbing the uncertainty of my status in American society, I assumed the role that I observed for myself—one of silence and invisibility. I enjoyed school and, following my father's example, studied hard and performed well academically, but I consciously avoided bringing attention to myself and rarely spoke up, even on matters related to me.

For example, there was Mrs. George. From second grade until I graduated from John F. Kennedy High School, Mrs. George was my physical education teacher. She was the aunt of Olympic track star Carl Lewis and was always kind to me. But for those ten years, Mrs. George called me Zi, as though it rhymed with "eye." One day, when I was in twelfth grade, she yelled over at me, "Zi, come over here." A classmate standing nearby said, "Mrs. George, Helen's name isn't Zi, it's Zia." Mrs. George looked at me and let out a huge laugh. "Zi," she said, then corrected herself. "I mean, Zia, how come you never told me how to say your name after all these years?"

I didn't know how to answer. It had never occurred to me to correct my teacher. In the Confucian order of the world, teachers were right up there with parents in commanding respect and obedience. I simply had no voice to raise to my teacher.

Despite my deference to traditional Chinese behavior, the day finally came when I had to disobey my father. I had received several offers of full scholarships to attend college. Like the Chinese who lined up for the imperial civil service examinations in hopes of a new life, I viewed college as my means of escape from the narrow life of making flower shop baby novelties in our dull New Jersey town.

Though my father was proud of my educational achievement, he didn't want me to leave for college. He had already stated his desire for me to attend the closest school to home. When the time came for him to sign the college registration forms, he refused. "The proper place for an unmarried daughter is at home with her parents," he insisted. He wanted to keep me out of trouble until I found a husband to do the overseeing.

I could see the doors to my future slamming shut. At age seventeen, I had never knowingly disobeyed my father. I policed myself, turning down dates, invitations to parties, and even educational opportunities away from home, because I thought Dad would disapprove. I was caught between two conflicting Asian ideals. The Three Obediences demanded subservience from females, but the primacy of education taught me to seek advancement through study. My American side told me to heed my own call.

Somehow I mustered the courage to shout, "No! I'm going to college." I don't know who was more surprised by my outburst, my father or me. He said nothing more about the subject, and I continued my preparations to leave. I also finally learned that the world wouldn't end if I challenged authority, a lesson I would take with me to college.

The Forethought: Raw Skin

VIJAY PRASHAD

My sense of being an Indian in the world is mediated through the struggles of South Africans for liberation. So much are they a part of me that when Chris Hani, head of the South African Communist Party and a major figure in the ANC, was assassinated in 1994, I was brought to tears. As a teenager, I remember joining my classmates in emotional discussions about the battles against

Vijay Prashad, "The Forethought: Raw Skin," in *Everybody Was Kung Fu Fighting: Afro-Asian Connections and the Myth of Cultural Purity* (Boston: Beacon Press, 2001). Retrieved from http://zombie-popcom.com. Reprinted by permission.

apartheid. We talked about Gandhi's time in that far-off land and of the relation-ship between India and Africa. We sang, *"Amar raho, Nelson Mandela"* ("Be eter-nal, Nelson Mandela").

When I came to the United States, I fell into this tradition, first in the anti-apartheid movement of the early 1980s and then with El Salvador solidarity work. I and many of my immigrant friends put our shoulders to the wheel of these struggles, to join the diverse world of the U.S. Left. Names like Sanjay Anand, Anna Lopez, Noel Rodriquez, Karen May, Sid Lemelle, and so many others complicated our identification with the main fights of the day. Those of us who came from other nations found our America in the heart of the global fights for justice. This tendency to work across the lines that divide us continues in the fabric of the social justice movements in the United States, whether through the concept of "allies" in the queer liberation movement or else in cross-ethnic formations such as Asians for Mumia and the Center for Third World Organizing.

But all people of color do not feel that their struggle is a shared one. Some of my South Asian brethren, for example, feel that we should take care of our own and not worry about the woes of others, that we should earn as much money as possible, slide under the radar of racism, and care only about the prospects of our own children. To many of us from India, this is an uncomfortable bargain, but nonetheless it is one that is not unfamiliar in our times among all people.

White supremacy reigns, as it did then, and blackness is reviled. Who can begrudge the desire among people to seek fellowship in their new society, to throw themselves into the cultural worlds of the place in which they live? Since blackness is reviled in the United States, why would an immigrant, of whatever skin color, want to associate with those who are racially oppressed, particularly when the transit into the United States promises the dream of gold and glory? The immigrant seeks a form of vertical assimilation, to climb from the lowest, darkest echelon on the stepladder of tyranny into the bright whiteness. In U.S. history the Irish, Italians, Jews, and—in small steps with some hesitations on the part of white America—Asians and Latinos have all tried to barter their var-ied cultural worlds for the privileges of whiteness.

Yet all people who enter the United States do not strive to be accepted by the terms set by white supremacy. Some actively disregard them, finding them impos-sible to meet. Instead, they seek recognition, solidarity, and safety by embracing others also oppressed by white supremacy in something of a horizontal assimila-tion. Consider the rebel Africans, who fled the slave plantations in the Americas and took refuge among the Amerindians to create communities such as the Semi-noles'; the South Asian workers who jumped ship in eighteenth-century Salem, Massachusetts, to enter the black community; Frederick Douglass's defense of Chinese "coolie" laborers in the nineteenth century; the interactions of the Black Panther Party with the Red Guard and the Brown Berets in the mid-twentieth century; and finally the multiethnic working-class gathering in the new century.

When people actively or tacitly refuse the terms of vertical integration they are derisively dismissed as either unassimilable or exclusionary. We hear "Why do the black kids sit together in the cafeteria," instead of "Why do our institutions routinely uphold the privileges of whiteness?" There is little space in popular discourse for an examination of what goes on outside the realm of white America among people of color.

I have chosen to discuss the peoples who claim the heritage of the continents of Asia and Africa, not only because they are important to me, but because they have long been pitted against each other as the model versus the undesirable. I hope by looking at how these two cultural worlds are imbricated in complex and varied ways through five centuries and around the globe that I can help us rethink race, culture, and the organization of our society. This book is, if you will, a search for a new skin.

We begin our journey in the Indian Ocean region, with the destruction of the economic and cultural traffic that defined the premodern world. The birth of Atlantic racism superseded and (through fascism) transformed earlier xenophobic ideas into the cruelty of biological hierarchy. White supremacy emerged in the throes of capitalism's planetary birth to justify the expropriation of people off their lands and the exploitation of people for their labor. Of course, the discussion of the birth of racism begs the question of its demise: What is a useful antiracist ideological framework? The conservative theory of the color blind and the racialist theory of the indigenous, in their own way, smuggle in biological ideas of race to denigrate the creativity of diverse humans. The best liberal response to the color blind and to racialism comes from those who refuse to believe in the biological weight given to skin. This position, the liberalism of the skin, suggests that there are different skins, and we must learn to respect and tolerate one another.

Liberalism of the skin, which we generically know as multiculturalism, refuses to accept that biology is destiny, but it smuggles in culture to do much the same thing. Culture becomes the means for social and historical difference, how we differentiate ourselves, and adopt the habits of the past to create and delimit social groups. The familiar dichotomy between nature-nurture becomes the basis for distinction between the white supremacists and the liberals. Culture, unlike biology, should allow us to seek liberation from cruel and uncomfortable practices. But instead, culture wraps us in its suffocating embrace. If we follow liberalism of the skin, then we find ourselves heir to all the dilemmas of multiculturalism: Are cultures discrete and bounded? Do cultures have a history or are they static? Who defines the boundaries of culture or allows for change? Do cultures leak into each other? Can a person from one culture critique another culture? These are the questions that plague both social science and our everyday interactions. Those who subscribe to the liberalism of the skin want to be thought well of, to be good, and therefore, many are circumspect when it comes to the culture of another. The best intentions (of respect and tolerance) can often be annoying to those whose cultures are not in dominance: we feel that we are often zoological specimens.

To respect the fetish of culture assumes that one wants to enshrine it in the museum of humankind rather than find within it the potential for liberation or for change. We'd have to accept homophobia and sexism, class cruelty and racism, all in the service of being respectful to someone's perverse definition of a culture. For comfortable liberals a critique of multiculturalism is close to heresy, but for those of us who have to tussle both with the cruelty of white supremacy and with the melancholic torments of minoritarianism, the critique comes with ease. The orthodoxy of below bears less power than that from above, but it is unbearable nonetheless. We have already begun to grow our own patchwork, defiant skins.

These defiant skins come under the sign of the polycultural, a provisional concept grounded in antiracism rather than in diversity. Polyculturalism, unlike multiculturalism, assumes that people live coherent lives that are made up of a host of lineages—the task of the historian is not to carve out the lineages but to make sense of how people live culturally dynamic lives. Polyculturalism is a ferocious engagement with the political world of culture, a painful embrace of the skin and all its contradictions.

Paper Tigers: What Happens to All the Asian-American Overachievers When the Test-Taking Ends?

WESLEY YANG

Sometimes I'll glimpse my reflection in a window and feel astonished by what I see. Jet-black hair. Slanted eyes. A pancake-flat surface of yellow-and-green-toned skin. An expression that is nearly reptilian in its impassivity. I've contrived to think of this face as the equal in beauty to any other. But what I feel in these moments is its strangeness to me. It's my face. I can't disclaim it. But what does it have to do with me?

Millions of Americans must feel estranged from their own faces. But every self-estranged individual is estranged in his own way. I, for instance, am the child of Korean immigrants, but I do not speak my parents' native tongue. I have never called my elders by the proper honorific, "big brother" or "big sister." I have never dated a Korean woman. I don't have a Korean friend. Though I am an immigrant, I have never wanted to strive like one.

You could say that I am, in the gently derisive parlance of Asian-Americans, a banana or a Twinkie (yellow on the outside, white on the inside). But while I don't believe our roots necessarily define us, I do believe there are racially inflected assumptions wired into our neural circuitry that we use to sort through the sea of faces we confront. And although I am in most respects devoid of Asian characteristics, I do have an Asian face.

Here is what I sometimes suspect my face signifies to other Americans: an invisible person, barely distinguishable from a mass of faces that resemble it. A conspicuous person standing apart from the crowd and yet devoid of any individuality. An icon of so much that the culture pretends to honor but that it in fact patronizes and exploits. Not just people "who are good at math" and play the violin, but a mass of stifled, repressed, abused, conformist quasi-robots who simply do not matter, socially or culturally.

Wesley Yang, "Paper Tigers: What Happens to All the Asian-American Overachievers When the Test-Taking Ends?" *New York Magazine*, May 8, 2011. Reprinted by permission.

I've always been of two minds about this sequence of stereotypes. On the one hand, it offends me greatly that anyone would think to apply them to me, or to anyone else, simply on the basis of facial characteristics. On the other hand, it also seems to me that there are a lot of Asian people to whom they apply.

Let me summarize my feelings toward Asian values: Fuck filial piety. Fuck grade-grubbing. Fuck Ivy League mania. Fuck deference to authority. Fuck humility and hard work. Fuck harmonious relations. Fuck sacrificing for the future. Fuck earnest, striving middle-class servility.

I understand the reasons Asian parents have raised a generation of children this way. Doctor, lawyer, accountant, engineer: These are good jobs open to whoever works hard enough. What could be wrong with that pursuit? Asians graduate from college at a rate higher than any other ethnic group in America, including whites. They earn a higher median family income than any other ethnic group in America, including whites. This is a stage in a triumphal narrative, and it is a narrative that is much shorter than many remember. Two thirds of the roughly 14 million Asian-Americans are foreign-born. There were less than 39,000 people of Korean descent living in America in 1970, when my elder brother was born. There are around 1 million today.

Asian-American success is typically taken to ratify the American Dream and to prove that minorities can make it in this country without handouts. Still, an undercurrent of racial panic always accompanies the consideration of Asians, and all the more so as China becomes the destination for our industrial base and the banker controlling our burgeoning debt. But if the armies of Chinese factory workers who make our fast fashion and iPads terrify us, and if the collective mass of high-achieving Asian-American students arouse an anxiety about the laxity of American parenting, what of the Asian-American who obeyed everything his parents told him? Does this person really scare anyone?...

A few months ago, I received an e-mail from a young man named Jefferson Mao, who after attending Stuyvesant High School had recently graduated from the University of Chicago. He wanted my advice about "being an Asian writer." This is how he described himself: "I got good grades and I love literature and I want to be a writer and an intellectual; at the same time, I'm the first person in my family to go to college, my parents don't speak English very well, and we don't own the apartment in Flushing that we live in. I mean, I'm proud of my parents and my neighborhood and what I perceive to be my artistic potential or whatever, but sometimes I feel like I'm jumping the gun a generation or two too early."...

Mao has a round face, with eyes behind rectangular wire-frame glasses. Since graduating, he has been living with his parents, who emigrated from China when Mao was 8 years old. His mother is a manicurist; his father is a physical therapist's aide. Lately, Mao has been making the familiar hour-and-a-half ride from Flushing to downtown Manhattan to tutor a white Stuyvesant freshman who lives in Tribeca. And what he feels, sometimes, in the presence of that amiable young man is a pang of regret. Now he understands better what he ought to have done back when he was a Stuyvesant freshman: "Worked half as hard and been twenty times more successful."

Entrance to Stuyvesant, one of the most competitive public high schools in the country, is determined solely by performance on a test: The top 3.7 percent of all New York City students who take the Specialized High Schools Admissions Test hoping to go to Stuyvesant are accepted. There are no set-asides for the underprivileged or, conversely, for alumni or other privileged groups. There is no formula to encourage "diversity" or any nebulous concept of "well--roundedness" or "character." Here we have something like pure meritocracy. This is what it looks like: Asian-Americans, who make up 12.6 percent of New York City, make up 72 percent of the high school.

This year, 569 Asian-Americans scored high enough to earn a slot at Stuyvesant, along with 179 whites, 13 Hispanics, and 12 blacks. Such dramatic over-representation, and what it may be read to imply about the intelligence of different groups of New Yorkers, has a way of making people uneasy. But intrinsic intelligence, of course, is precisely what Asians don't believe in. They believe—and have proved—that the constant practice of test-taking will improve the scores of whoever commits to it. All throughout Flushing, as well as in Bayside, one can find "cram schools," or storefront academies, that drill students in test preparation after school, on weekends, and during summer break. "Learning math is not about learning math," an instructor at one called Ivy Prep was quoted in the *New York Times* as saying. "It's about weightlifting. You are pumping the iron of math." Mao puts it more specifically: "You learn quite simply to nail any standardized test you take."...

Somewhere near the middle of his time at Stuyvesant, a vague sense of discontent started to emerge within Mao. He had always felt himself a part of a mob of "nameless, faceless Asian kids," who were "like a part of the décor of the place." He had been content to keep his head down and work toward the goal shared by everyone at Stuyvesant: Harvard. But around the beginning of his senior year, he began to wonder whether this march toward academic success was the only, or best, path.

"You can't help but feel like there must be another way," he explains over a bowl of phô. "It's like, we're being pitted against each other while there are kids out there in the Midwest who can do way less work and be in a garage band or something—and if they're decently intelligent and work decently hard in school..."...

Mao was becoming clued in to the fact that there was another hierarchy behind the official one that explained why others were getting what he never had—"a high-school sweetheart" figured prominently on this list—and that this mysterious hierarchy was going to determine what happened to him in life. "You realize there are things you really don't understand about courtship or just acting in a certain way. Things that somehow come naturally to people who go to school in the suburbs and have parents who are culturally assimilated." I pressed him for specifics, and he mentioned that he had visited his white girlfriend's parents' house the past Christmas, where the family had "sat around cooking together and playing Scrabble." This ordinary vision of suburban-American domesticity lingered with Mao: Here, at last, was the setting in which all that implicit knowledge "about social norms and propriety" had been transmitted. There was no cram school that taught these lessons....

While he was still an electrical-engineering student at Berkeley in the nineties, James Hong visited the IBM campus for a series of interviews. An older Asian researcher looked over Hong's résumé and asked him some standard questions. Then he got up without saying a word and closed the door to his office.

"Listen," he told Hong, "I'm going to be honest with you. My generation came to this country because we wanted better for you kids. We did the best we could, leaving our homes and going to graduate school not speaking much English. If you take this job, you are just going to hit the same ceiling we did. They just see me as an Asian Ph.D., never management potential. You are going to get a job offer, but don't take it. Your generation has to go farther than we did, otherwise we did everything for nothing."

The researcher was talking about what some refer to as the "Bamboo Ceiling"—an invisible barrier that maintains a pyramidal racial structure throughout corporate America, with lots of Asians at junior levels, quite a few in middle management, and virtually none in the higher reaches of leadership.

The failure of Asian-Americans to become leaders in the white-collar workplace does not qualify as one of the burning social issues of our time. But it is a part of the bitter undercurrent of Asian-American life that so many Asian graduates of elite universities find that meritocracy as they have understood it comes to an abrupt end after graduation. If between 15 and 20 percent of every Ivy League class is Asian, and if the Ivy Leagues are incubators for the country's leaders, it would stand to reason that Asians would make up some corresponding portion of the leadership class.

And yet the numbers tell a different story. According to a recent study, Asian-Americans represent roughly 5 percent of the population but only 0.3 percent of corporate officers, less than 1 percent of corporate board members, and around 2 percent of college presidents. There are nine Asian-American CEOs in the Fortune 500. In specific fields where Asian-Americans are heavily represented, there is a similar asymmetry. A third of all software engineers in Silicon Valley are Asian, and yet they make up only 6 percent of board members and about 10 percent of corporate officers of the Bay Area's 25 largest companies. At the National Institutes of Health, where 21.5 percent of tenure-track scientists are Asians, only 4.7 percent of the lab or branch directors are, according to a study conducted in 2005. One succinct evocation of the situation appeared in the comments section of a website called Yellowworld: "If you're East Asian, you need to attend a top-tier university to land a good high-paying gig. Even if you land that good high-paying gig, the white guy with the pedigree from a mediocre state university will somehow move ahead of you in the ranks simply because he's white."

Jennifer W. Allyn, a managing director for diversity at PricewaterhouseCoopers, works to ensure that "all of the groups feel welcomed and supported and able to thrive and to go as far as their talents will take them." I posed to her the following definition of parity in the corporate workforce: If the current crop of associates is 17 percent Asian, then in fourteen years, when they have all been up for partner review, 17 percent of those who are offered partner will be Asian. Allyn conceded that PricewaterhouseCoopers was not close to reaching that bench-mark anytime soon—and that "nobody else is either."

Part of the insidious nature of the Bamboo Ceiling is that it does not seem to be caused by overt racism. A survey of Asian-Pacific-American employees of Fortune 500 companies found that 80 percent reported they were judged not as Asians but as individuals. But only 51 percent reported the existence of Asians in key positions, and only 55 percent agreed that their firms were fully capitalizing on the talents and perspectives of Asians.

More likely, the discrepancy in these numbers is a matter of unconscious bias. Nobody would affirm the proposition that tall men are intrinsically better leaders, for instance. And yet while only 15 percent of the male population is at least six feet tall, 58 percent of all corporate CEOs are. Similarly, nobody would say that Asian people are unfit to be leaders. But subjects in a recently published psychological experiment consistently rated hypothetical employees with Caucasian-sounding names higher in leadership potential than identical ones with Asian names.

Maybe it is simply the case that a traditionally Asian upbringing is the prob-lem. As Allyn points out, in order to be a leader, you must have followers. Associates at PricewaterhouseCoopers are initially judged on how well they do the work they are assigned. "You have to be a doer," as she puts it. They are expected to distinguish themselves with their diligence, at which point they become "super-doers." But being a leader requires different skill sets. "The traits that got you to where you are won't necessarily take you to the next level," says the diversity consultant Jane Hyun, who wrote a book called *Breaking the Bamboo Ceiling.* To become a leader requires taking personal initiative and thinking about how an organization can work differently. It also requires networking, self-promotion, and self-assertion. It's racist to think that any given Asian indi-vidual is unlikely to be creative or risk-taking. It's simple cultural observation to say that a group whose education has historically focused on rote memorization and "pumping the iron of math" is, on aggregate, unlikely to yield many people inclined to challenge authority or break with inherited ways of doing things.

Sach Takayasu had been one of the fastest-rising members of her cohort in the marketing department at IBM in New York. But about seven years ago, she felt her progress begin to slow. "I had gotten to the point where I was overde-livering, working really long hours, and where doing more of the same wasn't getting me anywhere," she says. It was around this time that she attended a sem-inar being offered by an organization called Leadership Education for Asian Pacifics.

LEAP has parsed the complicated social dynamics responsible for the dearth of Asian-American leaders and has designed training programs that flatter Asian people even as it teaches them to change their behavior to suit white-American expectations. Asians who enter a LEAP program are constantly assured that they will be able to "keep your values, while acquiring new skills," along the way to becoming "culturally competent leaders."

In a presentation to 1,500 Asian-American employees of Microsoft, LEAP president and CEO J.D. Hokoyama laid out his grand synthesis of the Asian predicament in the workplace. "Sometimes people have perceptions about us and our communities which may or may not be true," Hokoyama told the audience. "But they put those perceptions onto us, and then they do something that can be very devastating: They make decisions about us not based on the truth but based on those perceptions." Hokoyama argued that it was not sufficient to rail at these unjust perceptions. In the end, Asian people themselves would have to assume responsibility for unmaking them. This was both a practical matter, he argued, and, in its own way, fair.

Aspiring Asian leaders had to become aware of "the relationship between values, behaviors, and perceptions." He offered the example of Asians who don't speak up at meetings. "So let's say I go to meetings with you and I notice you never say anything. And I ask myself, 'Hmm, I wonder why you're not saying anything. Maybe it's because you don't know what we're talking about. That would be a good reason for not saying anything. Or maybe it's because you're not even interested in the subject matter. Or maybe you think the conversation is beneath you.' So here I'm thinking, because you never say anything at meetings, that you're either dumb, you don't care, or you're arrogant. When maybe it's because you were taught when you were growing up that when the boss is talking, what are you supposed to be doing? Listening."

Takayasu took the weeklong course in 2006. One of the first exercises she encountered involved the group instructor asking for a list of some qualities that they identify with Asians. The students responded: upholding family honor, filial piety, self-restraint. Then the instructor solicited a list of the qualities the members identify with leadership, and invited the students to notice how little overlap there is between the two lists.

At first, Takayasu didn't relate to the others in attendance, who were listing typical Asian values their parents had taught them. "They were all saying things like 'Study hard,' 'Become a doctor or lawyer,' blah, blah, blah. That's not how my parents were. They would worry if they saw me working too hard." Takayasu had spent her childhood shuttling between New York and Tokyo. Her father was an executive at Mitsubishi; her mother was a concert pianist. She was highly assimilated into American culture, fluent in English, poised and confident. "But the more we got into it, as we moved away from the obvious things to the deeper, more fundamental values, I began to see that my upbringing had been very Asian after all. My parents would say, 'Don't create problems. Don't trouble other people.' How Asian is that? It helped to explain why I don't reach out to other people for help." It occurred to Takayasu that she was a little bit "heads down" after all. She was willing to take on difficult assignments without seeking credit for herself. She was reluctant to "toot her own horn."

Takayasu has put her new self-awareness to work at IBM, and she now exhibits a newfound ability for horn tooting. "The things I could write on my résumé as my team's accomplishments: They're really impressive," she says.

The law professor and writer Tim Wu grew up in Canada with a white mother and a Taiwanese father, which allows him an interesting perspective on how whites and Asians perceive each other. After graduating from law school, he took a series of clerkships, and he remembers the subtle ways in which hierarchies were developed among the other young lawyers. "There is this automatic assumption in any legal environment that Asians will have a particular talent for bitter labor," he says, and then goes on to define the word *coolie*, a Chinese term for "bitter labor." "There was this weird self-selection where the Asians would migrate toward the most brutal part of the labor."

By contrast, the white lawyers he encountered had a knack for portraying themselves as above all that. "White people have this instinct that is really important: to give off the impression that they're only going to do the really important work. You're a quarterback. It's a kind of arrogance that Asians are trained not to have. Someone told me not long after I moved to New York that in order to succeed, you have to understand which rules you're supposed to break. If you break the wrong rules, you're finished. And so the easiest thing to do is follow all the rules. But then you consign yourself to a lower status. The real trick is understanding what rules are not meant for you."

This idea of a kind of rule-governed rule-breaking—where the rule book was unwritten but passed along in an innate cultural sense—is perhaps the best explanation I have heard of how the Bamboo Ceiling functions in practice. LEAP appears to be very good at helping Asian workers who are already culturally competent become more self-aware of how their culture and appearance impose barriers to advancement. But I am not sure that a LEAP course is going to be enough to get Jefferson Mao or Daniel Chu the respect and success they crave. The issue is more fundamental, the social dynamics at work more deeply embedded, and the remedial work required may be at a more basic level of comportment....

Sometime during the hundreds of hours he spent among the mostly untouched English-language novels at the Flushing branch of the public library, Jefferson Mao discovered literature's special power of transcendence, a freedom of imagination that can send you beyond the world's hierarchies. He had written to me seeking permission to swerve off the traditional path of professional striving—to devote himself to becoming an artist—but he was unsure of what risks he was willing to take. My answer was highly ambivalent. I recognized in him something of my own youthful ambition. And I knew where that had taken me.

Unlike Mao, I was not a poor, first-generation immigrant. I finished school alienated both from Asian culture (which, in my hometown, was barely visible) and the manners and mores of my white peers. But like Mao, I wanted to be an individual. I had refused both cultures as an act of self-assertion. An education spent dutifully acquiring credentials through relentless drilling seemed to me an obscenity. So did adopting the manipulative cheeriness that seemed to secure the popularity of white Americans.

Instead, I set about contriving to live beyond both poles. I wanted what James Baldwin sought as a writer—"a power which outlasts kingdoms." Anything short of that seemed a humiliating compromise. I would become an aristocrat of the spirit, who prides himself on his incompetence in the middling tasks that are the world's business. Who does not seek after material gain. Who is his own law.

This, of course, was madness. A child of Asian immigrants born into the suburbs of New Jersey and educated at Rutgers cannot be a law unto himself.

The only way to approximate this is to refuse employment, because you will not be bossed around by people beneath you, and shave your expenses to the bone, because you cannot afford more, and move into a decaying Victorian mansion in Jersey City, so that your sense of eccentric distinction can be preserved in the midst of poverty, and cut yourself free of every form of bourgeois discipline, because these are precisely the habits that will keep you chained to the mediocre fate you consider worse than death.

Throughout my twenties, I proudly turned away from one institution of American life after another (for instance, a steady job), though they had already long since turned away from me. Academe seemed another kind of death—but then again, I had a transcript marred by as many F's as A's. I had come from a culture that was the middle path incarnate. And yet for some people, there can be no middle path, only transcendence or descent into the abyss.

I was descending into the abyss.

All this was well deserved. No one had any reason to think I was anything or anyone. And yet I felt entitled to demand this recognition. I knew this was wrong and impermissible; therefore I had to double down on it. The world brings low such people. It brought me low. I haven't had health insurance in ten years. I didn't earn more than $12,000 for eight consecutive years. I went three years in the prime of my adulthood without touching a woman. I did not produce a masterpiece.

I recall one of the strangest conversations I had in the city. A woman came up to me at a party and said she had been moved by a piece of writing I had published. She confessed that prior to reading it, she had never wanted to talk to me, and had always been sure, on the basis of what she could see from across the room, that I was nobody worth talking to, that I was in fact someone to avoid.

But she had been wrong about this, she told me: It was now plain to her that I was a person with great reserves of feeling and insight. She did not ask my forgiveness for this brutal misjudgment. Instead, what she wanted to know was—why had I kept that person she had glimpsed in my essay so well hidden? She confessed something of her own hidden sorrow: She had never been beautiful and had decided, early on, that it therefore fell to her to "love the world twice as hard." Why hadn't I done that?

Here was a drunk white lady speaking what so many others over the years must have been insufficiently drunk to tell me. It was the key to many things that had, and had not, happened. I understood this encounter better after learning about LEAP, and visiting Asian Playboy's boot camp. If you are a woman who isn't beautiful, it is a social reality that you will have to work twice as hard to hold anyone's attention. You can either linger on the unfairness of this or you can get with the program. If you are an Asian person who holds himself proudly aloof, nobody will respect that, or find it intriguing, or wonder if that challenging façade hides someone worth getting to know. They will simply write you off as someone not worth the trouble of talking to.

Having glimpsed just how unacceptable the world judges my demeanor, could I too strive to make up for my shortcomings? Practice a shit-eating grin until it becomes natural? Love the world twice as hard?

I see the appeal of getting with the program. But this is not my choice. Striving to meet others' expectations may be a necessary cost of assimilation, but I am not going to do it.

Often I think my defiance is just delusional, self-glorifying bullshit that artists have always told themselves to compensate for their poverty and powerlessness. But sometimes I think it's the only thing that has preserved me intact, and that what has been preserved is not just haughty caprice but in fact the meaning of my life. So this is what I told Mao: In lieu of loving the world twice as hard, I care, in the end, about expressing my obdurate singularity at any cost. I love this hard and unyielding part of myself more than any other reward the world has to offer a newly brightened and ingratiating demeanor, and I will bear any costs associated with it.

The first step toward self-reform is to admit your deficiencies. Though my early adulthood has been a protracted education in them, I do not admit mine. I'm fine. It's the rest of you who have a problem. Fuck all y'all.

Whither the Asian American Coalition?

PAUL SPICKARD

By the 1980s the idea that Asian Americans were a single panethnic group whose members had a lot in common across lines of ancestral ethnic nationality had become a fairly unremarkable feature of life, not only on the West Coast but in communities all across the nation. Yet it was always the case that some peoples were closer to the heart of the Asian American coalition than others. In the 1970s the core ethnic groups were Chinese and Japanese Americans, with Filipino Americans relegated to a second circle.

The Immigration Act of 1965 removed the racial bar against Asian immigration, and the numbers of Asian immigrants soared. By the 1990s Asian Americans had become the fastest-growing American racial minority (in percentage terms), and the countries from which they or their ancestors came multiplied. Chinese and Filipinos continued to arrive in large numbers, but hundreds of thousands of others came from Korea, Taiwan, Vietnam, and other countries in Southeast Asia. The forces of globalization brought many more from India, Pakistan, and elsewhere in South and Southwest Asia. By the end of the twentieth century the Asian American coalition had grown in size and in the number of its constituent parts, but some groups were still generally regarded to be near the center of Asian American identity and others to be further away. Korean Americans had joined Chinese and Japanese Americans at the core of the Asian American coalition; Filipinos, Vietnamese, and some multiracial people of part-Asian parentage formed a second circle; and other Southeast Asians and South Asians were still more loosely connected to the coalition (Figure 1.1).

Spickard, Paul. "Whither the Asian American Coalition?" *Pacific Historical Review*, 76, no. 14 (November 2007). © 2007 by the Regents of the University of California. Published by the University of California Press.

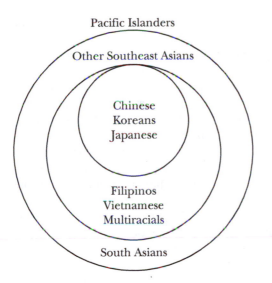

Pacific Islanders

Other Southeast Asians

Chinese
Koreans
Japanese

Filipinos
Vietnamese
Multiracials

South Asians

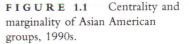

FIGURE 1.1   Centrality and
marginality of Asian American
groups, 1990s.

Are These Asian Americans?

Let us consider how four groups of people—Pacific Islander Americans, multiracial people of part-Asian descent, international adoptees, and Arab and other
Middle Eastern Americans—might or might not be regarded as members of, or
connected to, the Asian American coalition, now and in the years to come.

Pacific Islander Americans.   Pacific Island peoples in the United States have long
been lumped together with Asian Americans by non-Pacific Islanders. The U.S.
Census long included Hawaiians, Samoans, Tongans, Maori, Chamorros, and
other Pacific Island peoples in their aggregate numbers for Asian Americans.
Sometimes the lumping has been done by Asian Americans, but very seldom
by Pacific Islanders. Some histories, textbooks, and anthologies on Asian American subjects have routinely included treatment of Pacific Islanders. Others
have routinely ignored them. There were plenty of Pacific Islanders in the
United States when the Asian American coalition was founded, but they were
not then part of that coalition....

Early in the [21st] century, several Pacific Islander American scholars proposed to re-engage Asian America. Debbie Hippolite Wright called for a frank,
open, mutually respectful, and mutually supportive dialogue between Asian and
Pacific Islander Americans, with a goal to build a working coalition to support
each other's issues, from antiracism to immigration reform to Hawaiian sovereignty. Several scholars, noting that Hawaiians, Maori, Chamorros, Samoans,
and other Pacific Islanders had long been active in the Association for Asian
American Studies (AAAS), asked that the name of the scholarly association be
changed again, to include Pacific Islanders—but this time, to really include
them. Scholars like Vicente Diaz, Davianna Pomaika'i McGregor, Amy Ku'u-
leialoha Stillman, and Joanne Rondilla cited the long, intertwined history of

people who have conventionally been regarded as Pacific Islanders and those regarded as Asians. They pointed to the manifest linkages between how American colonialism has been experienced by some Pacific Island peoples such as Hawaiians, Samoans, and Chamorros, and how it has been experienced by some Asians (Filipinos, especially, but also Japanese, Vietnamese, and others). They pointed to the large numbers of Filipinos, Japanese, Chinese, and other Asians who have been in the Pacific in the modern era, as well as to ancient trade and cultural links between island and continental peoples.

The panethnic concepts "Asian" and "Pacific Islander" mask profound differences between some of their constituent groups. Punjabis and Koreans share very little history or experience, yet they are in the Asian American coalition. Hawaiians and Solomon Islanders likewise have very little common history or experience, yet they are both Pacific Islanders. On the other hand, Filipinos are considered to be in the Asian American coalition and Chamorros in the Pacific Islander coalition, despite the fact that Filipinos and Chamorros share vast amounts of common history, culture, and social placement. Not all the history between Asian and Pacific Islander Americans is common history; sometimes it has been a history of oppositional interests and actions, as the ongoing discussion of "Asian settler colonialism" in Hawai'i suggests. But Asian Americans and Pacific Islanders have had a great deal of intertwined history, and it will be useful as we go forward to explore the intertwining, even as we recognize that Pacific Islanders are not a subset of Asian America.

What would it mean for historians of Asian America consciously to ask ourselves: How do the issues that I think I am seeing in my study of Asian Americans look different if I consider the situations of Pacific Island peoples as well? I think we might well have a much greater appreciation for the flexible and contingent nature of ethnic coalitions, as well as for the role played by American (and perhaps other nations') colonialism. We might want to open up our inquiry to talk about the links between the American colonial projects in California, in Hawai'i, in the Philippines, and in Southwest Asia into the twenty-first century. We might want to think critically about Asian immigrants' complicity in Japanese colonialism in Micronesia and in American colonialism in Hawai'i.

Multiracial Asian Americans.   Multiracial people are also part of Asian America and have been from the beginning, although the monoracially framed histories of Asian America have generally lost sight of their existence. In the mid-1990s a tall, slim, pale, chestnut-haired, hazel-eyed student stood up and accosted the instructor of an Asian American studies class at a renowned West Coast university. The professor had been speaking about Asian Americans as if they were a racially pure people, as if there had been no mixing and blending between Asians and other Americans. The student declared: "Look at me. I am the face of Asian America."

The student had a point. Outmarriage by several Asian American groups—particularly Filipinos, Japanese, and Vietnamese—has been increasing since the latter 1940s. The rate now hovers around 50 percent for those three groups, and other groups are not far behind. Maria Root talks of an "interracial baby boom" following the *Loving v. Virginia* U.S. Supreme Court decision of 1967, which overturned state antimiscegenation laws....

In writing a book about skin-tone preferences among Asian Americans, my fellow researchers and I found that, when we asked almost any Asian American to go back in his or her family history more than a few generations, they were almost uniformly surprised to find out that there was someone two or three generations back who was mixed with another Asian nationality, or with someone White or Black or Latino, whose story had been erased from official family memory. Chinese have been mixing with most of the peoples of Southeast Asia for centuries, to the point where most Filipino, Cambodian, Vietnamese, Thai, Lao, and Burmese Americans have at least some Chinese ancestry. Many Vietnamese and Cambodian Americans have elements of the other group's ethnic ancestry within their family lines. Throughout the first half of the twentieth century, Punjabi men made families with Mexican American women in California's San Joaquin and Imperial valleys. Filipino and Mexican Americans have been living in the same towns and neighborhoods, working at the same jobs, and often being members of the same families since at least the 1930s. Most Pacific Islander Americans have multiple ancestries—mixed Tongan and Samoan, Maori and Pakeha, Hawaiian and Haole, Chamorro and Filipino, and so on and on.

What would it mean for historians of Asian America consciously to ask ourselves: How do the issues that I think I am seeing among Asian Americans look different if I consider the situations of multiracial Asian Americans as well? It may be that the options and ambiguities surrounding an individual's identity will be as important as the single-group commitments. It will surely be that the nature and prospects of any group will immediately look very much more complex. If we explore racial and ethnic multiplicity in Asian American history, we open ourselves up to thinking about connections between groups, and not just between groups that have traditionally been included in the Asian American coalition.

Adoptees.   One of the places in Asian American history where the multiracial story must be told is with respect to international and transracial adoption. According to the online adoption service Adoption.com, each year more than 20,000 people come to the United States as international adoptees—in 2005, more than 8,000 from China alone. By far the majority of such people become part of multiracial families; many of them join White families in the American heartland. At various times since World War II, Japan, Korea, and Vietnam have sent large numbers of multiracial adoptees—presumably the children of U.S. GIs—to the United States. The rule of thumb in Korean adoptee activist circles is that one in ten Korean Americans is an adoptee (I don't know of any authoritative figure on this). Yet no one has written the history of international adoptees as Asian Americans, nor even as immigrants. The field has been left to social workers, novelists, anthropologists, and adoptees themselves to tell their stories. Those stories, as told by such people, almost never explore whether and how such people might be considered part of Asian America. Certainly, none of the mainstream historians of Asian America treats adoptees as part of the Asian American story.

What would it mean for historians of Asian America consciously to ask ourselves: How do the issues that I think I am seeing among Asian Americans look different if I consider the situations of internationally and transracially adopted Asian Americans as well? Talking about Asian American adoptee history forces us to think transnationally, for the history of the birth country and its relationship with the United States is inevitably part of the adoptee story. As with Pacific Islanders and multiracial people, adoptee history invites us to think more deeply and critically about the implications of U.S. colonial involvement in Asia and in Asian America. What is more, considering adoptees as Asian Americans opens up the Asian American story to embrace multiple definitions of group membership. Does one need to have grown up in an Asian American family and community in order to be an Asian American? Or does Asian biological ancestry suffice? Ought adoptees from Korea be treated as part of Korean American history? Or should they be thought of, along with adoptees from Japan, China, and Vietnam, as part of a pan-Asian adoptee experience?

Arab and Middle Eastern Americans.   I don't know anyone who asserts that Arab, North African, Persian, or other Middle Eastern-derived Americans are a subset of Asian Americans. Yet growing numbers of Arab and Middle Eastern American scholars have regularly been part of the Association for Asian American Studies, have contributed to Asian American publications, and have wanted to talk about whether, and in what ways, Arab or other Middle Eastern Americans might connect with the Asian American coalition. Perhaps it is partly that, as with Pacific Islander Americans, there is nowhere else on the ethnic studies map for such people to find a home, and the Asian American coalition has always shown some flexibility and welcome.

Let me point to issues where the experiences of Asian Americans and Arab and Middle Eastern Americans have considerable resonance, even commonality. The first is Orientalism. Arab and other Middle Eastern Americans experienced the European-generated, eastward-looking Orientalism about which Edward Said wrote and that was defined mainly by images of Turkey, Arabia, and Persia. That is quite a different thing from the westward-looking Orientalism, built on contemplation of China and Japan, that focused American Orientalist thinkers. White Americans may call both Japanese Americans and Arab Americans Orientals, but they do not really think of them as the same sort of people, whereas they do think of Japanese and Chinese as pretty much the same. Yet the two Orientalisms overlap and come together in many places, not least in the study of Asian religions in America (which must be distinguished from the study of the religious experiences of Asian Americans).

A connected Orientalism contributes to the fact that Asian Americans and Middle Eastern Americans are the two largest immigrant groups who have never quite overcome their immigrant status, no matter how many generations they may have lived in the United States. Other Americans see Asians, Arabs, Persians, and other Middle Eastern peoples as eternal foreigners, much as White Americans treat U.S. citizens of East and South Asian descent as if they were from a foreign land. Vincent Chin was murdered because his attackers took him for a citizen of Japan. In 1996 a Seattle newspaper combed the records of contributors to American-born Gary Locke's gubernatorial campaign for non-citizen Chinese names; they did not look for non-citizen English or Scandinavian names in his opponent's contributor lists. Asian American scientists have lost their jobs, and one was incarcerated without cause, in a racist scare campaign in the 1990s that alleged Asian Americans were giving secrets to the People's Republic of China. Just as numerous are the cases of people of Middle Eastern ancestry being cast as foreigners by White Americans. If one asks the average American to describe an Arab, a Muslim, or someone whose ancestors are from the Middle East, out comes a chilling description of a terrorist or sinister oil baron. Almost no one talks about Ralph Nader, John Zogby, and Danny Thomas as Arab Americans.

Arab and Asian Americans have a linked history with regard to a series of court cases from the 1910s and 1920s that decided definitively who was White (and therefore allowed to become a naturalized citizen) and who was not. The answers then were different: George Dow, a Lebanese immigrant, was judged first not White, but then the federal court reversed the decision and ruled that he was White after all. The court never had any question about Japanese-born Takao Ozawa or Bhagat Singh Thind, an immigrant from India: They were not White. Yet in the years after the oil shocks of 1974, and especially after the rise of violence in the 1990s by people whom White Americans chose to call Muslim terrorists, Arab and Middle Eastern Americans grew darker and darker in the White American imaginary.

In recent years, especially since September 11, 2001, several South Asian and Arab American scholars have begun to explore commonalities between their groups' experiences and ways in which they might form intellectual and political coalitions. One aspect of both communities is the large minority of Muslims in each. Another has to do with the ways in which both Asians and Middle Eastern Americans have experienced American colonialism at home and abroad. Then there is the conflation in White American minds of Middle Eastern and South Asian-descended peoples. It is tragic, but not accidental, that several of the people murdered or attacked in hate crimes just after September 11 were not Muslims, nor Arabs, nor Middle Eastern Americans at all, but rather Sikhs. As journalist Tram Nguyen wrote of immigrants in the years since 9/11: "We are all suspects now."

What would it mean for historians of Asian America consciously to ask ourselves: How do the issues that I think I am seeing in my study of Asian Americans look different if I consider the situations of Arab and other Middle Eastern Americans as well? Surely, there is important historical work to do at the intersection of the experiences of Asian Americans and of Arab and other Middle Eastern Americans.

★ ★ ★

In the end, I suppose I am calling for a less essentialist, more flexible vision of who is an Asian American. The lives and experiences of Pacific Islander Americans have much in common with those of certain groups such as Filipinos who have long been part of the Asian American coalition. The multiracial aspect of many Asian Americans, and the persons of many multiracial people, have been for the most part unacknowledged in Asian American history. Adoptees from Asian countries have also been left out of Asian American history. Likewise, there is a good bit of common experience and current political positioning between Arab Americans, other Middle Eastern Americans, and South Asian Americans. The commonalities of inquiry may be tied to the politics of particular historical moments, whereas the Asian American coalition has up until now been quite durable and has evolved only slowly.

The one issue that seems to tie all these threads together is U.S. colonialism around the world, and its creation of racial hierarchies both abroad and at home. American colonialism, Orientalism, and racism may make it necessary that historical inquiry be made on the basis of larger and shifting coalitions, rather than the simpler Asian American coalition of old. If historians of Asian America take up a more complex and shifting idea of who is an Asian American, we will have to make conscious, explicit choices of who we will regard as an Asian American as we address each project.

What Is Transnational Asian American History?

ERIKA LEE AND NAOKO SHIBUSAWA

Beginning IN THE 1990s, THE TERM "globalization" became a catchall phrase to explain a multitude of economic, cultural, and political transformations taking place around the world in everything from finance markets and technologies to fast food and popular culture. Pundits and laypeople alike asserted that internet technology, cell phones, and faster and more frequent air travel made the world a smaller place. People were on the move, too, migrating not only along the older patterns of south to north and east to west, but also in newer and unpredictable patterns of remigration and secondary migration. Scholars generally recognized globalization as an intensification and acceleration of centuries-old patterns of trade and migration, and nearly everyone—regardless of whether they decried or celebrated globalization—saw it as a process that denied the centrality of the nation-state. In the age of globalization, consumer products, capital, and people supposedly traveled, or should be able to travel, across national boundaries "freely," without undue state hindrance.

Within academia, the call came loud and clear from many different fronts that it was time to examine and explain these changes by widening the traditional focus on the nation-state to a transnational framework. In the field of U.S. history, the Organization of American Historians sponsored a working group devoted to "rethinking American history in a global age." In 2000, the resulting LaPietra Report to the profession urged scholars to "extend our analysis of [national histories] to incorporate an awareness of larger, transnational contexts, processes, and identities." The *Journal of American History* encouraged the

Erika Lee and Naoko Shibusawa, "What Is Transnational Asian American History? Recent Trends and Challenges" *Journal of Asian American Studies* 8, 3 (October 2005), vii-xvii. Reprinted by permission.

field to consider transnational U.S. history with its special issue in 1999. Similarly, the American Studies Association sponsored conferences with themes emphasizing crossing borders and national, transnational, and postnational issues. In 2004, Shelly Fisher Fishkin noted the "transnational turn" in American Studies, explaining that the field was an "increasingly important site of knowledge ... a place where borders both within and outside the nation are interrogated and studied, rather than reified and reinforced." And as a sign of the growing scholarship on transnationalism within the field of Asian Studies, the *Journal of Asian Studies* also began to include a section on "Comparative and Transnational" work in its book review section beginning in 2001.

The term "transnational" has admittedly now become an academic buzzword. Scholars in different disciplines and areas of studies have used the term so loosely that its very meaning is in danger of being diluted. This special issue ... is an attempt to define what we mean by "transnational Asian American history," to give recent examples, and to start exploring its possibilities and challenges.

First, it is useful to think about the terminology more carefully. The terms "transnational," "global," "international," and "diaspora" are also often used interchangeably and often complement each other. But, they are best understood as describing distinct, though often related, processes and phenomena. As Nina Glick-Schiller explains, "global" refers to processes, such as the development of capitalism, that are "not located in a single state but happen throughout the entire globe." "Transnational," on the other hand, refers to "political, economic, social and cultural processes that extend beyond the borders of a particular state, include actors that are not states, but are shaped by the policies and institutional practices of states." David Thelen, editor of a special issue on transnational U.S. history in the *Journal of American History,* offers an even broader definition of "transnational" that would "interrogate, and not assume the centrality of the nation-state as an organizing theme in American history." Scholarship would explore how "people and ideas and institutions and cultures moved above, below, through, and around, as well as within, the nation-state." "Transnational" processes should also be understood as related to, but distinct from, "international" and "diasporic" ones. Daniel Mato defines "international" as referring to "those relations maintained between governments (or their agencies) which invoke the nation-states they are supposed to represent in the mutually supportive so-called international system." The term "diaspora," as it has been commonly used in recent academic writings, is less tied to the biblical, Jewish model of forced exile from a homeland and instead places emphasis on what Jigna Desai has explained as the "heterogeneous connections to both the homeland and to other diasporic locations through such forms as political commitment, imagination, memory, travel and cultural production."

Situated at the intersections of U.S. history, American Studies, and Asian Studies, Asian American historians have arguably always been transnational in outlook by integrating transnational, diasporic, and global perspectives into analyses of the Asian American past. Initially foregrounded in social history, Asian American histories have primarily focused on non-state actors—the Asian migrants and their descendants—as well as on transnational networks in which they participated, demonstrating that such processes are not only a product of our contemporary, globalized world, but in fact have deep historical roots. But during the first decades of Asian American Studies as a formal field of study, Asian Americanist historians emphasized the U.S. side of their narratives. This was an understandable strategy at a time when our professors and colleagues routinely confused Asian American Studies with Asian Studies. Although this problem has not entirely disappeared, the marked increase of campuses offering courses and even degrees in Asian American subjects and, quite significantly, the number of tenure-track and tenured Asian Americanist positions attest to its establishment as a legitimate and distinct field of study. We should thus consider this greater academic acceptance of Asian American Studies, as well as the larger trend of examining the rapid changes in our world, to account for the recent "transnational turn" in Asian American historiography.

Transnational Asian American history can and has taken many different forms, encompassing a huge variety of projects, ethnic groups, nations, questions, and methodologies, but we believe it would be useful to begin specifying and identifying the hallmarks of transnational Asian American history. These are works that incorporate some or all of the following characteristics:

- Relate histories about Asians in the Americas and their ongoing economic, cultural, ethnic, and political networks and relationships with those in Asia.

- Provide substantial focus on the stories and historical contexts in Asia as well as in the Americas. This characteristic presumes non-English language training and multinational archival research.

- Examine Asian migration to the Americas and its impact on Asia and on U.S.-Asia relations.

- De-center the state, but do so without ignoring state power.

- Investigate migratory circuits and border crossings—not only across the Pacific but also across the Atlantic and within the Western hemisphere.

- Emphasize the mutual, interactive nature of cultural, institutional, and economic flows. In this respect, transnational histories are not merely comparative, looking at parallel developments across national borders. They seek as well to illuminate the connections that bind people and places to each other.

Within the field of Asian American history, scholars have employed transnational frameworks to re-examine a multitude of issues. First, there is work that is explicitly and traditionally transnational in scope and methodology, meaning that it focuses on migrant social, economic, cultural, and political networks, processes, or institutions that transcend national borders. These works, researched in multiple locations and sometimes multiple languages, pay close attention to one immigrant group's ongoing negotiation between the U.S. and their homeland—or the ways in which developments in one nation are inextricably linked to migrant lives in another. One good recent example is Madeline Hsu's *Dreaming of Gold, Dreaming of Home,* which illustrates how Chinese immigrants lived interconnected lives between the United States and China, made possible through remittances and transnational communication and transportation systems. Hsu's work explicitly draws our attention to one of the key aspects of transnationalism: the migrants' simultaneous incorporation into their states of origin and settlement and the interconnected and transnational "social fields" that result. Similarly, Adam McKeown's work focuses on transnational migrant networks in order to understand how "social formations ... are directly embedded in social processes at a global scale."

Another type of transnational scholarship uses the international context—the state relations between two or more nations—to examine their impact on Asian Americans. Ji-yeon Yuh's study of Korean camptown prostitution, Korean military brides, and the unequal and "neoimperialist relationship" between the U.S. and South Korea is one excellent example that connects private lives to international relations. As Yuh argues, "Korean military brides have been on the front line of Korea-U.S. cultural and social contact for the past half-century." This type of work usually requires a methodology that Catherine Ceniza Choy calls a "two shores" approach. Her work on Filipina nurse migration employed extensive archival research, ethnographic fieldwork, and oral histories on both sides of the Pacific Ocean to explain how American colonialism in the Philippines shaped the migration of nurses to the U.S. beginning in the early twentieth century and continuing into the present.

The analysis in Christina Klein's *Cold War Orientalism* is also located in an international context. She illustrates how representations of Asia that promoted integration, adoption, and assimilation during the Cold War justified the growth of U.S. power in Asia. But while her work is definitely valuable, even complimentary, to Asian Americanists doing transnational history, should it be categorized as transnational? Klein thinks it should be, with good cause. Even though she looks at U.S. public discourse, culture, and foreign policies in her book, she explores "the idea of America in the world" and "America as it relates to other countries and peoples." Yet this argument still raises the issue of whether we should categorize cultural histories that look primarily—if not entirely—at one nation as transnational if the histories do not substantively study the reception of culture, ideas, or policies in other countries. Must transnational histories denote some sort of mutual exchange and influence? We are not decided about this question, but thought it important to raise this issue for further discussion.

One last category of transnational Asian American history is diasporic in nature and seeks to define and track migrant streams, networks, and cultural production, among other things, on a broad, even global scale. Encyclopedic projects, such as Lynn Pan's *Encyclopedia of the Chinese Overseas* (Harvard, 1999) or Akemi Kikumura-Yano's *Encyclopedia of Japanese Descendants in the Americas: an Illustrated History of the Nikkei* (Alta Mira, 2002) represent the first stage in simply documenting the various migrant communities and in interpreting these groups on larger geographic scales. Adam McKeown's work on the Chinese diaspora compares migrant networks within a global framework in order to serve as a corrective to Chinese-language scholarship that emphasizes enduring ties to China and to Asian American history, which he critiques as being "America-centered."

As the examples above show, a transnational framework deepens Asian American history and has allowed Asian Americanists to make their narratives more complex, nuanced, and historically accurate. There are many other works not mentioned here that have greatly contributed to our understandings of transnational Asian American history. The fact that we cannot survey all of them is evidence of the strength of the field.

The transnational framework, moreover, encourages Asian Americanist historians to ask and research different questions, as well as challenge presumptions inherent in U.S.-centric studies. Paying more attention to the story beyond U.S. borders forces us to rethink established narratives about the Asian American experience. Sucheta Mazumdar demonstrates, for example, that a transnational focus on the historical context in China and India disputes the notion that the existence of racist restrictions primarily explains why Chinese and Indian women did not emigrate to the U.S. in the nineteenth and early twentieth centuries. As Mazumdar points out, Chinese and Indian women were not emigrating in large numbers to any place at this time. Vital to household economies that would collapse without them, lower-class and lower-caste women were indispensable on Guangdong and Punjabi farms. But since men's labor was more replaceable, a common family strategy had sons—especially younger sons—sojourn abroad and send remittances to buy more land or ensure "survival in an economy where the cash nexus had been amplified through global economic processes." Thus, by analyzing historical contexts beyond a single nation-state, transnational studies have been heralding a paradigmatic shift about border flows and migratory circuits in Asian American history.

Although it has been important to encourage scholars to shift their perspectives away from the nation, there is a danger, however, in eschewing the salience of the nation and of national borders altogether. As Erika Lee has written elsewhere, prior to World War Two and during an era of increased regulation of international migration by nation-states, the maintenance of transnational migration patterns, ties, and networks by Asian migrants was certainly possible, but only under certain prescribed limitations." Sau-ling Wong has also criticized diasporic studies that celebrate the crossing of borders while ignoring the continuing salience of race and racism produced by nation-states.

An approach that considers diasporic communities and transnational migration, networks, and culture *within* an Asian American Studies framework recognizes the continuing importance of the nation on and to Asian American subjects. Here, lessons from the work of cultural studies scholars such as Jigna Desai are instructive. In *Beyond Bollywood,* Desai locates the South Asian diaspora and diasporic film in the "Brown Atlantic" between India (and other parts of South Asia), Britain, the United States, and Canada. Approaching the transnational through the lens of post-national American Studies, Desai calls for the "foregrounding of transnational and international dimensions of the United States and the Americas," rather than foregoing the nation-state altogether. She suggests that we should explore the relationship between racialization and transnationality in order to produce Asian American Studies scholarship that moves "beyond simple claims of nationalism or generalized disavowals of the nation-state," and instead "recognizes their mutual implications and dependencies."...

The challenge for Asian Americanists is clear. We must continue to preserve and reclaim lost and marginalized histories, placing them within a larger framework of race, class, gender, and sexuality in the United States. But whenever possible, we should also expand our vision beyond U.S. borders to explain why and how transnational linkages were maintained across the Pacific with Asia, north and south within the Americas, and around the world.

☾ FURTHER READING

"Asian American History in Transnational Perspective," research forum, *Pacific Historical Review* 76 (2007).

Campomanes, Oscar V. "New Formations of Asian American Studies and the Question of U.S. Imperialism," *Positions: East Asia Cultures Critique* 5 (1997): 3–18.

Chan, Sucheng, "Asian American Historiography," *Pacific Historical Review* 65 (1996): 363–399.

———. *Asian Americans: An Interpretive History* (1991).

Chang, Gordon H. "Asian Immigrants and American Foreign Relations," in *Pacific Passages: The Study of American-East Asian Relations on the Eve of the Twenty-First Century*, ed. Warren I. Cohen (1996): 103–118.

"Conversations on Transpacific History," special issue, *Pacific Historical Review* 83 (2014).

Cumings, Bruce. *Dominion from Sea to Sea: Pacific Ascendancy and American Power* (2009).

Daniels, Roger. *Asian America: Chinese and Japanese in the United States Since 1850* (1988).

———. "No Lamps Were Lit for Them: Angel Island and the Historiography of Asian American Immigration," *Journal of American Ethnic History* 17 (1997): 3–18.

Dirlik, Arif. "Asians on the Rim: Transnational Capital and Local Community in the Making of Contemporary Asian America," *Amerasia Journal* 22 (1996): 1–24.

Hing, Bill Ong. *Making and Remaking Asian America Through Immigration Policy, 1850–1990* (1993).

"Histories and Historians in the Making," special issue, *Amerasia Journal* 26 (2000).

Hune, Shirley. *Pacific Migration to the United States: Trends and Themes in Historical and Sociological Literature*, Research Institute on Immigration and Ethnic Studies, Smithsonian Institution (1977).

Jensen, Joan M. "Women on the Pacific Rim: Some Thoughts on Border Crossings," *Pacific Historical Review* 67 (1998): 3–38.

Lee, Robert G. *Orientals: Asian Americans in Popular Culture* (1999).

Lee, Shelley Sang-Hee. *A New History of Asian America* (2013).

Okihiro, Gary Y. *The Columbia Guide to Asian American History* (2001).

———. *Margins and Mainstreams: Asians in American History and Culture* (1994).

Ong, Paul, et al. *The New Asian Immigration in Los Angeles and Global Restructuring* (1994).

Parrenas, Rhacel and Lok C.D. Siu. *Asian Diasporas: New Formations, New Conceptions* (2007).

Takaki, Ronald. *Strangers from a Different Shore: A History of Asian Americans* (1989).

"What Is Transnational Asian American History? Recent Trends and Challenges," special issue, *Journal of Asian American Studies* 8 (2005).

Wong, Sau-Ling C. "Denationalization Reconsidered: Asian American Cultural Criticism at a Theoretical Crossroads," *Amerasia Journal* 21 (1995): 1–27.

Yanagisako, Sylvia. "Transforming Orientalism: Gender, Nationality, and Class in Asian American Studies," in *Naturalizing Power: Essays in Feminist Cultural Analysis*, eds. Sylvia Yanagisako and Carol Delany (1995): 275–298.

CHAPTER 2

Transpacific Crossings, 1688–1883

The narrative of Asian American history has three primary starting points. The earliest is in the sixteenth century, when large wind-powered Spanish ships (galleons) began transporting sailors, travelers, and captives from the Philippines to the New World. Another is two centuries later with the inauguration of trade relations between China and the new nation of the United States in the 1780s. And the third is in the mid-nineteenth century with the start of sustained labor migrations from Asia to the United States and Hawai'i. The common denominator for each of these starting points is the long-term global transformations set in motion by Christopher Columbus's historic voyages across the Atlantic Ocean, beginning in 1492. Columbus, who was seeking a new trade route from Europe to East and Southeast Asia, opened up the modern era of transoceanic exploration and commerce, which contributed to Europe's rise over and above the great civilizations of East Asia, Africa, Mesoamerica, Peru, and the Middle East. Asian American history was made possible by the development of this ocean world as it played out in and across the Pacific.

In colonizing what would be called the Philippine Islands, Spain created the conditions through which 40,000 to 100,000 peoples from Asia would end up in the country's New World territories. Some of these migrants came as slaves locked away in the holds of Spanish galleons crossing the Pacific to Mexico. Known collectively as "chinos" (Chinese), the slaves in Mexico were actually from diverse backgrounds, and included indigenous peoples and Muslims (Moros) in the Philippines, Southeast Asians, and South Asians. One of the most famous slaves, Catarina de San Juan, was originally from India. Soon after her death in 1688, the chinos were reclassified as "Indians" in Mexico, which ended their status as slaves. In death, Catarina became a beloved saint, known for originating the still renowned Mexican woman's dress—the colorful China poblana. *Legend has it that a few of the Filipinos who crossed with the galleons in the late eighteenth century made their way to what would become the state of Louisiana to establish what might be one of the first Asian American communities. While this community was real, evidence suggests that it originated from the mid-nineteenth century, much later than has been believed and decades after the galleon trade ended in 1815.*

After its founding in 1776, the United States looked to the Pacific as a key source of commerce. Americans played an active role in the China trade and Pacific whaling ventures, which made it possible for individual Chinese and Pacific Islander sailors to venture to the new nation on American ships. Beginning in the early nineteenth century, contract laborers from China and India were brought to work on Latin American and Caribbean plantations. Known as "coolies,"[1] these highly exploited laborers provided an alternative to African slavery, which before then had been abolished in the French empire and which, by the 1830s, would be banned in newly independent Latin American nations like Mexico and throughout the British Empire.

Some coolies were exported to Hawai'i sugar plantations. Brought into the transpacific world system in the late eighteenth century by the British explorer Captain James Cook, the Kingdom of Hawai'i underwent dramatic social, economic, and political changes after contact with foreigners. Like indigenous peoples everywhere, Hawaiians suffered from deadly diseases, which precipitated major population decline. In addition, they experienced resource depletion and the introduction of foreign enterprises, work routines, languages, life-styles, schooling, and religions. In Hawai'i, unlike in the United States, Asians, by the late nineteenth century, constituted a numerical majority.

The vast majority of Asian workers who came to the United States were free migrants, not coolies. The economic development of the nation's West Coast also spurred Asian migration, which for most of the nineteenth century came from China. Perhaps the best known of all the early Asian migrants were the Chinese attracted by the California Gold Rush and recruited to build the first Transcontinental, Railroad. These migrants created ethnic communities that became nodes in a network spreading across the Americas and back to southern China, from which almost all overseas Chinese descended. This Chinese diaspora (those living outside the homeland) also included communities in Australia, Japan, and especially Southeast Asia—the site of the largest and oldest Chinese diasporic communities. By the late nineteenth century, trade routes from California to China, which included refueling in Hawai'i, had become busy trans-pacific highways in which massive, reliable, and relatively fast steam-powered ships carried migrants and traders, as well as goods, ideas, and cultures. Such transportation networks provided the infrastructure that shaped Asian American history in the modern Pacific world.

☀DOCUMENTS

From 1565 to 1815, Spanish galleons circulated in the Pacific one or two times per year. The ships departed from Acapulco, Mexico, loaded with silver and gold mined in New Spain that Chinese traders in Manila exchanged as payment for spices, porcelain, ivory, lacquerware, processed silk cloth, and other valuable commodities that would make the return voyage back to Mexico. In Document 1, a seventeenth-century Spanish visitor, Jesuit Father Colín, describes the remarkable

---

[1] A term, which many scholars think originated in India and was put into currency by Portuguese traders in Asia, describing the lowest class of workers.

global port of Manila, where goods and slaves from across Asia and the Americas were exchanged. The growth of this thriving port city was due to the lucrative galleon trade that centered on the exchange of Mexican currency (silver and gold) for Chinese merchandise.

The transpacific China trade remained popular after the Manila galleons ceased operations. In the late eighteenth century, founders of the United States, such as Benjamin Franklin, were hopeful that a robust trade with China would give the new nation a solid economic foundation to compete with England's dominant East India Company. Document 2 is a report of the first U.S. vessel to trade with China, a voyage sponsored by private investors that carried national significance. While leaders during the early republic saw China as a great economic hope for their nation, they did not see the need for Chinese immigrants because the original thirteen colonies, now states, benefitted from the labor of African slaves, as well as from contract labor in the form of British and European indentured servants. Document 3 reveals that the nation's founders granted eligibility to U.S. citizenship only for a "free white person" of "good character." Such criteria were designed to exclude free blacks, white indentured servants, convicts, and the poor; they unwittingly also barred Asians.

The next two documents address the impact that heightened transpacific traffic had on the Hawaiian Islands. Some of the changes wrought by foreign trade were welcomed by the native Hawaiians, while others raised concerns, as Document 4 shows in the debate between the Hawaiian Privy Council and the common people. By 1848, the debate was settled in favor of foreign landholding through the enactment by King Kamehameha III of land redistribution (Mahele). Document 5 shows that American and other foreign ambitions to transform Hawai'i into a profitable sugar economy undergirded land reform efforts.

Given the diseases that decimated Native Hawaiian populations, foreign agriculture on the islands came to rely upon Chinese and other Asian labor. Labor shortages throughout the U.S. West also compelled the country's leaders to imagine developing this vast frontier region with Chinese immigrant workers. Document 6 offers the fantastic vision of one influential New York senator, William Seward, who, like Benjamin Franklin and others of the founding generation, saw Chinese trade, and now immigration, as key for enabling the United States to surpass the power of the almighty British Empire. How the Chinese immigrants felt about developing the western frontier was altogether different and is largely lost to history because of the lack of records left behind by those who ventured across the Pacific. Documents 7 and 8 are songs written by the Chinese that provide glimpses of the anxieties they and their wives left behind in China faced as they sought to get rich in "Gold Mountain."

Equally difficult to research are the supposed Filipino descendants of the Manila galleon trade who founded one of the first Asian American communities. Document 9, written in 1883 by a white journalist who was more interested in exotic adventure than historical accuracy, is one of the earliest accounts of Filipino Americans in Louisiana.

1. Spanish Visitor Describes the Philippine Market, 1663

Manila is the equal of any other emporium of our monarchy, for it is the center to which flows the riches of the Orient and the Occident, the silver of Peru and New Spain; the pearls and precious stones of India; the diamonds of Narsinga and Goa; the rubies, sapphires and topazes, and the cinnamon of Ceylon; the pepper of Sumatra and the Javas; the cloves, nutmegs and other spices of the Moluccas and Banda; the fine Persina silks and wool and carpets from Ormuz and Malabar; rich hangings and bed coverings of Bengal; fine camphor of Borneo; balsam and ivory of Abada and Cambodia, [...] and from Great China silks of all kinds, raw and woven in velvets and figured damasks, taffetas and other cloths of every texture, design and colors, linens and cotton fabrics, gilt-decorated articles, embroideries and porcelains, and other riches and curiosities of great value and esteem; from Japan, amber, varicolored skills, writing desks, boxes and tables of precious woods, lacquered and with curious decorations; and very fine silverware.

2. Manager of Cargo Reports on First U.S. Ship to Trade with China, 1785

On the 22 February 1784, the ship sailed from New York, and arrived the 21 March at St. Iago, the principal of the Cape de Verd Islands. Having paid our respects to the Portuguese Vice Roy, and with his permission, taken such refreshments as were necessary, we left those Islands on the 27th and pursued our voyage. After a pleasant passage, in which nothing extraordinary occurred, we came to anchor in the Streights of Sunda, on the 18th of July. It was no small addition to our happiness on this occasion, to meet there two ships belonging to our good Allies the French. The commodore, Monsieur D'Ordelin, and his officers, welcomed us in the most affectionate manner, and as his own ship was immediately bound to Canton, gave us an invitation to go in company with him. This friendly offer we most cheerfully accepted, and the Commodore furnished us with his signals by day and Night, and added such instructions for our Passage through the Chinese Seas, as would have been exceedingly beneficial, had any unfortunate accident occasioned our separation. Happily we pursued our route together. On our arrival at the Island of Macao, the French Consul for China, Monsieur Vieillard, with some other Gentlemen of his Nation came on board to Congratulate and Welcome us to that part of the World, and kindly undertook the introduction of the Americans to the Portuguse Governor. The little time that we were there was entirely taken up by the good offices of the Consul, the Gentlemen of his Nation, and those of the Swedes and

Excerpt from Evelyn Hu-DeHart and Kathleen Lopez, "Asian Diasporas in Latin America and the Caribbean: An Historical Overview," *Afro-Hispanic Review* 27, 1 (Spring 2008), p. 9.

From Samuel Shaw to John Jay, May 19, 1785, in *Papers of the Continental Congress*, item 120, v. 1, pp. 281–289 (letterbook copy); M40, reel 1, *National Archives*; reprinted, Mary A. Guinta (ed.), *Documents of the Emerging Nation: U.S. Foreign Relations, 1775–1789* (Wilmington, DE: Scholarly Resources, 1998), 241–245.

Imperialists, who still remained at Macao. The other Europeans had repaired to Canton. Three Days afterwards we finished our outward bound Voyage....

The Day of our arrival at Canton, August 30th and the two following Days, we were visited by the Chinese Merchants, and the Chiefs and Gentlemen of the several European Establishments and treated by them in all respects as a free and independent Nation. As such during our stay we were universally considered. The Chinese themselves were very indulgent towards us, though our being the first American ship that had ever visited China, it was some time before they could fully comprehend the distinction between English men and us. They styled us the *New People* and when by the map we conveyed to them an Idea of the extent of our Country, with its present and increasing population, they were highly pleased at the prospect of so considerable a market for the productions of theirs.

The Situation of the Europeans at Canton is so well known as to render a detail unnecessary. The good understanding commonly subsisting between them and the Chinese was in some degree interrupted by two occurrences, of which, as they were extraordinary in themselves, and led to a more full investigation of the American Character, by both Parties, than might otherwise have taken place, I will, with your permission, give a particular Account.

The Police at Canton is at all times extremely strict, and the Europeans residing there are circumscribed within very narrow limits. The latter had observed with Concern some circumstances which they deemed an encroach-ment upon their rights. On this consideration they determined to apply for redress to the Hoppo, who is the head officer of the Customs, the next time he should Visit the Shipping. Deputies accordingly attended from every Nation, and I was desired to represent ours. We met the Hoppo on board an English ship, and the causes of complaint were soon after removed.

The other occurrence of which I beg leave to take notice gave rise to what was commonly called the Canton War, which threatened to be productive of very serious Consequences. On the 25 November an English ship, in saluting some Com-pany that had dined on board, killed a Chinese, and wounded two others, in the Mandarine's Boat along side. It is a Maxim of the Chinese Law that Blood must answer for Blood, in pursuance of which they demanded the unfortunate Gunner. To give up this Poor man was to consign him to certain Death. Humanity pleaded powerfully against the measure. After repeated conferences between the English and the Chinese, the latter declared themselves satisfied, and the affair was supposed to be entirely settled. Notwithstanding this, on the morning after the last Conference, (the 27th) the supercargo [manager] of the Ship was seized, while attending his Business, thrown into a Sedan Chair, hurried into the City and committed to Prison. Such an outrage on personal Liberty spread a general alarm, and the Europeans unanimously agreed to send for their Boats with armed men from the shipping, for the security of themselves and Property, until the matter should be brought to a conclusion. The Boats accordingly came, and ours among the number; one of which was fired on and a man Wounded. All Trade was stopped, and the Chinese men of war drawn up opposite the Factories [trading posts]. The Europeans demanded the restoration of Mr. Smith, which the Chinese refused, until the Gunner should be given up. In the mean while, the Troops of the Province were collecting in the Neighbourhood of Canton—the Chinese servants were ordered by the Magistrates to leave the factories—the Gates of the suburbs were shut—all intercourse was at an end—the Naval force was increased—many Troops were embarked in boats, ready for landing—and every thing wore the appearance of War. To what extremities matters might have been carried, had not a negociation taken place, no one can say. The Chinese asked a conference with all the Nations, except the English. A deputation, in which I was included for America, met the *Fuen* who is the head Magistrate of Canton, with the principal officers of the Province—After setting forth, by an interpreter, the power of the Emperor, and his own determination to support the Laws, he demanded that the Gunner should be given up within three days, declaring that he should have an impartial examination before their Tribunal, and if it appeared that the affair was accidental he should be released unhurt. In the mean time he gave permission for the Trade, excepting that of the English, to go on as usual, and dismissed us with a present of two pieces of silk to each, as a mark of his friendly disposition. The other Nations, one after another, sent away their Boats, under protection of a Chinese flag, and pursued their Business as before. The English were obliged to submit—the Gunner was given up—Mr. Smith was released—and the English, after being forced to ask pardon of the Magistracy of Canton, in presence of the other Nations, had their Commerce restored. On this occasion, I am happy that we were the last who sent off our boat, which was not disgraced with a Chinese Flag; nor did she go until the English themselves thanked us for our concurrence with them, and advised to the sending her away. After peace was restored, the Chief and four English Gentlemen visited the several Nations, among whom we were included, and thanked them for their assistance during the Troubles. The Gunner remained with the Chinese—his fate undetermined.

Notwithstanding the treatment we received from all parties was perfectly Civil and respectful, yet it was with peculiar satisfaction that we experienced, on every occasion, from our good Allies the French the most flattering and substantial proofs of their friendship. "If, said they, we have in any instance been serviceable to you, we are happy—and we desire nothing more ardently than further opportunities to convince you of our affection." The harmony maintained between them and us was particularly noticed by the English, who more than once observed, that it was [a] matter of astonishment to them, that the descendants of Britains would so soon divest themselves of prejudices, which they had thought to be not only hereditary, but inherent in our Nature.

We left Canton the 27 December, and on our return refreshed at the Cape of Good Hope, where we found a most friendly reception. After remaining there five Days, we Sailed for America and arrived in this Port on the 11th Instant.

To every Lover of his Country, as well as to those more immediately concerned in Commerce, it must be a pleasing reflection, that a communication is thus happily opened between us and the Eastern Extreme of the Globe; and it adds very sensibly to the pleasure of this reflection, that the Voyage has been performed in so short a space of time, and attended with the loss only of one man....

Permit me, Sir, to accompany this Letter with the two pieces of silk, presented to me by the *Fuen* of Canton, as a mark of his good disposition towards the American Nation. In that view, I consider myself as peculiarly honored in being charged with this testimony of the friendship of the Chinese for a People, who may in a few Years prosecute a Commerce with the Subjects of that Empire, under advantages equal if not superior to those enjoyed by any other Nation whatever.

3. U.S. Bases Citizenship on Race, 1790

An Act to establish an uniform Rule of Naturalization.

SECTION 1. *Be it enacted by the Senate and House of Representatives of the United States of America in Congress assembled,* That any alien, being a free white person, who shall have resided within the limits and under the jurisdiction of the United States for the term of two years, may be admitted to become a citizen thereof, on application to any common law court of record, in any one of the states wherein he shall have resided for the term of one year at least, and making proof to the satisfaction of such court, that he is a person of good character, and taking the oath or affirmation prescribed by law, to support the constitution of the United States, which oath or affirmation such court shall administer; and the clerk of such court shall record such application, and the proceedings thereon; and thereupon such person shall be considered as a citizen of the United States. And the children of such persons so naturalized, dwelling within the United States, being under the age of twenty-one years at the time of such naturalization, shall also be considered as citizens of the United States. And the children of citizens of the United States, that may be born beyond sea, or out of the limits of the United States, shall be considered as natural born citizens: *Provided,* That the right of citizenship shall not descend to persons whose fathers have never been resident in the United States: *Provided also,* That no person heretofore proscribed by any state, shall be admitted a citizen as aforesaid, except by an act of the legislature of the state in which such person was proscribed.(*a*)

APPROVED, March 26, 1790.

4. Hawaiians Petition the Privy Council to Halt Foreign Influence in the Islands, and Council Replies, 1845

Translated from the Elele, for the Friend.

A PETITION TO YOUR GRACIOUS MAJESTY, KAMEHAMEHA III., AND TO ALL YOUR CHIEFS IN COUNCIL ASSEMBLED.

To His Majesty Kamehameha III., and the Premeir Kekauluohi, and all the Hawaiian Chiefs in council assembled; on account of our anxiety, we petition you, the father of the Hawaiian kingdom, and the following is our petition.

1. Concerning the independence of your kingdom.

2. That you dismiss the foreign officers whom you have appointed to be Hawaiian officers.

3. We do not wish foreigners to take the oath of allegiance and become Hawaiian subjects.

From *An Act to Establish an Uniform Rule of Naturalization*, March 26, 1790, in Public Laws, 1st Congress, 1 Stat. 103 (chapter 3).

From *The Friend*, August, 1845.

4. We do not wish you to sell any more land pertaining to your kingdom to foreigners.

5. We do not wish taxes in a confused obscure manner to be imposed in your kingdom.

6. This is the cause of our wishing to dismiss these foreign officers. On account of difficulties and apprehensions of burdens that will come upon us. There are your chiefs, who may be officers under you, like as their fathers were under your father, Kamehameha I., and good and intelligent men, in whom you have confidence; let these be officers.

Therefore we make known unto your most gracious Majesty, and to the Premeir Kekauluohi, and to all the chiefs of the Hawaiian kingdom, some of our thoughts relative to the above named articles.

1. Concerning the independence of the Hawaiian kingdom.

We assure your Majesty, and the Premeir Kekauluohi, and the Chiefs and all your common people that we understand your kingdom to be independent. You and your Chiefs perceived the perilous situation of the Hawaiian kingdom in reference to foreigners. Therefore you sent one of your own men and a foreigner, viz: T. Haalilio and Mr. Richards, respectfully to beseech large independent nations that your nation might be independent. These large nations, viz: the United States, Great Britain, France and Belgium, have declared your kingdom to be independent. By this distinct expression, that these large nations have declared the independence of the Hawaiian kingdom, therefore it is very clear to us, that it is not proper that any foreigner should come in and be promoted in your kingdom, among your Chiefs, and your people. But that it be according to the petition of the ministers, whom you sent to these large nations, praying that the Hawaiian kingdom might be independent by itself.

This is independence; that your gracious Majesty, Kamehameha III. be King, and the Chiefs of your kingdom be your assistants, and also your own people.

Thus may you and your Chiefs act, that your kingdom and all your people may be blessed.

On account of these our thoughts, we petition and beseech you and your Chiefs.—

We the common people of your kingdom hereby subscribe our names.

[It is said that over 1600 names were subscribed to this petition.]

———

REPLY OF THE COUNCIL ASSEMBLED TO THE PETITION.

JULY 3d, 1845.

To His Majesty and to the Nobles of the Council assembled, and to the delegates of the common people.

This is our reply to the petition of the common people of Lahaina, and Wailuku and Kailua, and it is submitted for your approbation or disapprobation.

1. "Concerning the independence of your kingdom."

This is the meaning of independence;— that Kamehameha III. be King of the Hawaiian Islands, and there be no other King over him. This is the reason of the independence; Great Britain and France, America and Belgium say that "the Hawaiian government are qualified to transact business with foreigners."

How can they transact business with foreigners? In this way only; let His Majesty select persons skilful like those from other lands to transact business with them.

2. "That you dismiss the foreign officers whom you have chosen to be Hawaiian officers."

If these shall be dismissed, where is there a man who is qualified to transact business with foreigners? There is no one to be found at the present time; hereafter perhaps the young chiefs will be qualified, when they have grown up to manhood, and shall have completed their education.

3. "We do not wish foreigners to take the oath of allegiance and become Hawaiian subjects."

Shall foreigners who become officers take the oath? If not, then they have a chief in another land, and Kamehameha III. is not their proper sovereign, and they will not act righteously between the King and their own countrymen. But if they take the oath of allegiance to Kamehameha III., will they not be faithful to him. And will they not cease to have regard for the chief they have forsaken!

Shall other foreigners take the oath of allegiance? This is a land which lies where ships in the Pacific ocean often come. Shall not foreigners come on shore? They do come on shore. Can they not be permitted to live on shore?— According to the treaties they can. Who shall be their proper sovereign? Will not difficulties arise between some of them and the Hawaiians? Difficulties will arise, for formerly there were many difficulties, and the land was taken; it was not taken because the government was really in the wrong, but because evil was sought. Here is the difficulty which ruins the government, viz: the complaint of foreign governments followed by the infliction of punishment. Foreigners who take the oath of allegiance can apply to only one sovereign, viz: Kamehameha III.; he will adjust their difficulties in a proper manner, and they will render important services to Hawaii, their land.

Some say, let none but good foreigners take the oath of allegiance. How then shall it be with those who are not good? Shall they not live on shore? How can they be driven off? Shall they be put on board another man's ship? If so, the owners will forsake the ship, and the government must pay the damages. Messrs. Bachelot and Short were thus treated, and the result was a fine of $20,000.

Let no one have apprehensions concerning those who take the oath of allegiance. It they conduct properly, then the land is blessed by them. If they transgress, here are laws to punish them, and there is no other nation which will interfere in behalf of wicked foreigners, when we punish them. Here is wherein other nations will favour us; they will not take the part of their people, who transgress our laws, neither will they punish us without a cause, as they did formerly.

4. "We do not wish you to sell any more land pertaining to your kingdom to foreigners."

This is our opinion; it is by no means proper to sell land to aliens, nor is it proper to give them land, for the land belongs to Kamehameha III.; there is no chief over him. But we think it is proper to sell land to his Majesty's people, that they may have a home. But if these persons wish to sell their lands again, they cannot sell to aliens, for there is only one sovereign over those who hold lands; but if the people wish to sell to those who have taken the oath of allegiance, they can do so, for Kamehameha III. is King over them. If his Majesty thinks it expedient to sell lands to his own people, is it proper for him to refuse another, who has forsaken the land of his birth, and his first chief, and become a Hawaiian subject? By no means, for this would be using partiality. There has not been much land sold, but foreigners have heretofore occupied lands through favor, without purchasing. It is better to sell. The people have not thought much about purchasing lands; but those who have been to the Columbia River [in the Pacific Northwest], see the advantage of purchasing land, and they will here-after wish to purchase lands....

This is our reply to the petition laid before you, with due reverence.

JOHN YOUNG.

JOHN II

This reply was corrected and approved by the assembly of chiefs and dele-gates of the common people in the hall of legislation, on the 8th of July, 1845, with no dissenting voice.

KAMEHAMEHA.

5. Foreign Experts Stress Optimism for Agriculture in Hawai'i, 1850

For years past the agricultural interests of these islands have been insignificant and their pursuit unprofitable. With an uncertain and distant market—with little or no encouragement or facilities given to foreign tillers of the soil, without proper knowledge of that soil, or sufficient capital to experiment upon its capabilities, most of the agricultural enterprises here have languished or utterly failed.

Within the last two years, however, a great nation has grown up, and a sudden change has taken place in the prospects of this group. The extension of the territory and government of the United States to the borders of the Pacific, the wonderful discoveries in California, and the consequent, almost instantaneous creation of a mighty state on the western front of the American Union has, as it were, with the wand of a magician, drawn this little group into the very focus of civilization and prosperity. We find ourselves suddenly surrounded by intelligent, enterprising neighbors who call loudly to us to furnish of our abundance and receive in exchange of theirs. Our coffee and sugar no longer remain piled in our warehouses. Our fruits and vegetables no longer decay on the spot where they were grown. We are not even compelled to seek for them a market, but clamorous purchasers come to our very doors and carry off our supplies with an eagerness that has caused us to feel a scarcity ourselves, and we are assured that not only for all these, but for any other products of the soil that we will raise, a ready and increasing demand may be relied

From Josephine Sullivan, *A History of C. Brewer and Company, Limited: One Hundred Years in the Hawaiian Islands, 1826–1926* (Boston: Walton Advertising and Printing, 1926), 104–105.

on from our enterprising neighbors. The native government is relaxing its former tenacious grasp on the arable lands of the islands, and even inviting and encouraging their cultivation by foreign skill and capital.

With these brilliant prospects suddenly opening to these islands ... we find the agricultural operations checked and embarrassed by the insufficiency of the four great requisites—capital, experience, proper implements, and labor.

It is a fact worthy of remark that as your committee believe, without a single exception, all the sugar plantations that have been commenced at these islands have been so commenced by persons possessing neither experience in the business they were undertaking, nor the requisite capital and knowledge of the soil, to carry it through to a successful result.

Large sums of money have been thrown away, experiments which the experience of persons acquainted with the business would have enabled them to avoid, and no system of intercourse between the planters has been established by which the experience of one could be rendered available to another. And these are the great drawbacks from progress now.

To meet these difficulties, to provide for these wants, to render the experience of other countries available to this, to supply by a combined action, facilities and information *to all*, which cannot be procured by individuals, to encourage and foster agricultural operations in every form, are the main objects of the proposed association.

The improvement of the breed of cattle, horses, swine, sheep, poultry, etc., is another great object of the [new agricultural] society. Stated annual exhibitions could be held, and encouragement given to farmers and planters, by premiums being awarded for superior specimens of their products.

Another subject of great importance before this association is that of *Labor*. The introduction of coolie labor from China to supply the places of the rapidly decreasing native population is a question that is already agitated amongst us, and should such a step become necessary, the aid of such an association in accomplishing this object would be of great benefit.

6. Senator Wants Millions of Chinese Laborers in the United States, 1852

Sir, have you looked recently at the China trade? It reaches already seven millions in value annually. Have you watched the California trade? Its exports in bullion alone already exceeds $50,000,000 annually, and as yet the mineral development of that State has only begun. The settlement of the Pacific coast is in a state of sheer infancy. There is, speaking relatively, neither capital nor labor there adequate to exhibit the forces of industry that might be employed in that wonderful region. Nor is California yet conveniently

From William H. Seward, "Commerce in the Pacific Ocean Speech," *Congressional Globe*, 32nd Congress, 1st Session, July 30, 1852.

accessible. The railway across Panama is not yet completed. The passage through Nicaragua is not perfect; that which leads through Tehuantepec [in Mexico] is not begun; nor have we yet extended, even so far as to the Mississippi, the most important and necessary one of them all, the railroad across our own country to San Francisco. The emigrant to the Atlantic coast arrives speedily and cheaply from whatever quarter of the world; while he who would seek the Pacific shore, encounters charges and delays which few can sustain. Nevertheless, the commercial, social, and political movements of the world are now in the direction of California. Separated as it is from us by foreign lands, or more impassable mountains, we are establishing there a custom-house, a mint, a dry-dock, Indian agencies, and ordinary and extraordinary tribunals of justice. Without waiting for perfect or safe channels, a strong and steady stream of emigration flows thither from every State and every district eastward of the Rocky Mountains. Similar torrents of emigration are pouring into California and Australia from the South American States, from Europe, and from Asia. This movement is not a sudden, or accidental, or irregular, or convulsive one; but it is one for which men and nature have been preparing through near four hundred years. During all that time merchants and princes have been seeking how they could reach cheaply and expeditiously, "Cathay," "China," "the East," that intercourse and commerce might be established between its ancient nations and the newer ones of the West. To these objects Da Gama, Columbus, Americus [Amerigo], Cabot, Hudson, and other navigators, devoted their talents, their labors, and their lives. Even the discovery of this continent and its islands, and the organization of society and government upon them, grand and important as those events have been, were but conditional, preliminary, and ancillary to the more sublime result, now in the act of consummation—the reunion of the two civilizations, which, having parted on the plains of Asia four thousand years ago, and having traveled ever afterwards in opposite directions around the world, now meet again on the coasts and islands of the Pacific ocean. Certainly no mere human event of equal dignity and importance has ever occurred upon the earth. It will be followed by the equalization of the condition of society and the restoration of the unity of the human family. We see plainly enough why this event could not have come before, and why it has come now. A certain amount of human freedom, a certain amount of human intelligence, a certain extent of human control over the physical obstacles to such a reunion, were necessary. All these conditions have happened and concurred. Liberty has developed under improved forms of government, and science has subjected Nature in Western Europe and in America. Navigation, improved by steam, enables men to outstrip the winds, and intelligence conveyed by electricity excels in velocity the light. With these favoring circumstances there has come also a sudden abundance of gold, that largely relieves labor from its long subjection to realized capital. Sir, this movement is no delusion. It will no more stop than the emigration from Europe to our own Atlantic shores has stopped, or can stop, while labor is worth there twenty cents and here fifty cents a day. Emigration from China cannot stop while labor is worth in California $5 a day, and in the West Indies $10 a month, and yet is worth in China only $5 for that period. Accordingly we have seen sixty-seven ships filled, in three months of the present year, with seventeen thousand emigrants in the ports of Hong Kong, Macao, and Whampao, and afterwards discharge them on the shores of California, and of Cuba, and other islands of the West Indies.

Sir, have you considered the basis of this movement, that this country and Australia are capable of sustaining, and need for their development, five hundred millions, while their population is confined to fifty millions, and yet that Asia has two hundred millions of excess? As for those who doubt that this great movement will quicken activity and create wealth and power in California and Oregon, I leave them to consider what changes the movements, similar in nature but inferior in force and slower in effect, have produced already on the Atlantic coast of America. As to those who cannot see how this movement will improve the condition of Asia, I leave them to reflect upon the improvements in the condition of Europe since the discovery and colonization of America. Who does not see, then, that every year hereafter, European commerce, European politics, European thoughts, and European activity, although actually gaining greater force, and European connections, although actually becoming more intimate, will, nevertheless, ultimately sink in importance; while the Pacific ocean, its shores, its islands, and the vast regions beyond, will become the chief theater of events in the world's great Hereafter? Who does not see that this movement must effect our own complete emancipation from what remains of European influence and prejudice, and in turn develop the American opinion and influence, which shall remould constitutional laws and customs in the land that is first greeted by the rising sun?...

Commerce is the great agent of this movement. Whatever nation shall put that commerce into full employment, and shall conduct it steadily with adequate expansion, will become necessarily the greatest of existing States; greater than any that has ever existed.

7. Song Captures Reasons for Chinese Sojourn to United States, 1852

In the second reign year of Haamfung [1852], a trip to Gold Mountain was made.
With a pillow on my shoulder, I began my perilous journey:
Sailing a boat with bamboo poles across the seas,
Leaving behind wife and sisters in search of money,
No longer lingering with the woman in the bedroom,
No longer paying respect to parents at home.

8. Two Songs Reveal Concerns of Wives Left in China, n.d. [late 1800s]

YIK JOOK, YEE JOOK [Song 1]

I beg of you, after you depart, to come back soon,
Our separation will be only a flash of time;
I only wish that you would have good fortune.
In three years you would be home again.

Also, I beg of you that your heart won't change,
That you keep your heart and mind on taking care of your family;
Each month or half a month send a letter home.
In two or three years my wish is to welcome you home.

[Song 2]
O, just marry all the daughters to men from Gold Mountain:
All those trunks from Gold Mountain—you can demand as many as you want!
O, don't ever marry your daughter to a man from Gold Mountain:
Lonely and sad—a cooking pot is her only companion!

9. Journalist Reveals Filipino Roots of American Community, 1883

For nearly fifty years there has existed in the southeastern swamp lands of Louisiana a certain strange settlement of Malay fishermen—Tagalas from the Philippine Islands. The place of their lacustrine village is not precisely mentioned upon maps, and the world in general ignored until a few days ago the bare fact of their amphibious existence. Even the United States mail service has never found its way thither, and even in the great city of New Orleans, less than a hundred miles distant, the people were far better informed about the Carboniferous Era than concerning the swampy affairs of this Manila village. Occasionally vague echoes of its mysterious life were borne to the civilized centre, but these were scarcely of a character to tempt investigation or encourage belief. Some voluble Italian luggermen once came to town with a short cargo of oysters, and a long story regarding a ghastly "Chinese" colony in the reedy swamps south of Lake Borgne.... In order to offer *Harper's* artist a totally novel subject of artistic study, the *Times-Democrat* of New Orleans chartered and fitted out an Italian lugger for a trip to the unexplored region in question—to the fishing station of Saint Malo. And a strange voyage it was. Even the Italian sailors knew not whither they were going, none of them had ever beheld the Manila village, or were aware of its location....

From "Yik Jook, Yee Jook," in ed. Tin-Yuke Char, *The Sandalwood Mountains: Readings and Stories of the Early Chinese in Hawaii* (Honolulu: University of Hawaii Press, 1975), 67; reprinted in Judy Yung, Gordon H. Chang, and H. Mark Lai (eds.), *Chinese American Voices: From the Gold Rush to the Present* (Berkeley: University of California Press, 2006), 8. Reprinted by permission of the University of Hawaii.

Lafcadio Hearn, "St. Malo: A Lacustrine Village in Louisiana," *Harper's Weekly*, March 31, 1883, 198–199.

Out of the shuddering reeds and banneretted grass on either side rise the fantastic houses of the Malay fishermen, poised upon slender supports above the marsh, like cranes or bitterns watching for scaly prey. Hard by the slimy mouth of the bayou extends a strange wharf, as ruined and rotted and unearthly as the timbers of the spectral ship in the "Rime of the Ancient Mariner." Odd craft huddle together beside it, fishing-nets make cobwebby drapery about the skeleton timber-work. Green are the banks, green the water is, green also with fungi every beam and plank and board and shingle of the houses upon stilts. All are built in true Manila style, with immense hat-shaped eaves and balconies, but in wood; for it had been found that palmetto and woven cane could not withstand the violence of the climate....

Such is the land: its human inhabitants are not less strange, wild, picturesque. Most of them are cinnamon-colored men; a few are glossily yellow, like that bronze into which a small proportion of gold is worked by the moulder. Their features are irregular without being actually repulsive; some have the cheek-bones very prominent, and the eyes of several are set slightly aslant. The hair is generally intensely black and straight, but with some individuals it is curly and browner. In Manila there are several varieties of the Malay race, and these Louisiana settlers represent more than one type. None of them appeared tall; the greater number were under-sized, but all well knit, and supple as fresh-water eels. Their hands and feet were small; their movements quick and easy, but sailorly likewise, as of men accustomed to walk upon rocking decks in rough weather. They speak the Spanish language; and a Malay dialect is also used among them. There is only one white man in the settlement—the ship-carpenter, whom all the Malays address as "Maestro." He has learned to speak their Oriental dialect, and has conferred upon several the sacrament of baptism according to the Catholic rite; for some of these men were not Christians at the time of their advent into Louisiana. There is but one black man in this lake village—a Portuguese negro, perhaps a Brazilian maroon. The Maestro told us that communication is still kept up with Manila, and money often sent there to aid friends in emigrating. Such emigrants usually ship as seamen on board some Spanish vessel bound for American ports, and desert at the first opportunity. It is said that the colony was founded by deserters—perhaps also by desperate refugees from Spanish justice....

There is no woman in the settlement, nor has the treble of a female voice been heard along the bayou for many a long year. Men who have families keep them at New Orleans, or at Proctorville, or at La Chinche; it would seem cruel to ask any woman to dwell in such a desolation, without comfort and without protection, during the long absence of the fishing-boats....

And nevertheless this life in the wilderness of reeds is connected mysteriously with New Orleans, where the head-quarters of the Manila men's benevolent society are—*La Union Philipina*. A fisherman dies; he is buried under the rustling reeds, and a pine cross planted above his grave; but when the flesh has rotted from the bones, these are taken up and carried by some lugger to the metropolis, where they are shelved away in those curious niche tombs which recall the Roman *columbaria*.

How, then, comes it that in spite of this connection with civilized life the Malay settlement of Lake Borgne has been so long unknown? Perhaps because of the natural reticence of the people. There is still in the oldest portion of the oldest quarter of New Orleans a certain Manila restaurant hidden away in a court, and supported almost wholly by the patronage of Spanish West Indian sailors. Few people belonging to the business circles of New Orleans know of its existence. The *menu* is printed in Spanish and English; the fare is cheap and good. Now it is kept by Chinese, for the Manila man and his oblique-eyed wife, comely as any figure upon a Japanese vase, have gone away....

The most intelligent person in Saint Malo is a Malay half-breed, *Valentine.* He is an attractive figure, a supple dwarfish lad almost as broad as tall, brown as old copper, with a singularly bright eye. He was educated in the great city, but actually abandoned a fine situation in the office of a judge to return to his swarthy father in the weird swamps. The old man is still there—*Thomas de los Santos.* He married a white woman, by whom he had two children, this boy and a daughter, *Winnie,* who is dead.

ESSAYS

The first essay, by Hawai'i-born, former University of California, Berkeley, historian Ronald Takaki, describes the development of the first sugar plantation in Hawai'i. Takaki, who died in 2009, shows how the islands' multiracial workforce, consisting mainly of Asian immigrants, by the late nineteenth century embodied U.S. attempts to control Hawai'i's political economy. In the second essay, former University of Hong Kong historian Elizabeth Sinn reveals the transpacific business and migration networks through which the Chinese diaspora extended to California.

Hawai'i and the Global Labor Market

RONALD TAKAKI

In Koloa, "a mere hamlet, seldom visited by even a missionary," the Hawaiian natives noticed in 1835 the arrival of William Hooper of Boston, Massachusetts. They had seen white men before: in 1778, some of them had travelled to Waimea, sixteen miles away, to get a glimpse of Captain James Cook, or had heard stories about the English explorer's momentous visit—how he had sailed into the bay in two huge ships with billowing white sheets, how his men had carried awesome weapons of fire and destruction, and how they had left behind them, with the native women, a dreadful disease. Many of the natives still

From Takaki, "An Entering Wedge: The Origins of the Sugar Plantation and Multi-ethnic Working Class in Hawaii," *Labor History* 23, no. 1 (Winter 1982): 34–46. Copyright © 1982 Taylor & Francis Ltd. Used with permission. www.tandf.co.uk/journals.

possessed souvenirs of Cook's visit, the iron nails they had ripped from his landing boats and the butcher's cleaver one of them had stolen.

As the natives curiously scrutinized their new visitor, they compared Hooper to the other white men at Waimea: the merchants shipping the fragrant sandalwood to China and supplying whaling vessels with water and provisions, and the missionaries building a new church there and spreading Christianity among the natives. But the people of Koloa did not realize that Hooper, more than the merchants and the missionaries, represented the beginning of a new era in the history of Hawaii. Sent to Koloa by Ladd and Company of Honolulu to establish the first plantation in the Sandwich Islands and to cultivate sugar cane as a cash crop, he was there to remake Hawaii in his own image: to advance American capitalism and civilization to a new Pacific frontier, undermining in the process the feudal society of Hawaii and the people's traditional relationship with their land.

During the next century, the Hawaiian sugar industry, which Hooper had initiated, transformed both the ethnicity of the people and the economy of the islands. In 1835, nearly the entire population was Hawaiian: foreigners constituted only .55 percent of the total, or only 600 out of a population of 108,000. In 1920, persons of Hawaiian ancestry made up only 16.3 percent of the population, while Caucasians represented 19.2 percent, Chinese 9.2 percent, Japanese 42.7 percent, Koreans 1.9 percent, Puerto Ricans 2.2 percent, and Filipinos 8.2 percent. Eighty years after Hooper had planted his first field of sugar cane, Hawaiian plantations produced 556,871 tons of sugar, representing the leading industry of the islands and providing the basis of five large and powerful corporations—American Factors, Castle and Cooke, C. Brewer and Company, T. H. Davies and Company, and Alexander and Baldwin.

While the relationship between the ethnic diversity of the people of Hawaii and the development of the sugar industry is readily apparent, little is known about the early origins of both of them. Fortunately, we have documents which can help to unshroud much of this history—the handwritten diary of Hooper and the extensive collection of his correspondence with Ladd and Company. Together they can enable us to reconstruct the critical early years of modern plantation Hawaii.

As a young man of twenty-six years, William Hooper keenly understood the significance of his enterprising venture in Koloa. Only two years earlier, he had landed in Honolulu with Peter Brinsmade and William Ladd; together they had opened a mercantile trading house named Ladd and Company. The company had leased from King Kamehameha III a tract of land, 980 acres on the east side of the Waihohonu Stream in Koloa, for 50 years at $300 a year, for the cultivation of sugar cane. The company had also secured permission to hire natives to work on the plantation. It had agreed to pay Kauikeouli, the King of Kauai, and Kaikioewa, the Governor of Kauai, a tax for each man employed, and to pay the workers satisfactory wages. The King and Governor, in return, would exempt the workers from all taxation except the tax paid by their employer.

As Hooper surveyed the newly leased land and the natives to be inducted into his work force, he must have thought Koloa was a fitting place for the beginning of the sugar industry in the islands, for the name itself meant "Great Cane"—"Ko" (cane) and "loa" (great). Everywhere, Hooper could see, wild cane flourished on the fertile land of Koloa, nourished by the rains falling first on towering Kahili Mountain, almost always shrouded in mist, and then sweeping toward the plains of Koloa and finally the beaches of Poipu. Far away from American civilization, Hooper lived initially in a grass hut and was obliged to eat taro, a root which the natives pounded into "poi"; he even jokingly described himself as becoming a *"real kanaka."*...

Within one year, the young man from Boston had transformed both the land and native society in Koloa. On September 12, 1836, he proudly listed his accomplishments. He had 25 acres of cane under cultivation; in addition, he had erected twenty houses for the natives, a house for the superintendant, a carpenter's shop, a blacksmith's shop, a mill dam, a sugar house, a boiling house, and a sugar mill. Pleased with the progress of his plantation, Hooper recorded in his diary his thoughts on the meaning of the Koloa experience:

> Just one year to day since I commenced work on this plantation, during which I have had more annoyances from the chiefs and difficulty with the natives (from the fact of this land being the first that has ever been cultivated, on the plan of *free* labour, at these islands) than I ever tho't it possible for one white man to bear, nevertheless I have succeeded in bringing about a place, which if followed up by other foreign residents, will eventually emancipate the natives from the miserable system of "chief labour" which ever has existed at these Islands, and which if not broken up, will be an effectual preventitive to the progress of civilization, industry and national prosperity.... The tract of land in Koloa was [developed] after much pain ... for the purpose of breaking up the system aforesaid or in other words to serve as an entering wedge ... [to] upset the whole system.

A sense of mission lay behind Hooper's energetic enterprise. More than profits were at stake. In building his plantation, Hooper viewed himself as a "white man," as a pathfinder or an advance guard of "other foreign residents," introducing the system of *"free* labour" in order to "emancipate" the natives from the miserable system of "'chief labour.'" For young Hooper, the Koloa plantation was the "entering wedge" of capitalism, designed to split apart, irrevocably, the ancient system of feudalism in Hawaii.

As they watched Hooper begin his enterprise, the natives of Koloa must have felt a profound ambivalence. They undoubtedly viewed his new operation very apprehensively, fearful of the negative effects the plantation system would have on their culture and way of life. They also saw him as a *haole,* an outsider, and identified him with the destruction of the sandalwood forests, the denuding of the *aina* or land, and with the sailors who were infecting native women with venereal diseases. But the natives also must have hoped Hooper would offer them an escape from the old Hawaiian system of exploitation and fear. Hawaii for the common people, the *makaainana,* was hardly paradise. The king owned all of the lands, and chiefs holding land did so in return for payment of feudal dues. Common people, in order to secure the use of small tracts of land, had to labor for the king or local chiefs, the *alii. Kapus,* or tabus, strictly enforced by the *ilamuku* or police, severely restricted their activities and ambitions. Commoners, reported the

Hawaiian historian David Malo who had been educated by missionaries and who was forty-two years old when Hooper founded the Koloa plantation, were subjected to hard labor, heavy taxation, and cruelty. If they were slack in performing labor for their chief, they were expelled from the land, or even put to death. They held the chiefs in "great dread," living in a state of "chronic fear." Theirs was a "life of weariness … constantly burdened by one exaction after another."

Seeking to improve their lot, twenty three natives went to work for Hooper on September 13, 1835. But two days later, they suddenly stopped working. "The kanakas having discovered the chiefs were to pay and not me," Hooper wrote in his diary, "concluded that 'all work and no pay' was poor business, therefore spent most of the forenoon in idleness." Apparently Hooper's workers thought they were to be paid through their chiefs and refused to work, doubting they would be paid at all. They were quickly offered an "inducement." They were promised to be paid directly "one real" or 12½ cents per day, and "they sprang to it, and at sundown finished their stint." Workers were also given food and shelter, in addition to their wages.

But Hooper did not pay his workers in reals or cash. Rather he issued coupons or script for 12½, 25, and 50 cents, which he wrote by hand on pieces of cardboard and which his workers could exchange for goods only at his plantation store. Thus Hooper was able both to pay his workers and to make a profit from their purchases.... In this process, he had created both a wage earning labor force and a consumer class dependent on a plantation-owned market which had to expand consumer needs constantly.

Native families, reported Hooper's neighbor James Jarvis, readily "volunteered" to have their taxes paid for them and to work for the Koloa plantation for wages. "The inducement of regular wages, good houses, and plenty of food, when compared with their usual mode of living," was one few natives resisted. Hooper's work force increased from twenty five in September of 1835 to forty in May of 1836. In March of 1838, Hooper noted that one hundred men, women, and children looked to him for their "daily Poe [poi]." By the end of the year, he counted four hundred workers in his employ.

Among Hooper's workers were native women. Employed to strip the cane and assist in grinding and boiling operations, they proved to be such effective workers that Hooper wrote to Ladd and Company on June 12, 1838: "I am in want of no more Sugar Boys. The women on the plantation now make good ones and it is best that I should keep them constantly at work." They were not only worked constantly; they were also paid less than the men, only six cents per day while the men received twelve and one half cents. Hooper justified this dual wage system by saying that it kept the women employed and allowed them to make "more than enough to support their families."

No longer peasants, Hooper's laborers found themselves in a new world of modern industrial agriculture. They no longer worked on their traditionally held small plots of land, sharing their crops with the *alii*. They no longer directed their own labors, making their own decisions regarding what to plant and when to work, rest, or go fishing. As plantation laborers, they found their time controlled by unfamiliar workday sounds, schedules, and rhythms....

As plantation workers, they performed a myriad of tasks. Under Hooper's direction, they first cleared grass from tracts of land for cane cultivation, and used a plough pulled by oxen to prepare the soil for the planting of cane cuttings. When one of the oxen died, "from the injury recd. by overwork," Hooper replaced the oxen with men. "At one time," Jarvis reported, "in lieu of cattle, he was obliged to employ forty natives, to drag a plough.".…

Drawn away from their feudal lands and traditional homes, Hooper's native workers entered a new plantation community. They lived on the plantation, in houses allotted to them by Hooper. Assigned plots of land to cultivate crops for their own food and allowed time on weekends to work their gardens, they also received from Hooper a barrel of fish every third week. This system in which the workers supplemented their own subsistence needs enabled Hooper to minimize both wages and production costs. On Saturday, Hooper's workers visited the plantation store to sell vegetables and crafts and to purchase goods with their coupons.…

Plantation workers not only labored, lived, and shopped on the Koloa plantation; they also received medical care when they became ill. Initially Hooper himself attended the medical needs of his workers. On April 29, 1836, he reported to Ladd and Company: "They are often ailing.… They are troubled with sore eyes etc etc which need & ought to have advice & medicine.".…

Though they were dependent on Hooper for their "daily Poe" and other needs, native workers refused to give him the control and loyalty he expected. Time and again Hooper found himself in a state of exasperation over his inability to exact from his workers satisfactory obedience and sustained labor. Throughout his Koloa diary, he described his workers with great disgust as undependable, as children, as "dull asses," and as "Indians." His letters to Ladd and Company chronicled the frustrations he felt as the supervisor of recalcitrant laborers.…

Hooper's laborers required constant surveillance or else they would not work. They became skillful pretenders, and Jarvis often "amusingly" watched them practice their art of deception. While working in the fields, natives were always ready to deceive their employer and escape from work. If an overseer left for a moment, down they would squat and pull out their pipes. Then the "longest-winded fellow" would begin a story, "a sort of improvisation" which would entertain everyone with "vulgar" humor and which would often "mimic the haole (foreigner)." As soon as the overseer came back within sight, they would seize their spades and quickly "commence laboring with an assiduity" that baffled description and "perhaps all the while not strain a muscle."

But Hooper did not find their behavior amusing. Irritated and impatient, he castigated his native workers for their inefficiency and doubted they would ever become useful as plantation workers. Their "habits and customs" which had been handed down to them from their forefathers and which they preserved so tenaciously would remain "the great obstacle to their employment" as agricultural wage laborers. Centuries, at least, Hooper lamented, would intervene before they would understand that it was a part of their "duty" to serve "their masters faithfully." He conceded that there were many good men among the natives who would take hold and turn themselves into "white kanakas" for one or two years. But he had no confidence that their patience would hold out. As long as the plantation depended on native labor, the superintendant would have to be a "*Slave Driver.*"

Frustrated because he could not convert the natives into docile and efficient modern agricultural workers, Hooper turned to the Chinese as a solution to his labor problem. He had first noticed their presence in Waimea: there a few of them were grinding wild cane, brought to them by natives, in a small sugar mill owned by William French. After visiting this mill in the spring of 1835, Hooper wrote to Ladd and Company:

> I have seen the Chinese sugar works in successful operations; although extremely crude, yet they are doing well. They have worked 6 days in the week ever since its first establishment, making abt 210 lb sugar per day & molasses by the cord. They could make four times as much by increasing the size of kettles. Mr. F. is much elated with its success and from what I learn from Mr. Whitney you may expect a Host of Chinese.... Mr. French's establishment at Waimea is a great eye sore to the natives. They have to work *all* the time—and no regard is paid to their complaints for food, etc., etc. Slavery is nothing to it.

Shortly after the completion of the construction of his own mill, Hooper projected the need for Chinese labor. "We may deem it," he advised Ladd and Company, "at a future day, necessary to locate some halfdozen Chinese on the land, if the establishment grows it will require them. The Supt. cannot feed the mill, boil the juice, make the sugar, etc etc, and to trust it to the natives is worse than nothing—they are alas, children, boys, and always will be."

In a letter to Ladd and Company on December 1, 1838, Hooper insisted that the Koloa plantation needed a source of labor from other countries, and that no other country offered itself but China. "A colony of Chinese would, probably, put the plantation in order, to be perpetuated, sooner and with less trouble than any other class of husbandmen." By this time, several Chinese were already working for Hooper: they had probably been recruited from French's mill which had been put out of business due to competition from the Koloa mill. A pattern of ethnic labor segmentation was already evident, for Hooper tended to assign his Chinese laborers to the mill and Hawaiian laborers to the fields. Unlike the native workers, who lived on the plantation with their families in individual houses, the Chinese workers seemed to be all male and were housed together in a barrack-type structure. In April 1838, Hooper informed Ladd and Company that a "large comfortable building" had been erected for the "Chinamen." "They are highly pleased," he added, "and by their fixtures on doors I should suppose they intend to spend their days in it." Thus, Chinese workers, too, now looked to Hooper for their "daily Poe." Early in 1839, Hooper ordered from Ladd and Company a supply of rice for them.

But the use of Chinese workers did not mean the end of labor difficulties. Hooper's workers, Hawaiian and Chinese, found new ways to resist management and avoid work. Some of the natives simply helped themselves to merchandise in the plantation store without paying for them. On January 28, 1837, Hooper angrily scribbled into his diary: "[Detected] the natives stealing—therefore paid out no goods to day." And three days later, he wrote: "5 natives taken before Hukiko [Hukiku, the headman at Koloa]—convicted of stealing and sentenced to work on the roads." But by this time, some of his workers had devised a more ingenious way to acquire goods from the plantation store: they used counterfeit coupons. As the natives learned how to read and write from a young schoolmaster in the village, some of them utilized their newly acquired knowledge and skills to make artful reproductions of Hooper's medium of exchange. The counterfeit coupons, according to Jarvis, were "so strikingly like the original, imitating the signatures with scrupulous exactness, that it was some time before the fraud was detected."

But the fraud was eventually discovered. On June 11, 1836, Hooper, surprised and dismayed, wrote in his diary: "Some native has attempted to counterfeit the papers which I issued for dollars." Some of the counterfeiters were Chinese. The problem caused Hooper much distress: unless it were checked, the counterfeit conspiracy could undermine his entire enterprise. His laborers would have little incentive to work, for they would have their own source of script. Determined to outwit his workers, Hooper asked Ladd and Company to have paper bills engraved in Boston. In its letter to the printer on November 15, 1837, Ladd and Company gave instructions to have the currency printed from a copper plate in order to be certain it could not be duplicated....

The founding of the Koloa plantation had been a very trying experience for Hooper. The new land did not yield easily. The rainy seasons, with their howling winds and pelting showers, forced him to stay indoors, and the enveloping dampness agitated his rheumatism. Cut off from family and friends and from the security and comfort of Boston, he suffered from intense isolation, finding his new life in Koloa "lonesome" and "dull as death." And the people of the new land had not been as pliant as he had hoped: they were difficult to manage and often drove him to dispair. They seemed to resist him at almost every point. They were also more intelligent than he had assumed, able to avoid work and to extract extra compensation in creative and devious ways. Psychically exhausted from his constant struggle with his workers, Hooper vented his frustrations to Ladd and Company in 1838: "No galley slave looks forward to the day when he is to be made free with half so much satisfaction as I do when I shall bid a *final* adieu to intercourse with Hawaiians! Gracious Anticipations!"

A year later, Hooper was granted his wish, but he left behind him, in Koloa, a place transformed. In a sense, Hooper may remind us of William Shakespeare's Prospero and Mark Twain's Connecticut Yankee: Prospero had settled on an island and inducted a native, Caliban, into his service, his work force; and Hank Morgan had travelled to another island, Arthurian England, where he had imposed a modern industrial order. Reflecting the expansionist culture portrayed in Prospero and Morgan, Hooper had removed himself to an island. There, employing native labor, he had cleared the wild grass from the land in order to plant ordered rows of cane; he had altered the very character of the tiny hamlet of Koloa, bringing to it the dark smoke and the loud and dissonant mechanical sounds of a modern factory. He had integrated economic and moral motives, seeking both to earn corporate profits for Ladd and Company and liberate natives from an oppressive feudalism. Converting them into free laborers, he had removed them from their farms and villages to his plantation where he offered them housing and paternal care. He had opened the way for the development of a corporate dominated sugar economy and a paternalistic racial and class hierarchy of social relations in the islands.

Setting in motion dynamic forces which would transform the ethnicity of Hawaii's population, he had initiated the making of a multiethnic and transnational plantation labor system which would draw into the plantation work force not only people from Hawaii itself but also from China, Japan, Portugal, Norway, Germany, Korea, Puerto Rico, the Philippines, and even Russia. Though he had been at Koloa for only four years, Hooper had proven it was possible to induce the natives to labor as wage earners and to produce sugar as a cash crop. His invoices for 1837-38 showed that he had shipped to Honolulu approximately 30 tons of sugar and 170 barrels of molasses—a small but nonetheless portentous beginning of a new plantation economy which would penetrate Hawaiian society like an "entering wedge."

Chinese Emigration to California

ELIZABETH SINN

The Pacific Ocean can be—and has been—represented in many different ways. Here, we will look at it in the context of Chinese migration. In the mid-nineteenth century, a series of stunning gold discoveries were made, first in California (1848), then Australia (1851), western Canada (1858), and New Zealand (1861). By coincidence, these places were all on the Pacific Rim, and tens of thousands of Chinese from the Pearl River Delta sailed across the immense watery expanse to reach the Gold Mountains. Until the California Gold Rush transformed it into a hot, happening ocean, the Pacific had been largely irrelevant to Hong Kong, despite its being situated on the ocean's very edge. Gradually, as Chinese migrants embarked at Hong Kong for the gold countries and disembarked there on their way home, the British colonial port became the gateway to the Pacific as well as a pivot in the Cantonese diaspora....

The flow of people with different interests and desires was accompanied by the flow of goods, money (as capital and remittances), communication, information, and the bones and coffins of deceased emigrants. These flows—intricately intertwined, multidirectional, and often circular—created all kinds of networks that in turn facilitated further movements and transactions across the Pacific. "Network" can be a vague word, and too often projects a static image. To flesh out the networks, I examine how they operated on the ground and find that the transpacific networks were not only multidirectional, but also multileveled, interactive, interpenetrating, overlapping, and interlinked. Far from static, they were vibrant and constantly reconfigured....

Sinn, Elizabeth, "Highway to Gold Mountain, 1850–1900," *Pacific Historical Review*, 83, no. 2, (May 2014): 220–237. © 2014 by the Regents of the University of California. Published by the University of California Press.

Shipping networks and the flow and circulation of people

The story of transpacific shipping in the mid-nineteenth century is often told in terms of steamliners … The transpacific route was a circular one, reflecting the circular nature of Chinese migration in the nineteenth century. While in general the ultimate goal was to return to China, there was great variation in how migrants actually circulated. Some made a single trip to California and returned home after making a fortune (or when they could no longer bear the loneliness), while others made multiple trips across the Pacific, returning to China from time to time to visit parents, impregnate wives, and, for merchants, to buy and sell before returning to California once more.…

Flow of goods from China

The Chinese presence in California promoted a California–China trade, although it should not be assumed that the trade was only in Chinese hands. Some of the goods imported into California were specifically for Chinese consumption, such as prepared opium and opium pipes, rice, joss paper, bird's nest and shark's fin, salted eggs, fungus, pots and pans, clothing, and Chinese medicine. Impressarios even sent out Cantonese opera troupes and actors to entertain the Chinese there. Other goods from China were imported for sale to non-Chinese consumers as well, like tea and sugar, paintings, furniture, and all kinds of silk goods. The Chinese curio shop has been a Chinatown feature from the very earliest days.

We know very well that not every Chinese in California prospered, but, compared to Chinese in contemporary China or even Southeast Asia, even the most menial laborers enjoyed a much higher income in the United States. The Gold Rush created a stock figure in the minds of people in South China that resonates even today. He was the *gum saan haak* or "Gold Mountain sojourner," the high-income, big-spending Chinese emigrant in California. He was keenly sought after as a husband and son-in-law, but no less as a customer, investor, and business partner. The *gum saan haak*'s consumption pattern to a large extent dictated the composition and the value of the import-export trade between China and California, with far-reaching consequences for the transpacific economy. For example, his preference for Hong Kong's prepared opium, which was the most highly regarded and expensive opium, led directly to the high price of the opium monopoly in Hong Kong. His preference for no. 1 China rice led to the illegal export of the finest rice from Guangdong province, with the result that cheap rice had to be imported to Guangdong from Siam and Annam to feed the poor. This high-end consumption in California boosted the value of the China-California trade and other trades linked to it.

Flow of goods from California

In the early days of the Gold Rush, almost everything had to be imported to feed and clothe the emigrants arriving from all corners of the earth, but California was soon able to produce certain commodities for export, thus redressing somewhat the imbalance of trade. Abalone and dried shrimps, ginseng, quicksilver, flour, and treasure, both silver and gold, were major California exports....

Flow of *qiaohui*

Besides being a consumer, the Chinese migrant was also a sender of funds, either from savings or profits. Clearly migrants from other countries also sent money home, but the degree and scale of Chinese remittance practices were exceptional. The majority of Chinese emigrants sent money home as a primary duty. The image of the free-spending *gum saan haak* should not blind us to the fact that many Chinese in California were poor. Nevertheless, it was rare for a man, however poor, not to be scrimping and saving in order to send a few dollars home to China every month. The wealthy sent enormous sums to buy land and build houses, to make donations to public projects, and to invest in modern enterprises, such as railroads and electricity companies. Whether sent by poor or rich, the remittances collectively formed an enormous source of income for South China....

Funds could be remitted in different ways. Returning migrants could take their gold with them. Alternatively, the money could take a more tortuous journey. It was common for a Chinese laborer in California to take his few dollars to a shop that undertook to send the money for him, usually accompanied by a letter to his family. After a sizable amount had accumulated, the shopkeeper would send the funds onward to Hong Kong through a variety of means, including by a bank draft or in the form of goods to be sold on arrival. In Hong Kong, the money was converted to silver before being forwarded by couriers or other means to the sender's home. This sounds a lot easier than what happened on the ground, since the sender could live in some very remote part of California, and his home in China could be equally remote and isolated. It could take months before the money reached the recipient, and, in the process, many people had a chance to dip into it, using it either as capital or to ease their own cash flow. In some cases, the money might never have left California at all, as long as shops or firms in California and Hong Kong were able to settle their accounts against goods, passage money, chartering costs, commissions, or other assets.

All these import-export and remittance activities were undertaken by Chinese and non-Chinese firms of different sizes. Very often Chinese and non-Chinese merchants worked closely together; even though this article focuses on Chinese networks, it is important to remember that they were seldom exclusively Chinese.

Networks of firms and the circulation of capital

Chinese firms in Hong Kong (and Guangzhou) had always been closely connected with those in California. They collaborated in different ways. For example, in the early days Hong Kong firms extended credit on goods while the California firms collected the proceeds and other debts for their Hong Kong counterparts and collected *qiaohui*; they also acted as agents for each other's ships. A number of California firms started as branches and *lianhao* (explained below) of Hong Kong firms; as the California firms expanded, they in turn established branches and *liaohao* in Hong Kong and other cities in China, creating a counter-trend and making the transpacific connections more complex....

Let me illustrate such a network of firms with the story of Chiu Yu Tin's firm, Chong Wo. Chiu Yu Tin, a native of Nanhai, founded Chong Wo in Hong Kong around 1849, soon after the California Gold Rush. The firm was an active exporter, sometimes acting as agent for others, sometimes trading on its own account. Over time, the goods that Chong Wo exported included shawls, bed covers, lacquered ware that might be classified as "fancy Chinese goods" catering to Westerners, and also rice, opium, clothing, medicinal roots, vegetables, women's shoes, and so on, which were clearly for Chinese consumption. Through the 1850s, as Chong Wo's cargoes grew in value, the firm expanded its business through a series of *lianhao* and other associated companies in California and other localities.

There is reason to believe that Chong Wo originally set up a branch in San Francisco in the early 1850s, managed by a brother or close relative of Chiu's. Later, however, it formed a new firm in San Francisco called Wing Wo Sang with several partners and seems to have done a lot of its business through it. Chong Wo probably held shares in other firms in California as well. Together and separately, Chong Wo and Wing Wo Sang carried on a thriving and large-scale trade, with Chong Wo in Hong Kong frequently sending Wing Wo Sang large amounts of rice, opium, and cooking oil and Wing Wo Sang shipping flour and quicksilver in return. Wing Wo Sang was a major exporter of quicksilver and was listed as a shipper on almost every ship that carried the mineral. The establishment of Wing Wo Sang and other firms in which Chong Wo had an interest benefited Chong Wo in multiple ways, far beyond just facilitating its import-export trade. Through Wing Wo Sang, for instance, Chong Wo was able to invest in gold mines, an opportunity that many Chinese in Hong Kong must have craved but that would have been impossible without the proper agent.

Chong Wo's commercial network spread in all directions, and Chiu Yu Tin was credited with having assisted, through his generosity and connections, "over a thousand" relatives, neighbors, and friends to set up businesses abroad. Even assuming this to be an exaggeration, one can still imagine the pivotal position he must have occupied in a network that covered Hawai'i and spanned the east coast of the Pacific from California to Panama, Peru, and Chile. San Francisco no doubt played a major role in the expansion, serving as the springboard for Hong Kong trade with other parts of North and South America, in the same way that Hong Kong became San Francisco's gateway to China, Southeast Asia, and beyond. The Hong Kong-California corridor became the concourse from which many tributary corridors emerged, directed and re-directed by the movements of Chinese migration and attendant trades.

At the same time that he was looking east across the Pacific, Chiu Yu Tin was also busy trading with China and Southeast Asia through his Nam Pak Hong firm, Kwong Mou Tai. In China he had *lianhao* in many cities all along the China coast, including Shantou, Shanghai, Jiaozhou, Yingkou, and Dalian.

Such multidirectional operations, centering like spokes around Hong Kong's hub, created immense synergy.

In China, the trade with California was known as Gold Mountain trade and the firms as *gum saan jong*. It became an important and iconic trade in Hong Kong. Besides import and export, *gum saan jong* typically engaged in shipping, *qiaohui*, and, later in the century, insurance, and it offered a wide range of personal services to customers, especially migrants and their families.

The Wo Hang firm illustrates these myriad functions very well and shows how the network of firms achieved both vertical and horizontal integration. Besides the California trade, Hong Kong was also a major hub of the valuable Nam Pak trade. This was the trade between the north (North China and Japan) and the south (South China and Southeast Asia), a trade that covered an immense array of commodities. With these two important trading systems intersecting in Hong Kong, the East Asian economy was greatly stimulated....

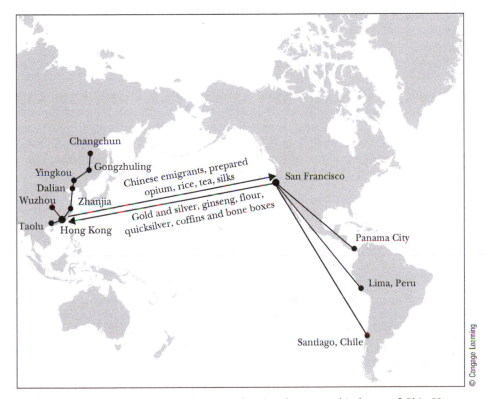

© Cengage Learning

FIGURE 2.1   An impressionistic map showing the geographical span of Chiu Yu Tin's commercial networks. Map created by Jacquelyn C. Ferry and used with permission.

The flow of coffins and bones

Profit and consumption were not the only impetus for transpacific flows. Let us look at another kind of flow. A distinctive activity among Chinese migrants in

California was the repatriation of the bones and coffins of those who had died abroad, an activity requiring not just money and labor, but also trust and goodwill. The work was often undertaken by native-place organizations, the *huiguan* (or "companies," as some of them were misleadingly called in California) on both sides of the Pacific.

Chinese migrants in the nineteenth century generally expected to return and spend their last days in comfort in their home villages, not to settle overseas permanently; even when they died overseas, they hoped to be buried at home. As a result, the practice of sending home the remains of deceased migrants emerged in California. The purpose was to let the deceased be buried among their descendants who would make offerings at their graves for generations to come; the greatest fear was that those left abandoned in graves in America would be unattended to and become wild and hungry ghosts.

When a Chinese migrant died in California, the body was usually first buried *in situ*; after five to seven years, the bones were exhumed, cleaned, and boxed for the voyage home. This was a labor-intensive exercise that frequently involved locating isolated graves in regions far from the main cities; on occasions when someone was known to have died but his burial place could not be found, the bone collector would summon the soul of the deceased and collect it in a *zhao-hun xiang* (spirit box) that would be sent home and buried just like the coffins and bone boxes. In the nineteenth century, thousands of deceased emigrants returned to China in these boxes. Yet, although the activity of bone repatriation was full of social, cultural, and emotional meaning, the complicated operational and financial arrangements were tightly intertwined with business and financial networks, reinforcing and deepening the transpacific connections. All these comings and goings kept the Pacific a busy highway.

Conclusion

When the Pacific Ocean turned into a highway for Chinese seeking Gold Mountain, it marked a new era for the history of South China, California, and the ocean itself. With the constant to-ing and fro-ing of people (dead and alive), goods, letters, and money, transpacific relationships became intricate and interdependent. The overlapping personal, family, financial, and commercial interests of Chinese and merchants in California and those in Hong Kong energized the connections and kept the Pacific busy and dynamic while shaping the development of regions far beyond the ocean's shores. It also makes the ocean an exciting historical site, full of opportunities for research.

☛ FURTHER READING

Beechert, Edward. *Working in Hawaii: A Labor History* (1985).

Borah, Eloisa Gomez. "Filipinos in Unamuno's California Expedition of 1578," *Amerasia Journal* (1995/1996): 175–183.

Chen, Yong. *Chinese San Francisco, 1850–1943* (2000).

Crouchett, Lorrain Jacobs. *Filipinos in California: From the Days of the Galleons to the Present* (1982).

Espina, Marina E. *Filipinos in Louisiana* (1988).

Haddad, John. *The Romance of China: Excursions to China in U.S. Culture, 1776–1876* (2006).

Hsu, Madeline Y. *Dreaming of Gold, Dreaming of Home: Transnationalism and Migration Between the United States and Southern China, 1882–1943* (2000).

Kame'elehiwa, Lilikala. *Native Lands and Foreign Desires: Pahoa La E Pono Ai?* (1992).

Kuykendall, Ralph S. *The Hawaiian Kingdom, 1778–1854, Foundation and Transformation* (1965).

———. *The Hawaiian Kingdom 1874–1893: The Kalakaua Dynasty* (1967).

Malo, David. *Hawaiian Antiquities* (Moolelo Hawaii) (1898).

Sinn, Elizabeth. *Pacific Crossings: California Gold, Chinese Migration, and the Making of Hong Kong* (2013).

Tchen, John Kuo Wei. *New York Before Chinatown: Orientalism and the Shaping of American Culture, 1776–1882* (1999).

Tinker, Hugh. *A New System of Slavery: The Export of Indian Labour Overseas, 1830–1920* (1974).

Wills, John E., Jr. "A Very Long Early Modern? Asia and Its Oceans, 1000–1850," *Pacific Historical Review* 83 (2014): 189–203.

Yun, Lisa and Ricardo Rene Laremont. "Chinese Coolies and African Slaves in Cuba, 1847–74," *Journal of Asian American Studies* 4 (2001): 99–122.

CHAPTER 3

Debating Chinese Immigration, 1860–1899

The new Republic's egalitarian creed, "all men are created equal," combined with its need for human capital to fuel its ever-expanding economy, fostered liberal immigration policies that welcomed anyone in the world, with the exception of convicts, paupers, and, after 1807, slaves. While Asian immigrants could not become U.S. citizens, U.S. employers, especially those seeking to develop Hawai'i and the Western frontier as discussed in Chapter 2, sought them out. White populations on the West Coast, however, bitterly opposed Asian immigration to that region. Californians, in particular, enacted numerous state and local public policies discriminating against Chinese immigrants in order to discourage their immigration and to encourage those who had already arrived to return home. These policies included special taxes charged upon arrival and on "foreign miners" in the state's gold mining regions; bans on Asians testifying in a court of law or intermarrying with whites; and prohibitions against Chinese businesses, group living quarters, and even the long ponytail or queue hairstyle required by the Qing dynasty.

In contrast to California, the federal government did little to lessen free Chinese immigration, and in some cases it overruled state laws, such as "head taxes" on arrivals from China, as interfering with international commerce. The pro-business Republican Party, which controlled the nation's politics from 1860 to 1877 during Civil War and Reconstruction, defended Chinese immigration as part of the nation's egalitarian creed and as necessary labor for developing the U.S. West. William Seward, who had lauded Chinese immigrants as a senator, brokered a historic U.S.-China accord in 1868 when he served as secretary of state. A key provision of this Burlingame Treaty was to grant China "most favored nation" status and to promise the Chinese the right to free immigration and travel within the United States and the protection of Chinese citizens. The Burlingame Treaty expressed a commitment to the principle of equality between the United States and China but, at the urging of a California senator, made an exception regarding naturalization rights so that Chinese immigrants still could not become U.S. citizens.

During Reconstruction, when southern states returned to the Union and in so doing boosted the power of the Democratic Party, the Republicans' inclusive immigration policies and friendship with China were tested. A major economic depression in the 1870s added to Republican woes as labor unions found in Chinese immigrants a scapegoat for the nation's ills. Western nativists joined Democrats and labor unions to push Congress to enact a series of immigration policies that singled out the Chinese for discrimination. A landmark act in 1882 overturned the spirit, if not the letter, of the Burlingame Treaty and restricted Chinese laborers from immigrating to the United States for a ten-year period. Subsequent legislation and treaty revision through 1904 transformed the restriction of laborers into the near total exclusion of all classes of Chinese immigrants.

Scholarship on the causes of Chinese exclusion has identified the relative significance of three factors: class, race, and politics. The class argument portrays Chinese immigrants as tools of big business used to undermine the rising power of labor unions. Exclusion, from this perspective, is seen as a victory for the white working class. The race argument, on the other hand, underscores the common class position of Asian and white workers and thus attributes exclusion to the race, not class, consciousness of the U.S. labor movement. The politics argument recognizes the importance of both class and race factors but casts exclusion as fundamentally rooted in party politics during a time when sparsely populated Western states like California came to have heightened power over national elections. Another dimension of the politics perspective looks at the implementation of Chinese exclusion through the policing of entry points, such as the Angel Island immigration station and the borders of Canada and Mexico. In these sites, a whole new set of actors emerged that reveal both the draconian enactment of racist policies by immigration and border patrol officers and the crafty maneuverings by lawyers, Chinese advocates, and the immigrants themselves to get around exclusion.

☭DOCUMENTS

While congressional efforts to restrict free Chinese immigrants did not come to fruition for over two decades after they began arriving in the United States, prohibitions against the coolie trade came earlier, in 1862, as part of the Republican Congress's anti-slavery stance. In Document 1, the *New York Times* describes two types of coolies. The good type are "Hindoos" brought to the British and French Caribbean to work on sugar plantations; the bad type are slave-like Chinese forced labor in Spanish-held Cuba and Peru. Note that the voluntary Chinese immigrants who came to California were not considered coolies and thus were not seen as a threat. But exclusionists in California firmly disagreed and pushed to ban Chinese free laborers as a form of coolie labor detrimental to white workers. By 1875, as Document 2 reveals, exclusionist concerns about unfree Chinese immigration grew to include Chinese prostitutes, who were banned because of a fear that they would "cause disease and immorality among white men." Document 3 shows that Chinese immigrant leaders accommodated the increased calls to exclude even free immigration from China by urging the Qing government to curtail the flow of laborers to the United States.

In 1879, Congress held hearings to study the causes of a severe economic depression that damaged businesses and labor opportunities for much of that decade. In Document 4, a white merchant in San Francisco blames Chinese immigrants for the depression in California, testifying to the congressional committee that Chinese do not assimilate to U.S. standards and, as a result, do damage to both white workers and businesses. The testimony was typical of the hearings, which were a decidedly anti-Chinese affair. Document 5, a graphic depiction of the Chinese as a tool of big business, captures the widespread fear at the time that these immigrants were contributing to a dystopian society in which monopoly capitalism was destroying the American Dream. As the Chinese Exclusion Act of 1882 was being debated on Capitol Hill, Massachusetts senator George Hoar denounced it as violating U.S. egalitarian principles and offending China and the spirit of the liberal Burlingame Treaty. Excerpted in Document 6, Hoar's speech is consistent with both the Burlingame Treaty and William Seward's earlier pro-China stance.

The push for Chinese exclusion in Congress reflected widespread anti-Chinese sentiment that was particularly acute in the U.S. West. Vigilante campaigns in that region murdered scores of Chinese immigrants and drove countless numbers of them from their homes and workplaces. Document 7 reports on one of the worst instances that occurred in the mining town of Rock Springs, Wyoming, where, in 1885, striking white workers rioted against Chinese laborers who refused to join their strike. The riot left twenty-eight Chinese dead and fifteen injured and forced the U.S. government to pay a substantial indemnity to China for the Chinese losses incurred. The indemnity proved a victory for the Chinese diplomatic corps, which worked closely with elite Chinese immigrant merchants in protesting acts of anti-Chinese discrimination. Much of the time, the merchants sought to appease Americans by declaring their love for the United States and even supporting the restriction of Chinese laborers as long as merchants and other elite classes of Chinese were permitted entry. Yet Document 8, a letter to the editor of the *New York Sun*, shows that some Chinese immigrants blamed white Americans, not Chinese laborers, for discrimination. The author of this document became disillusioned with the nation's egalitarian creed when he was asked to contribute money to building a pedestal for the Statue of Liberty.

The experience of discrimination for Chinese immigrants differed by gender as well as class. Document 9, written by a white investigative reporter, exposes the world of a Chinese woman who owned a brothel and was engaged in immigration smuggling and human trafficking. The predominance of men in Chinese immigrant communities (nearly seven for every woman in San Francisco Chinatown in 1910) created the conditions in which prostitution became a lucrative business controlled by organized crime and its henchmen ("highbinders"). Some poor or unfortunate families in China sold their daughters into slavery and some of these slaves were smuggled into diasporic communities in the United States.

1. Newspaper Distinguishes Between Good Coolies, Bad Coolies, and Free Asian Immigrants, 1860

The American Coolie-Trade

By a curious coincidence, which we trust may not be altogether unprofitable to the cause of humanity, the Legislatures of England and America have been

---

From "The American Coolie-Trade," *New York Times*, April 21, 1860, p. 4.

almost simultaneously called upon to consider the abuses of the Coolie-trade in the East. The report of Mr. ELIOT, of Massachusetts, upon this traffic, has just been laid before the House of Representatives, and through the press before the people of the United States. In this report it was proved with terrible distinctness that in the absence of any regulations weighted with the national authority to restrain them from violating the instincts of humanity, American merchants and ship-masters have been gradually drawn into the most atrocious practices in connection with the Coolie-trade on the coasts of the Chinese Empire. The traditional horrors of the African middle-passage have been reënacted, are indeed continually reënacting, under the American flag in the Chinese ports and on the Indian seas. Men are kidnapped by the agents of American mercantile houses, huddled into the unventilated holds of American clipper-ships, restrained of their liberty by force of arms, transported thousands of miles to foreign lands, there disposed of under instruments which they cannot comprehend to masters whose language they do not speak, and condemned to labors which in nine cases out of ten can have no end but death, and to a life from which death is a welcome and desirable release....

Nor is this all. We are even now preparing to receive with unwonted pomp the first embassy which any great Power of Eastern Asia has ever sent to a Christian State, since the then mighty empire of Siam dispatched its envoys to the Court of LOUIS XIV. The Japanese Ministers are to be welcomed as the forerunners of a wonderful expansion in the intercourse of maritime Asia with the United States; and we are already confidently counting upon our growing influence with the Chinese and Japanese nations, to give us certain immense future advantages over our European rivals in the opulent commerce of the Orient. It should be clear to the meanest capacity, that if we suffer our flag to become identified in the Eastern seas with the excesses and outrages now perpetrated almost exclusively under its starry folds, we shall seriously compromise our position in that quarter of the world. All considerations of Christianity and civilization apart, it may perhaps be doubted whether the profits which half-a-dozen reckless shipowners may make for themselves by selling the bodies and souls of a few thousand Mongols, yearly, to the sugar-planters of Cuba and the guano-workers of Peru, can compensate us for this national risk.

The Coolie-trade, upon which we now desire to see the energetic action of Congress concentrated, needs, perhaps, a clearer definition than it has yet received, to the popular apprehension. It has no sort of connection either with the voluntary Chinese emigration which has filled the ranches and cañons of California with the patient disciples of CONFUCIUS, or with the Hindoo Coolie-trade which has produced such marvelous results of prosperity in the English Colonies of the Mauritius, Guiana and Trinidad, and of which the French Emperor is now seeking to extend the advantages to the Indian and Caribbean Colonies of France. The Chinese emigrants to California and Australia, like the Irish and German emigrants to America, pay their own passage-money, command their own labor, and are the architects of their own good or ill fortune. The Hindoo Coolies, whose industry, honestly rewarded, has raised the sugar crop of the Island of Mauritius in a single year of freedom to five times the amount which it attained in the last year of Slavery, are persons engaged to labor for a term of five years in that colony, under the constant supervision of Government agents charged to protect their rights, to secure them the payment of their wages, a proper allowance of food and medical attendance in case of illness, and at the end of their stipulated term of service to provide them, if required to do so, with a free passage back to India. This emigration is not the ally, but the enemy of Slavery. It has been carried on with ever increasing results of good to all parties concerned, not only with the Mauritius, but with the remoter American Colonies of Great Britain; and so far as the jealousy of the Anglo-Indian Government would permit, with the French Antilles and the *Isle de la Réunion.*

The Chinese Coolie-trade, on the other hand, is prosecuted by entirely irresponsible persons, with no control from any Government, Asiatic or European; and is a creation of European shipping-agents, acting in combination with Chinese contractors, no more decent or scrupulous than the emigrant-runners of New-York. The Imperial Chinese Government in 1855 issued proclamations forbidding the trade to be carried on, under the severest penalties. But thanks to domestic rebellion and foreign intervention, the Chinese Government has been reduced to a state of practical paralysis; and its fulminations have been found powerless against the cruel greed of the Coolie-dealers. In the same year, 1855, the British Government was appealed to on the subject, and Parliament passed an act confiscating all British vessels found engaged in this traffic within the British jurisdiction in the China seas. The only effects of this act have been to drive the traffic from the open ports of China into the smuggling port of Swatow, about two hundred miles above Hong-Kong; and to transfer the burden of the business from British to American vessels. Our only present rivals of importance in the nefarious traffic are the Peruvians, Chilians and North Germans. Peru, in 1856, followed the example of China and England, and made the trade illegal. But, so long as the American flag covers this cruel and cowardly commerce, it must continue to be carried on with all its actual incidents of shame and sin. Immediate and vigorous action on the part of Congress must result in its almost instantaneous suppression; and that action should clothe our civil agents in China with authority to put the enormity down with all the power of our naval forces in those seas. Circumstances having finally shifted the responsibility of this great wrong mainly upon our shoulders, it rests with ourselves to vindicate our national reputation, by acting at once in the premises as becomes our Christianity and our civilization.

2. Congress Excludes Un-free Asians, Prostitutes, and Felons, 1875

Be it enacted by the Senate and House of Representatives of the United States of America in Congress assembled, That in determining whether the immigration of any subject of China, Japan, or any Oriental country, to the United States, is free and

An Act supplementary to the acts related to immigration, Congressional Record, 43rd Congress, Sess. 11, Ch. 141 (1875) 477–478.

voluntary, as provided by section two thousand one hundred and sixty-two of the Revised Code, title "Immigration," it shall be the duty of the consul-general or consul of the United States residing at the port from which it is proposed to convey such subjects, in any vessels enrolled or licensed in the United States, or any port within the same, before delivering to the masters of any such vessels the permit or certificate provided for in such section, to ascertain whether such immigrant has entered into a contract or agreement for a term of service within the United States, for lewd and immoral purposes; and if there be such contract or agreement, the said consul-general or consul shall not deliver the required permit or certificate.

Sec. 2. That if any citizen of the United States, or other person amenable to the laws of the United States, shall take, or cause to be taken or transported, to or from the United States any subject of China, Japan, or any Oriental country, without their free and voluntary consent, for the purpose of holding them to a term of service, such citizen or other person shall be liable to be indicted there-for, and, on conviction of such offense, shall be punished by a fine not exceeding two thousand dollars and be imprisoned not exceeding one year; and all contracts and agreements for a term of service of such persons in the United States, whether made in advance or in pursuance of such illegal importation, and whether such importation shall have been in American or other vessels, are hereby declared void.

Sec. 3. That the importation into the United States of women for the purposes of prostitution is hereby forbidden; and all contracts and agreements in relation thereto, made in advance or in pursuance of such illegal importation and purposes, are hereby declared void; and whoever shall knowingly and willfully import, or cause any importation of, women into the United States for the purposes of prostitution, or shall knowingly or willfully hold, or attempt to hold, any woman to such purposes, in pursuance of such illegal importation and contract or agreement, shall be deemed guilty of a felony, and, on conviction thereof, shall be imprisoned not exceeding five years and pay a fine not exceeding five thousand dollars.

Sec. 4. That if any person shall knowingly and willfully contract, or attempt to contract, in advance or in pursuance of such illegal importation, to supply to another the labor of any cooly or other person brought into the United States in violation of section two thousand one hundred and fifty-eight of the Revised Statutes, or of any other section of the laws prohibiting the cooly-trade or of this act, such person shall be deemed guilty of a felony, and, upon conviction thereof, in any United States court, shall be fined in a sum not exceeding five hundred dollars and imprisoned for a term not exceeding one year.

Sec. 5. That it shall be unlawful for aliens of the following classes to immigrate into the United States, namely, persons who are undergoing a sentence for conviction in their own country of felonious crimes other than political or growing out of or the result of such political offenses, or whose sentence has been remitted on condition of their emigration, and women "imported for the purposes of prostitution." Every vessel arriving in the United States may be inspected under the direction of the collector of the port at which it arrives, if he shall have reason to believe that any such obnoxious persons are on board; and the officer making such inspection shall certify the result thereof to the master or other person in charge of such vessel, designating in such certificate the person or persons, if any there be, ascertained by him to be of either of the classes whose importation is hereby forbidden.

3. Chinese Immigrant Leaders Discourage Further Immigration from China, 1876

The Chinese Six Companies is asking our fellow clansmen not to make the long sea voyage to the United States so as to avoid bringing trouble on the community. The reason we have been subjected to all kinds of harassment by the white people is that many of our Chinese newcomers are taking jobs away from them. And yet, if we take a look at the wages of the Chinese workers in the various trades, we can see that they are shrinking day by day. This is also due to the large number of our fellow clansmen coming here. If up to 10,000 people come here, even if they do not take away 10,000 white men's jobs, they will still drive down the wages of 10,000 workers in various trades. It's inevitable. If this trend is not stopped, not only will the white men's harassment continue, causing a great deal of trouble for our community, but even skilled Chinese workers will have difficulty finding jobs and will lose their livelihood. If it is hard for the Chinese who are already here, imagine how much worse it will be for the newcomers.

Therefore, in an effort to prevent disaster before it strikes, the members of the Six Companies believe that the best course of action is to have each person in California write a letter home exhorting his clansmen not to come to America. And who would doubt such advice when it originates from a kinsman? This is much better than our posting thousands and thousands of notices. If the trend should cease and fewer clansmen come here, first, further trouble from the white people would be avoided; second, wages will stop shrinking; third, there will be no worry about newcomers being detained. Everyone will benefit. Just a single word from you will do a world of good. For this reason we are urging every one to write home.

The Chinese Six Companies
15th day of the 3rd month, Guangxu 2nd year [April 9, 1876]

4. White Merchant Testifies Against Chinese Immigration, 1879

Mr. JOHN F. SCHAEFER came before the committee. He said in reply to preliminary questions: I am a resident here [San Francisco, CA]; I crossed the plains in

Reprinted in Judy Yung, Gordon H. Chang, and H. Mark Lai (eds.), *Chinese American Voices: From the Gold Rush to the Present* (Berkeley: University of California Press, 2006), 25.

From House Select Committee, *The Causes of the General Depression in Labor and Business. Chinese Immigration*, San Francisco, CA, August 15, 1879 (Washington, D.C.: Government Printing Office, 1879), 263–264.

1850, when I was but twelve years of age. We are manufacturing clothing in New York and selling it here. We also sell piece goods, woolens, & c.

The CHAIRMAN. Give us your views in reference to the question of Chinese labor as brought into competition with your own.

Mr. SCHAEFER. My views are that the Chinese are going to ruin the country. They will not only ruin the Pacific States, but as soon as they get through here they will go to the East. I have fought for the Chinese for ten years. I thought that they would make good American citizens, that they would be like other people and would adapt themselves to American customs, but I find that I was mistaken. Even the Chinese merchants and the Chinese millionaires who are here are just as much Chinese to-day as they were when they came here. I know one Chinaman who dresses in American clothes. He talks English pretty well. I said to him some time ago, while the excitement on this subject was high, "Why do you not tell your intelligent people to wear American clothes and to adapt themselves to American customs? They all look like stuffed monkeys in their clothes." "To tell you the truth," said he, "I wear American clothes because I make my living here, but the other Chinamen look upon me as a degraded slave, and they do not admit me into their houses and families because I wear American clothes."

The CHAIRMAN. In your intercourse with them as a merchant, have you learned that there is any affinity or any common feeling between them and the American people, or whether the feeling that exists between them is a feeling of hostility?

Mr. SCHAEFER. I do not know one white man to-day who is in favor of the Chinese coming here.

Mr. CHAIRMAN. Why?

Mr. SCHAEFER. Because he has found out by experience that the Chinese will drive us out by starvation. It is a question of starvation. I talked not long ago to a Chinaman. I said, "Chinaman, you must go." He said, "Me no go; white man go." The Chinese drive us out by degrading labor. Even the manufacturers of cigars and of boots and shoes who employed them at first find out that the Chinese have taken away their business, and that the Chinese can sell at 25 per cent. less than they can. It is merely a matter of time. Chinatown is increasing, and the property of the white people in the vicinity is depreciating. The rich people lose much more by the Chinese than the poor do, on account of the depreciation of property. I have a good deal of property here which I cannot sell for half what it cost me ten years ago.

The CHAIRMAN. Does the presence of the Chinese here prevent immigration from other parts of the United States?

Mr. SCHAEFER. Most assuredly. People cannot get anything to do here. I know young men who are offering to work for me at almost any price. I have got a clerk in the store whom I keep out of sympathy. He has the best of recommendations, and yet he works for me at $2 a day as clerk and bookkeeper, because he cannot get a better situation. I knew another man, a telegraph operator, who ran around unemployed for six months, and who finally went to work at $1 a day in a sawmill, and he had to pay one of those intelligence offices to get that place. Last week I begged a friend of mine who has a mill in the country to take that man, and he says that when he has a vacant place he will let me know. He employs seventy men. Practical miners get $3 a day, but they have got a society which prevents any man working under that rate....

The CHAIRMAN. What do you think ought to be done with the Chinese?

Mr. SCHAEFER. That is a hard question to answer. I have been thinking that as the people East do not know and will not learn the merits of the question, we ought to send all these Chinese East, and give the people of the East a trial of them. I have been always a steady Republican, but this idea of wanting to sell out (as I may say) our country and homes to the Chinese goes against my grain.

The CHAIRMAN. Have you ever met with a Chinaman whom you could make a citizen of so that he would be creditable to the American standard?

Mr. SCHAEFER. You might just as well try to Christianize the Chinaman. A Chinaman once said to me, "If you give me four bit I will play to Jesus, and for four bit more I will take it all back." It is so in regard to Americanizing them. They will not even leave their bones here. They come out under contract that they shall be sent back to China, or if they die here that their bones shall be sent back.

The CHAIRMAN. Then it is your conviction that you cannot make a civilized American out of a Chinaman?

Mr. SCHAEFER. I thought at first that you could, and I have fought for them many a time and quarreled about them, but I find out that I was mistaken. As to making them American citizens, it is impossible. In different islands in the South Pacific Ocean, where the Chinese have been for one hundred years, the natives have had to clear them out, but the Chinese came back, and the natives did not drive them out a second time. And now the Chinese have these countries, and there are just as many Chinese there as there were one hundred years ago. They will stick to their ideas and their religion just as long as they live.

5. Graphic Comic Depicts Chinese Labor Threat, 1881

Choy, Philip P., Lorraine Dong, and Marlon Hom. *The Coming Man: 19th Century American Perceptions* of the Chinese © 1995. Reprinted with permission of the University of Washington Press.

6. U.S. Senator Declares Chinese Exclusion Un-American, 1882

Nothing is more in conflict with the genius of American institutions than legal distinctions between individuals based upon race or upon occupation. The framers of our Constitution believed in the safety and wisdom of adherence to abstract principles. They meant that their laws should make no distinction between men except such as were required by personal conduct and character. The prejudices of race, the last of human delusions to be overcome, has been found until lately in our constitutions and statutes, and has left its hideous and ineradicable stains on our history in crimes committed by every generation. The negro, the Irishman, and the Indian have in turn been its victims here, as the Jew and the Greek and the Hindoo in Europe and Asia. But it is reserved for us at the present day, for the first time, to put into the public law of the world and into the national legislation of the foremost of republican nations a distinction inflicting upon a large class of men a degradation by reason of their race and by reason of their occupation.

The bill which passed Congress two years ago and was vetoed by President Hayes, the treaty of 1881, and the bill now before the Senate, have the same origin and are parts of the same measure. Two years ago it was proposed to exclude Chinese laborers from our borders, in express disregard of our solemn treaty obligations. This measure was arrested by President Hayes. The treaty of 1881 extorted from unwilling China her consent that we might regulate, limit, or suspend the coming of Chinese laborers into this country—a consent of which it is proposed by this bill to take advantage. This is entitled "A bill to enforce treaty stipulations with China."

It seems necessary in discussing the statute briefly to review the history of the treaty. First let me say that the title of this bill is deceptive. There is no stipulation of the treaty which the bill enforces. The bill where it is not inconsistent with the compact only avails itself of a privilege which that concedes. China only relaxed the Burlingame treaty so far as to permit us to "regulate, limit, or suspend the coming or residence" of Chinese laborers, "but not absolutely to prohibit it." The treaty expressly declares "such limitation or suspension shall be reasonable." But here is proposed a statute which for twenty years, under the severest penalties, absolutely inhibits the coming of Chinese laborers to this country. The treaty pledges us not absolutely to prohibit it. The bill is intended absolutely to prohibit it....

Here is a declaration made by a compact between the two greatest nations of the Pacific, and now to be re-enforced by a solemn act of legislation, which places in the public law of the world and in the jurisprudence of America the principle that it is fit that there should hereafter be a distinction in the treatment of men by governments and in the recognition of their rights to the pursuit of happiness by a peaceful change of their homes, based not on conduct, not on character, but upon race and upon occupation. You may justly deny to the

From George Hoar, "Chinese Immigration," *Congressional Record*, 13: 200, March 1, 1882.

Chinese what you may not justly deny to the Irishman. You may deny to the laborer what you may not deny to the scholar or to the idler. And this declaration is extorted from unwilling China by the demand of America. With paupers, lazzaroni [beggars], harlots [prostitutes], persons afflicted with pestilential diseases, laborers are henceforth to be classed in the enumerations of American public law.

Certainly, Mr. President, this is an interesting and important transaction. It is impossible to overstate or to calculate the consequences which are likely to spring from a declaration made by the United States limiting human rights, especially a declaration in a treaty which is to become the international law governing these two great nations. As my friend from California [Mr. MILLER] well said, it is of the earth earthy. The United States within twenty years has taken its place as the chief power on the Pacific. Whatever rivalry or whatever superiority we may be compelled to submit to elsewhere, our advantage of position, unless the inferiority be in ourselves, must give us superiority there. Are we to hold out two faces to the world, one to Europe and another to Asia? Or are we to admit that the doctrine we have proclaimed so constantly for the first century of our history is a mere empty phrase or a lie?

For myself and for the State of Massachusetts, so far as it is my privilege to represent her, I refuse consent to this legislation. I will not consent to a denial by the United States of the right of every man who desires to improve his condition by honest labor—his labor being no man's property but his own—to go anywhere on the face of the earth that he pleases....

The number of immigrants of all nations was 720,045 in 1881. Of these 20,711 were Chinese. There is no record in the Bureau of Statistics of the number who departed within the year. But a very high anti-Chinese authority places it above 10,000. Perhaps the expectation that the hostile legislation under the treaty would not affect persons who entered before it took effect stimulated somewhat their coming. But the addition to the Chinese population was less than one-seventy-second of the whole immigration. All the Chinese in the country do not exceed the population of its sixteenth city. All the Chinese in California hardly surpass the number which is easily governed in Shanghai by a police of one hundred men. There are as many pure blooded Gypsies wandering about the country as there are Chinese in California. What an insult to American intelligence to ask leave of China to keep out her people, because this little handful of almond-eyed Asiatics threaten to destroy our boasted civilization....

The Chinese are in many particulars far superior to our own ancestors as they were when they first came forth into the light of history. Our British forefathers, at a time far within the historic period, remained in a degradation of superstition and a degradation of barbarism to which China never descended. Centuries after the Chinese philosopher had uttered the golden rule, and had said, "I like life and I like righteousness; if I cannot keep the two together I will let life go; and choose righteousness," the Druids of Britain were offering human sacrifices to pagan deities. We must take a race at its best in determining its capacity for freedom. This race can furnish able merchants, skillful diplomatists, profound philosophers, faithful servants, industrious and docile laborers. An eminent member of the other House told me that he had dealt with Chinese merchants to the amount of hundreds of thousands, perhaps millions, and that they had never deceived him....

Humanity, capable of infinite depths of degradation, is capable also of infinite heights of excellence. The Chinese, like all other races, has given us its examples of both. To rescue humanity from this degradation is, we are taught to believe, the great object of God's moral government on earth. It is not by injustice, exclusion, caste, but by reverence for the individual soul that we can aid in this consummation. It is not by Chinese policies that China is to be civilized. I believe that the immortal truths of the Declaration of Independence came from the same source with the Golden Rule and the Sermon on the Mount. We can trust Him who promulgated these laws to keep the country safe that obeys them. The laws of the universe have their own sanction. They will not fail. The power that causes the compass to point to the north, that dismisses the star on its pathway through the skies, promising that in a thousand years it shall return again true to its hour, and keeps His word, will vindicate His own moral law. As surely as the path on which our fathers entered a hundred years ago led to safety, to strength, to glory, so surely will the path on which we now propose to enter bring us to shame, to weakness, and to peril.

7. Chinese Laborers Report on Race Riot at Rock Springs, Wyoming Territory, 1885

From a survey of all the circumstances, several causes may be assigned for the killing and wounding of so many Chinese and the destruction of so much property:

1. The Chinese had been for a long time employed at the same work as the white men. While they knew that the white men entertained ill feelings toward them, the Chinese did not take precautions to guard against this sudden outbreak, inasmuch as at no time in the past had there been any quarrel or fighting between the races.

2. On the second day of September 1885, in Coal Pit No. 6, the white men attacked the Chinese. That place being quite a distance from Rock Springs, very few Chinese were there. As we did not think that the trouble would extend to Rock Springs, we did not warn each other to prepare for flight.

3. Most of the Chinese living in Rock Springs worked during the daytime in the different coal mines, and consequently did not hear of the fight at Coal Pit No. 6, nor did they know of the armed mob that had assembled in "Whitemen's Town." When twelve o'clock came, everybody returned home from his place of work to lunch. As yet the mob had not come to attack the Chinese; a great number of the latter were returning to work without any apprehension of danger.

4. About two o'clock the mob suddenly made their appearance for the attack. The Chinese thought that they had only assembled to threaten, and that some of the company's officers would come to disperse them. Most of the Chinese, acting upon this view of the matter, did not gather up their money or clothing, and when the mob fired at them they fled precipitately. Those Chinese who were in

From "Memorial of Chinese Laborers at Rock Springs, Wyoming Territory, to the Chinese Consul at New York," September 18, 1885; reprinted in *"Chink": A Documentary History of Anti-Chinese Prejudice in America*, ed. Cheng-Tsu Wu (New York: World Publishing, Times Mirror, 1972), 152–159.

the workshops, hearing of the riot, stopped work and fled in their working clothes, and did not have time enough to go home to change their clothes or to gather up their money. What they did leave at home was either plundered or burned.

5. None of the Chinese had firearms or any defensive weapons, nor was there any place that afforded an opportunity for the erection of a barricade that might impede the rioters in their attack. The Chinese were all like a herd of frightened deer that let the huntsmen surround and kill them.

6. All the Chinese had, on the first of September, bought from the company a month's supply of provision and the implements necessary for the mining of coal. This loss of property was therefore larger than it would be later in the month.

We never thought that the subjects of a nation entitled by treaty to the rights and privileges of the most favored nation could, in a country so highly civilized like this, so unexpectedly suffer the cruelty and wrong of being unjustly put to death, or of being wounded and left without the means of cure, or being abandoned to poverty, hunger, and cold, and without the means to betake themselves elsewhere.

To the great President of the United States, who, hearing of the riot, sent troops to protect our lives, we are most sincerely thankful.

In behalf of those killed or wounded, or of those deprived of their property, we pray that the examining commission will ask our minister to sympathize, and to endeavor to secure the punishment of the murderers, the relief of the wounded, and compensation for those despoiled of their property, so that the living and the relatives of the dead will be grateful, and never forget his kindness for generations.

Hereinabove we have made a brief recital of the facts of this riot, and pray your honor will take them into your kind consideration.

(Here follow the signatures of 559 Chinese laborers, resident at Rock Springs, Wyoming Territory.)

8. Chinese Immigrant Objects to the Hypocrisy of the Statue of Liberty, 1885

Sir:

A paper was presented to me yesterday for inspection, and I found it to be specially drawn up for subscription among my countrymen toward the Pedestal Fund of the Bartholdi Statue of Liberty. Seeing that the heading is an appeal to American citizens, to their love of country and liberty, I feel that my countrymen and myself are honored in being thus appealed to as citizens in the cause of liberty. But the word liberty makes me think of the fact that this country is the land of liberty for men of all nations except the Chinese. I consider it as an insult to us Chinese to call on us to contribute toward building in this land a pedestal for a statue of Liberty. That statue represents Liberty holding a torch which lights

From Saum Song Bo, *Letter to the New York Sun*, n.d., 1885, reprinted in *American Missionary*, Oct. 1885, 290.

the passage of those of all nations who come into this country. But are the Chinese allowed to come? As for the Chinese who are here, are they allowed to enjoy liberty as men of all other nationalities enjoy it? Are they allowed to go about everywhere free from the insults, abuse, assaults, wrongs and injuries from which men of other nationalities are free?

If there be a Chinaman who came to this country when a lad, who has passed through an American institution of learning of the highest grade, who has so fallen in low with American manners and ideas that he desires to make his home in this land, and who, seeing that his countrymen demand one of their own number to be their legal adviser, representative, advocate and protector, desires to study law, can he be a lawyer? By the law of this nation, he, being a Chinaman, cannot become a citizen, and consequently cannot be a lawyer.

And this statue of Liberty is a gift to a people from another people who do not love or value liberty for the Chinese. Are not the Annamese and Tonquinese [Tonkinese] Chinese, to whom liberty is as dear as to the French? What right have the French to deprive them of their liberty?

Whether this statute against the Chinese or the statue to Liberty will be the more lasting monument to tell future ages of the liberty and greatness of this country, will be known only to future generations.

Liberty, we Chinese do love and adore thee; but let not those who deny thee to us, make of thee a graven image and invite us to bow down to it.

9. Journalist Exposes Activities of Chinese Brothel Owner, 1899

SUEY HIN, a Chinese slave-owner, who has been importing Chinese girls into San Francisco for years, has just been converted to Christianity. To show her sincerity she has freed the seven girls in her possession, valued by her at $8,500, and will endeavor to see them safely married. Several of the girls were kidnaped and they will be returned to their parents. In the light of her new faith, Suey Hin uncovers the whole nefarious Chinese girl slave trade in San Francisco, and describes how the girls are sold here among the Chinese for a few hundred dollars. She herself when only five years old was sold into the trade by her own father, and lived out the whole dreadful life to the time when she adopted Christianity.

Suey Hin, importer, seller, keeper of slave girls, has become a Christian. She says her seven girls may go free if they will live a right life. She is the first woman slave-keeper in Chinatown ever known to give up her business for the Christian religion.

She did not intend to become a Christian. She wanted the "white teachers" to be friends because sometimes her girls were sick, sometimes they were kidnaped. Then, shrewd Chinese believe that the white teachers are good friends to have in a contest with highbinders. Suey Hin reasoned that way, and she went about gaining their friendship in the usual shrewd Chinese way.

She went to the lassies of the Salvation Army and asked them to come and pray for her. She returned with them to her little sitting-room, with its great carved and canopied bed, with its shrine and burning punk sticks and prayers on scarlet paper pasted at the side of the altar. "May honorable guests constantly visit this house," and the punctured red paper which makes the money god happy. Only two of the seven slave girls were in the room, and they knelt while the lassies prayed. They could not understand English, so their slaveowner thought the prayers could not hurt them, but it was a way to gain the good will of the lassies. Suey Hin did not understand the prayers herself at first, but the more she did understand them the better she remembered her mother and the old home in Shantung, and how life was before she began to buy and sell young girls....

It took Suey Hin five months to "get" so much conversion that she reached the point where she could give up her trade. Then she went back to her home where the seven girls had been under the care of a woman she called her sister.

It was in this home I listened to her story, partly in her own pigeon English and the rest from the lips of an interpreter. And this is the story she told me in her broken pigeon English:

"I am old, very old, too old to be an American. I like Americans, and if I were younger I would be one. Long, long ago I was born in Shantung, where the flowers are more beautiful and the birds sing more sweetly than in any other place. But my people were poor. There was not enough for all our stomachs. Two baby girls had been left exposed—that is, to die, you know. They were born after me and my father said often, 'She is too many.'

"Once there was an old woman came to our house and she looked at me. I was 5 that year, 6 the next. When she looked at me I was afraid and I hid myself behind my mother. My father told the old woman to go away.

"But that night she came back again and talked to my father and mother. She put a piece of gold money in my hand and told me to give it to my father. I did, for I wanted nothing to do with her. I had enough; yes, I had plenty to eat!

"But that night the old woman carried me away, and I kicked and screamed and said I would not go. I do not remember much more about the beginning. I remember the ship, and I remembered playing with other little girls. We were brought to San Francisco, and there were five or ten of us and we all lived with a woman on Ross alley. Every little while some one would come and see us, and as we grew older the girls were sold.

"One day it was my turn. They said I was 14 years old, but I was really 12. I don't know how much I cost, but I know both my hands were filled three times with all the gold they would hold. The money, you know, is always put in a girl's hand when she is sold.

"Well, then I was a slave for ten years. There was a man who loved me, but he was a poor washman, and he worked eight years and saved all, all the time. I saved all I could get, too, but it took eight years before we had saved $3000. Then we bought me from my owner and we were married.

"Then, ah, it's all of my life I like to think about. It wasn't but two next years, three years. My husband got sick and didn't get any better, and then he died. I didn't have anything but just myself, and I had to live, and I could not live on nothing. No, I had to have things, so I got a little house; you know, one with a little window over the door.

"Then pretty soon I went back to China, but I did not go to my own village. No, my parents would not want to see me. I went to Hongkong and I bought three girls. Two of them are dead, but Ah Moy, that's Ah Moy, she was a baby, and I paid her father 50 cents for her. After I had returned here a few months I went back to China again. I wanted to see my village, always I wanted to go back to my home. So I went, but I didn't let anybody know I was there. I went to the place where they put the babies to die. There was a baby there. A little bit of a brown baby, and she didn't look much good anyway. But I wanted some one from my own village, and so I took the baby, and she is Ah Lung. Don't you think she is a pretty girl now? She's not a slave you know. She's a good girl, just the same as white girls. She comes from Shantung, so I say she shall never be like the others. Slave girls most all die soon. It's bad, yes, and only the girls who want to be good and the dear Jesus knows about that. You see she is a girl and her people sold her, so what can she do?

"That trip I brought home four girls besides Ah Lung. You see it was not hard to smuggle the girls into this country then. You can't do it so easy now. Sometimes they come, only sometimes now. You see the Hop Sing tong fix it with the Custom House. They swore to the officers that the children were born here and went to China to visit. Some witnesses come and they say they knew the girl who wants to land was born here, and they tell all about it. Then they say they know she is the same because they saw her when they went back to China. It was not hard to swear them into this country.

"Then I went back once more. That was only a year ago and I brought back six girls. They did not seem to be with me when we got to the landing, but I watched them. I made the girls learn the answers to the questions the highbinders said would be asked by the Custom House. I told the girls if they made any mistakes the white devils would get them. I said white men liked to eat China girls, they like to boil them and then hang them up to dry and then eat them.

"Oh, the girls didn't make any mistakes when the inspector asked them questions and when they were landed they didn't want to run away. I told them that the girls only stayed at the missions till they got very fat and then Miss Cameron and Miss Lake sold them. Oh, I was bad—wasn't I bad? But I love Jesus now.

☾ ESSAYS

In the first essay, Princeton University historian Beth Lew-Williams examines the causes of Chinese restriction in 1882 and explains how and why Chinese labor migration to the United States did not end until more draconian exclusion policies were implemented later. The ambiguities of anti-Chinese discrimination are also revealed in the second essay, in which Massachusetts Institute of Technology historian Emma Teng describes representations of mixed-race Chinese Americans. Some of the depictions, she argues, supported popular racial theories at the time that saw such race mixing as detrimental as detrimental to the individual and society. Yet others saw them as a sign of "hybrid vigor" and the benefits of race mixing.

From Chinese Restriction to Exclusion

BETH LEW-WILLIAMS

Re-examining the Chinese Restriction Act of 1882

Although West Coast sinophobes began demanding the end of Chinese immigration in the 1850s, it took decades before the federal government enacted immigration restriction, both because of diplomatic entanglements and because the electorate was highly divided on the advisability of banning the Chinese. Three primary groups argued in favor of Chinese immigration: Radical Republicans, who opposed exclusion on the grounds of racial equality; Protestant missionaries, who believed exclusion would undermine their conversion efforts; and capitalists, who argued that "cheap" Chinese labor was essential to the development of the West. These constituencies had clout in Congress and made exclusion far from a foregone conclusion. However, the largest impediment to legislation barring Chinese immigration came not from interest groups on American soil, but from U.S. diplomatic agreements with China.

Through the first half of the nineteenth century, Americans habitually likened immigrants to imports and assumed that the governance of migration was a diplomatic matter. American treaties with European nations routinely granted the free movement of people between nations, along with the free movement of goods. In 1868 the United States negotiated a similar relationship with China in the Burlingame Treaty, whereby it recognized China as "an equal among the nations" and agreed to "free migration and emigration" between the two countries. The surprisingly egalitarian nature of the treaty derived from American economic anxiety. As U.S. territorial expansion slowed and industrial expansion increased in the mid-nineteenth century, industrialists believed that finding overseas markets for their products was imperative. Through this agreement with China, U.S. diplomats curried favor with the Chinese in order to secure a vast market, provide U.S. capitalists with a flow of inexpensive labor, and give U.S. missionaries access to millions of potential converts. At the time, the treaty had widespread support: The Senate unanimously ratified it, and the press lauded its "vast commercial importance."

Although well received in 1868, the Burlingame Treaty—and the sentiment behind it—ceased to have unanimous support in the 1870s as it became a stumbling block for congressional attempts to restrict Chinese immigration. In 1879 Congress passed the Fifteen Passenger Bill, which proposed to limit the number of Chinese immigrants who could disembark from a given vessel in the United States to fifteen. But President Rutherford Hayes vetoed this attempt at restriction, explaining that "our treaty with China forbids me to give the bill my approval." Hayes recognized Congress's prerogative to abrogate a treaty, but he argued that Congress should contravene treaties only in times of "highest necessity." Furthermore, he argued, Congress could not strike out one section of the treaty and leave

Lew-Williams, Beth, "Before Restriction Became Exclusion: America's Experiment in Diplomatic Immigration Control," *Pacific Historical Review*, 83, no. 1 (February 2014): 24–56. © 2014 by the Regents of the University of California. Published by the University of California Press.

the rest in place, because this would undermine executive diplomatic power. In his judgment, Congress could not restrict Chinese immigration without abrogating all diplomatic agreements with China, so Hayes pushed to secure a new treaty with China. After contentious negotiations, the 1880 Angell Treaty provided that the United States "may regulate, limit, or suspend" Chinese immigration but "not absolutely prohibit it." The treaty also stated, "the limitation or suspension shall be reasonable and shall apply only to Chinese who may go to the United States as laborers." The treaty contained another key limitation: "Chinese laborers who are now in the United States shall be allowed to go and come of their own free will and accord." The Angell Treaty permitted the United States to begin closing the gate that the Burlingame Treaty let open.

Soon after the new treaty was ratified, more than a dozen anti-Chinese bills were introduced in Congress, but it was California's Republican Senator John Miller's bill that got the attention of the Senate. Senate Bill 71 suspended the immigration of Chinese laborers for twenty years. To avoid violating treaty stipulations, Senate Bill 71 made an exception for Chinese workers currently residing in the United States and for Chinese who were present in the United States before November 17, 1880 (the day that the Angell Treaty was signed). All future Chinese immigrants—whether laborers or not—would be required to secure a passport from the Chinese government and approval from a U.S. diplomat before embarking from China. Any Chinese found entering illegally would be convicted of a misdemeanor, fined up to $100, subject to one year in prison, and then deported by the U.S. government. Chinese found to have forged their passports could be fined $1,000 and imprisoned for up to five years.

Most Democrats and western Republicans supported the bill, passionately repeating that the Chinese degraded American labor and contaminated white American civilization. But a sizable minority—mostly Republicans from northeastern and Atlantic states—opposed the legislation, arguing that it was an "extreme... sweeping and oppressive" bill that breached the new Angell Treaty with China. Congress claimed a constitutional right to contravene the treaty, but most Republicans feared that unilateral abrogation of a treaty would jeopardize America's national honor and relations with China. Connecticut Republican Orville Platt reminded the Senate, "We made this contract which we call a treaty with the Chinese Government.... We must keep it or stand forever disgraced in the eyes of the world." Some congressmen went further, questioning Congress's unilateral right to exclude Chinese immigrants. Senator George F. Hoar (Republican of Massachusetts) pointed out that the United States had described immigration as an "inalienable right of man" in the Burlingame Treaty....

Although they did not defend the merits of Chinese immigration, these Republican holdouts fought to amend the bill to make it less severe. They argued that the length of twenty years should be shortened and the passport section dropped, or that the law should only apply to certain undesirables (such as contract laborers, criminals, paupers, and the diseased). This fight for amendments reveals that by 1882 the vast majority of congressmen agreed that some form of restriction was needed, but there was no consensus for complete exclusion. In the end, Republicans did not appreciably weaken the bill. "An Act to Execute Certain Treaty Stipulations relating to the

Chinese" passed the Senate with Democrats voting in favor (twenty to one) and Republicans divided (nine to fourteen). Soon after, the House also passed the bill. Again, Democrats united in favor of the act, and Republicans split their votes, with sixty in favor and sixty-two opposed.

But Republican President Chester Arthur vetoed Senate Bill 71, explaining to Congress that the legislation was "a breach of our national faith" and threatened U.S. commercial interests in Asia. Arthur wrote to Congress, "Experience has shown that the trade of the East is the key to national wealth and influence.... It needs no argument to show that the policy which we now propose to adopt must have a direct tendency to repel Oriental nations from us and to drive their trade and commerce into more friendly hands." Although Arthur vetoed Senate Bill 71, he made it clear that he would favor a more limited form of Chinese restriction that did not threaten the U.S. relationship with China. In his veto message, he argued that the twenty-year suspension was unreasonable, but he encouraged Congress to consider "a shorter experiment." Congress might have had the constitutional right to unilaterally abrogate the Angell Treaty and exclude Chinese laborers, but President Arthur, like President Hayes, denied them the power to do so.

Given the sizable number of Republican holdouts, Congress could not hope to pass the law over Arthur's veto....

Only a few weeks after President Arthur's veto, Congress considered a new Chinese bill that was a watered-down version of its predecessor. The vetoed Bill 71 had already made significant efforts to avoid angering the Chinese government: Chinese who were not laborers were free to come and go as they pleased, and Chinese laborers who had arrived before the 1882 act or had visited the United States before the 1880 treaty were also allowed free entry. The new bill went further to place diplomatic concerns above the desire to limit Chinese immigration. Not only did Congress shorten the term of restriction to ten years, it also eliminated section seven, which instituted an internal registration and passport system, and section fourteen, which made illegal immigration a crime punishable by imprisonment and a fine. Some congressmen, especially those representing the West Coast, may have earnestly hoped the bill would stop the immigration of Chinese workers. For others, however, this was clearly a temporary solution that they hoped would placate western sinophobes without eliciting retribution from the Chinese government. With additional Republican support, Congress passed the weakened bill. On May 6, 1882, President Arthur signed the Chinese Restriction Act into law.

Documented Immigration during Chinese Restriction, 1882–1888

The Restriction Act was not the "near total victory for the exclusionists" that some scholars have claimed. Tempered by Republicans' fears of violating U.S. treaties with China, the Restriction Act was deliberately narrow in scope. Without an internal passport system to register and identify Chinese in America, it was nearly impossible to determine whether a Chinese immigrant was legal or illegal. Furthermore, Congress virtually ensured the act's failure by appropriating a paltry $5,000 per year to implement its provisions. Inadequate enforcement mechanisms and inadequate funding guaranteed that the act would have only limited effect on the flow of Chinese immigration. No law could have suddenly and completely closed the borders to Chinese workers, but it is striking that the 1882 act left the doors intentionally propped open....

After 1882, tens of thousands of Chinese workers continued to enter California by claiming to be members of the exempt classes (i.e., a merchant, diplomat, tourist, or student), travelers who were merely "in-transit" across the United States, or workers who had previously resided in America. Some Chinese presented real or fabricated certificates to make these claims, but admission did not even require such papers. The Restriction Act, in compliance with the Angell Treaty, allowed free entry to Chinese who had resided in the United States before the Restriction Act went into effect. This meant that Chinese workers could claim they had resided in the country before 1880 and had left before the customs department started issuing return certificates. Congress had deliberately created the category of "return immigrant" as a diplomatic concession that would respect U.S. treaty stipulations and

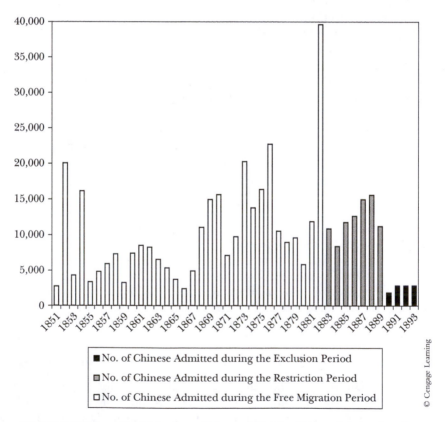

© Cengage Learning

F I G U R E   3.1   Total Number of New and Return Chinese Admitted to the United States by Year, 1851–1893. This figure offers a visual representation of the flow of documented Chinese immigration when Chinese were allowed free migration (1851–1882), when the Chinese Restriction Act was enforced (1883–1889), and when the 1888 Chinese Exclusion Act was enforced (1890–1893).

avoid antagonizing China. The law intended to hold the gate open for cyclical immigrants who had resided in the United States before, but it ended up also allowing many who were newcomers who had learned how to bypass the law. California Congressman William Morrow complained, "The practical effect of leaving our doors open to Chinamen who will assert and prove this claim of prior residence is to defeat the whole purpose of the treaty stipulations and legislation." During the Restriction period, the primary way that Chinese entered the United States was by claiming they were returning immigrants....

When returning immigrants are included in the annual totals of Chinese arrivals, the ineffectiveness of Restriction becomes clear. During the period of free Chinese migration, between 1851 and 1882, the mean annual number of Chinese entries was 10,388. During the period when Restriction was enforced (1883–1889), the mean number was 8,746. This represents only a 16 percent decrease in the annual number of Chinese immigrants as a result of the law....

Undocumented Immigration during Chinese Restriction, 1882–1888

The most visible stream of Chinese immigrants came through San Francisco, but the Chinese had another major illegal avenue into the United States. When drafting the Restriction Act, congressmen had conceived of western border control in terms of discrete points of entry at seaports, like San Francisco, where all immigrants could be stopped and questioned. They failed to appreciate the porous nature of thousands of miles of land and sea borders. This made little difference in California, because relatively few Chinese entered across the Mexican border in the 1880s. But in the north, thousands of Chinese lived in British Columbia and crossed into Washington Territory, which had a more robust economy at the time. Congress's failure to address the vast northern border made the U.S.-Canadian boundary an open back door into the United States. No law could have completely closed this long border, but the specifics of the 1882 act undermined a credible attempt.

The Restriction Act was impossible to enforce.... In 1884, the head U.S. immigration officer for the Northwest, summarized his desperate situation to his superiors: "This Chinese immigration is no fiction now. I believe they are coming over to our side every day, by water and by land, and by boats and canoes ... between British Columbia, and this country, it seems to me the Restriction Act is almost worthless."...

From Restriction to Exclusion

The failure of Restriction was clear not only to local customs officials, but also becoming clear to Congress, the President, and the general American public. In 1886 the *Philadelphia Press* observed:

> A trial of nearly four years of the restriction act has shown that it is little better than a rope of sand as a bulwark against the Mongolians. The frauds that can be practiced under it are numerous and the wily Chinese

were not slow to find the loopholes and take advantage of them. The knowledge of these facts has aroused the people of the Pacific slope as they were never aroused before on the subject.

In 1885 and 1886, the U.S. West erupted in violent local crusades to drive out the Chinese, and anti-Chinese vigilantes vehemently petitioned Congress to finally pass an exclusion law. The violence drew attention on both sides of the Pacific. In June 1886, in the wake of the violence, Congress debated the future of Chinese Restriction and its funding.... varied from $5,000 to $5,500. He complained, "The insufficiency of this appropriation compelled the Treasury Department to exercise such rigid economy in providing the machinery for executing the provisions of the act that the law has been evaded in a most shameful manner."

As Congress united against Chinese immigration, the treaty with China remained a roadblock to exclusion. But the anti-Chinese violence and the failings of the Restriction Act had also gained the attention of the Chinese government. In 1886, Cheng Tsao Ju, the Chinese minister stationed in Washington, D.C., wrote to the U.S. Secretary of State, Thomas Francis Bayard, "to bring ... immediate and urgent attention" to the fact that "Chinese have been driven by violence out of many places, their dwellings burned, their property robbed, and, in some instances, the people murdered, without any serious attempt being made by the authorities to prevent these acts or afford protection." Cheng demanded an end to the violence and redress for all financial losses. After months when complaints about the violence had drawn little response, Chinese diplomats tried a new tactic. They proposed a treaty (later called the Bayard–Zhang Treaty) designed to reduce attacks on Chinese by self-prohibiting the emigration of Chinese workers. Economically and politically subjugated by western countries, China did not have the power to force the United States to follow treaty stipulations and protect Chinese citizens. The Chinese government hoped that self-prohibition—preventing Chinese workers from boarding ships bound for the United States—would provide an alternate way to end anti-Chinese violence, increase American respect, and construct Chinese exclusion on Chinese terms.

The Bayard–Zhang treaty finally had the potential to prohibit Chinese workers from immigrating to America. The treaty would have excluded all Chinese laborers for the following twenty years, unless the laborer had a return certificate *and* either $1,000 in property or a direct relative (wife, child, or parent) in the United States. The United States eagerly ratified the treaty in May 1888, but in September rumors crossed the Pacific that the Chinese government was backing out of the accord. This news came two months before a highly contentious presidential election, and the Democratic administration rushed to contain the fallout. Through connections in Congress, President Grover Cleveland pushed forward a bill that would unilaterally exclude the Chinese even though it abrogated existing treaties. With his eyes likely trained on the swing state of California, Cleveland wished "to answer the earnest popular demand for the absolute exclusion of Chinese laborers."

Before 1888, fear of diplomatic and commercial repercussions had tied the U.S. government's hands. But now, from the perspective of the U.S. government, the Chinese had blinked. By proposing the Bayard-Zhang treaty, the Chinese government had revealed that it would be willing to accept some form of exclusion. Cleveland and Congress thus had reason to hope that they could close the door to Chinese workers while continuing to pursue an open door in China. Signing the 1888 Exclusion Act (also known as the Scott Act) into law, President Cleveland openly acknowledged that the law abrogated U.S. treaties with China. He justified this bold action, stating that "the unexpected and disappointing refusal of the Chinese Government" to ratify the Bayard-Zhang Treaty at the eleventh hour had driven the United States to act in "self-defense by exercise of legislative power."

Despite the long U.S. history of bilateral negotiations of immigration law through treaties with foreign nations, Cleveland now asserted that immigration control was a sovereign U.S. right. In his official message to Congress, he argued that "exclud[ing] from its border all elements of foreign population which for any reason retard its prosperity" was "the admitted and paramount right and duty of every Government" and "must be regarded as a recognized canon of international law and intercourse." Cleveland drew on the precedent of seventeenth-century international law, but the sovereign right of exclusion had not been explicitly part of U.S. law until Cleveland signed the Exclusion Act and the Supreme Court upheld its constitutionality the following year. In *Chae Chan Ping v. United States* (1889), the Supreme Court held that "the power of exclusion of foreigners" was an "incident of sovereignty belonging to the government of the United States as a part of … the Constitution" and that this right "cannot be granted away or restrained on behalf of any one." The Court's ruling recognized Congress's absolute power to exclude foreigners.

The United States had violated the spirit of Sino-American treaties before, but it had never blatantly and knowingly abrogated a treaty with China through federal legislation. Other western powers openly wondered if the United States were trying to provoke war with China in order to advance U.S. imperial ambitions. The Chinese minister in America expressed shock and dismay, writing, "I was not prepared to learn that there was a way recognized in the law and practice of [the United States] whereby your country could release itself from treaty obligations without consultation or consent of the other party." But the Chinese government did little but lodge protest after protest. The Exclusion Act of 1888 cemented into law the imbalance of power between the United States and China.

The 1888 Exclusion Act also represented a dramatic shift in the objectives of U.S. immigration policy and achieved a significant tightening of U.S. borders. Whereas the Restriction Act had allowed Chinese laborers who resided in the United States to return, the Exclusion Act ended this exception. It declared null and void approximately 30,000 return certificates that had been issued to Chinese laborers since 1882, leaving tens of thousands of men and women who had temporarily left the United States unable to return. By ending the use of return certificates, the law also closed a major avenue of immigration fraud. The only diplomatic concession the law retained was unrestricted immigration for upper-class Chinese, including students, diplomats, and merchants.

The Exclusion Act also dramatically slowed documented Chinese migration. Between 1888 and 1893 when the act was in place, the mean annual number of Chinese admitted to the United States dropped to 2,527, which represented a 75 percent decrease from pre-1882 admission levels.

As documented avenues of entering the country narrowed, Chinese migrants turned to illegal entry, increasing undocumented immigration along U.S. borders with Canada and Mexico. The Exclusion Act failed to close these illegal avenues (a failure repeated in many immigration laws since) or eliminate the possibility of fraud, but it is noteworthy that Congress intended the law to erect a new level of border control. The appropriations committee allocated $50,000 to enforce the Exclusion Act during its first year—ten times the yearly appropriation for the Restriction Act—and this allocation doubled in subsequent years. Along the U.S.-Canadian boundary, this meant the customs service could employ and train specially designated "Chinese inspectors" for the first time. These inspectors began to monitor the movement of Chinese on both sides of the border, with the help of their Canadian counterparts.

The funding also meant a change in the U.S. ability to punish illegal immigrants. Starting in 1890, the Department of the Treasury stopped deporting convicted Chinese in the Pacific Northwest to Canada and began sending them to China, regardless of the additional cost. In addition, the new language of the law, according to Attorney General William Miller, put "the burden of proof upon the Chinese applicant for admission [and] the evidence must be convincing." With the Exclusion Act came a change in federal attitude that made "exclusion the rule and admission the exception."

The tightening of U.S. immigration policy did not end with the Exclusion Act. Once Congress had breached its treaties with China without consequence, it became easy to do so again. Chinese officials and immigrants launched protests of the Exclusion Act of 1888, but they did little to disrupt U.S. trade or diplomatic relations with China. Without the approval of China, the United States passed additional legislation in 1892, 1902, and 1904 designed to constrain further the immigration of Chinese to the United States. In 1888 the federal government made exclusion its goal, marking a major shift in its conception of U.S. sovereignty and immigration law, but it continued to work out the practicalities of achieving full exclusion for years to come.

Debating Mixed Marriage in the United States and China

EMMA JUNHUA TENG

The most famous Eurasian in America during the 1890s was a criminal. A notorious pickpocket and "green-goods man," George Washington Appo (1856–1930) regularly appeared in newspaper stories of the time. After he testified in the sensational Lexow Committee investigation of New York police corruption,

Emma Junhua Teng, *Debating Mixed Marriage in the U.S. and China*. From Teng, *Eurasian: Mixed Identities in the United States, China, and Hong Kong, 1842–1943* (Berkeley: University of California Press, 2013).

the *New York Times* dubbed George "one of the country's most picturesque criminals," while the [Chinese-friendly] *Hartford Courant* unfailingly chronicled the "half-breed's" trials and testimony. George Appo even turned up on the stage, playing himself in George Lederer's theatrical melodrama, *In the Tenderloin*, to national acclaim. To cap it all off, the *World* voted him among "the People Who Made the History of 1894."

Journalist Louis J. Beck devoted a chapter to this colorful character, son of Quimbo Appo, the infamous Chinese tea merchant turned murderer, in his *New York's Chinatown: An Historical Presentation of Its People and Places* (1898). Part tourist guidebook, part amateur ethnography, part muckraking exposé, Beck's volume was the first full-length book on New York's Chinese Quarter and would in time become a frequently quoted source for Chinatown history. Beck promised his audience that his book would shed light on the vexed Chinese Question by presenting the city's Chinese residents through the unbiased lens of the reporter. At the heart of the Chinese Question was this: Could the Chinese in time become assimilated, and patriotic, American citizens, or did their "racial traits" render this impossible, warranting their exclusion from the nation? Beck offered George Appo's biography as food for thought: "George Appo was born in New York City, July 4, 1858 [*sic*], and is therefore an American citizen, and should be a patriotic one, but he is not. His father was a full-blooded Chinaman and his mother an Irishwoman. He was an exceedingly bright child, beautiful to look upon, sharp-witted and quick of comprehension. For ten years he was the pet of the neighborhood where his parents dwelt.... At the age of ten he became a pickpocket."

Beck's decision to dedicate an entire chapter to the celebrity criminal can be explained not only by sensationalism, but also by the special significance he saw in George Appo's life story. Beck considered this "noted Chinese character" a valuable case study in "heredity and racial traits and tendencies," one well worth investigating, he claimed, for he was only the first of the emerging "new hybrid brood" to come to popular notice. As such, Beck argued, "The question which naturally presents itself to the thinker is, 'What part will the rest of his tribe take in our national development?'"

It was a question that was on the minds of many journalists, social reformers, travelers, and others as they toured America's Chinatowns and saw growing numbers of "half-castes" on the streets and in doorways. Indeed, by the late nineteenth century, such "mixed" children could be found in virtually every Chinese American community, from Boston to Chicago and San Francisco (see introduction). When pioneering Chinese American journalist Wong Chin Foo reported on the New York Chinese for the *Cosmopolitan* in 1888, he asserted that there were more than a hundred "half-breed" Chinese children in that city alone. Although their absolute numbers were small, their anomalous looks drew attention and aroused curiosity. Observers attached a special significance to these children that went beyond their numbers. For many, they represented the future shape of the Chinese American population, for better or worse. Some regarded these "hybrids" as living specimens who offered a chance to see firsthand the biological consequences of race mixing, a subject of intense scientific debate and social concern.

This essay examines discourses on Chinese Eurasians as a "problem" in late nineteenth-century American society. Using Louis Beck's account of George Appo as a starting point, I explore the ways in which racial theories regarding the consequences of racial amalgamation (which were overwhelming dominated by discussions of white–black miscegenation) informed perceptions of Eurasians as a potential threat to the nation's development. George Appo's case reveals that while the figure of the "half-caste" was frequently connected to dystopian visions of the future—the threat of the Yellow Peril or the specter of mongrelization—representations of Eurasians from this era were not always uniformly derisive, as has often been assumed. Rather, as we will see from a closer reading of Louis Beck's account of Appo, such representations often reveal an underlying ambivalence toward this "half-white/half-Chinese" figure. This ambivalence made the Eurasian a locus of anxiety and desire in an age of increasing global interpenetration and migration....

The Eurasian as Problem

From the very beginning of Chinese immigration to the United States, nativists warned against miscegenation as an inevitable outcome of the Chinese presence in American society.... John Kuo Wei Tchen's study of the Chinese in pre-Exclusion era New York reveals that intermarriage between Chinese men and Irish women ... was prevalent in the early years of Chinese immigration. By 1900, Chinese immigrants in New York were marrying women of diverse backgrounds, but intermarriages still greatly outnumbered Chinese-Chinese marriages, 82 to 51. Indeed, owing in large part to the strictures on the migration of Chinese women to the United States during this era, interracial marriage would remain the predominant marriage pattern for Chinese in New York City until 1925.

The children of mixed couples increasingly drew the attention of journalists and reformers. In 1890, a *Harper's Weekly* feature on New York's "Chinese Colony" included a description of Chinese–Irish intermarriages, as evidenced by the sight of mixed-race children: "Around the gutters, playing on terms of equality with the other gamins, may be seen a few boys whose features betray their mingled blood." The writer pondered the fact that "it is only about 12 or 15 years since these marriages began, so that the children are all yet young. What kind of people the hybrids will prove to be is yet an unsolved problem." When Harry Wilson reported on the "Children of Chinatown" for the *New York Times* in 1896, he similarly represented mixed children as a "problem." Such children, he wrote, present "a view that is at once bewildering—a problem for which there is no solution.... They were the result of marriage between a Chinaman and an American woman." For those who perceived these "hybrids" as a problem, Beck's account must surely have been alarming. According to Beck, there were only thirty-two "full blooded Chinese children" in Chinatown, compared to forty-seven mixed children. This was the "new hybrid brood" that Beck warned the public would "hear more from ... as time rolls on."

Why was the Eurasian a problem for American society? A problem for which there was no solution? In Wong Chin Foo's eyes, the "half-breed children" were successful examples of Chinese assimilation into American society. As he wrote, "[They] speak the English language, adopt the American ways and dress." In sharp contrast, the two journalists cited displayed particular anxiety concerning racial mixing as an unknown. Although the *Harper's* writer confidently described the "Chinaman" and "Hibernians" as racial types, it remained for him an open question "what kind of people the hybrids will prove to be." What would be the effects, biological and cultural, of "mingled blood"? Building on long-standing American concerns over white–black and white–Native American interracialism that dated back to the colonial era (see introduction), such were the questions that the Eurasian "half-breed" frequently raised in the minds of curious observers.

Despite the long history of Euro–Asian interracialism in Asia, the New York press generally tended to look close at hand for answers, portraying Eurasian hybridity as a "new" phenomenon and an unknown, a rhetorical move that had the effect of sensationalizing this offshoot of the Chinese Question. The visual scrutiny of Eurasian faces and bodies was part of the anxious search for clues. The *Harper's Weekly* article of 1890, for example, was accompanied by a full-page illustration of a scene on Mott Street: the focal point is an Irishwoman standing next to her Chinese husband, holding a baby in her arms, two older mixed-race children playing beside them. Vividly visualizing the mixed character of Chinatown life, the illustration prompted readers to consider the yet "unsolved problem" of what such hybrids would become as they matured. Similarly, Wilson's *New York Times* article was illustrated with photographs of "Chinese Half-Castes." Wilson found one girl, a "Red-Headed Chinese-American Girl," to be a particular curiosity, and she was featured in several of the photographs. The "half-caste" as visual spectacle thus emerged as a feature of this time period.

With a naturalist's eye for hereditary patterns, Wilson ventured some curious rules as to the effects of this "Chinese-American" intermixing. "Half-caste" boys, he claimed, invariably looked Chinese, but the girls might "incline in resemblance toward their mothers." Mentally, he asserted, the children inherited "the qualities of both nations." Hence Wilson depicted these interracial households as "mixed up" and eclectic. In one family, the younger son wears American dress while the older son wears Chinese. Bilingualism is similarly presented as a strange curiosity of the "mixed" family. As a reporter for the *New York Daily Tribune* had written in 1869, "It is very curious to hear the little half-bred children running about the rooms and alternately talking Irish to their mothers and Chinese to their fathers." For some, the bilingualism/biculturalism displayed by the interracial family was more than a simple curiosity, for it represented a threat to the idealized homogeneity of American society.

Eurasians thus presented a problem in part because of their indeterminacy and liminal [in-between] status. At once Chinese and European, Sinophone and Anglophone, what place could they be assigned in the American hierarchy of race and ethnicity that was evolving at the turn of the twentieth century?

Straddling the boundary between white and non-white, Eurasians were trouble-some for, like others of "mixed race," they disrupted the notion of a clearly delineated color line. The ambiguity of Eurasian identity during this era is sug-gested in the story of one child encountered by a reporter for the *World* in 1877: "'Joe is his name,' said the proud [Irish] mother. 'He don't look like a Chinaboy, does he, when he's asleep! His eyes show it, though, when he's awake.'"

One can only imagine the confusion faced by census enumerators con-fronted with a child like Joe: Should such a child be classed as "white"? Or "Chinese"? It is perhaps no wonder that the New York census displayed the inconsistencies that John Kuo Wei Tchen first identified regarding the classifica-tion of Eurasian children, who were sometime categorized as "Chinese," some-times as "white," and sometimes as "mulatto." These inconsistencies would persist well into the twentieth century despite the Census Bureau's attempt to formulate rules regarding persons of "mixed-race". If Eurasians could manage to fool census enumerators into classifying them as "white," was there a danger that such racially indeterminate peoples would attempt "racial migration" ("crossing the color line")? Or, even worse, "play both sides"?...

The "Human Hybrid": Amalgamation in Western Racial Theory

Even before the advent of "human hybridity" as a scientific concept in the mid-nineteenth century, racial intermixing was long associated with anomalies, abnormalities, and monstrosity. In 1799, for example, British surgeon Charles White reported numerous instances of "irregularities" in the offspring of white-black unions, including piebald children, twins of opposite racial phenotype, and children who were quite literally half-black and half-white—one white on the right side of his body and black on the left, another white from the navel upward and black on his lower body. While such associations with monstrosity or physi-cal abnormalities did not disappear, the nineteenth century ushered in a new body of scientific racial theory on the question of amalgamation and related dis-courses on the historical effects of "race mixing" on civilizations. As demon-strated by George Stocking and Robert Young, the issue of so-called human hybridity was at the center of nineteenth-century debates over race, pitting monogenists against polygenists, abolitionists against slaveholders—positions that again can be seen as inclusionary versus exclusionary discourses. Young identifies five possible positions that emerged from these debates: (1) the polygenist denial that productive crossing could occur between human races; (2) the amalgamation thesis that racial intermixing produces a new mixed race; (3) the decomposition thesis that mixed-race progeny inevitably revert to parental type; (4) the variable hybridity thesis that unions between "proximate" races are fertile, whereas unions between "distant" races are infertile or degenerate; and (5) the mongreli-zation thesis that miscegenation produces "raceless chaos."

I add to this list a sixth thesis: that of hybrid vigor. As Nancy Stepan has demonstrated, although this position was a minority one, it nonetheless remained a constant in debates on racial amalgamation throughout the nineteenth century, playing a central role in Quatrefages's discussions of racial hybridity, for example, and even surfacing in Darwin's *The Descent of Man* (1871) among other texts. Indeed, the notion of what Stepan calls "constructive miscegenation" assumes greater historical importance when we extend our attention beyond the Anglo-American sphere to French colonial debates concerning acclimatization; to Latin American eugenics as studied by Stepan; and to Chinese racial theorists, as the next chapter will show. Among Anglo-American theorists, the idea that racial amalgamation was dysgenic remained the dominant view between the 1850s and the 1930s, Nonetheless, it is important to take stock of hybrid vigor as an alternative thesis, as we will see following, for the continuing (if submerged) influence of this viewpoint—which was made plausible through commonplace experiences with plant and animal breeding—helps to explain the deep-seated ambivalence toward the miscegen as a symbol alternatively of mongrelization or of assimilation.

One of the most prominent early proponents of hybrid degeneracy was American polygenist Josiah Nott, who warned of the "Probable Extermination of the Two Races If the Whites and Blacks Are Allowed to Intermarry" in the *American Journal of the Medical Sciences* in 1843. Theorizing the "laws" of human hybridity, Nott declared that "the Mulatto or Hybrid is a degenerate, unnatural offspring, doomed by nature to work out its own destruction." Edinburgh anatomist, Robert Knox, a polygenist like Nott, elaborated the laws of human hybridity in his influential book *The Races of Men*, declaring that "the hybrid was a degradation of humanity and was rejected by nature." Asserting that hybridity was unviable, Knox argued that miscegens either were infertile or reverted to one of the parental types after a few generations. From New York, the polygenist physician John H. van Evrie asserted in 1864 that the "facts" proved "the crossing of distinct races produces a mongrel population, which ... has less powers of virility, greater tendency to disease, and hence is shorter lived ... that the condition is an abnormalism, and one of unspeakable wrong and suffering." If unchecked, van Evrie warned, miscegenation would lead to the inevitable downfall of American civilization.

Demonstrating its staying power, Stepan writes, the theory of hybrid degeneracy even survived the revolution of evolutionary biology. The opinion that "crossed races of men are singularly savage and degraded" found support in no less a man than Darwin himself, who speculated that the "degraded state of so many half-castes is in part due to reversion to a primitive and savage condition, induced by the act of crossing, even if mainly due to the unfavorable moral conditions under which they are generally reared." Although Darwin explained "half-caste" degradation in terms of *both* environmental *and* biological factors, it was the latter notion that found most traction during his time.

Nativists in California and elsewhere invoked pseudoscientific ideas of the horrors of biological degeneracy to justify segregating, and ultimately excluding, Chinese immigrants, as we saw from chapter 1. At the Constitutional Convention of the State of California in 1878 delegates warned that "the result of the amalgamation [of Chinese and white] would be a hybrid of the most despicable, a mongrel of the most detestable that has ever afflicted the earth." Decades later the authors of a pamphlet *For the Re-enactment of the Chinese Exclusion Law* (1901) would similarly declare that "the offspring [of intermarriages] has been invariably degenerate. It is well-established that the issue of the Caucasian and the Mongolian do not possess the virtues of either, but develop the vices of both. So physical assimilation is out of the question." Hybrid degeneracy was thus taken as final proof of the unassimilability (biological and cultural) of the Chinese. Even scientific authorities like Herbert Spencer expressed approval for Chinese exclusion in light of the question of amalgamation. Spencer saw only two possible outcomes of Chinese immigration to the United States: either the Chinese would "remain unmixed" and thereby constitute a separate and slave-like class, "or if they mix they must form a bad hybrid." Either scenario would be damaging for American national development....

The Worst of Both Worlds: The Dual Nature of the Hybrid

By far the most popular expression of a belief in hybrid degeneracy was the pithy saying, "The half-caste inherits the vices of both parents, and the virtues of neither." Although its origins are obscure, this cliché had become well worn by the time *New York's Chinatown* was published—and even given the stamp of scientific authority by men like van Evrie. Beck certainly resorts to this chestnut in his portrait of George Appo, identifying specific traits and vices that the "half-breed" inherited from his Chinese father and Irish mother, respectively. From his father, Beck asserted, George inherited "mental cunning and duplicity" and a "cynicism which is particular to the Eastern character"; from his mother, a general "flyness," which also served him well as a professional thief. Combining the worst of (stereotypical) Chinese and Irish vices, Appo was set from birth to become a larger-than-life criminal.

One particular threat embodied by "half-castes" like George Appo was their putative ability to play both sides. Beck asserts that the "young halfbreed" carved out a role for himself as a go-between or interpreter between "Americans" and Irish, on one hand, and Chinese on the other. He worked for a time as a Chinatown guide, catering to sightseers eager to taste the exotic vices of the Quarter, but under the safety of an escort. Beck claimed that Appo's racial inheritance enabled him to function as the perfect inside guide to this mysterious and inscrutable world: "Appo had always, by virtue of his blood on his father's side, enjoyed to a certain extent the confidence of the Chinese—a confidence which the strange, secretive people seldom give to any one not of their own race." If Appo served as a cultural interpreter, in Beck's eyes he was also an agent of transmission of Chinese vices to the non-Chinese community. Indeed, Beck blamed Appo, with his specialized "Chinese" knowledge of the art of cooking opium and his familiarity with the Chinatown "joints," for introducing a taste for the drug to the "New York roughs and crooks" who soon came to frequent Chinatown's opium dens, bringing other white patrons in their wake. Hence the "half-caste" represents not only a corruption of white racial purity, but also a corrupting moral influence. Racial pollution, moral contamination, vice unbalanced by virtue—such were the associations of "half-caste" status. In fact,

Timothy Gilfoyle's detailed study of George Appo's criminal career demonstrates that he did have connections, and even financial backing, from criminal establishments both within Chinatown and beyond. According to Gilfoyle, however, it was the latter that played the major role in Appo's life.

The idea of the Eurasian's dual nature had earlier served as the premise for T.S. Denison's comedic drama, *Patsy O'Wang: An Irish Farce with a Chinese Mix-up* (1895). The play centers on the character of Patsy O'Wang, a.k.a. Chin Sum, a Eurasian of Chinese-Irish descent. As the playwright directed, "The key to this capital farce is the remarkable transformation of which Chin Sum is capable. Born of Irish father and Chinese mother and brought up in barracks in Hong Kong he has a remarkable dual nature." The transformation is effected when Chin Sum imbibes whiskey, "the drink of his father," and undergoes a metamorphosis into a "true Irishman." Strong tea, "the drink of his mother," restores Patsy's "Chinese character," which is that of a sober and industrious Chinese cook. The ideas of hybrid reversion and latent racial traits (blood will tell) are thus enacted in this farce through the bifurcated character of Patsy/Chin Sum, who reverts to parental type based on the drink he consumes.

Hybridity may be farcical, but it is also a cause of chaos, confusion, and disorder—a case for the police and a psychiatrist. In the final act, Patsy/Chin Sum's frustrated employer crossly asks him, "What are you now? Irish or Chinese?" When Patsy declares his choice to be Irish, he is immediately dismissed, roundly castigated for his "ambition" by the doctor's Irish assistant. The ultimate message of this ludicrous comedy is that the races should stay in their place....

Degenerate but Beautiful? Hybrid Vigor and Strains of Ambivalence

Given that his work is a case study in "heredity and racial traits and tendencies," Beck may have intended the lesson of George Appo as a warning. Yet, even as he portrayed Appo as the embodiment of hybrid degeneracy, degradation, and monstrosity, Beck also expressed a grudging respect for the man—a man who was, in fact, as Gilfoyle demonstrates, an inside informant who assisted the journalist in the compilation of *New York's Chinatown*. In particular, Beck lauds Appo's intelligence and cleverness, even if these traits were not put to good uses. As evident in the opening of Beck's biographical sketch, one of the first things he tells us is that George "was an exceedingly bright child, beautiful to look upon, sharp-witted and quick of comprehension." While Beck goes on to narrate Appo's fall from grace, he nonetheless repeatedly insists on the man's physical beauty. Seemingly unable to let go of this point, Beck returns to Appo's unusual attractiveness again paragraphs later: "The reference to his beauty is no exaggeration. Throughout his long and varied career of crime he retained the handsome features and charming manners which characterized him as a boy, and were it not for the scars of knife and bullet wounds that are visible on his face he would now be a handsome man of striking appearance."

This assertion of Appo's particular beauty, as one whose face showed the "characteristics of both his parents," confirmed yet another stereotype of the racial hybrid, one that paradoxically coexisted with that of racial degeneracy. As Robert Young points out, at the same time "as being instanced as degenerate, and literally, degraded (that is, lowered by racial mixture from pure whiteness, the highest grade), those of mixed race were often invoked as the most beautiful human beings of all." French racial theorist Quatrefages, for example, praised the beauty of "women of colour, mulattoes and quadroons," who exercised a peculiar charm on European travelers. For Quatrefages, this beauty was compelling evidence that mixed races were not inferior to the "pure" in all respects and actually exhibited a degree of hybrid vigor.

While Beck's offhand references to Appo's beauty strike a chord of dissonance with his dominant theme of hybrid degeneracy, this very dissonance calls our attention to a motif that figures in Beck's text as an instance of what we might regard as the "return of the repressed." What is repressed in Beck's sketch is the attraction exerted by the figure of the hybrid—an allure epitomized by the lovely Afong girls, daughters of the "Chinese Merchant Prince of Honolulu."

In the second half of the nineteenth century, boosters were promoting Hawaii's image as a paradise of harmonious intermixing, which some extended even to the notion of constructive miscegenation. This idea would become so compelling that by the first decades of the twentieth century American sociologists were treating the islands as a virtual "living laboratory" of racial fusion (see chapter 5). Already in the 1880s, the American press were lauding the Afong girls, widely said to be "beautiful and intelligent," as testaments to the success of constructive miscegenation as a vehicle for assimilation—cultural and biological. As the *New York Times* described the girls in 1885: "The mother and the daughters maintain a rigid adherence to the rules of fashion, and appear in the dress of white ladies and girls. When occasion demands, the lady and her older daughters are clad in as elegant raiment as the wealthiest lady on the islands ... as the family is received cordially into the best society in Honolulu.... A close observer of the merry quintet on their afternoon drive could not tell that they were not the off-spring of some wealthy Caucasian."

Wealthy, beautiful, cultured, and by this account virtually "Caucasian" to the eye (echoing early depictions of George Appo as a veritable Yankee boy), the Afong girls were frequently depicted by mainland media as "very much sought after," several distinguished for having married "prominent men." When Henrietta, the "belle of the islands," was wed to Naval Commander William Henry Whiting in 1893, the marriage shook Honolulu naval society but was acclaimed by Sanford Dole, head of Hawaii's provisional government, as a symbol for the potential union of Hawaii and the United States. Indeed, the beauty and eligibility of the Afong girls loomed so large in American press coverage of the family that when the "merchant prince" died in 1906, the *New York Times* gave his obituary the following title: "AFONG DIES IN CHINA; FATHER OF 13 [*sic*] BEAUTIES—Chinese Merchant Made Millions in Honolulu. DAUGHTERS MARRIED WELL."

The juxtaposition of the Afongs in Hawaii and the Appos in New York demonstrates the complex intersections of class, gender, and place in representations of Eurasian mixed race. If we consider place, in particular, the difference between Honolulu and the world of Manhattan's lower wards is striking. By comparison to New York's Five Points in particular, where anxieties surrounding social and sexual intercourse across racial, religious, and linguistic lines ran high during Appo's age, the discourse of constructive miscegenation came much more readily to the fore in Hawaii, where intermarriage was connected to U.S. imperial aspirations.

Hawaii was clearly a different context from New York, and yet we find that the discourse of constructive miscegenation is not entirely absent from representations of Chinese–white intermixing in the great metropolis, especially in the era before Chinese exclusion. Indeed, as we have seen, Beck was not alone in his portrayal of Appo's physical attractiveness, a trait commonly taken by racial theorists as evidence of hybrid vigor. As mentioned previously, the *New York Times* reporter who chronicled George's birth described him as a handsome boy, as white as his mother. Journalists also described other New York–born Eurasians in a similar fashion. An article in the *New York Daily Tribune*, for example, asserted, "As a rule the children [of Chinese fathers and Irish mothers] are decidedly well looking, which is more than one can say for their fathers." When a reporter for the *World* investigated that city's "Celestial colony" in 1877, he expressed surprise at finding a number of young Irish women married to Chinese. Unnerved by the phenomenon, the reporter nonetheless gave a favorable physical description of one of the babies: "It was sleeping in a tidy crib, and was certainly a beautiful child, being fair and chubby and healthy in appearance." Noticeably, all these descriptions associate the Eurasians' beauty with their partial whiteness: their fair skin, their fashionable "white" dress, their maternal inheritance. It is an "infusion of whiteness" that produces the good looks of Eurasian children, an infusion that overcomes the homeliness of Chinese fathers and their racial Otherness, transforming their offspring toward Sameness. In contrast to Quatrefages, who clearly valued the exotic and dusky beauty of the mulatto, these press accounts indicate that the notion of exceptional mixed-race beauty also contains within itself a privileging of whiteness. The mysterious charm exerted by mixed-race figures thus stems from their not-white/like-white physiognomy.

Here is where ambivalence rises to the surface in Beck's account: where the journalist cannot let go of Appo's beauty, despite his monstrous wickedness. Beck may regard Appo "better off dead," but he remains enthralled by his "striking appearance," unable to write him off entirely. In the end, George Washington Appo was a paradigmatic example of the contradiction Robert Young identifies in nineteenth-century Western racial theory: that is, the degenerate racial hybrid who is simultaneously invoked as a creature of great beauty. It is this doubleness that rendered the hybrid a figure of fascination and horror, of desire and anxiety.

Without a doubt, hybrid degeneracy is the dominant theme in Beck's biographical sketch of Appo, as it was among Anglo-American scientific discourses of the time. Yet I have emphasized the notion of underlying ambivalence even within this demonizing portrait in order to draw attention to alternate discourses of hybrid vigor that also circulated during this era. The notion of "constructive miscegenation" may have been a minority position, but hybrid vigor was taken seriously as an issue of scientific *debate* by men of no less stature than Gobineau, Quatrefages, and Darwin and continued to inform lay representations like Beck's even if only as an undercurrent of ambivalence. Hence, this counter-discourse should not be dismissed too readily from our readings of the period, as, I argue, is the case in Jayne O. Ifekwunigwe's characterization of the nineteenth century as the Age of Pathology in mixed-race studies. Harriet Ritvo has compellingly cautioned against monodimensional understandings of the past, which highlight dominant opinions of the age while obscuring alternative opinions and intense disagreement among experts, and in doing so force us to lose sight of the true variety of thought from the time. Such would be the danger for the intellectual genealogy of "mixed race" if we were to see in Beck's sketch of Appo nothing more than a case study of hybrid degeneracy without its complicating ambivalence.

FURTHER READING

Aarim-Heriot, Najia. *Chinese Immigrants, African Americans, and Racial Anxiety in the United States, 1848–1882* (2003).

Barth, Gunther. *Bitter Strength: A History of the Chinese in the United States, 1850–1870* (1964).

Chan, Sucheng, ed. *Entry Denied: Exclusion and the Chinese Community in America, 1882–1943* (1991).

Chang, Gordon H. *Fateful Ties: A History of America's Preoccupation with China* (2015).

Coolidge, Mary Roberts. *Chinese Immigration* (1909).

Gyory, Andrew. *Closing the Gate: Race, Politics, and the Chinese Exclusion Act* (1998).

Hunt, Michael H. *The Making of a Special Relationship: The United States and China to 1914* (1983).

Jung, Moon-Ho. *Coolies and Cane: Race, Labor, and Sugar in the Age of Emancipation* (2008).

Lee, Erika. *At America's Gates: Chinese Immigration during the Exclusion Era, 1882–1943* (2003).

McClain, Charles J. *In Search of Equality: The Chinese Struggle against Discrimination in Nineteenth-Century America* (1994).

McKeown, Adam. *Melancholy Order: Asian Migration and the Globalization of Borders* (2011).

Miller, Stuart Creighton. *The Unwelcome Immigrant: The American Image of the Chinese, 1785–1882* (1969).

Paddison, Joshua. *American Heathens: Religion, Race, and Reconstruction in California* (2012).

Peffer, George Anthony. *If They Don't Bring Their Women Here: Chinese Female Immigration before Exclusion* (1999).

Pfaelzer, Jean. *Driven Out: The Forgotten War against Chinese Americans* (2007).

Salyer, Lucy E. *Laws Harsh as Tigers: Chinese Immigrants and the Shaping of Modern Immigration Law* (1995).

Saxton, Alexander. *The Indispensable Enemy: Labor and the Anti-Chinese Movement in California* (1971).

CHAPTER 4

Pacific Empires and New Migrations, 1894–1919

The United States was a late-developing imperial power. In 1898, it annexed Hawai'i, and later that year claimed the Philippines, Puerto Rico, and Guam from a decaying Spanish Empire. These moves fit widely held beliefs that the Pacific Ocean would become the center of global economic activity in the twentieth century and that nations needed to protect Pacific shipping lanes. Consequently, the United States developed military bases in the Caribbean to oversee traffic flowing through the Panama Canal, which opened in 1914. By this time, the British Empire stretched across much of the Asia-Pacific region, including the prized colony of India, while the French and Dutch were also major players in this imperial Pacific World. Meanwhile, Germany developed into an imperial power as it shared the islands of Samoa with the United States, took over other Pacific Islands, and competed for control in northeastern China.

Japan was another late-developing imperial power. Japan staked its claims in the Pacific by taking Taiwan in 1895 and later claiming Korea and strategic areas of the Chinese mainland. Fresh off the victory over China in 1895, Japan was the first Asian nation to overcome the unequal treaties that Western powers imposed throughout Asia. Significantly, the United States and Britain gave Japan most favored nation status as a sign of mutual respect; this was the status that the United States had taken away from China in order to exclude its immigrants. In their stead, Japanese immigrants became the principle labor force in Hawai'i and were also counted on by growers and businesses on the West Coast.

Although Americans were new to colonialism, they were old hands at territorial expansion and managing subordinated populations within North America. In light of the Indian Wars of the late nineteenth century, U.S. imperialists, like President Theodore Roosevelt, portrayed Filipinos as another group of Indians to be subdued and, if possible, Americanized. The imperialists, however, faced powerful opponents within the U.S. who branded as un-American the conquest of territory that would be held in perpetuity as colonies and not incorporated into the United States. Catalyzing the opposition was the Anti-Imperialist League, which reported having over half a million members including the famous writer Mark Twain, editor E.L. Godkin, labor leader Samuel Gompers, and African American scholar and activist W.E.B. Du Bois. It was through the league that Americans learned about atrocities committed by U.S. soldiers in military campaigns to suppress armed insurrections by Filipinos struggling against U.S. colonization.

The Anti-Imperialist League signaled that some Americans were coming to accept the principle of national self-determination that President Wilson in 1919 would formalize as a general philosophy in the peace settlement ending World War I. This anti-imperialist sentiment was also evident among Indian and Korean immigrants in the United States. They saw the United States as a safe place from which to draw the world's attention to the repressive colonization of their homelands. In India, the anticolonial movement featured Mohandas Gandhi, who, after leading successful opposition to white rule in the British colony of South Africa, sought Indian independence through nonviolent means. Meanwhile, in Korea, millions of people proclaimed their nation's independence in March 1919, only to face violent repression by Japanese colonial authorities.

DOCUMENTS

Japan's leading proponent of Westernization, Yukichi Fukuzawa, encouraged his countrymen to migrate across the Pacific so as to prove to Americans that the Japanese were a first-rate people. Document 1 is an article from Fukuzawa's newspaper *Jiji Shimpo* that gives reasons for Japanese immigrants to be proud of their country and not to feel inferior to Westerners. Document 2, a comic strip drawn by a Japanese immigrant, shows the nationalist fervor among a group of ambitious students who came to San Francisco to work their way through school. Their optimism stands in stark contrast to the glimpse they get of the repressive experience of Chinese immigrants through poems written on the walls of the Angel Island immigration station in the San Francisco Bay.

The next three documents address U.S. colonization of the Philippines. In Document 3, Senator Albert Beveridge argues that taking the islands was both an economic necessity for U.S. trade with Asia and a moral imperative because the "barbarous" Filipinos were incapable of self-government. Document 4 is a song sung by U.S. soldiers detailing the torture of Filipino insurgents. Anti-imperialists exposed such brutality to turn the U.S. public not only against the war in the Philippines but also against the entire project of U.S. colonization there. In the face of anti-imperialist activism, U.S. officials in the Philippines cast their mission as uplifting, not subjugating, Filipinos. Document 5 reveals how a U.S. colonial official condemned racial prejudice exhibited by the U.S. military and civilians in the Philippines.

Documents 6 and 7 are taken from a book written by Indian exile Tarnaknath Das, who opposed the colonization of his homeland. The book's foreword, Document 6, is a broad plea by Das for Asians to resist the Western colonization of their countries, while the book's introduction, Document 7, was written by a Chinese leader who builds on Das's pan-Asianism in calling for Asian peoples to unite in overthrowing Western rule. Such calls for Asian unity, while pipe dreams that went unfulfilled, revealed frustrations with colonialism that were common across Asia.

The final two documents focus on Korea and Korean immigrants. Document 8 is a transcript from the Korean Congress in 1919, which brought delegates from around the world to Philadelphia's Independence Hall to draw attention to the plight of colonial Koreans. The main speaker is Dr. Syngman Rhee, one of the best-known leaders within the Korean immigrant community and the first Korean to receive a PhD from Princeton University. Document 9 provides an intimate look at the Korean independence movement following the experience of a Korean immigrant from Hawai'i who returns to her homeland to participate in the uprisings of March 1, 1919.

1. Japanese Newspaper *Jiji Shimpo* Views Emigration as Sign of Japan's Military Power, 1896

The recent victory in war not only demonstrated to the world the military power of Japan but it has convinced the Japanese people that in vitality and spirit, they are outstanding by far among Eastern nations and are among the outstanding races of the world. If the politicians and leaders, as such, give guidance to this deeply held belief of the people and draw up a major plan, they will probably realize that, right before their eyes, there are new homes for the Japanese race, everywhere in the Orient and in the South Seas. The dreams of people in olden times of expanding overseas need no longer end as dreams, but can now be certainly realized. This is indeed the one chance in a thousand years. We can hardly bear the happiness in our heart.

Though it is an incontrovertible fact that the Japanese race is not inferior to the peoples of the West in ability and vitality, the Japanese are unable to free themselves of narrow-minded propensities simply because by accident of nature their country is positioned in a distant corner of the Far East and thus was delayed in riding the currents of modern civilization. They view the civilized nations of the West as the penniless do the extremely rich; outwardly they talk big, saying they are people and we are people, but if their innermost thoughts are probed, they fear Western capability, power and knowledge and are resigned to the thought that they possibly cannot ever win in competition with them....

To urge a weakling who has no confidence in his own strength to cross the boundless seas to set up a new home is like urging a cripple to run. Thus, in spite of the earnest debate to date over emigration, it is no coincidence that it has not succeeded. However, the single fact that Japan has defeated the ancient and great country of China has opened the minds of the conservative, diffident Japanese people and has convinced them that in capability and in vigor, they are not inferior to any race in the world....

Jiji Shimpo, Feb. 3, 1986; reprinted in Yasuo Wakatsuki, "Japanese Emigration to the United States, 1866–1924: A Monograph," *Perspectives in American History* 12 (1979): 443.

2. Japanese Immigrant Comic Reveals Reasons for Emigration, 1904 (1929)

From Henry (Yoshitaka) Kiyama, *The Four Immigrants Manga: A Japanese Experience in San Francisco, 1904–1924*, trans. Frederik L. Schodt (Berkeley, CA: Stonebridge Press, 1998), 30–31.

3. Senator Albert Beveridge Champions Philippine Colonization, 1900

Mr. President, the times call for candor. The Philippines are ours forever, "territory belonging to the United States," as the Constitution calls them. And just

From Congressional Record, Senate, January 9, 1900, 704–711; reprinted in *The Philippines Reader: A History of Colonialism, Neocolonialism, Dictatorship, and Resistance*, ed. Daniel B. Schirmer and Stephen Rosskamm Shalom (Boston: South End Press, 1987), 23–26.

beyond the Philippines are China's illimitable markets. We will not retreat from either. We will not repudiate our duty in the archipelago. We will not abandon our opportunity in the Orient. We will not renounce our part in the mission of our race, trustee, under God, of the civilization of the world. And we will move forward to our work, not howling out regrets like slaves whipped to their burdens, but with gratitude for a task worthy of our strength and thanksgiving to Almighty God that He has marked us as His chosen people, henceforth to lead in the regeneration of the world.

Philippines Command the Pacific

This island empire is the last land left in all the oceans. If it should prove a mistake to abandon it, the blunder once made would be irretrievable. If it proves a mistake to hold it, the error can be corrected when we will. Every other progressive nation stands ready to relieve us.

But to hold it will be no mistake. Our largest trade henceforth must be with Asia. The Pacific is our ocean. More and more Europe will manufacture the most it needs, secure from its colonies the most it consumes. Where shall we turn for consumers of our surplus? Geography answers the question. China is our natural customer. She is nearer to us than to England, Germany, or Russia, the commercial powers of the present and the future. They have moved nearer to China by securing permanent bases on her borders. The Philippines give us a base at the door of all the East.

Lines of navigation from our ports to the Orient and Australia; from the Isthmian Canal to Asia; from all Oriental ports to Australia, converge at and separate from the Philippines. They are a self-supporting, dividend-paying fleet, permanently anchored at a spot selected by the strategy of Providence, commanding the Pacific. And the Pacific is the ocean of the commerce of the future. Most future wars will be conflicts for commerce. The power that rules the Pacific, therefore, is the power that rules the world. And, with the Philippines, that power is and will forever be the American Republic.

Value of China's Trade

China's trade is the mightiest commercial fact in our future. Her foreign commerce was $285,738.300 in 1897, of which we, her neighbor, had less than 9 per cent, of which only a little more than half was merchandise sold to China by us. We ought to have 50 per cent, and we will. And China's foreign commerce is only beginning. Her resources, her possibilities, her wants, all are undeveloped. She has only 340 miles of railway. I have seen trains loaded with natives and all the activities of modern life already appearing along the line. But she needs, and in fifty years will have, 20,000 miles of railway.

Who can estimate her commerce, then? That statesman commits a crime against American trade—against the American grower of cotton and wheat and tobacco, the American manufacturer of machinery and clothing—who fails to put America where she may command that trade.... The Philippines command the commercial situation of the entire East....

Resources and Immense Size of the Islands

But if they did not command China, India, the Orient, the whole Pacific for purposes of offense, defense, and trade, the Philippines are so valuable in themselves that we should hold them. I have cruised more than 2,000 miles through the archipelago, every moment a surprise at its loveliness and wealth. I have ridden hundreds of miles on the islands, every foot of the way a revelation of vegetable and mineral riches.

No land in America surpasses in fertility the plains and valleys of Luzon. Rice and coffee, sugar and cocoanuts, hemp and tobacco, and many products of the temperate as well as the tropic zone grow in various sections of the archipelago. I have seen hundreds of bushels of Indian corn lying in a road fringed with banana trees. The forests of Negros, Mindanao, Mindora, Paluan, and parts of Luzon are invaluable and intact. The wood of the Philippines can supply the furniture of the world for a century to come. At Cebu the best informed man in the island told me that 40 miles of Cebu's mountain chain are practically mountains of coal. Pablo Majia, one of the most reliable men on the islands, confirmed the statement. Some declare that the coal is only lignite; but ship captains who have used it told me that it is better steamer fuel than the best coal of Japan.

I have a nugget of pure gold picked up in its present form on the banks of a Philippine creek. I have gold dust washed out by crude processes of careless natives from the sands of a Philippine stream. Both indicate great deposits at the source from which they come....

Nothing is so natural as trade with one's neighbors. The Philippines make us the nearest neighbors of all the East. Nothing is more natural than to trade with those you know. This is the philosophy of all advertising. The Philippines bring us permanently face to face with the most sought-for customers of the world. National prestige, national propinquity, these and commercial activity are the elements of commercial success....

Character of the People

It will be hard for Americans who have not studied them to understand the people. They are a barbarous race, modified by three centuries of contact with a decadent [Spanish] race. The Filipino is the South Sea Malay, put through a process of three hundred years of [Spanish] superstition in religion, dishonesty in dealing, disorder in habits of industry, and cruelty, caprice, and corruption in government. It is barely possible that 1,000 men in all the archipelago are capable of self-government in the Anglo-Saxon sense.

My own belief is that there are not 100 men among them who comprehend what Anglo-Saxon self-government even means, and there are over 5,000,000 people to be governed....

But, Senators, it would be better to abandon this combined garden and Gibraltar of the Pacific, and count our blood and treasure already spent a profitable loss, than to apply any academic arrangement of self-government to these children. They are not capable of self-government. How could they be? They are not of a self-governing race. They are Orientals, Malays, instructed by Spaniards in the latter's worst estate.

They know nothing of practical government except as they have witnessed the weak, corrupt, cruel, and capricious rule of Spain. What magic will anyone employ to dissolve in their minds and characters those impressions of governors and governed which three centuries of misrule has created? What alchemy will change the oriental quality of their blood and set the self-governing currents of the American pouring through their Malay veins? How shall they, in the twinkling of an eye, be exalted to the heights of self-governing peoples which required a thousand years for us to reach, Anglo-Saxon though we are?...

People Indolent—No Competition with Our Labor

No one need fear their competition with our labor. No reward could beguile, no force compel, these children of indolence to leave their trifling lives for the fierce and fervid industry of high-wrought America. The very reverse is the fact. One great problem is the necessary labor to develop these islands—to build the roads, open the mines, clear the wilderness, drain the swamps, dredge the harbors. The natives will not supply it. A lingering prejudice against the Chinese may prevent us from letting them supply it. Ultimately, when the real truth of the climate and human conditions is known, it is barely possible that our labor will go there. Even now young men with the right moral fiber and a little capital can make fortunes there as planters.

But the natives will not come here [as immigrants]. Let all men dismiss that fear....

The Whole Question Elemental

Mr. President, this question is deeper than any question of party politics; deeper than any question of the isolated policy of our country even; deeper even than any question of constitutional power. It is elemental. It is racial. God has not been preparing the English-speaking and Teutonic peoples for a thousand years for nothing but vain and idle self-contemplation and self-admiration. No! He has made us the master organizers of the world to establish system where chaos reigns. He has given us the spirit of progress to overwhelm the forces of reaction throughout the earth. He has made us adepts in government that we may administer government among savage and senile peoples. Were it not for such a force as this the world would relapse into barbarism and night. And of all our race He has marked the American people as His chosen nation to finally lead in the regeneration of the world. This is the divine mission of America, and it holds for us all the profit, all the glory, all the happiness possible to man. We are trustees of the world's progress, guardians of its righteous peace. The judgment of the Master is upon us: "Ye have been faithful over a few things; I will make you ruler over many things."

What shall history say of us? Shall it say that we renounced that holy trust, left the savage to his base condition, the wilderness to the reign of waste, deserted duty, abandoned glory, forget our sordid profit even, because we feared our strength and read the charter of our powers with the doubter's eye and the quibbler's mind? Shall it say that, called by events to captain and command the proudest, ablest, purest race of history in history's noblest work, we declined that great commission? Our fathers would not have had it so. No! They founded no paralytic government, incapable of the simplest acts of administration. They planted no sluggard people, passive while the world's work calls them. They established no reactionary nation. They unfurled no retreating flag.

4. American GIs Sing About Using Water Cure Torture, 1902

Get the good old syringe boys and fill it to the brim
We've caught another nigger and we'll operate on him
Let someone take the handle who can work it with a vim
Shouting the battle cry of freedom

[Chorus]
Hurrah Hurrah We bring the Jubilee
Hurrah Hurrah The flag that makes him free
Shove in the nozzel [sic] deep and let him taste of liberty
Shouting the battle cry of freedom.

5. U.S. Civilian Officer Condemns Racial Prejudice in Philippines, 1902

Many people find in our occupation of the Philippine Islands the threat of a radical change in American character and ideals. Even if we look only on the evil side of things, it is hard to see how American character and social ideas can thus be radically altered. That it is a step of transcendent importance, involving new and various political difficulties, is true. But it draws us into a field in which ultimately our prejudices may broaden out, and in which our provincialisms must disappear.

Meanwhile, however, it must be admitted, the prospect of such beneficent results seems spoiled by two untoward phases of our new venture: we have carried into the Philippines a petty race prejudice, the offspring of past provincialism and the inheritance of slavery with its residue of unsettled problems; and we are betraying a tendency to swagger under the "white man's burden," sometimes in the garb of commercialism, sometimes in the raiment of science.

As might be expected, the petty prejudices are first to exhibit themselves, and are also, just at present, the more serious obstacles to a general good understanding in the Philippines. Relying upon the common sense of the reader not

From Paul Kramer, *The Blood of Government: Race, Empire, the United States, and the Philippines* (Chapel Hill: University of North Carolina Press, 2006), 141.

From James LeRoy, "Race Prejudice in the Philippines," *Atlantic Monthly* 90, 537 (July 1902).

to draw any hysterical conclusions of general "oppression" in the Philippines, it may be worth while to cite instances and facts to show how race prejudice has been doing us harm in the islands. Only instances for which I can personally vouch will be employed....

Before the arrival of the second Philippine Commission at Manila and the inauguration by Judge Taft and its other members of social gatherings in which the natives were in the majority, practically nothing had been done in the way of providing an informal meeting ground for representative Filipinos and Americans. The first Philippine Commission had given a ball in 1899, which was a landmark for Filipino matrons and belles in their discussions and misapprehensions as to what Americans were like socially. With two or three very notable exceptions, officers whose wives had joined them did not think of meeting any residents but some of the wealthy Spanish "left-overs" on anything like terms of social equality....

Force of circumstances has from the first, through the necessarily closer contact and the lack of other society, brought about more social mingling in the provincial towns. In general, however, the attitude of the army women in the islands is typified by that one in Manila who, in discussing affairs in her first call on the wife of a member of the Commission, exclaimed in horror: "Why, surely you don't propose to visit these people and invite them to your own home just the same as you would white people!" Time has perhaps brought a little more catholicity, at any rate the custom of entertaining natives has come to be received without a shock; but few army women in Manila have Filipinas on their calling list, and in the provinces they often take it on themselves to caution American women sent out as teachers against mingling with the people of their towns. This attitude is also that of the great majority of officers in the army, though the men, like men everywhere, are less formal about a social rule and less rigid in their likes and dislikes of persons.

An instance of this attitude was the attempt to exclude from the Woman's Hospital at Manila (founded by a donation of Mrs. Whitelaw Reid) all Filipinos as patients, as well as to keep off the list of patronesses the names of Filipino women. At about the same time the board of ladies to whose energy the American Library of Manila was due asked to have it made a public library, to be helped out by funds from the Philippine treasury, and made very strenuous protests against having it also thrown open to Filipinos for a share in its management and use. They contended that it had been established as a monument to American soldiers who lost their lives in the Philippines, and that it was unfitting that Filipinos should have anything to do with it, though Philippine taxes might support it....

This and the other instances do not, of course, reveal a prejudice grounded entirely on color, yet this is the chief factor. It may be worth while remarking that, judging by one man's personal observation, this attitude of contempt is less noticeable among officers from the South than among those from the North. Doubtless this is due to their having had closer contact with people of another color, and to a greater tolerance through the staling of custom, although the conviction of the other's inferiority may yet be deeper bred.

On the other hand, an experience to be remembered was hearing some Southern as well as Northern officers rate the Filipino higher than the American negro, greatly to the indignation of a colored chaplain of the army who overheard them. And these officers were rather more tolerant of the presence among the first-class passengers of an army transport of a Filipino mestizo from the Visayan islands than of the same chaplain, who was finally given a seat by himself because some very important young lieutenants would not sit next him....

The writer was one of a group of American civilians halted in the street of a Philippine town by an ugly sentinel and ordered, in gruff terms at the bayonet's point, to salute a minute American flag on the top of a fifty-foot pole. Not one, of course, had seen it. The pole had purposely been set some hundreds of feet from the barracks, almost in the street itself, and the order was enforced against every one who passed. A protest to the officer in command, a gray-haired captain, brought the reply that he was "teaching the niggers a lesson." This province was a leader in the revolt against Spain, first because of the friars, and second because of the abuses suffered at the hands of the Spanish civil guard. One need not add that the hatred felt toward our troops is intense....

Recent revelations have focused attention on the conduct of the army in the Philippines, and some have tried to make out that downright brutality was the rule of campaign there. Cases of actual inhumanity have been, I am convinced, the exceptional ones. It must be admitted, however, by any one who really knows things as they now are in the islands, that at least three fourths of the army, rank and file, entertain a more or less violent dislike for the Filipinos and a contempt for their capacity, moral and intellectual. This feeling in the army has grown during the past two years. Perhaps it may be dated back to the early days of 1900, when guerrilla warfare had begun, and our troops had to contend with ambushes and a foe who was an excellent masquerader, and who practiced the art of assassination on his own fellow countrymen in forms of the most refined cruelty....

Attacks on the character of the native are usually made the basis of the white man's plea in the Philippines. For this purpose the natives are all treated as identical in kind and character, grouped into one, as it were. Upon such a hypothesis one can argue that, because one native known to him was deficient morally and seemed incapable mentally, therefore the Filipinos are a dishonest and inefficient race. But thus baldly stated, the proposition seems too ridiculous to emanate from any educated person; yet it is remarkable how commonly it is set forth by persons who consider themselves very well educated. We all know how indignant we become when a European writer of short experience among us proceeds to cut one suit of clothes to fit us all; yet the Filipinos are hardly a more homogeneous people than we, and there are just as strongly marked individual types in the East as in the West....

That instances of real brutality on the part of our troops have been the exception has been stated to be the opinion of the writer. On the confession of the officer who conducted it, the campaign in the island of Sámar from October to March last must be excepted from this general statement. He has met the charge of violating the rules of civilized warfare with the counter-charge that the people of Sámar are savages, and that it was necessary to suspend many of these rules in order to restore peace and quiet to that part of the archipelago. By inference, it then became a war of extermination till one side or the other should cry quits. It is hard to deal with this matter as yet in a strictly impartial spirit, and full knowledge is one of the first requisites. One thing can at least be asserted, namely, that the classification of all the people of Sámar in one lump as savages will bear close scrutiny....

This digression as to matters of recent controversy will have been worth while if it shall serve to induce to a saner consideration of army conduct in the islands, and if it shall also emphasize the fact that the generally contemptuous attitude of army men and other Americans toward the natives—that feeling which gives itself vent in the term "niggers"—is what does us greatest harm. The Filipinos have grown, by hard experience, somewhat callous to measures that seem to us extreme, if not actually brutal. We do not make enemies for ourselves half so much by the occasional administration of the water cure or other forms of torture and barbarity as by a studied attitude of contempt, an assumption of racial and individual superiority, and the constant disregard of their petty personal rights and of the little amenities which count for so much with them....

It is wearisome to note how uniformly writers on the peoples of the Orient assume that they are inherently different from us in every respect,—that the ordinary Western ways of reasoning have no place in the East, must in fact be reversed. The familiar saying that the Chinese do everything backward is in point. Now, John seems to me one of the most unsparingly logical human beings in the world. [The British poet Rudyard] Kipling's jingles are responsible for much of that feeling that the Oriental is a wholly mysterious being, not given to be understood by other men, a curious psychological phenomenon. "Half-devil and half-child" comes trippingly to the tongue of many Americans in the Philippines, and their philosophy of the Filipino is thus summed up for them before their study of him has ever begun. What is less creditable, the same stock theory and a few facts, more or less, constitute the equipment of various university economists and world problem specialists.

6. Indian Nationalist Articulates an Anti-Imperial Vision for Asian Youth, 1917

To The Asian Youth

The idea of slavery as advocated by Aristotle and others is a dead-letter to-day. The idea of dominance of a European nation, however insignificant it may be, by any other Power to-day faces the strongest active opposition of the civilized world. We expect that a day will also come when the idea of dominance of Asia by Europe or America will be abandoned by the present aggressors. This can be brought about only through effective and vigorous assertion of Asia in all fields of human activity, especially Politics. Every Asian youth—male or female—who possesses even a tiny bit of the feeling of self-respect should strive to achieve the goal of Assertion of Asia to the fullest sense of its meaning. Our method of assertion should not be mere imitation of the West. Our ambition is to draw our inspiration from the glorious past of Asia and rising above its present degraded

From Taraknath Das, *Is Japan a Menace to Asia?* (Shanghai: Taraknath Das, 1917).

condition, preserving the best of our ancestral treasures from the attacks of vandals and assimilating the best of all that the modern world has to give to Humanity, to build up something higher than the best products of Modern civilization. It is your privilege to work for this noble cause.

7. Chinese Leader Urges Asian Unity, 1917

The future of Asia depends upon the ability of the Asiatic people to assert their rights politically. Political weakness of Asia has been the cause of many troubles and wars during the last century and a half. Asia as a whole, except Japan affords for the strong Powers unbounded natural resources, cheap labor, markets, defence-lessness, and inefficient governments which give every incentive for aggression. About the modern imperialism among the Great Powers, Mr. Walter Lippman in his book "The Stakes of Diplomacy" rightly says: "It is not enough to say that they are 'expanding' or 'seeking markets' or 'grabbing resources.' They are doing all these things, of course. But if the world into which they are expanding were not politically archaic, the growth of foreign trade would not be accompanied by polit-ical imperialism. Germany has expanded wonderfully in the British Empire, in Rus-sia, in the United States, but no German is silly enough to insist on planting his flag wherever he sells his dyestuffs or stoves. It is only when his expansion is into weak states—into China, Morocco, Turkey or elsewhere that foreign trade is imperialis-tic. This imperialism is actuated by many motives—by a feeling that political control insures special privileges, by a desire to play a large part in the world, by national vanity, by a passion for ownership, but none of these motives would come into play if the countries like China or Turkey were not politically backward."

Political backwardness is not inherent among the Asiatic people, though it is the current opinion among the western students. China in the past had her bright periods of history, her glorious days of Imperialism. In the field of culture and civilization China contributed her full share when she was politically strong. India of Asoka and Akbar was far ahead of any of the European countries of those ages. It is by contact with the Orient that Europe in the past has learnt many useful things for her present civilization. Prof. Benoy Kumar Sarkar in his excellent and critical work "The Chinese Religion Through Hindu Eyes" has very rightly said, The darkest period of European History known as the Middle Ages is the brightest period in Asiatic. For over a thousand years from the acces-sion of Gupta Vicramaditya to the throne of Pataliputra down to the capture of Constantinople by the Turks the history of Asia is the history of continuous growth and progress. It is the record of political and commercial as well as cul-tural expansion—and the highest watermark attained by oriental humanity.... It was the message of this orient that was carried to Europe by the Islamites and led to the establishment of mediæval universities....

Among other things the Concert of the Great European Powers have had one motive before them—exploitation of Asia and Africa to their advantage. This aggression of Europe in Asia can be stopped for the good of Asia and Europe by

---

From Taraknath Das, *Is Japan a Menace to Asia?* (Shanghai: Taraknath Das, 1917), i–vi.

a solid Asiatic unity not merely from a cultural standpoint but also from a political standpoint. This stupendous work of political regeneration of Asia by an Asian Concert has great moral and ethical aspects. There cannot be effective peace so long as one nation or a group of nations looks down upon the other as inferior and tyrannizes. Friendship and fellowship can be established on equal footing. Japan's demonstration of military strength forces the so-called superior nations to shake hands with her, though with great reluctance. Political assertion of Asia will make Europe and America more tolerant and respectful towards human rights.

Because Japan is politically strong, she is able to develop her country politically and culturally. China is struggling to be free and she should accept co-operation from any quarter that is truly friendly. Japan is China's disciple of the past and all far-sighted Japanese believe that "Japan without China and India, is, in the long run, without legs." I would say that China without Japan and India is without legs. The fulfilment of Indian aspiration depends upon a strong united Sino-Japanese Alliance....

Can there be anything more pathetic than the condition of the people of India, one-fifth of the population of the whole world? The cause of the three hundred and fifteen millions of the people of India is the cause of Asia and of Humanity. Japan and China, if far-sighted, should not be unmindful of the problems of the people of India, because a strong, free India will be a source of strength to them.

We have been tired of hearing that Japan is a menace to Asia. Now comes a Hindu scholar, Mr. Taraknath Das, well-versed in world politics, who tries to show that Japan is not a menace to Asia with Asian supremacy, but, rather, that Japan is a menace to European aggression in Asia. Some western author has recently said: "Japan is an international nuisance and she may easily grow to be an international peril." We, however, do not look at a rising Japan in the same spirit. We wish only that China and India be equally strong, that Japan hold her own on the Asiatic continent against European aggressors. Then the international nuisance, charged to Japan, but really traced to other outside forces, will cease to exist in Asia. The awakening of Asia is the most outstanding feature of the present age. The future of Asia is bright and glorious if the new spirit of Asia be rightly directed in co-operation with all the Asian people. We hope, though we may not live to see it fully accomplished, that Japan and China and India will work unitedly, standing for Asian Independence against all outside aggressions.

8. Korean Congress Declares Independence from Japanese Rule, 1919

An Appeal to America

We, the Koreans in Congress, assembled in Philadelphia, April 14–16, 1919, representing eighteen million people of our race who are now suffering untold

Korean Congress Declares Independence from Japanese Rule, 1919. From *First Korean Congress: Held in the Little Theatre, 17th and Delancey Streets* (Philadelphia), 1919 (Soul Tukpyolsi: Pomhan Sojuk Chusik Hoesa, 1986), 90–92, 31–36.

miseries and barbarous treatment by the Japanese military authorities in Korea, hereby appeal to the great and generous American people.

For four thousand years our country enjoyed an absolute autonomy. We have our own history, our own language, our own literature and our own civilization. We have made treaties with the leading nations of the world; all of them recognized our independence, including Japan.

In 1904, at the beginning of the Russo-Japanese war, Japan made a treaty of alliance with Korea, guaranteeing territorial integrity and political independence of Korea, to co-operate in the war against Russia. Korea was opened to Japan for military purposes and Korea assisted Japan in many ways. After the war was over, Japan discarded the treaty of alliance as a "scrap of paper" and annexed Korea as a conquered territory. Ever since she has been ruling Korea with that autocratic militarism whose prototype has been well illustrated by Germany in Belgium and Northern France.

The Korean people patiently suffered under the iron heel of Japan for the last decade or more, but now they have reached the point where they are no longer able to endure it. On March 1st of this year some three million men, mostly of the educated class composed of Christians, Heaven Worshipers, Confucians, Buddhists, students of mission schools, under the leadership of the pastors of the native Christian churches, declared their independence from Japan and formed a provisional government on the border of Manchuria. Through the news dispatches and through private telegrams we are informed that 32,000 Korean revolutionists have been thrown into dungeons by the Japanese and over 100,000 men, women and children have been either killed or wounded so far. The Koreans have no weapons with which to fight, as the Japanese had taken away from them everything since the annexation, even pistols and fowling pieces. What resistance they are offering now against the Japanese soldiers and gendarmery is with pitchforks and sickles. In spite of this disadvantage and the horrible casualty among the Koreans, these people are keeping up their resistance and this demonstration is now nation-wide, including nearly all provinces. Japan has declared martial law in Korea and is butchering by thousands these unfortunate but patriotic people every day.

The Koreans in the United States and Hawaii have sent their representatives to Philadelphia, the Cradle of Liberty, to formulate a concerted plan with a view to stop this inhuman treatment of their brethren by the "Asiatic Kaiser," and to devise ways and means to help along the great cause of freedom and justice for our native land.

We appeal to you for support and sympathy because we know you love justice; you also fought for liberty and democracy, and you stand for Christianity and humanity. Our cause is a just one before the laws of God and man. Our aim is freedom from militaristic autocracy; our object is democracy for Asia; our hope is universal Christianity. Therefore we feel that our appeal merits your consideration.

You have already championed the cause of the oppressed and held out your helping hand to the weak of the earth's races. Your nation is the Hope of Mankind, so we come to you.

Beside this, we also feel that we have the right to ask your help for the reason that the treaty between the United States and Korea contains a stipulation in article 1, paragraph 2, which states as follows:

"If other powers deal unjustly or oppressively with either government, the other will exert their good offices, on being informed of the case, to bring about an amicable arrangement, thus showing their friendly feelings."

Does not this agreement make it incumbent upon America to intercede now in Korea's behalf?

There are many other good and sufficient reasons for America to exert her good offices to bring about an amicable arrangement, but we mention only one more, which is a new principle recently formulated at the peace conference in Paris. We cannot do better than to quote President Wilson's words, who is one of the founders of this new international obligation:

"The principle of the League of Nations is that it is the friendly right of every nation a member of the League to call attention to anything that she thinks will disturb the peace of the world, no matter where that thing is occurring. There is no subject that touches the peace of the world that is exempt from inquiry or discussion."

We, therefore, in the name of humanity, liberty and democracy and in the name of the American-Korean treaty and in the name of the peace of the world, ask the government of the United States to exert its good offices to save the lives of our freedom-loving breathren in Korea and to protect the American missionaries and their families who are in danger of losing their lives and property on account of their love for our people and their faith in Christ.

We further ask you, the great American public, to give us your moral and material help so that our breathren in Korea will know that your sympathy is with them and that you are truly the champions of liberty and international justice.

9. Korean Immigrant Hee Kyung Joins the Korean Independence Movement, 1919 (1989)

Two years after she came to the new world Hee Kyung gave birth to her first child. She and her husband named her Chung Sook, meaning "straight and upright" and "clear and gentle like a brook." I was that daughter.

Although my father enjoyed learning his craft at the furniture shop, the wages he brought home still barely covered the necessities of life.

Home, church, and a society called the Youngnam Puin Hoe made up my mother's whole world. At her church she helped form the Methodist Ladies Aid Society, a powerful organization that provided a network of services reaching every Korean family in the community. Although the immigrants were all poor, so dedicated were the Society members that no family went without food or a roof over their heads (immigrant men often lost their jobs); a mother who became ill could depend on other mothers to help her; and a mother with a newborn baby did not have to rise from her bed until she was strong. All these

From Margaret K. Pai, *The Dream of Two Yi-min*, 7–9, 11, 17–21. © 1989 University of Hawaii Press. Used with permission.

services were rendered despite the fact that every woman was burdened with heavy responsibilities of her own.

The Youngnam Puin Hoe was a society that a good number of the immigrant women belonged to. The members were *yimin*, from a province in Korea called Kyungsangdo. These lively, bright-eyed ladies laughed easily and talked incessantly when they got together. They met once a month on Sunday afternoons (they observed the Sabbath by attending church and by not working that day). They helped the poor and the sick as an extension of the Methodist Society's work but looked for other projects as well.

A project that captured their fancy and enthusiasm soon appeared. The desire for freedom of their country from Japanese rule was always in their hearts. They spoke often of possible ways Koreans could win liberty, and of hopes for Japan's ultimate destruction. One day they heard a rumor from Los Angeles that spread to Hawaii, Shanghai, Manchuria—wherever Koreans lived.

It was a plan for a massive demonstration in Korea that would bring freedom and relief from Japan's rule. The purpose of the demonstration was to show the imperialists of Japan that Koreans were a strong, unified people, not the weaklings the oppressors made them appear to be. The public expression would attract the world's attention and cause nations to come to the rescue of Koreans suffering from oppression and humiliation.

Month after month as new details of the plan were received by the Youngnam Puin Hoe, the members' interest grew. The women declared they would go to Korea and participate in the demonstration.

However, it wasn't long before their enthusiasm diminished and their group plans collapsed when they realized they lacked the funds to cover the boat fare. Furthermore, who would care for their husbands and babies while they were gone?

My mother begged her friends to find a way to Korea and persisted in fanning the fire of fighting for freedom. She told them of the disturbing letters from her parents, who reported that more and more oppressive measures were being imposed on Koreans by the Japanese military. She urged, "Let us go and do what we can to help. We cannot let these measures continue unchecked!"

But the ladies shook their heads. They admired my mother for her unflagging patriotism and determination to take part in the plan. They said, "Hee Kyung, we think you should go and represent all of us. We will pay for your trip."

In the summer of 1918 my parents agreed that I, then three-and-a-half years old, should accompany my mother to Korea while my father stayed behind. Because I had been ill for months with the whooping cough, I was thin and frail.

"I'm concerned about Chung Sook," Father said. "Hee Kyung, don't you think you should wait until she's stronger?"

"But we may not reach Korea in time for the demonstration." She was torn. Finally she added, "My brother is a physician back home. You know, we can't afford a doctor here. But as soon as we get there I will put our daughter under his care."

The Youngnam Puin Hoe publicly announced to the immigrant community that Hee Kyung Kwon was their emissary to the demonstration, although the date for it was yet unknown. The Koreans responded with generous donations from their hard-earned wages to the cause, and the funds gathered were entrusted to my mother to take with her....

In September my mother decided to go to Seoul, the capital city. A week later she wrote to Grandmother that she was enrolling in Ewha College because that was where she found the people she needed to be with.

I did not know then that Ewha, a college for women, was seething with nationalism and that the majority of the students were revolutionaries. These young intellectual radicals detested the Japanese and were fomenting an over-throw of their rule. They secretly planned one day to join other political groups in the country in a massive show of patriotism.

"I don't know how long your mother will stay in Seoul," Grandmother said to me. "Shall we go and visit her?"

"Yes, yes," I answered. This was the first time I had been separated from my mother and I missed her.

One day in October when the weather was clear, with no anticipation of rain or snow, Grandmother and I, accompanied by one of the servant girls, Sook Cha, took the train to Seoul.

When we met my mother in her dormitory room, we found her in a blue military uniform. How strange she looked without her *chi-ma* and *cho-gori*. She removed the blue cap from her head and sat on the floor, crossing her legs as a man would. I wanted to be close to her and climbed on her lap.

"I'm so sorry you can't be with me every day, Chung Sook," she sighed, stroking my head.

"Please come home, Omoni," I begged.

Her chin grew hard. She looked tense. "Chung Sook, I can't. We're almost ready." She did not explain.

Grandmother seemed to understand. She did not say much. She did not try to persuade Mother to return home. She merely stared at her daughter with sad eyes....

The tense stillness of March 1 lingered through the next few days. Grandfa-ther stayed at home. No one dared to go out to the street. The military com-mander's curfew rule forced people to remain in their homes.

But our servants were able to tread the back alleys and gather information, and they reported what they heard to my grandparents. They learned that the demonstrations for independence had taken place all over Korea, even in the small towns and outlying provinces. The largest parade, it was believed, was in Seoul. Thousands had joined in the marches, waved flags, cried for justice and an end to Japanese oppression. When the police started shooting and slaughtering the marchers, the Koreans wildly destroyed or damaged custom houses, police stations, and court buildings, especially those in the outskirts of the capital. The Japanese angrily retaliated by setting fire to many Korean churches and schoolhouses.

How quickly and brutally the Japanese suppressed the revolutionists! During the parade in Seoul a young woman's hand, proudly waving the Korean flag, was cut off by a Japanese sword. But before the flag touched the ground, she caught it with her other hand. More than 2,500 Koreans were thrown in prison in Seoul alone that day. Among the women activists incarcerated was my mother, Lee Hee Kyung.

☀ ESSAYS

The first essay, by University of Pennsylvania historian Eiichiro Azuma, places the immigration of Japanese to the United States and Hawai'i within the context of Japan's effort to move away from its unequal power vis-à-vis the West. Azuma identifies three types of immigrants—merchants, colonists, and laborers. The first two types were fired with nationalism to have their migration serve the Japanese Empire, while the third type was driven by dreams of personal fortune that were sometimes at odds with building a stronger Japan. In the second essay, Vanderbilt University historian Paul A. Kramer addresses the significance of race for the U.S. colonization of the Philippines. Rather than dismiss Filipinos as simply racially inferior, U.S. officials promoted an "inclusionary racial formation" that emphasized the ability of especially elite Filipinos to absorb American ideals and practices. The *pensionados*, students sent to the United States as models of America's "benevolent assimilation," were the prime example.

Heterogeneous Origins of Japanese America

EIICHIRO AZUMA

Popularized after the Meiji Restoration of 1868, "emigration" and "colonization" were new concepts borrowed from the West, which the Japanese political elite and intellectual class came to use interchangeably in their discussion of the most pressing national tasks: national formation and expansion. The dissemination of these ideas to the emergent citizenry through the press, political organizations, and academia was central in the making of a modern empire in Japan. The very notion of emigration or colonization had not even existed under the closed-door policy of the Tokugawa feudal regime. The exodus of various classes of Japanese for Hawaii and the mainland United States after the 1880s prompted the intelligentsia for the first time to seriously contemplate the meaning of popular emigration in tandem with the nascent ideas of national expansion.

In order to explain the nature of early Japanese expansionism with which the practice of emigration was tightly intertwined, it is necessary to delve into three interrelated contexts: geopolitics in the Asia-Pacific region, Japan's incorporation into the international network of capitalist economies, and the formation of the modern nation-state. First, Meiji Japan's entry into modernity coincided with the era in which Western powers had been engaged in fierce colonialist competitions in East Asia and the Pacific Basin. During the 1880s, a new style of imperialism became the vogue as the West sought direct control of overseas territories, replacing the emphasis on hegemonic control in trade to link the metropolis and its colonies. In Southeast Asia, the French took over Indochina, and the British established footholds in Burma, while both powers

BETWEEN TWO EMPIRES: RACE, HISTORY, AND TRANSNATIONALISM IN JAPANESE AMERICA by Azuma (2005) 3400w from Chp.1 "Mercantilists, Colonialists, and Laborers: Heterogeneous Origins of Japanese America," pp. 17–34 © 2005 by Oxford University Press, Inc. By permission of Oxford University Press, USA.

scrambled for Africa. The Pacific and northeastern Asia subsequently emerged as another sphere of imperialist competition. During and after the Spanish-American War of 1898, the United States acquired Hawaii, the Philippines, and Guam, while the Germans took over the hitherto-neglected Spanish possessions of Pacific island chains in Micronesia and Melanesia. In the meantime, since the mid-1800s, China had become a major battlefield for Christian missionaries and merchants from Europe and the United States.

Meiji Japan, a latecomer, joined this international scramble for new territories and export markets, not only because its leaders felt that the "civilized" had to accept manifest destiny to partake in the practice of colonization, but also because they believed that proactive expansionist endeavors would be imperative in defense of Japan's fragile security. The nation had been on the receiving end of Western imperialism, when it had been forced to open to international commerce in 1854 by U.S. warships under Commodore Matthew Perry, but Japan had diverged from other Asian nations because of its quick "success" in acclimating to the geopolitical environment. No sooner had Emperor Meiji formed a new government in 1868 than imperial expansionism began internally and externally, resulting in the colonization of Hokkaido (1869) and Okinawa (1879); the seizures of Taiwan (1894), south Sakhalin (1905), and Kwantung Province (1905) in northern China; and then the annexation of Korea (1910). In the meantime, the country fought two successful foreign wars, first with China in 1894–1895 and then with Russia in 1904–1905....

Japan's late adoption of a capitalist economy further contributed to the blurring of the boundaries between emigration and colonization. Although the nation turned itself from a feudal society into a major military power within the span of a few decades, the development compounded the integration of Japan into the international capitalist network, rendering it perpetually dependent for markets and capital on more advanced industrial economies, particularly the United States. Given its relative underdevelopment, Japan often served as a source of cheap workers for the more advanced economies, transferring manual labor to Hawaii, the American West, and to a lesser degree, various European colonies in Southeast Asia and the plantation economies of Latin America. Insofar as it also enhanced the competitiveness of imperial Japan's economy, the cheapness of domestic labor dovetailed with Japan's own colonialist projects, leading to significant overlap in socioeconomic characteristics between Japanese immigrants in other countries and colonial settlers within the empire. Although the movement of Japanese across the Pacific transpired between the sphere of Japan's sovereign control and that of another nation-state, it was this overlap that caused U.S.–bound emigrants to be often confounded with colonialists who moved and lived "under the aegis of our national flag."

Tokyo's effort to consolidate state control over its populace provided the third context in which expansionism and emigration were interlocked. Aside from setting up formal state apparatuses and a unified capitalist economy, Meiji nation-building sought to make imperial subjects out of village-bound peasants, who would act voluntarily for the benefit of the emperor and the national collectivity. In accordance with this mandate, as the Meiji elite often stressed, emigrants were expected to obey the call of their nation as citizen-subjects. Just as the state dictated that the obligations of every imperial subject included such acts as paying taxes from meager income, working fourteen hours a day under hazardous conditions, and dying while fighting a foreign war, so Meiji leaders defined emigration as a patriotic duty in support of Japan's expansionist cause, whether commercial, political, or territorial. The colonialist discourse therefore usually assigned a nationalist meaning to the act of emigration on the premise that the masses shared the same dedication to the state's collective purpose. Importantly, while it created another point of intersection between colonialism and emigration, the nationalist presumption blinded the elite to the fact that most emigrants of rural origin viewed their endeavors from the standpoint of personal interest without much regard to the purported duties of the imperial subject. Subsuming popular individualism under nascent nationalism, the elite vision of emigration-led expansionism contradicted the logic of most ordinary emigrants and planted the seeds for discord, which would later grow among Japanese residents in the American West.

During the years between 1885 and 1907, when most male emigrants left for Hawaii and the United States, the ideological terrain of Meiji Japan was indeed a diverse one, with competing ideas developing in tandem with the political process of nationalizing the Japanese people. There were three major currents of emigration thought that directly affected the early development of Japanese America. Roughly corresponding with the class origins and mental worlds of the Issei, they were mercantilist expansionism, Japanese-style manifest destiny, and an ideology of striving and success. The heterogeneity of the Japanese emigrant population also provided a background for contentious relations and identities within their communities, based on how individuals, with varied degrees of national consciousness, understood their ties to the homeland, as well as their role and place in their adopted country.

Mercantilist expansionism helped form what was to become the core of urban Issei leadership in the Pacific Coast states. Rather than seizing colonial territories by military force, proponents of this position aspired to establish footholds of international trade at foreign locations, to which Japan could send its export goods while exercising indirect forms of economic domination. The leading advocate was Fukuzawa Yukichi, who took the lead in the learning of things Western and the development of entrepreneurial culture in Meiji Japan. In 1884, dreaming of British-style commercial hegemony in the Pacific, Fukuzawa promoted Japanese export business by the way of entrepreneurial migration to the United States. Through his private Keio academy and commercial newspaper, this foremost scholar of "Western studies" sought to impress his ideas upon the emerging urban bourgeoisie in Tokyo.

Fukuzawa believed that there was an imminent need to shore up the Meiji policy of "enrich the nation, strengthen the military." With a weak industrial base and a small domestic market, Japan in the mid-1880s badly needed to increase its exports to develop foreign exchange holdings. While propagating trade as essential to solidifying the fiscal basis of the state and its military,

Fukuzawa defined emigration as a cardinal means of promoting commerce with the United States. Specifically, he anticipated that Japanese immigrants in key American trade ports would serve as a "commercial linkage between their homeland and their new country of residence."...

Not everyone, however, was capable of taking up such an endeavor, in Fukuzawa's opinion. He restricted the practitioners of entrepreneurial migration to the United States to a narrow range of educated, middle-class Japanese, for the national "enrichment of Japan" was contingent upon whether or not emigrants possessed the dispositions with which to remain loyal imperial subjects even on foreign soil. Fukuzawa believed that such individuals should be given an opportunity to leave for "the land of boundless opportunities," because he felt that their intellect, talent, and "superior racial qualities" would ensure their ascendancy in American society. Focusing on people of warrior background, Fukuzawa's emigration discourse offered no room for common people of rural origin, whom he frequently ridiculed as lacking national consciousness and modern sensibilities....

A more colonialist discourse on emigration overtook mercantilist expansionism from the 1890s on, when the international scramble for colonies reached its nadir in the Asia-Pacific region. The main theme of the new position revolved around the control of a foreign land through mass migration. Historian Akira Iriye aptly summarizes this Japanese-style manifest destiny:

> The line between emigration and colonization was rather tenuous. Most authors, advocating massive overseas emigration, were visualizing the creation of Japanese communities overseas as centers of economic and social activities closely linked to the mother country.... Though the outright use of force was not envisaged, such a situation would be much closer to colonization than to mere emigration—like the massive English colonization of the North American continent. Thus, "peaceful expansionism" did not simply mean the passive emigration of individual Japanese, but could imply a government-sponsored, active program of overseas settlement and positive activities to tie distant lands closer to Japan....

Toward the late 1890s, a clear pattern of domestic entrepreneurship emerged from the expansionistic Issei intelligentsia. Seeking capital consolidation and ethnic mobilization, many looked to integrate common Japanese laborers, who had hitherto lived in a separate world. In San Francisco, Seattle, and Portland, as well as in smaller regional towns, this ushered in the formation of a class of professional Issei labor contractors. Not only did they promote the influx of additional laborers from Japan, but they also played a major role in increasing landed Japanese communities by facilitating settlement farming in rural districts. In this way, Issei expansionists were being incorporated into the agricultural economy of the American West, conveniently filling the labor vacuum created by Chinese exclusion, as suppliers of farm hands and tillers of undeveloped land....

Unlike the ideas of emigration tied to trade and colonization, the third current of emigration thought, an ideology of striving and success, fit into the mental world of many common emigrants. From the mid-1890s through the following decade, what contemporaries observed as a popular "success boom" swept Japanese society, and emigration to the United States was central to this new social phenomenon. As the print media exalted the American Dream, mass-produced magazines popularized stories of self-made white men, such as Andrew Carnegie, Theodore Roosevelt, Cornelius Vanderbilt, and John D. Rockefeller. Because "America" became synonymous with boundless opportunities in the Japanese vocabulary of the time, many unprivileged but ambitious youth projected onto these role models their own future trajectories. Portraying emigration to the United States as a crucial step, the success ideology catered to the aspirations of the indigent students to work their way through school in the American West and the desire of the rural farming class to make a quick fortune through manual labor there....

When addressed to student-emigrants, the ideology of striving and success was not divorced from the prevailing concern with the national whole that educated Japanese generally shared. Since it was urban literati ... who articulated the meaning of going to America, the success ideology was often worded in the familiar language of "extending national power."... Influenced by such an ideology, which subsumed self-interest under nationalism, it was not uncommon for many student-emigrants to merge into the earlier group of expansionist entrepreneurs once they arrived in the American West. Indeed, in the first two decades of the twentieth century, many immigrant farmers, business owners, and regional community leaders emerged from this population.

The ideology of success had another keen audience: Japan's rural masses. Unlike students, *dekasegi* emigrants of rural origin were mostly indifferent to the valorization of emigration beyond personal or family concerns. For example, a *dekasegi* returnee ascribed her family's emigration decision solely to the "rumor that [it] would pay off handsomely," while another sought to acquire land in his home village and build a "tile-roofed house"—a symbol of wealth in rural Japan. Upon his return from California, a migrant worker admitted that he had acted on the words of former migrant workers that one could "make a bundle of money in America." Despite his advanced age and family objections, the fifty-three-year-old took the journey to the unknown land, because he knew he could not have enjoyed "his fill of sweet *sake*" had he stayed put as a poor farmer in Japan. These accounts demonstrate no trace of concern for the state, or even for their village communities.

From the standpoint of the government elite and urban intelligentsia, rural Japanese were indeed a great trouble. When a large number of laborers crossed the Pacific for work, the process of molding them into imperial subjects had barely begun at home. Starting in the early 1870s, the Meiji state strove hard to integrate Japan's periphery into its centralized state apparatuses, while inculcating national identity in the population of feudalized peasants. This process entailed the development of suitable ideologies, such as state Shintoism, legally sanctioned patriarchy, and the orthodoxy of emperor worship, as well as the construction of corresponding institutions, including compulsory education and military service. The making of imperial subjects in rural areas was nonetheless uneven and incomplete due partially to the often-strained relationships between the central elite and grassroots leaders. Not until after the Russo-Japanese War of 1904–1905 did the state achieve any notable integration of village Japanese....

The departure of *dekasegi* laborers for Hawaii and the United States between 1885 and 1908 signified the zenith of popular pragmatism among ordinary Japanese. In the context of the nation's incorporation into the international network of capitalist economies, the decade of the 1880s ushered in a drastic reconfiguration of its rural economy. What helped to encourage the farming population to emigrate was the overarching effect of commercial agriculture, which alienated so many villagers from their chief means of production, the farmland. These displaced peasants formed a pool of working-class people in need of wage labor. At the same time, the intrusion of market forces into villages opened up the world view of rural residents, allowing some to dream of upward mobility beyond what they could have had under the feudal regime. Depending on varying economic, political, and social circumstances, these developments made some groups of rural Japanese more receptive than others to the idea of going abroad as a way to material fulfillment. The resultant emigrants divide into two major types: distressed contract laborers and entrepreneurial laborers.

Known initially as "government-contract emigrants" (1885–1894) and later as "private-contract emigrants" (1894–1899), *distressed contract laborers* consisted mainly of individuals of "landless or small landowning farming households," who looked to earn American dollars through contract labor in Hawaii. Transportation to Hawaii and other initial expenses were paid for by the employer. In the two phases, there were 29,069 and 40,230 such emigrants, respectively, who were recruited to work on sugar plantations on three-year contracts....

Between 1895 and 1908, more than 130,000 Japanese—the majority of them *entrepreneurial laborers*—left for the continental United States and Hawaii. The typical emigrant of this group originated from a better-off rural household, and he preferred to go to the continental United States without his wife. An average immigrant in California could earn twice as much as a field hand in Hawaii. Given that even a plantation worker was paid four to six times more than a common laborer in Hiroshima, the benefits of choosing labor on the U.S. mainland far exceeded that of going elsewhere and was well worth the initial expenses, which amounted to at least $100. For the same reason, many Japanese laborers in Hawaii, "liberated" from three-year contracts as a result of U.S. annexation, opted to go to the Pacific Coast states after 1900 instead of continuing to work on sugarcane fields or returning home. From 1902 to 1907, there were reportedly about 38,000 Japanese remigrants from Hawaii to the American West.

Unlike the contract labor scheme, the new pattern of labor emigration soon came into conflict with the diplomatic agenda of the Japanese state. The massive influx of common laborers from Japan incited anti-"Oriental" agitation among white Californians, who had excluded Chinese immigrants on the pretext of their economic, cultural, and racial danger. Quickly gathering political momentum, the anti-Japanese movement in the West became such a liability to Tokyo that the Foreign Ministry was compelled to stop the departure of Japanese for the

U.S. mainland altogether in August 1900. A partial relaxation of the ban was effected in June 1902, but it excluded "laborers" categorically from the right of passage. Following this change in emigration policy, when rural Japanese applied for passports, many farmers posed as "businessmen," "merchants," or even "industrialists"—a practice that continued until 1908 with some degree of success. Others went to Mexico and Canada, from which they entered the continental United States. Stringent administrative restrictions only led to widespread popular defiance. Viewed from the perspective of officials, such fraudulent passport applications presented a challenge not only to the diplomatic affairs of the state but also to the very authority of the central government.

Military service formed another notable area of popular defiance by entrepreneurial emigrants. Since the 1870s, rural Japanese had resisted conscription in a variety of ways ranging from mass protests to feigned illness. *Dekasegi* emigration offered many youths a safer means to avoid giving up several years of their lives for something other than their personal benefit and family interests. By virtue of their sojourns abroad, emigrant laborers were able to enjoy annual draft deferments; but in exchange they would be subject to mandatory induction into the army upon their return to Japan without a chance of obtaining reserve status. Yet even this restriction could not match the genius of many emigrants, who simply overstayed in the United States until after their eligibility for active duty expired at the age of thirty-two. The Japanese government was particularly concerned with this problem in the early 1900s, for officials considered it to be not only embarrassing but also inimical to national security. During the crisis of the Russo-Japanese War, Tokyo was compelled to order local offices to scrutinize passport applications from *dekasegi* laborers and crack down on draft evasions, noting that "more and more adolescents due to be draftable in 1905 and 1906 have been attempting to go abroad." Popular individualism seriously challenged the elite/national mandate, producing rebellious rural folks who hardly fit the image of the self-effacing imperial subject.

The Gentlemen's Agreement of 1907–1908 between Washington and Tokyo was a logical culmination of the struggle between the state and rural emigrants. It primarily addressed the problem of anti-Japanese agitation in San Francisco, which demanded immigration exclusion, but also offered the Tokyo elite a solution to the uncontrollable proliferation of the success ideology among labor emigrants. Under the bilateral agreement, the entry routes from Mexico, Canada, and Hawaii into the U.S. mainland were shut down under an executive order of President Theodore Roosevelt, and Tokyo limited the issuance of America-bound passports to specific classes of individuals. Aside from international merchants and students of higher education, the qualified emigrants included only spouses and minor children of bona fide U.S. residents. Until the total exclusion of Japanese in 1924, a smaller scale of labor migration continued in the form of family chain migration, including the so-called picture brides, but after 1908 the control of rural emigrants posed far fewer challenges to the central government.

Thereafter, the main stage of struggle between the commanding state and the defiant emigrant shifted from the domestic sphere of Japan to the society of

Japanese immigrants. In the American West, Tokyo's diplomatic agents and the local Issei elite, including expansionistic mercantilists, colonialists, and patriotic students, formed a coalition to keep the immigrant masses in line, while ordinary laboring men and women remained largely oblivious to the imposition of nationalist dictates. And behind this tug-of-war stood white Americans, who, as the chief force of political intervention, inadvertently furnished the framework for the intraethnic contestation and ensuing community-building efforts in early Japanese America.

Filipino Students and the Politics of Racial Inclusion

PAUL KRAMER

The opening and dedication of Manila's Santa Cruz bridge was pompously undertaken in March 1903, celebrating the "first outward and visible monument to American progress in the Philippines." By that year, the project was simply one element in the U.S. colonial regime's ongoing reform of the capital, aimed especially at commercial infrastructure, sanitary improvement, and police surveillance. But the bridge carried special symbolic weight that spoke to the peculiar predicaments of a colonial state still literally under construction. In reporting the occasion, Manila's English-language press and American colonial officials shared a somewhat obvious metaphorical vocabulary. The structure "not only bridges the Pasig," reported the *Manila American*, "but a chasm that has existed between the native Filipinos and their American fellow-citizens." The hope was for a one-way crossing, so that "over this bridge may come the hearts and minds of the former."...

The ritual would demonstrate how significantly the political, and racial, texture of American colonial politics had changed since the formal declaration of the end of the Philippine-American War. The new colonial state, with the Philippine Commission at its hub, would have civilians at its helm, although it would retain strong military elements. It would draw strength from, but also be challenged by, an American colonial civil society of merchants, businessmen, and adventurers. Most of all, it would be a regime of collaboration between Americans and Filipinos, one in which U.S. officials recognized provincial and metropolitan elites as unequal political partners. The process had, of course, begun during the war itself. Continued repression and the promise of amnesty had attracted both rural and urban elites away from the revolution and toward the U.S. military state. But the system of collaboration would become more extensive and formalized under the civilian regime, both more autonomous from Washington and more deeply rooted in Filipino social structures.

The new political configuration necessitated a new racial formation to organize and legitimate it. The broad-gauged, in some cases exterminist, racism of the U.S. military during the Philippine-American War was ill suited to the more subtle arts of compromise, feint, and manipulation that would characterize Filipino-American power-sharing under the Philippine Commission. What was needed was a racial formation that could somehow persuade its Filipino participants that they were "brothers" and not "serfs" and simultaneously explain to them why they were unready for the rigors and responsibilities of self-government. It must also be able to explain to racist anti-imperialists why the assimilation of Filipinos would be successful and pose no threat to the United States itself. The result was an inclusionary racial formation that brought metaphors of family, evolution, and tutelary assimilation into a gradualist, indeed indefinite, trajectory of Filipino "progress" toward self-government....

If the Filipino masses were superstitious, passive, and ignorant, if Filipino elites were venal, corrupt, and abusive, what was a colonial state to do? What was the inclusionary racial narrative of postwar colonialism in the Philippines to be about? Three interlocking narratives and metaphors went into the making of this inclusionary racism: familial, evolutionary, and tutelary-assimilationist. All three provided necessary frameworks for hierarchical participation and a progressive, if indefinite, time frame for political change. Each recognized Filipinos but predicated that recognition on Filipinos' demonstration of sociocultural features that only Americans could determine and evaluate. Each marked a path into the otherwise uncertain colonial future by drawing necessary, concrete calibrations. The unevenness of their deployment, and their inconsistencies when juxtaposed, were part of their collective power, if they also opened up spaces for resistance. At the same time, their underlying homologies—especially by promising and withholding authority—sustained the hegemony of inclusionary racism and the imperialism of process.

What made each of the narratives powerful was its success in colonizing the future. Filipino incapacities were deep obstructions in the present, but not immutable. "While there is to-day a palpable unfitness for self-government among [Filipinos]," Taft himself put it, "there is in them a capacity for future development, for future preparation for self-government." Each of these narratives came with its own progression into that future: children matured, the backward evolved, students learned. Each of these required outside authorities to accredit or deny progress. When asked to provide more specific timetables for U.S. colonialism, Taft and other colonialists drew boundaries far into the future. Filipinos would "need the training of fifty or a hundred years before they shall even realize what Anglo-Saxon liberty is," Taft wrote, for example. Oftentimes, American officials turned to an expansive language of "generation." There were, for example, Maud Jenks's necessary "fifty generations" of education. Taft believed it would take "at least two generations" to "educate" Filipinos for self-government. "Generation" used in this way combined an open-ended sense of time, a logic of family reproduction, and a neo-Lamarckian hope that self-government might be bred in.

Discourses of family were central to the new inclusionary racial formation. The idiom was encouraged, but not determined, by the arrival of American women and the establishment of new U.S. colonial domestic settings that included, in some cases, young children. Family was a metaphor of inclusion and belonging but also one of hierarchy, of natural inferiors and superiors.

In its elaborated form, the colonial state as "family" cast Filipinos on the whole as children; as such, they were credulous, irresponsible, undisciplined, unruly, and gendered as boys; they were also "educable," reinforcing the colonial state as "school." The colonial state sought graduated timelines for colonialism, which children's progressive maturation to adulthood could provide. But if they agreed Filipinos were "children," Americans in both the Philippines and the United States divided sharply over the broader organization of the colonial "family." Most Manila Americans, for example, especially those close to the military, defined Americans as Filipinos' metaphorical "fathers"; in this mode, the framing of colonialism as family was impelled by the desire to make the ongoing brutalities of war morally invisible by recasting them as legitimate, patriarchal, disciplinary family violence. Officials associated with the Philippine Commission, by contrast, represented themselves as Filipinos' elder "brothers"; the result was what might be called colonial fraternalism, most succinctly expressed in the term for Filipinos attributed to Taft, "little brown brothers." While often taken as a generic expression of colonial condescension, this term needs to be seen in the specific context of an emerging inclusionary Philippine-American racial politics. It invited Filipinos into an imagined household of U.S. empire; it remade them from "black"—the color often attributed to them during the war, into the softer "brown." The metaphor of "brotherhood" did not need to convey actual or potential equality, but it was nonetheless the most potentially subversive of the terms—a fact noted by the Morrison poem above—which made the two other modifiers necessary. While naturalizing and moralizing colonialism, familial metaphors were also problematic in racial terms; it remained unclear how American "fathers" ended up with Filipino "children," or how Americans became the elder siblings to "little brown brothers."

Of the three, evolutionary metaphors were the most abstract, confidently grounding the contested historicism of U.S. colonialism in widely held metanarratives of staged, progressive development. During the late nineteenth and early twentieth centuries, social-evolutionary historicism had reached the pinnacle of its authority within U.S. social science and public culture as a mode of narration and legitimation. But "evolution" had specific functions to achieve in the Philippines: most important, evolution grounded social processes in natural-historical time, which rooted U.S. colonialism in inescapable forces. Where anti-imperialists had challenged the legitimacy of colonialism as a violation of U.S. historical traditions, evolution promoted an alternative—and primordial—historical narrative. But as in other spheres, U.S. colonialists did not simply export existing U.S. social-evolutionary frameworks but rather reworked existing Philippine ones. U.S. colonialists drew on earlier wave-migration theories in casting Philippine history on the whole as a series of racial invasions by progressively more civilized elements; Spanish colonial history, for all its depravities, was recast as the steady, gradual retreat of savagery in the wake of a more progressive Christianity. Within the imagined present and future of U.S. colonial history, Filipinos as individuals would progress still further in evolutionary time. The specific axes of movement varied: they would "evolve" from ignorant peasants to English-speaking students; from filthy urban denizens to sanitary subjects; from recalcitrant to disciplined laborers. Philippine society would also evolve as a whole: from the tribal chaos and fragmentation that was said to have characterized pre-Hispanic and Spanish colonial time, to the emergence—far in the future—of a nation characterized by "homogeneity," forged by transportation and communications infrastructure and by English as a common language. Not all the inhabitants of the Philippines were placed on the same evolutionary track: while evolution was said to characterize U.S. colonial time, Christians and non-Christians were progressing not only at different rates but in different directions. Evolutionary colonial progress, in fact, might widen rather than diminish difference among the islands' inhabitants.

More than any other, the new colonial state's defining metaphor would be tutelary and assimilationist, one that cast the colonial state in its entirety as a school and made its task the active transformation of Filipinos in an unsteady and necessarily indefinite movement toward "Americanism." Tutelage and assimilation were anchored in the actual construction and organization of schools during the first years of the Taft regime and the increasing number of American teachers. By 1904, there were hundreds of new school buildings erected at the center of villages throughout the archipelago; voluntary contributions by local elites for construction purposes rooted these novel institutions in Filipino power structures. The metaphor's greatest practical beneficiaries were the private English-language schools that sprung up in Manila and other cities, promising to train bright and enterprising young Filipinos in English for the civil service exams. The state as school, in other words, made sense in part because attending school facilitated entree into the state as a civil servant.

But the metaphor's power far outstripped the existence of actual public or civil service schools. There was virtually no state arena of Filipino-American interaction—from office clerkships to forced road labor—that was not conceived of as "education." On one level, it sublimated the wartime hatred that had often justified violence in the name of "teaching" Filipinos "a lesson." But "tutelage" was also a shorthand for "benevolence" and "uplift," the very messages the regime wanted to send to both Filipinos and domestic U.S. audiences. Even U.S. soldiers, officials emphasized, had opened schools in the garrisoned towns they had occupied during the war. Education organized the colonial state's myriad tasks into a single one: providing Filipinos the necessary, if elusive, political rationality required for successful self-government. If assimilation was the regime's long-term goal, tutelage was its process and policy. This pervasive metaphor—colonialism as tutelage in self-government—applied equally well, if differently, to still "incapable" Filipino elites and masses. Collaborating Filipino elites would receive "practical instruction" from the U.S. officials with whom they would share power in provincial and insular governments. In the new, American-run public school system, children of the Filipino masses would gain the manual and industrial training, literacy, discipline, and work ethic with which they might eventually exercise responsible "citizenship."

English-language instruction was central to the metaphor of colonialism as tutelage. The decision for English as the primary language of the state was partly structural. On the ground, there were small numbers of Americans who could speak Spanish with the elites of Manila and other cities, and none who spoke any other Filipino languages that might take them farther into the countryside or further down the class scale. A regime so heavily reliant on Filipino collaborators, it might have been argued, should have opted to train the comparatively few Americans in Filipino languages, rather than the far more gigantic project of training Filipinos in English. But, as many observers pointed out, neither the U.S. government nor the academy had the capacity for training potential U.S. civil servants in Filipino languages.

The choice of English was also profoundly ideological, becoming invested with political and moral force in at least two ways. First was the notion of English as the linguistic counterpart of nation-building. What had been one of the central rationales of the U.S. invasion—that proliferating tribes were a sign of the impossibility of Philippine nationality—was now emerging as an organiz- ing regime problem. If the Philippine Republic had been merely a Tagalog conspiracy, as many Americans believed, a genuine Filipino nation could only be constructed through the inculcation of a common language. Spanish might have presented itself as a candidate for the language of Filipino nationality, as the second language of much of the Filipino elite, especially in urban areas. But here, a second ideology was essential, one that invested English with transforma- tive, liberating power. The inherent political superiority of English had been emphasized during the Anglo-Saxonist mobilizations that had proven so impor- tant during the annexation debate. English was not only the means to national unity but the necessary vehicle for tutelage. Only English could convey Anglo- Saxon morals and institutions of self-government, transforming its users.

English-language instruction became one element in the regime's broader national-exceptionalist claims. Explaining why American colonial civil servants were neither trained nor examined on Philippine languages, Everett Thompson, a civil service board examiner, noted the "radically different principle underlying the *raison d'etre* of the Philippine government" relative to India, Java, and Indo- china. These colonies were "governed as sources of strength and revenue to the home power" and lacked an impulse "magnanimously to uplift" or "train the inhabitants for citizenship or to change their language or customs." As a result, European officials in them, "to better administer the necessary affairs of govern- ment," became "thoroughly imbued with the genius, the language, the laws, and customs of the subject peoples." "With the Philippines," he wrote, "all this is different." Since the Philippine government existed "primarily for the Filipinos," the "permeating spirit of the Philippine civil service is the training of the Filipino in the best methods of government." Filipinos compelled to speak English might become "thoroughly imbued" with the Anglo-Saxon genius, rather than the other way around. English might also have the more mundane benefit of encouraging compliance with the colonial state. "In mastering the English lan- guage the Filipinos not only fill their minds with a knowledge of its literature," wrote Thompson, "but are thus the better prepared to appreciate the high aims and purposes of the present government."

There was no better condensation of the projects of tutelage and assimilation than the *pensionado* program, inaugurated in 1903, which would eventually send approximately 300 Filipino students to the United States for government-funded higher education. After receiving four years of college and living with American families, the *pensionados* would be required to return to the Philippines as teachers, engineers, or other civil servants for five years. The program arose out of the desire for higher-level Filipino civil servants and the complete absence of secular higher education in the Philippines capable of meeting American standards of expertise. It was also hoped that it would introduce "assimilating" Filipinos to the United States as advertisements for the regime's benevolence. It resembled empire-building educational programs elsewhere; indeed, U.S. officials compared it to "the efforts of the British Government to educate the people of India by sending them to England, and of the Japanese Government in behalf of its own people in sending them to notable foreign schools."

If the *pensionado* program was about reorienting the rising elite generation toward American customs and loyalties, it was also about putting forward the best and brightest Filipino youths before American eyes as symbols of successful assimilation. The requirement of high-school graduation, a goal achieved by only those few families that could sustain children in school, tended to deliver upper-class candidates. Where a poor but talented student might have squeaked through, Taft's instructions to provincial governors made clear that "[e]ach student must be of unquestionable moral and physical qualifications, weight being given to social status." William Sutherland, the program's first supervisor, would later recall that the program's goal was "to make a favorable impression" on Americans "who mostly thought theretofore that Filipinos wore gee strings and slept in trees."

If narratives of tutelage, family, evolution, and assimilation made headway in the Philippines, it was only because they were ideologies familiar and acceptable to select Filipino elites, some of whom emphasized that Filipino progress could only be achieved through U.S. colonialism. These elites were recognized and promoted by the colonial state and given a platform in official publications and in opinion journals in the United States. Such ideological congruence was most visible at the insular level, where collaboration between Americans and Filipinos allowed and required a mutual shaping of political discourses. T. H. Pardo de Tavera best represented the Filipino side of this dialogue in the early years of the Taft regime. His vision of Filipino progress through colonialism, and especially through U.S. secular education, was articulated, for example, in a 1906 address given before American and Filipino teachers entitled "The Filipino Soul." In it, Pardo criticized "conservatives" who would "preserve our customs and traditions" so that "our social conscience, poetically styled the Filipino soul, may remain unchanged." Only "uncivilized countries," he claimed, remained "immutable and petrified before the moving forces of history." As when barbarous Europeans long ago had become civilized by submitting to conquering Romans, Filipinos should submit to the tutelage of the "Anglo-Saxon race," the "trustee and the dictator of the highest civilization that we have ever known of."

Like the American architects of inclusionary racism, Pardo stated that he did "not believe that race-inferiority is a matter of permanence or of anthropology" nor "an inherent or a natural condition of any race." Indeed, it was those who advocated a "Filipino soul" that were overcommitted to "racial" thinking. These "anthropo-sociologists" failed to acknowledge the "absurdity" of essential racial hierarchy, denying, for example, the historical rise and decline of races between positions of superiority and inferiority. Japan presented Pardo a "striking example" of social transformation through adoption of European ways; he prophesied that the day was "not far distant" when Philippine progress would "present one more practical example to the sociologists who deny the existence of inferior races, because our culture will also shed a luster on this world side by side with that of Japan."

Also like his American counterparts, Pardo sought to legitimate the U.S. occupation by indigenizing it, making it the historic extension of the late nineteenth-century *ilustrado* diaspora and Propaganda reform movement. Filipinos abroad in that period had sought "to acquire a new spirit, a new mentality," rather than to cling to a "Filipino soul." There was a certain irony, then, that "now that the civilization which we want to seek outside our country" had "come to visit our own homes in the form of the Anglo-Saxon public school instruction, a strange reactionary spirit and puzzling attitude of mind struggle to drive it away." Those who claimed that colonial education would undermine Filipino nationalism had to deal with an awkward historical fact: colonial education had historically promoted nation-building. "The Filipinos educated in Spanish schools in the Philippines, under a strictly Spanish system," he noted, "were the individuals who brought about the revolution which ended Spanish sovereignty in the Philippines." While it might seem that the "movement for Philippinism" emerged from the "uneducated classes," it was in fact the work of the educated, "whose souls had been 'profoundly adulterated.'" It was European-educated Filipinos that had learned "to respect the race, venerate the customs of the ancestors, discover the beauties of Nature in the Islands (in which other people found nothing but objects of ridicule and scorn), admire the land, and dream of the country's redemption." Pardo believed U.S. colonialism would continue this process. English-language education would create an awareness of "the oneness of our rights, the singleness of our duties, the harmony of our aspirations, and the unanimity of our ideals." Communications networks would spread civilization across physically isolated provinces, and "in place of heterogeneity, there will spring a homogeneity of ideas." Interregional contact and communication would "give rise to a sentiment of national fellowship which, in truth, hardly exists today."

While tutelage and assimilation found some Filipino advocates, they also produced American skepticism and anxiety. It would remain one of the regime's central tasks to persuade doubting domestic U.S. publics that Filipinos could be Americanized. Tutelage and assimilation were both fantasies of one-way cultural connection without unanticipated reflux: the colonized would learn from the colonizers without, in turn, teaching them; the colonized would become more similar to the colonizers without transforming them. If the new regime empowered Filipinos who believed in assimilation, there were nonetheless many American skeptics who feared what it might mean for the United States itself, as in Rebecca Taylor's 1903 critical essay, "Disposition of the Philippine Islands." Taylor's piece can be seen as taking up where Henry C. Rowland's wartime account of the tragic "degeneration" of U.S. troops had left off. It evaluated the regime's policy of assimilation, which she defined as "nothing less than incorporation into the body politic." Pushing the metaphor to the point of extremity and dark satire, Taylor defined assimilation in digestive terms, in the process revealing just how important unincorporated status had been. Taylor redefined McKinley's "benevolent assimilation" to mean that the "Philippine prey must be captured by the great assimilating body, and devoured—ground to powder by the military force composing the strong teeth of that body; that Filipino mincemeat must be moistened by saliva of superior brand—spat upon, if you please, the mouth of the big assimilating body fairly 'watering' at the prospect of an Oriental meal. Down the American esophagus the mass must go."

Once devoured, the Philippines would become "'flesh of our flesh and bone of our bone.'" But the process would not merely change the Philippines. During actual, physical digestion, "[t]he assimilating body is also changed by the character of the substance assimilated. The purity of the blood, the strength of the muscles, the quality of the brain, the tension of the nerve, the texture of the skin, the temperature, and even the moral nature are strongly influenced by that which is assimilated." This would operate as well in the political sphere. In "assimilating the Filipino, the American people must accept the change that will be wrought in the national body by the very nature of the case." Continuing her striking description of digestive imperialism, she stated:

> This fine pulp must be passed through the Taft pylorus into the American duodenum, to be acted upon by the various superior fluids, notably American gall, after which the political villi will dip down into the Filipino-American chyle … and finally the refined emulsion, when mixed with American blood, will pass to the heart of the nation, whence it will be pumped through the American arteries to all parts of the assimilating body, building up the new America.

Taylor predicted that, before assimilation was completed, the United States would have had "several centuries of frightful indigestion." More seriously, the nation would itself have been fundamentally disfigured. Americans would "scarcely recognize" the nation "because of its Oriental diet, so foreign to our American system," she wrote. An empire of recognition might become unrecognizable to itself. "We will find ourselves Malayed Americans, even as they shall have become Americanized Malays. It remains to be seen how far the change will improve either."

☾ FURTHER READING

Charr, Easurk Emsen. *The Golden Mountain* (1961).

Go, Julian. *American Empire and the Politics of Meaning: Elite Political Cultures in the Philippines and Puerto Rico during U.S. Colonialism* (2008).

Hunt, Michael H., and Steven I. Levine. *Arc of Empire: America's Wars in Asia from the Philippines to Vietnam* (2012).

Ichioka, Yuji. *The Issei: The World of the First Generation Japanese Immigrants, 1885–1924* (1988).

Iwata, Masakazu. *Planted in Good Soil: A History of the Issei in the United States Agriculture*, 2 volumes (1992).

Jensen, Joan M. *Passage from India: Asian Indian Immigrants in North America* (1988).

Miller, Stuart Creighton. *"Benevolent Assimilation": American Conquest of the Philippines, 1899–1903* (1982).

Moriyama, Alan Takeo. *Imingaisha: Japanese Emigration Companies and Hawaii, 1894–1908* (1985).

Patterson, Wayne. *The Ilse: First-Generation Korean Immigrants in Hawai'i, 1903–1973* (2000).

———. *The Korean Frontier in America: Immigration to Hawaii, 1896–1910* (1988).

Posadas, Barbara M. *The Filipino Americans* (1999).

Rafael, Vincente L. *White Love and Other Events in Filipino History* (2000).

Rydell, Robert. *All the World's a Fair: Visions of Empire at American International Expositions, 1876–1916* (1984).

Thompson, Lanny. *Imperial Archipelago: Representation and the Rule in the Insular Territories under U.S. Dominion after 1898* (2010).

Wakatsuki, Yasuo. "Japanese Emigration to the United States, 1866-1924: A Monograph," *Perspectives in American History* 12 (1979): 387–516.

CHAPTER 5

New "Oriental Problems,"

1900–1918

Given the rising status of Japan as a world power, Japanese immigrants came to the United States expecting to receive better treatment than the excluded Chinese. But their hopes were dashed. U.S. workers viewed all Asian laborers as a threat to their jobs and standards of living, and they joined with nativists in preventing them from entering the nation. Making matters worse, according to the advocates of Japanese exclusion, was the fear that imperial Japan sought to use immigration as a nefarious means to conquer the United States in order to dominate the Pacific. In this scenario, Japanese immigrants were branded a "silent invasion" and "yellow peril." Such antagonism fueled a movement for Japanese exclusion that relied on many of the same arguments used against the Chinese, and California remained the hub of anti-Asian activity. In 1906, San Francisco officials approved the segregation of Japanese students in the city's public schools in an attempt to discourage Japanese immigration.

Leading federal officials opposed the discrimination of Japanese immigrants on the grounds that it was a violation of treaty rights and an offense to a nation with which the United States was on good terms. President Theodore Roosevelt genuinely respected Japan's military successes, especially after its defeat of Russia in 1905. He did not want nativists to damage trade relations in the Pacific or, even worse, to provoke an unwanted war with the formidable island nation. Consequently, Roosevelt tried to resolve the conflict in California through establishing the Gentlemen's Agreement in 1907 by which Japan agreed to restrict laborers from coming to the United States in return for San Francisco scrapping plans to segregate Japanese students. But the immigration of Japanese women and merchant classes, who were not restricted by the Gentlemen's Agreement, pushed the California state legislature in 1913 to discriminate against Japanese by preventing them from owning farmland. President Woodrow Wilson intervened at the behest of Tokyo officials, but to no avail. It took the eruption of World War I in Europe to calm tensions, as the United States and Japan found themselves fighting on the same side.

Preventing the immigration of Japanese laborers with the Gentlemen's Agreement created a need for workers along the West Coast that was met in part by immigrants from India. The newcomers followed the Japanese into agricultural labor and small farming.

But they too faced hostility from labor and nativist groups, and in some incidents, such as the 1907 riots in Bellingham, Washington, angry white mobs attacked them and drove them from their homes. In 1914, Congress held hearings to discuss the exclusion of Indian immigrants, and three years later sweeping legislation banned immigration from India and almost all of the Asia-Pacific region. In addition, the British government urged U.S. officials to keep close tabs on Indian nationalists, most of whom were students who used the United States as a base to advance the struggle for India's independence from British colonialism. During World War I, eight Indian independence activists were convicted in San Francisco for conspiring to engage in a military plot against British India.

Concerns about Asian criminal activity grew during this exclusion era. Foremost were ever-present fears that Asians were being smuggled into the country through schemes run by organized crime syndicates. As a result, immigration officers at West Coast stations like Angel Island placed Chinese newcomers under strict scrutiny as they searched to find false identities. Angel Island became more like a prison than a temporary immigration-processing center for many unlucky Chinese. Meanwhile, exclusionists saw Chinatowns throughout the West as notorious places for gambling, drugs, and prostitution.

DOCUMENTS

Documents 1 to 5 concern efforts to exclude Japanese immigrants. Author Jack London wrote Document 1 while serving as a newspaper correspondent for the Russo-Japanese War in 1904. Japan's victory in that war compelled London to alert the West of the potential for a Japanese–Chinese alliance that could menace the world. President Roosevelt dismissed such alarmism, and Document 2 is an excerpt of his State of the Union address in 1906 that extols Japanese civilization while condemning San Francisco exclusionists for irresponsibly damaging U.S.–Japan relations. Note that the president also wants to change the nation's naturalization law to allow Japanese immigrants to become U.S. citizens, a position from which he later retreated. Document 3, written by a leading exclusionist organization, captures the intense anti-Asian animosity that the president sought to defuse by defending Japanese immigrants, while Document 4 provides the perspective of Japanese immigrants regarding the approval of an exclusionist alien land law in California. In Document 5, a prominent Californian publisher compares the state's Japanese population to antebellum black slavery in the South. He argues that the Japanese should be excluded before their population grows and becomes permanent, lest the nation go down the same troubled road of Southern race relations that led to the Civil War, Reconstruction, and the seemingly perpetual oppression of African Americans.

Documents 6 and 7 show two sides of a debate over the exclusion of Indian immigrants, as expressed in a 1914 congressional hearing. In Document 6, an educated Indian immigrant defends the virtues of his community and countrymen, while assuring the committee that they are not Mongolians like the Chinese and Japanese. He also assures the committee that Indians can assimilate and become good Americans without needing to intermarry with whites. In Document 7, a U.S. immigration official disagrees with the testimony in Document 6, stating that the vast majority of Indian immigrants are uneducated workers who are not able to assimilate into U.S. society. His views are seemingly corroborated by findings from a Canadian report on Indian immigrants.

Documents 8 and 9 address Chinese immigrants. Document 8 consists of two poems carved into the wooden barracks at the Angel Island immigration station by Chinese waiting to learn whether they would be allowed to enter the United States or be returned home. Both poems convey the helplessness and desperation of those held at Angel Island. Document 9 is an editorial, published in Vancouver, British Columbia, that outlines the problems related to gambling in that city's Chinatown. Key here is the editorial's focus on a petition by Chinese merchants that did not protest against their discrimination in as much as it bemoaned the lawlessness by Chinese immigrants. This position is similar to the stances of earlier Chinatown leaders who supported the exclusion of Chinese laborers.

1. American Writer Decries the New Yellow Peril, 1904

HERE WE HAVE THE CHINESE, four hundred million of him, occupying a vast land of immense natural resources—resources of a twentieth century age, of a machine age; resources of coal and iron, which are the backbone of commercial civilization. He is an indefatigable worker. He is not dead to new ideas, new methods, new systems. Under a capable management he can be made to do anything. Truly would he of himself constitute the much-heralded Yellow Peril were it not for his present management. This management, his government, is set, crystallized. It is what binds him down to building as his fathers built. The governing class, entrenched by the precedent and power of centuries and ... by the stamp it has put upon his mind, will never free him. It would be the suicide of the governing class, and the governing class knows it.

Comes now the Japanese. On the streets of Antung, of Feng-Wang-Chang, or of any other Manchurian city, the following is a familiar scene: One is hurrying home through the dark of the unlighted streets when he comes upon a paper lantern resting on the ground. On one side squats a Chinese civilian on his hams, on the other side squats a Japanese soldier. One dips his forefinger in the dust and writes strange, monstrous characters. The other nods understanding, sweeps the dust slate level with his hand, and with his forefinger inscribes similar characters. They are talking. They cannot speak to each other, but they can write. Long ago one borrowed the other's written language, and long before that, untold generations ago, they diverged from a common root, the ancient Mongol stock.

There have been changes, differentiations brought about by diverse conditions and infusions of other blood; but down at the bottom of their being, twisted into the fibres of them, is a heritage in common—a sameness in kind

From Jack London, "The Yellow Peril" (1904), in *London, Revolution and Other Essays* (New York: Macmillian, 1910), 277–289; reproduced in S. T. Joshi, ed. *Documents of American Prejudice* (New York: Basic Books, 1999), 439–444.

which time has not obliterated. The infusion of other blood, Malay, perhaps, has made the Japanese a race of mastery and power, a fighting race through all its history, a race which has always despised commerce and exalted fighting.

To-day, equipped with the finest machines and systems of destruction the Caucasian mind has devised, handling machines and systems with remarkable and deadly accuracy, this rejuvenescent Japanese race has embarked on a course of conquest, the goal of which no man knows. The head men of Japan are dreaming ambitiously, and the people are dreaming blindly, a Napoleonic dream. And to this dream the Japanese clings and will cling with bull-dog tenacity. The soldier shouting "Nippon, Banzai!" on the walls of Wiju, the widow at home in her paper house committing suicide so that her only son, her sole support, may go to the front, are both expressing the unanimity of the dream.

The late disturbance in the Far East marked the clashing of the dreams, for the Slav [Russian], too, is dreaming greatly. Granting that the Japanese can hurl back the Slav and that the two great branches of the Anglo-Saxon race do not despoil him of his spoils, the Japanese dream takes on substantiality. Japan's population is no larger because her people have continually pressed against the means of subsistence. But given poor, empty Korea for a breeding colony and Manchuria for a granary, and at once the Japanese begins to increase by leaps and bounds.

Even so, he would not of himself constitute a Brown Peril, He has not the time in which to grow and realize the dream. He is only forty-five millions, and so fast does the economic exploitation of the planet hurry on the planet's partition amongst the Western peoples that, before he could attain the stature requisite to menace, he would see the Western giants in possession of the very stuff of his dream.

The menace to the Western world lies, not in the little brown man, but in the four hundred millions of yellow men should the little brown man undertake their management. The Chinese is not dead to new ideas; he is an efficient worker; makes a good soldier, and is wealthy in the essential materials of a machine age. Under a capable management he will go far. The Japanese is prepared and fit to undertake this management. Not only has he proved himself an apt imitator of Western material progress, a sturdy worker, and a capable organizer, but he is far more fit to manage the Chinese than are we. The baffling enigma of the Chinese character is no baffling enigma to him. He understands as we could never school ourselves nor hope to understand. Their mental processes are largely the same. He thinks with the same thought-symbols as does the Chinese, and he thinks in the same peculiar grooves. He goes on where we are balked by the obstacles of incomprehension. He takes the turning which we cannot perceive, twists around the obstacle, and, presto! is out of sight in the ramifications of the Chinese mind where we cannot follow....

We have had Africa for the Africander, and at no distant day we shall hear "Asia for the Asiatic!" Four hundred million indefatigable workers (deft, intelligent, and unafraid to die), aroused and rejuvenescent, managed and guided by forty-five million additional human beings who are splendid fighting animals, scientific and modern, constitute that menace to the Western world which has been well named the "Yellow Peril." The possibility of race adventure has not passed away. We are in the midst of our own. The Slav is just girding himself up to begin. Why may not the yellow and the brown start out on an adventure as tremendous as our own and more strikingly unique?

The ultimate success of such an adventure the Western mind refuses to consider. It is not the nature of life to believe itself weak. There is such a thing as race egotism as well as creature egotism, and a very good thing it is. In the first place, the Western world will not permit the rise of the yellow peril. It is firmly convinced that it will not permit the yellow and the brown to wax strong and menace its peace and comfort. It advances this idea with persistency, and delivers itself of long arguments showing how and why this menace will not be permitted to arise. To-day, far more voices are engaged in denying the yellow peril than in prophesying it. The Western world is warned, if not armed, against the possibility of it.

In the second place, there is a weakness inherent in the brown man which will bring his adventure to naught. From the West he has borrowed all our material achievement and passed our ethical achievement by. Our engines of production and destruction he has made his. What was once solely ours he now duplicates, rivalling our merchants in the commerce of the East, thrashing the Russian on sea and land. A marvellous imitator truly, but imitating us only in things material. Things spiritual cannot be imitated; they must be felt and lived, woven into the very fabric of life, and here the Japanese fails.

It required no revolution of his nature to learn to calculate the range and fire a field-gun or to march the goose-step. It was a mere matter of training. Our material achievement is the product of our intellect. It is knowledge, and knowledge, like coin, is interchangeable. It is not wrapped up in the heredity of the new-born child, but is something to be acquired afterward. Not so with our soul stuff, which is the product of an evolution which goes back to the raw beginnings of the race. Our soul stuff is not a coin to be pocketed by the first chance comer. The Japanese cannot pocket it any more than he can thrill to short Saxon words or we can thrill to Chinese hieroglyphics. The leopard cannot change its spots, nor can the Japanese, nor can we. We are thumbed by the ages into what we are, and by no conscious inward effort can we in a day rethumb ourselves. Nor can the Japanese in a day, or a generation, rethumb himself in our image....

The colossal fact of our history is that we have made the religion of Jesus Christ our religion. No matter how dark in error and deed, ours has been a history of spiritual struggle and endeavor. We are preëminently a religious race, which is another way of saying that we are a right-seeking race.

2. President Roosevelt Warns Against Anti-Japanese Racism, 1906

The countries bordering the Pacific Ocean have a population more numerous than that of all the countries of Europe; their annual foreign commerce amounts to over three billions of dollars, of which the share of the United States is some seven hundred millions of dollars. If this trade were thoroly understood and pushed by our manufacturers and producers, the industries not only of the Pacific slope, but of all our country, and particularly of our cotton growing States, would be greatly benefited. Of course, in order to get these benefits, we must treat fairly the countries with which we trade....

Not only must we treat all nations fairly, but we must treat with justice and good will all immigrants who come here under the law. Whether they are Catholic or Protestant, Jew or Gentile; whether they come from England or Germany, Russia, Japan, or Italy, matters nothing. All we have a right to question is the man's conduct. If he is honest and upright in his dealings with his neighbor and with the State, then he is entitled to respect and good treatment. Especially do we need to remember our duty to the stranger within our gates. It is the sure mark of a low civilization, a low morality, to abuse or discriminate against or in any way humiliate such stranger who has come here lawfully and who is conducting himself properly. To remember this is incumbent on every American citizen, and it is of course peculiarly incumbent on every Government official, whether of the nation or of the several States.

I am prompted to say this by the attitude of hostility here and there assumed toward the Japanese in this country. This hostility is sporadic and is limited to a very few places. Nevertheless, it is most discreditable to us as a people, and it may be fraught with the gravest consequences to the nation. The friendship between the United States and Japan has been continuous since the time, over half a century ago, when Commodore Perry, by his expedition to Japan, first opened the islands to western civilization. Since then the growth of Japan has been literally astounding. There is not only nothing to parallel it, but nothing to approach it in the history of civilized mankind. Japan has a glorious and ancient past. Her civilization is older than that of the nations of northern Europe—the nations from whom the people of the United States have chiefly sprung. But fifty years ago Japan's development was still that of the Middle Ages. During that fifty years the progress of the country in every walk in life has been a marvel to mankind, and she now stands as one of the greatest of civilized nations; great in the arts of war and in the arts of peace; great in military, in industrial, in artistic development and achievement. Japanese soldiers and sailors have shown themselves equal in combat to any of whom history makes note. She has produced great generals and mighty admirals; her fighting men, afloat and ashore, show all the heroic courage, the unquestioning, unfaltering loyalty, the splendid

From Theodore Roosevelt, "Sixth Annual Message," December 3, 1906, in *House of Representatives, Papers Relating to the Foreign Relations of the United States* (Washington, D.C.: Government Printing Office, 1909), XL.

indifference to hardship and death, which marked the Loyal Ronins; and they show also that they possess the highest ideal of patriotism. Japanese artists of every kind see their products eagerly sought for in all lands. The industrial and commercial development of Japan ... was accepted with gratitude by our people. The courtesy of the Japanese, nationally and individually, has become proverbial. To no other country has there been such an increasing number of visitors from this land as to Japan. In return, Japanese have come here in great numbers. They are welcome, socially and intellectually, in all our colleges and institutions of higher learning, in all our professional and social bodies. The Japanese have won in a single generation the right to stand abreast of the foremost and most enlightened peoples of Europe and America; they have won on their own merits and by their own exertions the right to treatment on a basis of full and frank equality. The overwhelming mass of our people cherish a lively regard and respect for the people of Japan, and in almost every quarter of the Union the stranger from Japan is treated as he deserves; that is, he is treated as the stranger from any part of civilized Europe is and deserves to be treated. But here and there a most unworthy feeling has manifested itself toward the Japanese—the feeling that has been shown in shutting them out from the common schools in San Francisco, and in mutterings against them in one or two other places, because of their efficiency as workers. To shut them out from the public schools is a wicked absurdity, when there are no first-class colleges in the land, including the universities and colleges of California, which do not gladly welcome Japanese students and on which Japanese students do not reflect credit. We have as much to learn from Japan as Japan has to learn from us; and no nation is fit to teach unless it is also willing to learn. Thruout Japan Americans are well treated, and any failure on the part of Americans at home to treat the Japanese with a like courtesy and consideration is by just so much a confession of inferiority in our civilization.

Our nation fronts on the Pacific, just as it fronts on the Atlantic. We hope to play a constantly growing part in the great ocean of the Orient. We wish, as we ought to wish, for a great commercial development in our dealings with Asia; and it is out of the question that we should permanently have such development unless we freely and gladly extend to other nations the same measure of justice and good treatment which we expect to receive in return. It is only a very small body of our citizens that act badly. Where the Federal Government has power it will deal summarily with any such. Where the several States have power I earnestly ask that they also deal wisely and promptly with such conduct, or else this small body of wrongdoers may bring shame upon the great mass of their innocent and right-thinking fellows—that is, upon our nation as a whole. Good manners should be an international no less than an individual attribute. I ask fair treatment for the Japanese as I would ask fair treatment for Germans or Englishmen, Frenchmen, Russians, or Italians. I ask it as due to humanity and civilization. I ask it as due to ourselves because we must act uprightly toward all men.

I recommend to the Congress that an act be past specifically providing for the naturalization of Japanese who come here intending to become American citizens. One of the great embarrassments attending the performance of our international obligations is the fact that the Statutes of the United States are entirely inadequate. They fail to give to the National Government sufficiently ample power, thru United States courts and by the use of the Army and Navy, to protect aliens in the rights secured to them under solemn treaties which are the law of the land. I therefore earnestly recommend that the criminal and civil statutes of the United States be so amended and added to as to enable the President, acting for the United States Government, which is responsible in our international relations, to enforce the rights of aliens under treaties. Even as the law now is something can be done by the Federal Government toward this end, and in the matter now before me affecting the Japanese, everything that it is in my power to do will be done, and all of the forces, military and civil, of the United States which I may lawfully employ will be so employed. There should, however, be no particle of doubt as to the power of the National Government completely to perform and enforce its own obligations to other nations. The mob of a single city may at any time perform acts of lawless violence against some class of foreigners which would plunge us into war. That city by itself would be powerless to make defense against the foreign power thus assaulted, and if independent of this Government it would never venture to perform or permit the performance of the acts complained of. The entire power and the whole duty to protect the offending city or the offending community lies in the hands of the United States Government.

3. Asiatic Exclusion League Argues Against Japanese and Korean Immigration, 1908

WHILE THE AMERICAN PEOPLE ARE BEING CHLOROFORMED BY DIPLOMATIC NEGOTIATIONS, PREPARATIONS ARE MADE TO OPEN THE GATES FOR THE COOLIE HORDES OF THE ORIENT.

Repeated efforts have been made to repeal or nullify the Chinese Exclusion Act.

Powerful influences, both in America and in China, have sought in past years to break down the barriers placed against the Oriental coolie. So far they have failed.

The infamous Foster bill was snowed under by the millions of protests from citizens, sent at the request of the Asiatic Exclusion League; President Roosevelt's message to the last session of the Fifty-ninth Congress, where he recommended the naturalization of Japanese, and threatened the people upon the Pacific Coast with all the power at his command, met with such a storm of protest that it aroused the entire nation.

As a result, the time established policy of the United States Government towards Chinese immigration has been rigidly maintained up to the present time, and promises have been made by the administration at Washington that this same policy would be extended to all Asiatic immigrants.

From *Proceedings of the Asiatic Exclusion League, 1907–1913* (New York: Arno Press, 1977), 10, 16–19, 22–24.

The Californians especially have accepted these promises in good faith, and behaved exceedingly well. In fact, some of the leading papers in the State have even told us that the entire Asiatic immigration problem was settled and that we really had extended the exclusion policy to all the Oriental people.

But in this firmly rooted security there lurks the greatest danger. The signs which have been displayed from Washington and Tokio within the last few weeks ought to act as danger signals to the American citizens who are standing guard for the Caucasian civilization on the western border of our country.

Secretary Straus recommends, in his report to the President, that the Chinese should be treated under the general immigration laws. That is virtually a recommendation to repeal the Chinese Exclusion Act, although the Secretary of Commerce and Labor denies that such was his intention.

Yet, if Straus' views should prevail every able-bodied Chinese coolie, not a criminal, pauper, or anarchist, or suffering from infectious disease, would have free admittance into our ports.

There are over four hundred millions of them in China, and ten, twenty, thirty, forty or fifty millions would hardly be missed in the Celestial Empire, but they would make themselves felt in America in a manner that no intelligent white man or woman can have any doubt of.

Uncle Sam has a real serious race problem in the South. Is he to have one ten times more aggravated in the West? If the people permit themselves to be chloroformed by promises and diplomatic negotiations, the "yellow peril" will in the future threaten Europe not only from Asia but from America.

Last Saturday, the House of Representatives passed a bill for the greater protection of aliens. It was carried by the vote of the Speaker, as the votes of the members stood 100 against and 100 for the measure on a recapitulation.

We have not seen the full text of this law, but from what has been learned it appears that it is not only an invasion of State rights, but also intended as a club whereby native and naturalized citizens may be kept in subjugation while the Chinese and Japanese swarm and bask in the sunlight of favored nation's treaty rights.

Some day we may perhaps find that if we fail to patronize a Chink or a Jap that we will be indicted by a Federal Grand Jury and thrown into prison; and if your sweet little girl should murmur in protest because she had to sit in school side by side with a courteous, courting Japanese study boy, whose proficiency in the American language manifests itself in the writing of obscene letters, she might run the risk of having the United States marshal drag her off to the dungeon.

Simultaneously with all this comes the news from Tokio that the Mikado's Government has decided to prohibit all immigration of Japanese labor to the main land.

That is nothing new; a similar edict went forth from the Mikado in 1900. There is absolutely nothing binding, not even a treaty agreement. It is simply an announcement by the Nipponese Government of its intentions. However, it should be noted that the Japanese laborers are only prohibited from immigrating to the main land. They can go in hundreds of thousands to our "insular possessions," the Philippines and the Hawaiian Islands, and from these halfway stations they can readily find a passage to California, Washington or Oregon, and then, there is nothing to stop them from coming in millions by way of Canada and Mexico.

These are among the danger signals that ought to arouse the American people to the peril that is threatening their existence and the fate of their children.

The conquest of a country can be effected more thoroughly by the spade and the hoe than by the sword or the musket.

4. Japanese Immigrants Oppose California Alien Land Law, 1913

The Proposed Land Bills: The Other Side

During the last half century or more the United States has sustained a peculiarly close relation to Japan, for she it was that opened the doors of the Island Empire, introduced her to Western civilization and Christian ideals, and taught her her first lessons of fairness, freedom and equality. She it was that first recognized Japan as a member among the civilized nations and proposed to treat her as such.

In view of these past pleasant experiences and the favorable sentiment of a large part of the American public relative to Japanese affairs, it is almost unthinkable that so many bills of discriminatory nature should be introduced at this session of the State Legislature.

Misunderstandings

Without doubt this is largely due to a misunderstanding of the condition of the Japanese in this State. To not a few examples, it has been said that the Japanese congregate themselves in one quarter and do not assimilate. And it has also been said, on the contrary, that the Japanese are unlike the Chinese in that they scatter everywhere. They mix with American people. They go to the public schools. They learn American methods, and are in sympathy with American institutions and ideals. In other words, they become assimilated. These two conflicting theories are working side by side in the support of the proposed measures in Sacramento. Again it is said that the Japanese can live on almost nothing and work very cheaply. On the other hand, we hear that the Japanese are a most extravagant people and demand enormous wages for their services. These two statements are diametrically opposed, but they have been used as the reasons for the Anti-Japanese legislation.

Some claim that the Japanese make money and send it home. Consequently, they are in no way helping American industry and business. At the same time another argument is advanced that the Japanese make money, save it, and invest it in this country: hence certain people fear that they are going to buy up all the land.

From Japanese Association of America, *The Proposed Land Bills: The Other Side* (San Francisco, CA: Japanese Association of America, 1913).

If one argument is right the other is wrong, but all these conflicting theories and reasons are working side by side to create sentiment against the Japanese. Why? Because there is a great deal of misunderstanding on the part of the American people.

Misrepresentation

The amount of land owned and leased by the Japanese in California is frequently greatly overstated. On page 633 of the latest, 1912, report of the State Bureau of Labor Statistics, we find that the total area of farm lands owned by Japanese is only 12,726 acres, cut up into 331 farms and assessed at $478,990. On page 635, we get the town lots so held as 218 in number and assessed at a beggarly $136,955. That is to say, there are 549 separate pieces of land, valued at $615,945. In all the years that Japanese have been coming here—and the number is decreasing—they have not acquired much more than half a million dollars' worth of California land.

Two years ago the State Legislature appointed a special commission to investigate Japanese conditions in California. The report was so favorable to the Japanese that it was suppressed from publication. The recently published Report of the United States Immigration Commission is equally favorable, and is well worthy of a careful study before final action is taken.

Small Politics

The real purpose of the proposed anti-alien land bills is clearly revealed editorially in the San Francisco *Wasp*, as quoted in the Los Angeles *Times* of April 20th. (San Francisco *Wasp*): "The ostensible purpose of this alien land law is to prevent Japanese from holding land in California. The real purpose is to create a new agitation and thus galvanize a lot of discredited professional agitators and decayed politicians. The anti-Japanese agitation in California has been kept alive by the efforts of a combination of professional politicians, known as the Anti-Japanese and Korean Society, of which that delectable patriot, Olaf Tveitmoe, has been the nerve center."

These men have been in political life sufficiently long to recognize that the resident Japanese, without the ballot, is a convenient subject for world-wide notoriety in connection with small politics, and further that there would be little political harm to the agitator himself.

Business Interests Opposed

Commercial interests are not advanced in this way, and far-sighted business men are opposing such legislation.

A recent United States Customs report shows that San Francisco's exports to Japan for 1912 were $18,182,316 or 33 per cent of the total, and that her imports from Japan were $25,844,698, or 41 per cent of the total.

At a conference of thirty-seven commercial organizations, covering the entire State, including Chambers of Commerce, Boards of Trade, Merchants Associations, etc., held in San Francisco February 20, 1913, action was taken opposing these land bills.

5. Californian Insists the Japanese Are a Race Problem, 1913

May 6, 1913.

WHILE IT IS SMALL.

The Columbia, South Carolina, "State" has an editorial on the Japanese question in California in which, while inclined to sympathize with any state on any race question, it tries to make out that the California problem is so much smaller than the South Carolina problem as to be ridiculous. California, according to the "State" has 10,000 Japanese and 2,300,000 white people, while South Carolina has 835,000 negroes and only 679,000 white men. All the negroes in South Carolina are voters, many of them are property holders and all of them have the right to be property holders. They constitute a majority of the whole population of the state. Their rights were given them by the bayonets of national troops, against the will of the white people of South Carolina, and the only reason they do not rule the state today is that South Carolina has managed, by a kind of peaceable secession, to defy the laws and the will of the United States. As compared with this problem the "State" says the California problem is too small to justify California in embarrassing the nation and the other states in their international relations.

Setting aside some errors in figures made by the "State", it still must be conceded that the California problem is insignificant as compared with that of South Carolina. But South Carolina's problem was insignificant once, also. The Chicago fire was once a spark. Every such problem has its small beginning, and some problems can be solved only while they are small. The "State" will not pretend that any solution whatever of South Carolina's problem is possible. It is not possible to solve it by dealing justly with the negroes, or by dealing unjustly with them; by educating them or by keeping them in ignorance; by methods of democracy or of aristocracy. Unanswerable arguments can be made against every possible course in South Carolina now and forever. It is simply and eternally a curse laid on that state by the forefathers who traded New England rum for African slaves and thereby imposed on that section forever a situation which offers no way out, and no way except the choice of wrong ways of staying in.

The very importance of California's problem is that it is now in a condition in which South Carolina's problem was in the sixteenth century, when it began. What would South Carolina now give if it could turn back the wheels of history and decree that the South Carolinans and their Massachusetts allies of three hundred years ago should have done for what was than a small problem what California now demands that the nation do for what is here still a small problem? If we deal with this race question now, our descendants will have no race questions to deal with. If Californians do not deal with it now, they, like, South Carolinans, will leave a race question which their descendants will have to deal with, and against which they will be helpless.

From Chester Rowell, "While It Is Small," *Fresno Republican*, May 6, 1913.

6. Indian Immigrant Claims Group Is Assimilable, 1914

Dr. Bose. Mr. Chairman and gentlemen of the committee, on behalf of this delegation, which has been sent here by the Pacific Coast Khalsa Diwan Society and the Hindustan Association of America, I wish to invite your attention to a few facts on the subject of legislation on Hindu labor immigration. I have often been asked why the Hindus come to the country at all. I wish to say that the Hindus come to this country precisely for the same reason as the millions that come to this country from other countries. To us America is another name for opportunity. We come here to this country because of the opportunities we have for social uplift, intellectual betterment, and economical advancement. If you will pardon a personal allusion, I wish to say that a few years ago I came to this country as a laborer and if I had been in any other country I would not have had the opportunity of education that I have received in this country.

I mention this fact not in a boastful spirit, but to express my appreciation and gratitude for what I have received in this country. I am deeply indebted to it for all that I am. Only a short time ago I was speaking with a gentleman in this city, a high Government official, a gentleman for whom I have great respect, and he stated to me that the Hindus of all people are most undesirable. In the course of the conversation I found out that this gentleman had never studied a page of Hindu philosophy, had never turned over the first page of Indian history, had not the remotest conception of the contribution of India to the world's progress and civilization; and yet this gentleman stated that the Hindus are the most undesirable people in the world. So I am inclined to think that there are other people who have also a good many misunderstandings as to the standing of our people in the world.

Now, in the few moments which you have kindly given me. I wish to take up a few of the principal objections that are raised against Hindu immigration and answer them as well as I can. First, it has been asserted that Hindus undersell the white labor. Now, practically, there is no competition whatever between the American labor and the Hindu labor, because the American laborers are skilled laborers and the Hindus are nearly all unskilled laborers: that is, the Hindus who come here come from the rice fields of India. Now, the economic thinkers ever since the days of Adam Smith and John Stuart Mill down to our own time of Walker, Hadley, and Tostig, all say that there can be no competition between skilled labor and unskilled labor....

Now, it has been contended here that the Hindus are too frugal and too economical. Of course, I am aware of the fact that when we go to church, no matter what church it may be, we are always exhorted by the ministers to be careful and not to be spendthrifts. While we may not be Christians, we always practice these Christian virtues. I do not suppose anybody will criticise us for that. Nevertheless, I wish to say that the Hindus are good spenders. They spend their money in observing the various national festivals. In this country where we have such a step-lively business civilization we have not many festivals, but the Hindus have a good many

From Sudhindra Bose, in Hindu Immigration, *House Committee on Immigration and Naturalization* (Washington, D.C.: U.S. Government Printing Office, 1914).

festivals and they observe them carefully. They cost a good deal of money to observe; in fact, the Hindus suffer from imprudence in this respect. At all events, the Hindus are hospitable entertainers, and only too anxious to spend their money with the people among whom it has been made.

Now, it has been alleged that the Hindus become public charges. Now, Mr. Chairman, that accusation is based upon insufficient evidence, we contend. The Hindus in their personal habits are cleanly people. They bathe every day. Their religion requires them to take two baths a day. My folks at home, even my aged mother who is now nearly 70 years of age, bathe three times a day....

There seems to be a prevalent impression that the Hindus are of the Mongolian race. While I mean no reflection upon members of any other race, I wish to say that of all races the Hindus do not belong to the Mongolians. They are not of Chinese stock. The Hindus belong to the great Aryan family. The authorities on India say that the Hindus are a branch of the Aryan family. Before the great Aryan migration took place in the dim past the ancestors of India and of Europe lived together as members of one family in central Asia. All great thinkers on this subject have accepted that theory....

Now, I am speaking in general terms, but it is absolutely certain that there is no connection whatever between the Mongolian people and the Aryan blood that runs in our veins. It is possibly quite true that many of us who are here in this country have not yet adopted your customs and your institutions. It is quite likely that they are slow in changing their habits and their institutions. Gentlemen, all growth is slow.... You can not expect that they will drop all their habits overnight. But that does not mean that they are not capable of adapting themselves to new circumstances and new environment of living. Many of them have taken to the American way of living.

Again, if you will pardon me for mentioning a personal incident, I will refer to my case. I do not like to speak in the first person, but I think this illustration is just as good as any other, and it is typical. After I came to this country from India, for two years I insisted on wearing my turban and keeping on my beard, and so forth and so on, because I knew no better. For 20 years I had lived that way in India; and how could I change that all of a sudden? It would be nothing short of a revolution; but gradually I laid aside the customs of my country, because I realized that I had come here to do the very best I could do and to mix with the people of this country as best I could....

My training and my education does not permit me to compare myself with other people, because comparisons, as has been said, are always invidious. Nevertheless I will give you the facts. In the first place, the Hindus are entirely different from the Chinese and Japanese in regard to their clannishness. I have attended five or six universities, and, being at the head of a national organization, the Cosmopolitan Club, with four or five thousand members, with a chapter in every country. I have occasion to meet students from all the world, and never have I found a more cosmopolitan student than the Hindu student. I am not bragging: but these are actual facts, and I think the observation and experience of various college professors and presidents will bear me out thoroughly. Wherever you go you will find that the Japanese and Chinese students live together in one room, but never do you find the Hindu students rooming together. They do not want to do that. If we stay among ourselves we will be liable to speak our own language instead of the English language, and we do not want to do that. I lived in one town where there were three or four Hindu students, and when I went to see them they never returned my visits. They said, "We are getting too much Hinduized: we are getting too much by ourselves. Let us absorb all we can while we are here....

Now, as to racial intermarriages. I do not think it is necessary to say much about that. Think of the Jews who have lived in Europe for hundreds of years and have contributed magnificently to European civilization, and they have never been detractors of European civilization. Of course, in this country there may be a racial prejudice—I do not know—but in India there is absolutely no barrier between a Hindu and an Englishman....

I do contend that assimilation is possible without racial intermixture. We will not try racial intermixture if it is not suitable. It is not our desire, and we do not ask for it, but we do know that those who have married into American families, as quite a few have done, have lived quite happy lives, and their children are a credit to this great nation and to India.

7. U.S. Commissioner General of Immigration Says Indian Immigrants Are Unassimilable, 1914

Mr. CAMINETTI. In relation to the able argument presented by Dr. Bose in behalf of his people, particularly his tribute to their good qualities, I will only say that he is possibly talking about a different class of people—a different race of people—from that which is now coming to our Pacific coast; and possibly, also, a different kind of people from those who have gone to British Columbia, because if they were of those of whom the doctor has so eloquently spoken ... possibly there might not be heard any objection here or elsewhere.

From what I know of the Hindu laborers who are in California they do not answer the description given here to-day....

At the time that this question first attracted attention on the Pacific coast of our country, in 1907 and 1908, the situation became acute in parts of Canada. The authorities there took it up in a very determined way; they did not allow politics or political conditions there or elsewhere to interfere with their endeavor to protect the people of British Columbia. One of the leading citizens of Canada, W. L. Mackenzie King, deputy minister of labor, was commissioned by the Governor General of Canada to go to England for the purpose of laying before the English Government the attitude and condition of the people and the dangers existing in the immigration of Hindus to the Provinces of Canada. This gentleman had been selected because of his experience in British Columbia in

---

Anthony Caminetti, in Hindu Immigration, *House Committee on Immigration and Naturalization* (Washington, D.C.: U.S. Government Printing Office, 1914).

investigating the subject of Hindu, Japanese, and Chinese immigration. By reason of that experience and the information he had thus gained he was peculiarly qualified for the mission. I have his report. All of it should be read in order to understand the question from the Canadian standpoint. Upon his authority I state that the distinguished gentleman's position [Dr. Bose's] is not well taken, because Mr. King speaks after four weeks of continued discussion and deliberation with those who represented the English Government at the very seat of the British Empire, and he came back to Canada and made a report sustaining the Canadian idea and the wishes and aspirations of the people of British Columbia in their endeavor to save their colony from these people.

Some of Mr. King's views and impressions are summarized in the following extracts from said report:

It was clearly recognized in regard to emigration from India to Canada that the native of India is not a person suited to this country; that, accustomed as many of them are to the conditions of a tropical climate, and possessing manners and customs so unlike those of our own people, their inability to readily adapt themselves to surroundings entirely different could not do other than entail an amount of privation and suffering which render a discontinuance of such immigration most desirable in the interest of the Indians themselves. It was recognized, too, that the competition of this class of labor, though not likely to prove effective, if left to itself, might none the less, were the numbers to become considerable (as conceivably could happen were self-interest on the part of individuals to be allowed to override considerations of humanity and national well-being and the importation of this class of labor under contract permitted) occasion considerable unrest among workingmen whose standard of comfort is of a higher order, and who, as citizens with family and civic obligations, have expenditures to meet and a status to maintain which the coolie immigrant is in a position wholly to ignore.

★ ★ ★

Whilst effective as a means of restricting a class of immigration unsuited to Canada, it will be apparent that the arrangement as herein set forth is one which finds its justification on grounds of humanity as strong as are the economic reasons by which it is also supported. The liberty of British subjects in India is safeguarded rather than curtailed, the traditional policy of Britain in regard to the native races of India has been kept in mind, and the necessity of enacting legislation either in India or in Canada which might appear to reflect on fellow Bristish subjects in another part of the empire has been wholly avoided. Nothing could be more unfortunate or misleading than that the impression should go forth that Canada, in seeking to regulate a matter of domestic concern, is not deeply sensible of the obligations which citizenship within the empire entails. It is a recognition of this obligation which has caused her to adopt a course which by removing the possibilities of injustice and friction, is best calculated to strengthen the bonds of association with the several parts, and to promote the greater harmony of the whole. In this, as was to be expected, Canada has had not only the sympathy and understanding, but the hearty cooperation of the authorities in Great Britain and India as well.

As a result additional safeguards have been established in Canada leading up to the present restrictive conditions enforced there. With few exceptions and with some modifications all of the British colonies ... had preceded Canada in enacting laws and regulations of that character....

Of course, we do not want to exclude men like Dr. Bose; we do not want to exclude men like that who come from India or elsewhere; but we do want the laborers, the men who are denominated in this country as of the coolie class, excluded for economic reasons. Those are the people that Canada is after. They are practically excluded to-day from Canada, as well as from practically all the British colonies that have been named here to-day.

I come from the Pacific coast, where we have had two race problems which we have had to fight, and the third one about to be thrown upon us out there, and I have known practically and personally the patience of our people in waiting for diplomatic negotiations upon the Chinese immigration question, and I have known practically and personally the patience of our people in waiting....

8. Poems Describe Chinese Detention by U.S. Immigration Authorities, n.d. (1910–1930)

Imprisoned in the wooden building day after day,
My freedom withheld; how can I bear to talk about it?
I look to see who is happy but they only sit quietly.
I am anxious and depressed and cannot fall asleep.
The days are long and the bottle constantly empty; my sad mood,
    even so, is not dispelled.
Nights are long and the pillow cold; who can pity my loneliness?
After experiencing such loneliness and sorrow,
Why not just return home and learn to plow the fields?

America has power, but not justice.
In prison, we were victimized as if we were guilty.
Given no opportunity to explain, it was really brutal.
I bow my head in reflection but there is nothing I can do.

9. Newspaper Issues Alert About Gambling in Chinatown, 1918

Gambling in Vancouver

When a petition signed by eighteen Chinese citizens is addressed to a Canadian city it suggests something unusual, and this is certainly the case with the appeal recently made to the people of Vancouver by representative Chinese citizens,

From H. Mark Lai, *Island: Poetry and History of Chinese Immigrants on Angel Island* (Seattle: University of Washington Press, 1991).

From *The Globe*, May 23, 1918, p. 4.

calling attention to the gambling evil which is said to be in full swing at the present time. The petitioners maintain that Chinatown is a menace to the health and morals of Vancouver, and they appeal for immediate and drastic action to be taken to clean up the Oriental quarters.

The signatories do not mince matters in their petition, as these words clearly show:

"We must confess that we cannot understand your methods of administering law, which permit our fellow-countrymen to conduct organized gambling dens. They merely laugh at your insignificant fines and the short jail terms imposed by the local courts, and go on again with their law-breaking."

They also say that Chinese merchants and others have already made attempts to bring this matter before the Mayor of Vancouver and the Chief of Police, but, in spite of proofs that open gambling is being carried on, nothing has yet been done to deal with an evil which is said to have gone on to "an alarming and almost unprecedented extent."

Here are some of the facts and figures adduced in support of this urgent appeal:

"(1) The men employed inside gambling dens, that is, men who give their whole time to the work inside the dens, and who are not otherwise employed in any kind of useful work, number no less than seven or eight hundred.

"(2) Over three thousand Chinese practise gambling constantly in Vancouver alone, many of whom spend all their earnings in this way.

"(3) Many representative Chinese who have given much time to the study of this problem state positively that there are over forty gambling dens in Chinatown to-day, and that many of these have advertisements in their windows for 'fantan' as above stated.

"(4) Within the last few months, we understand from the local Press, many new licenses have been issued by the Attorney-General for Chinese clubs, so-called in order to evade the law, but which in reality are mere make-believe institutions, the same sort of clubs which have ever been notorious violators of the gambling law.

"(5) Numbers of Chinese who, after many years of hard labor, have made good money in Eastern Canada, when they arrive in Vancouver in order to return to China, find the temptations of Pender street so great that they quickly lose every dollar they have earned.

"(6) There are many attendant evils and products of this gambling business, such as idleness, opium smoking, licentiousness, stealing, and even suicides.

"(7) Besides all these, gambling always draws crowds together and holds them in congested centres. Hence the unsanitary housing conditions with their appalling increase of tuberculosis, as reported by the Medical Health Officer of your city, are a direct result also of the gambling evil.

It is clear from these plain statements that a glaring and even gigantic evil is rampant in Vancouver and is ruining the bodies and souls of those who ought to be the objects of our special care. What is needed at once is a thoroughly stringent enforcement of Canadian laws among the Chinese of Vancouver, and at the same time, as the petition so well points out, "the time has arrived when a much greater interest should be taken by the Government of the Province and by the administrators of your city in the social betterment of our people, and that some constructive effort should be made to give the Chinese wholesome means of recreation and entertainment which would take the place of these harmful practices which now occupy their time."

Already the Churches are moving in the matter, and from two independent quarters, representing two of the most important denominations, appeals have come to call public attention in Eastern Canada to this evil. This is a matter affecting the whole Dominion. The urgency of the peril should meet with an instant and thorough response from those who are in authority in Vancouver.

ESSAYS

In the first essay, Rutgers University, Newark, historian Kornel Chang explains the process of constructing the U.S.–Canadian border as a means to keep Asian immigrants in check during the era of exclusion. The heightened border patrol and surveillance of Asian immigrants existed as one side of a cat-and-mouse game in which the immigrants came up with ingenious plans to evade the policing. The second essay, written by University of Southern California historian Nayan Shah, explores intimate bonds within bachelor societies in which Indian immigrant men interacted with a wide variety of Americans. His description of a sodomy trial reveals both the criminalization of same-sex relations and stereotypes of Indian families as bastions of male authority and female subservience.

Policing Borders in the Pacific Northwest

KORNEL CHANG

The rising emphasis on border control and surveillance in the Pacific Northwest was fueled by the intensifying migratory links between the North American West and the Asia–Pacific world. In 1907, the Northwest region experienced a record influx of Japanese and South Asian immigrants. From January 1, 1907 to September 12, 1907, more than eight thousand Asian immigrants landed at the British Columbia ports of Vancouver and Victoria, with more than half applying for admission to the United States. Among the Japanese arrivals, almost all were migrating from the recently U.S.-annexed territories of Hawai'i. In search of new sources of overseas labor, Japanese contracting firms in Seattle and

Chang, Kornel. "Enforcing Transnational White Solidarity: Asian Migration and the Formation of the U.S.-Canadian Boundary." *American Quarterly* 60:3 (2008), 671–696. © 2008 The American Studies Association. Reprinted with permission of Johns Hopkins University Press.

Vancouver imported thousands of migrants as contract workers from the sugar plantations of Hawai'i throughout the course of the year. Seizing on the opening created by U.S. imperial expansion into the Pacific, they generated new global circuits of labor cutting across multiple imperial and national boundaries.

For the Seattle-based Oriental Trading Company, this was a complex, multiple-step process necessitated by an executive order issued by President Theodore Roosevelt several months earlier that elaborated a new form of sovereignty in an attempt to exert control over Asian migrants crossing the empire. It authorized the immigration bureau to refuse entrance to Japanese and Korean laborers whose passports were issued for any destination other than the continental United States. U.S. immigration authorities hoped this would end the practice among Asian laborers of using alternate routes through the empire to enter the country. To circumvent this measure and the new boundaries it delineated, the firm had migrant laborers from Hawai'i first shipped to British Columbia, where they were processed for admission into Canada, and kept in boarding houses in Victoria and Vancouver until runners hired by the company were ready to guide them over the border. This elaborate labor-recruiting scheme brought Japanese migrant laborers from Hawai'i through Canada to different points in the American West where they performed seasonal work in railroad construction, fishing, and salmon canning.

Meanwhile, U.S. immigration officials in Seattle watched this new wave of immigration to British Columbia with concern, predicting quite correctly that many of the new Asian arrivals would attempt to enter the United States surreptitiously via the border. Moreover, they worried that the influx of Japanese and South Asian immigrants would generate public agitation and social unrest, especially among the white working-class, reproducing the tumultuous scenes from twenty years earlier. One U.S. Immigration Inspector warned that

> the number of Japanese and other aliens who are now in British
> Columbia and the state of public feelings on both sides of the border in
> this vicinity against these aliens is such that an emergency has arisen,
> whereby it is absolutely necessary to have additional men appointed, if the
> border is to be properly guarded." In August 1907, the bureau responded
> to this threat by hiring six temporary watchmen and forming a border
> detail led by Immigrant Inspector C.A. Turner. This newly created unit
> patrolled and guarded the border between Steveston, British Columbia,
> and Point Roberts, Washington, on a full-time basis....

The problem of Asian migration to the Pacific Northwest evolved into an international crisis with the race riots of September 1907. While anti–Asiatic racism was already a constitutive feature of Northwest borderland culture, it reached, in the words of one Canadian minister, "almost hysterical" proportions by this time. This racial hysteria culminated with upheavals and demonstrations in the borderland cities of Bellingham and Vancouver, occurring within days of each other in September 1907. These hostilities were fueled by the prevailing belief that the dominant social order, founded upon the notion of a "white man's country," was under siege. One British Columbia newspaper played to these racial anxieties and fears when it asked rhetorically: "Are we to have this great big province—a land virtually flowing in milk and honey—conserved for the best interests of the white British subject—English, Scott, Irish, Welsh, etc.—or must it be given over entirely to the yellow and brown hordes of China and Japan?"...

In Bellingham, tensions between white and South Asian laborers, already simmering for months, finally came to a spectacular head in the first week of September. Incited by sensational newspaper reports and the growing public hysteria over the so-called Hindu invasion, a mob of some four hundred to five hundred white men stormed the quarters of the South Asian community on the night of September 5 and proceeded to perpetrate acts of racial violence. This led to a mass exodus of South Asians from the city: some recrossed the border to the North traveling to Vancouver while others migrated southward to California. The following day, the Asiatic Exclusion League of Seattle sent an ominous letter to President Theodore Roosevelt threatening that "if something were not done soon the agitation started in Bellingham would spread all over the Sound country and massacres of the Eastern aliens were likely."

Two days later on September 7, the Vancouver branch of the Asiatic Exclusion League organized an anti-Asiatic demonstration in the city with the assistance of a number of white labor activists from south of border as well as across the Pacific world. Organizers hailed from Australia, New Zealand, Canada, and the United States. Assembled in front of City Hall, the protesters included about twenty-five thousand people and representatives from fifty-eight labor organizations. During the rally, several of the participants marched into the Chinese and Japanese districts in downtown Vancouver instigating a clash with Asian residents. This small flare up eventually led to several days of intense conflict between white laborers and Chinese and Japanese residents. When the dust finally settled, the Chinese and Japanese in Vancouver sustained tens of thousands of dollars in damages to their homes and businesses and several Chinese and Japanese reported physical injuries.

In an attempt to quell social unrest on the west coast, both the United States and Canada consummated agreements with the Japanese government, known as the "Gentleman's Agreements," which set numerical limits on immigrants coming from Japan. The Japanese government agreed to limit passports to certain categories of people including diplomats, merchants, students, and tourists. The U.S. Gentleman's Agreement became official policy in the summer of 1908 while the Canadian version, also known as the Hayashi-Lemieux Agreement, went into effect several months earlier.

As for the northern border, U.S. immigration officers lobbied for new powers and resources that would change the scale and nature of boundary policing in the Pacific Northwest. Efforts to control the boundary in a more systematic manner began with increasing the size of the border force and positioning them along the international line dividing Washington and British Columbia. Immediately following the riots, U.S. Commissioner-General of Immigration Frank Sargent secured funding for a new team of border inspectors. Sargent instructed the bureau in Washington to "utilize their services in guarding the British Columbia boundary, bending every effort towards preventing the illegal entry of Japanese." Despite this upgrade in border personnel however, local public opinion demanded even further state intervention....

A year after the anti-Asiatic riots and the initial augmentation of the border force, Inspector-in-Charge John Sargent wrote confidently to the commissioner-general of immigration that "the [northern] border is being better guarded than ever before." According to a 1910 roster, the immigration force in the Washington jurisdiction alone consisted of close to fifty full-time Immigrant and Chinese inspectors and border watchmen. To match the increase in the size of the force, the Service also expanded their facilities to include substations in almost every border town along the boundary.

The institutionalization of the border also involved the construction of a dense, state-organized system of surveillance. The bureau established regular contact with numerous government agencies in Washington and British Columbia regarding Chinese, Japanese, and South Asian communities. They also hired mobile informants who toured the borderlands—including Steveston, Vancouver, and Westminster on the Canadian side and Blaine, Anacortes, Bellingham, and the San Juan Islands on the U.S. side—in order to report on the movements and activities of Asian groups. Finally, the Service relied on the eyes and ears of the local population to help monitor the border. As one U.S. immigration inspector reported: "There are several thousand people living in Whatcom County ... many of whom are in possession of telephones and most of whom are willing to give our officers any information they may secure regarding aliens passing their residences or places of business." Similarly, in British Columbia, Canadian immigration authorities sought the cooperation of borderland residents by installing telephones along roads and byways thought to be traveled by illegal Asian migrants. Taken together, they formed an information network that enabled state bureaucrats to put Chinese, Japanese, and South Asian immigrants under surveillance with the objective of restricting their mobility....

The efforts to define and institutionalize the border invariably led to struggles between the state and the Chinese, Japanese, and South Asian immigrants who were intent on maintaining control over their mobility. Asian migrants, whether on their own or with the assistance of professional smugglers and guides, found creative ways to defy the borders and boundaries designed to keep them out. In one scheme, Japanese and South Asian immigrants in Washington State sold their passports to countrymen in British Columbia seeking to enter the United States. Once the Japanese or South Asian immigrant secured entrance, the individual would perpetuate the cycle by selling or circulating it to yet another immigrant across the border:

> Ten Japanese caught at the international boundary line in one week with bogus passports shows the wholesale extent to which coolie laborers of the Mikado's empire are attempting to deceive the United States Immigration department. The favorite system is that of the use of the same passport over and over again. Nine out of the ten men who were detained at the boundary last week and finally refused admittance to the United States confessed that they had been supplied with the passports of Japanese now in the United States. These had been mailed back to Vancouver and were resold at from five to twenty-five dollars each.

One of the more imaginative ploys to gain entry from Canada into the United States involved the complicity of unsuspecting border inspectors. Issei

Izo Kojima recounts how Japanese seeking entry from British Columbia deceived U.S. border inspectors into believing they were residents of the United States. "There were many iron bridges, and those who tried to get into America from Canada thought up many tricks to get across. There was the trick of walking backwards inconspicuously. Sooner or later such a walker would be discovered by the American guards, and when called he would turn around, as if trying to escape from America to Canada."

Border inspectors thinking that the Japanese immigrant was unlawfully crossing the border to Canada would apprehend the suspect and "return" the person to the United States. There was also the use of racial disguise in attempts to surreptitiously cross the border. "When questioned the Oriental gave his name as R. Abe and said he wanted to go to Seattle to look for work. Before crossing the line near Blaine, he smeared his face with grease and blackening, giving him the appearance of a Negro."

Some Asian transients in British Columbia relied on family and kinship networks to make it across the boundary. Take the case of Sahuro Iguchi, who traveled on the transpacific steamship liner "Athenian" and arrived in Vancouver on May 30, 1907. About a month later, he applied for admissions to the United States but was rejected on account of having contracted a degenerative eye-disorder known as trachoma. It is very likely that his intent all along was to immigrate to the United States, but Iguchi probably took the indirect route through Canada to avoid the stricter regulations of the U.S. Immigration Service. Unable to deport him back to Japan, the Service returned him to Vancouver where he received treatment for trachoma. He applied for admissions two additional times in October 1907 and March 1908 and each time U.S. immigration authorities denied him entry based on his medical condition. Desperate to gain entry, Iguchi contacted a friend in Seattle, Nada Tokujiro, "to find some way by which [Iguchi] could enter the United States." Tokujiro sent one Mr. Hashizume to Vancouver with the intention of having him escort Iguchi across the border and into Seattle, Washington. The plan comprised several steps. They took a train from Vancouver to Cloverdale, British Columbia and from there they walked by foot across the international line to Blaine, Washington and spent the night at a nearby hotel. In the morning, they left for Bellingham where they were supposed to take a boat to Seattle; unfortunately for them, U.S. border inspectors apprehended the Japanese migrants before they could complete the final leg of their journey.

Precisely because of cases like this, the U.S. government applied pressure on Canada to modify its immigration standards and regulations to conform to that of the United States. U.S immigration inspectors often complained that the less rigorous inspection standards encouraged Chinese, Japanese, and South Asian immigrants to exploit Canada as a back door into the United States. Eventually, the Canadian Immigration Bureau agreed to end the policy of allowing diseased Asian immigrants to receive treatment in their detention hospitals. In 1909, Canadian immigration authorities began to summarily reject Asian arrivals diagnosed with "loathsome disease" and prohibited them from landing at their ports of entry.

In the Pacific Northwest, professional smugglers and ethnic-labor contractors facilitated the cross-border trafficking of illegal Asian migrants. Prior to the boundary enforcement buildup in the late 1900s, Chinese, Japanese, and South Asian immigrants could pay a small fee to be navigated across the international line. Native Indians in British Columbia, for example, piloted Chinese and Japanese transients to the United States for as little as three dollars. By 1914, Special Immigrant Inspector Roger O'Donnell testified before the House Committee on Immigration that the Chinese were willing to pay anywhere between one hundred and one thousand dollars to be smuggled into the United States. While inspector O'Donnell may have exaggerated the figures, he was accurate in suggesting that Asian smuggling had become big business in the new era of the border. Noted Asian smuggler George Nelson told authorities that he charged between $125 and $150 per Chinese alien. Working as a fireman for the Great Northern, Nelson concealed his human contraband in the tool box within the engine tender, and once his train made it safely across the border, Nelson delivered the immigrants to a Chinese labor agent in Seattle.

Asian labor contractors contributed to the cross-border flow of illegal immigrants by importing them as workers from across the international line. Labor agent T. Sengoku unknowingly confided to an informant for the U.S. Immigration Service that he had "taken three hundred Japanese across the Border at Blaine" and "placed [them] at work in the state of Idaho in the building of the Great Northern Railway." In the same conversation, Sengoku boasted that "he would be able to get Hindoos across the border without examination provided they were first taken down and put to work on the Canadian side for a few days' time."...

The seemingly intractable problem of Asian migration brought together officials from the United States and Canada who were equally intent on preserving a "White Man's Country."...

A number of U.S. and Canadian bureaucracies including local law enforcement, customs houses, and immigration departments coordinated joint efforts to address the problem of illegal immigration across the border. One U.S. official described the working agreement with Canadian officials to the Congressional Committee on Immigration and Naturalization in 1913. "American immigration officers board boats and examine passengers landing in Canadian ports, join in border patrols, and obtain the assistance of Canadian immigration officers in investigating records of immigrants coming from Canada."

The transnational process of raising the border both reflected and engendered racial ideas and practices in the Northwest borderlands. While the boundary emerged as a barrier to Asian migrants, it remained porous and open to white Euro-Americans and Canadians during this time....

U.S. and Canadian immigration officials stationed in the Pacific Northwest treated the cross-border flow of white Americans, Canadians, and European immigrants mostly with benign neglect and in some cases outright support....

Race also played an important role in the construction of the border on the Canadian side. When designing their immigration and border policies, Dominion authorities in British Columbia considered how they could meet the demands of the labor market without compromising the racial ideal of whiteness. Indeed, they endeavored to attract immigrant laborers, who were essential to economic development and growth, while maintaining a "White Man's Province" at the same time.

In 1908, the Dominion passed what was known as the Continuous Journey Act which barred immigrants not traveling directly from their country of origin. The legislation was a subtle attempt to exclude South Asians, as there was not a single steamship line at the time traveling directly from British India to Canada. However, the act, unbeknownst to those drafting the law, also prohibited Euro-Americans in the United States from entering Canada. Dominion authorities remedied the situation by passing an Order-in-Council allowing non-Asians to emigrate from places other than their country of origin, and in doing, so reopened the border to Euro-American migration while keeping it closed to Asian immigrants.

The Immigration Bureau in British Columbia also implemented more explicit measures in order to promote the migration of "desirable" groups. Immigration authorities, for example, distributed a departmental circular to all boundary inspectors in 1914 encouraging them to allow European migrants from the United States to enter Canada. More specifically, it authorized Canadian inspectors stationed in Washington and other bordering states to issue letters of entry to European immigrants interested in settling in Western Canada....

The intensifying movements and linkages with the Asia-Pacific ... led Canada and the United States to consolidate their respective national-state sovereignty, giving rise to a new emphasis on border policing and surveillance at the turn of the twentieth century. Yet ... delineation of the U.S.-Canadian boundary was neither about drawing rigid lines of division, nor enforcing strict notions of national difference between Canada and the United States. Rather, the process of border formation in the Pacific Northwest was primarily concerned with defining an outer limit against the encroachment of an Asia-Pacific world. North American regimes adopted political, diplomatic, and legal measures to restrict and regulate the transpacific as well as the transborder movement of Chinese, Japanese, and South Asian migrants. This binational effort to systematically control transnational Asian migration involved the construction of transpacific borders—a process that included enforcing an imaginary line between the Asia-Pacific world and the North American West, as well as consolidating a territorial boundary between the United States and Canada.

Regulating Intimacy and Immigration

NAYAN SHAH

The churning of migrants through Vancouver and Seattle was directly related to the cycles of timber harvesting in locales spread like spiderwebs across the Pacific Northwest. In the nineteenth and early twentieth centuries, western North America was not only a site of convergence for global streams of workers but also drew massive capital investment from eastern Canada, the United States, and Europe. Capital investment to build the railroads, roads, and harbors necessary for agriculture and the extraction of natural resources produced the material contours of the social geography of migrants' lives and livelihoods. Railroads both brought workers and raw materials together and were sites of social contact. In the Pacific Northwest, men and boys found work in the instant towns that emerged along the main line and spurs of the Northern Pacific Railroad Line, which ran across the northern tier of the United States from Minneapolis–Saint Paul through North Dakota and Montana across the Cascade mountains and joined the line built in the late 1880s that hugged the coast of Puget Sound. The line ran from Blaine at the border with British Columbia, down through Bellingham, Seattle, Tacoma, and Lacey to Centralia and Portland, Oregon. In 1890, the Northern Pacific Railroad extended tracks south from Lacey to Centralia, and a train depot was built in Gate City, which became a thriving railroad center and mill town in the early twentieth century. Young European immigrant men eager for work in the lumberyards of Washington State came from Minnesota and Dakota towns in the early twentieth century. Asian immigrants traveled up and down the railroads of the Pacific Northwest coast looking for work in saw-mills and cordage factories. In 1912, South Asian workers who had worked in Port-land, Seattle, and Vancouver found work at the Gate City Lumber Company.

The circuit from train depot to bunkhouse was the social terrain that brought Clarence Murray, whose family had migrated from rural Minnesota, and Jago and Bram Singh, who came from India, together in Gate, Washington. On a Sunday afternoon in March 1912, Clarence Murray and his cousins Ed Murray and John McGuire got off the 2:30 passenger train at the depot at Gate. Clarence, nearly eighteen years old, worked at the Gate City Lumber mill for a couple of weeks. Standing at the rail depot, Clarence recognized two co-workers, twenty-three-year-old Jago Singh and thirty-two-year-old Bram Singh, among a group of "Hindu" men standing near the tracks. The two men invited Clarence and his cousins to their rooms to smoke and drink.

Since Gate had a local prohibition ordinance in effect, the men's retreat from the train depot to the bunkhouse was necessary to find a semi-private space to drink. The workingmen in Gate lived in hotels that had been converted to bunkhouses on either side of the railroad tracks, on the outskirts of the town-ship of Gate, about a mile from the center of town. The long narrow buildings were partitioned into small rooms, six feet by six feet, where two men often bunked together. In one of the hotels, one side of the building housed "Hindus" and the other side "white" men. Although such rooms did not, of course, pro-vide the privacy of a middle-class home, they served temporarily as domestic spaces and offered respite from the intrusive attention outdoors at the depot.

That Sunday afternoon, the South Asian and white men were in a revolving circuit of drinking, socializing, fighting, and reconciling, with different men com-ing in and out of the bunkhouse. Clarence Murray, his cousin Edward Murray and a friend, Clif Chamberlain, went into Bram's room on one side of the tracks. The white men were all from established families in Gate. The communal sharing of alcohol and the social encouragement of intoxication made the encounters between dissimilar males adhesive. The sharing of liquor enhanced social relations, freed submerged desires, and also made interactions between men fractious and violent. Their party broke up when a glass of whiskey broke and Bram chased Clarence out of the room, swearing that he had dropped the glass. Another of

Clarence's cousins, Jack McGuire, came upon the fight outside the "Hindu Camp" at about 3 P.M. Bram Singh was threatening to "lick" Clarence but Jago Singh and Don Singh held him back. In anger, Bram Singh ran off and began picking up rocks on the railroad track and throwing them aimlessly. Jago Singh reassured Clarence of his friendship and invited Jack and the others to their rooms for another drink, saying, "the other fellow couldn't do anything to him." They drank a quart of whiskey over about half an hour; then Jack, Ed and Clif prepared to leave, but Clarence decided to stay behind with the South Asian men. At 4 P.M. Dwight Murray, Clarence's older brother, saw Clarence outside the "Hindu Camp" and spoke with him. "The boy will be all right with me; I am his friend," Jago Singh assured Dwight, and so Dwight left Clarence with them. Dwight remembered that Clarence was "pretty well intoxicated but not drunk."

The men who gathered that afternoon over drinks and conversation saw themselves as social, convivial, passionate, liable to tease and fight, all in the process of "making friends." The intimacy between these strangers was enabled by the curiosity of working alongside one another and living nearby, allowing their social worlds to overlap. The men lived apart in "Hindu," Japanese, and white "camps" or bunkhouses by the depots, and the white single-family houses a half mile away from the tracks materially defined racial difference and spatial boundaries. The combination of liquor, desire, and violence would, however, rock the social gathering hours later.

In the court case that followed, the moral and ethical drama was between South Asian men. Rohmdlla and Aramo, two South Asian men who worked at the Gate City Lumber Company and boarded at the hotel, criticized Jago and Bram Singh's behavior that afternoon and alerted Clarence Murray's relatives to return to the hotel. Rohmdlla and Aramo observed a drunk Clarence Murray "crying" at about 4 or 5 P.M. Aramo claimed that Jago had pushed Clarence "by force," and that Bram had held his hand over Clarence's mouth to stifle any cries. At the court hearing, Aramo, intent to prove his morality and code of homosocial camaraderie, appealed to Bram Singh and Jago Singh "not to commit this crime ... I say it make us too unpopular in this country."

Three hours afterwards, both Aramo and Rohmdlla went to look for Dwight Murray after 8 P.M. in the evening. As Dwight followed the men to the bunkhouse, he met his cousins Ed Murray and Jack McGuire, who joined them in retrieving Clarence from the "Hindu camp." Each of Clarence's kin described discovering Clarence unconscious, partially undressed, and exhibiting telltale signs of sexual assault: "His pants were down, his shirt was pulled up, rolled up pretty nearly to the shoulder blades," and his clothes and body were "oily" and "all doped up with some kind of oil or grease" that seemed to "smell like Vaseline." In the same room, they found Don Singh laying on the bed asleep "with his pants open." While they were getting Clarence together to take him home, Bram Singh stormed in and allegedly yelled, "What the God Dam[n] business you fellows got in here.... Get to hell out of here and go home." They carried Clarence out, and he was vomiting on the way to the Company bunkhouse. Clarence remembered drinking with Jago and Bram, but he had lost consciousness and only could recall the trip back to the company bunkhouse at night. In the trial, the defense attorney brought no witnesses, and the jury swiftly returned a verdict of guilty of sodomy against Jago, Bram, and Don Singh.

P.L. Verma, who had served as a translator for part of the trial, orchestrated a campaign for clemency for Don Singh. In addition to raising questions about court procedure and unreliable eyewitness accounts of Don Singh's presence at the scene of the assault, Verma offered the Parole Board an explanation of the sexuality and morality of "Hindoo" men. Verma attempted to reframe the prosecution of Don Singh, which relied upon guilt by association and proximity to the passed-out victim, to redeem Don's reputation. Verma characterized sodomy as a "great and unnatural sin among Hindoos" and it was unlikely that "a good Hindoo citizen is addicted of that habit." He quickly set aside the disturbing affronts to white masculinity by the revelations of South Asian men sexually penetrating a white male to focus on the status and behavior of the one married man in their company. Verma defined a "good Hindoo citizen" as a religious observant, married man. Marriage was a deterrent to the "addictive habit" of sodomy: "Don Sing[h] is married and married men do not like things like that, they are never addicted to such unnatural habits. They have to look far into the future. They are tied down by the weight of marriage." Verma presented exemplary "Hindoo" married men as possessing sexual self-restraint and monogamous morality, much like the images of respectable white American manhood. The practice of sodomy was coded as a habitual practice that could be addicting for the unmarried man whose unregulated behavior was ruled by irrational passion. Verma produced a moral code for married male migrants, for whom future responsibilities at home loomed large, that contained injunctions to avoid the entanglements, distractions, and costs of transitory sexual encounters. The imperative against sodomy was less about steadfast heterosexual preference than about the need for containment within and for marriage and the legitimate progeny that it would produce.

Verma skillfully marshaled compassion for Don Singh and his predicament and invoked a sympathetic hearing for Don's wife, including a letter from her to bolster the appeal for his parole, in which she wrote, "Life to me is not worth living, I have no body to support me." The pitiful wife was an archetype; her letter was translated for the parole board, but she was never named except as Don Singh's wife, his dependent. However, the success of the appeal to pity and compassion necessitated that she appear to be a worthy and helpless dependent.... In his letter, Verma emphasizes the wife's "miserable condition" and her "cries for help," because she is without means of male support and will become destitute. Don Singh's "misfortune ... has fallen on her head. She will ... starve to death unheeded, if no steps are taken for granting Don Singh his liberty." She feared that his case was "hopeless" and his imprisonment could last twenty years. Her letter articulated both despair and powerlessness, inviting the assistance of the empowered, both Verma's advocacy, and the parole authorities' sympathetic judgment....

Verma's campaign for Don Singh was enhanced by the sympathetic portrait of the pitiable wife as well as by the rehabilitation of Don's public reputation. Verma enlisted testimonials from Don's white employers and landlords in Portland, who praised him as an "honest, well-behaving gentleman" and a "trustworthy," "reliable and industrious" worker with a gentle, unassuming disposition. Twenty men, who had signed their names in either Punjabi or English, endorsed a petition of the "Hindoos of Portland" for Don Singh, drafted by Verma. The petition characterized Don Singh as "always a law-abiding citizen," "from a good family," and possessing "temperate habits."

These qualities of honesty, temperance, and industriousness were certainly values that the warden and parole board would uphold as evidence of Don Singh's character. However, the petition of his friends also revealed Sikh communitarian values that may for them have demonstrated a different vision of his humanitarianism. His friends considered Don Singh to be a devout man, who worshipped regularly and was considered a "missionary" for the charitable work he did. His generosity was legendary in his community in Portland, and he was known to help others financially in times of distress. The support of the community of South Asian laborers and Singh's employers in Portland created a credible portrait of a civic-minded and responsible immigrant in the United States and became crucial to Don Singh's appeal. The other two men who were convicted, Bram Singh and Jago Singh, had no such local support in Gate, Portland, or elsewhere.

The final and perhaps most crucial element in making Don Singh a subject for compassion was the assessment prison authorities made of his advocate, Verma. Certainly, Verma's English education and resourcefulness in soliciting and collecting testimonials, creating petitions, and meeting with the prison warden, Reed, made such an appeal strategically plausible…. In addition to his formal dress and respectfully articulate communication, Verma demonstrated his sentiments of justice and equity. In the florid conclusion of his appeal, Verma invoked the ideals of "American Justice … Equality and Brotherhood" to win the intercession of the warden, whom he personally thanked for his "kind and philanthropic [sic] words that you love our nationality just as you love your own. Your words that Hindoos are treated by you as brothers still ring in my ears." The rhetorical invocation of American justice and cross-national brotherhood to dislodge racial antipathy appears to have assured the warden of Verma's integrity and shared values. If Verma could be trusted, then perhaps the warden and parole board could identify with the plight of Don Singh and his wife.

The moral empathy generated by Don Singh's good character and the pitiful condition of his incredulous wife in India may have loosened the suspicions of the warden and parole board about the trial testimony. Their decision was not based on Don Singh's character or Verma's sentiments, however, but on other legal criteria that Verma presented that disputed Don Singh's purported role in the crime. The board reflected on the conspicuous absence of eyewitness testimony that placed Don Singh in the bunkhouse room when the two other South Asian men were explicitly identified. Don Singh's participation in the crime had been implied because police had discovered him sleeping in the same room in which the unconscious "white victim" was found. The sympathetic treatment that Don Singh received from the prison warden and the parole board did not disrupt the judicial certainty that Clarence Murray had been sodomized, nor did it temper the conviction of Jago Singh and Bram Singh. In 1913, the Prison

Board determined that there was grave doubt that Don Singh had been present at the commission of the crime, and on October 14, Washington State Governor Ernest Lister commuted Don Singh's five-year sentence, of which he had served eighteen months.

Verma had succeeded in winning Don Singh's parole by casting the abstract category of "Hindu marriage" as producing moral and respectable manhood and then offering the canvas of Don Singh's public character as exemplary. Verma analogized the Hindu married man as the serial copy of the white (Christian) married man. He characterized such an individual as steadfastly faithful, circumspect, and responsible: a "good family man." The sympathetic judgment for Don Singh also protected the reputation of South Asian married men generally. His status as a married man offered Don Singh an alibi of respectable sexuality and morality. The power of "sympathy and morality," as Amit Rai has shown, both created and targeted the "heterosexual family" for compassionate assistance. It distinguished him from the two unmarried men, whose convictions were not in doubt. In rallying to support Don Singh, South Asian men in Portland distinguished reputable, moral men from disreputable men by ignoring the other two convicted men and disparaged the honesty of the South Asian eyewitnesses for falsely implicating Don Singh. Verma was able to present a unified reputation for Don Singh by emphasizing his personal commitment to his wife and his charity among his peers.

Verma's successful campaign enabled Don Singh to recover the property of a public self—his reputation. Singh's reputation was tied with the responsibilities of his overseas marriage and its demands of moral rectitude. His reputation's rehabilitation enabled the review of his conviction and his freedom from imprisonment. The public status of a married man, however, was contingent and uncertain in Singh's experience as a migrant laborer whose wife lived in India. In his file at the Washington State Penitentiary, there is a 1930 FBI report that catalogues a litany of public drunkenness and disorderly conduct convictions in Washington, Oregon, and California during the 1910s and 1920s. The spellings of the name of the man are different, but the FBI has catalogued them all as the same Don Singh who received clemency for a sodomy conviction in 1913....

The efforts by Verma to defend Don Singh and reclaim his married man's honor from lurid allegations and circumstances did not blunt the broader suspicions of South Asian unmarried men, and in particular Jago Singh's and Bram Singh's convictions. The campaign for Don Singh's clemency dissented against the overwhelming representation of South Asian immorality, but its horizons were limited. It did not directly contest hierarchies and in fact reinforced the public status hierarchies of married men over unmarried migrants. For Don Singh, the ensemble of his marriage, his suffering wife, and testimonials as to his spiritual devotion, piety, and charitable service provided a shield against suspicions of improper behavior. Verma's intercession to rehabilitate the reputation of Don Singh placed "Hindu" married men alongside Christian American men by challenging blanket suspicions of the immoral "Hindu sodomite." However, it could not completely dislodge police aspersions of interracial association with probable immorality and perversion.

In Gate during the 1910s, the police, immigration authorities and bystanders observed and acted upon interracial encounters in a spatial borderland where transient male workers converged....

The documented testimony in police court records reveal the texture and spaces of inter-ethnic social life, ranging from casual conversations begun in streets and alleys to bars, tram stations, and railroad depots. Public encounters and visibility enabled the street politics of public life. Men swiftly moved socializing from the streets to rented rooms, bunkhouses, and workers' shacks. These spaces were the settings for casual, fortuitous, and dangerous encounters between men and boys of different ethnicities and ages.

Through these encounters between strangers, South Asian migrants forged intimate possibilities around plural masculinities to engage in public life. They negotiated and assessed honor, reputation, authority, and strength in developing relationships between men. However it was social practices that gave the relationships substance. Men engaged in practices of gift-giving, visiting, mentorship, and sharing interests. Their forms of exchange encompassed buying drinks and their visits to bunkhouses and rooms, sharing observations and opinions, and transacting business deals. However, the exchange of money between working males became flagged as illicit transactions of hustling and prostitution. The jostling and confrontation of plural masculinities generated expressions of affection, friendship, care, and camaraderie in tension with feelings of distrust, duplicity, hostility, manipulation, and force. Males on the ground judged the ethics, conscience, and intentions of their peers. Court cases were rife with mens' and boys' assessments of trust, injustice, improper sex, violence, and fraud, with claims of robbery, extortion, duplicity, and entrapment, as well as companionship and sexual advances welcomed or rebuffed. The variety of social dependencies reinforced the fragility of male autonomy and the necessity of interdependence for survival.

☭ FURTHER READING

Azuma, Eiichiro. *Between Two Empires: Race, History, and Transnationalism in Japanese America* (2005).

Chang, Kornel. *Pacific Connections: The Making of the U.S.-Canadian Borderlands* (2012).

Daniels, Roger. *The Politics of Prejudice: The Anti-Japanese Movement in California and the Struggle for Japanese* (1962).

Hess, Gary R. "The 'Hindu' in America: Immigration and Naturalization Policies and India, 1917–1946," *Pacific Historical Review* 38 (1969): 59–79.

Hsu, Madeline Y. *Dreaming of Gold, Dreaming of Home: Transnationalism and Migration between the United States and Southern China, 1882–1943* (2000).

Ichioka, Yuji. *The Issei: The World of the First Generation Japanese Immigrants, 1885–1924* (1988).

Jensen, Joan, M. *Passage from India: Asian Indian Immigrants in North America* (1988).

Kim, Richard S. *The Quest for Statehood: Korean Immigrant Nationalism and U.S. Sovereignty, 1905–1945* (2011).

Lee, Erika. *At America's Gates: Chinese Immigration during the Exclusion Era, 1882–1943* (2003).

Lee, Mary Paik. *Quiet Odyssey: A Pioneer Korean Woman in America* (1990).

Lee, Shelley Sang-Hee. *Claiming the Oriental Gateway: Prewar Seattle and Japanese America* (2010).

Leonard, Karen Isaksen. *Making Ethnic Choices: California's Punjabi Mexican Americans* (1992).

———. *The South Asian Americans* (1997).

McClain, Charles J. *In Search of Equality: The Chinese Struggle against Discrimination in Nineteenth-Century America* (1994).

McKeown, Adam. *Melancholy Order: Asian Migration and the Globalization of Borders* (2011). ·

Modell, John. *The Economics and Politics of Racial Accommodation: The Japanese of Los Angeles, 1900–1942* (1977).

Shah, Nayan. *Contagious Divides: Epidemics and Race in San Francisco's Chinatown* (2001).

Wong, Scott K., and Sucheng Chan, eds. *Claiming America: Constructing Chinese American Identities during the Exclusion Era* (1998).

Young, Elliott. *Alien Nation: Chinese Migration in the Americas from the Coolie Era through World War II* (2014).

Yung, Judy. *Unbound Feet: A Social History of Chinese Women in San Francisco* (1995).

CHAPTER 6

Politics Between the World Wars, 1918–1937

After World War I, Asian immigrants experienced renewed hostility fueling vigilante vio-
lence, discrimination, and the push for exclusion. The Japanese remained the main focus of
attention. In 1920 California strengthened its alien land law, and in 1924 Congress
overrode the Gentlemen's Agreement by enacting Japanese exclusion through banning
the entry of "aliens ineligible to citizenship." Two Supreme Court cases that sought to
win naturalization rights for Asian immigrants failed as the Court upheld the nation's
discriminatory naturalization law that left Asians as the only racial group barred from
citizenship. The first Supreme Court case concerned a Japanese immigrant, Takeo
Ozawa, while the second one focused on an Indian immigrant and World War I veteran
Bhagat Singh Thind. The Court held that Ozawa, despite his assimilation to American
norms and standards, was not a member of the "white race." In Thind's case, it ruled
that while contemporary science viewed Indians technically as "Caucasian," the average
American did not.

Closing the gate to Japan in 1924 was part of a program of comprehensive immigra-
tion reform that capped total immigration to the United States at 150,000 per year, a
figure less than 12 percent of the roughly 1.3 million who had come during the peak
year of 1907. Congress assigned every nation in the world an immigration quota, which
varied depending upon the percentage of its people in the United States in 1890. This date
was chosen to lower the allowable number of "new immigrants" from southern and eastern
Europe. So while the national origins system excluded Asians entirely, it also discriminated
against others who did not meet the white, Anglo-Saxon, or Protestant standard.

The one exception to Asian exclusion was U.S. imperial subjects from the
Philippines. Filipinos, too, were ineligible for U.S. citizenship, but they were not subjected
to exclusion per the 1924 Immigration Act because technically they were not "aliens."
The United States followed the precedent that allowed colonial subjects free access to the
metropolitan center of the empire known as the "metropole." As a result, Filipino migra-
tion began amid the long controversy over excluding the Japanese, as growers in Hawai'i
and on the West Coast looked for alternative sources of labor. After 1924, Filipinos

became the main source of Asian workers. They also generated the same fears of Asian invasion that had targeted Chinese, Indian, and Japanese immigrants. In 1934, during the Great Depression, Congress granted independence to the Philippines (to begin ten years hence). In exchange for their country's freedom, the leaders of the Philippines agreed to the immediate exclusion of Filipino immigrants from the United States, which, to the leaders, was a small price to pay for independence. Thus Filipinos were excluded in 1934 when the timetable for independence began. Not long afterward, Congress sought to return unemployed and destitute Filipino residents in the United States to the Philippines through a repatriation program designed to lessen the burden on Depression-weary welfare agencies. This program failed as the vast majority of Filipinos opted to remain in the United States.

The expression of anti-Asian racism between the world wars stimulated opposition by a critical mass of educated white Americans. The leading edge of social scientists between the world wars rejected race-based science, and this allowed them to see Asians as capable of assimilation and thus able to become good Americans. Moreover, internationally minded Americans sought to overturn Japanese exclusion in order to prevent U.S.–Japan tensions from boiling over into a disastrous war in the Pacific.

DOCUMENTS

The multiethnic workforce in Hawai'i derived from the plantation owners expertise at dividing workers by ethnicity to exact more work and lower pay. The Great Strike organized in 1920 sought to overcome the divide-and-rule strategy as Japanese and Filipino workers joined forces against plantation bosses. Document 1 is a report written by an organization for the striking workers, while Document 2 provides a different view of race relations in Hawai'i in which the author, U.S. Official William Atherton Du Puy, praises the harmonious mixture of races in the islands as a positive indication of Hawai'i statehood.

Documents 3 to 8 focus on the issue of immigration exclusion. Document 3 presents perspectives on Japanese immigration written by prominent white Americans in response to a questionnaire sent by business leaders in Tokyo. The document reveals a diverse set of reasons for their supporting of Japanese exclusion and, in some cases, for opposing it. Document 4 is the U.S. Supreme Court decision regarding Bhagat Singh Thind, which upheld Indian immigrants' ineligibility for U.S. citizenship despite the Court accepting the scientific consensus that they are of the Caucasian race.

Documents 5 and 6 turn to the question of Filipino exclusion as debated at a congressional hearing in 1930. In Document 5, V. S. McClatchy, a prominent California exclusionist, testifies that the peoples on the West Coast fear Filipino immigrants in the same way they feared Japanese immigrants. He also alerts the committee to the sexual threat Filipino laborers pose to white women. McClatchy's push for exclusion took place in the shadow of the Watsonville Riots, in which a mob in Watsonville, California, angered by labor competition with Filipinos and intimate relations between Filipino men and white women, ransacked Filipino residences and killed one man. Document 6 is a congressional

testimony by Manuel C. Briones, member of the Philippines House of Representatives, who argues against the rationale for exclusion made by Californians
like McClatchy and contained in the proposed legislation (Welch bill).

Document 7 is a request by Filipino immigrants for Congress to offer free
passage back to the Philippines as a source of aide during the Great Depression,
when there were few jobs and harsh anti-Filipino sentiment. While the repatriation program, to exclusionists like McClatchy, operated as deportation in disguise, this document underscores the degree of desperation that many Filipinos
endured during this time.

1. Laborers Report on Hawai'i Sugar Strike, 1920

We are laborers working on the sugar plantations of Hawaii.

People know Hawaii as the paradise of the Pacific and as a sugar-producing
country, but do they know that there are thousands of laborers who are suffering
under the heat of the equatorial sun, in field and in factory, and who are weeping with 10 hours of hard labor and with a scanty pay of 77 cents a day?

Hawaii's sugar! When we look at Hawaii as the country possessing 44 sugar
mills, with 230,000 acres of cultivated land area, as a region producing 600,000
tons of sugar annually we are impressed with the great importance of the position which sugar occupies among the industries of Hawaii. We realize also that
50,000 laborers who, together with their families number about 160,000, are a
majority of the total population of 250,000 in Hawaii. We consider it a great
privilege and pride to live under the Stars and Stripes, which stands for freedom
and justice, as a factor of this great industry and as a part of the labor of Hawaii.

We love production. Fifty years ago, when we first came to Hawaii, these
islands were covered with ohia forests, guava fields, and areas of wild grass. Day
and night did we work, cutting trees and burning grass, clearing lands and cultivating fields until we made the plantations what they are to-day. Of course, it is
indisputable that this would have been impossible if it were not for the investments made by the wealthy capitalists and the untiring efforts of the administrators. But we believe that the impartial public will not only magnify and praise
the efforts of the capitalists, but will not hesitate to recognize the work of the
laborers who have served faithfully with sweat on their brows. We are faithful
laborers who love labor and production.

Look at the silent tombstones in every locality. Few are the people who visit
these graves of our departed friends, but are they not emblems of Hawaii's pio-
neers in labor? Turn your eyes to the ever diligent laborers. They are not beautiful in appearance, but are they not a great factor of Hawaii's production?

We are faithful laborers, willing to follow the steps of our departed elders
and do our part toward Hawaii's production. We hear that there are in Hawaii
over a hundred millionaires, men chiefly connected with the sugar plantations.

From Hawai'i Laborers' Association, "Facts About the Strike on Sugar Plantations in Hawaii," in
House Committee on Immigration and Naturalization, *Labor Problems in Hawaii* (Washington, D.C.:
U.S. Government Printing Office, 1921).

It is not our purpose to complain and envy, but we would like to state that there are on the sugar plantations which produced these fortunes for their owners a large number of laborers who are suffering under a wage of 77 cents a day.

When asked, "What is a laborer?" a certain plantation manager is said to have replied, "A laborer is an ignorant creature." We do not wish to believe such a statement, but when we look back over our own experience in Hawaii we regret to state that the above fact [of prejudice against laborers] is undeniable.

Impartial and just ladies and gentlemen, we are laborers working on the plantations of Hawaii. Certain capitalists may regard us as ignorant creatures, but as laborers working seriously and faithfully we wish it understood that we are willing to do our part toward Hawaii's production and welfare the best we know how, hoping for the progress of civilization and endeavoring to safeguard justice and humanity as members of the great human family....

The Demands—Resolutions of the Assembly of Representatives

1. The wages of common man laborers, which at present are 77 cents per day, shall be increased to $1.25, and those of the higher-salaried men shall be increased in proportion:

And minimum wages for women laborers shall be fixed at 95 cents per day:

However, it is to be understood that the present bonus system shall be retained with changes hereinafter mentioned, and same to be paid in addition to the wages already mentioned above.

2. The present bonus system shall be changed in the following particulars, viz:

(a) That the principal of the bonus system shall be made so that the laborers may claim the same in court of justice as of right if it is not already so.

(b) That all men laborers who shall work 15 days or more and all women laborers who shall work 10 days or more per month, shall be entitled to the bonus; and that all cane-growing contractors who may be employed by the plantations to do work for them, shall be paid their bonus irrespective of number of days they work for the plantations:

(c) Seventy-five per cent of bonus shall be paid to laborers every month, the remaining 25 per cent to be retained by the plantation to be paid at the end of each bonus year: *Provided, however,* That whenever the laborers shall leave the plantations because of their intention of returning to Japan, or change of place of work, or of discharge, they shall be paid at once the whole remainder of the bonus, which has been so retained.

3. Eight hours shall constitute a day's work, with the wages and bonuses hereinabove mentioned.

4. Women laborers shall be excused from their work for two weeks before and six weeks after their delivery [childbirth], during which time, however, they shall be entitled to their wages and bonuses as if they were actually at work.

5. For work on Sundays, legal holidays, or overtime services the laborers shall be paid double their regular wages and bonuses.

6. Regarding the cane-growing contract, it is requested that the same be so changed, after deducting the marketing expenses, that the share of companies shall be 40 per cent and that of the planters shall be 60 per cent of the gross value of the market price of sugar.

7. That the price of cane paid to the cane-growing contractors be increased in proportion to the increase of wages and bonus as outlined hereinabove.

8. That the planters shall further improve the provisions made for the health and amusement of laborers.

Resolutions Submitted to Planters' Association

The assembly of the representatives of Japanese laborers, which passed the above resolutions, submitted the same, accompanied by a letter, to the planters' association on December 4, 1919, through a delegation consisting of one representative from each island. It should be remembered that similar demands were also presented to the same association by the Filipino Laborers' Union on the same day.

It was our firm belief that a request so moderate in its nature as the one above referred to would naturally be accepted by the planters' association. This belief we held not without reason, for words and actions of the various plantation managers revealed in unofficial manner, the assurances that the demands would he accepted. But, contrary to our expectation, the annual meeting of the Hawaiian Sugar Planters' Association resulted in the total rejection of our demands, excepting that single clause relating to the bonus system.

It was an unexpected issue. However, we were not entirely disappointed. Believing that an honest explanation of our situation would cause our sincere desires to be acknowledged, we again submitted a similar request with the following reason in support of it on December 27, 1919.

Reasons in Support of Request for Higher Wages, Shorter Hours, etc., for Plantation Laborers of Hawaii

There is something astonishing in the price movement of living staples. In order to ascertain what effect the present high prices have had upon the life of the plantation laborers, our federation has chosen 45 articles of provisions, clothing, and kindred commodities, and has investigated the retail prices thereof. We find that the highest has increased as much as 207.70 per cent and even the lowest 40 per cent, averaging an increase of 115 per cent as compared with normal prewar prices....

Incomes of laborers.—Now, turning to the incomes of laborers at the present time, men earning $20 per month are common and there are not a few who are working at 77 cents per day. Of course there is a bonus which increases quite materially their earnings. But the bonus is not sufficient to supply the discrepancy between the increased cost of living computed at prewar rates and the low present wages. And for those who, from sickness or other reasons, can not obtain the benefit of the bonus, their difficulty is still more emphasized.

A laborer's wage should be sufficient to support him and his family in decency and in comfort. Only so can his physical energies be reasonably conserved. But a mere existence or subsistence is not enough, and the laborer who must spend his entire earnings for living expenses is insufficiently paid. There should always be available a reasonable margin of earnings in excess of necessary expenses to set aside as an insurance fund to provide against the hazards of misfortune and the approach of old age. To provide less than this for a laborer is to place him in a class beneath the beasts of burden which are used on the plantations, and to treat him with less consideration than is accorded to a working mule. The latter beast, whether from motives of selfishness or of humaneness, is fairly certain of not only adequate support during his working career, but of a humane provision for his needs when old age or accident shall have incapacitated him for further service. But where, let us ask, in the wages scale as now existing, can the plantation laborers in Hawaii find a guaranty or even a promise of provision for his maintenance when age or misfortune shall have placed a period upon his earning capacity? His condition in this respect compares unfavorably with that of the beasts of burden now in use upon your plantations. But if the laborer from the inadequate wage now in vogue should nevertheless endeavor to set aside something, even a trifle, each month to assist in such provision for the future, he can do so only at the sacrifice of his comforts, necessities, and even features of decency, of which he should not, upon grounds of morality and justice, be deprived. In short, then, and to epitomize the present situation, the plantation laborer is enabled to exist but not to live and support those dependent upon him in any just and reasonable sense of those terms.

2. American Official Extols Race Relations in Hawai'i, 1932

In continental United States the fundamental American stock has usually absorbed those elements that were introduced, except the Negro, and in the end they have become not noticeably different from it. In Hawaii, where the old American stock constitutes but some 6 per cent of the whole, this will, of course, be impossible. Here it would seem that there ultimately must be a fusion, and that in the end the Hawaiian-American will be a composite of all the peoples who have settled here as permanent residents. Careful examinations of these fusions by specialists at the University of Hawaii have refuted the old theory that unions of these unlike races produce inferior individuals. Careful mental and physical tests have shown that the results of these racial crosses come very near approximating a mean that is halfway between the two parents. So it seems safe to conclude that the ultimate

United States Government Printing Office, Washington, D.C., 1932

Hawaiian–American will come to rest at a point that represents the mean of the blood in his veins. On the basis of the present populations he, therefore, will be something near one-third Japanese, one-fifth Filipino, one-ninth Portuguese, one-tenth Hawaiian, one-twelfth Chinese, one-fifteenth Anglo-Saxon, with a sprinkling of Korean, Puerto Rican, and what-not. This American will be some seven-tenths oriental, two-tenths occidental, and one-tenth Polynesian. He will be about as swarthy as a Sicilian, straight-haired, stocky, physically fit, industrious, efficient, athletic, vain, dressy, given to gambling. His women will be known around the world for a peculiar beauty found no place else.

One very remarkable educational fact already has been quite fully demonstrated through more than three decades of the exposure of the sons and daughters of these oriental cane-field workers to the influences of the American school. They acquire education with a facility that lags little, if any, behind children of the white races. Almost none of the barefooted parents of these youngsters had known anything at all of education, even in their own languages. Transplanted to the land of opportunity, however, they were anxious that their children should take advantage of all the opportunities that presented themselves. It was the old story of downtrodden peoples, long denied such advantages as America offered, and, therefore, when they were presented, more appreciative of them than the native born. The children of Chinese and Japanese particularly never miss the opportunity for an hour in school, and spare no whit of drudging application to master whatever is taught there.

Among the psychologists there long have been two theories as to the inheritance of intelligence. One school has considered that the individual is the heir to the culture and the capacity of the race from which he comes, and that his mental capacity is directly inherited from those who have gone before him. Race traits and peculiarities would thus come down from father to son. Another school holds that these capacities are a result of environment, and that if a Fiji baby were taken at birth and brought up in a Back Bay Boston family its chance of making a scholastic record in Harvard would be as good as that of the child honestly born of this same family.

The first of these theories would not offer much to the coolie's son, born in the laborer's cottage by the sugar mill. The tests at the University of Hawaii tend to add weight to the latter contention. These children of contract laborers who had remained beaten, suppressed, unbelievably poor, through the centuries in their native lands, who had known only unremitting toil, bloom out in the public schools of Hawaii, pass readily through the high schools, go on to the university, and meet the psychological tests as well as do the blonde sons of Nordics whose ancestors have been educated since Chaucer. Japanese, Chinese, Hawaiian, and Anglo-Saxon youngsters show capacities for study and the acquisition of knowledge that come so near being on the same level that the differences are of little importance....

So the population status in Hawaii to-day is something like this: The introduced laborers and their families live on the sugar and pineapple plantations in company houses. There are 105,000 of them on sugar plantations alone.

Families have individual cottages, and bachelors live in group houses. These are likely to be scientifically worked-out units, and have running water, lights, and fuel free of charge. There is a hospital on each plantation, and medical care costs nothing at all. I stopped at one of these hospitals one day and a young surgeon showed me a bright little Japanese baby, son of a laborer, that he had just brought into the world, with no charge for the service, by the Cæsarean operation route....

White men are comparatively more numerous in the towns but still in an inconspicuous minority. Practically all the tasks from the operation of the garage to the collection of the taxes are carried on by nonwhites. When the militia turns out for drill, for example, Chinese, Japanese, Hawaiian, Portuguese, and white types will be indiscriminately mixed. I listened one night to a Chinese top sergeant explaining the mechanism of a machine gun to his squad in language which to me smacked of the Philadelphia water front. Japanese girls make excellent maids and run many a household in Honolulu. For the sake of local color they are often required to wear Japanese clothes. The visitor may make the mistake of talking pigeon English to these young women but is likely to be answered in the perfect speech, quite without any accent, of the high-school graduate....

There is much talk in the continental press of race antagonisms in Hawaii. This talk is based on a lack of understanding of the relations between the races over there. In the States race conflicts and race prejudices are often intense. In the islands they are practically nonexistent. The masses are of a common, lowly, and unpretentious origin. The whites through a century have felt sympathetic toward them. The social question of race has never been raised. It does not exist. It is never raised except by some outsider who brings his prejudices with him or some continental newspaper which bases its interpretation of events in Hawaii on race prejudices that exist where it is published.

If this outsider had an appreciation of the beauty of the interracial relations of these islands he would hesitate long before taking any step that would interfere with them. Race prejudice is a mad, intense, unreasoning thing, and arousing it where it does not exist is an act as malicious as the introduction of the plague.

There is much apprehension lest groups in Hawaii based on race should come into political dominance. No tendency of this sort has yet developed, but active minds conjure up possibilities. It has not been shown that such groups, if they came into dominance, would not provide satisfactory government. It can hardly be argued, under the American form of government, that, as a majority, they would not have the right to rule. And all that any of these groups know of government is based on the American model.

It is a part of the beautiful experiment, here in the mid-Pacific, that self-government is to be tried out under conditions and with human material that is new. There is nothing so far to indicate that the experiment will not turn out to be as successful as it is interesting. America, obviously, should have sufficient courage to see to a conclusion her most novel venture in that type of government which she originated.

3. Americans Provide Diverse Perspectives on Anti-Japanese Racism, 1922

Answers to the First Question

Question: "What do you consider the principal reasons of the present anti-Japanese agita-
tions in California: are they economic, social, or racial?" ...

1. MR. MILTON H. ESBERG, San Francisco, Cal.:

"Anti-Japanese agitation in California is largely due to the non-adoption of American standards of living, working, and working hours, together with the fact that there seems to be no discrimination on the part of the Japanese as to whether the men, or the women do the work, as the same basis seems to apply for both sexes." ...

2. PRESIDENT TULLY C. KNOLES, San Jose, Cal.:

"I have lived in California for thirty-three years and my judgment is that the principal reasons for the present anti-Japanese agitation in California are political. I do not think that the economic situation is so serious as it is set forth by the [anti-Japanese] agitators, particularly as the Japanese give evidence of spending most of their surplus profits in the United States of America. There seems to be little ground for the somewhat prevalent idea that the Japanese problem should ever arise to the dignity of a social or racial problem, such as we have with the negroes already here."

3. PROFESSOR H. A. MILLIS, Lawrence, Kan.:

"I should say that the principal reasons for the anti-Japanese agitation in California have been economic, racial, and political.... The political reason has increased in importance. On the one hand it has been good politics for candidates for office to stand for most anything anti-Japanese and the very fact that prominent politicians have done so has made for further agitation. On the other hand I find a very general feeling that the Japanese government stands for power very much as Germany did before the war, and that this was well shown when the peace treaty and the League of Nations were under consideration. Without question there is much more fear of Japan's attitude than there was four or five years ago."

4. REVEREND U. G. MURPHY, Seattle, Wash.:

"The principal reason is racial. Other nationalities are doing the very same that the Japanese are doing, have always done these things, and yet very little is said about it, because these other aliens are of the white race, which means that ultimate physical assimilation is possible. Because the opposition to the Japanese is almost altogether racial, there is, of necessity, some degree of social antipathy." ...

5. PROFESSOR ROBERT E. PARK, Chicago, Ill.:

"Racial competition, i.e., competition between peoples different in culture, language, and race. Where racial differences are as marked as they are in the case of the Japanese and the American, public sentiment opposes intermarriage. Where intermarriage does not take place assimilation is never complete and the difficulty of the two races mutually accommodating themselves to one another,

From Tasuki Harada (ed.), *The Japanese Problem in California: Answers (By Representative Americans) to Questionnaire* (San Francisco, CA: American Japanese Relations Committee of Tokyo, 1922), 14–31.

while maintaining each a separate racial existence, is bound to be very great. A racial group which is small in numbers, intimate, compact, and well organized, as is the case of the Jew and the Japanese, has, in the long run, great advantages in competition with a larger and less organized community. If there are already racial prejudices this kind of competition intensifies them." …

6. MR. WM. T. SESNON, San Francisco, Cal.:

"The principal reason for the present anti-Japanese agitation is the growth of a permanent population which is politically ineligible and which does not assimilate with our people. Naturally when the Japanese population grows to a sufficient extent and concentrates in colonies on our lands, and by its thrift and ability becomes competitively offensive, it furnishes a fertile ground for successful agitation upon the part of politicians and others who on conscientious and other grounds desire drastic and repressive legislation." …

Answers to the Second Question

Question: "Will you mention some of the more important objections or grievances against Japanese in California, or in the United States?"

1. PROFESSOR H. COOLEY, Ann Arbor, Mich.:

"It is my observation that nearly all Americans like the Japanese. It is generally admitted that they are personally delightful, and they are much more popular in this regard than, say, the Jews. But many think they are collectively dangerous, either as a nation or as groups of settlers in America. My own opinion is that they are in no way dangerous to us so long as they do not settle here in large numbers. There is a widespread belief, based on experience, that if they did they would form unassimilated groups, and thus destroy the homogeneity of our population. Why this should be the case with Orientals more than with Europeans it is hard to say, but it seems to be a fact, and we must be guided by facts. Much as I like the Japanese I am opposed to their immigration." …

2. DOCTOR DAVID STARR JORDAN, Palo Alto, Cal.

"Most of the criticisms are grossly exaggerated. It is true that the farmer-Japanese came generally from Hawaii; having been, then, serfs and coming originally from the homeless farmer class in Yamaguchi and Okayama, Japan, they are ignorant and perforce clannish, and non-naturalization keeps them so. The children are readily 'assimilated,' except in looks." …

3. PRESIDENT TULLY C. KNOLES, San Jose, Cal.:

"The objection most frequently heard to the increase of the number of Japanese in California is that they are securing such large quantities of desirable agricultural and horticultural land by the process of purchase and leasing in the name of their children who are already citizens of the United States by virtue of the fourteenth amendment, and if their success in these fields continue, their standard of living, being lower than that of the American, will tend to racial competition disastrous for the higher standard of living.

"In the second place, the objection is quite seriously raised to the continuance of the Japanese picture-bride arrangement. I understand, however, that this project has been abandoned, but it must be met by earnest argument for many years.

"Incidentally, we hear the fact mentioned that all aliens are debarred from the ownership of real estate in Japan, and occasionally the objection is made that even though Japanese children born in the United States are technically citizens of the United States, attempts are being made to give them in Japanese schools such a training as will prejudice them against the United States and lead them as they approach their majority to continue their relations as citizens of the mother country of their ancestors."

4. REVEREND F. M. LARKIN, San Francisco, Cal.:

"First, economic competition growing out of the fact that unmarried men without families can underlive and consequently eliminate men with families. Social and racial differences which produce naturally race prejudice. I do not believe that any race naturally is without race prejudice. It is only overcome by the acceptance of the higher ideal as taught by Jesus Christ. The promotion of Buddhism among groups of Japanese which has essentially different standards of life from Christianity. I am not now asserting that one is better than the other, simply stating the fact that they are different and naturally the majority in any country think that they are right. History shows that whenever large groups of different races come together they quarrel." ...

5. MR. WM. T. SESNON, San Francisco, Cal.:

"I was one of the committee that went to Japan last spring and later had occasion to travel over the Orient. What I discovered there in the attitude of all races is so significant that I think the impression should be conveyed to you and your associates for what it is worth. This is done in no desire to offend the sensibilities of your people—quite the contrary, in the highest spirit of friendship. I honestly believe that the root difficulty is the military and commercial reputation which your nation is gaining throughout the world. However true or false this reputation may be, it naturally plays a large part in such an intense situation as exists in California, and as a sincere friend of your country I would earnestly urge you to address all your energies to the reëstablishment of good faith in the mind of the outside world." ...

6. MR. JULIUS WANGENHEIM, San Diego, Cal.:

"From the above it will be evident that I think the social objections are the only valid ones. These are based upon the fact that the Japanese, by their superior industry, thrift, and frugality, can overwork and underlive the average American so that in any section where he settles he is almost certain, sooner or later, to drive out the other inhabitants; and this is due to his virtues, not his vices."

4. *U.S. v. Bhagat Singh Thind*, 1923

MR. JUSTICE SUTHERLAND delivered the opinion of the Court.

This cause is here upon a certificate from the Circuit Court of appeals requesting the instruction of this Court in respect of the following questions:

"1. Is a high-caste Hindu, of full Indian blood, born at Amritsar, Punjab, India, a white person within the meaning of § 2169, Revised Statutes?"

"2. Does the Act of February 5, 1917 (39 Stat. 875, § 3) disqualify from naturalization as citizens those Hindus now barred by that act who had lawfully entered the United States prior to the passage of said act?"

The appellee was granted a certificate of citizenship by the District Court of the United States for the District of Oregon, over the objection of the Naturalization Examiner for the United States. A bill in equity was then filed by the United States seeking a cancellation of the certificate on the ground that the appellee was not a white person, and therefore not lawfully entitled to naturalization. The district court, on motion, dismissed the bill (268 F. 683), and an appeal was taken to the circuit court of appeals. No question is made in respect of the individual qualifications of the appellee. The sole question is whether he falls within the class designated by Congress as eligible.

Section 2169, Revised Statutes, provides that the provisions of the Naturalization Act "shall apply to aliens being free white persons and to aliens of African nativity and to persons of African descent."

If the applicant is a white person within the meaning of this section, he is entitled to naturalization; otherwise not. In *Ozawa v. United States*, 260 U.S. 178, we had occasion to consider the application of these words to the case of a cultivated Japanese, and were constrained to hold that he was not within their meaning. As there pointed out, the provision is not that any particular class of persons shall be excluded, but it is, in effect, that only white persons shall be included within the privilege of the statute.

"The intention was to confer the privilege of citizenship upon that class of persons whom the fathers knew as white, and to deny it to all who could not be so classified. It is not enough to say that the framers did not have in mind the brown or yellow races of Asia. It is necessary to go farther and be able to say that, had these particular races been suggested, the language of the act would have been so varied as to include them within its privileges"...

In the endeavor to ascertain the meaning of the [Naturalization Act] statute, we must not fail to keep in mind that it does not employ the word "Caucasian," but the words "white persons," and these are words of common speech, and not of scientific origin. The word "Caucasian" not only was not employed in the law, but was probably wholly unfamiliar to the original framers of the statute in 1790. When we employ it, we do so as an aid to the ascertainment of the legislative intent, and not as an invariable substitute for the statutory words. Indeed, as used in the science of ethnology, the connotation of the word is by no means clear, and the use of it in its scientific sense as an equivalent for the words of the statute, other considerations aside, would simply mean the substitution of one perplexity for another. But, in this country, during the last half century especially, the word, by common usage, has acquired a popular meaning, not clearly defined to be sure, but sufficiently so to enable us to say that its popular, as distinguished from its scientific, application is of appreciably narrower scope. It is in the popular sense of the word, therefore, that we employ is as an aid to the construction of the statute, for it would be obviously illogical to convert words of common speech used in a statute into words of scientific terminology when neither the latter nor the science for whose purposes they were coined was within the contemplation of the framers of the statute or of the people for whom it was framed. The words of the statute are to be interpreted in accordance with the understanding of the common man from whose vocabulary they were taken.

They imply, as we have said, a racial test; but the term "race" is one which, for the practical purposes of the statute, must be applied to a group of living persons now possessing in common the requisite characteristics, not to groups of persons who are supposed to be or really are descended from some remote common ancestor, but who, whether they both resemble him to a greater or less extent, have at any rate ceased altogether to resemble one another. It may be true that the blond Scandinavian and the brown Hindu have a common ancestor in the dim reaches of antiquity, but the average man knows perfectly well that there are unmistakable and profound differences between them today, and it is not impossible, if that common ancestor could be materialized in the flesh, we should discover that he was himself sufficiently differentiated from both of his descendants to preclude his racial classification with either. The question for determination is not, therefore, whether, by the speculative processes of ethnological reasoning, we may present a probability to the scientific mind that they have the same origin, but whether we can satisfy the common understanding that they are now the same or sufficiently the same to justify the interpreters of a statute—written in the words of common speech, for common understanding, by unscientific men—in classifying them together in the statutory category as white persons. In 1790, the Adamite theory of creation—which gave a common ancestor to all mankind—was generally accepted, and it is not at all probable that it was intended by the legislators of that day to submit the question of the application of the words "white persons" to the mere test of an indefinitely remote common ancestry, without regard to the extent of the subsequent divergence of the various branches from such common ancestry or from one another.

The eligibility of this applicant for citizenship is based on the sole fact that he is of high-caste Hindu stock, born in Punjab, one of the extreme northwestern districts of India, and classified by certain scientific authorities as of the Caucasian or Aryan race. The Aryan theory, as a racial basis, seems to be discredited by most, if not all, modern writers on the subject of ethnology. A review of their contentions would serve no useful purpose. It is enough to refer to the works of Deniker (Races of Man, 317), Keane (Man, Past and Present, 445, 446), and Huxley (Man's Place in Nature, 278), and to the Dictionary of Races, Senate Document 662, 61st Congress, 3d Sess. 1910–1911, p. 17.

The term "Aryan" has to do with linguistic, and not at all with physical, characteristics, and it would seem reasonably clear that mere resemblance in language, indicating a common linguistic root buried in remotely ancient soil, is altogether inadequate to prove common racial origin....

The word "Caucasian" is in scarcely better repute. It is, at best, a conventional term, with an altogether fortuitous origin, which, under scientific manipulation, has come to include far more than the unscientific mind suspects. According to Keane, for example (The World's Peoples 24, 28, 307 *et seq.*), it includes not only the Hindu, but some of the Polynesians (that is, the Maori, Tahitians, Samoans, Hawaiians, and others), the Hamites of Africa, upon the ground of the Caucasic cast of their features, though in color they range from brown to black. We venture to think that the average well informed white American would learn with some degree of astonishment that the race to which he belongs is made up of such heterogeneous elements....

It does not seem necessary to pursue the matter of scientific classification further. We are unable to agree with the district court, or with other lower federal courts, in the conclusion that a native Hindu is eligible for naturalization under § 2169. The words of familiar speech, which were used by the original framers of the law, were intended to include only the type of man whom they knew as white. The immigration of that day was almost exclusively from the British Isles and Northwestern Europe, whence they and their forebears had come. When they extended the privilege of American citizenship to "any alien being a free white person," it was these immigrants—bone of their bone and flesh of their flesh—and their kind whom they must have had affirmatively in mind. The succeeding years brought immigrants from Eastern, Southern and Middle Europe, among them the Slavs and the dark-eyed, swarthy people of Alpine and Mediterranean stock, and these were received as unquestionably akin to those already here and readily amalgamated with them. It was the descendants of these, and other immigrants of like origin, who constituted the white population of the country when § 2169, reenacting the naturalization test of 1790, was adopted, and, there is no reason to doubt, with like intent and meaning.

What, if any, people of primarily Asiatic stock come within the words of the section we do not deem it necessary now to decide. There is much in the origin and historic development of the statute to suggest that no Asiatic whatever was included. The debates in Congress during the consideration of the subject in 1870 and 1875 are persuasively of this character. In 1873, for example, the words "free white persons" were unintentionally omitted from the compilation of the Revised Statutes. This omission was supplied in 1875 by the act to correct errors and supply omissions. 18 Stat. c. 80, p. 318. When this act was under consideration by Congress, efforts were made to strike out the words quoted, and it was insisted, upon the one hand, and conceded upon the other, that the effect of their retention was to exclude Asiatics generally from citizenship. While what was said upon that occasion, to be sure, furnishes no basis for judicial construction of the statute, it is nevertheless an important historic incident which may not be altogether ignored in the search for the true meaning of words which are themselves historic. That question, however, may well be left for final determination until the details have been more completely disclosed by the consideration of particular cases as they from time to time arise. The words of the statute, it must be conceded, do not readily yield to exact interpretation, and it is probably better to leave them as they are than to risk undue extension or undue limitation of their meaning by any general paraphrase at this time.

What we now hold is that the words "free white persons" are words of common speech, to be interpreted in accordance with the understanding of the common man, synonymous with the word "Caucasian" only as that word is popularly understood. As so understood and used, whatever may be the speculations of the ethnologist, it does not include the body of people to whom the appellee belongs. It is a matter of familiar observation and knowledge that the physical group characteristics of the Hindus render them readily distinguishable from the various groups of persons in this country commonly recognized as white. The children of English, French, German, Italian, Scandinavian, and other European parentage quickly merge into the mass of our population and lose the distinctive hallmarks of their European origin. On the other hand, it cannot be doubted that the children born in this country of Hindu parents would retain indefinitely the clear evidence of their ancestry. It is very far from our thought to suggest the slightest question of racial superiority or inferiority. What we suggest is merely racial difference, and it is of such character and extent that the great body of our people instinctively recognize it and reject the thought of assimilation.

It is not without significance in this connection that Congress, by the Act of February 5, 1917, 39 Stat. 874, c. 29, § 3, has now excluded from admission into this country all natives of Asia within designated limits of latitude and longitude, including the whole of India. This not only constitutes conclusive evidence of the congressional attitude of opposition to Asiatic immigration generally, but is persuasive of a similar attitude toward Asiatic naturalization as well, since it is not likely that Congress would be willing to accept as citizens a class of persons whom it rejects as immigrants.

It follows that a negative answer must be given to the first question, which disposes of the case and renders an answer to the second question unnecessary, and it will be so certified.

5. Californian Testifies for the Exclusion of Filipino Immigrants, 1930

We had first the invasion by the Chinese, next the invasion by the Japanese, then by the Hindus, and now we are called upon to resist the invasion of the Filipinos.

The conditions with regard to the Filipinos are more serious than they were with regard to any of those other peoples, as will appear to you later, although they are less in number....

Hawaii offers herself as a terrible example of the penetration of colored races. Hawaii is hopelessly lost to the white race. Idealists may talk enthusiastically about the noble experiment being conducted in Hawaii, the melting pot

V.S. McClatchy and Victor K. Houston, House Committee on Immigration and Naturalization, Exclusion of Immigration from the Philippine Islands (Washington, D.C.: U.S. Government Printing Office, 1930).

and what it is producing; but the result is simply terrible to those who will look ahead....

There were about 60,000 Japanese in Hawaii in 1900. To-day the Japanese constitute two-fifths of the entire population of the Islands, and more than one half of the school registration is Japanese. The Filipinos constitute about one-fifth of the population. Only 6½ per cent of the entire population (not counting Portugese), are white. White labor is barred by conditions there. The American Federation of Labor posts a great notice on our West Coast warning all labor not to go to Hawaii, and telling them there is no place for a white man there in skilled or unskilled labor....

Let me impress upon the committee this thought: That continued Filipino and Mexican immigration into California will bring to California the condition which you now have in Hawaii. And, if California goes that way it will spread all over the United States. We are trying to maintain a white country in California for our own interests and for the interests of the Nation....

Now, why do we protest against Filipino immigration?

First, it is opposed to a basic principle of the restrictive immigration act of 1924. You will recall the provision of section 13, subdivision (c), excluding as immigrants all aliens ineligible to citizenship. The debates and hearings then held show that it was desired to restrict immigration materially in number and to exclude so far as possible unassimilable elements. Aliens ineligible to citizenship were held to be hopelessly unassimilable and therefore barred as a class. The principle thus established has been violated ... by a provision in section 28 of the act to the effect that citizens of tributary islands of the United States shall not be considered as aliens. That admitted the Filipinos....

The second reason for Philippine exclusion is that this violation to which I have referred is regarded as an act of bad faith by our friends the Japanese.

Congress in 1924 recognized Japanese immigration as an evil which must be remedied, but it was desired to do so without just offense to Japanese pride. Of all the plans suggested the one that best met the conditions was the one adopted, which made no mention of Japanese but simply declared that no alien ineligible to our citizenship should be admitted as immigrant. It was explained to the Japanese that the provision was not discriminatory and applied alike to all those ineligible to our citizenship.

As said before, the principle has been violated in wholesale manner in the case of Filipinos.... The matter has perhaps not come to the attention of this committee, nor has it perhaps been taken up diplomatically, but the violation is bitterly resented by the Japanese particularly, as is indicated by frequent reference thereto in their vernacular newspapers....

The third reason for Filipino exclusion is the extreme unassimilability of the Filipino people. I hope this will be taken by our Filipino friends in the spirit in which it is offered.

The Philippine Islands have about 12,000,000 population. Those inhabitants are of the Malay race which is an offshoot of the Mongolian, and they are ineligible to citizenship except where they have served in our Navy and hold honorable discharge. All the population of the islands is ineligible to citizenship. All are permitted to come in as immigrants and to come in without discrimination....

In addition to the discordant and diverse character of the population of the islands, all elements of which have full liberty to come here, your attention is directed to the fact that the worst class are entering. R. W. Kearney, who supervises for the State the labor camps of California says that the contractors of Filipino labor tell him that in going back to the islands for labor they deliberately choose the less intelligent, because they are more easily controlled. The Manila Tribune says it is the "riffraff" that comes. And now you see more clearly what I have in mind....

I do not want to reflect upon any members of the class that come over here from the Philippine Islands for the purpose of study. Mr. Kearney tells me that in the labor camps he has found young Filipinos who, after working all day in the fields, would spend a couple of hours twice a week in night school; and he says there is not another race in the labor camps that will do that. So, while all elements over there are unassimilable with our people yet the worst of them are coming here to a greater extent now than before.

I have reports showing they have clashes in Hawaii and in California not only with whites but with other races. In California a Filipino married a Japanese girl in Stockton, and the Japanese inaugurated a general boycott against the Filipinos. Both races seemed to resent it. They have also had clashes elsewhere in the State with Mexicans. I saw the other day that in the city of Manila there was a riot, and an attempt to kill a number of United States sailors. That may have been due to fault on the part of the sailors. These instances are quoted, not with the assumption that the Filipinos are always to blame, but to demonstrate that they do not mingle well with other racial elements, and therefore that a continuance of this character of immigration must make for more or less trouble.

I now come to the most serious phase of this question, and that is the sex problem. I will read a statement by Dr. David P. Barrows, for a number of years director of our educational system in the Philippines, for four years president of the University of California and still attached to that institution, a friend of the Filipino, which appeared in the Commonwealth Bulletin, at page 322:

> Their vices are almost entirely based on sexual passion. This passion in the Malay—which includes practically all types of Filipinos—is inordinately strong; and in accordance with native customs it is rarely directed into the right channels or restrained by custom or by individual will. The irregularity of his conduct, and the social problem in American life which his presence aggravates is, in my opinion, entirely based on this phase of his character.
>
> The evidence is very clear that having no wholesome society of his own, he is drawn into lowest and least fortunate associations. He usually frequents the poorer quarters of our towns, and spends the residue of his savings in brothels and dance-halls, which in spite of our laws, exist to minister to his lower nature. Everything in our rapid, pleasure-seeking life and the more or less shameless exhibitionism which accompanies it,

contribute to overwhelm these young men who, in most cases, are only a few years removed from the even, placid life of a primitive native barrio.

As I said, the Filipino does not bring his females with him. In 1929 only 3 per cent of those who came were females.

You can realize, with the declared preference of the Filipino for white women and the willingness on the part of some white females to yield to that preference, the situation which arises. It is one of the phases which is at the bottom of the racial trouble in the State of California. Take, for instance, the Watsonville riot, which threatened to be quite serious. There was one death in connection with that matter. There was one incident perhaps not known outside the State, of a young girl 17 or 18 years of age who associated with a Filipino, and her parents endeavored to stop it but without avail. She was missing for two or three days and they started to hunt for her, and she was found hidden in a Filipino hotel. She made complaint that she had been mistreated and she was taken to the detention home. That was only one of the incidents which inflamed the public....

6. Leader of Philippines House of Representatives Reveals Trade-Off Between Exclusion and Independence, 1930

The questions involved in this bill are of extremely delicate nature. Economic considerations are intermingled with those of racial character. The economic phase permits a wide latitude for discussion; the racial angle is narrowed by embarrassing sensibilities provocative of resentment. You will, therefore, understand why we come before this committee with a great deal of reluctance and diffidence. For it is not easy to assert one's dignity and self-respect in the face of similar feelings and sentiments of others.

Our peculiar relations with America, however, justifies us in presenting our side of this question. Were it not for such relations, unsought by the Filipinos and imposed upon them by America, it would indeed be very embarrassing, even bad taste, to come before you. This will explain at the outset why, in opposing this measure, we have frequently to appeal to the innate sense of justice and fair play of the American people.

In all due respect, we submit that the exclusion of the Filipinos from the United States as provided for in the Welch bill, which in effect places us in the same category as the Chinese under the Chinese exclusion act of 1882 and as the Japanese under the Japanese exclusion act of 1924, can not be justified by any of the reasons so far publicly given in support of the measure, among which are the protection of American workingmen against alleged cheap Asiatic labor and the preservation of the racial and social integrity of the American Nation.

From the political and moral point of view the passage of this bill is even less justified. The very author of this measure, in one of his recent addresses on the floor or the House, himself admitted that the Filipino in America does not

From Manuel Roxas, in House Committee on Immigration and Naturalization, Exclusion of Immigration from the Philippine Islands (Washington, D.C.: U.S. Government Printing Office, 1930).

compete with the American laborer when he stated that the Filipinos do not come here as colonists; in other words, they do not settle permanently. This may be demonstrated by the fact that they only engage in transient and seasonal occupations. The reason is obvious. The great majority of the Filipinos coming to the United States are young men whose primary object is to study and gain experience by direct contact with American culture and civilization. To them, therefore, employment is only secondary and incidental. They work only sufficiently to earn enough with which to maintain themselves in school and pay their tuition fees and other necessary expenses. As an example we have the thousands of Filipinos who go to Alaska during the salmon fishing season, after which they return to the cities on the Pacific coast where they reside to continue their studies. A great many of these young men come from families who, in our country, own a small parcel of land and a few work animals. In many cases, their parents have had to sell a piece of their land or one or two "carabaos" in order to provide the money necessary to send them to America and maintain them until they have become self-supporting. In vain they have not learned the lesson taught them in school about Lincoln, the self-made "rail splitter." Many of these young men who come here are near relatives or intimate friends who hail from the same community and they mutually help one another by paying for each other's expenses in school by turns; that is, while one goes to school the other works for the other's maintenance. When the one studying has finished his course he in turn goes to work so that the other may go to school. These mutual arrangements do not surprise those familiar with the compactness of the Filipino family and with the spirit of helpfulness which is innate among the Filipinos— characteristics which Dr. David P. Barrows, of the University of California, himself could not help but admit as an excellent quality of our race. Once they have finished their studies or have learned enough to have compensated for the sacrifices they incurred in coming to this wonderful land of opportunity, they return to the Philippines to help their parents or establish themselves in their various callings or occupations....

It will be seen from these considerations that Filipino immigration to the United States is not really a menace to the welfare of the American workingman, much less to the racial and social integrity of this Nation. It does not constitute a third race problem that is to be added to those that you already have—the problems of the colored and the red races. The sociologist in California exaggerates when he envisions such danger. The Filipinos in America constitute a race problem only if one or two things happen—either a sufficient number of Filipino women must come to the United States to make possible a normal and well balanced Filipino community, or, if Filipino women are not available, the Filipino residents would have to intermarry freely with the American women of the white race.

The first is not possible. Immigration of Filipino women to the United States in large numbers is out of the question because of the enormous distance between America and the Philippines and the high cost of transportation, not to mention other one thousand and one inconveniences. The other is unthinkable. Intermarriage between Americans and Filipinos will always be a rare exception, never a general rule. The radical differences in race will never be bridged.

Aside from the existence of a public opinion here against Filipino marital incursions into the nordic circle, individual inclinations and differences militate against the success of such unions. For the purpose of marriage and the creation of a family the Filipino, in general, will prefer to return to his country where he can find a women who can understand him and in whom he can find complete identity in custom, manner, desire, education, habits, religion, etc. Similarly, the American woman will always feel inclined to find a life companion from amongst her race. The world has advanced greatly, but the time is yet far distant when humankind shall have become one great family; it is as yet composed of various great families denominated races whose tendency is to isolate themselves from one another.

To Dr. David P. Barrows, whom I have already cited, has been attributed the statement that the Filipino has a weakness to sexual propensity which makes him a racial menace in America. As an anecdote or as a mirth-provoking post-prandial sally, this observation is contagiously humorous; as a scientific formula, it is sublimely ridiculous. The very records and statistics of this country as well as those of the Philippines show that the contrary is exactly the truth. The records of the Quarantine Service of Seattle, were they consulted, would show that the result of the physical examination given to thousands of Filipinos that journey to Alaska is better than that of a similar group of men of the white race of the same age. Of course, there are not lacking Filipino immigrants of low moral character, but to judge the entire Filipino community in America or on the Pacific coast by the low standard of this type of Filipinos would be like judging the mortality of the American people by the low standard shown by some of the sailors and soldiers of the United States stationed in Manila or those who arrive in ports of call after a prolonged abstinence....

I will now discuss the moral phase of this question which to me is the most important of its various aspects. The Congress is urged to solve this problem once and for all taking only into consideration the welfare of the American people. Supposing, for the sake of argument, that this question is really a matter of life and death to the States of the Union alleged to be affected by Filipino immigration, we ask: Should it be solved solely in compliance with the pressure of the inexorable laws of necessity? Would it not be more noble and more magnanimous for the American people and just to the Filipinos, first to settle the principal question in the relations between the two peoples of which the problem of immigration is only incidental?

We are aware of the fact that this committee is not the one called upon to deliberate on the problem of [Philippine] independence. Much as we would like to avoid this issue the force of circumstances makes it impossible for us to evade it. The truth is that the present situation is very much more undesirable than it looks on the surface. For the cause of all these conflicts is our present state of dependency. Give us our liberty, grant us our independence, and this immigration problem, as well as the other problems arising from our present relationship, will solve themselves automatically. If despite all, you still decide to close your doors to us, we shall endeavor to drown our anxiety to come to your country, much as we desire to do so. We will not even utter a single word of protest against your determination to exclude us. But may we be permitted to say, humbly but emphatically, that while we remain under political subjection; while American capital, American products, American citizens have free entry in our country, we believe that we are entitled to reciprocity [of immigration]. To do one and not the other is one sided, beneficial to one and prejudicial to the other.

7. Filipino Immigrants Petition Congress for Repatriation, 1932

Resolution of the Filipino Communities Under the Auspices of the Legionarios Club

Whereas in pursuant to a resolution adopted by the Filipino community in a mass meeting held under the auspices of the Legionarios Club, a duly incorporated California corporation, on November 13, 1932, in the city and county of Los Angeles, State of California, that a nation-wide relief movement for unemployed Filipinos in continental United States be started; and

Whereas attached hereto a set of resolution approved on the abovementioned date, which resolution is duly indorsed and subscribed to by 55 Filipino clubs and organizations and Filipino business men composing the great majority of Filipino residents in Los Angeles County, State of California, hereby make the same a part of this resolution; and

Whereas increasing unemployment is causing 65,000 Filipinos, native inhabitants from the Philippine Islands residing in continental United States have fallen into financial distress, are not employed; are in want for the necessities of life amidst a surplus of all things necessary to life and the maintnance of a high standard of living, is becoming a menace to the maintenance of orderly government; and is an indictment of our intelligence and capacity for self-government; and

Whereas practically all means of correction so far tried in government and industry have made the situation worse rather than better, by bringing about the curtailment of employment and reduction of wage scales, thereby further restricting buying capacity and causing further Filipino unemployment, who are now and have been beneficiaries of public and private charitable institutions; and

Whereas the owners of wealth and institutions which have control of a large volume of credit further complicate the situation by restricting credit and expenditures to 48,750 unemployed Filipinos; and

Whereas various small groups within the Filipino communities have devised ways and means to raise funds to defray the furnishing of food and shelter from those 16,250 employed Filipinos receiving meager income are without any success; and

Whereas the removal of these unemployed Filipinos of public and private charities would relieve the local burden now borne by the cities and communities in which they live; also will save these Filipino wards from the clutches of complete breakdown of their morale as well as the victims of degenerative

From House Committee on Immigration and Naturalization, To Return to the Philippine Islands Unemployed Filipinos (Washington, D.C.: U.S. Government Printing Office, 1933), 40–41.

crimes, thus insure peace and security and prevent riots and mob attacks in their respective localities, and

Whereas at this time 20,875 Filipinos who are unemployed and financially distressed are ready and willing to return to the Philippine Islands if a way could be provided for their passage, transportation, and maintenance en route from continental United States: Therefore be it

Resolved, That the Seventy-second Congress, second session, of the United States of America, now assembled, unanimously approve H. J. Res. 549 [a Filipino repatriation measure] introduced by the Hon. Samuel Dickstein and referred to the Committee on Immigration and Naturalization; and be it further

Resolved, That a copy of this resolution be sent to the honorable Secretary of War and the Philippine Resident Commissioners in Washington, D. C.; and both houses of the Philippine Legislature and the Governor General of the Philippine Islands; and also, be it further

Resolved, That President Roque E. de la Ysla of this Nation-wide relief movement be the representative and spokesman of our Filipino communities and to wait upon personally the honorable Committee on Immigration and Naturalization, House of Representatives, United States, for detailed facts of the Filipinos' economic, social, and political problems in continental United States.

[SEAL.]   ROQUE E. DE LA YSLA, *President.*
Attested by:
    FRANCISCO X. CARBONELL, *Secretary.*

ESSAYS

The first essay, by Oberlin College scholar Rick Baldoz, examines the politics of Filipino exclusion and repatriation, focusing particularly on congressional debate. While the significance of race is clear in this essay, so is the complicated politics of Philippine independence that cannot be reduced to racism alone. In the second essay, Maile Arvin critiques the myth of Hawai'i as a "racial paradise" that was advanced by a consensus of local politicians, plantation owners, and social scientists. An assistant professor of ethnic studies at the University of California, Riverside, Arvin maintains that such a rosy impression of the islands masked the complexity of interracial relations in the islands and the existence of Native Hawaiian peoples and their claims to sovereignty over their homeland.

Filipino Exclusion and Philippine Independence

RICK BALDOZ

By the time Congress held hearings on immigration from the Philippines, the desirability of Filipino exclusion was not really a matter of debate, with most

From Baldoz, *The Third Asiatic Invasion: Empire and Migration in Filipino America, 1898–1946* (New York: NYU Press, 2011), 156–193. Reprinted by permission.

senators and representatives accepting the premise that immigration from the islands constituted a serious social problem. There were, however, significant differences of opinion on how to resolve the matter. On one side were advocates of outright immigration restriction, who believed Congress should bar Filipinos from the United States irrespective of their status as American nationals. Hardcore exclusionists worried that the issue of Philippine independence was a political hot potato that was best dealt with as a separate legislative matter. On the other side were those who believed that exclusion could be implemented in a more diplomatic and honorable way, favoring independence as a means to curtail immigration. The granting of Philippine independence, they argued, would allow the United States to avoid a rather ugly diplomatic precedent—being the first imperial state to ban its own political subjects from entering their sovereign state. The passage of an independence bill, moreover, would yield the added bonus of placing Philippine imports under tariff quotas. This was a major concern of mid-western congressional representatives from states with large sugar-beet and/or dairy industries, who had long railed against the import of cheap Philippine goods such as cane sugar and copra (coconut oil) that competed with their products.

The Shortridge bill was first introduced on the Senate floor as a standalone exclusion bill (S. 4183) on April 16, 1930, but Shortridge quickly shifted tactics and reoffered his proposal a week later as an amendment (S. 51) to Senator William Harris's Mexican-exclusion bill, which already had significant support in Congress. The Shortridge amendment was modeled on the Chinese Exclusion Act of 1882. The senator explained that the "main and vital purpose" of his provision was to "prevent the coming of what may be called the laborer class," exempting students, merchants, and government officials from quota limits. The bill targeted only immigration to the "Continental United States," a proviso added to appease Hawaiian sugar planters, who opposed any legislation that would hinder the unfettered flow of Filipino labor to the islands....

Although many members of the Senate supported Filipino exclusion in principle, Shortridge had a difficult time securing votes for a stand-alone immigration bill that did not address the independence issue....

The Filipino-exclusion question received a more protracted deliberation in the House of Representatives, where Immigration Committee chairman Albert Johnson scheduled formal hearings on Representative Richard Welch's exclusion bill. This piece of legislation was even more malicious than the Shortridge amendment, seeking to reclassify Filipinos as "aliens ineligible to citizenship." This change was designed to strip them of their status as U.S. nationals, thereby subjecting them to the exclusionary quota system established by the 1924 Immigration Act. In Welch's speech introducing HR 8708, he warned his colleagues that Filipino migration and settlement in the United States constituted one of the "gravest problems that has ever faced the people of the Pacific Coast." He referenced the recent outbreaks of violence on the West Coast, which in Welch's view "reveal[ed] the intense jealousy and racial hatred which the Asiatic immigrants [in Watsonville, California and other sites] have aroused."...

The hearings on the Welch bill began on April 10, 1930. Among the witnesses invited to the proceedings were "distinguished Californians" U.S. Webb and V. S. McClatchy, as well as a number of other restrictionists such as John Trevor of the American Coalition of Patriotic Societies and William Hushing of the American Federation of Labor. Welch kicked off the hearings by stressing the unique burden that the citizens of California and the American West had borne when it came to dealing with immigration problems. Unlike other parts of the country, this region faced an unceasing onslaught of aliens from both the southern and Pacific borders. He argued that California had become a "dumping ground for Filipinos … and Mexicans" but promised that citizens of the western states were ready to play a vanguard role in shoring up the nation's borders as they had done in previous decades against the Chinese and Japanese.…

The Southern Strategy

Western nativists knew that they could not win passage of an exclusion bill without another large bloc of votes in Congress. Movement spokesmen saw southern Democrats as their natural allies on issues of racial exclusion, regularly invoking the specter of miscegenation in a bid to win support from the representatives from that region. Restrictionists portrayed Filipinos demands for social equality and minority rights in the United States as a thinly veiled smokescreen for their real agenda: interracial marriage with white women. This same accusation had long been levied by white leaders in the South to disparage the civil rights demands of African Americans, who, according to segregationists, possessed an irrepressible desire for conjugal access to white women. Nativist point men warned that Filipinos would soon be intermarrying with white women in the eastern and southern states if congressional leaders did not throw their support behind exclusion.

Restrictionists claimed that Filipino men had a peculiar talent for winning the affections of white women and had proven themselves adept at evading proscriptions on interracial marriage. J. Edward Cassidy reminded the committee that even though the number of Filipinos intermarrying with whites was small, the "mongrel stream" resulting from such unions multiplied rapidly, producing hybrid children "of the worst type." This point was underscored by V. S. McClatchy, who painted a grim picture of white racial decline in the face of unrelenting waves of Asian migration over previous decades. Admixture with Filipinos, he argued, violated the laws of nature and degraded the blood of the white race. The arrival of increasing numbers of Filipinos had pushed the situation to a crisis point, forcing western leaders such as McClatchy to demand from Congress "protection against the colored races of the Orient." He dismissed charges that recent campaigns to expel Filipinos from the West Coast were motivated by hate or malice, claiming instead that white citizens had acted in self-defense to reclaim their communities and their nation from an alien onslaught. The struggle to defend America's Pacific border was described as a high-stakes conflict that was already playing itself out in the Hawaiian Islands. McClatchy pointed to Hawaii as a "terrible example of the penetration of colored races" into an American domain. The demographic majority of Asians in Hawaii offered a cautionary tale that illustrated the dangers of laissez-faire immigration policy. Hawaii, according to McClatchy, was "hopelessly lost to the white race" due to the lax attitude of federal lawmakers. The nightmare scenario that had unfolded in Hawaii was likely to be repeated in "white man's country" if law-makers did not fortify the nation's western border. This scenario, he warned, was a matter of great urgency for American citizens, since if California went "col-ored," it would quickly "spread all over the United States."...

The Opposition Speaks

Filipinos testifying on the Welch bill had their own agenda for the hearings. They saw the forum as an opportunity to make the case for independence and to challenge racist claims made by their adversaries. The Philippine delegation included Manuel Roxas, speaker of the Philippine House of Representatives; Camilo Osias, Philippine resident commissioner; Manuel Briones, House major-ity leader; and Pedro Gil, House minority leader. Joining them in opposition to the bill was a representative from the U.S. War Department and lobbyists from the Hawaiian Sugar Planters Association. Filipino leaders had two main objec-tives at the hearings: The first was to challenge the political and legal propriety of the United States' excluding its own colonial wards. Their second goal was to steer the debate away from immigration restriction and back to the question of Philippine independence, a legislative solution that would allow both sides to claim a measure of victory. Philippine officials had pressed the case for national self-determination for decades without making much headway, so the immigra-tion hearings offered a timely, though somewhat awkward, opportunity to move their political aims forward....

Manuel Roxas laid out the key themes of the opposition strategy, engaging in a protracted back and forth with committee members, who at times seemed confused about the precise legal status of Filipinos in the United States. Roxas challenged a key premise of the Welch bill—that the U.S. Congress could legally reclassify Filipinos as aliens, as defined in the 1924 Immigration Act. Recalling earlier debates surrounding Filipinos' naturalization status in the United States, he pointed out that U.S. courts had definitively recognized that Filipinos were American "nationals" and not "aliens." To change their status now would give the term "alien" a "wholly arbitrary meaning" inconsistent with established legal precedent. Roxas reminded the committee members that American officials had always framed their role in the Philippines as a benevolent one, rooted in "prin-ciples of fair-play, righteousness, and justice." To enact restrictive legislation would call into question the "guiding norm[s] of American conduct" and would likely create resentment against the United States in the islands, upsetting cordial relations between the two governments. Roxas also drew on the rhetoric of American exceptionalism to defend the special status of Filipinos, noting that U.S. policymakers had always touted their brand of imperialism as a more munif-icent and progressive type of sovereignty, a tradition that could not be reconciled with the belligerent aims of the Welch bill.

Roxas spent significant time responding to nativists such as McClatchy and Webb, whose testimony was riddled with misinformation and specious claims.

He ridiculed Webb for suggesting that the United States might solve the problem of Filipino immigration simply by selling the Philippines to another imperial power. The notion that Filipinos were "owned as mere chattels, as a herd of oxen, and [might] be disposed of as such" was, according to Roxas, wholly inconsistent with political and moral norms undergirding American dominion in the islands. This was a compelling point, insofar as Filipinos had U.S. sovereignty imposed on them by force and were powerless to "disentangle themselves" from this imperial attachment. Other members of the Philippine delegation reminded the members of the Immigration and Naturalization Committee that Filipinos "owed allegiance" to the United States and lived under the American flag. Passage of the Welch bill, they argued, would set a troubling precedent, singling out the United States as the world's only imperial power to ban its own political subjects from entering the "mother country." Roxas drove this point home by highlighting the fact that Filipinos had never been excluded from Spain during its three centuries of colonial rule in the islands, even though Spain, unlike the United States, "was a selfish, imperialistic power!" This clever contrast between Spanish colonial policies and the ostensibly more humane character of American empire effectively communicated the odious nature of the Welch exclusion bill....

Independence from the Philippines

Over the next two years (1932–1933), Congress considered a variety of bills aimed at conferring Philippine independence. Senator William King, who hailed from the sugar-beet-producing state of Utah, proposed a bill granting immediate independence to the islands, a change in status that would subject Philippine cane sugar to tariff restriction....

Support for Philippine independence picked up new momentum in 1932 with the introduction of concurrent bills by Harry Hawes of Missouri and Bronson Cutting of New Mexico in the Senate and by Butler Hare of South Carolina in the House. The Senate and House bills shared the same basic outlines and eventually merged into a single legislative proposal after some back and forth between the two legislative bodies. The American Federation of Labor, powerful agribusiness interests, and Philippine delegates Sergio Osmena and Manuel Roxas all testified at hearings on the new bill. The initial versions of the Hare and Hawes-Cutting bills did not directly deal with the issue of immigration exclusion, due to concern that such a provision would offend the Filipino people and derail support for the legislation in the Philippines. California congressmen Hiram Johnson (Senate) and Richard Welch (House) considered this issue to be a deal breaker and quickly inserted an exclusion clause into the Hare-Hawes-Cutting bill. That the motivations of American lawmakers in pushing this legislation forward were less than noble was not lost on Filipino leaders, who remarked that congressional support for national autonomy was as much about "independence of America *from* the Philippines" (emphasis added) as it was about independence for the Philippines....

The bill's supporters were caught by surprise when the Philippine legislature, which had long demanded independence, vetoed the bill in early 1933 after

Manuel Quezon, president of the Philippine Senate, raised strong objections. Not surprisingly, Filipino leaders wanted to begin their sovereign status on the most advantageous terms possible and were not happy with key provisions of the Hare-Hawes-Cutting bill. The issue was also complicated by the fact that Quezon was locked in a power struggle with Sergio Osmena and Manuel Roxas, as both camps jockeyed for control of the postindependence regime. Most Philippine leaders had reservations about the tariff and immigration provisions in the bill but figured that this was the price to be paid for independence. Some opponents of the Hare-Hawes-Cutting bill also expressed concerns about the continued presence of U.S. military bases in the islands, which for many Filipinos symbolized a threat to national sovereignty. Quezon believed that he could negotiate a better deal with the incoming Roosevelt administration, one that would adjust the restrictive immigration and trade quotas laid out in the Hare-Hawes-Cutting bill. Roosevelt's representatives informed Quezon, however, that these issues were not negotiable and that restrictionists might demand even harsher terms if Filipinos continued to press the issue. This seemingly endless political maneuvering did not sit well with nativist leaders, who believed that Filipinos were getting cold feet about the exclusionary provisions contained in the bill. They criticized Filipino leaders for reneging on the deal and called on federal officials to settle the matter once and for all. California labor boss Paul Scharrenberg wrote an article entitled "What Do Filipinos Want?" which voiced the concerns of exclusionists....

The only area in which Philippine leaders were able to win any concessions was on the issue of military bases, with Quezon negotiating the withdrawal of U.S. Army bases and gaining a promise to revisit the issue of Navy bases during the Commonwealth period. The revised Hare-Hawes-Cutting bill was reintroduced in 1934 by its new sponsors, Senator Millard Tydings of Maryland and Representative John McDuffie of Alabama, and it was passed by Congress in March 1934. The Tydings-McDuffie Act mandated a ten-year probationary period under which a Commonwealth government supervised by the United States would assist in the transition to self-rule. The Philippine legislature was instructed to draft a national constitution patterned on the U.S. republican system. The Philippine Constitution was approved by President Roosevelt in March 1935.

The ten-year probationary period mandated by the Tydings-McDuffie Act revealed the separation anxiety of American officials, who believed that the Philippines would descend into chaos without another decade of paternal supervision. And though formal independence would not be enacted for ten years, two important exclusionary provisions prescribed by the act would be put into force immediately. Section 6 of the act established quotas for Philippine products such as sugar, coconut oil, and cordage, and graduated tariff duties were placed on other goods, slowly limiting the access of Filipino products to the American market. Not surprisingly, the act contained no provision allowing the Philippine government to reciprocally levy any duties or quota restrictions on the entry of U.S. products, allowing American goods unfettered access throughout the Commonwealth period. More important, Section 8 of the Tydings-McDuffie Act reclassified the Philippines as a "foreign country" vis-à-vis U.S. immigration law. American immigration authorities were now obliged to treat Filipinos "as if they were aliens" in all matters pertaining to their right to enter the United States. This change in status made them subject to the limitative restrictions established in the 1917 and 1924 Immigration Acts.

Federal officials granted the Philippines a quota of a mere fifty immigrants per year during the Commonwealth period. This meager quota reflected the lingering hostility to Filipino immigrants on the West Coast and was only half the number of entries allocated to other Asian nations such as China and Japan, which received one hundred slots per annum under the 1924 Immigration Act....

A Problem Not Solved

While nativist leaders celebrated the new restrictions on immigration from the Philippines, they still expressed concern about the problems posed by the tens of thousands of Filipinos already in the United States. Racial antagonism toward Filipinos remained strong on the West Coast and had spread to other parts of the country by the mid-1930s....

Widespread unemployment during the early years of the Great Depression added to resentment ... about the continued presence of Filipinos in the United States. In April 1932, eighty-seven Filipino laborers were "driven out" of Banks, Oregon, by white laborers and farmers. Filipinos had been hired to harvest the area's strawberry crop but were ordered to evacuate the district after a "mass meeting of whites" declared them a menace to the local economy. The next year, a bombing campaign was orchestrated by residents of the Yakima Valley to drive Filipino agricultural workers out of the region. A local white Citizen's Committee "requested" that Japanese truck farmers on the Yakima reservation stop employing and/or subleasing agricultural land to Filipinos. The committee cited "unfair competition with white labor and mingling with white women" as its principal objections to Filipinos. The Japanese initially refused to cooperate with this order, and during March and April 1934, nightriders tossed dynamite and planted bombs on farms that employed Filipinos.

The growing labor militancy of Filipino workers also remained in the spotlight. A series of large-scale strikes and labor actions disrupted the agricultural industry in California and reinforced perceptions of Filipinos as a disruptive force in American political life. A major strike in 1933 saw workers across the state engaged in simultaneous labor actions.

"A Disguised Form of Deportation"

Some of the key figures behind the campaign for Filipino exclusion launched a new campaign aimed at repatriating those immigrants still residing in the United States back to the Philippines. A mass deportation of Filipinos similar to campaigns carried out against Mexicans during the early 1930s was not practicable because of the unique political attachment between the United States and the Philippines. Congressional restrictionists and nativist leaders, however, got creative in their efforts to facilitate a mass exodus of Filipinos. Lawmakers came up with a novel legislative solution that might achieve the result of a large-scale deportation without the political fallout. U.S. officials set about crafting a federal policy aimed at convincing Filipinos to leave the country voluntarily, with Uncle Sam providing financial and logistical assistance to facilitate their departure.

Representative Samuel Dickstein, who chaired the House Immigration and Naturalization Committee, proposed an early version of this legislation in 1933. The bill, House Joint Resolution 549, was specifically aimed at repatriating "unemployed" Filipinos back to the Philippines, with government assistance. The federal government would provide logistical support for transportation to the islands and a financial appropriation from Congress would pay for their one-way passage back to the islands. Dickstein's proposal was couched in humanitarian terms as an effort to help indigent Filipinos return home during a time of economic distress. Lawmakers also believed that the departure of large numbers of Filipinos would help to quell the racial antagonism on the West Coast, which continued to flare up on a regular basis through the mid-1930s. Among the notable witnesses appearing at the hearings in favor of the resolution were U.S. Secretary of Labor William Doak....

William Doak heartily endorsed HJ 549 and sent a special assistant, Murray Garsson, to Southern California to do some "heavy investigation" of the Filipino situation and then report his findings at the hearings. Garsson's testimony asserted that the number of Filipinos had reached epidemic proportions in California, a situation that reinforced the need for aggressive government action on the matter. He introduced wildly inflated estimates of the Filipino population in the United States and of the total number of those who were unemployed to inflate the scale of the problem. Garsson suggested that there were as many as 150,000 Filipinos living on the U.S. mainland and 60,000 residing in Los Angeles County alone, figures at odds with the Census Bureau's count of 45,000 total living in the continental United States. He estimated that 80 percent of the Filipinos in the United States were unemployed, a situation that caused severe hardships for the communities in which they resided. Garsson drove this point home by telling the committee about the dire conditions he discovered while investigating a "Filipino colony" in Los Angeles. He described visiting a Filipino home where fifteen or sixteen men lived together in a single room, "sharing beds in shifts of three" and rotating sleepers twenty-four hours a day. These practices, according to Garsson, were typical among Filipinos and posed a possible public-health risk to the communities around them. Other witnesses at the hearings on the Dickstein bill assured committee members that there was widespread support for repatriation among Filipino leaders, who recognized that economic and social competition in the United States had reached a crisis point. Committee members discussed the logistics and costs of a repatriation operation, even though Filipino leaders criticized the bill as a thinly veiled deportation act. Advocates of the Dickstein measure suggested that as many as thirty thousand Filipinos would voluntarily repatriate if their travel was subsidized by the federal government....

Although support for repatriation on the committee was unanimous, HJ 549 was eventually tabled, unable to secure a spot on the legislative calendar. The bill was reintroduced again a few months later, with some minor revisions, as HJ 118. The proposal, however, did not contain a clear provision barring Filipino repatriates from returning to the United States, which became a sticking point for restrictionists, who wanted assurances that there would be no right of return.... On March 6, 1935, the indefatigable Richard Welch sponsored HR 6464, which contained clear-cut language prohibiting the return of Filipinos who had been "deported." Immigration and Naturalization Committee members Martin Dies of Texas and Thomas Jenkins of Ohio applauded Welch for putting together a bill that would "make it impossible for Filipinos to return to the United States." The only weakness of the legislation, according to Dies, was that it made repatriation "voluntary," a problem that allowed Filipinos to stay in the country even though they were no longer welcome. A final amended version of the bill, cosponsored by Hiram Johnson in the Senate, was signed into law on July 10, 1935.

Media observers extolled the virtues of the new policy, suggesting that the mass departure of the islanders was in the best interest of both Americans and Filipinos....

The Filipino Repatriation Act was extended two times through December 31, 1940, in a last-ditch effort to convince Filipinos to leave the country. A mass exodus of Filipinos, however, never materialized. By the end of 1938, *Time* magazine called the repatriation program the "Philippine Flop," characterizing the $237,000 spent on the operation as a disappointment. The magazine speculated that the campaign had failed because the "boys [were] loathe to leave a country, where as a California judge remarked, they boast of enjoying the favors of white girls because they are a very superior grade of lovers." This did not surprise renowned labor journalist Carey McWilliams, who predicted that very few Filipinos would apply for the act since they viewed the Welch bill as a "trick, and not a very clever trick, to get them out of the country" because of their labor militancy and political activism. The program officially ended during the fiscal year 1941, having repatriated 157 Filipinos in 1936, 580 in 1937, 502 in 1938, 392 in 1939, 425 in 1940, and 134 in 1941, for a total of 2,190. These numbers fell far short of the thirty to forty thousand predicted by exclusionists.

Challenging the Construction of Hawai'i as America's Racial Laboratory

MAILE ARVIN

Beginning in the late 1920s, sociology solidified ideas about Hawai'i as a place of racial mixture.... The noted Chicago school of sociology at this time was particularly interested in Hawai'i as its many different races seemed to provide a

From Maile Renee Arvin, "Pacifically Possessed: Scientific Production and Native Hawaiian Critique of the 'Almost White' Polynesian Race" (Ph.D. diss., University of California, San Diego, 2013). Reprinted by permission.

perfect site for modeling their theories about immigration and assimilation. This literature perpetuated viewing Native Hawaiians as largely a race of the past and routinely slotted Native Hawaiians as only a minor segment of Hawai'i's many races. Sociologists were interested in Native Hawaiians only insofar as they made up a piece of Hawai'i's racially patch-worked population and the heralded "neo-Hawaiian," which would be a new, uniquely American, "raceless" race....

Though the sociology of this period largely portrayed Hawai'i as an exceptionally racially harmonious place, there is ample evidence that many people (Native Hawaiian and non-Hawaiian, white and non-white, residents of Hawai'i and residents of the continental United States, academic and laymen) found Hawai'i anything but harmonious. For example, historian Christine Manganaro has demonstrated in her analysis of the sociological interviews of Hawai'i residents produced by graduate student researcher Margaret Lam in the early 1930s that many Hawai'i residents, even or especially those who were themselves in interracial marriages, found Hawai'i to have a great deal of "race prejudice" and generally disapproved of racial mixing. In the popular media of the United States in the early 1930s, images of Hawai'i as a "racial nightmare" were in fact being splashed over countless newspapers and magazines in response to the so-called Massie affair. The Massie affair involved a series of highly publicized court cases originating from the claims of Thalia Massie, the white wife of a naval officer stationed at Pearl Harbor, that she had been assaulted and raped by a group of Native Hawaiian and Asian American men in 1931. When these men failed to be convicted due to lack of evidence, enraged white Navy men engaged in vigilantism. One Japanese American man, Horace Ida, was severely beaten. Further, Massie's husband and mother along with two other Naval officers kidnapped, shot, and killed Joseph Kahahawai—a Native Hawaiian man identified as the "darkest" of the accused. Stopped on their way to dump Kahahawai's body in the ocean, they were caught and arrested. Massie's mother and husband were subsequently convicted of killing Kahahawai, but ultimately, under great pressure from the Navy and the yellow journalism of the U.S. mainland, the governor of Hawai'i commuted their sentences and they served only an hour under arrest—and not in jail but at tea in the governor's office.

The Massie case was widely reported on throughout the United States and the world, shocking readers with depictions of Hawai'i as a terrifying place where "roads go through jungles, and in those remote places bands of degenerate natives lie in wait for white women driving by." Some have argued that the furor over the Massie case and the racial fears brought on by the widespread media coverage of it were even responsible for delaying Hawai'i's entry into the United States as a state [though hearings on Hawai'i's statehood were held in the 1930s, it would not be secured until 1959]. This new image of Hawai'i as a "racial nightmare" was completely at odds with the idyllic, carefree image that local government officials of the Territory of Hawai'i wished to promote. It also flew in the face of social scientists' existing views ... of the Pacific as a benign and controlled "racial laboratory" for human biology. However, instead of destroying the racial laboratory ideal, after the Massie affair such sociological accounts only seemed to gain further importance....

Romanzo Adams was specifically hired by Hawaii Territorial officials to head the University of Hawai'i's studies of race relations, officially titled a "Station for Racial Research," which, beginning in May 1926, was funded by the Rockefeller Foundation. Accordingly, unlike eugenics studies that focused on the Pure and Part Hawaiian almost exclusively, Adams looked to Hawai'i's population as a whole as a model of race relations that had the potential to provide insights into racial problems on the U.S. mainland. Adams's research focused on what he defined as two central aspects of race relations in Hawai'i: first, the so-called Japanese Problem (his focus in the late 1920s) and second, interracial marriage (his focus in the 1930s).

Where sociologists on the U.S. mainland were eager to solve the "Negro Problem," that is, prevalent antiblack attitudes and the failure of black Americans to be integrated into mainstream society, the "Oriental Problem" or, more specifically, the "Japanese Problem," in Hawai'i was defined as anti-Japanese attitudes (those who, before during, and after World War II viewed Japanese as potential spies and traitors to the United States) and the Japanese's inability or unwillingness to assimilate to American norms. Adams's writing sought to answer the Japanese problem by illustrating that Hawai'i's Japanese population was not in fact a barrier to Hawai'i's Americanization. Through analyses of demographic shifts, he emphasized that though Japanese residents of Hawai'i were by far the least likely to intermarry with other races, they would likely follow the example of other Asian groups like the Chinese and eventually intermarry with whites and Native Hawaiians. Thus, Adams's scientific view backed up other nonacademic [accounts] of Hawai'i at this time as, in Honolulu minister Albert Palmer's words, "a bridge between Japan and America." Palmer concluded his 1924 book *The Human Side of Hawaii* thus: "After all that is just what Hawaii means—a human bridge of international good will and understanding between East and West!"

Given the Chicago School's understanding of race relations as primarily about attitudes and feelings, rather than [social] structures, interracial marriage between "East and West" was seen as a key bellwether of lessening racial prejudice. For Adams, Hawai'i's rates of racial intermarriage were exceptionally high relative to the mainland United States, and thus race problems seemed to him practically nonexistent there. Hawai'i's high rates of racial intermarriage also seemed to uniquely prove the achievement of assimilation (according to the Chicago race relations cycle) into American society....

Thus, though Hawai'i was exceptional, like the broader ideology of American exceptionalism, Adams thought Hawai'i should be used as racial laboratory because it promised a universal model for race relations everywhere. In his influential 1937 book *Interracial Marriage in Hawaii*, Adams argued "Hawaii presents an exceptional opportunity for the observation and study of a type of social process [namely, racial amalgamation] that has been going on in many parts of the world for a long time.... Since Europeans and Asiatics began to come to Hawaii there has been sufficient time to permit of many interesting changes...."...

Adams was interested in Native Hawaiians only insofar as they made up a piece of Hawai'i's racially mixed population. He took for granted the findings of eugenics literature that Native Hawaiians were quickly dying out and that all residents of Hawai'i were therefore becoming part of a new mixed race of "Hawaiians" (non-Native, but unmarked as such). In this way, we might say that he could not think beyond the logic of possession through whiteness that had been formulated in the Polynesian Problem and eugenics literature that came before him. This stance was abundantly evident in a 1926 address Adams gave to the Pan-Pacific Research Institution, titled "Hawaii as a Racial Melting Pot." Subsequently published in the Mid-Pacific Magazine, Adams's address explained the import of racial intermarriage in Hawai'i by describing a hypothetical demographic equation:

> Take the 13 Japanese women who married other Caucasians, and if in the next 50 years they have 30 children, it will be more natural for them to marry out than for their parents, and finally you get 1/4 and 1/8 strains and finally the racial boundaries are obscured and within 3 or 4 hundred years people will not know what blood they have in their veins. In fact nearly everyone here will be entitled to go to Kamehameha Schools.
>
> In my own case, I hardly know what combinations I have represented in my ancestry. I found out on a trip to Ohio that I had German, Irish, English, Scotch and Dutch, and many of you are probably the same.

In this quote, we can see that although the racial and ethnic groups that Adams mentions do not include Native Hawaiians, he sees all of these races (and his Pan-Pacific Research Institution audience) as eventually being "entitled to go to Kamehameha Schools...." Kamehameha Schools was set up for Native Hawaiian children (as determined by genealogy, not by blood quantum fractions) and has retained a Native Hawaiian first admission policy. By projecting that in "3 or 4 hundred years people will not know what blood they have in their veins," Adams assumes that everyone will be fairly counted as Native Hawaiian, making Kamehameha Schools open to all. Adams therefore assumed that specific Native Hawaiian Indigenous ties to culture, land, ocean, and sovereignty in Hawai'i would naturally transfer to all settlers of Hawai'i. Although this transfer was ostensibly to be universal, including to Asian immigrants to Hawai'i, Adams's final emphasis of his "German, Irish, English, Scotch and Dutch" roots as a commonality with the audience (his quip that "many of you are probably the same") highlights the fact that white men would hold a particularly important kind of entitlement to Native Hawaiian-ness. In this way, the logic of possession through whiteness is also quite baldly a logic of commensurability—an understanding that everyone would eventually be the same, and racial or ethnic distinctions would cease to matter.

Yet this desired commensurability would benefit white settlers and dispossess Native Hawaiians of their own identities, along with their lands.... [S]ettler colonialism required not only the assimilation of Native Hawaiians into the United States but also relied upon changing the category of "Hawaiian" into something that white Americans who had settled or aspired to settle in Hawai'i would be able to inhabit, perform, and possess.... Thus, the "Hawaiian" was implicitly or explicitly redefined as always, at base, a "Part Hawaiian"; someone who was always part something else too. And though that part something else could be Asian, it was the being part white that really mattered. Because, though ... [the image of Hawai'i as a melting pot] uses Hawai'i to show a unique fulfillment of America's foundational ideals of racial equality and democracy, it also shows that its ideal of multiculturalism was premised on the assimilation of "other" races into the white race.... Indeed, the discourses about racial mixture in Hawai'i were never fixed on the result of an even mix of racial, physical, and moral characteristics. Rather, as Pacific Islands Studies scholar Damon Salesa puts it in the context of racial amalgamation policies in colonial New Zealand:

> A proper amalgamation did not combine two races into a "new" race that was substantially mixed or intermediate; rather the process of amalgamation projected, very baldly, the disappearing of one race into another.... Yet, although the other race would then no longer exist as a race, race itself would still pertain, still visible in individuals.

Thus, if individuals in Hawai'i still demonstrated "threatening" racial characteristics or an affinity for identifying as "Native Hawaiian," this was not sufficient evidence to deny that the category of "Hawaiian" was becoming universal and that Hawai'i overall was becoming truly American. It also allowed a racial hierarchy to implicitly remain even as such multicultural equations seemed to gesture toward the end of racial distinctions altogether....

Adams encouraged a public image of Hawai'i as a racially harmonious place, actively publishing in popular journals and teaching classes not just for university students but the public (especially businessmen) in Honolulu. Even his most academic work, his text *Interracial Marriage in Hawaii*, he understood as important to nonacademic audiences. Manganaro notes that he planned:

> to send *Interracial Marriage in Hawaii* to all plantation managers first; then to principals of all schools, public and private, that had four or more teachers including language schools; territorial officers; members of the University of Hawai'i faculty; members of the Institute of Pacific Relations; universities on the department exchange list; pastors of churches; directors of sugar and pineapple companies; and members of the Hawaii Sugar Planters Association.

Adams's advocacy of Hawai'i as a model of race relations undeniably took on significance beyond academia; then—he saw his research as directly relevant to the economy, projecting that Hawai'i's lack of racial conflict would maintain social stability and encourage the growth of business.

Adams's views may have even influenced Hawai'i's eventual incorporation into the United States as a state. He submitted expert testimony to the first hearing on Hawai'i's statehood in 1935, where he pointedly deflected fears about the "Japanese problem," noting that the Japanese population in Hawai'i was declining. Okamura further notes the legacy of Adams's ideas in the persistent image of the "Hawai'i multicultural model," which first emerged in popular and academic literature of 1980s and continues to exert an influence today. The repetition of tropes about Hawai'i as "the 'ethnic rainbow', 'positive example', and 'melting pot'" in the news media, Okamura argues, has influenced a "countless" audience of people around the world to understand Hawai'i in such simplistic, and erroneous, terms....

[For example,] The U.S. Department of the Interior published a booklet called Hawaii and Its Race Problem in 1932 [in response to the racial fears sparked by the Massie affair of 1931], which sought to reassure the public that "race antagonisms" in the islands were "practically non-existent." This booklet concluded:

> There is much apprehension lest groups in Hawaii based on race should come into political dominance.... It is a part of the beautiful experiment, here in the mid-Pacific, that self-government is to be tried out under conditions and with human material that is new. There is nothing so far to indicate that the experiment will not turn out to be as successful as it is interesting.

The rhetoric of Hawai'i as a racial laboratory or experiment station closely mirrored the sociological work of those like Romanzo Adams and is deployed in this government document to underline the fact that the United States was in charge of all "experimenting" and that the white population of Hawai'i had the racial masses under control.

In sum, ... Hawai'i's enduring image as a place of racial mixture and racial harmony was [first] constructed in the work of sociologists, trained in the Chicago School of Sociology and based at the University of Hawai'i from the late 1920s ... who understood Hawai'i as a racial laboratory.... While such accounts sought to prove Hawai'i's suitability, even destiny, to be American, ... discourses proclaiming the virtues of the coming "neo-Hawaiian-American race" were used to cover the continued existence of Native Hawaiian people and claims to sovereignty.

⊙ FURTHER READING

Baldoz, Rick. *The Third Asiatic Invasion: Migration and Empire in Filipino America, 1898–1946* (2011).

Bulosan, Carlos. *America Is in the Heart: A Personal History* (1943).

Daniels, Roger. *The Politics of Prejudice: The Anti-Japanese Movement in California and the Struggle for Japanese* (1962).

Delgado, Grace. *Making the Chinese Mexican: Global Migration, Localism, and Exclusion in the U.S.-Mexico Borderlands* (2012).

Hirobe, Izumi. *Japanese Pride, American Prejudice: Modifying the Exclusion Clause of the 1924 Immigration Act* (2002).

Kramer, Paul A. *The Blood of Government: Race, Empire, the United States, and the Philippines* (2006).

Ngai, Mae. *Impossible Subjects: Illegal Aliens and the Making of Modern America* (2004).

Okihiro, Gary Y. *Cane Fires: The Anti-Japanese Movement in Hawaii, 1865–1945* (1992).

Salyer, Lucy E. "Baptism by Fire: Race, Military Service, and U.S. Citizenship Policy, 1918–1935," *Journal of American History* 91 (2004): 847–876.

Shah, Nayan. *Contagious Divides: Epidemics and Race in San Francisco's Chinatown* (2001).

Young, Elliott. *Alien Nation: Chinese Migration in the Americas from the Coolie Era through World War II* (2014).

Yu, Henry. *Thinking Orientals: Migration, Contact, and Exoticism in Modern America* (2002).

CHAPTER 7

Americanization and the Second Generation, 1924–1941

The process of becoming American, or Americanization, has been a perennial concern in U.S. society and politics. Scholars, like the general public, have understood Americanization from three different perspectives. First is the conception of the melting pot, which at its most literal connotes the mixing of various peoples and cultures to create an entirely new one—the American. Related to, and often confused with, the melting pot is the idea of Anglo conformity, which has meant that newcomers must give up their cultures and adopt the mainstream culture. Note that one must pay close attention to what is meant by assimilation, because this term can mean either the melting pot or Anglo conformity. A third perspective, cultural pluralism, is best recognized in today's society. It casts the United States as a mosaic of irreducible ethnic, racial, and cultural differences. There are two versions of pluralism: a soft variety celebrates differences as a source of the nation's strength, while a hard one views such differences as the basis for persistent conflict, discrimination, and inequality.

An important interest among historians has been how Asian Americans have engaged the issues of Americanization. How could the immigrants prove to the white majority that they could become good Americans? As the documents and essays in Chapter 6 show, the answer to this question continued to evade Asian Americans into the 1920s. At this time, a profound demographic change—the coming of age of the immigrants' children, the U.S.-born second generation—was under way. This change would come to have major historical significance. As U.S. citizens, the second generation was legally immune from policies like exclusion or land laws that discriminated against immigrants. Another crucial difference from their parents was that the second generation usually had no cultural or linguistic handicaps to evoke misunderstanding and mistrust between themselves and whites. The foundation of their Americanization was public schooling, in which the second generation was taught to think and behave like Americans often by white teachers who were convinced they were good citizens.

The Americanization of the second generation did not shield its members from racial prejudice. Many abhorred the fact that the general society saw them as no more trustworthy than their immigrant parents. But it was no coincidence that the second generation played a decisive role in dismantling anti-Asian racism after the start of World War II. The roots of this revolution in race relations reached back to the 1920s and 1930s.

DOCUMENTS

Documents 1 to 4 reveal the experiences and perspectives of various Asian American women. Document 1 is an excerpt of a transcribed interview conducted as part of a scholarly study in 1924 researching the conditions of race relations on the West Coast. Here the American-born Flora Belle Jan projects an image of iconoclastic youth rebellion that was popular at the time. While rejecting her parents' Chinese traditions, she is also rejected by mainstream white society. Document 2 excerpts an essay extoling the virtue of racial tolerance and cultural pluralism written by the celebrated novelist Pearl S. Buck, a white American who was born and raised in China and thus identified as a particular type of Chinese American. Buck's essay was written amid growing international sympathy for China. The United States opposed Japan's growing imperial conquests in China, and although the United States was technically neutral at the outbreak of the second Sino-Japanese War in 1937, President Franklin Roosevelt and the mainstream press supported the Chinese. Another source of sympathy for China came from the success of Buck's novel, *The Good Earth*, which won the Nobel Prize in Literature in 1938. This novel offers a heroic depiction of Chinese peasants that contradicted the then-popular stereotypes of Chinese coolies in the United States.

The 1930s was a decade in which Filipino and Korean immigrants were putting down roots in the United States. In Document 3, Connie Tirona reflects wistfully upon her childhood in close-knit Filipino immigrant communities, while also addressing the race and class prejudice she experienced growing up in the San Francisco Bay area. In Document 4, the American-born Dora Yum Kim, a Korean American, looks back on her life growing up among Chinese and Japanese Americans. Unlike her Korean immigrant parents, Kim mixed easily with other Asian Americans; international conflicts in Asia did not prevent her from being friends with either Japanese or Chinese Americans. She had a harder time, however, gaining the trust of white classmates.

Documents 5 to 7 focus on the Americanization of Japanese Americans. Document 5 is a letter to the editor of the *New York Times* in which Sidney Gulick, a leading opponent of Japanese exclusion, supports the naturalization of Asian immigrants who served in the U.S. military during World War I. These men were promised citizenship upon their enlistment, but after the war they were denied it. The government finally made good on its promise of citizenship through an act of Congress in 1935, and Document 6 is an excerpt of congressional testimony related to this act. Here the leading proponent of granting citizenship to the immigrant veterans, Tokutaro Slocum, underscores his own Americanization as a Japanese who was raised by a white American family. Finally, Document 7 is an editorial in a Japanese American newspaper that bemoans the lack of job opportunities for second-generation Japanese Americans or Nisei, as they were called. Nisei were, by far, the largest cohort of American-born Asians during the period, and they benefitted from working in the agricultural businesses of Japanese immigrants. But they were often frustrated because their schooling (some had college degrees) prepared them for work in the mainstream economy that was denied to them because they were not white.

1. American–Born Chinese Woman Longs for Unconventionality and Freedom, 1924

Interview with Flora Belle Jan, Daughter of Proprietor of the "Yet Far Low," Chop Suey Restaurant, Tulare St., and China Alley, Fresno

Miss Jan is a graduate of the Fresno High School and has taken two years in the Fresno State College. She is a leader among the native born Chinese, very much interested in writing, dramatics and social life.

She entertained me in her father's upstairs restaurant for about an hour. My first approach was through Miss Purcell, but was unsuccessful and I finally saw her by presenting my card directly.

She said, "Would you like to hear something about my life? I will tell you if you are interested. I was born here in Fresno Chinatown and attended the city schools and graduated from the High School and have had two years in the State College. When I was a little girl, I grew to dislike the conventionality and rules of Chinese life. The superstitions and customs seemed ridiculous to me. My parents have wanted me to grow up a good Chinese girl, but I am an American and I can't accept all the old Chinese ways and ideas. A few years ago when my Mother took me to worship at the shrine of my ancestor and offer a plate of food, I decided it was time to stop this foolish custom. So I got up and slammed down the rice in front of the idol and said, "So long Old Top, I don't believe in you anyway." My mother didn't like it a little bit.

As I grew older I came to see that American life is also full of conventionality and foolish customs and it has become a fad of mine to study these things and to write about them. I long for unconventionality and freedom from all these customs and ideals that make people do such ridiculous and insincere things.

I have written a good deal in local papers about Chinese life. Much of this had displeased the Chinese people of Fresno. My article on "The Sheiks of Chinatown," (a description of the young sports of China Alley), was a takeoff on certain well known native born Chinese. It made a terrible fuss in Chinatown. I have had three blackmailing letters sent me for writing so openly about Chinese life. One of the Chinese students from North China became very angry at my article on the Sheiks and wrote me a very long, fat letter attacking me and

From "Interview with Flora Belle Jan…," June 5, 1924, Box 28, Folder 225, Survey of Race Relations Collection, Hoover Institution on War, Revolution, and Peace. Stanford University, Stanford, CA.

picking to pieces everything that I had said. He thought that I was trying to disgrace China, which I distinctly was not, but only trying to have a little fun with my Chinese friends. All Chinatown got very excited and two of the boys, one from North China and the other from South China fought a kind of a duel over it. North boy said that I had disgraced China. South boy said No, that we should [not] be too proud to let a little dust like this hurt us. A delegation of Chinese students met me at college and I challenged them to show what I had said that disgraced anybody or anything. They put on their spectacles and after ten minutes could not find anything. I said, "Ta ta, Kiddos, when you find any disgrace you just put me wise. I can't wait all day."

It is very funny to watch the snobbishness of the girls at the state college. I listen to the Sorority girls talk over possible candidates to membership in their sorority. "It runs something like this, "Girls, what do you suppose, Jane Smith whom we've been rushing, is impossible. We've just found out that her father once drove a delivery wagon. They live in such a nice house and she wears such pretty clothes, who would have dreamed it. My, she's such a nice girl, it is really too bad." I happen to know that some of these very girls have families where the men are working at shop work and day labor and where the mothers do their own work. They judge people entirely by the clothes they wear and the amount of money they spend, and they get awfully stung in this way sometimes. Of course being a Chinese girl, I'm not eligible to membership in a sorority, but some of the girls are awfully good to me.

I have written a sketch of American girls, called, "Old Mother Grundy and her brood of unbaptized nuns," which takes off some of the characteristics of the modern flapper in American society.

At the Community House last week our Chinese Club gave a play called, "Miss Flapper Vampire," that I wrote. I was the leading character and about five young men played in it with me. There was a large audience of Americans. Afterward we danced and the American girls danced with the Chinese boys and I danced with American young men.

2. Author Pearl Buck Identifies as Immigrant from China, 1937

I HAD LIVED ALL MY LIFE AN AMERICAN AWAY FROM America. Then I returned, a sort of immigrant among immigrants, except that I came to my native land. But it was as new to me as though I came from Sweden or from Italy or Greece. I knew almost as little what to expect before I landed.

But we all have pictures, we immigrants, of what the America is to which we come. They must be pleasant pictures, or we would not have come. People do not easily leave all they know unless they hope for something much better. Of course I suppose most of us hoped for a better chance for a living, for more

From Pearl S. Buck, "On Discovering America," *Survey Graphic* 26, no. 6 (June 1937). Reprinted by permission.

money, for more education, for more room. Some of us came for freedom, freedom to think as we liked, to be ourselves unhampered by family and traditions. Some of us, like me, came because we wanted to come home, never having known what it was like to be at home, having lived always among an alien race, spoken a foreign tongue and walked the streets and roads of every day as a foreigner. We have all come to the America we each thought we saw.

I wish I could find out what other people have found in America. But I only know what I have found. I came from China, a land of long homogeneity and of unity, except perhaps for that least important of all, political unity. The Chinese are of the same general race. They have had an unbroken history of thousands of years. Their religions are the same, organized into three great types, mutually tolerant, non-evangelical, and mellowed by long human experience to a philosophy of humanism. Social customs are firmly fixed and such impacts as come from modern usages come against a solid whole which they can penetrate only gradually and therefore without great upset. Even the language is not really diversified, because three fourths of the people speak one language, or some form of it. Out of this great security of long established unit I came to America.

Now I had my picture of America, too. It was made up of visual images of my mother's much loved country home, of which she told me many stories, of a land of great plenty and ease, from which came money for the poor Chinese, because all Americans were rich and Christian. It would not have occurred to me that there were illiterate Americans, or unwashed or poor Americans, or criminals. As I grew older and understood better inevitable human nature this picture was modified and reason did indeed compel me to understand that heaven existed nowhere. But still something of this early picture persisted.

I BELIEVED, FOR INSTANCE, THAT IN LEAVING CHINA I WAS leaving forever the sight of hungry people whom I was powerless to feed. I thought I was leaving behind the sight of wasting floods and dried and sun-baked, treeless lands, swept by dusty winds. I thought I was coming to a country which had organized itself into economic plenty and moral clarity. I had heard all my life that America was rich, and I did not think of these riches as being selfishly gained or used. Money was poured generously out of America into China for famine relief, for Christian propaganda, for many and endless causes. Americans, then, though they were rich were generous, interested in a world culture, international-minded. I longed to meet my countrymen, whose idealism seemed almost fantastic to the materialistic philosophy of China.

When I first came here, then, I endeavored to find this recognizable country of my own. I looked first for Americans. But I could not find them. It seemed to me the country was full of foreigners. I found delightful people, for I came home under the best possible circumstances, having done a sort of work of my own which somehow made me friends. The people were wonderfully kind to me, but they seemed to me like English people, or Europeans. I kept thinking, "Where are the Americans?" It was very puzzling. I bored everybody by asking continually, "Where does one find the real Americans? What would *you* consider the typical American?" To my bewilderment everyone replied the same way—that is, *he* was American, his ancestors had come over in the Mayflower or before the Revolution or before the Civil War or something, and *he* was the typical American if there ever was one....

I came to see that these true Americans I had been looking for did not exist at all, and there are no typical Americans. I have come indeed to feel that if there is a typical American it is the one least typical of anyone except himself. The one hundred percent American, for instance, is one hundred percent nothing except himself, and represents nothing else....

And everywhere I was hurt and confounded by the amazing hatred among all these Americans for each other. I have heard such hatred for black Americans from white Americans, such venomous sullen hatred for white Americans from black Americans, that in another country I would have been afraid of immediate race war. And the hatred burns like wildfire in a hundred different directions. There is the hatred of the Jew and the Christian, of the native-born and the foreign-born, of the Protestant and the Catholic, and these are only a few of the greater hatreds. It is true also that combating each separate hatred, like a leash upon a beast, is an organization of people working for peace between any two opposing groups. But it is a question whether the leash is strong enough for the beast. At least, a sensitive mind at first cannot but be frightened and oppressed by the fearful prejudices of race and creed which possess the feelings of the average American.

Thus afraid and oppressed, therefore, I began to delve into these dark feelings which few Americans, it seems to me, are willing to face and acknowledge. For feeling is the basis of these hatreds which take such strange and violent open expressions as lynching, as unjust treatment of aliens, as inhuman deportation laws. With my Chinese training, I cannot get excited over a particular individual or over a particular bill in Congress, but I can get deeply excited over why people should want to commit murder by lynching, or why people should want to deport, wholesale, persons who are honorably fulfilling their places as human beings in our country, if not as citizens. The reasons why we hate each other are very important indeed, and there is no cure for individual injustices until those causes are clearly understood.

From whence, then, do all these diversities of hatred come in our country.... Why then, do we Americans so hate each other and especially so hate those whom we consider aliens among us? I will not here dwell upon my complete astonishment in discovering that we, who are so generous to foreigners in their own lands, who rush relief to Belgium and Czechoslovakia and China and Japan, are so ruthless to the same foreigners who find themselves aliens in our own country. It must have bewildered others than I. A hundred reasons are given me for it. I am told by many that the chief one is economic. But I do not believe people hate each other in groups fundamentally because of economic conditions. Poverty and stress merely augment already existing hatreds. What I want to know is, why do the hatreds exist at all, and why do they burn with such fearful heat in America, still the richest country in the world?

I HAVE GONE BACK IN MY SEARCH, "CHINESE FASHION," TO our beginnings. I find we are all immigrants, we Americans. Not one of us is really native in any profound sense. Everybody in the United States, except the Indians, is now or was once, foreign-born. I find it ridiculous to hear a man whose great-grandfather came to this country look down on a man who comes in now, and call him "alien." For what is a hundred or two hundred years in the life of a nation? The nation is and will be for centuries to come made up of the foreign-born, that is, people from all countries. And looking at all these people, I discover in them all the diversities of the world in race, in culture, in religion. They have only one thing in common with which to become Americans. They are all restless....

BUT I KNOW VERY WELL THAT WHEN I THINK OF OUR America a thousand years from now and five thousand years from now that I am thinking Chinese and not American. The Chinese thinks instinctively in terms of centuries and he sees himself as a particle in time. But the American stretches his imagination to pain if he thinks two generations ahead to the grandchild that is an actuality or a possibility. That is a trait of the restless. We cannot and will not wait, though the truth remains that the only true view is the long one, and the present will not be right if it is an end in itself instead of being as well a foundation for the future. We Americans, that is, cannot and will not think of our nation as a whole in time and space and so choose nationally, though perhaps at immediate inconvenience, what permanent stuffs we want in our making. We demand to know what we shall do now, in our momentary situation, with "aliens," as we call them, in our jobs, on our relief rolls, and sending good American money out of the country.

Unfortunately for me as an American, I cannot froth about any of these things. I see these "aliens" first as human beings, and I observe that many, indeed most of them, are honest and industrious, or as honest and industrious as the upstarts who dare, at this early date in our history, to call themselves, "the Americans." Citizens or not, I cannot see why these good people should be deported. We need honesty and industry. No nation can have too many people with these qualities. I cannot see why they should not be relieved if they starve, nor why they should not send money back to Italy or anywhere else. I should think the more money circulates the better. The richer the Italians are, the better for American markets. And in return for this money the people have given good hard labor on roads and bridges and buildings and the money is theirs when they have earned it, my American spirit tells me. And America is still the richest country in the world and likely to remain so.

Nor can I get excited over the differences between us. Hatreds, yes—they are stupid and wrong. It is senseless to hate a man because he is different, and the fault is in our education which has not made us enough above the beast to see this. For though men hate each other when they come here, they should be taught as the basis for American citizenship that here we may differ each from the other, and that diversity is our strength and our nature, and each man is to believe what he feels true, and our one common belief is this.

3. American–Born Filipina Connie Tirona Recalls Growing Up in Immigrant Community, 1930s and 1940s (1995)

Childhood Memories of the Manongs

When my parents landed on Angel Island in San Francisco Bay, their friends were in the Delano area working in the grape fields. My parents did not know where Delano was. A Japanese grower from Stanford decided to hire them. (Part of Stanford at one time was all a nursery owned by this Japanese farmer.) So my parents had a place to stay.

But their friends from Delano contacted them again and asked them to join them there, where they could earn more money. So my parents decided to move to Delano to be near their *kababayans* (countrymen) from Hawaii. My father said there was a lot of Bombays (East Indians) but not as many Mexicans in Delano. However, the Bombays were moving on to El Centro. My parents stayed in that area for quite some time, until I was born, and then my father decided to move the family back to northern California.

I was born in 1929 in Selma, which is right next to Fresno. I remember many Filipinos as I was growing up. They still had their cockfights. The cockpit arena was really the gathering place for all the Filipinos. Even if some didn't like to bet on the cockfights, everybody was there. I remember the women having little stalls, with their little tables filled with individual special delicacies they had cooked. And of course, the men who were single at the time were so happy to have Filipino food because they lived in these barracks, while the families lived in cottages and could prepare their own food. These cottages were really dilapidated shacks, but they were always kept neat and immaculate.

Even when they were following the seasonal crops, all of them—there were three families in my parents' group—would pitch in to buy a car so they could travel from camp to camp. And we would all go in that car, and I can remember sometimes there was not enough work for everyone, and the ones who got the work would buy the groceries. And everyone would pitch in to get a small place where we all lived together. It was somewhat crowded, but we always kept it clean. Everybody would cook and help.

I can remember one time, they were down to their last fifty cents. They were going to another place where there was an opening for pruning grapes. So, the other two families would stay behind in the place that they had rented, while the rest would go seek jobs. Well, they only had fifty cents. Two chickens crossed the road. Let me tell you, those chickens did not stay alive for very long. They plucked them and cleaned them that night. They gathered vegetables from their garden; they always had a garden wherever they went. They threw everything in a pot. Those two chickens fed three families that night. Soon they were able to get jobs again. Not one of us ever went hungry.

From Connie Tirona, "Sometimes, I Am Not Sure What It Means to Be an American," in *Filipino American Lives*, ed. Yen Le Espiritu (Philadelphia, PA: Temple University Press, 1995), 66–71. Reprinted by permission.

When I was about four or five years old, my parents moved up to Oakland. With his experience working in the shipyard in Hawaii, my father eventually got a job at a shipyard. So he was able to leave the agricultural job environment. He was a rigger and retired from the Mare Island shipyard after twenty years. And guess what? He went back to work as a foreman in the fields again. I think he was one of the first who wanted to organize a union against the growers. He was always fighting for the rights of workers.

In the 1930s, most of the *manongs* were still on the farms. The *manongs* were those men who came here from Hawaii without any families. They were bachelors. And they were the best dancers, the best dressers. There was just something very suave about them....

There were about thirty *manongs* in the labor camps in the Sacramento—San Joaquin area that we would visit. Sometimes the *manongs* would come and visit us. They were so homesick for family. They always looked up to my father because he had a "government job" in the shipyard. We went to see them almost every week or every other week. My mother would bake all her delicacies all week long for such visits, and the *manongs* enjoyed eating them.

It was so beautiful there when we visited them. They built what looked like a Japanese bathhouse. They installed a huge metal tub with hot coals underneath to warm the water. Of course, you had to bathe outside first. That was the biggest treat! And the *manongs* would fix up their rooms immaculately. They scrubbed their place because "the families were coming!" They picked fresh corn and cooked good, wholesome food. Their big thing was fishing in the delta's rivers. We would go up there and fish, and they would be roasting pigs.

After eating they would play guitars and mandolins, and we, as little children of the families, would sing and dance. The *manongs* liked to hear the little kids sing. They had a small makeshift stage for us, and we would go up there with our curly hair and cute little dresses. And they would throw coins at us. It was the biggest thing for them. You could just see tears of joy on their faces. They would come up and hug us. And I was thinking, "Gosh! Just a little joy that we brought to them." But they were so happy.

I especially remember when we sang the Visayan songs. You could see the tears on the faces of those grown men. Usually, Filipino men are not like that. I don't think Asian men really show their feelings. I remember my younger sister had a beautiful soprano voice, and she would sing this one Visayan song that said something about how hard life was in a strange land. It was like a love song. As they listened to her song, tears would form and slowly flow from their eyes. They would drink their wine and cry softly. They would say to my parents, "Thank you for teaching your daughter to sing that song."

Soon it was time for us to go to bed. As I was drifting off to sleep, I could hear them laughing as they started to sing nostalgic songs from the Philippines. Lying on a small cot, it just lulled me to sleep. The next morning, we would go fishing again and do the same thing. Breakfast was prepared and served. We would leave for home on Sunday evening. After such weekends, the *manongs* prepared for another grueling week of hard work.

The *manongs* bought me my first bike. They wanted to have snapshots taken so they could send them back to their families in the Philippines. When they received mail from the Philippines, they would ask me to read it to them. Some of them did not read well. Their families probably had someone write the letters in English for them. One of the letters said, "Thank you for the picture of your adopted daughter with the bicycle you got her. Thank you for the money that you sent." And I would end up writing back to them. The *manongs* would keep the mail they received until it became so frayed and torn because of so many readings. You could tell that they read it at night when loneliness overcame them.

I wish for those days again. If I could relive one day in the past, I would love to see them again.

Growing up in the 1930s and 1940s

At this time, Filipinos were experiencing much prejudice and discrimination. We could not buy homes in certain areas. My parents bought a home in Vallejo on the other side of town by the waterfront, where all of the people of color lived. We would take walks on Saturday nights to pass the time away. We could not afford anything else. We just wanted to see people. We could see all the Filipinos all dressed up with no place to go, except the dance halls. My mother would say, "No, no! We don't go this way," as if I didn't know what was down there.

Where we lived there was one certain block that you could go up to and feel comfortable. You could go to this one theater, and that was all right because that was where all the people of color would go. But if you went beyond to the next block, people would stare at you. They would look at you when you went into a department store. My father would say to us, "Well, we don't have to go there. Things are so expensive up there anyway."

Being foolhardy, I told my sister, "Well, I am going up there." She told, me that I should not. When I asked her why, she told me what had happened to her. She had gone into a department store because it fascinated her. The manager told her she did not belong in there and to get out. She told the manager she was just looking around and was not doing anything wrong.

I guess that when you are a child and curious, you would do anything. Since I could not go into that department store, I remembered that there was a Sees candy store in the same block. So I went there to buy a piece of candy. The lady in the store asked if I had any money. When I showed her my money and pointed to the piece of chocolate candy I wanted, I remember her taking double pieces of paper so she wouldn't touch my hands. Being the child that I was, I purposely dropped the money on the floor. She had to come around the counter to pick it up. I was about eight at the time.

Then I decided I would be more adventurous, so I went down to another block and into another department store. Again, I was kicked out. Then I went into a Chinese-owned store, and they welcomed me with open arms. They asked me what I was doing at that end of town. I told them I was just curious and wanted to find out what it was like, since we were told that we could not go there.

Of course, I got a spanking afterward because I disobeyed my parents. My father sat me down and asked, "Well, what did you learn?" I replied, "Everything you said was true, Papa." He said, "I just wanted you to know that you can do these things. You can go anywhere; it's just that you may not be treated as good as other people. So you have to learn how to respond and react in that situation." I told him about dropping the money on the floor in the candy store, and he laughed.

I went to a Catholic school. The reason we were able to attend this school was because the sisters said that we only had to pay so much. Our home was five miles away from the school I attended. But that was all right, since I had many friends that I picked up on my way to school. I can remember walking to elementary school and being taunted at times.

My sister and I were the only ones of color in the school. But that never bothered me because I thought I could play just as well as anyone could, and I was equally as bright as the other students, if not brighter. I used to bring rice and fish to school for lunch because I love to eat both. It was a great meal for me. The little girls would not sit by me, and I wondered why, because their lunch was not as good as mine. The nuns would come over and say, "They don't understand."

In high school, some of my friends were Greeks and Italians. They were white people but never thought about color. The only problem that I had was when they had a school dance. They did not allow people of color to attend. My friend, who was the captain of the basketball team, invited me. I told him I could not go, and he said he would not go either. All my friends said they would not go also, but I told them it was the rule and rules are not made to be broken.

4. American-Born Korean Dora Yum Kim Recalls Growing Up in Chinatown, 1920s–1940s (1999)

I started going to school at Lincoln Grammar School in Oakland. Then we moved back to San Francisco when I was in second grade, where I started going to the Jean Parker School. When I started going to school, my mother told us that she had tried to take English lessons. She had gone to the ESL classes they had at a Chinese church located a block down from where we lived. But she said it just wouldn't go into her head, and so, … I knew I was on my own. I ended up translating for my mother…. I don't remember how old I was, but I think by the time I was in second or third grade I was writing notes for my mother excusing me from school when I and, later, my brothers were sick.

When I was in grammar school, my mother had two Korean friends who spoke good English. And this one woman was just beautiful. This family

From "Coming of Age" in *Doing What Had to Be Done: The Life Narrative of Dora Yum Kim* by Soo-Young Chin (Philadelphia: Temple University Press, 1999). Reprinted by permission.

owned a cleaning shop, and she sewed, so she dressed up her four daughters just beautifully. And her English … I think I used to envy the girls because their mothers would come to the PTA meetings and talk with the teachers. My mother couldn't do that. She was so busy at the business that she probably couldn't have come anyway. But even if she did come, she couldn't communicate with anybody. In fact, most of the parents from Chinatown couldn't speak English and were fully engaged in minding their businesses. And I remember envying these girls because their mothers spoke English. When I was older, I learned that they spoke such good English because they were raised in Christian orphanages in Korea. But I didn't know that as a child. All I felt was the envy....

What did going to school teach you about where you fit in America?

Going to school was a real eye-opener. When I was young, before I went to school, I never thought about what I was or anything like that. But when I started going to school in Oakland, I realized I was different from most of the other kids at school—I was Oriental. But they never taught us about Orientals in America. I suppose by the time I was in second grade I already knew not to expect that. But what they did teach us about was China and Japan. I came to realize that there was no mention of Korea in geography or history. I couldn't find out anything about my background. So as a Korean I was invisible outside the small Chinatown Korean community. At that time the Koreans in the area were so actively involved in events in Korea, yet there was no mention of it in school.

I was really curious about my heritage, so I started cutting out anything I read in newspapers or magazines that had anything to do with Korea. These articles are where I learned how to talk about Korea and being Korean. I recall one picture of two Korean girls standing, instead of sitting, on a seesaw. I showed it to my mother, and she said, "I used to be real good at this. I could jump really high." …

I'm confused. Why did you rely on newspaper and magazine articles? I thought you said that your parents taught you about Korean heritage.

My parents did teach us about Korea. I think they did a pretty good job of it. When I was growing up, I wanted to visit Korea because I felt proud to be Korean. But I wasn't quite sure what being Korean meant because we were different from our parents. Our parents' ideas of being Korean had to do with their experiences growing up and living in Korea. But we American-born Koreans didn't have that experience; all we had was secondhand information about it. Since I am Korean and not Chinese or Japanese, I found myself having to explain what I was at a young age. When I was in grammar school, it was hard for me to explain where Korea was and what the people were like. The articles and clippings I saved in my scrapbook helped me explain these things in English to my classmates.

There are other differences between my parents' perspectives and mine. They were anti-Japanese because of the situation at home, but for the children it was different. It's different to be American. You know that your parents hate the Japanese, and that it's a sore point with them, but if your own experience doesn't support the hatred, it's all hearsay. Your parents tell you that in Japan the Japanese hate the Koreans and they still fingerprint them even though they have Japanese names and all that. But within the community of people we knew, we had a Japanese doctor, Dr. Clifford Uyeda, who went to Japan to try to fight against that. It didn't do any good, but as Americans we have different feelings than we're supposed to have. You can't tell what people believe based on appearance.

I also had close Japanese girlfriends. But as far as having Japanese friends, I was restricted. I couldn't bring a Japanese friend home. And I understood, and I just didn't bring them home. But I associated with lots of Japanese people.

I know you can read and write Korean. When did you learn that?

By the time I was in second grade, I could read and write Korean even though I couldn't understand everything I read. I don't actually remember learning to read and write, but I think my parents must have initially taught me. You know, from 1924 to 1965, when immigration laws were relaxed, no Koreans could come over except missionaries or students. The missionaries or students who did come over didn't have any money. So when they came to the restaurant, my parents felt so sorry for them and fed them. Anyway, I guess my dad must've made a deal with them. "Hey I'll feed you free if you'll teach my children Korean." So that's where I got some additional training in Korean. A few of them did come by to say hello after they got their Ph.D.'s.

I also remember going to Korean school with other Korean children. There were only about half a dozen kids of school age at any given time since there were no more than half a dozen total families here. I used to think that it was pretty terrible that the children would always cut classes. You would think that since we knew each other and their families they wouldn't just cut classes like that.... We had what they call *kuko hakyo* [Korean language school] at the church. The class was actually an organized tutorial. We tried to have that during summer vacations and other breaks. I don't remember studying very hard, but I remember all my Korean. In fact, even now I run into people who used to teach there. Not so long ago I ran into this man, and when we were introduced to each other, this guy says, "I taught her Korean." I remember reciting *kakya kokyo koekyoe ku kyu keu ki* [literally, the manner in which children recite the vowels with the first consonant (k/g) of the Korean alphabet] and all the other basics. I'm glad it stuck with me because I can read the Korean paper now and get the gist of it.

Can you tell me more about going to school?

In Chinatown we all went to the same grammar school, Jean Parker, school. It was on Broadway. We had the same teachers. I remember all the old maid teachers: Miss

Miller, the principal, Miss Guinasso, Miss Crowley, and all the other Misses. They were all old maid teachers in those days. We saw them as rather mean women who were strict and meted out punishment when you were bad. If you did something really bad, you were sent to Miss Miller. And we thought she was really mean! She would ask you to put out your hand and hit you with a ruler.

Actually, they were all nice when I think about it now. There was this Italian girl and myself who were Miss Valsangiacomo's pets. We used to clean up after school and we used to get a nickel and we all looked forward to that just for that nickel. It was amazing how much that nickel bought in those days. We used to run to a candy store called Splendid's, where you got five of this for a penny, five of that for a penny, and for a nickel you got a whole bunch of candy. Those were fun days.

At the Jean Parker school one student was always chosen to be captain of the traffic patrol they had at school, and one year my brother George was chosen to be the captain. He was the first Asian captain ever. You know, things like that are important. So many people today say, "What's so big about that?" It was a big deal. At that time they didn't hire Orientals even if you were born here, and our parents couldn't even buy property. Even in the schools, honors like valedictorian, which are supposed to go to the top student, weren't given to Asians. If you were an Oriental, you couldn't be a top student at that time. Forget it. Valedictorian? Are you kidding?

The Jean Parker school was the only school the kids from Chinatown could go to, and despite the limitations we faced as Oriental children, we had good teachers. When my three older children were in grammar school, they had all my teachers. Can you imagine? By then some of the teachers had gotten married, but they still remembered me. They taught my three kids before we moved out of Chinatown.

What did you do after school and weekends other than work?

Growing up in Chinatown, most of my girlfriends were Chinese, and they had to go to Chinese school after school. All the Chinese kids went to the Hip Wo school after school. So there wasn't really time to play with them. I have wondered if it's because they had to go to Chinese school every day that many of the Chinese who were born here still had accents. I actually think it's because the Chinese kids went to Chinese school that many of them really didn't have much time to study for American school.

In terms of the Korean girls, there were very few, and I was the youngest of the girls around my age. Often they wouldn't bother with me because I was younger than they were. So I didn't play with them much either. There were just a few girls who were younger, but they were much too young for me to play with.

So when I was growing up, I lived in the library. None of my girlfriends really used the library because they didn't have the time. But I would sometimes go twice a day. I'd read one book, bring it back, bring another book home. I was drawn to books. I enjoyed reading about other people's lives because I would get so absorbed when I read that I lived the parts. I still do. I remember being Jo in

Louisa May Alcott's *Little Women*. Maybe it was because there was nothing else to do in Chinatown in those days. The library was right down on Powell Street, where it still is. I used to like Nancy Drew books, the whole set, then the Five Peppers. I remember reading all of those. That's what I did after school when I didn't go down to my parents' restaurant ...

During high school ... [m]y social life was affected by discrimination. When I was at Girls' High School, there were dances. The girls used to be invited to dances at all boys' high schools. So my Chinese girlfriend and I decided to attend one of these dances just to see what it would be like. We talked about the fact that nobody was going to ask us to dance, but we decided to go just to see. Sure enough, every white girl was asked to dance, but this girl and I were never asked.

I didn't feel inferior or anything like that. I knew that not being asked to dance was part of discrimination and that it was a learned thing. And I knew that all those white boys were not going to have anything to do with Asians. I mean, my girlfriend and I were disgusted. I'm really glad I went with my girlfriend because imagine how I would have felt if I had gone there alone as the only Asian girl, being ostracized like that. It also could have been worse if we didn't know that we would be hurt. But we knew. We just went to see what it would be like anyway. And it hurt anyway. Back then I didn't think too long on being hurt. I thought it was just a part of life. We knew that we were Asians, and we couldn't do the things Caucasians did. We accepted that fact. And we were sheltered from the worst of the discrimination in Chinatown. But now I often think about these kinds of incidents that we had growing up when I read about the different effects of discrimination. When you grow up with it, it stays with you.

I didn't go to any more Girls' School functions. Instead, we went to the Chinese dances every Saturday night. I used to go around with a Chinese girl. All the high schools like Galileo High School, George Washington High School, Lowell High School, Commerce High School, Balboa High School, Polytechnic [a couple of those are no longer in existence] had a Chinese club with all Chinese members. And each week one club would give a dance with a live band. They, Chinatown, had a good band that played at the dances, and everybody [all the Asian teenagers] would look forward to that. It was mostly Chinese, and all the Koreans went, what few there were. Then toward the end of high school all the Japanese started to come because they didn't have anything like that. I would dance with any of the boys who would ask me—Chinese, Korean, Japanese.

5. Activist Supports Naturalization of Asian Veterans of World War I, 1925

On May 25, the United States Supreme Court handed down a judgment to the effect that Japanese who volunteered and served in the American Army during the World War are not entitled to the privileges of immediate citizenship on honorable discharge granted to other aliens under similar conditions.

From Sidney L. Gulick, "Men Without a Country," *New York Times*, July 12, 1925.

An act of Congress, it seems, provided (May 9, 1918) that "any alien serving in the military or naval service of the United States during the time this country is engaged in the present war may file his petition for naturalization without making the preliminary declaration of intention and without proof of the required five years' residence within the United States."

This act was generally understood to be all-inclusive, free from any trace of race discrimination. On the basis of this law many thousands of aliens who had served in our armies secured citizenship papers from the appropriate courts. Among these were a few hundred Japanese.

The Court now declares that it was not the intention of Congress to extend these special privileges of naturalization to any except "free white persons" and persons of "African nativity" and "African descent" and that, therefore, all soldiers of other races serving in our army who have become American citizens have done so illegally. It follows that they are now to be deprived of this citizenship.

The Chief Justice dissented from the decision, but it is now the policy of our land to say that, though a Japanese or Chinese [or person from India] may serve in our army and may even give his life in support of our Constitution and our flag, he is not worthy to be an American citizen.

This surely is a reductio ad absurdam of the law passed by Congress. Reactions are beginning to come from Japan. The Yamato of June 2, 1925, discussing America's Immigration law, declares, as translated by the Japan Advertiser:

"As long as America assumes such an insolent attitude toward this country, the outbreak of war may be beyond our control. Our relations will be gravely jeopardized. The United States deceived the Japanese who joined the expeditionary forces and unjustly deprived them of the citizenship she once willingly granted them." ...

The seriousness of the situation is increased by the fact that these Japanese who became American citizens in so doing renounced allegiance to their former Government. What, it may be asked, is their status when their American citizenship is taken away? Will the Japanese Government accept them back again? Can she in good face receive back a man who has renounced allegiance and does not voluntarily return to it?

Should not Congress pass a law covering such cases—where citizenship was both given and taken in good faith? Should the judgment of the Supreme Court be in effect retroactive?

6. Japanese Immigrant Veteran Argues for U.S. Citizenship, 1935

Mr. SLOCUM: Honorable Mr. Chairman and honorable members of the committee, I come to you to appeal in behalf of oriental veterans, who served honorably during the late war in the American

From Tokutaro Slocum, *House Immigration and Naturalization Committee*, Oriental Veterans (Washington, D.C.: U.S. Government Printing Office, 1935).

forces, for the recognition of the certificates of naturalization which were granted to us.

I do not know, sir, that there is much more that I could say other than what has already been said by those that are in favor of the appeal that I am making. I appeal to you, members of the committee, to kindly consider this in a favorable light. The less I say the better, but I certainly will be grateful and I will do my very best to justify your faith in us.

The CHAIRMAN: Do all of these veterans speak English as well as you?

Mr. SLOCUM: Most of them speak English, sir. Perhaps I do not speak very good English. I am from North Dakota. [Laughter.] I think we try to put the spirit of sincerity in our language instead of correct English, but we mean well and we certainly would like to get citizenship, and we certainly appreciate it if you vote on this favorably.

I am too full of emotion to tell you how I feel, but I sure am grateful, particularly in view of the fact that such initiative as this was taken in the spirit of fairness and a gesture of good will from the very State that has been against the people of my native country. Well, I am just too full of gratitude for expression, but I sure would appeal to you for favorable consideration. That is all I can say, Mr. Chairman.

Mr. BLACKNEY: How long have you been working on this?

Mr. SLOCUM: I have been working on this for a long time, sir; I reckon about 7 years.

The CHAIRMAN: You went to school in this country?

Mr. SLOCUM: Yes, sir; I went to school in this country. I have done everything, because I had to cover 48 States, and every State said, "I am in favor of you, Slocum, but you have to go to California and get their O. K." So I had to go to California.

The CHAIRMAN: Since when does California control this committee?

Mr. SLOCUM: But then the opinion of California must be respected, as you know, sir. That is the reason I went to California.

Mr. KRAMER: You do not mean that because there is a member from California on this committee that controls the committee?

Mr. SLOCUM: No, sir; but I respect your views, too, Mr. Kramer.

Mr. MILLARD: You are a professional man?

Mr. SLOCUM: I have been for this work. I had to do almost anything and everything, because you cannot take very good job in order to carry on appeal from one State to another. I have done everything.

Mr. MILLARD: Are you a college graduate?

Mr. SLOCUM: No, sir; I am not a college graduate, but I attended college 5 years.

Mr. MILLARD: What college?

Mr. SLOCUM: Minnesota and Columbia.

Mr. KRAMER: How long were you in the service?

Mr. SLOCUM: I was in the service not quite 2 years; I served in the same regiment with Sergeant York of Tennessee. I am proud to say I had the honor of being the only oriental sergeant major in the A. E. F. I did not abuse your confidence and I do not intend to abuse it now if you trust me in the future.

I speak in behalf of a few hundred orientals. They look rather forlorn. I told them, "Have faith; perhaps some day the American people will vindicate our faith in them and give us our citizenship." So I kept on.

I am mighty grateful to California, the Veterans of Foreign Wars, to the American Legion, and particularly to Mr. Lea, who believed in me, and Mr. Nye in the Senate, who believed in me, and at least gave me a break to be heard. I sure would like citizenship.

Mr. MILLARD: You would give up your citizenship in Japan if you become an American?

Mr. SLOCUM: We have already given up our citizenship, when we went in the American Army.

Mr. MILLARD: You have no responsibility to Japan, then?

Mr. SLOCUM: No, sir; no, sir. When we went into the American Army, we swore allegiance to America. We have given up our allegiance to Japan.

Mrs. O'DAY: How old were you when you came over?

Mr. SLOCUM: I was 10 years old.

Mr. MILLARD: You have been released by Japan, have you, so that if you become an American citizen you are released?

Mr. SLOCUM: Yes, sir. The law of Japan says that the minute you take allegiance to another country you are automatically released.

The CHAIRMAN: That is a good, sensible law.

7. American–Born Japanese Bemoans Limited Job Opportunities, 1937

I am a fruit stand worker. It is not a very attractive nor distinguished occupation, and most certainly unappreciated in print. I would much rather it were doctor or lawyer ... but my aspirations [were] frustrated long ago by circumstances, social and financial.... I am only what I am, a professional carrot washer.

From Taishi Matsumoto, "The Protest of a Professional Carrot Washer," *Kashu Mainichi* [newspaper] (Los Angeles), August 4, 1937, English Language section, editorial page.

My work can be very pleasant at times. That is, if [I] make no complaints of long hours and little pay, thereby impressing my subdued qualities upon my employer who so approves of this virtue among his employees. He often goes out of his way to humor me, for he realizes that I am of a rebellious nature. He approaches me beaming, and plants a hearty slap on my shoulder … attempting to create a comradely atmosphere. He attributes this familiarity to his and my parent's prefecture, Hiroshima, of which he may take advantage once too often. After all, what is Hiroshima ken [prefecture] to me? It is a mere name without meaning only that my parents had drifted from thence seeking a livelihood here in America. What so important connection is there here that my employer should make so much of it? I can almost say without due contempt that the man [i]s exploiting my labor in the name of an alien country. What sort of spineless fool am I to be accepting this daily hypocrisy?…

Disillusioned men, well on in their years, work with me side by side. They make no complaints; they make no progress; they accept the days as they unfold, following [in their] wake as though it were their undisputable lots. Yet what can they expect and what can be expected of them with their underdog complexes? Will I, and the rest of the nisei youths contract their attitude and inherit their lot?

I grit my teeth at the drudgery, the unending hours of the hopelessness of fruit stand work, and its meagre compensation. This cannot go on forever, much less can I go on.

It seems that I started out in life on the wrong foot. I feel [like] a square peg in a round hole.… An optimist would undoubtedly make the best of it, but even the most optimistic, after several years of market work[,] will begin to notice the hole.

I understand my position and realize that I am stagnating; that I am making no progress, and most keenly do I realize that … I am getting older.

The little optimism that is left in me refuses to accept my ever increasing conviction that market work may have to be my career after all. It goads me on with the hope that when I have a few shekels saved that I can call my own, and only God knows when that will be, I will invest it in an enterprise which will be, through habit and familiarity rather than choice, most likely another market.

But until then, and it will be a long time till then, [are] there no inspired Messia[h]s, no strong organizations to whom I can appeal not only for myself, but for others like me, so that life will be less miserable, that we may bear fewer blisters on our hands and less corns on our toes?

☕ E S S A Y S

The first essay, by Arizona State University historian Karen J. Leong, explores the complicated ethnic identity of film actor Anna May Wong. Leong reveals how Wong crafted a particular image as a Chinese American that was meant for Hollywood and her fans, while keeping her personal identity private. In the second essay, University of Southern California historian Lon Kurashige addresses another type of biculturalism intended for public consumption—a festival in Little Tokyo. He argues that this event was a means for the Nisei to define themselves as good Americans while compelling their generation to shop in Little Tokyo.

The Racialized Image of Anna May Wong

KAREN J. LEONG

Hollywood's Narrative of White Heterosexual Romance

Hollywood's most established and popular plot narrative is that of the white heterosexual romance—white boy meets white girl, loses girl, wins girl back, and lives with her happily ever after. According to Hollywood's racial logic, and that of American society in general, nonwhites naturally desired whites, while those whites who desired nonwhites were obviously morally and emotionally deficient. Interracial erotic attraction—which was never honest, but based on deception, threats, or violence—inevitably complicated the plot. This diversion from the ultimate "happy ending" consummation of white heterosexual romance was only temporary, however. The white male protagonist's discipline—his mastery over his own or the nonwhite male's deviant desires—ultimately would triumph, demonstrating his moral right to the white female protagonist. As a Chinese American, Anna May Wong was not able to participate fully in portrayals of American femininity and whiteness; true womanhood continued to be defined as white and virtuous, and American orientalism assumed that Chinese (American) women lacked virtue.

Such was the case in Paramount's *Forty Winks* (1925), in which Anna May Wong earned a feature role as the pivotal character, Annabelle Wu. Wu's desire to be white and to win the love of a white man is a central theme in the story, further emphasizing whiteness as fundamental to the central romance between the American heroine and English hero. The screenplay makes stunningly clear the author's perception of a "typical" Asian woman in the scene where Annabelle Wu first appears:

> We intend to characterize Anna as a girl who would give her last drop of blood to be considered a "white" girl. She loves to think of herself as looking thoroughly American. To point this [out], we must make certain that all her dress (negligees, etc.) and her head-dress, in fact everything intimate and personal about her be done in American fashion. [But h]er instinctive reactions are *always* Oriental.

Karen J. Leong, "Anna May Wong," in *The China Mystique: Pearl S. Buck, Anna May Wong, Mayling Soong, and the Transformation of American Orientalism* (Berkeley: University of California Press, 2005), 57–67. Reprinted by permission.

These "Oriental" reactions, according to the screenplay, include wanting to be white and acting in a conniving and duplicitous matter. Yet no matter how much she strives to fashion herself as American in dress and makeup, Anna—as Annabelle appears in the scenario—will always remain innately Oriental.

In one revealing scene, Anna peers into the mirror, then looks intently at the magazine on her dressing room table. An advertisement on the open page promises. "For the thoroughbred American GIRL—a skin as white as milk! You can have it!," and features a full-length figure of the "Typical" American young woman on the margin. Her gaze drawn back to her reflection, Anna frowns at her "brown" arm and, directing her attention again to the mirror, attempts to "massage out her Oriental lines." Finally she reaches for a bottle of lotion, "Mal-hofsky's Milk White Magic." Gazing in the mirror, she imitates the pose of the "Typical American girl" pictured on the lotion's label. Annabelle Wu hopes that by achieving whiteness she will also win the love and adoration of Le Sage. But this cannot be. After Le Sage realizes she has failed him in his attempt to black-mail the heroine into marriage, he is furious. "You yellow fool! Do you know what this means to me? It means prison—for life!" When Anna hysterically indi-cates that they should flee together, his response, as written in the scenario, is to fling her from himself and out of the picture. "You! I hope I may never see your stupid, slant-eyed face again—you damned Chink!"

As the scenario suggests, definitions of femininity and whiteness mutually reinforce each other. White females—with the aid of cosmetics, fashion, and women's magazines—demonstrate femininity in their appearance, dress, and manners. The culmination of white femininity is to be desired by a white Euro-American male who is equally accessible for a heterosexual, romantic rela-tionship and the security of marriage. The screenplay also exemplifies the racial violence that Wong, as the Oriental subject of the camera's gaze, regularly expe-rienced. One film critic ruefully observed that Wong's complexion directly reflected the character of the women she portrayed: "Miss Wong is invariably conscripted when a moving picture demands Oriental intrigue. Her dark beauty appeared sinister by contrast with Nordic fairness of Laura La Plante in *The Chi-nese Parrot* and Dolores Gatella in *Old San Francisco*. She has been a villainess and a vampire, *but her appearance will never let her be heroine, although occasionally she manages to achieve a sympathetic role.*"

The Intertextual Oriental

The celebrity-making apparatus of Hollywood extended Wong's romantic life offscreen to "an existence already laid out in films." Wong's hybrid identity formed the basis of her unique star personality: she was the one recognizably Chinese American female in films during the twenties and thirties. Her publi-cized "personal" life, an essential ingredient of celebrity, only confirmed and entrenched expectations from producers (and possibly even audiences) of the characters Wong could convincingly portray. Wong's conflict of cultures and her attempt to reconcile her American and Chinese backgrounds were central to her picture personality as developed in movie magazines and in her film roles. Articles about Wong in film magazines, then, emphasized similarities, or intertextuality, between Wong's celebrity personality and the characters.

By the 1920s movie magazines marketed at movie fans constituted a particularly important mechanism for perpetuating personalities. Articles about film personalities promised their readers a glimpse into the real life of celebrity and a virtual relationship with particular actors inside and outside the movie theater. Interviews and articles "revealed" personal details of the star's ostensibly private life, individualizing his or her identity.… Hence publicists serve up stories to fulfill the audience's perceived desire to focus on, and identify with, the celebrity, to find out what made the individual unique and what kept her ordinary.

In this way, they projected onto Wong's private life Americans' fascination with Oriental exoticism and the stereotypical "all-American" (heterosexual) girl's desires of love, romance, and marriage. Discussions of her "real-life" cultural conflict set up a divergence of Chinese and American identities for Wong and the fanzine reader. For example, Wong discussed her family's reaction to her rather un-Chinese choice to become a film actor. "[My father] said I was disgracing his family and all that sort of thing, but I told him that I was determined to be independent some day, that I just couldn't be like the girls who live in China and it was no use trying to make me over." On the one hand, readers might partly identify with Wong's story of wanting to make choices independent of her parents. On the other hand, few readers could identify with the object of Wong's conflict—her Chinese ancestry.

These publications consciously appealed to middle-class and white adolescent women, who constituted the target audience for their advertisers' health and beauty products. Features about Wong affirmed white privilege and heterosexual same-race romantic relationships. The authors—many of them Euro-American women—implied that not being white resulted in suffering, and that any subsequent interracial relationships would be unfulfilling and tragic. In contrast to most movie magazine features, which focused on successful romances, features about Anna May Wong emphasized her romantic failures. A magazine article titled "The Tragic Real Life Story of Anna May Wong," was subtitled "Oriental Beauty Compelled to Choose Between Heritage of Race and Her Preference for an American Husband." Throughout this article the question of why Wong had to choose between race and nationality never presented itself. A caption in the same article read, "Anna May Wong finds it difficult to keep *her real Chinese self* separate from her westernized personality.

The conspicuous absence of publicized romance, a topic that immediately connoted a private life, became the core of Wong's public image. Discussions about Wong's romantic life emphasized gendered difference between the cultures of the West and those of the East. Helen Carlisle of *Motion Picture Magazine* reported Wong's conjectures about her marital status, heightening her privileged status as confidante and Wong's Oriental status. "In a burst of confidence, exceedingly rare among her people, she said to me one day: 'I don't suppose I'll ever marry. Whom could I marry? Not a man of your race, for he would lose caste among his people and I among mine.'" Another writer noted that this "strange problem," which "seemingly has no solution," fastened itself to Wong's image. "Yet, Hollywood wonders, what true romance—and romance should go hand in hand with youth—can come to this girl who is a part, yet not a part?" Melodramatic articles portrayed her as continually divided and terribly lonely. The taboo against interracial romance offscreen translated into the prohibition of on-screen interracial romance and suggested that Hollywood's form of fulfillment was accessible only within the discourse of whiteness.

Performing Orientals

Wong herself recognized a key distinction between her own embodiment of difference and Euro-American actors who performed Asians. Discussing her desire to portray the Asian wife of an Englishman in *Java Head*, she explained, "I know I will never play it. The captain, you see, *marries* the woman.... But no film lovers can ever marry me. If they got an American actress to slant her eyes and eyebrows and wear a stiff black wig and dress in Chinese culture, it would be allright. But me? I am really Chinese. So I must always die in the movies, so that the white girl with the yellow hair may get the man." As Wong acknowledged, her presence in a film as a publicly and visibly Chinese American actor maintained the distinctions of white/nonwhite in the midst of a perpetual play on appearance and served as a reminder that markers of Oriental exotica might adorn a non-Asian actor's body bur not ultimately affect his or her innate identity or character.

Hollywood's practice of *yellowface*, or making up Euro-American actors to "look Oriental," manifests another way in which whiteness constrained her opportunities in film. The ideology of whiteness as manifested in the film industry assumed that Euro-American actors were talented enough to perform roles that did not reflect their own identities or experiences: it also assumed that nonwhite actors could not perform roles beyond their social identities and lived experiences. In addition to competing with Euro-American actors for any Asian female protagonist roles, Wong also confronted the devaluation of her performance. For example, when Loretta Young played the Chinese ingenue and protagonist in First National's *The Hatchet Man* (1932), *Photoplay* featured a full-page photo spread, "Loretta Goes Oriental." "Intimate portraits of a smart, young American girl being turned into a Chinese woman" showed Young with adhesive and "fish skin" pulling back her eyes. The caption suggested, "The finished job might make you think Loretta was Anna May Wong." Additional captions explained that it was not necessary to cast a real Chinese "girl" like Anna May Wong because Loretta, who was already under contract with Republic, had made "tests ... as excellent as the make-up, so they thought you wouldn't know the difference." Yet "they"—the studio—clearly wanted "you"—the audience—to know the difference. The magazine hence discussed and displayed the two-hour process for its readers, differentiating the actor—"a smart, young American girl"—from the Chinese woman she portrayed on screen. Silk robes and a fan complemented Young's makeup of slanted eyes, pale skin, and black hair. These pan-Asian cues—music, lighting, scenery, costumes, and accents—all conveyed an Oriental aesthetic. The feature thus emphasized Young's acting capabilities as an actor and her embodiment of white femininity while simultaneously undermining Wong's acting ability by focusing on her racial identity, implying that Anna May Wong could not overcome the limitations of her racial identity but Young could....

The use of yellowface continued the film industry's tendency to cast Euro-American actors as persons of African, Asian, or Latino heritage. The notion that Euro-American actors could reproduce any culture and ethnicity also presumed cultural superiority; members of "more civilized" cultures could pass as racialized others, but members of "primitive" or "backward" cultures could only *attempt* to do so, with either tragic or comic results, as was the case with Annabelle Wu. Indeed, one of Wong's greatest frustrations was repeatedly witnessing how the few female Asian roles available were awarded to Euro-Americans. For example, although Anna May Wong reportedly was the leading contender for the starring role in the screen adaptation of *The Son-Daughter*, the role was awarded to Helen Hayes.

Moreover, even when Wong gained a role, she was pressed to play it according to directors' preconceptions of Asian mannerisms. Bessie Loo, a Chinese American woman who also worked in the film industry during the thirties and forties, recalled, "there were no important parts ... for Chinese because they thought Chinese were passive, they did not have any emotions." In most of her speaking roles Wong appeared stiff, her expressions inscrutable, and her voice a monotone. Perceptions about Asian behavior influenced how non-Asian actors portrayed Asian characters as well. Myrna Loy portrayed an "Oriental" slave girl opposite Wong, her fellow inmate of the House of a Thousand Daggers, in the silent film *Crimson City* (1928). Loy, who is not at all inanimate in other roles, appears to have been directed to express little feeling. One reviewer even observed, "Miss Loy has the sloe eyes, the exotic feature which, it would seem, would make her well suited for her role. However, she is strangely unemotional."

American expectation about "Oriental" behavior thus reached beyond casting decisions to restrain Anna May Wong's moving and talking image onscreen. In silent films like *Piccadilly* or *Toll of the Sea*, Wong's expressiveness had distinguished her performances. A change in her carriage and presentation accompanied Wong's transition to the talkies. Wong's acting ability is undeniable in *Shanghai Express*, which provided one of Wong's few sympathetic, complex, and almost heroic roles. Paramount invested this film with the time and resources that would befit a celebrated actor, Dietrich, and an equally respected director, von Sternberg. As a result, Wong's character is more fully developed, providing Wong with the material for one of her best performances.

The Global Politics of Film Representations

The glowing reviews Wong enjoyed for her work in *Shanghai Express* came from American film critics comfortable with China as a space of marginal morality. Wong confronted different reviews from Chinese already critical of Hollywood and American attitudes toward China. Chinese nationalism became even more internationally focused in the aftermath of the Mukden (Shenyang) Incident of

1931, when Japan occupied Manchuria in northeastern China. In January 1932 the United States, deeply mired in the Depression and isolationism, stated its "Non-Recognition Doctrine," asserting that it would not take sides. In March, Japan created a puppet state called Manchukuo (Dongbei) and even displayed Pu Yi, the last Qing emperor, as the head of state. While the League of Nations did not recognize Manchukuo as an independent state, the league did not actively oppose Japan's aggression.

Demonstrations against imperialism increasingly pointed out the presence of Western culture that depicted China in less than flattering ways. Chinese world-wide angrily sought to halt the film depictions of China's civil strife as a back-drop to foreign romance and adventure. Demonstrations took place in the streets of Chinese cities, and in the campuses of schools, and in movie theaters. During the filming of *Shanghai Express* one 1932 Chinese newspaper editorial decried that the film, "when completed, will further expose all evils of Chinese society, and as the Occident knows very little of Chinese and always entertains a con-tempt for things Chinese, the pictures always exaggerate the truth." This article entitled, "Paramount Utilizes Anna May Wong to Produce Picture to Disgrace China," reserved its most scathing criticism for Wong. "The Oriental star in Hollywood, Anna May Wong, is working as a featured player in America. Her specialty is to expose the conduct of the very low caste of Chinese, such as when she played the part of a half-robed Chinese maid in *The Thief of Bagdad [sic]*. Although she is deficient in artistic portrayal, she has done more than enough to disgrace the Chinese race."

Chinese officials had long complained about China's depiction by Holly-wood (as early as Harold Lloyd's work in silent films), but Anna May Wong was the target of particular ire because she herself was Chinese. Chinese speak-ing the language of nationalism were particularly fluent in translating the effect of gendered images. Half-dressed women prostitutes reflected on a nation's morals. Just as imperialism relied on ideas of proper feminine behavior to legiti-mize colonization as a civilizing project, some Chinese Nationalists—many themselves the products of Western education and thus doubly inculcated with norms of "proper civilization"—sought to legitimize the new, modern China through the representation of Chinese women. As Cynthia Enloe has noted, many communities seeking to affirm their national stature assign "ideological weight" to women's clothing, behavior, and sexuality, precisely because women are viewed as possessions of community, transmitters of culture, and mothers of the nation.

Hollywood and British film executives assumed that audiences expected a certain representation of Asian women. Because she was of Chinese descent, however, some Chinese interpreted Wong's representation, specifically her sex-uality and ethnicity, as a reflection on China. According to Chinese officials, Wong's roles onscreen perpetuated negative stereotypes of Chinese women and damaged China's international reputation. Stereotypes propagated by missionar-ies in China—that the Chinese hated baby girls, abused and exploited women, and were immoral—flourished in Americans' imaginations. When asked how Wong was perceived in China, General Tu, the Chinese government's official advisor to MGM for *The Good Earth*, replied, "Very bad. Whenever she appears in a film, the newspapers print her picture with the caption: "Anna May Wong again loses face for China." The general himself added, "I feel sorry for her … because I realize that she has to play the part assigned her. It is the *parts* China objects to. She is always a slave—*a very undressed slave*. China resents having its womanhood so represented."

As a Chinese American woman performing American orientalism, Wong was caught in crosscurrents of nationalism, racism, and sexism. Paralleling the imperial culture that Helen Callaway describes as functioning through "its cognitive dimension," the American film industry circulated its hierarchy of race and nationhood worldwide through the technology of mass culture and the dominant status of its government. In an attempt to refute negative historical perceptions and images, some Chinese critics further entrenched the gendered division of a masculine nationalism and a feminine propriety and civility.…

Travel

Anna May Wong first discovered travel's transformative potential in the late 1920s. According to Wong's account, she met Dr. Karl Vollmoller, a German author, in Hollywood. After he returned to Berlin in 1927 Vollmoller arranged for a German studio to hire her for a feature role. Wong traveled outside the United States for the first time in 1928 when she sailed to Germany. There she starred in three silent films. After completing those films, Wong sailed to England in late 1928 to star in *Piccadilly* for British International.…

Yet unlike Americans, who viewed her Chinese American identity as a liability, European audiences seemed to appreciate the complexity of her identity. When she made her London stage debut in *Circle of Chalk* in 1929 and was criticized for her flat voice, Wong worked with a vocal coach to improve her speaking voice and adopted a cultured English accent in the process. During Wong's return to England in 1930 the columnist Margery Collier observed that Wong combined stereotypes of both Chinese and American women and featured "the face and figure of a Chinese girl and the mind of an American flapper." The novelty of exotic appearance, careful speech, and carefree manner contributed to Europeans' fascination with Anna May Wong. Ironically, while Wong's celebrity inspired Oriental fashions in England, with women powdering their faces to "get the 'Wong complexion'" and "[g]orgeously-embroidered coolie coats" became the rage among the theater set, Wong herself wore "the smartest Paris clothes." Photographs of Wong in Berlin and in London show her continental attire and elegant companions; her scrapbooks indicate an avid social life, attending sports events and the theater. She was a modern cosmopolitan whose hybridity could not be easily categorized.

Whereas audiences in Europe marveled at her ability to be simultaneously American and Chinese, those in the United States perceived her as more cultured, sophisticated, and Western after her sojourn in Europe. Wong confided to American movie magazine writers how people told her she had "changed so much since my European experience, and that I don't look like a Chinese girl anymore.… My face has changed because my soul has changed. I think like the people of the West." Another article credited Europe with transforming her. "The Chinese flapper has an English accent now. She thinks in Western terms. Her manners, her dress, her humor, her attitude, are Western. She loves tea— but an English brand. Her face no longer looks very Chinese." …

Oriental Mystique

Wong consciously chose to exoticize herself even more as an "Oriental" celebrity. After *Picturegoer* reported that Wong received (but refused) an offer from "an Eastern plastic surgeon, who said he could take the slant out of her eyes, thereby allowing her to play European roles," perhaps it made sense to transform what some perceived as her "liability" into marketability. One of her mentors, Rob Wagner, had suggested that Wong could actively increase her value in the culture of film and celebrity by "being different." "Among other things," Wagner recalled, "I urged her to 'can' her Hollywood feathers and be Chinese. I suggested that she even burn incense in her hotel room, to add to her exotic charm." Wong followed Wagner's advice and, by all accounts, provoked curiosity, attention, and acclaim in Europe.

Rejecting the pathologies the American public associated with the Chinese, Wong drew on more exotic qualities in her self-representation. Vivien North described for the British readers of *Picturegoer Weekly* the mysterious quality surrounding the actor, "sitting there against the Oriental background of her room, with its bowls of big flowers, its mirrors and soft lighting, her hands—with their lacquered finger nails matching the Chinese red of her jumper—folded, her ankles crossed and every feature composed—almost physically feeling her complete stillness." John K. Newnham noted Wong's ability to emphasize both the American and Chinese aspects of her identity in her self-promotion and suggested that Wong's unique combination of American initiative and Asian allure enabled her to "play Hollywood's game well. She retains a deliberate atmosphere of subtle mystery. There is always a faint aroma of perfume about her. But in her conversation and outlook on life, she is smartly Western. No genuine Chinese woman could boast the attribute she possesses: women haven't been emancipated long enough in China. So you can see," Newnham continued, "why Anna May Wong is so unique and why she can always step back to starring roles. She has a corner which is uniquely her own."

Newnham's shrewd analysis suggested that Wong succeeded because she could use her multiple identifications to locate herself in the unique position of representing Chinese even as she maintained a Western outlook. Presenting herself in self-consciously orientalist fashion, Wong relied on a racialized identity to establish the uniqueness of her star persona. Although this strategy appears to contradict her earlier claims of realistically portraying China, Wong may also have persuaded herself that the exotic China she evoked was indeed authentic. Wong's willing participation in the Occident's orientalism provided her with a public platform in London from which to critique the treatment and perceptions of Chinese Americans in the United States.

The Problem of Japanese American Biculturalism

LON KURASHIGE

Buy Cultural

A surge of advertising was the first sign that Nisei Week was about to begin. Little Tokyo merchants flooded the vernacular press with sales announcements and redesigned display windows to appeal specifically to the second generation. In 1934 one retailer proclaimed that preparations were done "All for the Satisfaction of the Nisei!" Such appeals masked a fear among Little Tokyo merchants that the second generation had developed consumption tastes that lured them outside the enclave, particularly to department stores whose economies of scale allowed them to undercut small businesses. Some shop owners criticized Nisei who, they said, were embarrassed to wear clothing made in Japan. Others simply bemoaned the loss of an estimated half a million dollars a year that could be spent by Nisei shoppers. How would the merchants stop the hemorrhaging of money from the ethnic enclave?

That was the question that pushed the Issei leadership to place unproven second-generation businessmen in charge of Nisei Week. Never before had Little Tokyo been turned on its head, with the Nisei—albeit temporarily—in command. Sei Fujii, an Issei leader and newspaper publisher, challenged the JACLers "to show their old folks how much of an asset they are instead of being [a] burden as they used to be." The youngsters, for their part, welcomed the chance to run what they called the "greatest civic project undertaken by a second generation group." Nisei Week was a rite of passage that continued the JACL's initiation into community leadership. With solid Issei backing, the organization was founded in 1930 and mirrored the extensive and tightly organized network of Japanese immigrant associations throughout the West Coast. By 1936 thirty-eight chapters, governed by a national headquarters in San Francisco, supported the older generation's economic endeavors and efforts to fight anti-Japanese discrimination. "The early devices of the rising Nisei organization," one member observed, "were in many instances mild imitations of the Issei."

While the JACLers patterned themselves after the immigrant leadership, they differed significantly from the bulk of their own generation. They were overwhelmingly male despite equal numbers of Nisei women in Los Angeles and were about a decade older than the majority of their peers in the second generation. Moreover, they were almost twice as likely to have attended college and to be in management positions than most of the Nisei men their age. Thus the organization was made up of the second-generation elite—lawyers, dentists, medical doctors, and entrepreneurs who relied upon the ethnic enclave for their businesses and practices and therefore had vested interests in enhancing and protecting Little Tokyo. The exceptional status of the JACLers was doubly

From Lon Kurashige, "The Problem of Biculturalism: Japanese American Identity and Festival Before World War II," *Journal of American History*, 86, no. 4 (March 2000): 1636–1640, 1650–1654. Copyright © 2000 Journal of American History. Used by permission.

true for the organization's leaders. Consider the success story of Keiichi "Kay" Sugahara, the first president of the Los Angeles chapter. Born in 1909, Sugahara was thirteen when he and his younger siblings were orphaned. To help provide for his brother and sister, he worked at a fruit stand from junior high through his years at the University of California, Los Angeles (UCLA). In 1932, as a senior, the young Sugahara teamed with white partners to launch the first customs brokerage firm in Little Tokyo. As someone who could bridge American and Japanese cultures, he capitalized on the needs of businesses importing goods from Japan. The success of this venture, he claimed, made him a millionaire before the age of thirty.

Under Sugahara's command, the theme of the first Nisei Week festival was "Buy in Lil' Tokyo." Sugahara's brother, Roku, promised his generation that Little Tokyo stores would have the lowest prices and the highest-quality Japanese and American merchandise. Just in case competitive prices and products were not enough, the JACLers linked enclave purchases with Nisei Week participation. Admission to festival events required receipts from Little Tokyo stores, and by the late 1930s, purchasing merchandise enabled shoppers to cast votes for their favorite beauty contestants.

But even the most successful of such gimmicks ended with Nisei Week. In order to secure year-round patronage, the organizers of Nisei Week strove to give the second generation a stake in the future of the immigrant enclave. The logic was straightforward: If the Nisei benefited materially from Little Tokyo, they would have more reason to shop there. The most compelling incentive Issei merchants could offer the younger generation was employment. While free to patronize white-owned businesses, Nisei usually could not work for them. Most white employers refused to hire Japanese Americans, and major labor unions denied them membership. One field open to the Nisei was higher education, but only a select few followed this route since even college graduates faced racial barriers that forced them back to the restricted world of the ethnic enclave. On the eve of World War II, most Nisei were working in the ethnic enclave's primary sectors: agricultural production, retail enterprise, and domestic service. While Issei leaders looked to them to calm anti-Japanese antipathy in white America, the Nisei relied upon the older generation for employment opportunities.

Yet most Little Tokyo retailers refused to hire Nisei for sales positions because of their inability to meet the needs of Japanese-speaking clients. To spur Nisei employment, Nisei Week organizers persuaded enclave merchants that Nisei salespersons would boost their businesses by attracting second-generation shoppers. In 1934 the festival's employment bureau placed thirty-five workers in just three days, and although their jobs, like the sales and the beauty pageant, typically ended with Nisei Week, the employment agency attained a permanent place in Little Tokyo.

The strongest appeals for Nisei patronage relied upon a sense of fictive kinship. According to Roku Sugahara, Little Tokyo offered a pleasanter shopping experience than the stores outside its protective borders. There was, he suggested, "a better understanding, a feeling of freedom and congeniality, and friendliness" because the "seller knows the background and characteristics of the buyer much better." The winner of the Nisei Week essay contest in 1938 also viewed Little Tokyo as an ethnic sanctuary. Answering the question "Why I should buy in Little Tokyo," he listed the enclave's unique benefits for Nisei customers:

> Japanese can serve Japanese people with good taste. They know what type of clothing or merchandise would be best suited, whereas an American firm naturally would not. And, too, they are inclined to be more personal and understanding, as there are no barriers of speech or race. This results in friendly, sociable business tactics, and not cold ruthless negotiations.

Festival leaders used ethnicity as both carrot and stick to attract Nisei shoppers. While they played up the "natural" affinities among Japanese Americans, they also stressed the obligations that such ties entailed. "If the Nisei expect to see Lil' Tokio exist and rise out of its present depression," the *Rafu Shimpo* newspaper commanded, "they must cooperate and help build Lil' Tokio by putting some funds into the businesses" and "buy all necessities at Japanese stores and only buy those things which are not carried in Lil' Tokio at American stores." The result of "this extensive trading," explained the 1938 essay contest winner, "will be a closer union of our race—drawn together by the cohesive force of economic and social dependency." Roku Sugahara's do-or-die scenario best characterized the invocation of group obligation: "It all depends on the nisei, whether they will aid in strengthening our economic foundation or will stand idly by while it crumbles into oblivion."

Despite these appeals, Nisei Week leaders were aware of the pitfalls of attempts to attract second-generation customers. The *Kashu Mainichi* newspaper cautioned against any business strategy that promoted ethnic insularity as not only unfeasible, but "un-American." During the depression, the paper insisted, hoarding money within Little Tokyo was "un-American," since the nation's recovery required pumping money into the broader economy. Carl Kondo, the runner-up in the Nisei Week essay contest in 1935, criticized the futility of the "buy in Lil' Tokio" campaign. He warned that Japanese merchants should not rely on Nisei consumption because their mom-and-pop establishments could not compete with the department stores in nearby downtown Los Angeles. Even if prices were slashed in Little Tokyo, Kondo argued, the Nisei were too influenced by American culture to be interested in Japanese merchandise or to be swayed by invocations of racial responsibilities.

Kondo maintained that Japanese businesses should cultivate external, rather than internal, markets. He believed that the nation's increasing interest in Japan as a rising world power and United States trading partner created a favorable climate for purveying Japanese artifacts, services, and cultural displays to the exotic tastes of white America. The *Kashu Mainichi* also championed the benefits of the tourist market. It pointed with envy to Chinatown and the Mexican-inspired Olvera Street as two of Los Angeles's successful ethnic attractions and lamented that "one cannot immediately feel the foreign atmosphere or distinction upon entering Lil' Tokyo."

Nisei Week proved the optimal occasion to dress up Little Tokyo for white consumption. Here the Oriental-styled street displays, decorations, music, dance, and fashions assumed dual meanings: symbols of ethnic pride for Japanese Americans but also exotic enticements for outsiders. The kimono, in particular, attracted so much interest that Nisei Week leaders in 1936 added a second fashion show, where those Japanese garments were modeled exclusively for white Americans. The festival booklet billed the event as "an exhibition of Japanese pajamas and lounging clothes" with refreshments served by "petite Japanese maidens in picturesque kimonos." The JACLers invited hundreds of "leading women in Los Angeles society" and selected kimono styles that would "appeal particularly to American women."

Enclave merchants also proposed that Nisei women wear kimonos while serving as tour guides who provided a "night of adventure to Americans in Little Tokyo." The hostesses were to greet tourists as they entered the enclave, answer questions about Japanese culture, including flower arrangements and the tea ceremony, and assist them in purchasing merchandise. Nisei Week leaders in 1940 redesigned the festival booklet to increase the enclave's tourist appeal. A glossy full-page advertisement especially greeted white Americans. "WELCOME TO LITTLE TOKYO" appeared in orientalized script inserted within a photograph of the community's main thoroughfare. The night scene featured a group of well-groomed, entertainment-seeking white Americans chaperoned by four smiling, kimono-clad women. Fluorescent Little Tokyo storefronts, particularly the Fujikan Theater's elaborate neon marquee, in front of which the group stood, radiated an energy and enthusiasm that seemed to overwhelm the tourists. The smiling Japanese women reflected the enclave's warmth and hospitality, while the flood of bright lights and signs symbolized its entrepreneurial vigor—a shopper's paradise....

American Front

The economic motives that began Nisei Week and the concerns about Little Tokyo's Americanization were inexplicably tied to the demonstration of the second generation's civic virtue and political allegiance. "Through the medium of this festival," John Maeno declared in 1936, "the JACL hopes to present, acquaint, and connect you directly with the young Japanese American citizen, his life and environment." Maeno, the organization's second president, was one of the few Nisei lawyers in Little Tokyo. A graduate of the University of Southern California, he used his college ties to make inroads into Los Angeles political circles. He explained that as a "new American," the Nisei was a "true and loyal citizen of the United States" who sought to take "part in civic development and community progress."

The JACLers used the Nisei's citizenship to gain advantages in the political arena. They, like the leaders of African Americans and many urban immigrant groups, attempted to gain electoral power by combining Japanese American votes into one large ethnic bloc. This way, as increasing numbers of Nisei came of age, they could expand their impact on local elections. A flock of white office seekers took the Nisei vote seriously and showed up at the festival's inauguration in 1934, their large numbers even raising concerns in Little Tokyo that the festivities would turn into a "political rally." Nisei Week was also an occasion to pay respects to the highest elected official in Los Angeles. In the opening ceremony in 1936 a colorful procession moved through the streets of Little Tokyo on its way to Los Angeles's city hall two blocks away. The ethnic community's "leading citizens" accompanied the Nisei Week queen and "her pretty and charming attendants" as they were carried along in Japanese rickshaws. The ceremony concluded with these "kimono-clad, dark-eyed beauties" presenting the mayor of Los Angeles "with an official invitation to attend this gala event in Lil' Tokyo."

Such a visible display of goodwill toward the Los Angeles community illustrated the type of citizenship the JACLers espoused. Being American, to them, meant not just possessing legal entitlements, but performing a wide range of civic duties. The winner of the JACL's oratorical contest in 1938 placed the responsibility of resolving "our race problem" squarely on the Nisei's shoulders. He encouraged the Nisei to engage in "active citizenship" by voting and involving themselves in public affairs. Civic involvement, he asserted, would prove that the Nisei are a "racial group worthy of being accepted on an equal plane" because "it will show to the white citizenry that we are not a culturally or mentally inferior race …, that we are beneficial to America's social and economic welfare, and that we desire to cooperate with the white race in solving our community and national problems." The ultimate significance of active citizenship, the orator explained, was that eventually it would compel "the white race, themselves, to take down the racial barriers that have been erected against us."

But the JACLers did not equate proving loyalty to the United States with severing ties to Japan. Despite America's opposition to Japanese imperialism, they sided with their parents, who, like most expatriates, reveled in the military victories of their homeland. The formal declaration of the second Sino-Japanese war in 1937 heightened ties to the motherland, as both generations sent money, supplies, and well-wishes to Japanese soldiers. Issei leaders called upon the JACLers to counteract the American public's overwhelming support for the Chinese (President Franklin D. Roosevelt, in fact, disobeyed his own policy of neutrality in foreign wars by sending American arms to Chinese troops). The older generation, with assistance from the Japanese consulate, briefed the young leaders on the necessity and righteousness of Japan's foreign policies and helped to establish a Nisei "speakers bureau" to inform Americans about Japan's side of the story. Togo Tanaka, writing in the 1940s, confirmed that the English section of his newspaper, *Rafu Shimpo*, based its editorials and coverage of the Sino-Japanese war on information provided by Issei who blamed Japan's negative image on Chinese propaganda. The staff of the paper's Japanese section prepared pamphlets for their Nisei colleagues about Japan's plight in the West—the subtitle of one read, "How about Giving Japan a Break?" Thus Tanaka concluded that the JACLers, despite their strong commitment to American political institutions, were mindful "not to disparage the cultural values of Japan, nor to antagonize Issei feelings in the latter's sympathies for Japan. JACL leaders even rationalized their Americanism as being rooted in Japanese culture."

But opposition in the United States only grew when Japanese troops captured Beijing and pressed on to victory. In 1939 FDR abrogated the treaty that had safeguarded United States—Japan trade and, a year later, in response to Japan's Tripartite Alliance with Germany and Italy and its apparent movement into Southeast Asia, threatened to cut off the shipment of about 80 percent of the island nation's war supplies. The growing opposition to Japan buoyed antagonism to Japanese Americans. By 1938 Lail Thomas Kane was in the habit of sharing his opinions with *Rafu Shimpo* editor Togo Tanaka, who duly noted them as an alarming indication of popular sentiment. "By this time," Tanaka later noted, "Kane's attitude toward the Nisei as 'Jap-stooges' appears to have crystallized." This was evident in Kane's telling Tanaka, "I'm rapidly being convinced that the JACL which represents the Nisei leadership is nothing more than an instrument of the Issei. You really take your orders from Japan." Thus Kane, still backed by the American Legion, continued to lobby for legislation against Japanese American fishermen. He told Tanaka that if the JACLers, whom he referred to as "jackals," were really loyal "you would support this fishing bill which is a national defense, patriotic proposal"— "you should know that the security of the United States is menaced by the presence of fishing boats manned by naval reserve officers of the Imperial Japanese Navy." These fears reached a national audience through Kane's publications, including an article in the *Saturday Evening Post*, and spread beyond the issue of Japanese American fishermen. The immediate problem for Little Tokyo was that increasing anti-Japanese sentiment gave rise to boycotts against Japanese businesses that placed the depression-weary enclave in even further jeopardy.

"A direct correlation exists," asserted Togo Tanaka in an analysis of JACL history he wrote in the 1940s, "between the growing intensity of America-Japan friction and the increasing frequency of Nisei and even Issei loyalty pledges." The Issei old guard responded to anti-Japanese affronts as they had done before: they had the Nisei reassure Americans that their support for Japan was in no way at odds with their commitment to living and raising their children in the United States. But mounting United States—Japan hostility forced Nisei Week's leaders to retreat from the idea of biculturalism. The *Rafu Shimpo*'s English-language staff, for example, veered away from Japanese nationalism. Togo Tanaka claimed that the decision was based on both the fallout from the rescinding of the trade agreement and the results of a survey that revealed the impressive Nisei commitment to the United States. The English section split from the paper's Japanese staff to launch an editorial policy encouraging the Nisei to drop biculturalism in favor of a "single American political loyalty." The Nisei were urged to support the JACL's Americanism, buy United States defense bonds, and forgo dual citizenship with Japan.

Nisei Week now became a forum to ensure that Japanese Americans would not be confused with their relatives overseas. The *Kashu Mainichi* in 1940 assured the people of southern California of the Nisei's eagerness to participate "in the building of this great country, to assume responsibility for its defense against all enemies and to safeguard its great institutions." A year later the Nisei Week crowd was steered away from dressing in Japanese garb. "From the American point of view," the leading vernacular newspaper asked, "how can one be expected to be impressed by any profession of loyalty via a 'native Japanese kimono'? The two don't jibe." The call for patriotic expression was especially evident in the festival's parade. Old Glory replaced the "rising sun" flags so prevalent at earlier celebrations, while beauty contestants, draped in white evening gowns, floated through the streets of Little Tokyo perched beneath a replica of the Capitol dome. A sedan resplendent with red, white, and blue streamers carried a flowered marquee that left the Nisei's identity unambiguous. Displayed beneath the facsimile of a spread-winged dove were the words "USA, Our Home."

It was difficult to gauge the extent to which these patriotic activities paid off. No amount of flag-waving or swearing of loyalty oaths could convince Kane and other die-hard racists that the Nisei were trustworthy. But the JACL's patriotism made such a favorable impression on Kenneth Ringle, the naval intelligence officer responsible for assessing the loyalty of the ethnic community, that he concluded "the entire 'Japanese Problem' has been magnified out of its true proportion, largely because of the physical characteristics of the people." Japanese Americans also received support from the *Los Angeles Times*, which encouraged its readers to attend Nisei Week because its sponsors "had no part in and no responsibility for causing war clouds to gather in the Orient." Fletcher Bowron, the mayor of Los Angeles in 1941, echoed this sentiment. In the speech that opened what became the last Nisei Week before World War II, the mayor not only implored Japanese Americans to show their patriotism but reassured them, "we know you are loyal."

Yet after the bombing of Pearl Harbor and the United States' declaration of war on Japan, Bowron did not hesitate to call for the mass evacuation of 110,000 Japanese Americans from the West Coast. The mayor, along with most public officials in California and other western states, confessed his utter distrust of Japanese Americans and did not think twice about denying them their constitutional rights. In early February 1942, he warned a radio audience about the Japanese American threat: "Right here in our own city are those who may spring into action at an appointed time in accordance with a prearranged plan wherein each of our little brown brothers will know his part in the event of any possible attempted invasion or air raid." Two weeks later, despite intelligence reports that deemed the overwhelming majority of Japanese Americans loyal to the United States, President Franklin Roosevelt signed Executive Order 9066, sanctioning their removal to concentration camps. Not long after that, over 33,000 Japanese Americans were forcibly removed from southern California, and with their departure ended a chapter in Nisei Week history.

During World War II the JACLers took control of the ethnic community precisely because they had failed to fulfill Nisei Week's twin goals of ameliorating anti-Japanese racism and securing the future of the ethnic enclave. While neither biculturalism nor the switch to Americanism could prevent the internment, the latter identity proved more pragmatic amid the extreme anti-Japanese sentiment that gripped the nation during World War II. The JACLers, pushed by government officials, adopted a new language of identity predicated on the eradication, not celebration, of ethnic difference. To prove their loyalty to the nation, they, as an organization and individually, cooperated with American intelligence agencies by informing on "suspicious" elements within the ethnic community. Their surveillance activities, which the ethnic press highlighted often, generated deep animosities against the JACL (particularly its most boisterously anti-Japanese leaders) that led to the intimidation, beating, and attempted murder of JACLers within the internment camps. While military authorities saw the ethnic group as a monolithic (enemy) race, Japanese Americans experienced World War II more divided than ever.

❂ FURTHER READING

Chin, Soo-Young. *Doing What Had to Be Done: The Life Narrative of Dora Yum Kim* (1999).

Conn, Peter. *Pearl S. Buck: A Cultural Biography* (1998).

Hayashi, Brian Masaru. *"For the Sake of Our Japanese Brethren": Assimilation, Nationalism, and Protestantism among the Japanese of Los Angeles, 1895–1942* (1995).

Ichioka, Yuji. *Before Internment: Essays in Prewar Japanese American History*, eds. Gordon H. Chang and Eiichiro Azuma (2006).

Imai, Shiho. *Creating the Nisei Market: Race and Citizenship in Hawai'i's Japanese American Consumer Culture* (2010).

Matusmoto, Valerie. *City Girls: The Nisei Social World in Los Angeles, 1920–1950* (2014).

———. *Farming the Home Place: A Japanese Community in California, 1919–1982* (1993).

Modell, John. *The Economics and Politics of Racial Accommodation: The Japanese of Los Angeles, 1900–1942* (1977).

Siu, Paul. *The Chinese Laundryman: A Study of Social Isolation*, ed. John Kuo Wei Tchen (1988).

Spickard, Paul R. *Japanese Americans: The Formation and Transformations of an Ethnic Group* (1996).

Takahashi, Jere. *Nisei/Sansei: Shifting Japanese American Identities and Politics* (1997).

Tamura, Eileen H. *Americanization, Acculturation, and Ethnic Identity: The Nisei Generation in Hawaii* (1994).

Yoo, David K. *Growing Up Nisei: Race, Generation, and Culture among Japanese Americans, 1924–1949* (2001).

Yoshihara, Mari. *Embracing the East: White Women and American Orientalism* (2002).

Yu, Renqiu. *To Save China, to Save Ourselves: The Chinese Hand Laundry Alliance of New York* (1992).

Yung, Judy. *Unbound Feet: A Social History of Chinese Women in San Francisco* (1995).

CHAPTER 8

The Mass Removal and Detention of Japanese Americans, 1942–1948

Japan's destruction of Pearl Harbor on December 7, 1941, incited public calls for revenge against the "treacherous" Japanese and unleashed a new wave of anti-Japanese racism in Hawai'i and on the West Coast. President Franklin Delano Roosevelt authorized martial law in Hawai'i, and for nearly three years residents of Japanese ancestry in Hawai'i endured curfews, property loss, restrictions on travel and work, and the internment of nearly 2,000 individuals. The military commander of Hawai'i and business leaders, however, resisted calls to remove all Hawaiian Japanese from the islands because, as more than a third of the population, they were vital to the islands' economy. On the West Coast, anti-Japanese groups and prominent politicians campaigned for the mass removal and incarceration of Japanese Americans. California's attorney general and future civil rights icon Earl Warren even went so far as to claim that the lack of espionage and sabotage by Japanese Americans on the West Coast was evidence of a vast conspiracy. Repeating this illogical charge, Lieutenant General DeWitt, the military commander on the West Coast, justified mass exclusion by stating, "The very fact that no sabotage has taken place to date is a disturbing and confirming indication that such action will be taken."

On February 19, 1942, President Roosevelt signed Executive Order 9066 authorizing the designation of areas as military zones and clearing the path for the forced removal of Japanese Americans. Most were given less than a week's notice before they had to report for what the government euphemistically called an "evacuation." Allowed to bring only what they could carry, Japanese Americans were taken to "assembly centers" and then transferred to more permanent camps, called "relocation centers," in remote areas of the country with extreme temperatures, harsh conditions, barbed wire, and armed guards.

The mass incarceration of 40,000 immigrants and 70,000 American-born citizens without evidence or trials violated Japanese Americans' civil liberties. Japanese Americans responded to this forced detention in different ways. Some advised the War Relocation Authority (WRA), the government agency that managed the internment camps, through channels of internee governance or as camp researchers into internee life. Some second-generation

Nisei fought along with the WRA for their right to join the armed forces to demonstrate their patriotism and improve the public image of Japanese Americans. Japanese American Citizens League (JACL) leaders lobbied the War Department for more than a year to reclassify Nisei from "enemy aliens," prohibited from serving in the nation's armed forces, to citizens who could fight for their country. The outstanding training record of Japanese Americans in the 100th Infantry Battalion and the Varsity Victory Volunteers, both from Hawaii, contributed to President Roosevelt's decision on March 23, 1943, to establish the all-Nisei 442nd Regimental Combat Team. While nearly 10,000 young men volunteered for the unit from Hawaii, only about 1,500 volunteered from the internment camps. Nevertheless, the 442nd, reinforced by the 100th, became the most decorated U.S. military unit for its size and length of service during World War II.

In contrast to the backers of the 442nd combat team, other Nisei protested against the internment by refusing to sign a loyalty questionnaire, failing to comply with draft procedures, and in some cases even renouncing their U.S. citizenship. Conflicts between pro- and antiadministration groups among the internees led to mass demonstrations, violence, and an incident at the Manzanar camp that ended with a group of soldiers firing into a crowd of protesters, killing two and injuring many others. Dividing families and groups within the ethnic community, the internment left deep wounds.

DOCUMENTS

These documents present different views of Japanese American loyalty, patriotism, and citizenship during World War II. In Document 1, written two weeks after Pearl Harbor, naval intelligence officer Kenneth Ringle argues against mass removal based on evidence from the surveillance of the Japanese American community, a network of ethnic informants, and a break-in at the Japanese Consulate in Los Angeles. In Document 2, West Coast military commander John L. DeWitt urges the War Department in February 1942 to remove all Japanese Americans from the West Coast because he assumes that racial ancestry determines loyalty. Document 3 presents selections from the 1942 congressional testimony of Nisei Mike Masaoka, national secretary of the ultrapatriotic JACL, urging the recognition of Japanese Americans' citizenship rights and pledging cooperation with the government's removal order.

Documents 4 and 5 provide two Japanese American responses to internment. Document 4, an anonymous poem circulated at the Poston camp, constructed on the Colorado River Indian Reservation in southwestern Arizona, evokes the frustration and anger many internees experienced at being imprisoned behind barbed wire. In Document 5, immigrant leader Yamato Ichihashi, a Stanford University professor interned at the Tule Lake camp in northern California, writes department colleague Payson Treat a critique of the camp director's inability to understand internee decision making. Ichihashi explains why some internees deemed "loyal" choose to remain at this camp after it is converted into a segregated facility for supposedly disloyal Japanese Americans. He also criticizes as racist and hypocritical the government's refusal to let loyal internees leave the internment camps and return to their homes.

Documents 6 and 7 address Japanese Americans and military service. Document 6 recounts how the 442nd rescued a "Lost Battalion" from Texas after two other units failed. The five days of intense combat cost the 442nd several times the number of men they rescued, but the unit's heroism made headlines back home and improved the public image of Japanese Americans. Inside the internment camps, however, alienated Nisei men denounced government attempts to draft them into the military. In Document 7, the "Fair Play Committee," led by Kiyoshi Okamoto, Frank Abe, and other internees at the Heart Mountain camp, condemns the mass incarceration and the recruitment for the 442nd combat team. Urging the draftees to defend the constitution and democracy "here at home," the committee calls on them to protest the violation of their citizenship rights by resisting the draft. Document 8 reveals that the Heart Mountain protesters were not the only ones to stand up for the Nisei's rights as U.S. citizens. In a searing dissent to the 1944 Supreme Court opinion upholding the constitutionality of the mass removal, Associate Supreme Court Justice Frank Murphy argued that the removal and incarceration denied Japanese Americans' constitutional rights.

Document 9 examines the experiences of Japanese Americans after leaving the camps. The WRA advised them to resettle in midwestern states like Illinois, Michigan, and Ohio. The American Friends Service and other charitable agencies helped find jobs and housing for Japanese Americans who relocated to Chicago and other cities, where many resettlers found the people to be much friendlier than on the West Coast. Anti-Japanese antagonism in the West is the subject of Document 9, an oral interview conducted in 1999 in which Esther (Takei) Nishio recounts the hostility, threats, and media frenzy she encountered when she became the first Japanese American student to return to California in September 1944. Nishio remembers how certain liberally minded white Americans were instrumental in sponsoring her return and enrollment in college. They also paved the way for the return of many other Japanese Americans once President Roosevelt rescinded West Coast exclusion orders on December 17, 1944.

1. Chief of Naval Operations Kenneth Ringle Reports on Japanese American Loyalty on the West Coast, December 30, 1941

From:	Lieutenant Commander K.D. RINGLE, USN.
To:	The Chief of Naval Operations.
Via:	The Commandant, Eleventh Naval District.
Subject:	Japanese Question, Report on.

Serial No. 01742316 30 December 1941, Navy Department Library, http://www.history.navy.mil/library/online/jap intern.htm

The following opinions, amplified in succeeding paragraphs, are held by the writer:

(a) That within the last eight or ten years the entire "Japanese question" in the United States has reversed itself. The alien menace is no longer paramount, and is becoming of less importance almost daily, as the original alien immigrants grow older and die, and as more and more of their American-born children reach maturity. The primary present and future problem is that of dealing with these of whom it is considered that least seventy-five percent are loyal to the United States. The ratio of these American citizens of Japanese ancestry to alien-born Japanese in the United States is at present almost 3 to 1, and rapidly increasing.

(b) That of the Japanese-born alien residents, the large majority are at least passively loyal to the United States. That is, they would knowingly do nothing what ever to the injury of the United States, but at the same time would not do anything to the injury of Japan. Also, most might well do surreptitious observation work for Japanese interests if given a convenient opportunity.

(c) That, however, there are among the Japanese both alien and United States citizens, certain individuals, either deliberately placed by the Japanese government or actuated by a fanatical loyalty to that country who would act as saboteurs or agents. This number is estimated to be less than three per cent of the total, or about 300 in the entire United States.

(d) That of the persons mentioned in (c) above, the most dangerous are either already in custodial detention or are members of such organizations as the Black Dragon Society, the Kaigun Kyokai (Navy League), or the Heimusha Iai (Military Service Men's League), or affiliated groups. The membership of these groups is already fairly well known to the Naval Intelligence service or the Federal Bureau of Investigation and should immediately be placed in custodial detention, irrespective of whether they are alien or citizen.

(e) That, as a basic policy tending toward the permanent solution of this problem, the American citizens of Japanese ancestry should be officially encouraged in their efforts toward loyalty and acceptance as bona fide citizens that they be accorded a place in the national effort through such agencies as the Red Cross, U.S.O., civilian defense, and even such activities as ship and aircraft building or other defense production activities, even though subject to greater investigative checks as to background and loyalty, etc., than Caucasian Americans.

(f) That in spite of paragraph (c) above, the most potentially dangerous element of all are those American citizens of Japanese ancestry who have spent the formative years of their lives, from 10 to 20, in Japan and have returned to the United States to claim their legal American citizenship within the last few years. These people are essentially and inherently Japanese and may have been deliberately sent back to the United States by the Japanese government to act as agents. In spite of their legal citizenship and the protection afforded them by the Bill of Rights, they should be looked upon as enemy aliens and many of them placed in custodial detention. This group numbers between 600 and 700 in the Los

Angeles metropolitan area and at least that many in other parts of Southern California.

(g) That the writer heartily agrees with the reports submitted by Mr. Munson [Curtis B. Munson].

(h) That, in short, the entire "Japanese Problem" has been magnified out of its true proportion, largely because of the physical characteristics of the people; that it is no more serious that the problems of the German, Italian, and Communistic portions of the United States population, and, finally that it should be handled on the basis of the individual, regardless of citizenship, and not on a racial basis.

(i) That the above opinions are and will continue to be true just so long as these people, Issei and Nisei, are given an opportunity to be self-supporting, but that if conditions continue in the trend they appear to be taking as of this date; i.e., loss of employment and income due to anti-Japanese agitation by and among Caucasian Americans, continued personal attacks by Filipinos and other racial groups, denial of relief funds to desperately needy cases, cancellation of licenses for markets, produce houses, stores, etc., by California State authorities, discharges from jobs by the wholesale, unnecessarily harsh restrictions on travel, including discriminatory regulations against all Nisei preventing them from engaging in commercial fishing—there will most certainly be outbreaks of sabotage, riots, and other civil strife in the not too distant future.

2. Lieutenant General John L. DeWitt Recommends the Removal of Japanese Americans from the West Coast, 1942

The area lying to the west of the Cascade and Sierra Nevada Mountains in Washington, Oregon and California, is highly critical not only because the lines of communication and supply to the Pacific theater pass through it, but also because of the vital industrial production therein, particularly aircraft. In the war in which we are now engaged racial affinities are not severed by migration. The Japanese race is an enemy race and while many second and third generation Japanese born on United States soil, possessed of United States citizenship, have become "Americanized", the racial strains are undiluted. To conclude otherwise is to expect that children born of white parents on Japanese soil sever all racial affinity and become loyal Japanese subjects, ready to fight and, if necessary, to die for Japan in a war against the nation of their parents. That Japan is allied with Germany and Italy in this struggle is no ground for assuming that any Japanese, barred from assimilation by convention as he is, though born and raised in the United States, will not turn against this nation when the final test of loyalty comes. It, therefore, follows that along the vital Pacific Coast over 112,000 potential enemies, of Japanese extraction, are at large today. There are indications that these are organized and ready for concerted action at a favorable

From United States Department of War, *Final Report: Japanese Evacuation from the West Coast, 1942* (Washington, D.C.: U.S. Government Printing Office, 1943), 34–37.

opportunity. The very fact that no sabotage has taken place to date is a disturbing and confirming indication that such action will be taken.

Disposition of the Japanese

(1) *Washington.* As the term is used herein, the word "Japanese" includes alien Japanese and American citizens of Japanese ancestry. In the State of Washington the Japanese population, aggregating over 14,500, is disposed largely in the area lying west of the Cascade Mountains and south of an east-west line passing through Bellingham, Washington, about 70 miles north of Seattle and some 15 miles south of the Canadian border. The largest concentration of Japanese is in the area, the axis of which is along the line Seattle, Tacoma, Olympia, Willapa Bay and the mouth of the Columbia River, with the heaviest concentration in the agricultural valleys between Seattle and Tacoma, viz., the Green River and the Puyallup Valleys. The Boeing Aircraft factory is in the Green River Valley. The lines of communication and supply including power and water which feed this vital industrial installation, radiate from this plant for many miles through areas heavily populated by Japanese. Large numbers of Japanese also operate vegetable markets along the Seattle and Tacoma water fronts, in Bremerton, near the Bremerton Navy Yard, and inhabit islands in Puget Sound opposite vital naval ship building installations. Still others are engaged in fishing along the southwest Washington Pacific Coast and along the Columbia River. Many of these Japanese are within easy reach of the forests of Washington State, the stock piles of seasoning lumber and the many sawmills of southwest Washington. During the dry season these forests, mills and stock piles are easily fired.

(2) *Oregon.* There are approximately 4,000 Japanese in the State of Oregon, of which the substantial majority reside in the area in the vicinity of Portland along the south bank of the Columbia River, following the general line Bonneville, Oregon City, Astoria, Tillamook. Many of these are in the northern reaches of the Willamette Valley and are engaged in agricultural and fishing pursuits. Others operate vegetable markets in the Portland metropolitan area and still others reside along the northern Oregon sea coast. Their disposition is in intimate relationship with the northwest Oregon sawmills and lumber industry, near and around the vital electric power development at Bonneville and the pulp and paper installations at Camas (on the Washington State side of the Columbia River) and Oregon City, directly south of Portland).

(3) *California.* The Japanese population in California aggregates approximately 93,500 people. Its disposition is so widespread and so well known that little would be gained by setting it forth in detail here. They live in great numbers along the coastal strip, in and around San Francisco and the Bay Area, the Salinas Valley, Los Angeles and San Diego. Their truck farms are contiguous to the vital aircraft industry concentration in and around Los Angeles. They live in large numbers in and about San Francisco, now a vast staging area for the war in the Pacific, a point at which the nation's lines of communication and supply converge. Inland they are disposed in the Sacramento, San Joaquin and Imperial Valleys. They are engaged in the production of approximately 38% of the

vegetable produce of California. Many of them are engaged in the distribution of such produce in and along the water fronts at San Francisco and Los Angeles. Of the 93,500 in California, about 25,000 reside inland in the mentioned valleys where they are largely engaged in vegetable production cited above, and 54,600 reside along the coastal strip, that is to say, a strip of coast line varying from eight miles in the north to twenty miles in width in and around the San Francisco bay area, including San Francisco, in Los Angeles and its environs, and in San Diego. Approximately 13,900 are dispersed throughout the remaining portion of the state. In Los Angeles City the disposition of vital aircraft industrial plants covers the entire city. Large numbers of Japanese live and operate markets and truck farms adjacent to or near these installations....

I now recommend the following:

(1) That the Secretary of War procure from the President direction and authority to designate military areas in the combat zone of the Western Theater of Operations, (if necessary to include the entire combat zone), from which, in his discretion, he may exclude all Japanese, all alien enemies, and all other persons suspected for any reason by the administering military authorities of being actual or potential saboteurs, espionage agents, or fifth columnists. Such executive order should empower the Secretary of War to requisition the services of any and all other agencies of the Federal Government, with express direction to such agencies to respond to such requisition, and further empowering the Secretary of War to use any and all federal facilities and equipment, including Civilian Conservation Corps Camps, and to accept the use of State facilities for the purpose of providing shelter and equipment for evacuees. Such executive order to provide further for the administration of military areas for the purposes of this plan by appropriate military authorities acting with the requisitioned assistance of the other federal agencies and the cooperation of State and local agencies. The executive order should further provide that by reason of military necessity the right of all persons, whether citizens or aliens, to reside, enter, cross or be within any military areas shall be subject to revocation and shall exist on a pass and permit basis at the discretion of the Secretary of War and implemented by the necessary legislation imposing penalties for violation.

3. Japanese American Mike Masaoka Vows to Cooperate with Government Removal Plans, 1942

We have been invited by you to make clear our stand regarding the proposed evacuation of all Japanese from the West coast. When the President's recent Executive order was issued, we welcomed it as definitely centralizing and coordinating defense efforts relative to the evacuation problem. Later interpretations of the order, however, seem to indicate that it is aimed primarily at the Japanese,

---

From Testimony of Mike Masaoka, House Select Committee Investigating Defense Migration, 77th Cong. 2nd Sess. (1942), 1137. Reprinted in *Asian Americans: Opposing Viewpoints*, ed. William Dudley (San Diego, CA: Greenhaven Press, 1997), 151–154.

American citizens as well as alien nationals. As your committee continues its investigations in this and subsequent hearings, we hope and trust that you will recommend to the proper authorities that no undue discrimination be shown to American citizens of Japanese descent.

Our frank and reasoned opinion on the matter of evacuation revolves around certain considerations of which we feel both your committee and the general public should be apprised. With any policy of evacuation definitely arising from reasons of military necessity and national safety, we are in complete agreement. As American citizens, we cannot and should not take any other stand. But, also, as American citizens believing in the integrity of our citizenship, we feel that any evacuation enforced on grounds violating that integrity should be opposed.

If, in the judgment of military and Federal authorities, evacuation of Japanese residents from the West coast is a primary step toward assuring the safety of this Nation, we will have no hesitation in complying with the necessities implicit in that judgment. But, if, on the other hand, such evacuation is primarily a measure whose surface urgency cloaks the desires of political or other pressure groups who want us to leave merely from motives or self-interest, we feel that we have every right to protest and to demand equitable judgment on our merits as American citizens....

We Cherish Our American Citizenship

I now make an earnest plea that you seriously consider and recognize our American citizenship status which we have been taught to cherish as our most priceless heritage.

At this hearing, we Americans of Japanese descent have been accused of being disloyal to these United States. As an American citizen, I resent these accusations and deny their validity.

We American-born Japanese are fighting militarist Japan today with our total energies. Four thousand of us are with the armed forces of the United States, the remainder on the home front in the battle of production. We ask a chance to prove to the rest of the American people what we ourselves already know: That we are loyal to the country of our birth and that we will fight to the death to defend it against any and all aggressors.

We think, feel, act like Americans. We, too, remember Pearl Harbor and know that our right to live as free men in a free Nation is in peril as long as the brutal forces of enslavement walk the earth. We know that the Axis aggressors must be crushed and we are anxious to participate fully in that struggle.

The history of our group speaks for itself. It stands favorable comparison with that of any other group of second generation Americans. There is reliable authority to show that the proportion of delinquency and crime within our ranks is negligible. Throughout the long years of the depression, we have been able to stay off the relief rolls better, by far, than any other group. These are but two of the many examples which might be cited as proof of our civic responsibility and pride.

In this emergency, as in the past, we are not asking for special privileges or concessions. We ask only for the opportunity and the right of sharing the common lot of all Americans, whether it be in peace or in war.

This is the American way for which our boys are fighting.

4. An Anonymous Poet Denounces the Incarceration of Japanese Americans, 1943

THAT DAMNED FENCE
(anonymous poem circulated at the Poston Camp)

They've sunk the posts deep into the ground
They've strung out wires all the way around,
With machine gun nests just over there,
And sentries and soldiers everywhere.

We're trapped like rats in a wired cage,
To fret and fume with impotent rage;
Yonder whispers the lure of the night,
But that DAMNED FENCE assails our sight.

We seek the softness of the midnight air,
But that DAMNED FENCE in the floodlight glare
Awakens unrest in our nocturnal quest,
And mockingly laughs with vicious jest.

With nowhere to go and nothing to do,
We feel terrible, lonesome, and blue;
That DAMNED FENCE is driving us crazy,
Destroying our youth and making us lazy.

Imprisoned in here for a long, long time,
We know we're punished–though we've committed no crime,
Our thoughts are gloomy and enthusiasm damp,
To be locked up in a concentration camp.

Loyalty we know, and patriotism we feel,
To sacrifice our utmost was our ideal,
To fight for our country, and die, perhaps;
But we're here because we happen to be Japs.

Anonymous

We all love life, and our country best,

Our misfortune to be here in the west,

To keep us penned behind that DAMNED FENCE,

Is someone's notion of NATIONAL DEFENCE!

5. Yamato Ichihashi Writes a Letter Describing the Segregation of Supposedly "Disloyal" Japanese Americans at Tule Lake, 1943

YAMATO ICHIHASHI TO PAYSON TREAT

July 25, 1943

Dear Payson:

A mention has been made, in a previous report, of the newly adopted WRA policy of segregation between those who are "loyal" and "disloyal" to the United States among the Japanese who are now residing in the various WRA projects. This note is a continuation of the same report on what has followed since then, but let me repeat briefly as a preliminary what has already taken place. On July 15th, seven of the Japanese "leaders" were called in by [Camp Director Harvey] Coverley to meet in a conference with him and three of his colleagues who hold the key positions. It was stated by Coverley that about 4,500 were directly affected by the definition of the "disloyal," or roughly one-third of the entire population of this project. Thus numerically alone it is a big problem.

On the following Monday, July 19th, Coverley was informed by the chief director of the WRA, Dillon Myer, that the Tule Lake Project was designated as the camp for the segregates or black-sheep; this was more or less anticipated by some of us, but nonetheless it proved to be a bomb shell to the majority, especially to those who are "loyal" and who are compelled to move again. On the 22nd, a second conference was held between the same groups already indicated, to inform one another concerning reactions of the residents at large and to discover the best method of meeting the situation, which will likely lead to the development of a series of troubles.

At this conference the following facts, observations, opinions, etc., were revealed:

(1) Why was it that the changes made so far in the WRA policy always resulted in imposing beatings on the loyal ones, the present case being no exception? These loyal ones constitute two-thirds of the population, and will be forced to move again. These are indignant because the disloyal ones not only escape inconveniences and hardships attending a mass movement, but also suffer no real restrictions, the declared restriction being that they will not be allowed to re-settle outside for the duration. Herein is found the source of dissatisfaction on the part of loyal ones; let me make this point clear.

Letter from Yamato Ichihashi to Payson Treat, July 25, 1943, ed. Gordon H. Chang, *Morning Glory, Evening Shadow: Yamato Ichihashi and His Internment Writings, 1942–1945* (Stanford, CA: Stanford University Press, 1997), 241–244. Reprinted by permission.

(2) The restriction to be imposed on the disloyal ones is interpreted by the WRA as a stigma of the worst kind, but the Japanese do not see it in that light. By far the great majority of the issei are now too old to adventure again; they had worked hard from 30 to 45 years to build up such foundations which they had been capable of; but they were mercilessly and completely uprooted from these foundations. They have no hope, are afraid of strange and hostile environments, and they are now physically and mentally incapable to repeat what they were able to do in the prime of their life. These are the reasons why they do not wish to re-settle outside, and therefore the so-called stigma is no stigma at all to such people. Such being the case, the issei whether loyal or disloyal are united in disagreeing with the WRA interpretation.

(3) Moreover, the people have lived in this project for a year or more, striving to re-adjust themselves, and have succeeded remarkably well in this respect. The surrounding nature and the prevailing climatic condition have previously been described: barren, monotonous, desolate and without vegetation to speak of, and yet many have created "gardens" with such available rocks, weeds, sage-brush, etc.; they have converted their bare and furnitureless one-room tenements into somewhat decent and habitable "homes" by improvising all sorts of household articles out of scrap-wood. They have developed new friendships. They have even adjusted themselves to an unnatural, communistic, community life, and have created a more or less tolerant human society. Consequently they have become attached and devoted to their own created "city," and they do not want to be broken up again and scattered in small numbers among the nine remaining projects which are to them strange lands; wherever they go, they will be treated as green-horns, and they do not like it. Sentiments? Maybe, but their feeling is intense.

(4) From the foregoing observations, you may easily surmise that the proposed policy as it affects this project is apt to cause a general rebellion on the part of the loyal people even to the point of deliberately making themselves disloyal because of their intense desire to remain here or of avoiding the necessity of going elsewhere. The local administration has emphatically been told of such a possibility, and this time it appears that the administration appears to be sympathetic with the Japanese stand. In fact, its personnel seem to dislike to see this project made into the segregation camp, but of course because of their own selfish interests. Black-sheep will not be easy to manage.

(5) So they asked for our advice in order to present effectively their/our case at the conference to be held at Denver on the coming Monday–Tuesday, at which will gather delegates from the ten projects to thresh out various problems attendant on the policy. Therefore our delegates, all the administration men, may work for some modifications of the policy, but my own personal feeling is that they will not succeed in modifying the policy so as to make this project other than the black-sheep camp.

(6) But to me by far the worst implication of the segregation policy, which was no doubt adopted because of the pressure brought about by cheap politicians and interested parties, appears as follows:

a) The wholesale evacuation of the Japanese as a people was carried out by a military necessity, and because there was no time for the differentiation of individuals. At the same time, those who were suspected of being hostile or dangerous to the interests of this country, were thrown into concentration camps. These are called internees, but the meaning of which has never been clearly defined except in a negative sense. For that matter, the status of evacuees, Japanese citizens and aliens, remains undefined to this day, resulting in technical confusion between municipal and international law. Citizens are denied their constitutional rights and aliens of their international legal protection. In this respect, prisoners of war and internees are better off because they are being governed according to the provisions of the Geneva Protocol.

b) When the segregation is effected, how could the American government continue to justify the present policy of keeping the loyal citizens and aliens in the relocation centers? It conflicts with the fundamental reason given for the wholesale evacuation. Why are those who have proved themselves to be loyal to the American interests to be denied their right of returning to their respective homes wherever they may be, and be allowed to resume their legitimate trades, businesses or professions? Such desire and aspiration are quite natural with any people, and thus they can make contributions to America; the gains resulting from such treatment are mutual and avoid the necessity of wasting public money which should not be wasted in a meaningless enterprise. What rational reasons are there of further subjecting the poor devils to an unnatural communistic life, the life [abhorrent] to Americans and to any normal peoples?

c) If the policy is continued, there can be [but] one explanation, but which, in principle, has been denied and is now being denied everyday, namely, [there is] no discrimination because of color, race or religious belief. Why [then] are Italians and Germans (aliens) given such freedom and rights or privileges, and why are loyal Japanese citizens and aliens denied the same freedom, etc.? Obviously, as individuals, Japanese are no different from Italians or Germans. Surely the American government cannot afford to be so glaringly inconsistent; a few days ago, an appeal came from the Army to Japanese citizens and their parents that the former join the Army Language School, denying racial discrimination as an established principle. What are the Japanese people to do in such circumstances? Besides, the present treatment of the Japanese on racial grounds carries bad implications for all the colored peoples of the world, including Chinese and Indians.

6. Nisei Soldiers Help Rescue A Lost Battalion, 1944

WITH SEVENTH ARMY IN FRANCE, Nov. 6, (U.P.)—A combat unit made up of Japanese American fighting men, who already had distinguished

Nisei Soldiers Help Rescue Lost Battalion, *Los Angeles Times*, November 7, 1944. Reprinted by permission.

themselves in the bitter Italian campaign, was disclosed today to have led the drive which resulted in the rescue of the "lost battalion" behind the German lines in France.

These Japanese—Americans, members of the 442nd Regimental Combat Team, had been in action in the central area of the 7th Army front for only three weeks when they launched an attack on Oct. 15 through a forest three miles west of Bruyeres [France] where the "lost battalion"—270 infantrymen of the 36th (Tex.) Division—had been trapped for more than a week.

Foodless for Days

For five days the Texans had been without food until rations and medical supplies were dropped by low-flying Thunderbolts and they had all but given up hope when the 442nd unit and other American groups broke through Nazl lines to capture Bruyeres and reach the encircled infantrymen.

Members of the lost battalion left no doubt that the 442nd rated as their favorite regiment and a strong move was afoot to declare them all honorary Texans.

Southlanders in Action

The 7th Army disclosed that Pfc. Nakada of San Bernardino Cal., whose parents live at the Gila River Relocation Center, and Staff-Sgt. Pak Senvaki of Los Angeles, whose parents are at another relocation center at McGeehee, Ark., were among the first to reach the encircled battallion.

7. The Fair Play Committee Calls on Nisei, Second-Generation Japanese Americans, to Resist the Draft Within the Heart Mountain Internment Camp, 1944

We, the Nisei have been complacent and too inarticulate to the unconstitutional acts that we were subjected to. If ever there was a time or cause for decisive action, IT IS NOW!

We, the members of the FPC are not afraid to go [to] war—we are not afraid to risk our lives for our country. We would gladly sacrifice our lives to protect and uphold the principles and ideals of our country as set forth in the Constitution and the Bill of Rights, for on its inviolability depends the freedom, liberty, justice, and protection of all people including Japanese? Americans and all other minority groups. But have we been given such freedom, such liberty, such

From Frank Abe, "One for Al—All for One," 1944; reprinted at www.resisters.com. Reprinted by permission of the author.

justice, such protection? NO!! Without any hearings, without due process of law as guaranteed by the Constitution and Bill of Rights, without any charges filed against us, without any evidence of wrongdoing on our part, one hundred and ten thousand innocent people were kicked out of their homes, literally uprooted from where they have lived for the greater part of their life, and herded like dangerous criminals into concentration camps with barbed wire fences and military police guarding it, AND THEN, WITHOUT RECTIFICATION OF THE INJUSTICES COMMITTED AGAINST US NOR WITHOUT RESTORATION OF OUR RIGHTS AS GUARANTEED BY THE CONSTITUTION, WE ARE ORDERED TO JOIN THE ARMY THRU DISCRIMINATORY PROCEDURES INTO A SEGREGATED COMBAT UNIT! Is that the American way? NO! The FPC believes that unless such actions are opposed NOW, and steps taken to remedy such injustices and discriminations IMMEDIATELY, the future of all minorities and the future of this democratic nation is in danger.

Thus, the members of the FPC unanimously decided at their last open meeting that until we are restored all our rights, all discriminatory features of the Selective Service abolished, and measures are taken to remedy the past injustices thru Judicial pronouncement or Congressional act, we feel that the present program of drafting us from this concentration camp is unjust, unconstitutional, and against all principles of civilized usage. Therefore, WE MEMBERS OF THE FAIR PLAY COMMITTEE HEREBY REFUSE TO GO TO THE PHYSICAL EXAMINATION OR TO THE INDUCTION IF OR WHEN WE ARE CALLED IN ORDER TO CONTEST THE ISSUE.

We are not being disloyal. We are not evading the draft. We are all loyal Americans fighting for JUSTICE AND DEMOCRACY RIGHT HERE AT HOME. So, restore our rights as such, rectify the injustices of evacuation, of the concentration, of the detention, and of the pauperization as such. In short, treat us in accordance with the principles of the Constitution. If what we are voicing is wrong, if what we ask is disloyal, if what we think is unpatriotic, then Abraham Lincoln, one of our greatest American President[s,] was also guilty as such, for he said, "If by the mere force of numbers a majority should deprive a minority on any Constitutional right, it might in a moral point of view justify a revolution."

Among the one thousand odd members of the Fair Play Committee, there are Nisei men over the draft age and Nisei girls who are not directly affected by the present Selective Service program, but who believe in the ideals and principles of our country, therefore are helping the FPC in our fight against injustice and discriminations.

We hope that all persons whose ideals and interests are with us will do all they can to help us. We may have to engage in court actions but as such actions require large sums of money, we do need financial support and when the time comes we hope that you will back us up to the limit.

ATTENTION MEMBERS! FAIR PLAY COMMITTEE MEETING SUNDAY, MARCH 5, 2:00 P.M. BLOCK 6?30 MESS. PARENTS, BROTHERS, SISTERS, AND FRIENDS INVITED.

8. Justice Frank Murphy Criticizes the Supreme Court's "Legalization of Racism," 1944

Mr. Justice MURPHY, dissenting

This exclusion of "all persons of Japanese ancestry, both alien and non-alien," from the Pacific Coast area on a plea of military necessity in the absence of martial law ought not to be approved. Such exclusion goes over "the very brink of constitutional power" and falls into the ugly abyss of racism.

In dealing with matters relating to the prosecution and progress of a war, we must accord great respect and consideration to the judgments of the military authorities who are on the scene and who have full knowledge of the military facts. The scope of their discretion must, as a matter of necessity and common sense, be wide. And their judgments ought not to be overruled lightly by those whose training and duties ill-equip them to deal intelligently with matters so vital to the physical security of the nation.

At the same time, however, it is essential that there be definite limits to military discretion, especially where martial law has not been declared. Individuals must not be left impoverished of their constitutional rights on a plea of military necessity that has neither substance nor support. Thus, like other claims conflicting with the asserted constitutional rights of the individual, the military claim must subject itself to the judicial process of having its reasonableness determined and its conflicts with other interests reconciled....

The judicial test of whether the Government, on a plea of military necessity, can validly deprive an individual of any of his constitutional rights is whether the deprivation is reasonably related to a public danger that is so "immediate, imminent and impending" as not to admit of delay and not to permit the intervention of ordinary constitutional processes to alleviate the danger.... Civilian Exclusion Order No. 34, banishing from a prescribed area of the Pacific Coast "all persons of Japanese ancestry, both alien and non-alien," clearly does not meet that test. Being an obvious racial discrimination, the order deprives all those within its scope of the equal protection of the laws as guaranteed by the Fifth Amendment. It further deprives these individuals of their constitutional rights to live and work where they will, to establish a home where they choose and to move about freely. In excommunicating

From Korematsu v. United States, 323 U.S. 233, 235, 239–242; reprinted in *Racism, Dissent, and Asian Americans from 1850 to the Present a Documentary History*, ed. Philip S. Foner (Westport, CT: Greenwood Press, 1993), 254–257.

them without benefit of hearings, this order also deprives them of all their constitutional rights to procedural due process. Yet no reasonable relation to an "immediate, imminent, and impending" public danger is evident to support this racial restriction which is one of the most sweeping and complete deprivations of constitutional rights in the history of this nation in the absence of martial law.

It must be conceded that the military and naval situation in the spring of 1942 was such as to generate a very real fear of invasion of the Pacific Coast, accompanied by fears of sabotage and espionage in that area. The military command was therefore justified in adopting all reasonable means necessary to combat these dangers. In adjudging the military action taken in light of the then apparent dangers, we must not erect too high or too meticulous standards; it is necessary only that the action have some reasonable relation to the removal of the dangers of invasion, sabotage and espionage. But the exclusion, either temporarily of permanently, of all persons with Japanese blood in the veins has no such reasonable relation. And that relation is lacking because the exclusion order necessarily must rely for its reasonableness upon the assumption that *all* persons of Japanese ancestry may have a dangerous tendency to commit sabotage and espionage and to aid our Japanese enemy in other ways. It is difficult to believe that reason, logic or experience could be marshalled in support of such an assumption.

... The main reasons relied upon by those responsible for the forced evacuation, therefore, do not prove a reasonable relation between the group characteristics of Japanese Americans and the dangers of invasion, sabotage and espionage. The reasons appear, instead, to be largely an accumulation of much of the misinformation, half-truths and insinuations that for years have been directed against Japanese Americans by people with racial and economic prejudices—the same people who have been among the foremost advocates of the evacuation. A military judgment based upon such racial and sociological considerations is not entitled to the great weight ordinarily given the judgments based upon strictly military considerations. Especially is this so when every charge relative to race, religion, culture, geographical location, and legal and economic status has been substantially discredited by independent studies made by experts in these matters.

The military necessity which is essential to the validity of the evacuation order thus resolves itself into a few intimations that certain individuals actively aided the enemy, from which it is inferred that the entire group of Japanese Americans could not be trusted to be or remain loyal to the United States. No one denies, of course, that there were some disloyal persons of Japanese descent on the Pacific Coast who did all in their power to aid their ancestral land. Similar disloyal activities have been engaged in by many persons of German, Italian and even more pioneer stock in our country. But to infer that examples of individual disloyalty prove group disloyalty and justify discriminatory action against the entire group is to deny that under our system of law individual guilt is the sole basis for deprivation of rights. Moreover, this inference, which is at the very heart of the evacuation orders, has been used in support of the abhorrent and despicable treatment of minority groups by the dictatorial tyrannies which this nation is now pledged to destroy. To give constitutional sanction to that inference in this case, however well-intentioned may have been the military command on the Pacific Coast, is to adopt one of the cruelest of the rationales used by our enemies to destroy the dignity of the individual and to encourage and open the door to discriminatory actions against other minority groups in the passions of tomorrow.

No adequate reason is given for the failure to treat these Japanese Americans on an individual basis by holding investigations and hearings to separate the loyal from the disloyal, as was done in the case of persons of German and Italian ancestry.... It is asserted merely that the loyalties of this group "were unknown and time was of the essence." Yet nearly four months elapsed after Pearl Harbor before the first exclusion order was issued; nearly eight months went by until the last order was issued; and the last of these "subversive" persons was not actually removed until almost eleven months had elapsed. Leisure and deliberation seem to have been more of the essence than speed. And the fact that conditions were not such as to warrant a declaration of martial law adds strength to the belief that the factors of time and military necessity were not as urgent as they have been represented to be.

Moreover, there was no adequate proof that the Federal Bureau of Investigation and the military and naval intelligence services did not have the espionage and sabotage situation well in hand during this long period. Nor is there any denial of the fact that not one person of Japanese ancestry was accused or convicted of espionage or sabotage after Pearl Harbor while they were still free, a fact which is some evidence of the loyalty of the vast majority of these individuals and of the effectiveness of the established methods of combatting these evils. It seems incredible that under these circumstances it would have been impossible to hold loyalty hearings for the mere 112,000 persons involved—or at least for the 70,000 American citizens—especially when a large part of this number represented children and elderly men and women. Any inconvenience that may have accompanied an attempt to conform to procedural due process cannot be said to justify violations of constitutional rights of individuals.

I dissent, therefore, from this legalization or racism. Racial discrimination in any form and in any degree has no justifiable part whatever in our democratic way of life. It is unattractive in any setting but it is utterly revolting among a free people who have embraced the principles set forth in the Constitution of the United States. All residents of this nation are kin in some way by blood or culture to a foreign land. Yet they are primarily and necessarily a part of the new and distinct civilization of the United States. They must accordingly be treated at all times as the heirs of the American experiment and as entitled to all the rights and freedoms guaranteed by the Constitution.

9. Esther (Takei) Nishio Describes Returning to the West Coast, 1944

ESTHER (TAKEI) NISHIO: Organizations like the American Legion, Daughters of the American Revolution, Sons and Daughters of the Golden West, that sort of organization would all protest my return. But I never ran into anyone in particular. But I did run into ordinary citizens, and they would spit at me or call me "Jap" or something in that order. But my friends would ask them, "Why are you doing that?" They would say because— well one person said, "Well, when I went to a vegetable stand before the war and bought cauliflower or something, it made me sick!" It was very stupid! So it was just ignorance.

And there was one little old lady, in particular, who[m] I would run into at the bus stop. She would always call me, "Jap", and [say,] "Get out of here!" And one day she slapped me. One of my school friends said, "Why did you [do] that!" She said, "Because she's a Jap!" And he said, "Well, she's a better American than you are!" So there were people who stood up for you. And I understand that the other girls who came after me to school had the same experience. Some people would stare at them, call them names, and slap them. One girl said she even received a threatening phone call. So I guess things still hadn't settled down yet

DARCIE IKI: So about how long do you think the controversy continued after you first—?

ESTHER NISHIO: Well, I'm not sure. It didn't last too long, maybe a month or so. And there were letters pro and con, and a lot of servicemen would write to me and they would encourage me. I understand that when the American Legion was in Glendale it announced that they would march on Pasadena and protest. The Pasadena American Legion ordered them to stay away because their veterans—some of them had served in the Pacific—and they said they had fought for the rights of people like us. And they didn't want anybody interfering with citizen's rights.

IKI: And this is the Pasadena American Legion?

ESTHER NISHIO: Um hm. Well they were against my returning at the beginning but I think, after all this controversy, they came to realize that they were fighting the wrong war. I guess when things were really hot and heavy, students who had been in the South Pacific that returned to school were in an organization called the Amvets. And they kind of acted as a—not an honor guard, but they would escort me from class to class just to be sure that I was safe during that time.

IKI: Mmm. That's amazing.

ESTHER NISHIO: Mmhm. And, I guess, during that time Mr. [Hugh] Anderson's family had received many threatening calls. One of the papers in Pasadena had apparently printed their home address in every issue. So there would be streams of cars driving past their home to catch a glimpse of me, or Mr. Anderson's family, and so they had a very rough time. Dr. [John] Harbeson, who was the principal of the school, also received threatening calls. According to Mr. Anderson, Dr. Harbeson called one night [and said] that he received a bomb threat, and would I please—would he please ask Esther Takei to leave Pasadena, and go to Nebraska to attend school. He said, "I'll arrange it so they'll accept her there."

IKI: This is what Mr. Harbeson said?

ESTHER NISHIO: Dr. Harbeson asked Mr. Anderson. And so during that period, I guess when it was really bad, Mr. Anderson had his family visit relatives in another city. I stayed with another family [that] happened to be Mr. Walt Raitt's family. He was the advisor of the Student Christian Association. So I stayed with him for about five to 10 days, during the worst time.

IKI: So what is this like for you? You're nineteen years old and all of this is happening all around you? And, I mean it must have been such an adjustment on so many different levels?

ESTHER NISHIO: Well, I can't remember exactly, but it must have been difficult to study and go to school (laughter). It was interesting reading the articles and seeing how they would argue about having someone like me coming back, because they would consider me an alien. And it took servicemen to point out that there is a difference. [They pointed out] that they were treating an American citizen in a very terrible way, and they were fighting for all citizens. They were trying to protect the rights of people like us to, you know, go to school where they wanted to go to school.

IKI: That's really great. I mean that's really amazing, because at the same time, there were veterans in other parts of the country who had a completely opposite reaction to the situation.

ESTHER NISHIO: I was really impressed. Because a lot of these servicemen had served, or were serving, in the South Pacific—fighting the Japanese. Yet they were standing up for my rights. And I thought that was so wonderful. I don't remember their names, but lots of servicemen would read about my story. They would either call the Anderson family to see how I was doing, or they would hitch a ride and come to visit me, to protect me. They thought I was being overrun by all these protesters. They were really great!

IKI: Can you tell more about that one young soldier?

ESTHER NISHIO: Well, there was one gentleman who decided he was going to come and rescue me, and so he hopped on a train. I thought he was from the Midwest, but he was from the East Coast, and he came all the way to LA. I met him at the Union Station, and I reassured him that I was fine. I took him to lunch at Philippes* for a beef dip sandwich, and put him back on the train, and he went home. (laughter)

IKI: How did you know he was coming? He had written you?

ESTHER NISHIO: Well, I think he had either written or called me, so we had this date. And then another gentleman that I didn't get to meet was stationed up [in] northern or central California, along the coast. I forgot the name of the station, but he hitchhiked all night and came to Pasadena. Since I was asleep, he met Mr. Anderson. Mr. Anderson reassured him that I was fine, and he hitchhiked his way home again. So there were soldiers like that who really believed in protecting the rights of American citizens. I was so lucky that they were like that!

IKI: And these are—are these Japanese Americans?

ESTHER NISHIO: No, these were Caucasian soldiers. And then, also, I met a lot of 442nd soldiers who had been wounded and were recuperating at a hospital in Pasadena. It was formerly a very ritzy hotel called the Vista Del Arroyo Hotel, right by the Colorado Street Bridge, but they had converted it into an army hospital. So we would go visit these soldiers there. And there were other soldiers who had been wounded and were recuperating. I think they were from Palm Springs or somewhere in that area. They would come to town to see me and encourage me, and then I would, you know, try to take them to see a movie or something while they were in Pasadena.

IKI: Well that must have been incredibly encouraging for you to have all these people—

ESTHER NISHIO: Well, it was uplifting, really, to learn of the human spirit and how people will help you. There were so many people who were so brave. You know, during the war, it was not popular to be pro-Japanese or pro-Japanese American. Yet Mr. Anderson and Mr. [William] Carr who had founded The Friends and the American Way and their group—I think they had about twenty members—they went against public opinion to help the Japanese Americans. And they, I understand wrote letters to all the former Pasadena Japanese families in all the camps and offered to send them whatever they needed. [It was] just to let them know and they would provide it.

---

*Philippe's Original Sandwich Shop was established in 1908.

And, you know, they did things like that and they were—when I was having my problems on my return, conscientious objectors would write letters to the editor [of] all the papers in support of my going to school here. So a lot people were so good to me. I've said it before, but when I first returned, the members of the black community were so kind to me, and they made things so easy for me to come back. And the Latino churches were so welcoming. It was really nice. I went to the Pasadena Methodist Church. They had all been so good to us.

IKI: So what types of things did the African-American community do?

ESTHER NISHIO: They would invite me to their potluck suppers and things like that. They made me feel welcome. They were really nice.

IKI: That's so great. Were there other organizations or individuals—?

ESTHER NISHIO: The Quakers were very, very cognizant of the plight of the Japanese American, and they were very, very helpful.

ESSAYS

The following two essays examine the multiple perspectives of Japanese Americans during World War II. The first essay, by Alice Yang, a University of California, Santa Cruz, historian, examines the causes and consequences of Japanese American internment. Yang discusses the role of anti-Asian racism and hysteria following Pearl Harbor in the decision to incarcerate Japanese Americans, and she describes the tense and conflicted conditions within the camps. The second essay, by Michael Jin, an assistant professor of history at the University of Illinois, Chicago, examines the transnational experiences of Kibei, Japanese American citizens born in the United States and educated in Japan, who were branded by U.S. government officials and JACL leaders as disloyal supporters of imperial Japan. While some Kibei protested the mass removal and internment, others cooperated fully with these government orders and were some of the most patriotic internees within the camps. Jin notes that over generalized suspicion of Kibei influenced debates on Japanese American loyalty, the development of internment policies, the creation of a segregation center, and government attempts to strip Kibei of their U.S. citizenship.

The Internment of Japanese Americans

ALICE YANG

From Pearl Harbor to Mass Incarceration: A Brief Narrative

On the morning of December 7, 1941, Japanese Americans learned the shocking news that Japan had attacked Pearl Harbor in Hawaii. Like most Americans, they

From "What Did the Internment of Japanese Americans Mean?" by Alice Yang Murray. Copyright © 2000 by Bedford/St. Martin's. Used with permission of the publisher.

were stunned by the surprise assault that destroyed America's Pacific fleet. As Americans of Japanese ancestry, however, these immigrants and their children, American citizens by virtue of their birth in the United States, also feared retaliation. Even before the smoke had cleared from the ruins at Pearl Harbor, Federal Bureau of Investigation agents began rounding up suspected "enemy aliens" throughout Hawaii and the West Coast. Most of those arrested were male immigrants put under surveillance a year before the attack because they were leaders of the ethnic community—Japanese Association officials, Buddhist priests, Japanese-language teachers, and newspaper editors. In the weeks following the declaration of war, the FBI arrested more than two thousand of these Japanese immigrants and ten thousand immigrants from Germany and Italy suspected of belonging to pro-Nazi or fascist organizations.

The FBI interrogated these immigrants and sent those considered "dangerous" to internment camps administered by the Department of Justice.... The largest of these camps, the one in Crystal City, Texas, also interned many of the 2,264 Japanese Latin Americans deported from their countries so that the United States might exchange them for Americans held by Japan in 1942 and 1943.

The Justice Department camps held about 10 percent of all Japanese immigrants from the West Coast. Many of these immigrants questioned the fairness of their hearings.

All hopes of returning home, however, were dashed when they learned in March 1942 that all Japanese Americans on the West Coast would be interned in separate camps run by the War Relocation Authority (WRA).

Ultimately, 120,000 Japanese Americans, two-thirds of whom were citizens, were interned in one of ten WRA camps. Why did the U.S. government decide to remove and confine people from the West Coast solely on the basis of their Japanese ancestry? Most scholars now agree that this decision was not simply the product of wartime hysteria but reflected a long history of anti-Japanese hostility fueled by economic competition and racial stereotypes....

The attack on Pearl Harbor and the rapid succession of victories by Japanese forces in the Pacific rekindled the embers of anti-Japanese sentiment.

As Americans struggled to make sense of these losses, news accounts of the attack on Pearl Harbor fanned the flames of hatred against Japanese Americans. Secretary of the Navy Frank Knox told the press of an effective "fifth column"* in Hawaii, even though his official report contained no such charges. The report remained classified, and the government did nothing to allay the fears spawned by Knox's remarks as headlines blared "Secretary of Navy Blames Fifth Column for the Raid" and "Fifth Column Treachery Told." Further misleading the public and contributing to the "official" validation of sabotage suspicions were declarations by a committee of inquiry on Pearl Harbor, led by Supreme Court Justice Owen J. Roberts, that Japanese spies had helped the enemy during the "sneak" attack. Newspapers began reporting wild rumors about the bombing of Pearl Harbor as "facts." The *Los Angeles Times*, for example, announced that

---

* *fifth column*: a covert group or faction of subversive agents.

Japanese fliers shot down over Pearl Harbor were wearing class rings of the University of Hawaii and Honolulu High School. The paper even claimed that a Japanese resident painted himself green and "camouflaged himself so he could hide in the foliage and aid attacking Japs."

As reports of Pearl Harbor "treachery" proliferated, West Coast politicians stoked the fires of anti-Japanese prejudice and began clamoring for the removal of Japanese immigrants and citizens. In California, Congressman Leland Ford, Mayor Fletcher Bowron of Los Angeles, Governor Culbert Olson, and California Attorney General Earl Warren demanded that Washington take action to protect the West Coast from "Jap" spies. The advocates of internment found a receptive audience in the commander of the Western Defense Command, Lieutenant General John L. DeWitt. In charge of protecting West Coast security, DeWitt was more impressed by the dire warnings of California politicians and Allen Gullion, provost marshal general for the army, than by reports from Naval Intelligence, the FBI, and the Army General Staff dismissing any threat of sabotage, espionage, or invasion.

On February 14, 1942, DeWitt sent a memo to Secretary of War Henry Stimson recommending the removal of all immigrants and citizens of Japanese ancestry from the West Coast. DeWitt's memo declared, "The Japanese race is an enemy race," and "racial affinities are not severed by migration." Even second- and third-generation Japanese Americans who were citizens and "Americanized" could not be trusted, according to DeWitt, because "the racial strains are undiluted." Taking for granted that all "Japs" were disloyal, DeWitt concluded that the "very fact that no sabotage has taken place to date" was a "disturbing and confirming indication that such action will be taken."

Why did Washington accept DeWitt's recommendation? Members of the government who knew there was no need to remove Japanese Americans mounted a tepid response to the advocates of internment. FBI director J. Edgar Hoover wrote a memo to Attorney General Francis Biddle noting that the public hysteria was groundless. Biddle argued against mass exclusion at a luncheon conference with President Roosevelt. But neither one publicized their objections or criticized plans for mass removal on constitutional grounds. Once it became clear that the War Department and the president supported DeWitt's request, Biddle even proceeded to help implement the plans for mass removal.

President Roosevelt accepted Secretary of War Stimson's advice to endorse DeWitt's plans and ignored the advice of his own intelligence specialists.

Instead, Roosevelt signed Executive Order 9066 on February 19, 1942, authorizing the War Department to designate military areas from which "any and all persons may be excluded." Although this order never specifically named Japanese Americans, it soon became clear that they would be the only group targeted for mass removal. DeWitt also wanted to exclude German and Italian "enemy aliens" from the West Coast, but his civilian superiors at the War Department overruled him.

Individuals of Japanese ancestry in Hawaii were spared from mass exclusion despite the fact that the islands were more vulnerable to an invasion than the West Coast. The 158,000 people of Japanese ancestry in Hawaii were, however, viewed with suspicion and suffered special restrictions under martial law.

"Enemy aliens" in Hawaii were required to carry a registration card at all times and endured travel and work limitations. Almost fifteen hundred "suspects" of Japanese ancestry were arrested and interned in camps run by the U.S. Army or the Department of Justice because of their activities within the ethnic community. Yet General DeWitt's counterpart in Hawaii, General Delos Emmons, recognized that Japanese labor was critical to both the civilian and the military economies of the islands. Japanese Americans made up less than 2 percent of the population of the West Coast and could be removed without much difficulty. But removing more than 35 percent of the population of Hawaii not only would be a logistical nightmare but also would cripple many industries needed for the war effort.

DeWitt, by contrast, quickly implemented plans for mass exclusion on the West Coast. At first, he simply ordered Japanese Americans to leave Military Area 1, which consisted of southern Arizona and the western portions of Washington, Oregon, and California. Yet "voluntary evacuation" was short-lived because public officials in the mountain states condemned the prospect of their states becoming "dumping grounds" for California "Japs." If they were too dangerous to roam freely in California, why weren't they too dangerous to let loose in Idaho and Wyoming? With the exception of Governor Ralph Carr of Colorado, the governors of these western states unanimously opposed voluntary migration and urged that Japanese Americans be placed in "concentration camps."

Consequently, at the end of March, "voluntary evacuation" was replaced with what the government called a "planned and systematic evacuation." The government used such euphemisms to mask the fact that immigrants and citizens would be incarcerated behind barbed wire. Even the three thousand Japanese Americans who had moved from Military Area 1 to Military Area 2 in the eastern half of California, based on government assurances that this area would remain a "free zone," were forced into internment camps.

The Internment Camps

The government developed a two-step internment program. Japanese Americans were first transported to one of sixteen "assembly centers" near their homes and then sent to one of ten "relocation centers" in California, Arizona, Utah, Idaho, Wyoming, Colorado, or Arkansas. Most Japanese Americans had less than a week's notice before being uprooted from their homes and community. Instructed to bring only what they could carry, most had little choice but to sell businesses, homes, and prized possessions for a fraction of their value. Internment also disrupted educational and career plans. But for many Japanese Americans, the stigma of suspected disloyalty and the loss of liberty inflicted the deepest wounds. As one internee later recalled, "The most valuable thing I lost was my freedom."

A few Japanese Americans defied DeWitt's orders. Lawyer Minoru Yasui, still outraged by the internment of his father, Masuo Yasui, decided to walk the streets of Portland, Oregon, at night deliberately disobeying the curfew order. After failing to get a policeman to arrest him, he turned himself in at a police station so that he could contest DeWitt's authority in court. Yasui was soon joined by Gordon Hirabayashi, a twenty-four-year-old University of Washington student, who went to an FBI office to report his refusal to comply with removal orders. The third Japanese American to wage a legal challenge did not initially plan to be a protester. Fred Korematsu had simply wanted to remain in Oakland and San Francisco to be with his Italian American fiancée. But after he was discovered and arrested for violating the Army's exclusion order, Korematsu also decided to battle the government in court. Yasui, Hirabayashi, and Korematsu forced the Supreme Court to consider the constitutionality of the government's curfew and exclusion policies. When the Court affirmed the legality of the "mass evacuation," it established a legal precedent for the wartime removal of a single ethnic group that has never been officially overturned. Only in the case of Mitsuyé Endo did the justices acknowledge a limitation to the government's powers to detain Japanese Americans. On December 18, 1944, the Supreme Court ruled in the Endo case that camp administrators had "no authority to subject citizens who are concededly loyal to its leave restrictions" and made it possible for at least some Japanese Americans to return to the West Coast.

Although a few individuals went to court to fight the removal and detention orders, most Japanese Americans complied with DeWitt's instructions. Few had any idea of their destinations when they were labeled, like luggage, with numbered identification tags at designated departure points in April and early May 1942. Most of the "assembly centers" were located at racetracks and fairgrounds, and many families stayed in hastily converted horse stalls that reeked of manure. Then, at the end of May, they were sent to camps run by the WRA, where barbed wire, watchtowers, and military police reminded them that they were prisoners who could not leave without the administrators' approval. Even those who received permission to leave the camps could not return to the West Coast until the exclusion order was lifted in December 1944.

Most internment camps were located on desert or swamp-like terrain. In some camps, winter temperatures dropped to 35 degrees below zero, and summer temperatures soared as high as 115 degrees. The hot and humid summers in the Arkansas camps bred swarms of chiggers and mosquitoes. The assistant project director at Minidoka, a camp in Idaho, described the camp as "hot, dusty, [and] desolate" and remarked on the "flat land, nothing growing but sagebrush, not a tree in sight." A WRA official noted a common problem in many camps: "a dust storm nearly every day for the first two months.... Fine, choking dust ... swirled over the center. Traffic was sometimes forced to a standstill because there was no visibility."

Facilities differed from camp to camp, but all were spartan. Internees were assigned to a block consisting of fourteen barracks subdivided into four or six rooms. The average room for a family of six measured twenty by twenty-five feet. Privacy within the barracks proved elusive because room dividers often stopped short of the roof. Many internees, especially older women, were mortified by the lack of partitions in the communal bathrooms. Families constantly battled the dust that seeped through the barracks planks. The WRA supplied only canvas cots, a potbellied stove, and a lightbulb hanging from the ceiling. Resourceful internees later constructed makeshift furniture from scrap lumber and cultivated their own gardens to supplement the unfamiliar and unappetizing food served in the mess halls. Standing in line became an integral part of camp life. The WRA's assistant regional director once reported counting three hundred people waiting outside a mess hall.

At first, no internee could leave the center except for an emergency, and then only if chaperoned by someone not of Japanese ancestry. Regardless of education or training, Japanese American workers were subordinate to WRA personnel and received vastly lower wages of $12, $16, or $19 a month. For example, a WRA librarian might earn $167 a month, whereas her Japanese American staff members were paid only $16 for doing similar work. Moreover, wages and clothing allowances were often delayed, and the WRA failed to fulfill its promise to ship household goods to arriving internees. There were even rumors that WRA staff members at several camps stole food and other supplies.

WRA policies also exacerbated pre-existing tensions between Issei (first-generation) and Nisei (second-generation) community leaders. The government named Nisei leaders in the Japanese American Citizens League (JACL) as representatives of the entire ethnic community. Even though this middle-class, second-generation organization had fewer than eight thousand members before the war, government officials were pleased by JACL ultrapatriotic statements praising "American Democracy," vowing cooperation, and expressing gratitude for benevolent internment policies. Camp administrators accepted JACL advice to limit community government positions to citizens, to ban Japanese-language schools, and to prohibit the use of the Japanese language at public meetings. Whereas JACL leaders believed that cooperation, assimilation, and regaining the right to serve in the military were necessary to combat racism, many disgruntled internees, especially the disempowered Issei, derided JACL leaders as "inu" or dogs who collaborated with the government against the interests of the community.

As hostility toward the WRA grew, some internees vented their anger against JACL leaders suspected of being informers. The arrests of individuals accused of beating up suspected "inu" generated protests against the administration at the Poston and Manzanar Camps at the end of 1942. When the project director at Poston refused to release two men arrested for an attack, internees waged a general strike that shut down most camp services. Deciding to negotiate with the strikers, camp administrators agreed to release one suspect and to try the other within the camp rather than in an Arizona court. In return, strike leaders agreed to try to stop assaults against suspected "inu" and to promote harmony with the administration.

Similar protests at Manzanar, however, ended in bloodshed. The project director summoned the military police to put down a mass demonstration calling for the release of an arrested internee. When the crowd refused to disperse, military police sprayed tear gas, which was ineffective due to the wind. A member of the crowd started a car and aimed it at the police. While witnesses disagree about whether the police began firing before or after the car was started, all agree that they opened fire directly on the crowd, killing two people and wounding at least nine others. Even after the administration removed JACL leaders from the camp and moved suspected agitators to isolation camps, tensions remained high.

Turmoil enveloped all of the camps in February 1943, when the WRA instituted a loyalty review program with little or no notice and without a clear explanation as to how the information gathered would be used. All internees over the age of seventeen were told to fill out a "leave clearance" application, which included ambiguously worded questions that confused many internees. Ironically, the WRA mistakenly assumed that the internees would be grateful for this expedited "leave clearance" program, which would allow them to move to the Midwest or East and volunteer for military service. JACL leaders had fought for the opportunity to serve in the armed forces and praised the War Department's decision to allow Japanese Americans to volunteer for a segregated combat unit on January 28, 1943. But many other internees resented being asked to shed blood for a country that had imprisoned them.

Unaware of the depth of internee fear and anger, WRA officials were shocked by the controversy generated by two of the questions on the leave application. Question 27 required internees to say whether they were "willing to serve in the armed forces of the United States on combat duty, wherever ordered." Question 28 asked, "Will you swear unqualified allegiance to the United States of America and faithfully defend the United States from any or all attack by foreign or domestic forces, and forswear any form of allegiance or obedience to the Japanese emperor, or any other foreign government, power or organization?" Taking for granted that both questions would be answered positively, the WRA didn't contemplate how foolish it was to ask elderly Issei to serve in combat. Some Nisei suspected that question 28 was designed to trap them into admitting an "allegiance" to the emperor they never had. The injustice of asking immigrants ineligible for American citizenship to become stateless by forswearing "any form of allegiance or obedience to the Japanese emperor" was recognized only belatedly. But even after WRA officials rephrased these questions, some internees still refused to complete the "leave clearance" forms to avoid being forced to resettle. After losing their businesses and property and being told that they could not return to the West Coast, some embittered internees were skeptical that they could start over in predominantly white communities in the Midwest and East.

Although about some 68,000 internees answered the two loyalty questions with an unqualified yes, approximately 5,300 answered "no no" and about 4,600 either refused to answer or qualified their responses. One WRA staff member noted how difficult it was to distinguish

> the No of protest against discrimination, the No of protest against a
> father interned apart from his family, the No of bitter antagonism to
> subordinations in the relocation center, the No of a gang sticking

together, the No of thoughtless defiance, the No of family duty, the No of hopeless confusion, the No of fear of military service, and the No of felt loyalty to Japan.

Far from measuring "loyalty" to the United States or Japan, the questionnaire, another staff member noted, "sorted people chiefly into the disillusioned and the defiant as against the compliant and the hopeful."

Some of "the compliant and the hopeful" followed WRA procedures to leave camp for military service, jobs, or college programs. But of the almost 20,000 men in the camps who were eligible for military service, only 1,200 actually volunteered from behind barbed wire. Later, at the beginning of 1944, the Selective Service began drafting Japanese Americans. More than 300 men refused to comply with the draft while they and their families were still incarcerated. Many of these draft resisters served prison terms of two to four years, but they were pardoned by President Harry Truman in 1947. Other Japanese Americans agreed to offer "proof in blood" of their loyalty to the United States. Ultimately, approximately 23,000 Nisei, more than half from Hawaii, served in the 100th Infantry Battalion, the 442nd Regimental Combat Team, and the Military Intelligence Service during World War II. Fighting seven major campaigns in Italy and France, the 442nd suffered almost 9,500 casualties (300 percent of its original complement) and became the most decorated unit in American military history for its size and length of service.

Other Japanese Americans left the camps through the WRA's "seasonal leave" program, developed in the summer of 1942 to address a shortage of farmworkers. In 1942 and 1943, more than eight thousand internees obtained work release furloughs. The WRA encouraged internees who passed the "loyalty test" to resettle in the interior states after February 1943. By December 1943, the National Japanese American Student Relocation Council was able to place more than two thousand Nisei in colleges in the Midwest and East. Then, on December 17, 1944, officials announced the termination of mass exclusion one day before the Supreme Court declared in the Endo case that the United States could no longer detain loyal citizens against their will. Once allowed to go back home, more than two-thirds of the internee population chose to return to the West Coast.

A significant number of "the disillusioned and the defiant," however, remained in camps even after the war ended in August 1945. The Tule Lake camp in northern California, which had been transformed into a "segregation center" for "disloyals," did not close until March 1946. Approximately one-third of the eighteen thousand residents at Tule Lake were people the WRA deemed "disloyal"; another third were members of their families; and the final third were "Old Tuleans," who, when the camp was designated as a segregation center in 1943, chose to remain with the "disloyals" rather than be forced to move a second time. The combination of this diverse internee population and a repressive administration created an explosive atmosphere at the segregation center. On November 4, 1943, the Army was called in to quell a demonstration, took over the camp, and declared martial law, which remained in effect until January 15, 1944. In the last half of 1944, the WRA allowed "resegregationists," who demanded a separation of those wanting to leave the United States for Japan and those at Tule Lake for other reasons, to dominate the camp. Using rumors, beatings, and in one case murder, the resegregationists intimidated inmates considered "fence-sitters" or "loyal" to the United States. By the time the WRA brought the camp back under control, seven of every ten adult Nisei had renounced their citizenship.

The Department of Justice received more than 6,000 applications for renunciation of citizenship and approved 5,589 of them. This number represented 12.5 percent of the 70,000 citizens interned during the war. But even before many of these applications were processed, most of the "renunciants" tried to withdraw their requests. In fact, 5,409 citizens attempted to rescind their applications but the government ignored these attempts and proceeded with plans to deport these people to Japan. In August and September 1945, the renunciants who wanted to fight for their citizenship rights organized the Tule Lake Defense Committee and hired attorney Wayne M. Collins to represent them. Collins resisted pressure from the national American Civil Liberties Union to withdraw from the case and spent more than a decade fighting on behalf of the renunciants. In his suit, Collins argued that the Nisei had been coerced into renouncing their citizenship. He said that the government's forced removal and incarceration of Japanese Americans had subjected internees to "inhuman" treatment and extreme duress. To compound this injustice, the government had known about but had done nothing to restrain a small group of Japanese Americans at Tule Lake who terrorized many of the Nisei until they renounced their citizenship. Finally, after fourteen years, citizenship rights were restored to 4,978 Nisei.

Perhaps the most tragic example of "defiance" against the authorities was opposition to the closing of the camps. Instead of celebrating the prospect of freedom, many demoralized internees demanded that the government continue to provide for them or at least increase the amount of assistance given to resettlers. Many were afraid to leave the camps after hearing reports of how Japanese Americans outside of camp were subjected to arson, vandalism, and even gunfire. Many Issei men in their sixties didn't relish the prospect of starting over and felt that they were "entitled to receive compensation from the Government for the losses which they experienced at the time of evacuation." Rejecting these calls for substantive redress, the WRA gave recalcitrant internees $25 and put them on trains back to their hometowns.

Japanese American Citizenship, Loyalty, and the "Kibei Problem" During World War II

MICHAEL JIN

By the eve of the Second World War, thousands of second-generation Japanese Americans (*Nisei*) had lived and traveled outside the United States. Many Nisei had been sent to Japan at young ages by their immigrant parents to be

Essay by Michael Jin, written for this volume. Reprinted with permission of the author.

raised in the households of their relatives and receive a proper Japanese education. Many Nisei also sought opportunities for employment or higher education
in a country that represented an expanding colonial power in Asia especially during the 1930s. Although no official data exist to help determine the exact number of Nisei in Japan before the Pacific War, various sources suggest that about
50,000 Americans of Japanese ancestry spent some of their formative years in
Japan. Of these Nisei, 10,000-20,000 returned to the United States before the
outbreak of Pearl Harbor and became known as *Kibei* ("returned to America").

The Kibei who returned from Japan before the war and subsequently experienced the wartime incarceration along with the other 110,000 or so Japanese and
Japanese Americans from the West Coast have become controversial figures in both
the Japanese American community and scholarship. Because of their education in
Japan, many Kibei have been stigmatized as pro-Japan elements in the internment
camps. Both government and Japanese American Citizens League (JACL) wartime
documents reveal that the existence of Kibei was central to shaping the history of
Japanese American internment during the critical years of the Pacific War.

The presence of Kibei on the U.S. West Coast served the proponents of the
mass incarceration of Japanese Americans within the U.S. government as a justification of the "military necessity" to remove all Nisei from the West Coast without
due process of law. For instance, Western Defense Commander John L. Dewitt,
who had recommended forced relocation of Japanese Americans under military
supervision, found in Kibei convenient scapegoats and used their education in
Japan as evidence of their alleged pro-Japan attitudes. In *The Final Report: Japanese
Evacuation from the West Coast, 1942*, DeWitt claimed that Kibei were a "homogenous, unassimilated element" with unbreakable "ties of...custom and indoctrina-
tion of the enemy" that rendered the entire Japanese American community
vulnerable to ideological contamination. This assumption of the Kibei's cultural
and ideological homogeneity helped weave racial and military reasoning behind
the decision to incarcerate Japanese Americans. When there was no hard evidence
of Nisei's potential role as Japanese saboteurs, labeling Kibei as a dangerous pro-
Japan element would allow the proponents of the internment to argue that Americans of Japanese ancestry could be a national security threat.

Such extreme distrust of Kibei would shape the debate on Japanese American loyalty throughout the war, and ultimately, the wartime internment policies.
Identifying Kibei as a dangerous pro-Japan element became a pressing issue for
both government authorities and Japanese American community leaders. The
term Kibei simultaneously emerged as a political and cultural construct that
would transform the issue of wartime loyalty from a "Japanese problem" to a
"Kibei problem." Multiple parties involved in the development of wartime
internment policies took part in shaping the "Kibei problem." When the War
Relocation Authority (WRA) took over the management of the internment
camps in 1942, the agency devoted considerable effort to dealing with the
presence of Kibei within the camps. Some of the most vocal and prominent leaders of the emerging Nisei community organization Japanese American Citizens
League also targeted Kibei as scapegoats that would help spare the rest of the
Nisei from mass evacuation. Many JACL-oriented Nisei worked vigorously to

promote the image of loyal Nisei and used the image of disloyal and trouble-making Kibei as the antithesis of Americanized Nisei.

Kibei and the Japanese American Community during World War II

The historical narrative of the Japanese American internment emphasizing Nisei loyalty to the U.S. has had little room for the experiences Kibei during WWII. Although the existence of Kibei was central to shaping the internment policies, the "Kibei problem" has received little scholarly attention largely due to a general misunderstanding of the Kibei as transnational individuals. Many Kibei had received their education in Japan in the 1930s when Japan's political path was steered increasingly by the militarist wing of the government. Under this circumstance, it was easy for American policymakers and military leaders like DeWitt to claim that the Kibei who returned to the U.S. had been indoctrinated with Japan's imperialist agenda as a result of their education in Japanese public schools. Even those within the U.S. government who opposed the mass intern-ment of Japanese Americans in 1942 accepted the notion of Kibei as a pro-Japanese faction among Nisei without much criticism.

Instead of challenging this public indictment of Kibei's alleged loyalty to Japan, JACL leaders in the United States during WWII chose to distinguish them-selves and the Japanese American community from the negative Kibei image. As the JACLers opted for wartime cooperation with federal authorities to demonstrate Nisei loyalty, they saw the hostile reports on Kibei as a threat to the image of patriotic Japanese Americans. Soon after Pearl Harbor, JACL's national leaders determined that policing the thought and behavior of Kibei would be among the priorities in their campaign to promote Nisei Americanism.

For instance, in February 1942, the JACL National Headquarters issued a "Kibei survey" and directed each regional chapter to collect responses from local Kibei residents. National Director Mike Masaoka insisted that the survey was voluntary, but suggested that his organization would scrutinize the loyalty of any Kibei who failed to complete the questionnaire. He also warned local JACL chapters that a failure to administer the survey would be "reported to the authorities." The Kibei survey questions looked tailor-made for a report that could be furnished to the FBI, as they solicited detailed per-sonal information that revealed the level of each respondent's cultural and ideological connection to Japan. In this way, the Kibei survey served as a lesser-known prelude to the following year's loyalty questionnaire in the internment camps, which all of the incarcerated Japanese Americans were required to complete. Emerging Nisei leaders might have felt that a sacrifice forced upon Kibei would improve the fate of the majority of the Japanese American community in time of war. However, such extreme measure employed by JACL's loyalty campaign would exacerbate the alienation and stigmatization of many Kibei throughout the internment years and leave many more in the community to feel bitter in the years to come.

The WRA's "Kibei Problem"

Since the War Relocation Authority took over the management of the internment camps in mid-1942, what the agency's paternalistic director Dillon S. Myer described as the "Kibei problem" would emerge as an issue that shaped the internment policies. Myer was determined to prove his agency's ability to mold the Japanese American character and struggled with the question of what to do with Kibei. He faced pressure from the military to segregate Kibei from the rest of Nisei before the transfer of evacuees from the Army to the WRA was complete on October 31, 1942. Lieutenant General John L. DeWitt in August 1942 reiterated his point in the *Final Report* by asserting that Kibei remained a threat to national security and to "large numbers" of loyal Nisei. He insisted that segregation of Kibei would be necessary in the absence of military supervision after the Army's complete release of its jurisdiction over Japanese American internees. He went further by recommending not only the segregation of all Kibei in a separate facility, but also stripping them of their U.S. citizenship.

Despite the pressure from the War Department to swiftly deal with Kibei, Myer was not keen on branding a significant portion of Japanese Americans disloyal and segregating them. Also, rather than military intelligence, Myer placed more trust in his social scientific experts at the Community Analysis Section (CAS), who monitored the behaviors and attitudes of the Japanese American internees. The WRA in 1942 established CAS in each camp to assess grievances among the internees, but more importantly, Myer used the CAS reports as scientific proof of Nisei Americanization. The CAS ethnographers, many of whom were academics with advanced degrees, evaluated and reported on "what the evacuees are thinking on all subjects." Throughout his tenure, Myer turned to the Community Analysis Section to study Kibei behaviors and simultaneously to promote Nisei loyalty. The CAS reports served this purpose by categorizing "pro-Japan" constituents from the rest of the internees. These reports suggested that the majority of Japanese American internees were anti-Axis, but identified adult male bachelor Kibei as a group mostly sympathetic to the cause of Japanese empire. Rather than targeting all Kibei, the WRA's focus throughout the internment would be on this gender- and age-specific group of Kibei.

Reports on the internees' reactions to the WRA's infamous "loyalty questionnaire" in 1943 compounded the negative public perception and sweeping generalization of bachelor Kibei as the most dangerous fifth column. In February 1943, the WRA required all adult evacuees to complete the questionnaire as proof of their readiness for permanent relocation out of the internment camps. Designed initially to register male evacuees for military service, this program was adopted by the WRA in an attempt to punctuate Japanese American assimilation and loyalty. Myer hoped that positive results of registration would accelerate the "loyal" evacuees' release from the Relocation Centers and acceptance by the general American public. The WRA staff and JACLers expected the vast majority of the adult population to answer positively to the loyalty questions. However, Questions 27 and 28 on the questionnaire proved to be problematic, as they asked citizens and non-citizens, male and female, and young and old to prove their "unqualified allegiance" through their willingness to serve in the

U.S. military and renounce any loyalty to the Japanese emperor. Evacuee reactions to these questions varied, from confusion to outrage to enthusiastic support. To Myer's surprise and dismay, these diverse reactions to the loyalty questionnaire sparked a series of unrest at a number of camps.

While some evacuees answered no to one or both of these questions and others refused to answer at all, many "loyal" Nisei and WRA administrators had the impression that young Kibei men were leading the charge to sabotage the registration program. There were indeed a few Kibei among those who adamantly opposed registration, but such a wide belief in the Kibei men's role in instigating trouble did not emerge out of a vacuum. The term Kibei had come to carry such a negative connotation that it was not uncommon for many Nisei to simply refer to leading camp agitators as Kibei. According to CAS researcher John F. Embree's report from the Topaz Relocation Center, the most vocal opposition to registration allegedly came from a group of Kibei. A group of young Nisei complained to Embree that many Kibei were attempting to disturb the registration process because the Kibei had no will to fight against Japan. Other Topaz Nisei accused the Kibei gang of being cowards who feared becoming combat casualties.

The JACLers were also quick to blame Kibei for any camp disturbance, as attacks on the JACLers by troublemakers were reported during the registration period. Eric L. Muller has found that after a half century since the conclusion of the war, many old JACLers have continued to express their suspicion of those who opposed the registration program. Some Nisei critics of resistance, according to Muller, continue to believe that any attempt to interfere with registration was an act of "laziness" and "cowardice." Disturbances during the registration also contributed to the WRA staff's perception of all Kibei as "citizens in name only," who had "almost nothing in common with other second generation Japanese Americans."

As signs of agitation increased, the WRA began to consider more seriously the immediate segregation of "disloyals" in a separate Relocation Center and announced its plan in July 1943. Myer stated that the segregation program was to ensure the safety of "loyal American citizens and law-abiding aliens" in the camps and to expedite the process of preparing them for post-internment resettlement. Masaoka and the JACLers enthusiastically endorsed the segregation policy, which would isolate the "agitators from those who wanted to cooperate with the government." Male bachelor Kibei were high on the WRA's priority list of "disloyals" to be transferred to the WRA Segregation Center at Tule Lake, California in September 1943. The WRA's Administrative Instruction in July 1943 stipulated the agency's tentative plan to designate "bachelor Kibei" among the alleged disloyals in the internment camps to depart for Tule Lake before "all others." Dovetailing with a Community Analysis Section report from 1942, the instruction defined "bachelor Kibei" as a Nisei man who spent "a total of three or more years in Japan since January 1, 1935."

However, the WRA would reverse its policy in August 1943 and eliminate the Kibei category in its official publication explaining the segregation policy, instead using the neutral term "persons." Myer and his staff had to consider the fact that despite the negative public perception of Kibei, it was becoming increasingly difficult for them to cast all Kibei as potential troublemakers, as many Kibei within the camps had established themselves as some of the most cooperative and patriotic evacuees. For example, California Kibei and Communist Party member Karl G. Yoneda enthusiastically advocated Japanese American support for the U.S. war against what he described as the "fascist militarists" in Japan. The Glendale, California-native had returned to the U.S. after spending his formative years in Japan and become an influential labor organizer and a vocal critic of Japanese militarism in the 1930s and 1940s. During World War II, Yoneda not only rallied for the American war effort against Japan, but also cooperated with the U.S. government's internment policies. He did not even hesitate to report on the activities of other Kibei in the camp to the FBI. Many Kibei at Manzanar resented how the war had turned Yoneda's internationalist idealism into radical patriotism, as they called him "*inu*" ("dog"), a traitor of his own people.

To the paternalistic Myer who wanted to be remembered as the "great white father" that helped all Japanese Americans assimilate successfully, the words and actions of patriotic Kibei served as the most compelling evidence of Nisei Americanism. In summer of 1943, a number of Kibei internees stepped forward to announce their desire to fight for the United States. Some Kibei in fact demonstrated that their experiences abroad had armed them with a sense of internationalism that allowed a more sophisticated expression of patriotism. A young Kibei volunteer at Topaz Relocation Center who volunteered to serve in the U.S. Army declared, for example, "I am thinking not only of defending American democracy against all foes," but also of protecting the "common people of Japan." He claimed that while in Japan he had "learned the meaning of fascism" and "to fight against its oppressive measures."

Many Kibei proved especially useful in the U.S. intelligence warfare in the Pacific Theater. In 1943, the U.S. Army trained an increasing number of Nisei and Kibei to serve in the Military Intelligence Service (MIS). Brigadier General John Weckerling, who was instrumental in establishing the Military Intelligence Language School, praised the Kibei servicemen's role in the Pacific campaigns and insisted that any belief in Kibei's pro-Japan tendency was a mistake. In fact, white officers valued the service of Kibei linguists not only because of their Japanese proficiency, but also because of their knowledge of Japan as a result of their transnational experiences. The increasing number and usefulness of Kibei volunteers, collaborators, and servicemen meant that the WRA could no longer treat internment camp troubles simply as "Kibei problems."

Despite these complexities, the notion of Kibei's alleged disloyalty continued to shape the American public's misunderstanding of this subgroup within the Nisei community as a dangerous pro-Japan element. The mainstream press, such as the *Los Angeles Times* and the *San Francisco Examiner* continued to depict all male Kibei as militant troublemakers. The WRA attempted to counter this view by using its CAS study in January 1944 to recast Kibei's transnational identity and their nationalism. The report depicted Kibei as "new immigrants" subject to assimilation, despite their U.S. citizenship by birth. The literal meaning of the term Kibei—"returned to America"—notwithstanding, the report called for a "narrowed" definition in order for it "to have much use as designating a distinct type of Japanese American." The CAS report suggested that bona fide Kibei should have spent "anywhere from two to twenty years" in Japan to have been "influenced in important ways by [their] stay [in Japan]." Such an artificial definition used by the WRA has further reinforced the generalized image of Kibei as perpetual, if not dangerous pro-Japan, outsiders and the antithesis of the Americanized Nisei.

The "Kibei Problem" and the Question of Nisei Loyalty

Thus, by the late 1943 the question of Kibei loyalty was becoming increasingly complex in the WRA-JACL identity politics. However, while policymakers and Nisei elites could no longer label all bachelor Kibei as troublemakers, they nevertheless failed to adequately understand that the question of loyalty had affected Kibei in different ways because of their diverse transnational experiences. To many Kibei, the internment was a critical extension of their transnational movement, and the stigma of disloyalty had a profound impact on their internment experiences. The U.S. government's policies of relocation and resettlement involved close scrutiny of the internees' self-professed and perceived loyalty and Americanization. However, just as Kibei are not a culturally and economically homogenous group, their wartime experiences varied significantly. Many among the Kibei internees actively cooperated with the JACL and the War Relocation Authority's campaign to promote the loyal Nisei image. The exemplary service of Kibei volunteers and draftees in the Army between 1943 and 1945 defied the previously unchallenged notion of their Japanese nationalism and further complicated the WRA and JACL's dealings with the question of Kibei loyalty. Yet, others actively criticized and resisted the U.S. government's treatment of Japanese Americans as enemy aliens. In short, the history of Kibei internment experiences is as complex as that of the Japanese American internment as a whole.

FURTHER READING

Brooks, Charlotte. "In the Twilight Zone between Black and White: Japanese American Resettlement and Community in Chicago, 1942–1945," *Journal of American History* 86 (March 2000), 1655–1687.

Chang, Gordon. *Morning Glory, Evening Shadow: Yamato Ichihashi and His Internment Writings, 1942–1945* (1997).

Collins, Donald E. *Native American Aliens: Disloyalty and the Renunciation of Citizenship by Japanese Americans during World War II* (1985).

Daniels, Roger. *The Japanese American Cases: The Rule of Law in Time of War* (2013).

———. *Prisoners without Trial: Japanese Americans in World War II* (2004).

Fujitani, Takashi. *Race for Empire: Koreans as Japanese and Japanese as Americans during World War II* (2011).

Hayashi, Brian Masaru. *Democratizing the Enemy: The Japanese American Internment* (2004).

Hirabayashi, Lane Ryo. *Japanese American Resettlement through the Lens: Hikaru Iwasaki and the WRA's Photographic Section, 1943–1945* (2009).

Howard, John. *Concentration Camps on the Home Front: Japanese Americans in the House of Jim Crow* (2008).

Ichioka, Yuji. "The Meaning of Loyalty: The Case of Kazumaro Buddy Uno," *Amerasia Journal* 23.3 (Fall 1997), 45–71.

Inada, Lawson Fusao. *Only What We Could Carry: The Japanese American Internment Experience* (2000).

Kurashige, Lon. *Japanese American Celebration and Conflict: Ethnic Orthodoxy, Options, and Festival, 1934–1990* (2002).

Lyon, Cherstin. *Prisons and Patriots: Japanese American Wartime Citizenship, Civil Disobedience, and Historical Memory* (2011).

Matsumoto, Valerie J. *City Girls: The Nisei Social World in Los Angeles, 1920–1950* (2014).

McCaffrey, James M. *Going for Broke: Japanese American Soldiers in the War against Nazi Germany* (2013).

Muller, Eric L. *American Inquisition: The Hunt for Japanese American Disloyalty in World War II* (2007).

———. *Free to Die for Their Country: The Story of the Japanese American Draft Resisters in World War II* (2001).

Odo, Franklin. *No Sword to Bury: Japanese Americans in Hawai'i during World War II* (2004).

Okihiro, Gary Y., and Leslie Ito. *Storied Lives: Japanese American Students and World War II* (1999).

Robinson, Greg. *After Camp: Portraits in Midcentury Japanese American Life and Politics* (2012).

Spickard, Paul R. *Japanese Americans: The Formation and Transformations of an Ethnic Group* (2008).

Sterner, C. Douglas. *Go for Broke: The Nisei Warriors of World War II Who Conquered Germany, Japan, and American Bigotry* (2015).

Tamura, Linda. *Nisei Soldiers Break Their Silence: Coming Home to Hood River* (2012).

Yang Murray, Alice. *What Did the Internment of Japanese Americans Mean?* (2000).

Yoo, David. *Growing Up Nisei: Race, Generation, and Culture among Japanese Americans of California, 1924–49* (2000).

CHAPTER 9

War and Asia-Pacific Allies,

1941–1950

Chinese and Korean immigrants in the United States, whose home countries were being victimized under Japanese colonialism, rejoiced when the United States declared war against Japan in December 1941. Chinese Americans had called for boycotts of U.S.–Japan trade after Japan invaded Manchuria in 1931 and again when Japanese troops massacred and raped civilians in Nanjing in 1937. Korean Americans had been publicizing the abuses of Japan's colonization of Korea ever since 1910 and were especially vocal after the Japanese crushed a Korean independence movement uprising in 1919. To avoid being confused with the supposed Japanese American enemies after Pearl Harbor, Chinese Americans and Korean Americans wore buttons identifying their ethnicity. White Americans' inability to distinguish between different Asian people led Life Magazine to publish an essay on "How to Tell Japs from the Chinese" that presented racialized depictions of the skin color, facial features, and ostensible personality characteristics of "friendly Chinese allies" and "enemy alien Japs."

To counter Japan's military propaganda about American racism and to acknowledge China's contributions as a U.S. ally, Congress repealed Chinese exclusion in 1943 after a rousing U.S. tour by the First Lady of China, Soong May-ling, who backed such a repeal. No longer denounced as a yellow peril, Chinese Americans embraced new educational and occupational opportunities that became available as the wartime draft and new defense factories created a major labor shortage. Their new rights, however, were based on perceptions of Chinese Americans as foreign allies rather than as fellow citizens.

Filipino Americans, too, distinguished themselves sharply from the Japanese enemy and during World War II fought to liberate the Philippines from Japan's control. After evacuating from Manila and holding out on the Bataan Peninsula for three months, over 75,000 sick and starving U.S. and Filipino soldiers surrendered unconditionally to the Japanese in April 1942. As many as 10,000 Filipino and 1,000 American troops died on the Bataan Death March because they were starved, beaten, and bayoneted during the 65-mile trek to a prisoner of war camp. Between 500,000 and 1,000,000 Filipinos

died during the Japanese occupation. Filipinos suffered mass rape, massacres, and atrocities against POWs and suspected Allied supporters. Praised by Americans as "little
brown brothers," the Philippine Commonwealth Army was conscripted into the U.S.
forces, and Filipino Americans served as naval stewards and in segregated Filipino
army regiments. The U.S. government promised Filipino soldiers naturalization rights
and full veterans' benefits but allowed only a small number of them to become U.S.
citizens after the war.

In the U.S. territory of Guam, the indigenous Chamorros also suffered under
Japanese occupation. The Japanese seized private homes, initiated a strict curfew, forbade
the speaking of English, and required Chamorros to learn Japanese language and
customs. In 1944, the Japanese army closed schools and coerced the population to serve
the needs of the Japanese forces. Public executions of individuals suspected of supporting
the Americans terrorized the local population. Without notice, the Japanese occupiers
forced approximately 10,000 to 15,000 Chamorros to march to concentration camps in
Guam's central and southern jungles. The prisoners were allowed to bring only what
they could carry. Other Chamorros were forced to labor at bayonet point, tortured,
raped, massacred, and killed during battles or during American bombing campaigns before
the Japanese finally surrendered on August 10, 1944.

DOCUMENTS

Documents 1 to 8 provide different views of loyalty, patriotism, and citizenship
during World War II. Document 1 is an excerpt from "How to Spot a Jap," a
1942 U.S. War Department comic strip that was included in the *Pocket Guide to
China* booklet distributed to U.S. army and navy personnel in China. Drawn
by Milton Caniff, illustrator of the *Terry and the Pirates* comic strip, the guide
identifies Japanese enemies by emphasizing racialized differences in height, eye
slant, and feet. In marked contrast, Chinese allies are depicted as loyal supporters of the U.S. war effort. In Document 2, Rose Hum Lee, a sociology graduate student at the University of Chicago, describes how Chinese Americans
found well-paying jobs in the defense industry and the private sector. They
also enlisted in the U.S. military, and as American patriots and allies called for
the repeal of Chinese exclusion.

Soong May-ling, the wife of China's leader Chiang Kai-shek, proved to be
one of the most effective advocates for winning American public support for
China and Chinese Americans. A graduate of Wellesley College, the cultured
and glamorous Madame Chiang Kai-shek became the first Chinese and only
the second woman to address a joint session of Congress on February 18, 1943.
Her speech, excerpted in Document 3, persuaded Congress to provide more
support for the Chinese nationalists' struggle against Japan. In Document 4, President Franklin Delano Roosevelt asks Congress to repeal Chinese exclusion laws
to recognize China's important role in the war against Japan. However, he made
clear that no "flood" of Chinese immigrants would be unleashed since the quota,
based on a percentage of the total population of Chinese Americans in the
United States in 1920, would amount to only around 105 immigrants per year.

Document 5 attests to the way the repeal of Chinese exclusion in 1943 set a precedent for repealing the exclusion of Indian immigrants. Indian immigrants received a small quota in 1946 that reflected the U.S. commitment to cultivating anticommunist allies in South Asia during the Cold War. This document includes testimony calling for the repeal of Indian exclusion and the provision of naturalization rights in 1945.

Documents 6 to 8 address the conditions of the Philippines and Guam under Japanese occupation. In Document 6, drawn from a 1943 edition of *Asia and the Americas* magazine, Filipino regiment member Manuel Buaken celebrates American ideals, notes the failure of the United States to live up to those ideals, and recounts his feelings as one of 1,200 Filipino soldiers who became U.S. citizens in a wartime ceremony at Camp Beale in northern California. Rosa Roberto Carter addresses the harsh conditions Chamorros suffered in Guam during the war in Document 7. During testimony presented in 2003 to the Guam War Claims Review Commission, she details how she and her family experienced starvation, interrogation, forced labor, napalm burns, and the forced march to a concentration camp. In Document 8, Ben Blaz reflects on the fiftieth anniversary of the liberation of Guam and pays tribute to the Chamorro spirit during and after the war. He also criticizes American colonial rule and calls for self-determination for Guam.

1. The U.S. War and Navy Departments Tell U.S. Soldiers "How to Spot a Jap," 1942

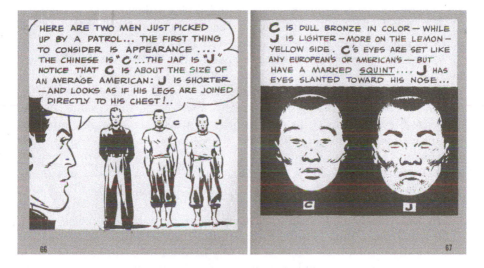

Source: U.S. War and Navy Departments, "How to Spot a Jap," *Pocket Guide to China* (Washington, D.C.): U.S. Government Printing Office, 1942, 66–67, 70–71.

2. Sociology Graduate Student Rose Hum Lee Describes How World War II Changed the Lives of Chinese Americans, 1942

One hundred and thirty million Americans were very little aware on December 7 of the eighty thousand Chinese in the United States. But by noon of December 8, the country's declaration of war on Japan and similar action by the Republic of China had made the two nations allies. Since then the outlook of the Chinese living in this country has been considerably changed by Pearl Harbor.

One half of our Chinese population lives on the West Coast. San Francisco and the Bay Region have approximately 30,000, Los Angeles 4,500, Seattle 3,500, Portland 2,000. Most of the others are located in large cities in the East and the Midwest; New York, Chicago, Cincinnati, Detroit, and Cleveland have sizeable Chinatowns. In out-of-the-way towns are lonely laundrymen silently washing and ironing. Wherever the Chinese are, it has been possible to count the variations in ways they can earn their living on the fingers of the hand—chop suey and chow mein restaurants, Chinese art and gift shops, native grocery stores that sell foodstuffs imported from China to the local Chinese community.

In San Francisco's Chinatown, merely from force of habit, signs saying, "This is a Chinese Shop" are still displayed. But they no longer are needed; the section today is completely Chinese. The fifty Japanese shops fringing upon or in Chinatown have had to liquidate and Chinese have rented the stores. One of the most attractive shops is being run by a second generation Chinese-American young woman.

Throughout the Chinatowns in the United States there is a labor shortage. For the first time since Chinese labor exclusion began, absorption of the Chinese into American industry has been significant. Whether in New York, Los Angeles, San Francisco, Chicago, or in Butte, Mont., the service in Chinese restaurants is slow. Four restaurants in New York's Chinatown have closed their doors in the past few months. The proprietor of Li Po, an up-to-date cocktail-chop-suey place located in "Chinatown on Broadway" in Los Angeles, said sadly: "I was just ready for another venture. But I can't now. No men to run it."

They have gone in the army and navy, into shipbuilding and aircraft plants. Even the girls are getting jobs. A personal column of the *Chinese Press* notes: "The newest on the defense payrolls are Jane Sai, stenographer; Rose Hom, timekeeper; Jimmy Hom, welder; J. Eric Hom, carpenter." And another item says; "In Fresno, Chinese boys and girls are training at the NYA resident project for employment with Consolidated Aircraft."

The same issue carried the announcement that the associate editor, William Hoy, is donning a uniform. This brilliant young inductee is one of the best informed persons on the history of the Chinese in California.

In War Industries

In Portland, Ore., the Chinese Consul, Silwing P. C. Au, and his wife have done much to promote interracial understanding. For three years they have worked to get Chinese assistants and cooks into the hospitals at Vancouver Barracks. The Chinese make good workers: they are taciturn, orderly, and perform their duties well. Meetings with the union leaders have smoothed out some labor difficulties and paved the way for absorption of many Chinese-Americans into war industries. Recently the restaurant unions invited the Chinese restaurant employees to join their ranks. Although very few Chinese have joined so far, the invitation is significant. Mrs. Au is active in the League of Women Voters, the American Association of University Women (she was recently invited to be the program chairman for the coming season), in the National Federation of Women's Clubs, as well as in the Chinese-American Women's League, and in all organizations aiding in relief for China.

Only a handful of stores dot the so-called Chinatown in Minneapolis. In June, when the city turned out to welcome fifteen war heroes from the East Coast, tiny Chinese-Americans wearing their gay costumes waved welcome to the visiting celebrities. The flag of the Republic of China elicited thundering applause. The proprietor of the city's only Oriental gift shop liquidated his business last winter at the height of a busy Christmas season and entered a war industry. His wife, likewise a Chinese-American, works in the same plant. An American-born University-of-Minnesota-trained master in architecture found work in a war industry—the first technical job he has held since his graduation fifteen years ago. Previously he had to be satisfied with managing his father's restaurant, but now, his American-born, business-trained wife is doing that.

In the Pittsburgh and Philadelphia communities, shortage of help has been acute for so long that not even labor imported from other cities can ease the situation. In New York, students who used to earn money as "extra waiters" during the weekends have found employment in industries working on lease-lend material for China. The China Institute in America has placed many trained young men in American industry as technicians, chemists, and engineers.

An officer of the China Institute, Dr. B. A. Liu, has been making a tour of the large universities to get in touch with Chinese students, many of them stranded in this country as a result of the war. The Department of State announced in April that such students would be given opportunities to gain practical experience or be assisted financially to complete their technical training. The response of American industry has been heartening. Industrial, transportation, and scientific organizations have absorbed many scientific and technical students. Other students hope for employment in educational institutions, libraries, foundations, hospitals, publishing houses; and as translators....

In the Armed Services

Portland's Chinese community sent a contingent of thirty-three trained pilots to Generalissimo Chiang Kai-shek before December 7. With America in the war as an ally, those now in training will be pilots in the United States Air Force. The Generalissimo has urged Chinese men here to enlist in the armed forces of the United States as a demonstration of China's complete cooperation with the United Nations. The removal of restrictions in the United States Navy and Naval Reserve has started a drive for 500 Chinese as apprentice seamen. Heretofore, Chinese were restricted to enlistment as messmen and stewards. The recent requirements for enlistment are American citizenship; ability to pass the navy's physical examination; age seventeen to thirty-one for the navy and seventeen to fifty for the naval reserve.

New York's Chinatown cheered itself hoarse when the first draft numbers drawn were for Chinese-Americans. Some below-age boys tried to pass on their "Chinese age," which is often a year or two older than the American count. Since their birth certificates told a different tale, they had to be patient and wait.

There are only eleven Chinese-Americans of draft age in Butte, Mont., and all have enlisted or are serving Uncle Sam in some other way. One in the army was promoted to be sergeant, and has gone overseas. A family with three sons has one in the medical corps, another in the army air corps, the third in the navy. In another family with three sons one, an engineer, is in the East in a lease-lend organization, and the other two, both engineering students, are reserves in the air corps until they graduate.

K. S. Jue, president of the Shiu [Sue] Hing Benevolent Society, speaking of home front activities, said: "San Francisco has gone over the top in its recent Red Cross drive. We raised $18,000 for the campaign. In the Defense Bond Drive, we bought over $30,000." This is in addition to all the war relief the

Chinese here have been sending to China and in response to the demands of relatives across the Pacific.

Civil Rights for Our Chinese Allies

This year, at the recent convention of the California League of Women Voters in San Francisco, the following resolution was passed:

> Recognizing the racial discrimination shown in several Asiatic Exclusion Acts passed by our government over a period of sixty years, the California League of Women Voters accepts its responsibility for education as to the history and effects of the Exclusion Acts leading toward effective opposition to racial discrimination in immigration laws, and asks that the National League send material to all State Leagues.

It is significant that this step towards righting an old wrong should come from California, where the Chinese exclusion movement first saw birth as a state issue, gradually to become national policy. While the exclusion sections of the Immigration Act of 1924 were aimed primarily at rapidly increasing immigration of Japanese picture-brides in the early years of the twentieth century, they worked even more hardship among the Chinese immigrants. The solution to the problem of Oriental immigration promises to be not exclusion by law, but intelligent restriction and selection of those who desire admittance into the country. It seems to the Chinese that those of us not born here should be eligible to become citizens through a process of naturalization as do those who come from other lands; and that the right to own property as citizens should be acknowledged. Surely racial discrimination should not be directed against those who are America's Allies in the Far East and are helping here in every way to win the war.

It has long been recognized that "cheap labor" was not eliminated by the series of exclusion laws. Immediately after the passing of those laws, "cheap labor" was supplied by incoming Mexicans and Filipinos.

Every thinking Chinese in this country and in China hopes that the American people will advance the social, political, and economic status of the Chinese in the United States. To be fighting for freedom and democracy in the Far East, at the cost of seven million lives in five years of hard, long, bitter warfare, and to be denied equal opportunity in the greatest of democracies, seems the height of irony. With the absorption of the Chinese in industry and the proof that they are good workers, loyal citizens, and faithful to the United Nations' cause, racial barriers and prejudices should break down now and for all time.

In California, today, there are fourth generation Americans—Chinese-Americans who speak no Chinese. They live on close terms with their American neighbors, enjoy the same recreation and health facilities offered to their fellow citizens. For them the present crisis is another stepping stone toward complete assimilation. No longer do Americans think of the Chinese as mysterious Orientals from a little known land. Most of these Chinese living among them are fellow citizens. The rest of them, as well as their cousins in the old country, are Allies. The crisis of December 7 has emancipated the Chinese in the United States. It is up to the American people to effect the emancipation by law.

3. Madame Chiang Kai-Shek Speaks to Congress on the Need to Provide Military and Economic Aid to China, 1943

You, as representatives of the American people, have before you the glorious opportunity of carrying on the pioneer work of your ancestors, beyond the frontiers of physical and geographical limitations. Their brawn and thews [muscles] braved undauntedly almost unbelievable hardships to open up a new continent. The modern world lauds them for their vigor and intensity of purpose, and for their accomplishment.

You have today before you the immeasurably greater opportunity to implement these same ideals and to help bring about the liberation of man's spirit in every part of the world. In order to accomplish this purpose, we of the United Nations must now so prosecute the war that victory will be ours decisively and with all good speed.

Sun-tse [Sun Tzu], the well-known Chinese strategist, said: "In order to win, know thyself and thy enemy." We have also the saying: "It takes little effort to watch the other fellow carry the load."

In spite of these teachings from a wise old past, which are shared by every nation, there has been a tendency to belittle the strength of our opponents.

When Japan thrust total war on China in 1937, military experts of every nation did not give China even a ghost of a chance. But, when Japan failed to bring China cringing to her knees as she vaunted, the world took solace in this phenomenon by declaring that they had overestimated Japan's military might.

Nevertheless, when the greedy flames of war inexorably spread in the Pacific following the perfidious attack on Pearl Harbor, Malaya and lands in and around the China Sea, and one after another of these places fell, the pendulum swung to the other extreme. Doubts and fears lifted their ugly heads and the world began to think that the Japanese were Nietzschean supermen, superior in intellect and physical prowess, a belief which the Gobineau(s) [Arthur de Gobineau] and the Houston Chamberlain(s) and their apt pupils, the Nazi racists, had propounded about the Nordics.

Again, now the prevailing opinion seems to consider the defeat of the Japanese as of relative unimportance and that Hitler is our first concern. This is not borne out by actual facts, nor is it to the interests of the United Nations as a whole to allow Japan to continue, not only as a vital potential threat but as a waiting sword of Damocles, ready to descend at a moment's notice.

Let us not forget that Japan in her occupied areas today has greater resources at her command than Germany.

Let us not forget that the longer Japan is left in undisputed possession of these resources, the stronger she must become. Each passing day takes more toll in lives of both Americans and Chinese.

Let us not forget that the Japanese are an intransigent people.

Delivered in House of Representatives, Washington, D.C., February 18, 1943, *Vital Speeches of the Day*, Vol. IX, pp. 301–303, http://www.ibiblio.org/pha/policy/1943/1943-02-18a.html

Let us not forget that during the first four and a half years of total aggression China has borne Japan's sadistic fury unaided and alone.

The victories won by the United States Navy at Midway and the Coral Sea are doubtless steps in the right direction—they are merely steps in the right direction—for the magnificent fight that was waged at Guadalcanal during the past six months attests to the fact that the defeat of the forces of evil, though long and arduous, will-finally come to pass. For have we not on the side of righteousness and justice stanch allies in Great Britain, Russia and other brave and indomitable peoples? Meanwhile the peril of the Japanese Juggernaut remains. Japanese military might must be decimated as a fighting force before its threat to civilization is removed.

When the Seventy-seventh Congress declared war against Japan, Germany and Italy, Congress, for the moment, had done its work. It now remains for you, the present representatives of the American people, to point the way to win the war, to help construct a world in which all peoples may henceforth live in harmony and peace.

May I not hope that it is the resolve of Congress to devote itself to the creation of the post-war world? To dedicate itself to the preparation for the brighter future that a stricken world so eagerly awaits?

We of this generation who are privileged to help make a better world for ourselves and for posterity should remember that, while we must not be visionary, we must have vision so that peace should not be punitive in spirit and should not be provincial or nationalistic or even continental in concept, but universal in scope and humanitarian in action, for modern science has so annihilated distance that what affects one people must of necessity affect all other peoples.

The term "hands and feet" is often used in China to signify the relationship between brothers. Since international interdependence is now so universally recognized, can we not also say that all nations should become members of one corporate body?

The hundred and sixty years of traditional friendship between our two great peoples, China and America, which has never been marred by misunderstandings, is unsurpassed in the annals of the world. I can also assure you that China is eager and ready to cooperate with you and other peoples to lay a true and lasting foundation for a sane and progressive world society which would make it impossible for any arrogant or predatory neighbor to plunge future generations into another orgy of blood.

In the past China has not computed the cost to her manpower in her fight against aggression, although she well realized that manpower is the real wealth of a nation and it takes generations to grow it. She has been soberly conscious of her responsibilities and has not concerned herself with privileges and gains which she might have obtained through compromise of principles. Nor will she demean herself and all she holds dear to the practice of the market place.

We in China, like you, want a better world, not for ourselves alone, but for all mankind, and we must have it. It is not enough, however, to proclaim our ideals or even to be convinced that we have them. In order to preserve, uphold and maintain them, there are times when we should throw all we cherish into our effort to fulfill these ideals even at the risk of failure.

The teachings drawn from our late leader, Dr. Sun Yat-sen, have given our people the fortitude to carry on. From five and a half years of experience we in China are convinced that it is the better part of wisdom not to accept fail-ire [failure] ignominiously, but to risk it gloriously. We shall have faith, that, at the writing of peace, America and our gallant Allies will not be obtunded [dulled] by the mirage of contingent reasons of expediency.

Man's mettle is tested both in adversity and in success. Twice is this true of the soul of a nation.

4. Franklin Delano Roosevelt Calls on Congress to Repeal Chinese Exclusion, 1943

To the Congress:

There is now pending before the Congress legislation to permit the immigration of Chinese people into this country and to allow Chinese residents here to become American citizens. I regard this legislation as important in the cause of winning the war and of establishing a secure peace.

China is our ally. For many years she stood alone in the fight against aggression. Today we fight at her side. She has continued her gallant struggle against very great odds.

China has understood that the strategy of victory in this world war first required the concentration of the greater part of our strength upon the European front. She has understood that the amount of supplies we could make available to her has been limited by difficulties of transportation. She knows that substantial aid will be forthcoming as soon as possible- aid not only in the form of weapons and supplies, but also in carrying out plans already made for offensive, effective action. We and our allies will aim our forces at the heart of Japan—in ever increasing strength until the common enemy is driven from China's soil.

But China's resistance does not depend alone on guns and planes and on attacks on land, on the sea, and from the air. It is based as much in the spirit of her people and her faith in her allies. We owe it to the Chinese to strengthen that faith. One step in this direction is to wipe from the statute books those anachronisms in our law which forbid the immigration of Chinese people into this country and which bar Chinese residents from American citizenship.

Nations, like individuals, make mistakes. We must be big enough to acknowledge our mistakes of the past and to correct them.

By the repeal of the Chinese Exclusion Laws, we can correct a historic mistake and silence the distorted Japanese propaganda. The enactment of legislation now pending before the Congress would put Chinese immigrants on a parity with those from other countries. The Chinese quota would, therefore, be only

Franklin D. Roosevelt: "Message to Congress on Repeal of the Chinese Exclusion Laws," October 11, 1943. Online by Gerhard Peters and John T. Woolley, The American Presidency Project. http://www.presidency.ucsb.edu/ws/?pid=16325

about 100 immigrants a year. There can be no reasonable apprehension that any such number of immigrants will cause unemployment or provide competition in the search for jobs.

The extension of the privileges of citizenship to the relatively few Chinese residents in our country would operate as another meaningful display of friendship. It would be additional proof that we regard China not only as a partner in waging war but that we shall regard her as a partner in days of peace. While it would give the Chinese a preferred status over certain other Oriental people, their great contribution to the cause of decency and freedom entitles them to such preference.

I feel confident that the Congress is in full agreement that these measures— long overdue- should be taken to correct an injustice to our friends. Action by the Congress now will be an earnest of our purpose to apply the policy of the Good Neighbor to our relations with other peoples.

5. Indians in America Call for Repeal of U.S. Exclusion Laws, 1945

U.S. Congress. House. Committee on Immigration and Naturalization. *To Grant a Quota to Eastern Hemisphere Indians and To Make Them Racially Eligible for Naturalization.* 79th Cong., 1st sess., March 7-14, 1945, excerpts.

Dr. Haridos T. Mazumdar, Professor of Sociology and Economics, William Penn College; Vice President, National Committee for India Freedom; Editor, Voice of India: "This particular bill of Mr. Lynch attempts to bring relief to a group of people who are in a very especially underprivileged position. They have been in this country for a number of years. They have participated in American culture, American activities. They have rendered their contributions to the well-being of America. They have paid taxes. They have carried on their part of the work in the business of this land. To all intents and purposes they have been Americans in everything except in the exercise of the rights of American citizenship. They are here. They are going to die here. They are doing their duty in everything as American citizens, except in the one vital fact of the exercise of the rights of American citizenship.

It would seem to me that America has an obligation to do the right thing, to rectify a serious wrong, by giving them the right to become American citizens ...

Those who are eligible to go into the armed services have gone into the armed services, regardless of whether they were born here, or have come here ... These people are perfectly willing to render service to Uncle Sam, and I think *it,* is only fair to expect Uncle Sam to do a little for them.

... I think it is better that we establish a general principle as to what is what, and the principle I should like to see established is that the people of India be put on a par with the people of Europe and the people of China in regard to

House Committee on Immigration and Naturalization. Hearings on Bills to Grant a Quota to Eastern Hemisphere Indians and to Make Them Racially Eligible for Naturalization. 79th Cong., 1st sess., March 7–14, 1945.

immigration and naturalization. I am convinced it would not do any harm. On the other hand, I suspect, and I humbly submit that it may do a great deal of good, both for India and for America."

Ramlal B. Bajpai, Vice President, India Welfare League: "India is not a small island, but a vast territory containing one-fifth of the world's population. Let us remember, further, that the people of India are predominantly of the same race as the Greeks, the Romans, and the Americans, i.e., Indo-Europeans or Aryans; though their skin has been browned by the tireless suns, that India was the mother–land of the Aryan race and Sanskrit the mother of European languages.

America has been the haven of free institutions and asylum for the disowned and oppressed of the human race. In view of this noble heritage of this great democracy it would seem inconsistent indeed to find that people from India who have entered the United States and lawfully resided for periods of 15 to 25 or more years, engaging in the free and legitimate pursuits of life and sharing in the blessings as well as difficulties peculiar to this land, are subjected to a legal discrimination that denies them the privilege of naturalization.

Today, American citizenship, which is open to every European, Syrian, Armenian, the Negroes, and now the Chinese, is not open to Indians.

This microscopic minority of about 3,000 Indians includes farmers, machine workers, writers, and at least 10 scientists of note—men whose achievements are considered top rank. The contributions of these people is out of all proportion to their numbers.

Since July, 1924, these people of ancient race and culture were barred from American citizenship. Those who suffer most from ineligibility to American citizenship are the Indian farmers of California, Nevada, Oregon, Texas, and Arizona, who by their labor improved what was considered worthless alkali swamps by making them into profitable rice, wheat, vegetable, and cotton fields. These experienced Indian farmers contributed so much to the prosperity of the States...

Like all peoples from other lands, natives of India in the United States have shown qualities of cultural adaptation and social assimilation and have proved themselves to be law abiding and loyal to the democratic institutions of the United States.

Since these Indian residents have voluntarily given up their former domiciles and cast their lots for better or worse with the land of their adoption, in the name of human justice and American sense of fair play it is only just that they be granted the right to become naturalized and saved from discriminating limitations due to the national origin clause."

J.J. Singh, President, India League of America: "… That brings me to the present bill, and if this bill is passed—and there is a tremendous amount of excitement in India at the present moment about this bill—it is front-page news. I have seen some of the recent papers in India, and there is quite a lot of excitement going on there. They're watching this as a test case of the professions of democracy and equality, and the Yalta Conference and the San Francisco Conference, and the new world order."

Rep. [A. Leonard] Allen (R-LA): "I think what is coming is the thing that Mr. [Ed] Gossett (D-TX) pointed out a few minutes ago, the predictions of what would happen when we passed the Chinese bill, that that bill would be followed by other bills, to let in Hindus, Koreans, people of Siam, and all other Orientals ... My personal conviction is that we have gone too far already ... we have got to call a halt ... You are breaking down barriers, and when you break down too many barriers, you get a flood like the floods on the Mississippi River ... We know that a crawfish may crawl through the levee and break the levee, and that is what we are called upon to do here. We are called upon to break the levee and I am not willing to break the levee any further."

6. Filipino Regiment Member Manuel Buaken Fights for Freedom, 1943

THE EYES OF THE WORLD were upon us that day of our world première as citizens of the United States. We were spotlighted before the cameras and microphones of the nation. The place of our debut was the parade ground of Camp Beale, on the wet red clay of northern California. The time, February 20, 1943.

We are soldiers, members of the First Filipino Infantry, United States Army. We are Mount Mayon's men, as you can see by our insignia symbolizing our oath of vengeance against the invaders of our homeland—a brilliant yellow disk upon which is the volcano Mount Mayon in black, erupting black smoke, with three bright stars shining through, to represent the three principal islands of the Philippines.

While we, the twelve hundred candidates for citizenship, stood proud and silent in a V formation, Colonel Cowley began the ceremony, saying in part, "Officers who returned from Bataan have said there are no finer soldiers in the world than the Filipinos who fought and starved and died there shoulder to shoulder with our troops. I can well believe it as I look at the men before me. On those faces is quiet determination and a consciousness of training and discipline with a definite end in view. I congratulate them on their soldierly appearance and on their approaching citizenship."

The post's public relations officer, Captain Sprague, described the scene to the radio audience "... fine looking, well disciplined Filipino soldiers. Their faces are immobile but their eyes are gleaming with anticipation. In exactly eight minutes they will become officially what they have long been in their hearts—Americans. They are waiting at this moment for the only reward they have asked—citizenship—real live nephews of the Uncle Sam they revere."

Next to come to the microphone was Colonel Offley, who simply said, "They are fine soldiers and I am proud to be their commander."

The concluding speech was made by Judge Welsh: "Citizenship came to us who were born here as a heritage—it will come to you as a privilege. We have

From Manuel Buaken, "Our Fighting Love of Freedom," *Asia and the Americas* 43, no. 6 (June 1943): 357, 359.

every faith you will become and remain loyal, devoted citizens of the United States, and we wish you. God speed and success."

Then the oath was solemnly administered by Judge Welsh, and as solemnly pledged by us.

Came the singing of "On to Bataan," our stirring regimental song, then "The Star Spangled Banner" and our salute to the flag. And we were citizens of the United States.

We have not taken this step lightly, but with serious consideration, and much debate among ourselves. We did not renounce our citizenship in the Philippines. We have accepted a wider citizenship, a greater responsibility. As Pfc. Jose Trinidad said, in one of our discussions in our barracks, "I cannot give up my citizenship in the Philippines, it is in my heart. But America is also in my mind. I wish to have both loyalties." One phase of this wider responsibility was voiced by Corporal Manuel Luz, of Company I, when he said, "This is a step toward our dream of a world citizenship, of a United States of the Orient. And we are preparing now the pattern of this citizenship, by this leadership that America has set for us, and has taught us."

That is the consensus of our convictions—that America has set the pattern this day, with this grant of citizenship to us, as we have granted it to Americans in the Philippines long ago—on a dual basis—*giving you full participation in our country's political and economic life without asking you to renounce your share in America.*

So you ask me, what is the Philippine interpretation of the meaning of citizenship?

With us, it is a growth, a summary of all our traditions, our folk-lore—it has taken elements of meaning from all our diverse racial strains, it has been molded by all our history....

Our citizenship concept has been tolerant—we have assimilated Chinese, modern Malayans, Spanish and other Europeans such as the Portuguese. And in some ways our citizenship standards are higher than yours. We have begun our national life with the protection of all our natural resources from exploitation and ruthless destruction. We shall have no denuded forests as you have, no exhausted lands or heavy concentration of wealth in the hands of the ruthless few. Our citizenship is foresighted.

More than that, we have taken your best ideals and made them our own. These twelve hundred Filipino soldiers, now citizens of America, are here because they were fired by American ideals and determined to learn the best democratic principles and practices, to make them a part of our country's heritage. We are here because we have studied your books, have made your patriotic leaders our heroes—Washington, Lincoln, Woodrow Wilson and, not least, Franklin Delano Roosevelt.

What Captain Sprague said is true: we have long been Americans in our hearts. We are thankful now for the privilege of becoming legally entitled to participate in your democracy. To us it is the fruition of Filipino-American friendship. It is the flower of a bloodless freedom, an achievement almost unparalleled in history.

But, alas, how many Americans are truly sincere in granting us this privilege? We know that you have long denied it to us and that military expediency is a large factor in the gift you have made to us.

But you must know us by our unwavering loyalty to you. We came to the United States to learn the best, and we found that our place here was in the blind spot of America. We believed in your ideals, we expected you to practise them. But we were barred from the best in your society, we were barred from economic advancement, held to the most menial of your unwanted tasks, kept from labor unions, denied access to skilled jobs or professions, prevented from learning those things that would be of value to our country when we returned home, condemned here for our dark skins, the light of our high ideals ignored and shunned. Yet we have not become bitter. No Filipino in the United States harbors hatred against the Americans in spite of all the stupidities with regard to race prejudice. We have always been loyal to your ideals to the extent of tolerating the un-American dealings of some Americans. We have held to the hope in our hearts that some day you would know us for what we are—*and now that day has come*. It came by way of Bataan—but it is here—this citizenship ceremony proves it.

It was to perfect our citizenship that we came to America. And the work done by Filipinos on California ranches, in Alaskan fisheries and canneries, in the movie industry, on railroads, in mills, factories and in homes all over America has been a contribution to the economic welfare of the United States, but primarily apprenticeship for us in service and useful arts. Here, as well as in your American schools and colleges, we have absorbed the lessons of America. Now we advance another step. We are soldiers now, soldiers of freedom, who go to take back a free citizenship to our country. When this war ends, when reconstruction comes to our homeland, the Filipino citizen of the United States will go back home, not to renounce his oath to the American people, but eager to fulfill his duty to the Philippines. The Philippines will need men who have been trained in your modern ways to rebuild the shattered Orient, to be the leaders of the new order. All that we learn now will one day be put to use for our country.

We are taking on a broad responsibility, a triple responsibility, really. We are responsible for our loyalty to the United States. Our duty to the Philippines means that we must take the leadership there. And we must also lead in the rebuilding of the new Orient. The Malayan lands, freed, must have leadership they trust and understand. We Filipinos must have trade and cooperation with our neighbors: we cannot live isolated from the rest of the Orient. The United States has already set up trade barriers against us. Furthermore, America has taught us well: now it is our duty to pass the teachings on to these other lands that will be freed from the Japanese invader, and freed also from European "colonizers," by the same army of the United Nations.

All this was bound up in the oath that we took at Camp Beale, as we stood in our Victory formation, as we saluted the American flag, proud American soldiers!

We are the Advance Echelon of the Army of the United States of the Orient.

7. Rosa Roberto Carter Recalls Starvation and Loyalty Interrogation in Guam, 1941–5 (2003)

When Japan occupied Guam 62 years ago, I was 12 years old, the oldest child in our family. My mother would have another child during the occupation, and her last one after the war, for a total of nine of us who made it through childhood. In regard to physical damage from the war, I am sure the effects of malnutrition on my parents, as well as nine of us kids, was severe in both the near term and over the following years.

There's no way to know all the negative effects of the two years of malnutrition we were forced to experience during the occupiers who confiscated our food for themselves. In the last two weeks, they forced us into more difficult situations involving a forced march and virtual imprisonment in a squalid camp, where there was no food at all. We older kids foraged for our family, searching wild lands for many miles. We nearly starved to death at that time.

In regard to immediately visible physical damage, most of us suffered wounds from being forced into the jungle, where we contacted scarring napalm from the United States bombing of the Japanese. When the bombing stopped, we were forced to go back to clearing bushes, which were dripping with this napalm. And in a proper setting, I could show you some scars, which have irritated me for 60 years. One of my brothers lost parts of two fingers, as well, from the live ammunition scattered over so much of Guam after the fighting in 1944.

And at one time, I found myself clinging to a large breadfruit tree while American planes attacked. Human limbs, arms and legs, flew through the air on their own. People screamed in the grip of hysteria. I saw people going berserk.

My own forced labor consisted, at first, of clearing fields in the Mangilao area. My brother Juan was also forced to do this too. At this time I was singled out by the Japanese soldiers, locked up in a tiny room at the old Price Elementary school house, and interrogated about my loyalty to the United States. It may have had something to do with my slightly lighter skin color, but the terrifying experience is still vivid in my mind. Also, at this time, I was given the extra duty of carrying their lunches to Japanese soldiers located at the present site of the Father Duenas Memorial School.

Our forced march started for me late one afternoon, when my brother and I returned from working in the fields to find my parents and my siblings loading our bull cart with as much food and personal belongings as possible. People congregated at the Mangilao school areas, where the trek to Manenggon concentration camp started around twilight. We trudged along on foot all night. Weak people fell by the way side. I do not know what happened to them.

From Real People. *Real Stories*, the Guam War Claims Review Commission public hearing held in Hagåtña, Guam, December 8, 2003, http://guamwarsurvivorstory.com.

In regard to the constant terror of being an occupied people, earlier in Mangilao, many of us were forced to line up in orderly rows to witness the beating of a family for the crime of trying to hide some of its food from the Japanese occupiers. If we showed any emotion, we would have been beaten too. We practiced a code of silence because that means collaborators might be anywhere at any time.

Near the end of the war out here in Guam, because tomorrow men were being forced to the front lines where they were to be sacrificed as human targets, my father went into hiding. As a survivor, immediately he led his entire family back to Mangilao. The regimentation of our lives extended to digging our own graves in the last days at Manenggon.

8. Ben Blaz Describes the Lessons of the Liberation of Guam, 1945 (1994)

My generation was caught between childhood and adulthood. The unexpected and violent interruption of our lives and the common adversity that we shared gave our parents and elders an unusual opportunity to inculcate in us much more vital learning than we could have received in calmer times.

Challenged by the threatening experience of war and pressed to our limits, we learned things about human nature and ourselves that we might never have been able to grasp in peaceful, less demanding, times.

We learned: to be tolerant when conditions were intolerable; to be generous when there was so little to give; to be patient when our deepest desire was to end our bondage; to be ourselves, preserving our language and culture while the enemy was trying to impose his on us.

Life seemed more endangered, more tentative, and therefore, more precious then. We learned through toil the sweetness of the saltiness of the sweat that trickled down our faces at the peak of a hard day's work.

We clearly saw and keenly appreciated the basic choices of life, between freedom and bondage; justice and oppression; hope and despair; surviving and perishing. Through the heat and dust and smoke, we saw ourselves and what we stood for.

There were many painful experiences in that dark period in our history. But there were also many pleasant memories:

—The long hours on a log with our parents sharing their thoughts and experiences with us much like the generations before them had done; but with greater urgency as the winds of war swirled around the island;

—The groups of neighboring farmers who pooled their strength to push back the jungle so we could plant; The women caring for the sick, working the gardens preparing food over open fires;

—The men echoing each other's folksong at twilight as they cut tuba [coconut tree sap used to make liquor];

Ben Blaz, "Chamorros Yearn For Freedom," in *Liberation: Guam Remembers* (Agana, GU: Golden Salute Committee, 1994), 92–94.

—The labor camps where we realized how we had to protect each other, how we had to care for one another as an island family;

—The devout men and women who emerged as our natural leaders and who would always lead us in prayer during our most trying and fearful moments as we labored to finish our forced labor projects under incredible duress;

—There was the young Japanese officer who taught me elementary Japanese in exchange for my father teaching him English and who, after getting to know us, innocently asked my father why we were at war;

—There was this same officer who came to say good-bye and as he left to defend against the invasion, I felt an indescribably mixed emotion of seeing a new friend leaving to fight those coming to liberate us;

—There were the U.S. Marines, the soldiers, the sailors and the Coast Guardsmen who, after hopping from island to island, liberated one of their own and seemed as glad as we were that they had come back to Guam;

—And there were the joyous faces of my fellow Chamorros, 23,000 strong, who had endured 31 months of harsh enemy occupation, including internment in concentration camps, in a war they had no part in starting.

As excruciating and as harrowing as the occupation was, our people did not surrender without a fight and did not stop fighting after the surrender. In the face of an overwhelmingly larger enemy force, a handful of U.S. sailors and Marines stood their ground. Standing beside them, with equal valor and courage but even with greater pride and determination, were the members of the Navy Insular Force Guard.

For these men, Chamorros all, the defense of Guam meant the defense of home, family and honor. Although they wore the same U.S. Navy uniforms, their pay was exactly one-half that of the stateside comrades. Although they fought under the same U.S. flag, they were considered only half-brothers in the patronizing, colonial society on Guam at that time.

Yet, when it came time to shed blood against foreign invaders, the Chamorros of the Navy Insular Force demonstrated their loyalty to the United States in the same way they demonstrated their love for the U.S. principles of freedom and democracy: not halfheartedly, but totally and wholeheartedly.

It is that commitment to home, family and honor that has sustained us over the years as a people. In the years since [Ferdinand] Magellan landed on Guam, our people have been colonized, proselytized, Catholicized, and subsidized. Guam has fallen under Spanish, American, Japanese and again American rule.

But never have we been asked what we as a people wanted. Progress, whatever there was of it, moved at a pace of the administering authority. It was his choice to uncover or cover at his will what he wished to know about us, and it was our lot to remain mute to the process. The attitude developed that the foreigners' right to dominate the land was established by their finding it, and the people - like the flora and fauna - had no alternative but to acquiesce in silence.

The Spaniards made Guam their own, but never did they ask the Chamorro people, the Old People, what relationship should be forged with them. Nor, centuries later, when the United States took control of the island did it ask the descendants of those Chamorros and those Spaniards what association should be formed.

We must wonder why the colonizing forces never asked this most fundamental question. Perhaps they felt that the new order they were bringing was so progressive that the people could not help but be overjoyed to embrace it. Or perhaps the ugly hand of racism was at work, and they believed the people could not tell the difference between freedom and subjugation.

Whatever the case, with the close of the war and with increased education opportunities becoming available to the people of Guam, those of my generation realized the disparities we had accepted without question for so long did not have to be the case. It was as if we had been born blind and then miraculously had been given sight.

It came as a shock to realize that darkness was not inevitable nor the natural state of the world. And so it was we who realized that we were not a second class people. Invisible barriers were just that—invisible and without reason. New horizons revealing incredible vistas began to open before us. We had been told for generations, for example, that should we join the Navy, we were worthy to serve as servants, as stewards. My generation began to ask: And why not officers? There was no reply.

And so slowly at first, and then with accelerating force, we set out on a quest to achieve our self-determination as a people—economically, culturally, and politically. Genuine self-determination, if the word is to have any meaning, is a self-help program. If you truly want it, if it truly means anything to you, you must reach out for it and grasp it as your own. That we have done.

During the 25th anniversary celebration in 1969, one of the most distinguished officers in the Marine Corps, Gen. Lemuel C. Shepherd, was our guest of honor. Having commanded one of the major units that liberated Guam, Gen. Shepherd had a very special place in his heart for the people of Guam and, in particular for those under his command who were killed in action during the fighting. I remember still his closing remarks before a full house at the Guam Legislature: "When I get to heaven," he said, "my men who died here during the war will be at the gate waiting for me with this question: 'Lem, was dying for Guam worth it?' My answer to them will be that having just visited Guam recently, the answer is, you damn right it was."

In closing my recollections of this very auspicious occasion, I cannot resist the urge to share an exchange I had with my own father as I was about to leave Guam after spending a week's leave following my graduation from Notre Dame and my being commissioned a second lieutenant in the U.S. Marines.

Departing with me that day was a group of young Guamanians who had just been recruited in the Army and on their way to basic training. As with me, most of them would eventually find themselves serving in Korea. Unlike me, however, some of them would die there and others would return home with lives and limbs shattered forever.

It made for a large group, the recruits and their mothers and fathers, brothers and sisters, aunts and uncles, and me and my family. We made our way to the tarmac for our final good-byes, and as I gathered my things for boarding, my father grabbed my arm.

In his eyes was the old fierceness, and despite his failing health, he was the robust and feisty man who had been a boxer and a fighter for equality. To my utter amazement, he said to me, "Since you are now an officer of the United States, Lieutenant, answer me this. Why is it that we are treated as equals only in war but not in peace?"

Still holding my arm, he pulled me to him and said, "You don't have to answer now. Just remember that the quest must endure."

My chest was tight as I said, "Yes, Sir."

As I finished kissing him good-bye, he whispered, "By the way, you never did return the salute I gave you when you first arrived." I stepped back from him, and standing ramrod straight, I brought my hand to my forehead in a crisp salute but my arm was trembling from the unexpected and affectionate admonition from my Navyman father.

To this day, my father's question continues to haunt all of us, but at least we now have that question formalized and on the Congressional table – the Commonwealth of Guam.

On this, the 50th anniversary of our liberation, we will be shedding a few tears—of gratitude to our liberators; of remembrance of our brothers and sisters who suffered with us but are unable to join us; and of thanksgiving as we thank Almighty God for all the blessings that have come our way during these golden years.

But after those tears have stopped and have become a precious memory for us all, we must remember that the work begun by the Liberators in 1944 is not yet complete. The people of Guam picked up the torch of freedom passed to them on July 21, 1944. All who call Guam home have worked so hard and so determinedly that the entire world can see the island and its people have come so far from that terrible time of long ago.

But true self-determination and equality still evade our people. Thus, the quest endures.

ESSAYS

These two essays address how World War II improved the status and treatment of Asian Americans whose homelands had joined the United States in fighting Japan. In the first essay, Xiaojian Zhao, a professor of Asian American Studies at the University of California, Santa Barbara, shows how the lives of approximately 500 to 600 Chinese American women in the San Francisco Bay area were transformed when they left Chinatown to become well-paid defense workers. Helping to shape a new positive image of Chinese Americans, many of these second-generation women were proud of their contributions to the war effort, even though discriminatory policies denied them promotions and supervisory positions. In the second essay, Jane Hong, an assistant professor of history at Occidental College, situates the repeal of Asian exclusion laws within the context of U.S. military intervention in Asia. Hong discusses how white lobbyists countered Chinese exclusionists by presenting the repeal as a necessary measure to defeat Japan. The repeal of Chinese exclusion established a model other groups could use to mobilize American geopolitical interests in Asia and counter anti-American propaganda about racism, discrimination, and colonialism in the United States. Indian activists won the repeal of exclusion laws not because they were considered desirable immigrants but because the U.S. government wanted to establish a Cold War alliance with India.

World War II and Chinese American Women Defense Workers

XIAOJIAN ZHAO

In February 1945, *Fortune Magazine* published an article on the Kaiser shipyards in Richmond, California, including eight photos of the shipyards workers. One of the captions for the photos says, "Chinese Woman: she hasn't missed a day's work in two years." This woman was Ah Yoke Gee, a welder in Kaiser Richmond Shipyard Number Two. The weekly magazine of the Kaiser Richmond shipyards, *Fore 'N' Aft*, described her as one of the oldest crew members of the Richmond shipyards. From July 31, 1942, when she started to work in the shipyard, to April 20, 1945, Ah Yoke Gee had missed only one day of work to spend time with her oldest son, a serviceman who was passing through San Francisco on his way to the Pacific front. At a time when there was a shortage of labor, Ah Yoke Gee's story was apparently useful for the Kaiser company's public relations. Here, a middle-aged Chinese American woman was being recognized as a patriotic, hardworking defense worker, who was doing her best to contribute to the nation's war effort.

Ironically, this model shipyard worker had been deprived of citizenship by her own government. Born in 1895 on the Monterey Peninsula in California, Ah Yoke Gee was a second-generation Chinese American for whom U.S. citizenship was a birthright. Her legal status changed, however, after she married a Chinese immigrant from Hong Kong. During the period of Chinese exclusion from 1882 to 1943, Ah Yoke Gee's husband, an alien from China, was racially ineligible for naturalization. Moreover, the Cable Act of September 22, 1922, stipulated that women citizens who married aliens ineligible for citizenship could no longer be citizens themselves. Though Ah Yoke Gee worked for the nation's defense industry, she could not vote as a citizen. Her daughters recalled that she had been very upset about losing her citizenship because she always considered herself an American. At age forty-six, she finally had the opportunity to work in a defense industry to demonstrate her patriotism to her country. It was also during the war that Congress repealed the Chinese exclusion laws and made it possible later for Ah Yoke Gee to regain her citizenship through naturalization. Unfortunately, her husband, who died before the war, did not live to see the happy day. Ah Yoke passed away in 1973.

Xiaojian Zhao, "Chinese American Women Defense Workers in World War II," *California History*, 75, no. 2 (Summer 1996): 138–153. Reprinted by permission.

World War II marked a turning point in the lives of Chinese Americans. For the first time, Chinese Americans began to be accepted by the larger American society. Chinese American women not only had a chance to work at jobs traditionally held by men, but were also allowed to show their loyalty to their country....

Since the United States and China were allies against common enemies during the war, American images of Chinese began to change from negative to positive ones. Whereas, once, negative stereotypes of the Chinese had dominated popular culture, the American mass media now described the Chinese as polite, moderate, and hard-working. On December 22, 1941, *Time* magazine, for example, published a short article to help the American public differentiate their Chinese "friends" from the Japanese. The facial expressions of the Chinese, according to the article, were more "placid, kindly, open," while those of the Japanese were more "positive, dogmatic, arrogant." Also, because World War II was considered by the American public as a "good war" against fascists who had launched a racist war, it was important for the United States itself to improve its domestic race relations....

After decades of isolation imposed by the larger American society, the Bay Area Chinese American communities lost no time in seizing this opportunity. In various meetings and social gatherings, community leaders and organizations urged Chinese American residents to participate in the war efforts. Because military service would qualify immigrants for U.S. citizenship and some Chinese immigrants had been granted citizenship while in the Army, it was considered a breakthrough in challenging the exclusion acts. *Jinshan shibao* (Chinese Times) published a number of articles regarding the advantages of defense jobs. First, defense jobs were well paid. Second, these jobs could be used for draft deferment. Third, defense employees could apply for government-subsidized housing, which provided a great opportunity for Chinese Americans to move out of their isolated ethnic ghettos....

Given the social isolation of the immigrant generation, it is not surprising that the Chinese American women who worked in defense industries were mostly the second-generation daughters of immigrant women....

Since most of them were already living in the Bay Area before the war, these younger Chinese American women were among the first American women to join the Bay Area's defense labor force. As early as May 1942, the *Chinese Press* reported that young Chinese American girls were working in most of the defense establishments in the region. At the Engineer Supply Depot, Pier 90, eighteen-year-old Ruth Law was the youngest office staff member in the company. Her co-worker, Anita Lee, was an assistant to the company's chief clerk. Fannie Yee, a high school senior at the time, won top secretarial honors for her efficiency at work at Bethlehem Steel Corporation in San Francisco. She worked with two other young women, Rosalind Woo and Jessie Wong. The major defense employers in San Francisco for Chinese American women at the time, according to the *Press*, were the Army Department and Fort Mason. In Oakland, the Army Supply Base recognized Stella Quan as a very capable clerk. The first two Chinese American women who worked at Moore Dry Dock Company were Maryland Pong and Edna Wong. The State Employment Bureau also had Chinese American women on its staff. Before Kaiser's Richmond shipyards and Marinship began production work, many young Chinese American girls worked at Mare Island Navy Shipyard. Among them were Anita Chew, Mildred Lew, and Evelyn Lee of Oakland. Both Jenny Sui of San Francisco and Betty Choy of Vallejo started as messenger girls in the yard, but they were soon promoted to clerk-typists....

Unlike single young women, it was much more difficult for married Chinese American women to take defense jobs unless they did not have small children at home. After she married, Ah Yoke Gee spent most of her time at home taking care of her six children. She kept her sewing machine running whenever she was free from household chores. One of her daughters remembered that sometimes she woke up at two o'clock in the morning and could still hear her mother sewing. By the time the war started, Ah Yoke was widowed. Two of her older children had left home and the rest of them were in either high school or college. Although she still cooked for her family, her children had their own routines and did not expect to be served in a formal way. Every morning before leaving for her swing shift job in the shipyard, Ah Yoke would cook enough food for the whole family for the day. On weekends she shopped, washed, and cleaned.

Maggie Gee, Ah Yoke Gee's daughter, was born in Berkeley....

On December 7, 1941, Maggie was spending the afternoon studying in the campus library. She found many students there talking very emotionally. Maggie sensed that something unusual had happened. To Chinese Americans, World War II had begun on September 18, 1931, when the Japanese invaded Manchuria in northeastern China. Maggie had been in the fourth grade at the time. Her mother had planned to send her and her sister to China to study, and they had to cancel the trip after the Japanese occupied Chinese territory. After July 7, 1937, when the Japanese attacked Chinese troops at Lugou Bridge near Beijing, the war against Japan became a nationwide effort in China. Overseas Chinese were actively involved in supporting their fellow countrymen. Maggie often went with her mother to San Francisco's Chinatown to attend rallies and fund-raising activities. She remembered how badly she felt when she learned about the outrageous atrocities during the 1937 Nanjing Massacre, but she was surprised to notice that her American classmates knew very little about what had happened in China. Not until Pearl Harbor did everyone seem involved in the war effort. The Berkeley campus offered classes for defense employment, in which Maggie and many other students received training. While still a full-time student at Berkeley, she got a graveyard-shift job at Richmond Shipyard Number Two.

Wartime employment provided tangible benefits to many Chinese Americans. "For people who used to have very little money," recalled Aimei Chen, "the war was a time of great economic opportunity." She started to buy things for her family—food, kitchen-ware, and other household items. Aimei's mother also got a job in a cannery in Stockton, where many former employees had left for defense jobs. Yulan Liu, meanwhile, made $65 a week, four times more than she had made before the war. She gave some money to her mother and saved the rest for herself. On her day off, she went to the movies and bought herself candies and pastries. As for Ah Yoke Gee, her family endured great difficulties for many years after she lost her husband. During the war, with both her and her daughters working in the shipyard and her son in the service, the living standard of the family improved significantly....

Although Chinese Americans were accepted in defense industries, they had little chance to be promoted to supervisory positions. Many companies simply assumed that white employees would not follow orders given by Chinese....

Ah Yoke Gee loved her job in the shipyard so much that she would not leave it for anything else. She knew that other jobs would not pay as well. Aimei Chen also wanted to stay at her defense job. Since so many white women were then also job-hunting, the chances for her to find a good job were slim. By late 1945, however, most of the Bay Area's defense establishments were about to shut down, and large-scale lay-offs began. With limited training and skills, these women could not find jobs in other industries; they had to look for jobs that were traditionally held by women.

These Chinese American women's wartime work nevertheless had important consequences: their lives were no longer restricted within their ethnic communities. Most of them found jobs outside Chinatowns as race relations and the economy improved in the postwar years. Ah Yoke Gee took a job at a post office in Berkeley, where she worked until her retirement. Meanwhile, she became actively involved in Berkeley's Chinese American community. Aimei Chen married and moved with her husband to Berkeley. Under the GI Bill, her husband became an engineering student at the University of California. Aimei found a job as an office clerk in a small firm, where she worked until her first child was born....

While acknowledging that World War II brought significant changes to their lives, many Chinese American women noticed that racial discrimination and prejudice did not disappear after the war. They continued in subtle ways. When Maggie Gee and her sister tried to find an apartment in Berkeley in the early 1950s, they knew that some people would not rent their properties to Chinese Americans. So they told people their ethnic identity when they first inquired over the telephone. At least in one case, a landlady refused to show the sisters the apartment when she learned that they were Chinese....

The young Chinese American women who participated in defense work had had fresh memories of discriminatory practices in American society before the war, and they were fully aware of the political implications of taking defense jobs. Although very few of them were able to keep their jobs after the war, and some of them might not necessarily have cared about the limited skills that they acquired, what they had accomplished was far more significant than the jobs themselves. They were accepted, for the first time, as Americans, even though most of them were born in the U. S. and had been Americans since birth. To a large extent, the war provided an entry for Chinese American women into the larger American society, something for which their ancestors had struggled a hundred years.

The Movement to Repeal Asian Exclusion

JANE HONG

The 1943 Magnuson Act marked both an end and a beginning. Popularly known as the "Chinese Exclusion Repealer," the legislation overturned all Chinese Exclusion legislation passed between 1882 and the early 1900s, gave China a race-based immigration quota of 105 persons per year, and made Chinese persons eligible for U.S. citizenship for the first time in U.S. history. On the one hand, the 1943 Act followed decades of activism by Chinese, Chinese American, and white American advocates to end America's exclusionary policies against Chinese people. On the other, the Magnuson Act provided a roadmap to success for groups of Indians, Filipinos, and Japanese and their advocates and allies to seek repeal legislation benefiting their own communities.

Understanding the Chinese repeal effort as part of a longer movement to end Asian Exclusion as a whole that extended from 1943 to 1965 reveals it as a the first of several legislative campaigns that together dismantled the exclusionary regime. This essay focuses on the Chinese and Indian campaigns of the World War II years. The Magnuson and Luce-Celler Act lobbies built upon the Chinese effort's success, adapting lessons from its organization, argumentation, and strategy. Chief among these was the leveraging of geopolitics. Throughout successive campaigns for repeal, advocates crafted their appeals to capitalize on the political cachet of U.S. foreign policy interests in Asia, as the region became a major site of Cold War conflict. The longer movement culminated in the 1965 Immigration Act, which overhauled the immigration system, replacing the national origins quota system with preferences based on occupational skills and family relationships.

World War II provided a confluence of international and domestic developments that made the repeal of the Chinese Exclusion laws politically viable as never before. For decades, U.S. and Chinese officials agitated against the Exclusion laws as an impediment to Sino-American diplomacy, but U.S. Congressional lawmakers felt little need to address them in light of China's weakness on the world stage. Japan's surprise attack on Pearl Harbor war changed their minds. America's entry into the war made the United States and China, led by the Nationalist regime of Chiang Kaishek, military allies and partners for the first time as the United States joined the Pacific War against Japan. Never before had Americans fought alongside an Asian power as formal allies, and never before had U.S. policymakers had such incentive to maintain a strong relationship with China. Washington's top priority to defeat Germany on the war's Western front, known in shorthand as the "Europe First" policy, threatened this partnership. Throughout 1942, Washington diverted the bulk of U.S. troops and resources to Europe, leaving the war-weary Chinese to bear the brunt of Allied casualties in Asia. As U.S. promises of aid and supplies repeatedly failed to materialize, Chinese morale and goodwill toward the United States suffered.

Jane Hong, "The Movement to Repeal Asian Exclusion," from Reorienting America: Race, Geopolitics, and the Repeal of Asian Exclusion, 1940–1952 (PhD diss., Harvard University, 2013). Reprinted by permission.

Japan sought to exploit the strain in the Sino-American alliance with radio campaigns singling out America's history of exclusionary laws against Asians, and Chinese in particular. In messages aired throughout occupied Asia, Japanese-controlled radio derided American claims to democracy, while calling on Asian audiences to unite under Japanese leadership against the forces of white, Western imperialism. The special publication and distribution of a pamphlet excerpting similar Japanese broadcasts for the House Committee on Immigration and Naturalization in 1943 ignited alarm among Congressional lawmakers. Its contents identified America's exclusion laws as a major impediment to U.S. wartime goals in the Pacific.

More than any other single factor, these attacks on America's anti-Chinese and anti-Asian laws strengthened the case for repeal of Chinese exclusion. Impressed with the necessity of keeping China in the war against Japan at all costs, Roosevelt and the U.S. State Department turned to concessionary, symbolic gestures to reassure Chinese officials of America's commitment to the Pacific front. In January 1943, Washington renounced its extraterritoriality privileges in China with an official abrogation of the unequal treaties. One month later, Congressional sponsors timed the introduction of the first Chinese repeal bills in February 1943 to coincide with a U.S. visit by Soong Meiling, Chinese Nationalist leader General Chiang Kaishek's Wellesley-educated wife. Soong became a media sensation, unleashing an outpouring of public support for America's Chinese allies. On a stop in Washington, DC, she addressed a joint session of U.S. Congress to request more American aid to China in the Pacific War against Japan. America and the other Allied powers had it wrong, she suggested, if they believed that Germany was a greater threat than Japan; such a belief was "not borne out by actual facts," as Japan had far "greater resources at her command than Germany." Working behind the scenes, Soong and Chinese consular officials seized the opportunity to express their support for the repeal measure through private diplomatic channels. They emphasized the boon it promised as a means to restore and strengthen the Sino-American alliance.

The Citizens Committee to Repeal Chinese Exclusion and Place Immigration on a Quota Basis, the white American group that spearheaded the public lobby for repeal through the spring and fall of 1943, made the argument the focus of its campaign. Framing Chinese exclusion repeal as a war measure had several advantages. Above all, war-related arguments were politically powerful during a time when winning the war was paramount both in the minds of Washington officials and the American public at large. Even the most reluctant Congressional lawmakers felt hard-pressed to deny a Chinese ally under duress lest it undermine or otherwise delay the objective of Allied victory. Furthermore, war arguments had broad appeal to an anxious American public, enabling supporters to market the cause to a general American audience beyond China enthusiasts alone. If repeal was primarily about the war, the logic flowed, it was a matter that concerned all Americans committed to an Allied victory on the Pacific front, and not simply those who took a personal interest in the Chinese.

Founded by New York-based publisher Richard Walsh, the Citizens Committee brought together some of the most powerful white American friends of

China around a common cause. As political scientist Fred Riggs has shown, the group did not generate new public interest in China so much as it coordinated the efforts of those already seeking repeal, including religious and liberal groups. Within government circles, U.S. State Department officials and other internationalists in the executive branch joined a small bipartisan core of Congressmen and women to draft and sponsor legislation, petition committees, and secure powerful endorsements in the effort to convince lawmakers to vote for repeal. Under Walsh's leadership, these diverse forces launched a broad publicity campaign using churches, direct mailings, radio broadcasts, and strategically placed editorials to rally public support for the Chinese cause.

Far from challenging the racial ideas and prejudices that underwrote exclusion, the Citizens Committee relied on a strategy of political expediency and pragmatism to win the support of U.S. lawmakers. This included a policy of restricting membership to white American citizens only. Thus, even as Chinese American activists agitated and editorialized in support of repeal, they largely did so behind the scenes and in Chinese-language forums, downplaying their public involvement for fear of inciting backlash or creating the impression that repeal was a Chinese cause. Chinese Americans also provided financial support, contributing a significant portion of the Citizens Committee's overall budget.

The Citizens Committee capitalized upon public support for China to push the Magnuson bill through a conservative coalition of restrictionist Southern Democrats and Western Republicans who maintained a majority on the U.S. House and Senate Immigration Committees. Citizens Committee members also strategically neutralized the opposition of groups that had long opposed Chinese immigration, including veterans' organizations, West Coast interests, and self-described patriotic societies. These groups took special issue with Congress passing the Chinese repeal bill on the grounds that doing so would invite "hundreds of millions of other Asiatics" to "ask for that same thing."

Their fears were prescient. Other Asian groups took the passage of the Magnuson bill through Congress on December 17, 1943 as a rallying cry. While President Franklin Roosevelt called the bill a "manifestation on the part of the American people of their affection and regard" for the Chinese people, declaring that the "war effort in the Far East [could] now be carried on with a greater vigor and a larger understanding of our common purpose," activists introduced a flurry of legislation proposing similar rights for Indians, Filipinos, and Koreans, among other groups, confirming the law's critics were right. No longer compelled to be discreet lest they jeopardize the Chinese campaign, Indian and Korean advocates began lobbying for their own communities in earnest.

World War II ultimately did not enable the passage of additional repeal legislation, but its conclusion brought an era of decolonization in Asia that would be the backdrop for the next phase of the repeal movement. As in the Chinese campaign, Indian and Korean advocates looked to the language of geopolitics as a political tool, but the problem of colonialism made their task fundamentally different. The Magnuson Act reflected a negotiation between sovereign states; the question of granting rights to Asian colonial groups involved their struggle for independence and the United States' relationship with their colonial oppressor.

The campaign for the rights of Indians would find success soon after World War II. As Indian independence from Great Britain looked increasingly likely, advocates in the United States (and in India) successfully pointed to the claims of a soon-to-be independent India that could ally with the United States—or its adversaries. They argued that legislation giving rights to Indians would invite support. It would also uphold Washington's claims, as articulated in the 1941 Atlantic Charter, to support self-determination. The result was the Luce-Celler Act of 1946. Among its provisions, the Act granted India an annual immigration quota of 100, to take effect upon the subcontinent's independence from Great Britain. In addition, it made Indians racially eligible for U.S. citizenship as exceptions to the blanket ban on naturalization for Asian peoples. (It also extended U.S. citizenship eligibility to Filipinos, whose status had changed from "American nationals" to "aliens" when the Philippines became a U.S. protectorate in 1935.)

Anti-colonial struggles made the approach Indian lobbyists took to legal victory fundamentally different from the approach of Chinese activists and their advocates, in spite of the fact that several key figures such as Richard Walsh participated in both efforts. While some Indians living in the United States sought immigration and naturalization rights as a path to domestic incorporation, others framed the legislative struggle as an instrument to advance their India's independence struggles. The New York-based India League of America (ILA), under the leadership of Sikh merchant J.J. Singh, embodied this approach. He explicitly stated that he had no interest in becoming a U.S. citizen. The Luce-Celler legislation would have symbolic power in the fight for Indian independence. If India's future lay in achieving equal status and recognition in the international community, he and other India League advocates argued, an American bill granting Indians nominal parity with European peoples under U.S. immigration and naturalization advanced the goal of Indian independence as a goodwill gesture affirming the nationalist aspirations of Indians everywhere.

This argument represented a continuum with the ILA's founding principle; it also brought conflict with another New York-based organization called the India Welfare League of America (IWL). Indian elites living in New York City had founded the ILA in 1937 to "interpret India and America to each other." By contrast, a group of Indian factory and blue-collar workers had created the IWL as a relief organization for unemployed members of their community. The IWL had been advocating since at least 1939 for an Indian citizenship bill that would provide U.S. naturalization eligibility to longtime Indian residents of the United States; unlike the ILA-endorsed Luce-Celler bill, the IWL's version made no mention of Indian immigration. In keeping with the IWL's focus on the practical needs of its members, it traded symbolism for the ability to maintain residency and a livelihood in the United States.

The India League proved the victor, ultimately, as Washington officials remained more interested in cultivating the goodwill of Indians in India than that of Indian immigrant communities stateside. But the success of drawing a connection between repeal and independence was by no means assured as the bill made its journey through Congress. Critics of the legislation also opposed passage on geopolitical grounds, saying it would strain the Anglo-American relationship. One

U.S. lawmaker, for example, objected that the British might interpret passage of the act as an American attempt to "alienate the affections of some of their oppressed Empire people." Others claimed that conscience barred them from voting for the Luce-Celler measure in advance of a formal statement from Whitehall [the British government]. While the voting records of a number of these lawmakers suggest that they would have opposed any bill to liberalize immigration on principle, India's colonial status offered ready grounds for opposition.

Just as Chinese officials working in the background had been decisive in the passage of the Magnuson Act, Indian officials within the British colonial government at Delhi, working mainly through diplomatic channels and outside of the public eye, proved critical to the success of the Luce-Celler bill. In the spring of 1945, when restrictionists tabled the bill in the House Immigration Committee, it was the private lobbying of Delhi's representative to Washington, Sir Girja Bajpai, that revived the legislation. Most critically, Bajpai secured an official endorsement for the Luce-Celler bill from the British Government at Whitehall. Recognizing that tensions with the Indian Congress threatened the war effort in the Pacific, British officials expressed support for the Luce-Celler bill as a "gesture of friendship" honoring India's past military contributions and anticipating its future role in finishing the fight.

With British support assured, the ILA and its advocates moved quickly to expedite another hearing on the Luce-Celler bill before the Congressional session ended. The U.S. House Committee on Immigration convened within weeks and reported the measure out favorably in late June 1945. One month later, British parliamentarian Clement Attlee replaced staunch imperialist Winston Churchill as the British Prime Minister; Attlee accelerated the decolonization process and U.S. policymakers soon recognized Indian independence as imminent. That fall the Luce-Celler bill passed the full U.S. House of Representatives by a vote of nearly three to one. While restrictionists on the Senate Immigration Committee proved a roadblock, President Truman's personal intervention prevented a stall and the measure proceeded to the Senate floor for a vote in June 1946, where it passed easily. Truman signed the Luce-Celler bill into law on July 2, 1946.

The passage of the Luce-Celler bill unleashed a wave of congratulatory and jubilant reports in both the United States and Indian media. Upon Pakistan's creation in 1947, Congress quietly extended the immigration quota and citizenship eligibility given to Indians to Pakistanis as well. The wholesale repeal of restrictive race-based Asian quotas would not come until 1965, however, when the Hart-Celler Act (or Immigration Act of 1965) abolished the national origins quota system once and for all.

☙ FURTHER READING

Baldoz, Rick. *The Third Asiatic Invasion: Empire and Migration in Filipino America, 1898–1946* (2011).

Camacho, Keith. *Cultures of Commemoration: The Politics of War, Memory, and History in the Mariana Islands* (2011).

Chung Simpson, Caroline. *An Absent Presence: Japanese Americans in Postwar American Culture, 1945–1960* (2001).

Cordova, Fred. *Filipinos: Forgotten Asian Americans* (1983).

Espana-Maram, Linda. *Creating Masculinity in Los Angeles's Little Manila: Working-Class Filipinos and Popular Culture, 1920s–1950s* (2006).

Espiritu, Augusto. *Five Faces of Exile: The Nation and Filipino American Intellectuals* (2005).

Espiritu, Yen Le. *Home Bound: Filipino American Lives across Cultures, Communities, and Countries* (2003).

Kim, Richard S. *The Quest for Statehood: Korean Immigrant Nationalism and U.S. Sovereignty, 1905–1945* (2011).

Lai, Him Mark. *Chinese American Transnational Politics*, ed. Madeline Y. Hsu (2010).

Lee, Marjorie, ed. *Duty and Honor: A Tribute to Chinese American World War II Veterans of Southern California* (1998).

Lee, Robert G. *Orientals: Asian Americans in Popular Culture* (1999).

Leong, Karen J. *The China Mystique: Pearl S. Buck, Anna May Wong, Mayling Soong, and the Transformation of American Orientalism* (2005).

Leong, Karen J., and Judy Tzu-Chun Wu, "Filling the Rice Bowls of China: Staging Humanitarian Relief during the Sino-Japanese War," in *Chinese Americans and the Politics of Race and Culture*, eds. Sucheng Chan and Madeline Y. Hsu (2008).

Lim, Christina, and Sheldon H. Lim. *In the Shadow of the Tiger: The 407th Air Service Squadron* (1993).

Marchetti, Gina. *Romance and the "Yellow Peril": Race, Sex, and Discursive Strategies in Hollywood Fiction* (1993).

Ngai, Mae M. *Impossible Subjects: Illegal Aliens and the Making of Modern America* (2014).

San Juan, E. *From Exile to Diaspora: Veterans of the Filipino Experience in the United States* (1998).

Shibusawa, Naoko. *America's Geisha Ally: Reimagining the Japanese Enemy* (2006).

Spickard, Paul, Joanne L. Rondilla, and Debbie Hippolite Wright, eds., *Pacific Diaspora: Island Peoples in the United States and across the Pacific* (2002).

Ting-Yi Lui, Mary. "Rehabilitating Chinatown at Mid-Century: Chinese Americans, Race, and U.S. Cultural Diplomacy," in *Chinatowns in a Transnational World: Myths and Realities of an Urban Phenomenon*, eds. Ruth Mayer and Vanessa Kunneman (2011), 81–100.

Wong, K. Scott, and Sucheng Chan, eds., *Claiming America: Constructing Chinese American Identities during the Exclusion Era* (1998).

Wu, Judy Tzu-Chun. *Doctor Mom Chung of the Fair-Hair Bastards: The Life of a Wartime Celebrity* (2005).

Yung, Judy. *Unbound Feet: A Social History of Chinese Women in San Francisco* (1995).

Yung, Judy, Gordon Chang, and Him Mark Lai, eds. *Chinese American Voices: From the Gold Rush to the Present* (2002).

Zhao, Xiaojian. "Disconnecting Transnational Ties: The *Chinese Pacific Weekly* and the Transformation of Chinese American Community after the Second World War," in *Media and the Chinese Diaspora: Community, Communications, and Commerce*, ed. Wanning Sun (2006), 26–41.

CHAPTER 10

Asian Americans and the Cold War, 1945–1965

After World War II ended, international affairs continued to impact Asian Americans who, regardless of their generation, were still viewed as foreigners by the majority of Americans. Once a hated foe and an occupied country, Japan became a vital friend of the United States and the site of bases strategic to the U.S. effort to contain Communist aggression in Asia. China, on the other hand, went from being a World War II ally to a feared adversary after Mao Zedong and his Communist troops took over the country in 1949. Tension escalated during the Korean War (1950–1953) when Chinese Communists joined North Koreans in combat against South Korean and U.S. forces. American popular media resurrected exclusion era images of "yellow hordes" bent on world conquest. While the U.S. government distinguished between the "bad" Communist China on the mainland and Chiang Kai-shek's "good" Chinese nationalist forces now on the island of Taiwan, the FBI and the Immigration and Naturalization Service suspected all Chinese Americans of being Communist spies. They kept Chinatowns under surveillance, harassed leftists, and evoked fears that Chinese Americans might suffer the internment Japanese Americans experienced during World War II.

The intense ideological war between communism and capitalism during the late 1940s and 1950s also affected American immigration and naturalization policies. Mindful of Communist indictments of American racism, U.S. politicians called for the removal of racial barriers to immigration and naturalization. The 1952 McCarran–Walter Act provided a mixed response to these reform efforts. The act failed to eliminate the national origins quota system that severely limited immigration from non-Western countries. In addition, it counted Asian immigrants, unlike other immigrants from Europe, not by their place of birth but by their racial ancestry. Thus an individual of half Indian ancestry who was born in Britain was included in India's immigration quota. The legislation also instituted loyalty tests to prevent "subversives" from entering the United States, expanded the ideological and moral criteria for preventing admission, and facilitated the deportation of "undesirable" immigrants.

At the same time, Japanese Americans praised the McCarran–Walter Act for ending Japanese exclusion by granting Japan a token annual immigration quota of 185 and for granting Japanese immigrants the right to become U.S. citizens. As a result of this and other changes in national and state laws, Asian immigrants were no longer relegated to the status of "aliens ineligible to citizenship" and therefore were no longer subjected to alien land laws that denied them the right to own property.

Refugees from the Korean War began migrating to the United States during the 1950s. Often called the "Forgotten War," the civil war in Korea became the first "hot war" of the Cold War. Beginning in 1950, just five years after liberation from Japanese colonial rule, the war permanently divided Korea into North and South, separated nearly 10 million people from family members, and produced, in 1953, an armistice that denied a definitive victory to either side. One million civilians in the South and two million civilians in the North died during the war and left numerous orphans. The division and militarization of Korea spurred many migrants—including military brides, adoptees, political exiles, job seekers, and international students—to leave South Korea. In 1955, evangelical Christians Harry and Bertha Holt started an adoption service for babies fathered and abandoned by U.S. soldiers. By the 1960s, many of these supposed "orphans" were in fact children given up for adoption because their mothers were unwed or their parents were poor.

☻ DOCUMENTS

Documents 1 and 2 illustrate the intense conflict within Asian American communities generated by the Cold War. In Hawai'i, business leaders and conservative politicians used fears of communism to attack the growing labor movement in the islands by charging that strikes were instigated and controlled by Communists. The House Un-American Activities Committee held hearings in Honolulu in 1950 and a year later indicted seven people for violating the Smith Act by advocating the overthrow of the U.S. government. In Document 1, radical labor journalist Koji Ariyoshi, one of the seven arrested, denounced the indictment as an assault on union activism. Although the seven were convicted, the verdict was overturned in 1958 after the U.S. Supreme Court ruled that the First Amendment protected a person advocating for revolution or government change.

During the Cold War, white Americans' impression of Asian Americans improved because the United States was firmly allied with Asian countries in the fight against communism. The McCarran–Walter Act, excerpted in Document 2, embodied the new appreciation of Japanese Americans by ending Japanese exclusion and providing immigrants from Japan with naturalization rights. In Document 3, a *Life Magazine* editorial worries that Asians will view the discrimination against a Chinese American family in South San Francisco as a failure of democracy that could threaten American geopolitical interests in Asia.

Documents 4 and 5 illustrate how the U.S. occupation of Japan after World War II and the expansion of military bases throughout Asia affected

American perceptions of race and gender. Document 4 provides Setsuko Kamei Amburn's account of how she went from being the daughter of a Japanese samurai to a war bride in the United States. After finding well-paying jobs with the occupation forces, she began socializing with Americans, fell in love with one, married him, and moved to the United States. Popular culture reinforced acceptance of these interracial couples in the United States. In James Michener's popular 1953 novel *Sayonara*, Major Ace Gruver jilts his American sweetheart for being too independent and is drawn toward an exotic and passive Japanese woman who is eager to fulfill his every desire, even though Americans killed her father and brother during World War II. Document 5, a 1957 poster for the movie adaptation of *Sayonara*, shows Hollywood's depiction of a strong, virile, and masculine white American man rescuing a submissive and feminine Japanese woman.

Document 6 testifies to the enduring legacy of the Korean War on Korean Americans. It presents a public television interview with filmmaker Deann Borshay Liem about family, loss, and identity after the Korean War. Adopted by an American family when she was eight years old, Liem left South Korea for California in 1966. Her adoptive mother told her she was a Korean War orphan named Cha Jung Hee, but recurring dreams and vague memories of her family led her to investigate her past. In South Korea, she discovered her birth family and introduced them to her adoptive parents. After chronicling this journey in her film *First Person Plural*, Liem made another film, *In the Matter of Cha Jung Hee,* about her return to Korea to find the girl whose identity she assumed in the United States.

1. *Honolulu Record* Editor and Labor Leader Koji Ariyoshi Describes the Arrest of Seven Suspected Communists in Hawai'i, 1951 (2000)

The early morning arrest of seven members of this community, including the editor of the *Record*, raises the curtain in Hawaii on the intensified campaign to stifle independent thinking and free speech, a suppression which is becoming more urgent in the whipped-up war program, highly profitable to the big employers but not popular with the great masses of the people.

The attack upon the constitutional rights of the seven individuals who are charged under the notorious Smith Act of advocating certain ideas, but not of committing any overt act of crime, comes at the crucial moment of the sugar negotiations between Hawaii's Big Five and the ILWU [International Longshore and Warehouse Union]. On Lanai, 750 workers are on strike, and have been now for more than half a year, and Hawaiian Pineapple Company is letting a $25,000,000 crop rot to break the union.

From *Kona to Yenan: The Political Memoirs of Koji Ariyoshi* by Koji Ariyoshi, 1–5, © 2000 University of Hawaii Press. Used with permission.

One of the seven is the ILWU regional director. The others have been alleged by fingermen, stool pigeons and disgruntled former labor leaders to have influenced the policies of the union, a union in whose democracy its participating members take great pride.

As the longshoremen from Maui have already said, this is a move to discredit the ILWU which, nationally and locally, has not kow-towed to the war mobilization program that results in higher taxes and less pork chops, while destruction and death take place far from our shores to keep the pumps primed for the highly profitable war industry that benefits only big employers.

The arrest of the seven is said to fall into the "national pattern" by Justice Department propagandists. It is significant that the top publicity man of the Justice Department was brought here to drum up the allegation of "conspiracy" and the teaching of the overthrow of the government by force and violence.

Such preparation of the propaganda barrage was necessary to strike fear into the people, even after all these years of red-baiting the labor movement, particularly the ILWU, in order to isolate the leadership of the union from the membership, and the union itself from the rest of the island community.

A large segment of the people who have had close association with the seven must realize from their own experiences that the allegation of teaching the overthrow of the government by force and violence is fantastic. Subscribers to the *Record* have read views of the editor as expressed in the editorial column week after week for more than three years....

What is this "national pattern"? Those who ride the bandwagon of the witch-hunters say it is the arrest and incarceration of Communists, alleged Communists and non-conformists.

Let us look at the picture from the other side and ask a few questions: "Why the arrests?" "What crime or crimes harmful to the populace have these people committed?" "What purpose and whom do the arrests serve?"

Actually, the "national pattern" today is the attack against trade unions, the buying off of some top leaders, attempting to crush militant unions that do not conform, loyalty purges, a war scare to condition the people for continued mobilization, unprecedented profits for big industrialists and financiers whose key men run the government. We have big steals in war contracts, corruption and graft in government even involving the President's immediate staff—now the chairman of the National Democratic Party is implicated.

All these go on as the industrialists, who postponed a recession setting in two years ago by the war program, grab profits in the most ruthless manner. They dodge taxes, get plants built free with taxpayers' money, and constantly fight to raise taxes of the low-income earners, 10,500,000 families of whom live, according to a recent government report, on less than $2,000 a year.

More and more people are beginning to realize that the war program is a phony, despite the increasing attempts to instill fear and timidity to voice their disapproval....

Now, what has the *Record* done to bring similar attacks upon its editor? It is not a Big Five controlled newspaper. Last week, for instance, it reported that Davies & Company is laying off its 25-year men, all of Japanese ancestry. No other newspaper has reported this major news in the community where job security is disdainfully ignored by big employers. The *Record* has criticized plantation conditions and has brought about improvements in housing on certain plantations. And the *Record* is the only newspaper that supports unions and the workers in the Territory.

The jailing of its editor will not suspend its publication. There will be others to carry on, and there being no monopoly of ideas, there are many more coming up who will see the injustices in these islands and raise their voices against them in order to improve conditions....

The hope lies in the people, here and on the Mainland. We have deep faith in them to struggle for progress. It is the duty of those who understand the situation, including those who have been silenced, to awaken the conscience of the whole populace.

2. Congress Expands Immigration and Naturalization Rights for Asian Immigrants, 1952

Chapter 1—Selection System/Numerical Limitations

Sec. 201. (a) The annual quota of any quota area shall be one-sixth of 1 per centum of the number of inhabitants in the continental United States in 1920, which number, except for the purpose of computing quotas for the quota areas within the Asia-Pacific triangle, shall be the same number heretofore determined under the provisions of section 11 of the Immigration Act of 1924, attributable by national origin to such quota area: *Provided*, That the quota existing for Chinese persons prior to the date of enactment of this Act shall be continued, and, except for as otherwise provided in section 202(e), the minimum quota for any quota area shall be one hundred....

[Sec. 202. (b)] (4) such immigrant born outside the Asia-Pacific triangle who is attributable by as much as one-half of his ancestry to a people or peoples indigenous to not more than one separate quota area, situate wholly within the Asia-Pacific triangle, shall be chargeable to the quota of that quota area....

Sec. 203. (a) Immigrant visas to quota immigrants shall be allotted in each year as follows:

(1) The first 50 per centum of the quota of each quota area for such year, plus any portion of such quota not required for the issuance of immigrant visas to the classes specified in paragraphs (2) and (3), shall be made available for the issuance of immigrant visas (A) to qualified quota immigrants whose services are determined by the Attorney General to be needed urgently in the United States because of the high education, technical training, specialized experience, or exceptional ability of such immigrants and to be substantially beneficial prospectively to the national economy, cultural interests, or welfare of the United

From Act of June 27, 1952: The Immigration and Nationality Act, 66 Stat. 163: reprinted in *U.S. Immigration and Naturalization Laws and Issues: A Documentary History*, ed. Michael Lemay and Elliot Robert Barkan (Westport, CT: Greenwood Press, 1999), 220–223.

States, and (B) to qualified quota immigrants who are the spouse or children of any immigrant described in clause (A) if accompanying him.

(2) The next 30 per centum of the quota for each quota area for such year… shall be made available for the issuance of immigrant visas to qualified immigrants who are the parents of citizens of the United States, such citizens being at least twenty-one years of age or who are unmarried.…

(3) The remaining 20 per centum of the quota … shall be made available… to qualified immigrants who are the spouses or unmarried sons or daughters of aliens lawfully admitted for permanent residence.…

(e) Every immigrant shall be presumed to be a quota immigrant until he establishes to the satisfaction of the consular officer, at the time of application for a visa, and to the immigrant officers, at the time of application for admission, that he is a nonquota immigrant. Every quota immigrant shall be presumed to be a nonpreference quota immigrant until he establishes to the satisfaction of the consular officer… that he is entitled to a preference status under paragraph (1), (2), or (3) of subsection (a) or to a preference under paragraph (4) or such subsection.…

Chapter 2—Nationality through Naturalization

Sec. 311. The right of a person to become a naturalized citizen of the United States shall not be denied or abridged because of race or sex or because such a person is married. Notwithstanding section 405(b), this section shall apply to any person whose petition for naturalization shall hereafter be filed, or shall have been pending on the effective date of this Act.

Sec. 312. No person except as otherwise provided in this title shall hereafter be naturalized as a citizen of the United States upon his own petition who cannot demonstrate—

(1) an understanding of the English language, including the ability to read, write, and speak words in ordinary usage in the English language.…

(2) a knowledge and understanding of the fundamentals of the history, and of the principles and form of government, of the United States.

Sec. 313. (a) Notwithstanding the provisions of section 405(b), no person shall be naturalized as a citizen of the United States—[the act lists subsection (1) through (6) which prohibit the naturalization of anarchists, communists, totalitarians, and those who believe or publish such, etc.].…

Sec. 316. (a) No person, except as otherwise provide for in this title, shall be naturalized unless such petitioner, (1) immediately preceding the date of filing his petition for naturalization has resided continuously, after being lawfully admitted for permanent residence, within the United States for at least five years and during the five years … has been physically present therein for periods totaling at least half of that time, and who has resided within the State in which petition is filed for at least six months, (2) has resided continuously within the United States from the date of the petition up to the time of admission to citizenship, and (3) during all the periods referred to in this subsection has been and still is a person of good moral character, attached to the principles of the Constitution of the United States, and well disposed to the good order and happiness of the United States.

3. *Life* Magazine Condemns Southwood's Denial of Housing to Sing Sheng, 1952

Mr. Sing Sheng placed a bet on American democracy and lost it. In Asia they will therefore be asking whether American democracy is worth betting on. It still is.

Sheng, a U.S. college graduate and a former Nationalist Chinese intelligence officer, is an airline mechanic in south San Francisco. He wanted to buy a small house for his growing family in Southwood, a suburb near the airport where he works. When he learned that some of the all-Caucasian residents of Southwood did not want a Chinese neighbor, he proposed that the question be put to a vote. To all residents he wrote, "We think so highly of democracy because it offers freedom and equality. America's forefathers fought for these principles and won the independence of 1776.... Do not make us the victims of false democracy. Please vote for us." The other side was summed up by a builder who said, "People must stick together to protect their property rights." Sheng lost, 174 to 28, with 14 abstentions. Said he bitterly, when the votes were counted, "I hope your property values will go up every three days."

The response to the Sheng case has been strong and nationwide. Other cities have offered him a job and a home; there is a move in south San Francisco itself to make amends. Since Sheng's original purpose was not to put democracy on the spot but simply to find a better place to live, the outcome for him is likely to be satisfactory. That is one minor count for American democracy.

Another is the fact that Sheng could have moved into the Southwood house if he had wanted to make an issue of it. The restrictive covenant is legally unenforceable; so says the Supreme Court. But Sheng made what he calls a "gentleman's agreement" to abide by the outcome of the balloting. In other words he tactfully asks more of our democracy than law can provide. He asks what the U.S. at present merely aspires to, namely complete absence of prejudice between man and man.

In fact the people of Southwood were less prejudiced against Sheng than against losing money. The market value of group prejudice is the key to the segregation problem in the U.S. During the last 10 years the U.S. has made revolutionary progress toward racial equality. If this progress continues, prejudice should eventually even lose its market value. It had better, for the national costs of discrimination are exceedingly high. Segregated slums yield only about 6% of the typical city's taxes, but use a third of its fire and almost a half of its police protection. The underemployment of Negro talents and skills is even more wasteful. According to the Urban League the total economic cost of discrimination in a city like New York is at least $1 billion a year.

Sing Sheng v. Southwood, 1952, excerpt.

This loss is at least as real as the one the calculating householders of South-wood think they have avoided. When we outgrow group prejudice in this country, the Southwood type of property loss would be inconceivable, and the present cost of discrimination will be turned into a big gain for all.

4. Setsuko Kamei Works at a U.S. Army Camp and Becomes a War Bride, 1952

Because of the war, the farm land was devastated, and not enough food was distributed by the government. People in Japan were starving. On October 4, 1945, the U.S. Occupation forces took over Hokkaido to reestablish the country, and the American soldiers poured into Sapporo. Two years later, the U.S. Occupation forces set up Camp Crawford, ten miles from Sapporo.

"Why don't you work at the army camp because the payment is good," said her brother, Toshio, who was a student and was also working as a boiler man for the officers of the Occupation forces.

The U.S. camp offered good-paying jobs to women. The pay was twice as much as the local jobs in Sapporo. From 1948 to 1952, Setsuko worked as a housemaid at five houses for American families in Sapporo.

"You are samurai descendant, so I do not want you to work as a house-maid," Setsuko's mother said. Her mother thought it was a menial job. Setsuko persuaded her mother, saying, "The war was over, and we had to change as our country changed."

Setsuko started working for American families. "It was a good experience because I learned American cooking, table setting, house-cleaning, and English," she said....

Antifraternity Rules in the American Camp

While working for Americans, she lived in the dormitory in Camp Crawford with other Japanese women. The dormitory in the camp had strict antifraternity rules and regulations.

"When I stepped in the dormitory on the first day, I noticed a big sign written in Japanese ink," she recalled. The sign said if you talk to an American soldier, you will be handed over to the Japanese police. "We Japanese women were ordered not to speak to American soldiers," Setsuko said. "Since I was not interested in men, including American men, I did not care about it." To her, Americans and the English were still devils, as she was taught during the war. To her surprise, Setsuko found that American soldiers were nice to Japanese girls. "They were so friendly, and they said 'Hello' to us whenever we met them in the camp," Setsuko recalled.

Japanese War Brides in America: An Oral History by Ward Crawford, Miki; Kaori Hayashi, Katie; Suenaga, Shizuko. Reproduced with permission of Praeger in the format Republish in a book via Copyright Clearance Center.

As the Korean War started, more and more young soldiers were sent to Japan from the United States. Young men who were looking for social opportunities with women sometimes visited brothels and ended up contracting venereal diseases. It became a big issue in the camp. To discourage the men from going to brothels, the antifraternity rules were loosened. The authorities thought that young soldiers needed recreation and relaxation, so they held a dance party every weekend....

One of Setsuko's two roommates in the dormitory asked her to go with her to the dance. Setsuko hesitated because she was not interested in going to dances. "You can learn English," said her roommate. Setsuko decided to go to the party because she wanted to improve her English.

At the dance, she talked with several Americans, and she noticed that they were nice and courteous. She could see they were not "devils and beasts," as she and other Japanese were told during the war.

"It was fun to talk to American men," she said. She thought American young men were cheerful and naïve. She started taking an interest in going to the dances and talking to Americans in English....

She Met Him

During the Korean War, the American soldiers in Camp Crawford were transferred to Camp Hachinohe or Camp Sendai on Honshu Island. Setsuko decided to move to Sendai for work. At Camp Sendai, she applied for telephone switchboard operator, a professional job.

While working in Camp Crawford, her English was getting better. She thought she could work as an English operator. The pay was better than that of a housemaid. The pay in the camp was also better than the pay outside the camp. She was paid 15,000 yen in the camp, and the same job paid 7,000 yen outside the camp.

Her American boss was not able to pronounce Japanese names. The boss gave her an American name, Betty.

In Sendai, Setsuko again lived in a dormitory on the camp. Her roommate, who was dating an American soldier, set up a date for Setsuko in the spring of 1952. "It started as a blind date," she said. "My roommate said a surgeon was waiting for me at the gate."

When she first met Joe, she did not think that it would develop into a romantic relationship. He was 5 feet 9 inches and 120 pounds. He had a moustache like Clark Gable's. When she saw his moustache, she thought that his affectations were annoying. Setsuko was a small woman. Her height was 4 feet 11 inches and her weight was ninety pounds.

On the second date, Joe had shaved off his moustache because she had told him on their first date that she did not like it. He was doing his best to make a good impression on Setsuko. However, she thought that he was not her type.

Joe was born in December 1931, in Duck Town, Tennessee, to Charles Rufus and Cora Roslee Amburn. His grandfather was German-Scottish, and his grandmother was German-Irish. "His eyes were so blue, and his skin was so fair," said Setsuko. He looked good, but he often misbehaved.

"I can give him 100 points right now, but at that time I could give him only 30 points out of 100 points," she said. He drank a lot, liked to gamble and sometimes lied to Setsuko. He was a harmless drunk. He often fell asleep after drinking, but he was quick to get in fights at the bars.

In his hometown, he was a delinquent. His mother thought he would end up in jail, so she decided to enlist him in the army at the age of sixteen....

Sayonara

In December 1952, Joe's enlistment ended. He was discharged from the army, and he returned to his hometown in Tennessee. Setsuko thought it would be the end of their relationship. "He would never go back to Japan," she thought. She heard a lot of sad stories of Japanese women deserted by American soldiers, and she thought that she might be one of them.

After he left Japan, she thought about him. When he drank, he sometimes got involved in useless fights in Sendai. He did not like fighting, but he got involved. She worried about him. "I simply cared about him, and I wanted to make sure he was okay in the United States," she said.

Setsuko sent a five-page letter to his mother in Tennessee, asking her to "train" him and take good care of him. After reading Setsuko's letter, Joe's mother sensed that Setsuko would be an ideal wife for Joe.

Within a couple of months after sending the letter, Setsuko received a call from Joe, who had just arrived in Yokohama, Japan. He had reenlisted in the army and gotten himself assigned to Sendai. Setsuko and Joe started dating again in Sendai. "We loved each other, so we decided to get married," she said.

In May 1953, Joe was transferred to Sapporo, where her mother lived. Setsuko's mother started looking for a house for them; however, it seemed to be difficult to rent a house. "I do not want to rent out a house to an American soldier," a landlord said. Setsuko and her mother grew tired of rejection from the Japanese landlords.

When Setsuko was walking with him in Sapporo, a Japanese man called her a *panpan*, which means "whore" in English. Joe got angry and tried to hit him. Setsuko asked him not to, even though she was shocked and offended by the remark. In the 1950s, many Japanese did not respect the women who were with American soldiers. They simply regarded them as prostitutes.

Setsuko had some difficulty living in Japan as the wife of an American soldier. She was tired of being discriminated against in Japan. She dreamed about a new life in the United States.

For their first Christmas, they invited Setsuko's family and people from Joe's military unit to dinner. Setsuko's mother brought a Christmas tree to celebrate the first memorable event for them. She felt that her mother accepted their marriage.

On January 1, 1954, they celebrated the first New Year, the most important holiday in Japan, at her mother's house in Sapporo. She wore a kimono given to her by her mother.

On May 13, 1954, their daughter, Cora Kayo Amburn, was born. Cora is Joe's mother's name, and Kayo is Setsuko's mother's name. Both families celebrated their daughter's birth. It was one of their happiest memories.

"Joe said he did not like kids, but he became a good father and changed her diaper and even ironed it," Setsuko said. After their marriage, as their life settled, he started changing. Setsuko felt that she really "trained" her husband.

To the United States

With their baby, Setsuko and Joe decided to go to America. She was excited with the new life in the United States. To most Japanese, America was a dream country with wealth and modernization. She was tired of being harassed by bigots in Japan.

Joe's tour of duty ended at the close of 1954, so Joe, Setsuko, and Cora left Camp Crawford to start their life in the United States. Their ship arrived in San Francisco on December 30, 1954. Joe's eldest sister, Edith, and Joe's mother, Cora, were waiting for them. They had driven from Tennessee to California to pick them up. The five of them headed to her house in Tennessee, and the trip took a few days. Setsuko felt she was welcomed by his family.

His mother, Cora, was so happy because Joe married Setsuko, as she had wanted.

Joe's relatives and friends in Tennessee also welcomed Setsuko. Most of Joe's relatives and friends were white. "His mother and sisters were nice to me, so I tried to be nice to Joe," she said. "I tried to be nice to Joe more to repay them. They did not discriminate against me because of my nationality and race." In Japan, Joe was not accepted because of his nationality and race, and Setsuko and Joe had been discriminated against as a mixed couple by some bigots. They were excited in their new life in the United States.

After his thirty-day leave was over, the three left for his new assignment at Fort Niagara, New York, in January 1955. Six months later, Joe was assigned to Fort Monmouth, New Jersey, and he went to the Signal Corps School to get promoted in the army. Then he was transferred to Darmstadt in West Germany in 1956.

While he was in West Germany, Setsuko and Cora went to his mother's house because housing was not provided for them by the military. At that time, she decided to become an American citizen. On January 16, 1956, she passed the test and became an American citizen. She felt secure to live in the United States.

5. A Hollywood Poster Sells Interracial Love and the Exoticism of Japan in the Film *Sayonara*, 1957

FIGURE 10.1   *Hollywood sells interracial romance and the exoticism of Japan in this poster for* Sayonara *(1957). Still courtesy of Jerry Ohlinger.*

6. Korean Adoptee Deann Borshay Liem Looks for Her Birth Family, 1966 (2010)

POV [Point of View]: *In the Matter of Cha Jung Hee* **is the second of two autobiographical films you've made about your adoption. The first film,** *First Person Plural,* **aired on POV in 2000. Can you refresh our memory of** *First Person Plural* **and talk about how you came to make** *In the Matter of Cha Jung Hee?*

Deann Borshay Liem: *First Person Plural* tells my story of being adopted by an American family. I was adopted by Arnold and Alveen Borshay from Fremont, California, when I was about 8 years old. When they adopted me, they thought I was a girl named Cha Jung Hee and that I was an orphan. I also grew up thinking that I was Cha Jung Hee and that I was an orphan. But when I was grown up, I discovered that I had a birth family in Korea. First Person Plural follows the journey of discovering the existence of my birth family, meeting my birth family and taking my adoptive parents to Korea for a meeting of the two families. It explores my relationship to both families, my sense of divided loyalties and divided identities and the paradox of living in two different worlds, being pulled in two different directions.

As for making *In the Matter of Cha Jung Hee*, I had always been curious and haunted by this identity that was never mine. Over the years, Cha Jung Hee has always been in the back of my mind. She was a girl I never knew; she was someone who apparently was at the orphanage with me, but someone I had never met. To this day, I have her identity, her birth date, her name and her legal papers. The clothing I was wearing when I came to the United States was hers; the shoes that I wore were hers. I have all the letters that she had written to my adoptive family from Korea. So in *In the Matter of Cha Jung Hee* I go back to Korea to look for her, to put this matter to rest once and for all.

In the film, I meet a number of women named Cha Jung Hee, and through the process I explore the history of international adoptions from Korea and uncover the deceptions and lies that took place within the process of my adoption. I also explore memory, amnesia and what it means kind of to live someone else's life.

POV: The shoes that you wore on your arrival to the United States and that you kept your whole life are one of the strongest symbols in *In the Matter of Cha Jung Hee.* **They play a major role in the film, triggering memories and becoming a part of this lost history. Can you talk about the role of those shoes?**

Liem: When I came off the plane in America as an 8 year old, I was wearing these shoes that didn't fit me. They were long and narrow, whereas my feet were short and wide. My adoptive mother couldn't figure out why the shoes didn't fit me properly, because she had bought them according to the tracings of Cha Jung Hee's feet. Well, it turned out I wasn't Cha Jung Hee, so that's why they didn't fit.

"In the Matter of Cha Jung Hee," Interview, "In the Matter of Cha Jung Hee," *American Documentary | POV, PBS,* September 14, 2010, http://www.pbs.org/pov/chajunghee/interview.php. Reprinted by permission.

The shoes have always been with me. Whenever I've moved to a different house, I've always taken with me baggage that included Cha Jung Hee's clothes and her shoes and all these documents and things. The shoes, in a literal fashion, represented walking into her life—I literally walked into the life that she would have had. In this film, I wanted to find the real Cha Jung Hee and give back her shoes and all her letters and be free of this identity.

My actual journey turned out to be a bit different. But the shoes are symbolic: They represent how any of us might have had a different life. What are the possibilities of living someone else's life or walking in someone else's shoes?

POV: There's a bit of ambiguity at the end of the film about whether you find the woman you're seeking. Do you think it matters whether or not you find the "real" Cha Jung Hee?

Liem: I do think that the woman I meet at the end of the film is Cha Jung Hee, the one I've been looking for, although there is some ambiguity about that, in part because she herself isn't entirely sure. Many of the facts about her adoption match [information about] the person I was looking for, yet some things don't match. In the end I've come to realize that there were untruths involved not only in my adoption, but in other children's adoptions as well. Cha Jung Hee served as a kind of template; she became a kind of ideal orphan. She was a marketing vehicle that was geared to the desires of adoptive parents abroad, and facts were made up to suit those desires.

For me, it does matter whether the woman I met was the "real" Cha Jung Hee, but in the end I discovered that it wasn't so much about finding her, that it was really more about finding myself. I had to wade through the layers of who I thought I was and embrace my life in the United States.

POV: *In the Matter of Cha Jung Hee* is one of three films that POV is broadcasting this year about adoption. What are your feelings about international adoption?

Liem: Every situation is different, but I think it's best when a child can be raised in a family, preferably in his or her native country. In Korea specifically, it's probably no longer necessary to have a huge number of international adoptions and they should stop.

International adoption is often seen as the first choice in a situation. And I don't think it's the best first choice. When there are various possibilities, the first choice ought to be to keep families together—whether it's a single mother or a single father or a grandmother raising a child. The first priority, in terms of policy, should be to create opportunities within the country to keep those families intact.

POV: Ultimately, what is *In the Matter of Cha Jung Hee* really about for you?

Liem: The film is a journey to find the real Cha Jung Hee and, through that process, work through this case of mistaken identity. Meeting all the Cha Jung Hees in Korea really enabled me to imagine my own life if I had stayed in Korea. So in part it's an attempt to walk in their shoes and discover who I might have become. At the same time, I wanted to explore my own adoption, the ethics of adoption, international adoption and my own experiences with memory, identity and adoption.

I wanted to explore the personal impact of living a lie. I've had Cha Jung Hee's identity for more than 40 years. It's been eating away at me for all these years, and it has impacted who I've become. So this additional layer in the film looks not only at the impact of carrying this person's identity on myself and my relationship with my adoptive family, but also the way in which memory and amnesia have played a role in how I've resolved that history and come to understand that history.

☾ ESSAYS

These two essays examine how Cold War politics and the importance of U.S.–Asian military alliances shaped the treatment of Asian Americans in the United States. The first essay, by Cindy I-Fen Cheng, associate professor of history and Asian American studies at the University of Wisconsin, Madison, analyzes how the U.S. public viewed racial equality as vital for demonstrating the superiority of democracy over communism. The perceptions and depictions of Chinese women as good wives and mothers helped Chinese Americans move from segregated urban Chinatowns into formerly white suburbs. In the second essay, Arissa Oh, a Boston College historian, describes the symbolic transformation of Korean War orphans from desperate, illegitimate, foreign waifs to beloved, grateful female beneficiaries of American benevolence during the Cold War. Adoption advocates portrayed Korean adoption as a kind of Christian missionary work that could help counter Soviet propaganda about American racism and win support from potential Asian allies.

Chinese Americans and the Politics of Cultural Citizenship in Early Cold War America

CINDY I-FEN CHENG

In 1951, *Life* magazine featured a look at "America's Chinese" through a New York Chinatown that was internally fractured and polarized between East and West. To capture this social and cultural rift, the article ran a photographic spread highlighting various segments of the Chinese population. This spread, which centered on a sequence of three photographs, depicted an elderly Chinese bachelor smoking alone in a dark apartment, a beaming war bride surrounded by her children, and lastly, a plump eight-year-old boy. Organized in part by the age of its subjects, these pictures generated a temporal narrative in which the passing of the old ushered in the new. Their accompanying captions also underscored the cultural difference separating the elderly bachelor who "spoke nothing but Chinese" from the eight-year-old boy who was "completely Americanized by the New York public school system." As these characterizations followed the temporal arrangement, the contrast of cultures emerged into a narrative of progress wherein a new generation

Cheng, Cindy I-Fen. "Out of Chinatown and into the Suburbs: Chinese Americans and the Politics of Cultural Citizenship in the Early Cold War America." *American Quarterly* 58:4 (2006), 1067–1090. © 2006 The American Studies Association. Reprinted with permission of Johns Hopkins University Press.

presumably moved away from the culture of the East only to advance into the culture of the West. Their nationality, moreover, shifted from Chinese to American. Notably, sandwiched between the two representative male figureheads was the war bride; her central placement reinforced her symbolic role in mediating the passage of time and bringing about a new generation of Chinese Americans. As wife and mother, she made possible the cultural citizenship of the Chinese.

Similarly, the *Los Angeles Times* in a 1959 article examined the cultural division of the city's Chinese population. It relied on spatial designations to convey the social and cultural differences among the Chinese and mapped these ideas onto specific locales. The article, for example, juxtaposed the caricature of an elderly Chinese man shuffling down the drab sidewalks of Old Chinatown with an image of an eight-year-old Chinese boy holding hands with his sister and skipping down Mei-Ling road, one of the main thoroughfares of New Chinatown. The two Chinatowns thus highlighted not only the disparity between the young and the old but also a change from the old to the new. The *Times*, however, did not limit its analysis of this transformation within the confines of the two Chinatowns. Instead it contrasted Chinatown from the suburbs to make known and bring coherence to the differences in culture, race, and nationality.

The *Times* cautioned its readers not to be deceived into thinking that New Chinatown was in fact the place of residence for this new generation. Not only was it merely "a glittering façade, a place dressed up" for the tourists' amusement, but it also acted as a smoke screen, masking the fact that the actual place of residence for this new group was in the suburbs, far removed from this tourist trap. According to the *Times*, "of a population of 22,000 only a few hundred remain in Chinatown. The others have moved to the suburbs." It further insisted that "there is nothing startling about this," for the Chinese "are Americans. As such, they wish to live as Americans—to own homes and breathe the fresh air of the suburbs, where there is greenery for their children to play." While the *Times* may not have considered this change "startling," it nevertheless recognized the significance of this resettlement in distinguishing the Chinese as Americans. But just as this transformation hinged upon a movement out of Chinatown, it also necessitated that the suburbs signified the place of Americans. Moreover, it elicited the symbolic effect of Chinese women to mediate the terms of assimilation. Since the new generation of Chinese consisted not of bachelors but of heterosexual nuclear families, they became like Americans, possessing similar values and goals. In particular, the Chinese, like Americans, desired to own homes with yards for their children to play in. Assimilation or conformity to the domestic ideal thus successfully overcame racial differences to convey a sense of both the possibility and the attainment of social equality between Chinese and Americans. The diminishing population in the Los Angeles Chinatown attested to the effectiveness of Americanization. The terms of becoming an American therefore entailed not only the ability to live as an American but also to live where Americans lived.

Sing Sheng and the Test of Cold War Democracy

In January 1952, Sing Sheng, his wife, Grace, and their two-and-a-half-year-old son, Richard, decided to move out of their apartment in San Francisco and placed a $2,950 deposit for a house in the Southwood suburb of South San Francisco. Shortly after, Southwood residents instructed Sheng and his family not to move into this restricted area. They claimed that their decision stemmed not from any personal prejudices against Sheng but from a desire to maintain the economic viability of their suburban tract. They also insisted that it was in Sheng's best interest not to take up residence in Southwood since he would only be targeted for acts of vandalism by neighborhood kids. Undaunted by these concerns, Sheng decided to fight for his right to live in Southwood, and for many weeks the Sheng case captivated the public's attention nationally and internationally.

Despite its racial restrictions, South San Francisco was a prime location for working-class families. Since 1895, South City, as this area was commonly called, had established an image of being a working-class family town whose livelihood depended on the area's factories, the main one being the Western Meat Company. At the turn of the twentieth century, the town became known for its ethnic diversity, consisting of Irish, Portuguese, and Italian immigrants. Chinese settlers were also found at the edge of town, but a fire in 1912 destroyed this small settlement. During World War II and the immediate postwar years, South San Francisco experienced a population boom as well as a rise in the number of industries, thus living up to its self-proclaimed moniker, "The Industrial City." Residential tracts also proliferated. Since the U.S. census during this time did not survey the racial composition of cities in the San Mateo County, a systematic breakdown of South San Francisco's population by race cannot be obtained. The *San Francisco Chronicle*, however, in its coverage of the Sheng case, provided a sense of the racial makeup of Southwood. The *Chronicle* reported that during a neighborhood meeting about the Sheng case, homeowner Belmar B. Shepley voluntarily confessed to being a "hapa haole," or a half Hawaiian, and to his wife being Polynesian. Although the headline quipped, "Southwood finds out it isn't an 'all-white' community, after all," this racial outing indicated the prevalence of white residents, or at the very least, how the white ideal regulated who resided in Southwood. It also crucially exposed a rupture in the adherence to this ideal underscored more pointedly by Sheng's battle to reside in Southwood.

The broad appeal of the Sheng case captured in part the growing interest that Americans had in Asia, Asians, and Asian Americans following U.S. military expansion in Asia from 1945 to 1961. Of great concern was the social status of Asians in the United States as it came to calibrate the credibility of U.S. democracy abroad; the need to ensure housing rights for Sheng thus became connected to the fight against communism in Asia. The manner in which Sheng went about challenging his exclusion from Southwood also contributed to the public's interest in this case. While Sheng in 1952 could have settled this matter in the district courts of San Francisco, especially since the U.S. Supreme Court had ruled in 1948 that state enforcement of racial restrictive covenants was unconstitutional, he nevertheless opted to abide by the social judgment of Southwood residents. He asked Southwood to administer a vote whereby residents could choose democratically whether to allow him and his family to move into their neighborhood. Sheng rallied support by distributing a letter explaining why they should vote on his behalf. Newspapers reprinted the following excerpt:

> Before you reach any decision as to how you will vote in this ballot, allow us to tell you our opinion. The present world conflict is not between individual nations, but between Communism and Democracy. We think so highly of Democracy because it offers freedom and equality. America's forefathers fought for these principles and won the independence in 1776 ... We have forsaken all our beloved China and have come to this country seeking the same basic rights. Do not make us the victims of false Democracy. Please vote in favor of us.

As this excerpted plea looked to contest racial restrictions in housing, it linked the fight against residential segregation to the fight against communism. More specifically, it argued that the best way to combat communism was not through the exclusion of Chinese from the United States or the rejection of Communist China. Rather, the inclusion of the Chinese spoke to the capacity of cold war democracy to entice China away from communism. The movement of Chinese into the suburbs therefore extended beyond mapping a national and cultural shift from China to America and from Chinese to American; it also marked a political progression from communism to American democracy. As this plea scrutinized the credibility of U.S. democracy, it also pitted the ideal of whiteness against a racially inclusive model of national belonging. Sheng's fight to live in Southwood therefore not only exposed the contradiction in the meaning of Americanness but also called into question the authority of whiteness to determine national citizenship.

As newspapers dubbed this vote "a test of democracy," they framed the significance of the Sheng case as proof of the claims of cold war democracy. Despite appeals to the broader political implications of this case, residents voted on February 16 to prohibit Sheng and his family from living in Southwood: 174 people voted against Sheng, 28 for, and 14 had no opinion. The outcome of this vote, however, did little to end this "test." It instead incited a public dialogue over the meaning, validity, and effect of cold war democracy. The *San Francisco Chronicle* ran a full-page editorial highlighting the outbursts of public dismay at the outcome of this vote just days after the results were published. It detailed the "floodtide" of telephone calls along with letters and telegrams all expressing "their indignation at such a desecration of democracy and American principles" while other correspondences sought to validate these ideals by offering Sheng a home elsewhere. The editorial also noted the vote's damaging impact on U.S. cold war policies in Asia:

> The ultimate effects cannot yet be known—but, like ripples in a pool, the effects of the Southwood plebiscite seem likely to spread to the outermost corners of this cold-war-torn globe. Already, public and private groups that spend great treasure and labor in wooing Asia to the side of the free world are complaining that Southwood has undone the long and tedious

work of the Voice of America, of Radio Free Asia and even of American men who have been fighting in Korea. They say: "We cannot sell freedom to Asia unless we can deliver freedom at home.

Arguing that America must "deliver freedom at home," the editorial participated in efforts to restore the credibility of U.S. democracy. The prescribed solution, which connected Sheng's acceptance by Southwood to the ability of cold war democracy to achieve a world order in which nations coexisted equally, crucially authorized the United States to be the leader of this new world order.

Additionally, the *Chronicle* examined how newspapers in Asia reacted to the Sheng vote. It discussed an editorial in the *Hong Kong Standard*, for example, which declared Sheng's actions reckless given the assault of propaganda attacks against the United States in Asia. The editorial also asserted that one can never "test democracy," since its espousal likened to "one's faith in religion, has to be intuitive and not lightly put to the test." Interestingly, the *Chronicle* expressed that it did not share the *Hong Kong Standard's* judgment of Sheng. Instead, it placed blame on Americans swayed by the unfounded fear that nonwhite residents depreciated property values of suburban homes. Their failings, nevertheless, did the United States a service as it imbued the nation with a "resolve to do better." As the *Chronicle* juxtaposed its interpretation of Sheng's actions with that of the *Hong Kong Standard,* it unveiled the desired subject position of Asia and America in promoting cold war democracy. Whereas Asia supplied "faith," America provided "resolve." By refusing to add to the *Hong Kong Standard's* criticism of Sheng, the *Chronicle* also affirmed the moral superiority of American democracy, which never blamed others for its own failings but rightfully took responsibility for its own mistakes.

Efforts to reclaim the validity of cold war democracy further relied on Sheng's racial identity as nonwhite to demonstrate democracy's triumph over racism even though being nonwhite had disqualified him from living in the place of Americans. Christina Klein has examined in *Cold War Orientalism* how the "dual identity" of Chinese in the United States, or an identity that contained recognizable albeit constructed Chinese and American elements, enabled their social position to signify the political relationship between the United States and China and to an extent Asia. Klein thus asserts that "the foreignness of Chinese Americans gave them value as Americans" and that this desire for the foreign resisted the complete assimilation of "Asian differences into a homogenous sameness of postwar American whiteness." The Sheng case supports this analysis since Sheng's Chineseness was the foreign element that helped to calibrate the effectiveness of American democracy in Asia. Additionally, his Chineseness served as a nonwhite trace that showcased the capacity of cold war democracy to bring about racial equality *and* to transform immigrants into assimilated Americans. Incorporating Sheng within early cold war America therefore necessitated that he be depicted as nonwhite and as conforming to white middle-class norms. His status of being like other Americans captured how cultural membership in the nation regulated race to convey a sameness and difference from whites.

The *San Francisco Chronicle*, for instance, focused on attributes that Sheng had in common with white Americans in order to construct him as fit for residence in the suburbs. While most articles highlighted the fact that Sheng was a veteran of the Second World War, only a few bothered to mention that his veteran status stemmed from service in the Chinese Nationalist army. The way in which Sheng was often casually absorbed into a nationally unmarked category of the "veteran," implicitly understood as a U.S. veteran, spoke not only to the allied relationship between China and the United States during the war but also to the conflation of Sheng's Chinese nationality with an American nationality. This characterization was further reinforced by repeated references to the fact that his wife, Grace, was born, raised, and educated in the United States and that their son was also American-born. Additionally, articles emphasized that Sheng completed college in the United States and worked as an airline mechanic for Pan-American Airlines.

A widely circulated image of Sheng that showed him sitting with his wife on their living-room couch staring lovingly at Richard captured the defining characteristics that cast Sheng as similar to white Americans. His role as father and husband, more than his identity as a middle-class, college-educated veteran, had narrowed the gap separating him from white Americans. His American-born wife, Grace, and their son, Richard, facilitated this cultural enfranchisement by distancing him from popular representations of the lone and aged Chinese bachelor whose inability to procreate had ghettoized him within the confines of Chinatown. Depictions of Sheng properly performing his assigned gender role also helped establish his Americanness. According to the *Chronicle*, Sheng expressed the impact that the vote had on him and his family by saying: "You know how women are. She [Grace] had it all worked out in her mind how she was going to decorate the house." Noting that he said this "with an understanding smile," the *Chronicle* depicted Sheng as like any typical family man looking after the interests of his family. The purchase of the suburban home was therefore not for his benefit but for that of his wife, who wanted a place to decorate, and his son, who needed a backyard to play in. The status of being like other Americans thus spoke to Sheng's successful assimilation. But Sheng's position as an assimilated American preserved a sense of difference from the original. This distance, rather setting the terms of exclusion, signified a capacity for inclusion and the ability of cold war democracy to bring about racial integration.

While most newspaper and magazine coverage of the Sheng case developed its significance within the context of U.S. cold war politics, a few accounts stressed its relevance outside the demands of cold war democracy. An editorial in the San Francisco–based *Chinese Pacific Weekly*, for example, argued that without "this strange voting procedure, the Western newspapers would not be interested in covering this story." It also criticized Sheng for unduly subjecting himself to the judgment of Southwood residents and asserted that "we [the Chinese in the U.S.] need to have more confidence in the belief that we have the right to choose where we want to live . . . Sing Sheng should not have suggested that a vote be administered. Does he not already have this right? Why allow others to determine his right?" By issuing this defiant critique against relinquishing power to white society to select who to integrate, the editorial tapped into other ideologies, mainly those espoused by black civil rights activists during the late nineteenth and early twentieth centuries, and not cold war democracy, to advocate for the rights of Chinese in the United States. Hence despite the attempts of cold war democracy to make use of civil rights reform to establish its own legitimacy, it did not completely limit all articulations of racial equality to the promotion of American democracy over communism. In other words, cold war democracy could not link antiracist senti- ments exclusively to a cold war agenda. As exemplified in the analysis of the *Chinese Pacific Weekly* editorial, the Sheng case extended beyond documenting the setback of U.S. cold war policies abroad, and significantly historicized the "gradual liberalism of the American press and the gradual liberalism of public opin- ion against discrimination."

The observation that the Sheng case captured the growing liberalism of U.S. press and public opinion against discrimination was well substantiated by the pro- liferation of press coverage of this case. Stories appeared in the *San Francisco Chron- icle*, the *New York Times*, the *New York Herald Tribune*, the *Chicago Tribune*, and *Time* and *Newsweek* magazines, to name a few. National radio and TV stations also took an interest in this story. Outside the United States, the Sheng case was reported in the *Manila Chronicle* and in Hong Kong newspapers. The majority of these accounts sympathized with Sheng. Additionally, key state and political lea- ders, along with national and community organizations, issued public statements in support of Sheng. They included the San Francisco City Council, the city attor- ney, the mayor, California governor Earl Warren, U.S. senators, the national Committee for Free Asia, and local church groups. The *Chronicle* further docu- mented the pervasive public dialogue over the Sheng case by publishing numerous letters from across the nation. It even administered its own vote, mimicking the one Sheng issued before Southwood residents. The results of this vote, gathered from tallying up the number of letters for and the number of letters against Sheng between February 16 and 23, indicated a landslide "victory" for Sheng supporters. The *Chronicle* headlined the results, "266 for Sheng, 16 on the Other Side." In doing so, the *Chronicle* effectively minimized the ability of Southwood residents to reflect public opinion and showed how the "public" had in fact supported Sheng's efforts to break race-based restrictions in housing. It also noted that "more letters were received on the Sheng affair than on any other single issue in many months" and that only the Shengs had received more letters than the *Chron- icle*, all, except for one unsigned letter, were sympathetic.

Against this overwhelming display of public support for Sheng, the American Homes Development Company of Burlingame issued a statement upholding the practice of racial restrictive covenants. Not only was this statement one of the few published in newspapers against Sheng but it also posed a rationale that was at odds with cold war democracy. It asked home owners to "hold fast to the principles of restrictive covenants in all their housing transactions" and explained how this prac- tice had "set forth salutary and beneficial restrictions on the land for those purchasers desiring ownership in a community where they would welcome their neighbor and live in equality." Exclusion and restriction, instead of inclusion, thus set the terms of equality. The effect of this belief in exclusion as equality entered and reentered pub- lic discourse when newspapers reported how Southwood residents had in fact remained steadfast against racial incursions into their neighborhood. Even though the Shengs later successfully purchased a home in the northern California region of Sonoma, reports on their exclusion from Southwood sparked a negotiation within public discourse over which account of American democracy would be dominant. The proliferation of media coverage of Sheng, in addition to documenting the growing liberalism of the U.S. press, also exposed attempts to recover the credibility of U.S. democracy by promoting its commitment to racial equality.

In light of the outpouring of public support for Sheng, his exclusion from Southwood did not necessarily point to the failure of cold war democracy, but neither did his admission into the suburbs of Sonoma indicate its success. Rather, the Sheng case, significantly, documented the negotiations taking place within public discourse over the meaning of American democracy. Its relevance was thus not as a test case for democracy but rather how it historicized the emergence of questions over the credibility of American democracy and the attempts to restore its legitimacy. Lisa Lowe has argued in *Immigrant Acts* that definitions of the American citizen have "cast Asian immigrants both as persons and populations to be integrated into the national political sphere and as the contradictory, confusing, unintelligible elements to be marginalized and returned to their alien origins." The discourse on postwar suburbanization played out this contradiction. Whether the Chinese were depicted as assimilated subjects to be integrated or as nonwhites to be excluded, they made known the values that informed the making of the U.S. national identity. During the early cold war years, a rupture occurred in the adherence to the white ideal, thus transforming this contradiction into a competing vision of Americanness. It allowed the assimilated nonwhite to challenge his systematic exclusion from the suburbs even as he affirmed the ability of the suburbs to include him. The assimilated subject's acceptance of white norms as the standards of society had compromised its potential to unsettle the privilege of whiteness. Even still, the assimilated did not become white, nor were the suburbs all white. Rather, early cold war America engaged in sustained discussion over the place of race in the making of the national identity.

The Cold War Transformation of the Korean Orphan

ARISSA OH

The figure of the Korean "orphan" was central to the development of Korean and intercountry adoption. Proponents of Korean adoption used this term to access deep cultural understandings and mythologies of the innocent, victimized child. In truth, the category of orphan was both capacious and easily manipulated. A child could be—and often was—made into an orphan through a simple administrative act by an orphanage director or a social worker. Alternatively, a child could be made a "social orphan" when released for adoption by a living parent, which subverted common understandings of the orphan as a parentless child.

Adoptive and would-be adoptive parents used the terms "son" or "daughter" to emphasize their kinship with these children. Media coverage of adoptions reinforced the transformation from orphan—the dirty, hungry, homeless waif—

Journal of American Ethnic History 31, no. 4 (Summer 2012), 34–55.

to adoptee—the well-dressed, beloved son or daughter grinning in the midst of domestic plenty. Adoptive parents used the language of transfiguration to describe how their children had flourished in American homes: from "undernourished waif," "emotional misfit," and "frightened, hopeless, little things" to "happy, healthy, well-adjusted," "bright-eyed," and a "roly-poly sunbeam." Many parents continued to campaign for new orphan laws even after they had completed their own adoptions. The letters they sent to members of Congress included snapshots of their thriving adopted children and reports that they "fit into our family circle perfectly" and were doing well in school.

Whether actually true or not, orphanhood was an essential precondition to adoption, not just legally but narratively. I have argued elsewhere that advocates of Korean adoption promoted it using the rhetoric of a specifically Cold War American civic religion that I call Christian Americanism. Coupling a diluted form of Christianity with values identified as particularly American, Christian Americanism viewed Korean adoption as an act that was at once personal and political. Through Korean adoption, Americans could simultaneously add to their families and support their nation's Cold War agenda by demonstrating American racial democracy abroad and by helping to fulfill America's moral obligations towards Koreans—especially those fathered by irresponsible American servicemen. The conflation of global politics and domestic family concerns—what scholar Mark Jerng calls the "collapsing of home and world"—in Christian Americanist discourse, and its sentimental narrative of rescue, required that the children be figured as orphans; in the words of adoption advocate Pearl S. Buck, as "piteous lonely children whom no country claims."

Indeed, Korean orphans could be thought of as a metaphor for Korea itself. Deemed irrelevant to American security interests, it had been abandoned by the U.S. in 1948 and emerged from civil war completely dependent on U.S. aid. During and after the Korean War, the U.S. mainstream and military media showcased the many ways GIs cared for Korean children: for example, by building orphanages, throwing Christmas parties, and distributing warm clothes and food sent by Americans. If GI humanitarianism offered a way for Americans to salvage a moral victory out of the stalemate of the Korean War, then adopting a Korean orphan was a way for Americans to atone for abandoning—for orphaning—the land of her birth. Furthermore, the relationship between American parents and Korean children mirrored geopolitics by enacting the asymmetry that has characterized the neocolonial U.S.–Korea relationship since World War II. Anthropologist Eleana Kim has suggested how that imbalance was mediated in part by "intimate diplomacy" conducted through the bodies of adopted Korean children: "the sentimentalization and depoliticization of children as orphans and pure humanity ... made them available to be dispatched as sons and daughters who could link people and nations in their roles as ambassadors and bridges."

The fantasy of the bereft orphan in need of rescue lay at the heart of American imaginings about the Korean child, when in fact she might have had living parents or relatives. The vision of themselves as rescuers led American adopters and their supporters to construct Korean children into victims: of poverty; homelessness; lovelessness; Communism; and, for GI babies, racism. While it is true that many were vulnerable to these forces, the conversation about Korean adoption provided no room for the possibility that these children could avoid grim fates without being saved by Americans.

The Korean child served a powerful function in Cold War America. Like the politically symbolic children that Karen Dubinsky has discussed, the Korean child served to "smooth out or even submerge complicated political issues under the veneer of sentiment." That veneer was central to the hegemonic narrative of Korean adoption, which claimed that love could conquer all divisions of race and nationality and that the adoption of a Korean child by an American family signified nothing more than the uncomplicated mutual completion of a homeless orphan and the parents who wanted her. The narrative erased birth mothers and ignored histories of imperialism, militarism, racism, and patriarchal sexism, as well as any suggestion of exploitation in an emerging adoption market.

A deeply contradictory figure, the Korean child altered intertwined American understandings of race, nation, and family but did so in ways that reaffirmed certain existing definitions and structures. The adoption of the visibly different Korean child demonstrated the racial liberalism of white Americans while at the same time rein-scribing racial boundaries. After all, it was the very visibility of Korean adoption that made it such powerful evidence of American racial liberalism. But that colorblind-ness had its limits. Korean-black children, rendered black by American "one-drop" thinking, languished in orphanages in Korea. Meanwhile, in a reversal of that "one-drop" rule, Korean-white children became white (though still considered Asian for immigration purposes). A kind of geneticism rendered Korean-white GI babies "our" babies in American eyes; a belief in the power of nurture suggested that their racial mixture could be overcome with the proper environment and upbring-ing. These feelings of sympathy for, and identification with, certain mixed-race Korean children paved the way for the later adoption of full-blooded Korean chil-dren. The logic of racial triangulation drastically altered the fate of Korean-white and full-blooded Korean children. Once labeled "unadoptable" because they were not white, they became "adoptable" because they were not black.

Likewise, the Korean child disrupted ideas of the monoracial (white) American family while also reaffirming its power as a "normalizing institution." Her adoption was revolutionary, for her obvious racial difference upended con-ceptions of family rooted in blood and biology and challenged the dominant social work doctrine of using careful matching to create "as-if begotten" adop-tive families. But Korean adoption was also deeply conservative, for the Korean child shored up "an idealized notion of kinship": the Cold War heterosexual nuclear family. She verified her adoptive parents' worthiness for inclusion in the nation at a time when status as a parent was equated with citizenship. These conservative underpinnings—the reinforcing of hierarchies of heteronor-mativity and race and the containment of the Korean child's otherness within conventional family forms—suggest one reason why some conservative evangel-ical Americans embraced the seemingly radical cause of Korean adoption.

Korean adoption highlighted the ambivalent relationship of many Americans with the state even as it exposed the falseness of the distinction between private and public spheres. Adoptive parents often resisted the incursions of social workers into their homes and families, insisting that the state had no business in their intimate matters. Yet they could not and did not completely sever themselves from state power, since they needed orphan laws to admit their adopted children. They appealed to lawmakers to enact adoption-friendly laws, deploying the language of Christian Americanism to present their desire to adopt as furthering national goals. Some adopters emphasized that adoptions helped the national cause but without public funds. Adoptive parents and their allies sought to protect their vision of family as, in Nancy Cott's terms, "personally chosen private freedoms" while at the same time tapping into the institution's symbolic importance as "public emblem of the nation." The way in which adoptive families used national concerns to gain support for Korean adoption demonstrates the deep mutual imbrication of public and private spheres.

Indeed, the adopted Korean child embodied the inextricable linkages between the private and the public. Simultaneously selected to be a member of both a nuclear American family and the national American family, her adoption resonated with old and enduring ways of thinking of the family as a microcosm of the nation and the hope that social and racial unity within the family could lead to the same in the community and the nation. One prominent supporter thought even more grandly than this, arguing that intercountry adoption would "prove a solid contribution to the culture and strength of our Nation and to the welfare of mankind as a whole." Many proponents of Korean adoption celebrated the horizon-broadening advantages of having a Korean child in their midst. An adoptive father declared that his Korean daughter had "helped to remove prejudice, and fear, and increased the understanding and vision of the people," which were "vital to our nations [sic] future." As adults, however, Korean adoptees did not always have positive memories of integrating their communities.

Adoption transformed the Korean child from "needy object" to "treasured subject," from a "pathetic" child to "our precious" child. With the spread of intercountry adoption and the rise of a market for Korean children, she became what Korean adult adoptee and filmmaker Deann Borshay Liem has called a "precious object of desire." Whether object or subject, the Korean child was nonetheless a child—without agency, but powerful as a cultural, social, ideological and political symbol. Imagined as an orphan, she was a tabula rasa, allowing politicians, adoptive parents, journalists, and social workers to project a multitude of ideals and burdens onto her: victim of Communism, herald of multiracial harmony, and ideal citizen.

Korean Adoption and the Refiguring of Asianness

Asian American and Korean American histories usually overlook intercountry adoption and adoptees, but adopted Korean children were instrumental to the larger refiguring of Asianness that occurred in the U.S. in the 1950s and 1960s. This process began during World War II, when Congress repealed the Chinese exclusion laws and offered token quotas to Filipinos and Asian Indians. It continued after the war as both the U.S. government and Asian American communities worked to transform the former image of alien, unassimilable Chinese and Japanese into "model" citizens—from Oriental alien to Asian American citizen—or, as historian Ellen Wu describes, from definitively not-white to definitively not-black.

Recasting Asians in America as model citizens was a central part of this transformation. Although standard accounts locate the origins of the model minority image in the 1960s, new historical research suggests that this stereotype started emerging earlier, in the immediate aftermath of World War II. The upheavals of global war, the Cold War imperatives of racial liberalism, and a nascent Civil Rights Movement led to broad changes in racial thinking. Against this shifting racial terrain, Asian Americans positioned themselves as a model minority: hardworking, family- and education-oriented, capitalist, and therefore superlatively equipped to be good American citizens.

These domestic shifts in ideology mirrored geopolitical developments, which were presented in familial terms that emphasized relationships of love and care. As the U.S. established new ties with Asian nations, war brides and war orphans from those countries allowed individual Americans to participate in these new relationships at the level of the everyday and perhaps reconsider the assimilating potential of Asians. As Christina Klein has shown, makers of middlebrow culture encouraged Americans to feel bonds of kinship with Asia and Asians, which were then enacted in part through sponsorship programs like Christian Children's Fund and the moral adoptions promoted by the *Saturday Evening Post*.

In these new configurations, the hypermasculinity that had been central to constructions of the Japanese Yellow Peril during World War II was replaced by feminization in America's embrace of East Asians during the Cold War. Americans imagined the rehabilitation of a deeply hated former enemy, Japan, in gendered terms, with Japan as compliant, willing wife to her dominating, masculine American husband. As American GIs began bringing home Japanese wives, resistance to these marriages competed with accounts that romanticized them as concrete ways to demonstrate American racial liberalism. War brides and war orphans replaced older images of the male Oriental laborer with more appealing women and children who affirmed colonial and Orientalist tropes of Asians as childlike and feminine. It is true that the war bride was not a wholly unproblematic figure, for she presented the specter of miscegenation and raised questions about whether she was actually a cunning prostitute using marriage to gain access to America. Children, however, were beyond such suspicions.

Despite this refiguring of Asianness, enduring anti-Asian sentiment delayed the liberalization of U.S. immigration law affecting Asians more generally. The 1952 INA [Immigration and Nationality Act] had established an Asia Pacific Triangle and imposed immigration quotas of one hundred per year to each country within it, with an overall limit of two thousand for the entire region. As [Mae] Ngai notes, "liberals believed strongly that the Asia Pacific Triangle, with its global race quotas, was racist policy that damaged America's reputation and interests in Asia." Yet eliminating it was not considered an option by conservatives like the powerful U.S. representative Francis Walter, who was openly hostile toward Asian immigration. In 1961, the same year that provisions for foreign-born adopted children became a permanent part of the INA, Walter "flatly declared his commitment to preventing a horde of Asiatics from overrunning the United States."

Yet mixed-race and full-blooded "Asiatic" babies and children, otherwise inadmissible under the American race-based immigration quotas, were not only acceptable but were idealized in conversations about immigration and refugee policy. The State Department declared openly that "orphans make the best possible immigrants from the standpoint of their youth, flexibility, and lack of ties to any other cultures." Although not ideal from a racial point of view, the mixture of Korean-white GI babies made them more palatable even to those opposing Asian immigration. As children, they posed no economic or national security threats, an important quality given how powerfully fears about Communist infiltration shaped refugee policy and its administration. Adoptive parents presented their children as being aware and proud of their special status as U.S. citizens. The mother of a three-year-old Korean-white girl described her as saying "I'm a 'cinzen'" and reciting the pledge of allegiance. A father in California described his two Korean daughters as "the most enthusiastic loyal Americans I have ever met" and claimed that they and other Korean children would "become wonderful citizens of our country." As lucky recipients of American citizenship—"the greatest gift to be given them!"—these children would one day give back by contributing to the nation, and eventually the world.

Together, the war orphan, war bride, and model minority offered a new image of Asians in the United States: anti-Communist, assimilable, conforming to American values, and therefore contributing to a stronger nation. Of these, the Korean orphan was the best kind of immigrant. Free of the taint of the potentially subversive adult refugee or the sexual threat of the war bride, and full of the promise of childhood, she was the worthiest of immigrants, deserving of entering the "circle of care" provided by both the nuclear and the national American family. She was the ideal future citizen, at once a model minority and a model immigrant.

☀ FURTHER READING

Bow, Leslie. *Partly Colored: Asian Americans and Racial Anomaly in the Segregated South* (2010).

Brooks, Charlotte. *Alien Neighbors, Foreign Friends: Asian Americans, Housing, and the Transformation of Urban California* (2009).

———. "Sing Sheng vs. Southwood: Residential Integration in Cold War California," *Pacific Historical Review* 72 (2004), 463–494.

Chan, Sucheng, and Madeline Y. Hsu, eds. *Chinese Americans and the Politics of Race and Culture* (2008).

Choy, Catherine Ceniza. *Global Families: A History of Asian International Adoption in America* (2013).

Chun, Gloria Heyung. *Of Orphans and Warriors: Inventing Chinese American Culture and Identity* (2000).

Cox, Susan Soon-Keum. *Voices from Another Place: A Collection of Works from a Generation Born in Korea and Adopted to Other Countries* (1999).

Cumings, Bruce. *The Origins of the Korean War: Liberation and the Emergence of Separate Regimes* (1981).

Dower, John W. *Embracing Defeat: Japan in the Wake of World War II* (1999).

Eng, David. "Transnational Adoption and Queer Diasporas," *Social Text* 21.3 (Fall 2003), 1–37.

Fong, Timothy. *The First Suburban Chinatown: The Remaking of Monterey Park, California* (1993).

Holmes, Michael T. *The Specter of Communism in Hawaii* (1994).

Horne, Gerald. *Fighting in Paradise: Labor Unions, Racism, and Communists in the Making of Modern Hawai'i* (2011).

Hsu, Madeline Y. "Befriending the 'Yellow Peril': Chinese Students and Intellectuals and the Liberalization of U.S. Immigration Laws, 1950–1965," *Journal of American-East Asian Relations* 16.3 (Fall 2009), 139–162.

———. "The Disappearance of America's Cold War Chinese Refugees, 1948–1966," *Journal of American Ethnic History* 31.4 (Summer 2012), 12–33.

Kim, Eleana J. *Adopted Territory: Transnational Korean Adoptees and the Politics of Belonging* (2010).

Kim, Jodi. *Ends of Empire: Asian American Critique and the Cold War* (2010).

Klein, Christina. *Cold War Orientalism: Asia in the Middlebrow Imagination, 1945–1961* (2003).

Kurashige, Scott. *The Shifting Grounds of Race: Black and Japanese Americans in the Making of Multiethnic Los Angeles* (2007).

Ngai, Mae M. "Legacies of Exclusion: Illegal Chinese Immigration during the Cold War Years," *Journal of American Ethnic History* 18 (Fall 1998), 3–37.

Oh, Arissa H. *To Save the Children of Korea: The Cold War Origins of International Adoption* (2015).

Shukert, Elfrieda Berthiaume, and Barbara Smith Scibetta. *War Brides of World War II* (1988).

Spickard, Paul R. *Mixed Blood: Intermarriage and Ethnic Identity in Twentieth-Century America* (1989).

Yuh, Ji-Yeon. *Beyond the Shadow of Camptown: Korean Military Brides in America* (2002).

Zhao, Xiaojian. *Remaking Chinese America: Immigration, Family, and Community, 1940–1965* (2001).

CHAPTER 11

The Rise of Asian American Identity, 1965–2012

During the political turmoil of the 1960s, politicians and the mainstream media began to portray Chinese Americans and Japanese Americans as "model minorities" who were able to overcome racism and discrimination through hard work, love of education, and patriotism. Declaring Chinese Americans a "Success Story," U.S. News and World Report *praised the ethnic group for overcoming a history of discrimination by emphasizing cultural traditions, family values, and self-reliance rather than government welfare. Contrasting satisfied and successful Asian Americans with angry and militant African American activists sent a clear message: while other minorities complained about racism, Asian Americans pulled themselves up by their own bootstraps.*

A critical mass of college students organized the Asian American movement, which challenged these model minority accounts. Movement leaders often were urban, middle-class, first- or second-generation Chinese Americans or third-generation Japanese Americans. Inspired by the civil rights, antiwar, and ethnic pride movements, these activists tried to transcend the ethnic and national differences among Asian Americans by emphasizing the need for a common bond of struggle against white racism. They were inspired by black power activists and Third World revolutionary leaders like Mao Zedong who championed grassroots mobilization, political protest, self-determination, and cultural pride. Some Asian American activists advocated policy reforms, while others worked toward socialist revolution, but all encouraged resistance to racial oppression. They tried to cultivate cultural pride by organizing artistic, musical, and theatrical programs; they also developed journals and magazines and joined global protests against the Vietnam War. Members of the Asian American Political Alliance, for example, denounced U.S. actions in Indochina as a racist war that massacred civilians; they also celebrated the goals and struggles of Vietnamese Communists. Asian Americans for Action, another activist organization, mobilized to fight imperialism abroad and "internal colonialism" at home that its members believed caused Asian Americans to feel inferior to white Americans. Other examples of activism include student strikes for the development of Asian American studies; demonstrations against urban renewal programs that evicted the poor and the elderly; the creation of health, vocational, and childcare programs within ethnic enclaves; and the successful campaign to repeal Title II of the Internal Security Act, a policy that allowed for the use of internment camps to quell social unrest.

While the Asian American movement demonstrated the power of pan-ethnic solidarity, it also experienced conflicts over issues of ethnic leadership, class, gender, sexuality, and mixed race heritage. Korean American and Filipino American activists challenged the prioritization of Chinese American and Japanese American causes. While proliferating on college campuses throughout the nation, pan-Asian groups were barely visible in Asian ethnic enclaves. Women often found that they were shut out of leadership roles and charged with betraying the community or being assimilationist if they brought up the topic of sexism within the movement. Some women formed separate feminist groups to address the "triple oppression" of intertwined race, class, and gender discrimination. Lesbian, gay, bisexual, and transgender (LGBT) activists drew attention to prejudice within Asian American communities based on sexual orientation.

Definitions of Asian American identity have changed as the population has grown to include large numbers of children of interracial marriages. After the 2000 census allowed participants for the first time to mark one or more of sixty-three racial classifications, nearly 7 million individuals identified themselves as having a mixed race background. While some associated more with a single racial or ethnic group, others embraced a variety of ancestral heritages. The professional golfer Tiger Woods, for example, proclaimed himself a "Cablinasian" to celebrate the Caucasian, black, American Indian, and Asian components of his identity. Some called for a stand-alone multiracial category in the census. Others opposed this addition because it would reduce the representation of traditional racial groups, decrease their political clout and funding for educational programs and healthcare facilities, and cut grants for community development.

DOCUMENTS

Documents 1 to 4 illustrate how Asian American activists challenged popular media portrayals of Asian Americans as uncomplaining model minorities. In Document 1, Malcolm Collier and Dan Gonzales recount how Asian American students, faculty, and community members participated in the San Francisco State strike to establish courses and programs on ethnic studies. Joining the Third World Liberation Front, the students went on strike in 1968 and organized a sit-in protest at the office of university president S. I. Hayakawa. The students won the strike, and as a result the university established a school of ethnic studies. In Document 2, an excerpt from an article published in 1969, Amy Uyematsu defines "yellow power" consciousness as emulating black power in demanding militant demonstrations against racism. Uyematsu's article and Document 3, a photograph of activists protesting the Vietnam War in the late 1960s, demonstrate the Asian American movement's commitment to anti-imperialism and revolutionary policies. Document 4, a poem by Filipino American Al Robles, pays tribute to the International Hotel, known as the

I-Hotel, which was the last remnant of San Francisco's Manilatown. Activists battled for nine years to save the hotel from being torn down due to urban renewal plans before the elderly Filipino residents were physically removed from the building in 1977. Robles participated in these protests, and he uses his poem to honor the *manongs*, older migrant laborers, and to celebrate their Filipino heritage.

Documents 5 to 9 discuss examples of more recent Asian American activism. Althea Yip recounts in Document 5 the story of Vincent Chin, a Chinese American engineer, who in 1982 was beaten to death in Detroit with a baseball bat because he was mistaken for a Japanese person. Yip argues that Chin's murder inspired Asian Americans to develop new advocacy organizations to fight for civil rights, lobby politicians and the press, and monitor hate crimes. In Document 6, Urvashi Vaid, an attorney and LGBT activist, speaks at a 1999 Michigan State University conference about the need for racial justice movements to address structural economic inequality and sexism. Calling for a re-evaluation of heterosexism, patriarchy, and discriminatory notions of family, Vaid maintains that an inclusive and anti-homophobic movement requires a transformation of conceptions of Asian family and culture. In Document 7, activists Annalisa V. Enrile and Jollene Levid describe how GABRIELA in the Philippines and GABRIELA Network (GABNet) in the United States developed a transnational alliance to promote public awareness about the trafficking of women and children in the Philippines. Document 8, by journalist Jeff Yang, explores how multiracialism has reconfigured Asian American identity. Noting that multiracial Asian Americans are projected to comprise more than a third of the population by 2050, Yang looks at how these individuals connect with their multiple heritages. Document 9 disputes the Pew Research Center's 2012 model minority portrayal of Asian Americans as a homogenous and successful group because of their "emphasis on traditional family mores." Citing critics of the report, sociologist C.N. Le, argues that biased survey questions misrepresented the diversity of Asian Americans, ignored continuing prejudice, and disregarded income differentials within the community.

1. Malcolm Collier and Dan Gonzales Recount the Origins of the San Francisco State Strike, 1968 (2009)

Three Asian American student organizations formed in 1967 and 1968: the Intercollegiate Chinese for Social Action (ICSA, 1967), the Philippine (later Pilipino) American Collegiate Endeavor (PACE, 1967), and the Asian American Political Alliance (AAPA, 1968), the latter of which had a largely, but not exclusively, Japanese American membership at San Francisco State. Unlike preexisting student groups, these were politically-charged organizations....

"Origins: People, Times, Place, Dreams," in *At 40, Asian American Studies at San Francisco State University*, eds. Malcolm Collier and Dan Gonzales (San Francisco, CA: Asian American Studies, 2009). Reprinted by permission.

Most of the Chinese American students in ICSA were nominally "second generation": they were born in the United States, the children of families formed by the arrival of wives from China, who were sometimes accompanied by older children. These wives joined husbands who had come earlier, often twenty years or more, usually as "paper sons." Some ICSA members, however, were third, fourth, and even fifth or more generation Chinese Americans. Some were born in China, having come to San Francisco in the 1950s....

Most had parents who worked in sewing factories, restaurants, and small stores, or ran small businesses. Only a few had parents with better paying jobs in mainstream employment. All were the first generation in their families to attend college, most were working their way through school, and many still lived with their families in their local community.

PACE members had somewhat similar backgrounds: most were children of men with earlier histories in the United States who, because of changes in immigration laws in 1946 and their US military veterans' status, were able to bring wives from the Philippines and start families after World War II. In 1968, there was a near even distribution in PACE between members born in the Philippines and those who were second generation.... Like their Chinese American counterparts, they too had an awareness of the earlier "bachelor society" Filipino American experience. Most were also working their way through college.... Their activism was informed by the farm labor movement which was, as is now often forgotten, started by groups with Filipino leaders and majority members (the Agricultural Workers Organizing Committee) that were later joined by the better-known Mexican American union (the National Farm Workers Association) to form the United Farm Workers. They were also intensely curious about the colonial history of the Philippines and the impact of America's relatively recent colonial control on Philippine and Filipino American culture and society....

AAPA was mainly, though not totally, a Japanese American organization. Unlike PACE and ICSA, most AAPA members were [third generation] sansei and their family backgrounds were more varied in economic status, occupations, and schooling, although almost all their families had the World War II "camp experience" in common. AAPA members seemed often more ideologically grounded and were more likely to espouse a pan-ethnic "Asian American" perspective (as reflected in the name of the organization) than the other two groups.

The three organizations saw themselves as community-focused, not simply traditional campus student groups. Prior to the Strike for example, ICSA was primarily concerned with community activities and engaged in a variety of social service endeavors. These included academic tutoring programs, social and recreational work with youth groups, and issue-based community advocacy intended to draw public and governmental attention to needs for improvements in public housing and the development of more social services in Chinatown. Consequently many ICSA members were more involved with the community service element of the organization than with on-campus activities.

AAPA members were developing community-based concerns and activities related to redevelopment and issues associated with wartime internment. They were also involved in the then very new concept, "Asian American," and the related developments of cultural and political consciousness and the growing movement stemming from them.

PACE actively supported the I-Hotel resistance to eviction that began in 1968 and advocated for community opposition to the destructive effects of business-oriented development both north and south of Market Street. They encouraged intergenerational political activism and organized youth groups.... Some PACE members developed a critical perspective of the Philippine government, particularly the Marcos administration – well before the 1972 declaration of martial law – while the Marcos family enjoyed tremendous popularity in the Philippines and among Filipino communities the world over. When anti-Marcos critics, including some members of PACE, began to voice their criticisms publicly, they were soon labeled "communist-inspired" radicals by the conservative leadership elite of their own ethnic community.

Community activism and service had substantial formative influence on all three organizations, which, despite the overlay of ideological rhetoric, were shaped by the pragmatic needs and immediate issues of their respective communities. ICSA, PACE, and AAPA members tended to identify as community people who were going to college, and not as college students who were going back to the community....

Ideology

The public language of those involved in the Strike, including many from the Asian American student groups, was often phrased in the ideological style of the time, with references to Mao Zedong (spelled Mao Tse-tung at the time), Frantz Fanon, and Malcolm X. This language, together with the radical nature of some of their demands, disguised the actual diversity of political perspectives within the three Asian American student groups. There was something of a shared "Third World" perspective, an identification of racism as a major problem in American society, and a strong emphasis on development of a "social consciousness," but the ideological forms expressed and applied by the student organizations and their members differed among and between them.

The demand for and eventual creation of an Asian American Studies program with Chinese, Filipino, and Japanese American components reflected an element of cultural nationalism that was largely driven by the desire for more knowledge about their own communities and cultures that had been previously denied them. This produced a clear "anti-assimilation" perspective, which conflicted not only with the very real pressures to assimilate and acculturate in the United States but also with universalistic tendencies within Marxism that promise superficial recognition of cultural minorities while limiting their access to power. Our ideological perspectives were correspondingly complex.

Some members of the three groups saw themselves as revolutionaries, influenced by international Marxism or domestic militant socialist groups. Others were inspired by the Civil Rights Movement and related traditions, by political movements in Asia, by local activism around issues affecting their own communities and families, or by familial environment.

None of the three groups forced a strict orthodoxy on their members, instead tolerating a range of eclectic personal political perspectives and beliefs. The core standard was a commitment to community and to the particular goals of the organizations. At San Francisco State, whatever the rhetoric, the reality was that the dominant ideological perspective was idealistic, democratic pragmatism....

The Strike

As the fall term opened in 1968, the skeleton of an agenda shared among the student organizations in the TWLF [Third World Liberation Front] directly addressed the deficiencies of SF State. The immediate triggers of the Strike were disputes over treatment of Black lecturers working in support programs for EOP students. The Black Student Union (BSU) and TWLF quickly articulated a wider range of issues that reflected collective anger and frustration caused by the inability or unwillingness of the institution to deal with the needs of minority students and communities....

The most important demand was the first TWLF demand that "a School of Ethnic Studies for all of the ethnic groups involved in the Third World Liberation Front be set up with the students in each particular ethnic organization having the authority and control of the hiring and retention of any faculty member, director, or administrator, as well as the curriculum in a specific area of study." At that time, a "school" was a separate academic administrative unit within the larger San Francisco State College. What the demand sought was the establishment and enabling of an academic unit with a substantial degree of control and autonomy over its internal processes. This demand for a "school" flowed from the TWLF's core principle of self-determination. More importantly, the demand demonstrates that the TWLF member groups understood the need for as much autonomy and independence as they could acquire within the larger college structure. It is this demand and its ultimate partial acceptance by the administration that made the development of Ethnic Studies programs, especially Asian American Studies, unique in comparison to related efforts at other colleges and universities....

Although alternately and appropriately called the "Third World Student Strike," not all third world students supported or participated in it. For a variety of reasons, many continued to go to class and, conversely, the greater number of students who did strike and walk the picket lines were white, as were the great majority of faculty who supported the strike demands. It was a complex affair in complex times.

The many communities of the Bay Area were also very much involved in the Strike, though most treatments of Strike history focus disproportionately on campus activity. At the start of the Strike, the TWLF immediately moved to seek outside support. ISCA, PACE, and AAPA engaged in meetings and held forums intended to cull support from individuals and organizations in their respective ethnic communities. Some of these forums, especially those held in Chinatown, drew large crowds and significant press coverage. Community leaders supporting the Strike, and student strikers themselves, presented the Strike to the public as being far more than a student-versus-college administration affair. Growing numbers of leading community figures began to show up on the campus picket lines. Several unions also publicly supported the Strike and sent members to join the picket lines. The intent, which was successful, was to define the issues to the public in larger political terms and to prevent the students from being isolated and vulnerable to police attacks.

The college administration and the TWLF both experienced many internal disagreements. Neither had full control of their supporters' actions....

The TWLF experience was positive in many respects, providing important practical learning and an exciting sense of collective effort and success that many participants remember with considerable fondness and which have continued to shape their political perspectives to the present. The camaraderie and productive interactions with people from different student groups enriched inter-group understanding and provided very valuable lessons in the building of a political movement. Collaboration among the students and community activist groups, however conflicted and imperfect, demonstrated a potential for future collective actions.

Conversely, it sometimes seemed that the operative word in "Third World Liberation Front" was "front" – behind which discord, mutual misperceptions, and other problems festered.... Each group had its own agenda and frequently had only limited understanding of the needs and positions of the other groups....

There were also obvious and serious gender issues. The leadership of TWLF and the public leadership of the various student organizations were overwhelmingly male and some of the men did not treat the women with respect. This led to conflict and frustrations for the women activists during the Strike. There was a general failure to address their concerns and to recognize the full extent, substance, and value of their contributions....

The gains of the Strike came with substantial cost. Many strikers and some community supporters were arrested, spending varying amounts of time in jail and in court. Others were beaten by the police. One unfortunate member of ICSA was overlooked in the chaos following a day of mass arrests and languished in jail for weeks as his relatives refused to bail him out and the student organizations assumed he had been bailed out by relatives. This is just one example of tensions with family that some members of ICSA, PACE, and AAPA experienced as they were castigated and ostracized by family members for their activism. While the student organizations received some community support, they were also subject to extreme criticism from many other segments of their communities who encouraged the authorities in their attempts to suppress the Strike by whatever means....

The Relevance and Legacy of the Strike Today

On a broad scale we wanted the college to become a place in which Asian American history, culture, and communities – which is to say the realities of the Asian American experience – would be accepted as legitimate areas of study at the university level. This was a dream, a push for inclusion and redefining what is American. We wanted Asian Americans to be seen as Americans, not at the price of assimilation and "acceptance" but through a change in the conception of America to one that was broader and more varied in its character. We saw this as an issue of equity; if college is intended to provide students with knowledge and understanding of their society and culture, then it should include ours. But there was a pragmatic aspect to this dream too. We believed that if Asian American students could be provided with a solid understanding of Asian American realities, past and present, that they/we emerge both better individuals and better prepared to help provide for the needs of our communities....

We were seeking a change in the character and focus of the college, of academia in general. We wanted a connection between college and communities, believing, hoping, that such connections would be to the long-term benefit of the communities and, secondarily, the college. We wanted the college to serve the communities, not to remove or "rescue" students from their communities.

2. Activist Amy Uyematsu Proclaims the Emergence of "Yellow Power," 1969

Within the past two years, the "yellow power" movement has developed as a direct outgrowth of the "black power" movement. The "black power" movement caused many Asian Americans to question themselves. "Yellow power" is just now at the stage of "an articulated mood rather than a program—disillusionment and alienation from white America and independence, race pride, and self-respect." Yellow consciousness is the immediate goal of concerned Asian Americans.

In the process of Americanization, Asians have tried to transform themselves into white men—both mentally and physically. Mentally, they have adjusted to the white man's culture by giving up their own languages, customs, histories, and cultural values. They have adopted the "American way of life" only to discover that this is not enough.

Next, they have rejected their physical heritages, resulting in extreme self-hatred. Yellow people share with the blacks the desire to look white. Just as blacks wish to be light-complected with thin lips and un-kinky hair, "yellows" want to be tall with long legs and large eyes. The self-hatred is also evident in the yellow male's obsession with unobtainable white women, and in the yellow female's attempt to gain male approval by aping white beauty standards. Yellow females have their own "conking" techniques—they use "peroxide, foam rubber, and scotch tape to give them light hair, large breasts, and double-lidded eyes."

The "Black is Beautiful" cry among black Americans has instilled a new awareness in Asian Americans to be proud of their physical and cultural heritages.

Yellow power advocates self-acceptance as the first step toward strengthening personalities of Asian Americans.

Since the yellow power movement is thus far made up of students and young adults, it is working for Asian–American ethnic studies centers on college campuses such as Cal and U.C.L.A. The re-establishment of ethnic identity through education is being pursued in classes like U.C.L.A.'s "Orientals in America." As one student in the course relates:

"I want to take this course for a 20–20 realization, and not a passive glance in the ill-reflecting mirror; the image I see is W.A.S.P., but the yellow skin is not lily white… I want to find out what my voluntarily or subconsciously suppressed Oriental self is like; also what the thousands of other (suppressed?) Oriental selves are like in a much larger mind and body—America… I want to establish my ethnic identity not merely for the sake of such roots, but for the inherent value that such a background merits."

The problem of self-identity in Asian Americans also requires the removal of stereotypes. The yellow people in America seem to be silent citizens. They are stereotyped as being passive, accommodating, and unemotional. Unfortunately, this description is fairly accurate, for Asian Americans have accepted these stereotypes and are becoming true to them….

The yellow power movement envisages a new role for Asian Americans:

"It is a rejection of the passive Oriental stereotype and symbolizes the birth of a new Asian—one who will recognize and deal with injustices. The shout of Yellow Power, symbolic of our new direction, is reverberating in the quiet corridors of the Asian community."

As expressed in the black power writings, yellow power also says that "When we begin to define our own image, the stereotypes—that is, lies—that our oppressor has developed will begin in the white community and end there."

Another obstacle to the creation of yellow consciousness is the well-incorporated white racist attitudes which are present in Asian Americans. They take much false pride in their own economic progress and feel that blacks could succeed similarly if they only followed the Protestant ethic of hard work and education. Many Asians support S.I. Hayakawa, the so-called spokesman of yellow people, when he advises the black man to imitate the Nisei: "Go to school and get high grades, save one dollar out of every ten you earn to capitalize your business." But the fact is that the white power structure allowed Asian Americans to succeed through their own efforts while the same institutions persist in denying these opportunities to black Americans.

Certain basic changes in American society made it possible for many Asian Americans to improve their economic condition after the war. In the first place, black people became the target group of West Coast discrimination. During and after World War II, a huge influx of blacks migrated into the West, taking racist agitation away from the yellows and onto the blacks….

The other basic change in society was the shifting economic picture. In a largely agricultural and rural West, Asian Americans were able to find employment. First- and second-generation Japanese and Filipinos were hired as farm laborers and gardeners, while Chinese were employed in laundries and restaurants. In marked contrast is the highly technological and urban society which today faces unemployed black people. "The Negro migrant, unlike the immigrant, found little opportunity in the city; he had arrived too late, and the unskilled labor he had to offer was no longer needed." Moreover, blacks today are kept out of a shrinking labor market, which is also closing opportunities for white job-seekers.

Asian Americans are perpetuating white racism in the United States as they allow white America to hold up the "successful" Oriental image before other minority groups as the model to emulate. White America justifies the blacks' position by showing that other non-whites—yellow people—have been able to "adapt" to the system. The truth underlying both the yellows' history and that of the blacks has been distorted. In addition, the claim that black citizens must "prove their rights to equality" is fundamentally racist.

Unfortunately, the yellow power movement is fighting a well-developed racism in Asian Americans who project their own frustrated attempts to gain white acceptance onto the black people. They nurse their own feelings of inferiority and insecurity by holding themselves as superior to the blacks....

A united black people would comprise over ten percent of the total American electorate; this is a significant enough proportion of the voting population to make it possible for blacks to be a controlling force in the power structure. In contrast, the political power of yellows would have little effect on state and national contests. The combined populations of Chinese, Japanese and Filipinos in the United States in 1960 was only 887,834—not even one-half percent of the total population.

However, Asian Americans are not completely weaponless, in the local political arena. For instance, in California, the combined strength of Chinese, Japanese, and Filipinos in 1960 was two percent of the state population. Their possible political significance lies in the fact that there are heavy concentrations of these groups in San Francisco and Los Angeles....

In city and county government, a solid yellow voting bloc could make a difference....

Although it is true that some Asian minorities lead all other colored groups in America in terms of economic progress, it is a fallacy that Asian Americans enjoy full economic opportunity. If the Protestant ethic is truly a formula for economic success, then why don't Japanese and Chinese who work harder and have more education than whites earn just as much? ...

The myth of Asian American success is most obvious in the economic and social position of Filipino Americans. In 1960, the 65,459 Filipino residents of California earned a median annual income of $2,925, as compared to $3,553 for blacks and $5,109 for whites. Over half of the total Filipino male working force was employed in farm labor and service work; over half of all Filipino males received less than 8.7 years of school education. Indeed, Filipinos are a forgotten minority in America. Like blacks, they have many legitimate complaints against American society.

A further example of the false economic and social picture of Asian Americans exists in the ghetto communities of Little Tokyo in Los Angeles and

Chinatown in San Francisco. In the former, elderly Japanese live in rundown hotels in social and cultural isolation. And in the latter, Chinese families suffer the poor living conditions of a community that has the second highest tuberculosis rate in the nation.

Thus, the use of yellow political power is valid, for Asian Americans do have definite economic and social problems which must be improved. By organizing around these needs, Asian Americans can make the yellow power movement a viable political force in their lives.

3. Asian Americans in Los Angeles Protest Against the Vietnam War, Late 1960s

Asian Americans protest against the Vietnam War.

4. Al Robles Celebrates the Manongs and the International Hotel, 1970s (2002)

International Hotel—in the mongo [mung beans] heart & isda mind of the Philippines—where old & young Pilipinos live, hang, & roam around all day like carabaos [water buffalos] in the mud: eating, sleeping & working. Pilipinos scattered all over—brown faces pied high, moving like shadows on trees, concrete doorways, pool halls, barber shops. Guitar music echoes thru—down deer

---

"Coming Home to Manilatown, International Hotel," *Amerasia Journal* 28, no. 3 (2002): 181–194. Reprinted by permission.

in your mongo heart & isda mind. Chinatown across the way. Sixty-thousand or more live in rooms the size of tea pots, stretching east, west, north & south. Thousands are crammed in damp basements, alley ways, behind run-down barrels of ancient Chinese mountain wine. Thousands of Chinese children run along soy sauce streets—long black hair glistening like a cool stream—a quiet moon watches. Short crop of hair—morning spring faces—underneath fresh-soaked clouds. All those tiny footsteps keep the winter belly warm.

> All night session—ocean of words
> Legaspi—Frank—Bob—Bill Sorro—Mee Har—Me
> & somebody else.
> Early start at Legaspi's UFA mountain fortress
> Put down your white mind
> with your eyes behind brown skin
> brown=brown=brown=brown
> fallen coconuts on a cold
> cold winter day.
> brown=brown=brown=brown
> fish drying
> in the hot summer sun
> Bill Sorro: "You know, when I go into the pool halls
> & see my Pilipino brothers, I want to say to them:
> 'you know I know how you feel; I know how you think.' I want to say to them,
> Manong [older brother], manong, manong, don't you know
> you are being fucked."
> "I am brown, I am together, I am beautiful"
> Come down from those white flaky hills
> the smell of the carabao shit stills
> the mind
> keeps the pampano [fish] swimming
> in your belly.
> Put down your knives & forks
> and eat rice & fish
> with brown winter-soiled hands.
> jump and wallow
> in the mountain-grass heap shit
> of the carabao.
> Ah, Pilipinos
> IF you only knew how brown you are
> you would slide down
> from the highest
> mountain top
> you would whip out your lava tongue
> & burn up all that white shit
> that's keeping your people down.
> Don't you know
> you smell like

the deep brown earth
if you only knew
if your eyes were
only opened
you would see the sun
come down

5. Althea Yip Remembers the Legacy of the Death of Vincent Chin, 1997

It was an unlikely place for a pivotal point in Asian American history. A young draftsman named Vincent Chin was attending his bachelor party at a suburban Detroit strip club called Fancy Pants. With the party in full swing, Chin and Ronald Ebens, a white autoworker, began trading insults across the bar. "It's because of you little motherfuckers that we're out of work," witnesses later remembered Ebens yelling at Chin.

Chin struck Ebens, and an altercation ensued. Ebens' stepson, Michael Nitz – who had been recently laid off from his job at an autoplant – jumped in. But it was soon broken up by a parking attendant. Chin and his friends left the bar and went their separate ways. Twenty minutes later, Ebens and Nitz caught up with Chin in front of a fast-food restaurant. Ebens grabbed a baseball bat and delivered a blow to Chin's leg. Nitz held the wounded Chin, while Ebens struck his head with the bat, bashing his skull in.

Before he slipped into a coma, Chin murmured to a friend, "It's not fair." Four days later – and five days before his wedding – Chin died as a result of the injuries he sustained during the beating.

The incident on June 19, 1982, seemed an almost perfect metaphor for anti-Asian sentiment in America. It was ignorant; Ebens and Nitz presumed Chin, a 27-year-old Chinese American, was Japanese. It was economically motivated; the two autoworkers blamed the Japanese – and, mistakenly, Chin – for the ailing U.S. auto industry and the consequential loss of jobs. And it was horribly violent; the use of a baseball bat as a murder weapon was a brutal act and an equally brutal reminder of Americana.

But if the beating itself was emblematic of the racial problems in America, the subsequent trial challenged many Asian Pacific Americans' faith in the American way.

Ebens and Nitz were charged with and pleaded guilty to manslaughter. For this, they each received a sentence of three years probation and a $3,000 fine – a sentence that many APA community leaders perceived as a slap on the wrist.

Later federal civil-rights cases brought against the two defendants were appealed, and the juries acquitted each of them. Neither served a jail sentence.

The first judgment against Ebens and Nitz outraged a group of APAs and motivated them to form American Citizens for Justice (ACJ), a pan-Asian American activist group that mobilized to demand a retrial against the two men....

"Remembering Vincent Chin: Fifteen Years Later a Murder in Detroit Remains a Turning Point in the APA Movement," *AsianWeek*, June 19, 1997, 12. Reprinted by permission.

Vincent Chin became a contemporary martyr of the APA movement. Fifteen years later, his death remains a turning point for many Asian Pacific Americans.

"I think that the Vincent Chin case ... was a watershed moment for all Asian Americans," said Helen Zia, a longtime community activist and ACJ co-founder. "Previously, there were mostly college and progressive activists who had taken up the name 'Asian American,' but as far as the average person in the Chinatowns, Japantowns, Koreatowns, they considered themselves their own ethnicity.

"For the first time, we considered ourselves as a race, a minority race in America that faced discrimination and had to fight for our civil rights. The Vincent Chin case marked the beginning of the emergence of Asian Pacific Americans as a self-defined American racial group." ...

The five-year legal battle that followed the shock of the initial verdict was conducted by APA advocates who had little experience dealing with national civil-rights cases, said Stewart Kwoh, executive director of the Los Angeles-based Asian American Legal Center, which was organized the same year the Chin case went to court....

In the first trial in Wayne County Criminal Court in 1983, the prosecutor of the case did not show up for the sentencing hearing; there were no advocacy groups present; and neither Lily Chin, Vincent's mother, nor any of the witnesses was called to testify.

With only the defense lawyer making a case for his clients, Judge Charles Kaufman handed down his verdict of a $3,000 fine, $780 in court fees, and three years probation for each of the men. Kaufman reasoned that Ebens and Nitz did not have criminal records and were not likely to violate the terms of their parole. And at the same time, Kaufman ignored the pre-sentence report that identified Ebens as an alcoholic with a history of alcohol-related problems. The report also recommended that in addition to incarceration, Ebens undergo detoxification and counseling for his problem.

The decision sent shock waves throughout the national APA community. Civil-rights leaders interpreted Kaufman's decision as judicially condoning anti-Asian violence.

"It was an intense time," said Henry Der, a longtime community activist and then-executive director of San Francisco-based Chinese for Affirmative Action (CAA). "Here these murderers were sitting out there literally smirking at the whole situation.

"Before Vincent Chin, people dealt with hate violence at the local level. But Vincent Chin galvanized the political consciousness among Asian Americans – that's the only way it can be described. The lack of a meaningful penalty for the murder was egregious. It was something that could not be ignored."

ACJ, with help from several other APA groups – including CAA, Japanese American Citizens League, Organization of Chinese Americans, Filipino American Community Council of Michigan, and Korean Society of Metropolitan Detroit – staged rallies, organized demonstrations, and launched a massive letter-writing campaign. They wrote to politicians, the press, and the U.S.

Department of Justice demanding that the two men be charged with violating Chin's civil rights.

Lily Chin, who barely spoke English, traveled the country raising money to pay the costs involved in bringing about a civil suit. Many credit her appeal to the APA community for bringing forth seniors and immigrants – who could identity with her – into the movement.

After an FBI investigation that was ordered by the Department of Justice gathered sufficient evidence, federal charges were filed and a federal grand jury indicted the men in November 1983 on two counts: one for the violation of civil rights, the other for conspiracy.

In June 1984, Ebens was found guilty only on the first count and sentenced to 25 years in prison. He also was told to undergo treatment for alcoholism, but was freed after posting a $20,000 bond. Nitz was cleared of both charges.

But in September 1986, Ebens' conviction was overturned on a legal technicality; one of the lawyers for ACJ had been accused of improperly coaching the prosecution's witnesses.

The Justice Department ordered a new trial in April 1987, but this time in a new venue: Cincinnati. But while the change in venue was meant to increase the chances of a fair trial, in some important ways it made that almost impossible.

Cincinnati was, in the early '80s, a city that had had little exposure to Asian Pacific Americans. Out of 200 prospective jurors interviewed, only 19 said that they had ever encountered an Asian American. They were quickly dismissed.

According to Zia, the actual jury had little if any understanding of the hostility people in Detroit harbored against Japanese cars and Japanese-looking people. The nation's trade imbalance with Japan had been blamed for the closing of or cutbacks at many auto plants in Detroit.

"The whole mood was total anti-Japanese," Zia said about Detroit, where she lived when Chin was killed.

"People who had Japanese cars were getting their cars shot at, and it didn't matter if they were white. And then if you were Asian, it was assumed that you were Japanese just like Vincent and there was personal hostility toward us.

"So, when Vincent was killed it was a confirmation to all Asian Americans there in Detroit, the antagonism that we were feeling. I felt totally like a moving target."

In May 1987, the jury of 10 whites and two African Americans acquitted Ebens of all charges. He never served a jail term for his crime.

The whole experience had taken its toll on Lily Chin. Disheartened, she left the U.S. and returned to her native village in the Guangzhou province in China.

Later in 1987, a civil suit ordered Ebens to pay $1.5 million to Chin's estate. But shortly before the verdict, Ebens had disposed of his assets and fled. He has been evading officials for the past 10 years....

Today, things are different, said Roland Hwang, current board member and former president of ACJ. Now the APA community has national lobbying organizations based in Washington, D.C., and several agencies throughout the country that investigate and follow hate crimes against APAs locally....

Cases that are currently on the radar screens of national APA advocacy groups include the recent assault on a group of APA students outside of a Denny's restaurant in Syracuse, N.Y.; the fatal shooting of a Chinese American man in Rohnert Park, Calif., by a police officer; and the stabbing death of a Vietnamese American man in Los Angeles....

For Karen Narasaki, who was in law school when Chin was killed, the case helped her decide to use her law degree to fight for civil rights.

"It was such a powerful story that brought home how fragile our existence here as Asian Americans is and the need to be vigilant," said Narasaki, executive director of the National Asian Pacific American Legal Consortium [NAPALC]. "I know that the incident shaped a lot of people who are currently involved in civil rights, including myself."

Liz Ouyang, a staff attorney at the New York-based Asian American Legal Defense and Education Fund, who was also inspired by the incident to work in the civil-rights field, felt a personal connection to the Chin case.

"When I heard about Vincent Chin, it made me think of my brothers," said Ouyang, who was a senior at the University of Michigan in 1982.

Growing up in Rochester, N.Y., Ouyang recalls the neighborhood bully taunting her brothers with racial slurs.

One day the bully attacked one of her brothers, tying a lasso around his neck and dragging him down the street when he tried to flee.

When the Chin case drummed up memories of what happened to her brother, Ouyang knew what she had to do.

"The legacy of Vincent Chin has left very deep impressions on my work today," she said. "It clearly has influenced me in what I am doing today, representing victims of anti-Asian violence and police brutality. And I tell my clients, 'I will represent you like you were my brother,' because, in a way, they are."

6. Urashi Vaid Criticizes Heterosexism and Patriarchy in Racial Justice Movements, 1999

I want to talk today about the limits of racial identity politics and the real challenge embedded in "including" sexuality. My talk uses examples from the immigrant Asian experience so bizarrely idealized and distorted last night by Dinesh D'Souza.

First, I believe that we are at a moment where the paradigm of ethnic and race based organizing needs to be examined and questioned – across the board, as does the framework of identity based to question the meaningfulness and even the racial content of concepts like "South Asian" and "Asian Pacific American" identity. Instead of a nationalist or ethnic based model, we need an economic model of organizing because that provides more fruitful opportunities to challenge racism and to start to connect in issues of gender, sexual orientation and the problem of challenging supremacy. Certainly, I believe that racism is a serious reality and obstacle for Asian Pacific Americans and for the political movements we are building in the US, but I think that immigrant communities and even the movement for racial justice in this country deploy ethnicity as a device to build a false racial solidarity, which conveniently ignores the currents of gender, sexuality, and class differences that run underneath. This deliberate strategic avoidance of anything but race was evident yesterday when Bill Wilson spoke about needing to stay away from issues that would divide the multi-racial coalition he proposed.

Second, the lessons of history teach us that on their own creating identity-based politics does not lead to liberationary outcomes. But this conclusion begs the question of what is the goal of an Asian Pacific American politics? Or a black-movement politics? What are we trying to achieve by attempting POC [people of color] movements? Do we agree on our goals and will we ever agree? Would the goals of ending economic and structural inequality be better served by organizing a movement that is not-identity based?

Third, I want to propose that in order to both address racism, structural economic inequality and sexism and in order to "include" sexuality in a racial justice movement at every level, people of color communities must be willing to engage in a drastic re-consideration of the heterosexism, of patriarchy in our communities, of our notions of family: for example, no inclusive, anti-homophobic Asian movement can emerge without such a re-visioning of Asian family and culture. And I am not at all confident that we are at a place where such questioning and revisioning and redefinition are possible or even taking place:

Overall what I want to argue is that while racial identity-based organizing and maintaining identity have been vital strategies that retain relevance, they are not on their own enough to end racism. The inclusion of sexuality within the POC context will engender a willingness to accept some discomfort and has encountered stiff resistance. The truth is – for those of you have been waging the effort in POC organizations and communities – in coalitions or in churches, or in APA organizations – that seeking inclusion and awareness are the easy parts. Transforming the institutions of family, relationships, gender and power dynamics in communities of color – which is what sexuality brings in the door still lie ahead of us.

As Dana Takagi has noted in her essay in the book Asian American Sexualities, the adding-on or adding-in of sexuality into the *melange* of Asian identities in America is on its own, not enough. If sexuality is submerged into the pre-existing, hierarchical ethnic based narrative, we are not redefining very much and not in fact opening up very much space for queer Asians like me, nor are we making real social change.

The Ethnic Model: APA Organizing

We live in a moment in which the effects of racism on people of color are visible everywhere, and yet we are urged to ignore them and re-interpret them from the lens of a libertarian ideology that argues that inequality is not a byproduct of the failure of an economic system, but the failure of an individual and the collapse of the "traditional" family structure that individual comes from. Racism in the disguise of "race-neutral" policies is dominant.

The goal of this resurgent racial bias is to re-impose white supremacy in the workplace, in the award of government contracts, in the allocation of public resources. Conservatives want you and me to believe that by erasing race, by getting rid of affirmative action, people of color will be "freer" but this nonsense obscures the truth about how institutionalized and embedded racial prejudice is and how linked racism is to class. Few of us are "free" to move up the ladder of success, business, and educational hierarchy on our merits alone – opportunity and freedom are conditioned by economic privilege. Few are "free" to go to college without financial assistance; few of us are "free" to break out of the class-lines assigned us by our race and our class-of-birth. Merit for POC in America is a cigarette, not the way the system works for us – the facts do not support the libertarian nonsense of people like D'Souza.

The idea of an Asian Pacific American political movement is rooted in the particular experiences of prejudice faced by Asians and immigrants in the US, and it borrows heavily from the model of ethnic based organizing that has characterized the civil rights struggle in the US. Ethnic or race based organizing has been an effective strategy in American politics to assert political power, to secure public policy solutions that meet the needs of the particular constituencies that are organizing and perhaps most importantly to develop a stronger sense of self and self-worth in a context that whitens all difference. Organizing as racial or ethnic based groups has been useful and it is this reason that many Asians are adapting the race based model of organizing today. There are very good reasons we are organized around and by ethnicity or nationality. But I remain skeptical of this strategy as a panacea or even the best model. My skepticism about ethnicity or nationality as the basis for organizing is best elaborated through the Asian Pacific American political movement that I see emerging around me.

The challenge I see about organizing as APAs comes in three forms. For one, economics as much as race conditions the experience of racism of APs in America. Our APA movement thus far has had little to say about economic justice. Second, the irony of the framework of APA is that American defines and unites us far more than 'Asian' or 'Pacific'. And third, the model of race-based or ethnic-based or even identity based organizing is very valuable in terms of definition, individual empowerment and community organizing. But it is of limited value as a transformational device.

My parents, like many Asian and South Asian and Pacific people came to America for "economic opportunity" – we came by choice but others came as economic slaves (laborers) building up American railways and infrastructure at the turn of the century and serving the households of immigrant families as indentured slaves today. Asians in this country have by and large completely bought into capitalism. This despite the fact that capitalism is now strip mining the economies of many of our countries of origin, has not provided relief to the millions in the world who are poor and living at subsistence levels; has created enormous disparities in freedom, opportunity and power between rich, middle class, working class and poor.

We are model minorities in our acquiescence to the system staying the same. So in this country, the same immigrants who are suffering from the racist immigration policies of the Republican right staunchly oppose health care reform or a social safety net. Indians in the US – at least of my parents' generation – are quite conservative and more often than not republican (although being democrat these days offers little solace to those of us who are progressive).

Many people I know believe that if you work hard, anyone can get ahead; that people who are poor and on welfare are shiftless; that economic security and property are the ultimate goals of life (all framed in the guise of providing for your family, but at its core no different from the insatiable greed that motivates all capitalists). Ironically, the condition of Asians and Pacific people in America is more linked to economic forces and the ups and downs of capitalism than they are to the deep well of racism that is a part of the American psyche. American labor is already resentful of immigrant labor. Pat Buchanan's message resonated well with many people in this country. If jobs tighten up in the US, the visas will dry up for immigrants. The boom in hi tech jobs which has created great opportunities for Asian engineers and programmers hinges on the success of speculative and volatile markets which have inflated the value of internet and computer stocks, creating a wealth that cannot last for most and will benefit only a very few. I do not see a progressive Asian Pacific American movement dealing with these and other economic contradictions and tensions.

A second reason I am skeptical of the term Asian Pacific American is that it means so little. We are more tied together by our shared experiences or marginalization in white America than we are by our Asian American-ness, or our links nationally, historically, linguistically or culturally. Most of us do not know a thing about each other's countries of origin or histories. For second and third generation Asians in America, it's enough of a challenge to learn about our own ethnic and cultural heritage. To forge a sense of common solidarity with each other has thus been difficult. I do not believe that the large numbers of Indians in America feel a sense of kinship with Japanese Americans or with Chinese Americans or with Filipinos. Instead, they feel kinship along the tradition bound lines we have always followed: family, caste, state or origin, language – the conventional links. Given this truth are we in fact trying to force on to our wildly diverse immigrant cultures a commonality that will never be shared? Is the commonality more about expediency in American politics – the need to be counted, to be able to marshal votes etc – than it is about reality: will we ever be able to deliver a voting bloc as Asians given our radical diversity?

And this brings me to a final point for us to consider as we think about the racial identity formulation from the perspective of the Asian experience in America today: does identity politics work? The answer is it depends on your goal in using it. For what does it work and for what does it fail? I think it works to create self-esteem, empowerment, and visibility in the American political system, and it works for community building and organizing. But it fails as a vehicle to revamp the social service system in this country. Ideology based movements are more valuable than identity based ones.

Lessons from the Queer Context

The queer movement is facing an analogous cross roads in its reliance on identity as the principle means of organizing. Structural heterosexism, or institutionalized racism explains why we have single-issue movements dedicated to the eradication of these forms of prejudice. Pervasive prejudice, violence and discrimination are why we have a GLBT movement. But the GLBT movement today confronts two dilemmas: on one hand is its profoundly radical challenge to the most basic and intimate forms of human life – desire and family. How do we make our selves appealing when we are indeed really unsettling to the order of heterosexism. On the other hand we confront the same limits of organizing along the ethnic-model of organizing – without an ideological unity, without an economic policy agenda, with only our sexual orientation to connect us to each other, we never seem to really get to the heart of the structural problems we encounter. Let me elaborate for one minute.

The queer movement is one whose full acceptance will require deep changes in society's treatment of sex, desire, gender, human relationship and family. It is a movement that raises the most extreme kinds of psychological reactions in people – because they can in some sense see themselves affected by desire, touched by it and it makes them uncomfortable. It is a movement condemned by some of the most powerful texts and contexts in America – religion. And in order for GLBT people to be fully accepted in America it will require what theologian Bob Goss calls the sexual reformation of the church. In short the GLBT movement is not a safe or easy or simple movement.

On the other hand, the queer movement, like the emerging APA movement has reached the same dilemma that confronts each civil rights movement today. We begin to approach the point of partial fulfillment, where the system accommodates somewhat to admit us, to change some laws, to open up a little bit, but the underlying prejudice and structural barriers to full equality remain in place. We create zones of freedom inside a fundamentally intransigent system – family, marriage, state and economic order. In terms of public policy, we end up working piecemeal on small solutions that benefit particular communities in the short run while not making systematic changes that could benefit society in the long run.

And that is because we do not have an ideological basis for our social justice movements.

We find ourselves at a crossroads as a gay and lesbian movement, and while both roads are legitimate, one leads farther than the other. Down one road lies the direction we have been pursuing – of working solely or exclusively within the lesbian, gay, bi, transgender context, on so-called gay rights issues working solely on issues that affect "us" as queers. Down the other road lies the project of not just trying to fit in, but trying to change the world and institutions we encounter. If we walk down this second road, we quickly realize that our fight to end discrimination on the basis of sexual orientation intersects with women's effort to overturn our second class status, with the struggle for racial justice and equality, and with the quest for a fairer economy and a cleaner environment. What we attempt in walking down the second road is the project of building a kind of political and social change movement than the civil rights movements we have built thus far – we must build a movement that is all about economic change and through that we will create massive social change.

Let me stress, neither choice – single-issue politics, nor multi-issue politics – is right or wrong: they are however quite different. Let me also stress that I am not arguing that we must abandon all the single-issue or identity based work we are doing – just that we have got to supplement it with new organizing that we are not doing. I want a movement that is not just focused on identity but that is engaged in defining what the kind of society we want to move into as we move into the 21st century.

Is this possible? I don't know. Is this necessary? Yes. Why? It is necessary to create this common movement because we face a totalizing right/opposition that is not capable of being defeated by anything but a systematic counter mobilization. Right wing ideas about public policy and the ordering of cultural life are not merely cyclical swings in the historic pendulum of policy ideas. They represent a serious effort to restore the very values and hierarchies that social justice movements have struggled to transform, and to construct something that has not before existed in America – a theocratic state. In place of gender equality, the right advocates male supremacy. In place of remedies aimed at addressing centuries of racial discrimination against African Americans, the right proposes policies blind to the impact race plays on economic opportunity. In place of a social welfare role for the state, the right proposes either the elimination or privatization of all government service programs. These ideas are antithetical to the policies and values of social democrats and to social justice movements.

How are we organized to deal with these huge and complex changes? If we are to be honest with ourselves, we must answer that we are not well organized and not handling these changed circumstances very well. Why? If we look at our work historically, we can understand that we have not paid attention to the most basic kinds of lessons: to thrive, every movement must have a strong and motivated base. And the organizing and motivation of such a base is not something that just happens by osmosis or on its own, or through a media campaign. It happens through systematic and creative grassroots community organizing – something that too few of our civil rights organizations do even to this day.

The problem that exists lies squarely in the realm of constituency support for these ideas. Because of the way we are structured – issue by issue, or identity by identity – social justice movements cannot boast the kind of ideological or political unity that is found on the conservative right. Because we have invested less time and skill to organizing, social justice movements seem to have less clout to deliver on our goals (as setbacks at the ballot box on affirmative action, immigration, gay rights suggest).

This is precisely the gap at which racial justice and civil rights movements of the 21st century must take aim. We can and we must rebuild a constituency for social justice. Tremendous and creative work can be done to expand the capacity of social justice movements in various fields to defend their policies and to increase their reach. New ways to forge constituency among social justice organizations working on discrete issues can be attempted. We can and must make a new structure out of the way we now operate to succeed nationally and locally. We can and we must have the courage of our values to take the risk of joint action and new cooperation. We can and we must take the leap of faith in order to build the trust that common purpose requires.

And constituency building to oppose the right requires us to not be limited to a movement built around racial identity, ethnic identity or gender or sexual orientation alone. My point is this, we cannot build a common movement unless we look honestly at both the good things and the bad things we get by organizing issue by issue, color by color, identity by identity.

Queering APA Organizing

This conference is to be commended for acknowledging that the only sexuality in Asian and Pacific communities is not heterosexual. This is a truth denied in most Asian contexts. All too often, one still hears the canard that homosexuality is a western thing or a corruption of truly Asian values. The histories of Asian sexualities in each of our countries of origin remain to be discovered and uncovered by scholars of your generation in the years ahead. The truth that I know is that of course there is a rich tradition of same-sex love and experience in every culture and continent of the world. Whether it understands itself as "gay" or "lesbian" or "transgender" or bisexual" is debatable but the existence of same-sex behavior and same-sex love the world over ought not to be obscure to any one. It is not just a western or white thing, never was.

Certainly you all know that queers in America face tremendous barriers to fully living our lives: discrimination, violence and prejudice is the pervasive and is the norm. Whether the context is employment discrimination, family recognition, criminal law, immigration, health care, HIV, military issues, hate violence – GLBT people face a lot of problems and challenges. I am quite able to detail the specific forms and statistics that document this and to cite you to volumes that will help you understand these realities. But I do not want to take my time to that right now.

The point I want make is two fold: (1) yes, indeed, a progressive racial justice movement ought to take up the challenge of being allies to the GLBT movement. We need to recognize that ending prejudice based on sexual orientation is a progressive stand and one that is integral to movements based on the values of justice. The unpopularity of homophobia does not justify anyone's silence. As you see embodied in me and the other panelists, for queers like us, a multi-issue movement is essential. This first level of inclusion is where we find ourselves today – still arguing for the most basic kind of recognition from communities of color. The specifics of the fight vary race and ethnicity by race – the level of visibility of queer poc varies in each community of color – for example South Asian GLBT people have only emerged in our communities in the past 9 years, while an organized African American GLBT movement has existed for arguably over 20 years.

The deeper challenge that queerness poses to POC communities, and to the society at large, it is similar to the challenge that feminism poses: and this is a challenge I am not so sure our people – even progressives are willing to take up. The challenge is to the notions of family that we are raised with and to their unyielding patriarchal, hetero-sexist and authoritarian terms.

If any of you read the *New Yorker* in mid February of 1999, you would have read a wonderful example of what I am talking about in the Asian context in the story of the 20-year-old Indian woman from Queens. Her struggle to determine a life for herself and to please her parents and fulfill their expectations for her is heartbreakingly familiar to each of us who are Asian in this room. She is expected to be married, to accept that without question, to settle on the person her father selects, to produce children, to be the good and obedient daughter, to be the subject of statements like this one from her father "When you are married, my life will be complete". This story is typical and it is contemporary. The Indian family exerts this kind of pressure and control inside it, and is coded with enormous heterosexist expectations. The Latino, Black and other family structures would have their own gender and heterosexist codes and norms.

What does it mean that we are all raised in families where compulsory marriage and compulsory heterosexuality (as Adrienne Rich named it so eloquently) is the unquestioned norm? Where to stand against that is to be ostracized by all family, community, and in some instances to be killed by one's own father for disobedience? Why do we tolerate and accept the blatant double standard in Asian families for girls and boys? Why do young Asians in America feel they must go along with this and that they have no recourse – short of radical rebellion and acting out? What does it mean that the dominant critique of family in the black community that is not feminist, but comes out of right wing or liberal think tanks? How can gay, lesbian bisexual or transgender person be accepted into this old conception of family?

We need to create ways to organize around the so-called private family issues – to publicize what has been privatized, questioning and take it as disrespect instead of frank interrogation and disagreement. But this to me is the undone work of "internalizing" the meaning of movements for women's liberation and sexual freedom into the APA (or any other context). There can be no more than token integration of these issues unless we are willing to examine the gender biases of the families and communities we come from.

Conclusion

Gandhi wrote that morality consists of doing what we ought to do. He argued that mere observance of custom and usage was not morality. That moral actions are those guided by justice and respect for the divine will. That moral acts involve no coercion and are not motivated by self-interest. If I help my neighbor because he is suffering, I commit a moral act. If I help my neighbor because I want credit for helping him through his suffering, my action may still be a good deed, but in Gandhi's argument it is not moral.

Merely by pursuing our own liberation and freedom we are not engaged in a moral course. If we place our liberation movement in the service of building a more just society then we will be a movement that is unstoppable because our course will be spiritually and politically just. Additionally, merely by adding sexual orientation as a category to the line-up of things racial or ethnic, we will not actually change a great deal at all.

7. Annalisa V. Enrile and Jollene Levid Describe GABRIELA Network's Transnational Sisterhood and Organizing, 2009

For decades, women's organizing has been predominately territorial-bound and geographically placed. However, since the 1990s there has been a shift to broader theorizing of global sisterhoods and the opportunity for solidarity, especially around gender justice and liberation movements. The United Nations Decade for Women (1976 to 1985) opened a dialogue of North/South and First World/Third World dichotomies. The 1995 Fourth United Nations Conference on Women and NGO [nongovernmental organization] Forum in Beijing, China brought the issue of solidarity practices to the forefront. The rise of international women's conferences has aided in the push for more transnational feminist organizing and the need to address economic, political, and social arenas of women's struggle.

Transnational feminism, or international feminism, began as collective actions found themselves crossing border-states and countries. However, transnational feminism has grown to transcend the familiar boundaries of nations and race, emphasizing instead, the common visions and goals of women engaged in political struggles. This border crossing reflects women's struggles against racism, sexism, colonialism, and imperialism, and recognizes interlinked inequalities rather than generic commonalities. What feminist theorists have thus called "imagined communities" have created a deep, horizontal comradeship. It is only within this praxis that solidarity may be achieved and global sisterhood achieved....

Members decided that GABNet would fulfill a dual role—that of a support network and a national mass organization comprised of chapters in the major cities of the U.S. (New York, Chicago, San Francisco were original chapters). While a national organization could operate on its own and provide material resources as well as launch political campaigns for its international counterpart; there was also a need for the women doing the work in the United States to be more than just a support group. Just as one would take precaution against falling into the role of a "rescuer," women must also avoid falling into the role of "provider" with no political growth and empowerment of their own. Thus, a plan for mass organizing was drafted which served as the foundation for chapters to be set up. A group of women organized into a chapter would then be mass organizing around women's own political education and training, campaigns, and movement building, as well as providing support for the Philippines. Local chapter organizing would address the immediacy of issues occurring at the local/city/community level and the recognition

GAB[riela]Net[work]: A Case Study of Transnational Sisterhood and Organizing, *Amerasia Journal* 35, no. 1 (2009), 92–107. Reprinted by permission.

that the concrete circumstances of each area might be vastly different from one city to another. Local chapters would have the autonomy to launch local campaigns. At the same time, national leadership would coordinate chapters and national campaigns as well as be the liaison for international relations with the Philippines. Notwithstanding its growing pains, the national leadership of GABNet reached an integrated work pace—balancing the need to address local issues, project a national character, and mediate international needs. This type of organizing model attracted women inside and outside of the Pilipino community committed to the idea of doing international work that was integral and tied to their own lives in the U.S. Women were also drawn to GABNet for their own development and empowerment.

Despite the quasi-autonomous nature of GABNet, the organization still carried the ideological line of its Philippine counterparts. Some points of unity included a strong anti-imperialist stance, while some points were specific to the Philippines, such as the call from the Philippine Left for national democracy. GABNet supported both. The distinctive feature of this political ideology is the "national" aspect, which underscored the issue of sovereignty and a removal of foreign control in all aspects of Philippine life. In other words, this ideological line determines a course of relationships that must be attuned to the nature of power, particularly sensitive to the threats of colonial mentality and practices. As stated earlier, if not, there is a threat of falling into the trap of colonial provider and overseer of work. It cannot be emphasized enough that transnational feminist activism faces the difficult task of historicizing and denaturalizing the values of global capitalism in order to expose the underlying exploitative social relations and structures.

Having grappled with the organizational structure and reaching consensus about the political ideology, GABNet was left to create a practice of transnational work which would manifest itself into solid campaigns, relevant to the Philippines and the United States. The system for work became this: an annual meeting with GABRIELA Philippines in which their current yearly plan of action would be shared. For example, they could indicate a need to do a campaign on militarism because of an upcoming policy that would activate U.S. military bases or a campaign on migrant labor because of a global trend of recruitment for Pilipina nurses. After their one-year plan was laid out, a discussion ensued as to what would be the best way for GABNet to carry out these campaigns in the U.S. Because GABNet is not a chapter formation of GABRIELA, the freedom to articulate and interpret international campaigns became the backbone for successful campaigns in the United States...

Purple Rose Campaign (1998 to present)

The Philippines is one of the top three source countries for trafficked women and children. Although there were existing anti-trafficking campaigns, especially around forced prostitution and mail order brides, no campaigns specifically targeted the general public. The Purple Rose Campaign thus aimed to raise public critical awareness of the commodification of women and children, to ask the public to consider the factors contributing to trafficking—including national sovereignty, patriarchy, and economic stability.

The Purple Rose was chosen as the icon of this campaign, because this flower was artificially created and exoticized, for no other purpose than to satisfy desire. It is no different from other roses and yet remains apart, because it does not exist in nature and is not a product of evolution. So are women in the sex trade: artificially created and exoticized and willed to be apart and different. A pin in the image of the purple rose icon is sold as a statement of support for the campaign. The campaign was conceived in the United Stated and tested out countrywide during 1998.

In the summer of 1998, GABNet formally presented the Purple Rose Campaign to GABRIELA Philippines and its allied organizations during an international women's conference. It was at this time that the Purple Rose Campaign was adopted internationally. The planning meeting in the Philippines was composed of actual concrete planning and actions to be coordinated in all countries on specific days (October 28—Philippine Women's Day of Protest; November 25—Day Against Violence towards Women; March 8—International Women's Day) as well as activities that could be held specific to each area. Activities ran the gamut from fundraising dinners, to movie showings, to community forums. The Purple Rose Campaign also launched a media blitz of public service announcements, testimonials via print media, and an online website.

The Purple Rose Campaign is incorporated into every major holiday. For example, purple roses were delivered for Valentine's Day, and supporters wore purple leis for graduation. A public service announcement on the Purple Rose Campaign has been distributed and shown on various television channels, including the Discovery Channel, Lifetime TV for Women, and TLC. Mainstream venues such as parties, poetry readings, and even beauty pageants have served as vehicles for the campaign to gain momentum.

The Purple Rose Campaign's success lies in its appeal to a broad range of concerns: violence towards women and children as well as the nature of its issues being at the same time political, economic, and social. Gloria Steinem wore the Purple Rose pin during a Baltimore meeting of the Feminist Majority. The campaign has helped organizations meet the challenge for innovative, groundbreaking campaigns that challenge the status quo as well as expose the sex industry....

Twenty Years of Struggle

In 2009, GABNet celebrates its twentieth anniversary. The past twenty years have been full of struggle and of sisterhood. Since its inception, GABNet has grown to over eleven chapters (Seattle, Portland, San Francisco Bay Area, Santa Barbara, Los Angeles, Orange County, San Diego, Chicago, Boston, New York, and New Jersey) with a membership of hundreds of women. The work of GABNet has been conducted with many lessons learned, the most salient of which is the ability to be independent and develop a course of work that best fits with the environment. In doing so, GABNet has been able to make a true contribution to the women of the Philippines, conceptualizing such campaigns as the Purple

Rose Campaign which moved the anti-prostitution and anti-trafficking issues of Pilipina women worldwide to new arenas and pushed the issue into the mainstream. The success of GABNet must be attributed to its ability to develop its own strategies for working within U.S. society, building new pathways and new formulations.

As U.S. imperialism tightens its grip on neocolonies like the Philippines, the talons of oppression will be felt all the way to immigrant communities in America. Therefore, the work of an organization like GABNet can never hesitate or turn complacent....

While GABNet will continue to do work in solidarity with the Philippine women, it cannot ignore its responsibilities to respond to shifting world contexts and situations, which demand the maximization of women's organizing to achieve liberation. The transnational sisterhoods GABNet has created must now transcend the U.S. and the Philippines, declaring, "For liberation, Women of the World unite!"

8. Jeff Yang Discusses Multiracialism and Asian American Identity, 2011

As multiracial identity becomes the Asian American mainstream – by 2020, it's projected that one out of five Asians in the U.S. will be multiracial; by 2050, that ratio will exceed one in three – the population of persons with one-fourth Asian heritage or less is poised to spike.

"I'm half Japanese, and my husband is all Irish," says sociologist Dr. Rebecca Chiyoko King-O'Riain. "Our kids have very Celtic coloration – pale skin and fair hair. They're not obviously Asian in appearance at all, and yet they still feel very connected with that part of their heritage. And that's becoming more common, particularly among Japanese Americans, where multiracial identity is so common. There's even a term for it I heard in California: 'Quapa.' If hapas are half Asians, quapas – like my kids – are quarter-Asians."

Quapas have an overwhelmingly non-Asian ancestry; many don't look Asian and don't have Asian surnames. Yet anecdotal evidence suggests that as Asian America becomes more multiracial, a growing number of quapa Asians are affirmatively reconnecting with their Asian heritage, and actively embracing a sense of Asian American identity – challenging society's conventional means of defining race in the process.

Japanese and Damn Proud

For rising folk-pop star Meiko – just the one name – embracing the culture of her Japanese grandmother Chikako was both an homage to a woman who'd played an outsized role in her life, and a way of turning her feelings of being different from a liability into an asset. The singer-songwriter, whose eponymous

"Mixing It Up: Multiracialism Complicates Asian American identity," *SF Gate*, February 11, 2011. Retrieved from http://www.sfgate.com. Reprinted by permission of Jeff Yang.

first album made her a critics' darling and a top iTunes download, grew up in Roberta, Ga., a tiny town in rural Crawford County.

"Roberta only had about 800 people, and it was pretty much split down the middle, half black and half white," says Meiko. "I think there was one Mexican girl who came in as an exchange student when I was in 9th grade; other than that, my sister and I were the only ones who didn't fit on either team. But my grandmother taught me that being a quarter Japanese was something that made me special, and that's what I always felt...."

Meiko asserted her Japanese American identity in other ways as well. "When I was in middle school, we had this Veteran's Day assembly, and these really old soldiers came to tell us war stories. Well, they kept using the word 'Jap,' and every time they did, I cringed," she says. "At the end of the assembly, it was question time, and I went up to the mike and I said, 'Yeah, I have a question: Why do you keep referring to Japanese people as 'Japs'?' It kind of blew things up, and I ended up getting suspended. They're being racist and I'm the one who gets in trouble! But you know, small town, small minds. I'm still happy I did that."

Meiko now lives in Los Angeles, a considerably bigger and more diverse place than her rural Georgia hometown (with better sushi) – and though she's no longer the only Asian girl for miles, she continues to find her Japanese heritage to be a source of strength and a creative inspiration....

Chinese in the Heart

Author Lisa See ("Snow Flower and the Secret Fan") has similar feelings about her heritage: Even though it's not evident in her strawberry-blonde, green-eyed features or obvious from her name – she notes that people are more likely to think she's connected to the candy business than Chinatown – her sense of being Chinese is still at the core of her self-identity.

"In my first book, I wrote a line that sums up what I feel: 'I don't look very Chinese, but I'm Chinese in my heart,'" she says. "And every interview, every book event I've ever done, that's still the first thing everyone asks about. But the fact is, even though I'm only one-eighth Chinese, I grew up as a part of a very large Chinese American extended family – I have around 400 relatives, and they're still my mirror; when I look inside myself, they look back."

See's great-grandfather on her father's side was one of the grand patriarchs of Los Angeles's Chinese community, and as a result, their family's store was a regular gathering place for Chinatown's most notable and colorful personalities....

Those stories eventually inspired See to write her first book, "On Gold Mountain," a memoir of her family's history. It took a lot of convincing to get her relatives to give her the permission to write it: Like many Chinese families that lived through the Exclusion Acts, the Fong See clan was forced to break America's laws simply to live as Americans – falsifying names in order to enter the country, purchasing land under the table to evade the ban against Chinese owning property, living without legal marriage because of the laws against miscegenation. "If those laws hadn't been broken, I wouldn't even exist, but there was still a lot of shame and fear about it," she says. "And my side of the family, the white side, felt that was something you had to keep absolutely secret."

But once See broke the dam holding them back, the stories flooded out. Many of them ended up in "On Gold Mountain"; others inspired her later novels, which have led her deeper into her ancestral culture even as they've scaled higher up the bestseller lists....

Inside but Out

Multiracial individuals note that mixed identity requires a constant negotiation of insider-outsider status; belonging to both can often mean feeling at home in neither. But for mixed-race individuals with less than half Asian ancestry, actual programmatic boundaries exist to inclusion. Some Asian American cultural and civic activities are restricted to those who have 50 percent Asian heritage or more – for example, San Francisco's Cherry Blossom Queen pageant, which has been a fixture of the Japanese American community in Northern California since 1968.

"Racial eligibility rules were originally put in place because Asian Americans faced discrimination – it was a way for these communities to say, hey, our women are beautiful too," says Dr. King-O'Riain, whose book "Pure Beauty" explores the history of Japanese American beauty pageants. "But now you have a problem, because on the one hand, there are fewer and fewer Japanese American girls who meet that 50 percent standard, and on the other, the community's old guard is concerned that throwing open the racial eligibility rules will lead to blond-haired *hakujin* women becoming Cherry Blossom Queen, and then where would you be? So even though there's this debate about lowering the racial percentage to 25 percent or getting rid of it entirely, I personally think the people running the pageant will shut it down before they do that."

Of course, these concerns sidestep the fact that not all multiracial Japanese Americans are blond, blue-eyed and white. Among the dozens of pageant participants Dr. King O'Riain interviewed were a handful whose mixed heritage was black or Latino. "I interviewed two girls who were half African American, whose mothers were from Japan, who'd lived in Japan, who spoke Japanese beautifully," she says. "They had a deeper sense of the culture than most of the 'pure' Japanese candidates. And yet they didn't win, and they felt there was unquestionably discrimination against them. In the Los Angeles Cherry Blossom pageant, there's actually a no-tanning rule – you have to stay out of the sun. And the reason they give is that dark skin doesn't look good with a kimono."

Sheena Quashie, a Chinese-Caribbean journalist who proclaims herself a "proud blasian," says that that sense of rejection is a fundamental part of black-Asian mixed-race identity. "You do sometimes feel very rejected," she admits. "I'm one-quarter Asian, but Asian people look at me and just see this big, tall black girl. And sometimes they'll actually ask me to defend my Asianness – like I need to present a receipt or something! And I'm like, 'Man, what golden treasure do I get for lying about being it?'"

Nevertheless, Quashie – whose family name was Au-Yeung before her father changed it – remains resolutely connected to her roots. "Who I am is who I am," she says. "I've been through my angry period, and I'm done with it. I'm Trinidadian, and I'm proud of that. And I'm Chinese, and I'm proud of that."

More than the Sum of Our Parts

The mainstreaming of multiracialism hasn't just made it harder to define identity; it's raised the question of whether it makes sense to try to define it at all. More and more mixed-race individuals are calling for an end to the tyranny of racial algorithms, of the blood quantum that measures us by inherited fractions.

They're not, however, suggesting that race should be erased entirely: Attempts at "colorblindness" miss the practical realities that lie behind racial identities — the historical narratives they recount in shorthand, the social and political challenges they serve to benchmark, the cultural contexts they illuminate and enrich. As Quashie points out, race may simply be a construct, but so is a brick wall — and you ignore either at your peril.

There are other ways, as my friend TzeMing Mok notes; in her native New Zealand, the Maori determine identity not by name, appearance or percentage, but by *whakapapa* — the act of narrating lineage.

To be accepted as Maori, you must be able to recount your ancestral line back up to an *iwi* — a tribe — and then beyond that, to the *atua,* the gods. You can be 1/1024th Maori by blood, but if you can speak the story of your family's descent from the Earth Mother Papatuanuku to the present, you're as Maori as anyone. It's a viral rather than dilutive interpretation of race; a way of looking at identity as a story, of which each individual is a chapter.

The bottom line: Race is complicated, and only getting more so. Why shouldn't it be an essay question, rather than multiple choice?

9. C.N. Le Criticizes the Pew Report's Depiction of Asian Americans as Model Minorities, 2012

For those who missed it, the Pew Research Center recently released a report titled, "The Rise of Asian Americans" that, among other things, attempted to provide a demographic, socioeconomic, and cultural summary of the Asian American population, using a combination of Census data and the Pew's own telephone survey of over 3,500 Asian American respondents. Some of the report's notable findings are:

- In terms of total population, there are over 18 million Asian Americans as of 2011 and they represent 5.8% of the total U.S. population.

- Asian Americans are the fastest-growing racial/ethnic group in the U.S. in terms of percentage growth. This is also reflected in the most recently-available data from 2010 that shows that 430,000 Asians (legal and undocumented) immigrated to the U.S., compared with 370,000 Latinos.

"Pew Report on Asian Americans: A Cautionary Tale," *The Color Line*, July 24, 2012. Reprinted by permission of Dr. C.N. Le.

- Confirming current patterns, Asian Americans also have the highest proportion of adults 25 years or older who have a college degree and have the highest median household income.

The Pew report also spends much of its time discussing the "cultural" characteristics of Asian Americans and unfortunately, it is at this point where things start to hit the fan. As the *New York Times* summarizes:

> In the survey, Asians are also distinguished by their emphasis on traditional family mores. About 54 percent of the respondents, compared with 34 percent of all adults in the country, said having a successful marriage was one of the most important goals in life; another was being a good parent, according to 67 percent of Asian adults, compared with about half of all adults in the general population.
>
> Asians also place greater importance on career and material success, the study reported, values reflected in child-rearing styles. About 62 percent of Asians in the United States believe that most American parents do not put enough pressure on their children to do well in school.

Soon after its release, numerous Asian American scholars, community organizations, and academic associations began roundly criticizing the report. For example, the Japanese American Citizens League stated, "While our community reflects diversity, this research does not; instead, it sweeps Asian Americans into one broad group and paints our community as exceptionally successful without any challenges. This study perpetuates false stereotypes and the model minority."

Another nationally-recognized Asian American group, the Organization of Chinese Americans, wrote:

> "What is particularly disturbing is that these types of broad generalizations can have serious implications in public policy, civil rights, as well as perpetuation of bias, discrimination, and racial tension between communities of color. Even though the study fills a void for more statistics and information on the APA community, the framing of the contextual data in the report is troublesome.... The assertions that our community enjoys an exaggerated level of privilege are simply and unfortunately not the case.

Other statements of criticism and even condemnation of the Pew report came from organizations such as the Association for Asian American Studies, the Asian American Pacific Islander Policy and Research Consortium, the Asian & Pacific Islander American Scholarship Fund, the National Commission on Asian American and Pacific Islander Research in Education, Leadership Education for Asian Pacifics, and numerous Asian American Studies departments and programs around the country, to name just a few.

Perhaps the best critique came from Professor Karthick Ramakrishnan, Associate Professor of Political Science at the University of California Riverside, and ironically, a member of the Pew's faculty advisory board on Asian American issues:

> Unfortunately, [the report] prioritized questions asked of Asian Americans— regarding their parenting styles and their own stereotypes about Americans—that

seemed more concerned with Amy Chua's Battle Hymn of the Tiger Mother than with the priorities of Asian Americans themselves, either as revealed in past surveys or as articulated by organizations serving those communities....

More concerning than the Pew report, however, was the sensationalist headline on the press release that introduced the study to news media: Asians Overtake Hispanics in New Immigrant Arrivals; Surpass US Public in Valuing Marriage, Parenthood, Hard Work. These few words carried sway in hundreds of newspaper articles in the first two days of the report's release, provoking outrage among broad swaths of the Asian American community, including many researchers, elected officials, and community organizations....

As one of 15 advisors to the project, I felt blindsided by the press release. Words failed me as I read it for the first time, as we had not gotten a chance to review it. The dominant narrative in the release reinforced the frame of Asians as a model minority, stereotypes that the advisors had strongly objected to in the only meeting of the group two months ago.

Generally, the Pew Research Institute produces useful, informative, and reliable data and reports. However, as Prof. Ramakrishnan points out in the full text of his critique, this is not the first time that Pew has mischaracterized, sensationalized, or even misinterpreted its own data. Further, as I pointed out before, on occasion, Pew has inexplicably excluded Asian American respondents in some of its previous studies.

With that point in mind, I suppose we should be somewhat thankful that Pew has been more inclusive of Asian Americans as a valuable source of study lately. Nonetheless, simply including Asian Americans is not the same as accurately representing our community.

Pew might argue that their methodology and data are valid. Technically, I suppose they are. But as the above-referenced criticisms consistently point out, many of the questions they asked were sensationalist and not representative of the real, substantive issues and concerns that the Asian American community have identified themselves.

In the end, this Pew report teaches us a couple of valuable lessons. First, that biases can come in many different forms. That is, most of us thinking of biases in the form of direct and blatant statements that clearly favor one ideological viewpoint over another. But the Pew report shows us that biases can also manifest themselves in the questions researchers ask and how they frame the results of their data, based on the misfocused questions, to emphasize certain interpretations over others.

Second, the Pew report shows us that even something that is initially framed as a positive portrayal of Asian Americans can turn out to be just the opposite—a skewed misrepresentation that actually reinforces negative and damaging stereotypes. This lesson is at the core of the model minority image of Asian Americans and how some naively think that they are paying Asian Americans a compliment by commenting how well-educated we are, or how we're so good at math or science, or how hard we tend to work. While there is obviously some truth to these observations, the problem is that such characterizations are easily and often generalized to the entire Asian American population. When that happens, they mask the demographic, socioeconomic, and cultural diversity among Asian Americans and marginalize the continuing discrimination, inequalities, and injustices we still experience.

The Asian American community deserves to be represented better than this and research organizations such as Pew need to do a better job at asking us about the issues that we, not they, care about.

ESSAYS

These two essays analyze how Asian American activists during the Vietnam War and more recently promoted different interpretations of the history of racial discrimination against Asian Americans. The first essay, by Judy Tzu-Chun Wu, a University of California, Irvine, historian, documents the foreign travels of antiwar activists to Vietnam and explores how exposure to Vietnamese people, politics, and culture shaped their perception of internationalism and solidarity with Third World nations. Providing a transnational, gendered, and racially comparative analysis, Wu discusses why antiwar activists viewed Asian revolutionary women as inspirational role models and exemplars of "radical Orientalism." The second essay, by Ellen Wu, an Indiana University, Bloomington, historian, recounts battles against government and media model minority depictions of self-sufficient, educated, family-oriented, and politically moderate Asian Americans. These activists drew attention to structural racism and urged Asian Americans to support victims of oppression within the community and to model themselves on African American civil rights, black power, and anti-imperial activists.

Journeys for Peace and Liberation: Third World Internationalism and Radical Orientalism During the U.S. War in Vietnam

JUDY TZU-CHUN WU

One of the greatest thrills of being a historian is to uncover a compelling and unexpected story while sifting through vast amounts of paper in an archive. I came across one such treasure during my last visit to the Swarthmore College Peace Collection. On January 19, 1973, the Washington, D.C., branch of the Women's International League for Peace and Freedom (WILPF) received an urgent cable from the Union of Vietnamese Women (VWU), an organization based in Hanoi. The message, written in French and translated into English, invited a small delegation from WILPF to visit the capital of North Vietnam for a week, beginning on January 27. WILPF, an international organization founded by Jane Addams in 1915 and dedicated to promoting peace, had a

Pacific Historical Review, 76, no. 4 (November 2007), 575–584.

history of corresponding with individual women and women's organizations in both North and South Vietnam. Members of WILPF also had visited both nations during the long and destructive U.S. war in Southeast Asia (1965–1973). Consequently, even though the American travelers had only eight days to prepare for their journey and were not provided with a reason for their visit, WILPF accepted the invitation. Upon their arrival, the delegates from WILPF discovered that they were joined by "five women representing the Women's International Democratic Federation, one each from Argentina, Russia, India, France, and the Republic of Congo. To our knowledge, we were the only two visiting Americans in Hanoi for the signing of the Peace Accord," which formally ended direct U.S. military involvement in the war.

This story is provocative in and of itself. The popular narrative of the American antiwar movement has tended to focus on the theatrics of the 1960s generation, particularly the long-haired and militant young men who burned their draft cards and refused to fight. Yet, this account of international solidarity indicates that the only American friends present in Hanoi to celebrate the ending of the U.S. war in Vietnam were women. Furthermore, they were elderly women affiliated with an organization widely regarded by baby boomers as "out of touch." Compared to a younger generation of women who became politically active through the Civil Rights Movement, the New Left, and Women's Liberation, WILPF members were viewed as "traditional," upper-middle-class, and, of course, predominantly white. Consequently, the 1973 journey to Hanoi becomes even more intriguing in light of the fact that one of the travelers was a Japanese American woman named Marii Hasegawa. While previous antiwar delegations to Hanoi attempted to include non–whites, particularly African Americans, Hasegawa's presence was not just a token gesture: She was actually the president of the U.S. Section of WILPF and consequently at the helm of arguably the most historically significant women's peace organization of the twentieth century.

Unexpected historical actors like Marii Hasegawa, who formed political relationships across racial and national boundaries, play a large role in my current research. Her life raises questions about how the experience of travel fostered and solidified a sense of internationalism, a conviction of political solidarity, with Third World peoples and nations among U.S. activists of varying racial backgrounds. Because antiwar protesters tended to be suspicious of government-issued reports and mainstream media representations of the war, they sought alternative sources of information. Traveling outside the United States and learning from those who had direct experience with the war became valuable avenues for those seeking greater knowledge about the Vietnam War. Furthermore, these journeys facilitated international exchanges of ideas that I believe fundamentally shaped the political understanding, identities, and agendas of American travelers. The reports of what they perceived in turn nurtured an antiwar movement that eventually helped to end the U.S. war in Vietnam.

Studies of politics and travel like mine build on recent trends in Asian American history and contribute to the scholarship on social movements during the "long decade" of the 1960s in four major ways. First, they offer an international interpretation of the antiwar movement. Along with a variety of other fields, Asian American Studies has increasingly sought to emphasize and analyze the flows of people, ideas, and goods across national boundaries. This transnational turn serves as the foundation for my study, which highlights the travels of U.S. protesters not only to Hanoi but also to South Vietnam, Cambodia, North Korea, the People's Republic of China, Canada, and Europe. One of the goals is to go beyond an American-centered perspective by illuminating the intentions of Asian representatives in establishing contacts with U.S. activists. The relationships that developed between these two groups suggest that the Asian opponents of the American government actively cultivated connections with members of the U.S. citizenry as part of their strategy to end the war. The Americans who traveled outside of the United States did not have the formal authority of state-designated diplomats. However, they either represented significant social, political, or religious organizations and movements or had the ability to mobilize these sectors of American civil society politically. My project, for instance, builds on the efforts to internationalize the study of American history by portraying the antiwar movement in the United States as part of a global political dialogue. I do so by exploring the travels of Americans abroad as well as of Asians to Europe and North America.

While I am interested in understanding how people build connections across borders, I also analyze the partial representations and misconceptions of such encounters. In other words, I examine how Asian anticolonial liberation struggles held a sense of "romance" for American antiwar activists. Even as U.S. organizers sought the "truth" about the military and political conflicts in Southeast Asia, they tended to idealize Ho Chi Minh, the National Liberation Front, and socialist Asia more generally. I propose the concept of *radical Orientalism* to describe the phenomenon of American activists of the baby boom generation continuing the practice of cultivating visions of the "Orient" as the polar opposite of the Occident.

Edward Said conceptualized Orientalism as a system of knowledge that the West developed about the East as the Occident engaged in a colonizing project of the Orient. Within this framework, the East historically has served as a contrasting and, not coincidentally, inferior image to the West. This polarization not only created the Orient in the Occidental imagination but also defined the West to itself. Asian American historians and American Studies scholars have increasingly utilized the concept of Orientalism to examine the ways in which Americans perceive, imagine, and understand Asia, its culture, and its peoples. Under this rubric, studies of Asia and Asian Americans are not as easily marginalized within the broader field of U.S. history. Instead, these topics assume more central prominence in defining what it means to be an American.

Especially for the Gold War era, Christina Klein has revised Said's thesis to provide an interpretation of American Orientalism in the context of containment politics. She has argued that middle-brow culture emphasized the similarities between the East and West in order to distance the United States from an overtly imperialist project and to evoke a sense of integration and connectedness between America and its potential Asian allies. The activists who constitute the focus of my own study wanted instead to name U.S. imperialism and oppose its destructive reach. They also sought an identification and connection with Asia but specifically with revolutionary Asia. In order to critique the perceived corruption of Western society, they highlighted the differences between "radical" Asia and mainstream America. However, instead of denigrating the East, they sought inspiration *from* Asian countries and peoples.

While the formation of Third World internationalism (a conviction of political solidarity) might be perceived as being at odds with radical Orientalism (a romantic projection of revolutionary desire), I want to argue that these two phenomena are actually intertwined. The perceptions of the "Radical Orient" were not necessarily accurate or complete depictions of these dynamic societies undergoing complex political, military, and social changes. By serving as a source for alternative cultural and political values, however, these idealized depictions of revolutionary Asia assisted American activists in imagining the possibilities of new political identities and new ways of organizing society.

In studying Third World internationalism and radical Orientalism, my project also offers an analysis of relational racialization and coalition formation by examining how individuals of diverse backgrounds interacted and understood one another in the context of 1960s activism. While Asian American history has increasingly gained academic recognition and institutionalization, popular and academic understandings of "race" still tend to be conceived in black and white. I hope to challenge the predominant image of the antiwar cause as a "white" movement and also go beyond the usual binary paradigm for understanding American race relations. The 1960s and 1970s witnessed the emergence of a variety of racial liberation movements that shaped the political discourses about equality and justice. It is especially valuable to highlight and contextualize the role of Americans of Asian ancestry in these efforts. Just as African Americans organized and made public demands for civil rights, economic justice, and political power during the mid-1960s, the popular media and sociological studies constructed an image of Asians in the United States as "model minorities"—passive, non-complaining, but nevertheless successful individuals whose achievements stemmed not from protest but from hard work and strong family values. By the late 1960s, however, an Asian American movement had emerged, modeling itself on Black Power and drawing political inspiration from the national liberation struggles in Vietnam and socialist Asia more generally.

My own work seeks to understand how the antiwar movement fostered multiracial coalitions and connected domestic aspirations for racial justice with global critiques of imperialism. Recent efforts by Max Elbaum, Daryl Maeda, Laura Pulido, and Cynthia Young likewise reinterpret the period of the late 1960s and 1970s. Their works challenge the depiction of this era as one of fragmentation and decline, an interpretation that lauded the Civil Rights and early New Left movements as the high points of the 1960s. Instead, these authors point to the continued political ferment during the latter part of the decade with the emergence of a "Third World left." This formation developed mainly among people of color in the United States who were inspired by one another and by socialist movements in the Third World. I hope to contribute to this growing literature by examining the efforts to build multiracial and international antiwar coalitions before, during, and after the rise of racial liberation movements. This entails an exploration of political and personal relationships between white and nonwhite activists as well as within the category of Third World people.

Finally, gender analysis provides insight into the dynamics of international and multiracial interactions. The antiwar movement has commonly been represented as male-dominated. In fact, feminist scholars point to the chauvinism within these circles as a catalyst for the emergence of a separate women's liberation movement. I seek to examine the gender dynamics between men and women who worked together to critique American foreign policies in socialist Asia. Specifically, how did women and men experience their politically motivated travels differently, and how did romantic encounters and sexuality shape their understandings of cross-cultural contact? In addition, I also stress women's peace efforts that were more independently enacted from men. Female activists from a variety of organizations and movements traveled internationally to dialogue with their counterparts in decolonizing Asian countries. These exchanges provide an opportunity to examine the dynamics of an international and multiracial movement based on the ideal of a "global sisterhood."

This concept has been critiqued by various Third World and First World feminists for masking inequalities between women of different racial, national, and class backgrounds. Certainly some North American women during the Vietnam War exhibited a sense of condescension toward their Third World sisters. They condemned the repressive gender hierarchies that they described as characterizing traditional Asian societies. In addition, they highlighted the roles that First World women could perform in rescuing their less fortunate Third World sister. During the Vietnam War, however, North American women of varying racial backgrounds also exhibited a deep sense of admiration for their Asian "sisters." Through travel and correspondence, they learned to regard Third World female liberation fighters as exemplars of revolutionary womanhood. This admiration was in turn communicated to the broader antiwar movement through activist newspapers. Throughout the late 1960s and early 1970s, the figure of the Vietnamese female peasant was widely circulated. Frequently depicted with a baby in one hand and a rifle in the other, she served as one of the primary symbols of Third World resistance against the most powerful and technologically advanced nation in the world. Furthermore, Asian women served as role-models due to their positions of leadership, not only in the military and the family but also in the government and the workplace.

These idealized depictions of Asian revolutionary womanhood were central to the phenomenon that I have identified as *radical Orientalism*. These female warriors countered classical Orientalist depictions of exotic, sexualized, and victimized Asian women. Nevertheless, these radical portrayals tended to serve an Orientalist purpose by representing a contrasting image to Western women's critiques of gender roles in North American societies. The dichotomy between the oppression that they identified in the West and the revolutionary hope that they perceived in the East helped North American women to redefine their own identities and political goals.

In this study of travel and politics, Asian American subjects are both fore-grounded and contextualized. Americans of Asian ancestry constitute significant historical actors in an ensemble cast. Their political activism and importance are analyzed in relation to individuals of varying racial, ethnic, and national identities. To understand why Marii Hasegawa was in Hanoi at the signing of the Peace Accords necessitates a reinterpretation of the history of WILPF, which, according to Hasegawa, was "one of the few organizations which had passed a resolution against the concentration camps in which Japanese and their citizen children were held in WWII" by the U.S. government. To help support Japanese American internees seeking to resettle outside of the designated intern-ment zones on the West Coast, WILPF supported a hostel in Philadelphia where Hasegawa found a place to stay after she left camp.

In addition to this historical narrative that ties the history of Japanese Americans and hence domestic racialization to WILPF, I suspect that Hasegawa's participation in the organization also is connected to the group's international agenda related to nuclear weaponry. Like other women's peace organizations and eventually like Asian American movement organizations, WILPF sponsored annual commemorations of the bombing of Hiroshima and Nagasaki. They sought to raise awareness of the destructiveness of the atomic age and facilitated international dialogue and exchanges with Japanese women's peace organizations. These reminders of Asia and Asian bodies as the victims of American for-eign policy most likely facilitated the political involvement and leadership of Asian Americans and helped lay the basis for WILPF's eventual peace campaigns on behalf of Vietnam and Vietnamese people.

However, before Hasegawa arrived in Hanoi in 1973, she also expressed her concerns about social injustice in the American context. In 1969, at the annual meeting of the U.S. Section of WILPF held in Atlanta, Georgia, she successfully introduced a resolution on racism. She called on WILPF to study the "Black Manifesto," a statement issued by James Forman demanding repara-tions for African Americans due to the history of slavery and institutionalized racism. Hasegawa also asked WILPF as a peace organization to understand seri-ously the "rhetoric of violence of the oppressed," explaining that "if in answer we say, 'Let them do their own thing,' without scrutinizing our own role in the struggle, we are acting in a racist manner. We have to stop the rhetoric of violence from becoming reality." Her words and the support that her resolu-tion received from the predominantly white, "traditional," upper-middle-class, and elderly membership of WILPF indicate that the standard narrative of 1960s movements and of their "fragmentation" and "decline" during the late 1960s needs to be reexamined.

These intertwined stories of multiracial and international political formation center Asia and Asian America in the historical narrative of Cold War America. They illuminate the ways the circulation of people and knowledge across various boundaries shaped the political imagination and identities of diverse American activists. In Benedict Anderson's now famous phrase, the nation is an "imagined community," because "all communities larger than primordial villages of face-to-face contact … will never know most of their fellow-members.… yet in the minds of each lives the image of their communion." My study seeks to analyze how individuals who experienced moments of heightened nationalism imagined themselves as members of communities that crossed national boundaries. A study on travel provides the opportunity to analyze the face-to-face contacts that inspired the international expansion of political communion.

Protest Against the Model Minority Myth

ELLEN D. WU

By the twilight of the civil rights era, the success stories of Japanese and Chinese America had themselves become success stories. The cross pressures of exigencies and desires both within and beyond the ethnic communities had effectively midwifed the rebirth of the Asiatic as the model minority. Since then, the model minority has remained a fixture of the nation's racial landscape, ever present yet constantly evolving to speak to a host of new imperatives in the late twentieth century and early twenty-first. Recent iterations depart from the original in notable ways, but retain many of the themes that first coalesced in the postwar period: self-reliance, valorization of family, reverence for education, and political moderation. The persistence of these features suggests that the model minority's durability—like its origins—is about more than just race. Its longevity derives from its ability to adapt to changing historical circumstances. Far from being an outdated vestige of the mid-twentieth century, its periodic resuscitation effectively commands attention because of its flexibility and capaciousness, shape-shifting to respond to the nation's most pressing questions. The reproduction of the model minority as racial truth has posed new obstacles to freedom and equality for Americans from all walks of life. Yet it has also contained the seeds of its own critique, paradoxically serving as a rallying point for the formation of an innovative racial identity—Asian American—grounded in dreams of a different kind of world.

The mid- to late 1960s witnessed the convergence of the postwar trajectories of Japanese and Chinese American racialization. World War II had set the two peoples on distinct, albeit imbricating, paths; both were remade from indelible aliens into assimilating Others in the crucibles of racial liberalism, cultural conservatism, and global wars, although their respective transformations were occasioned by circumstances unique to each. While their merging into definitive not-blackness was neither predictable nor predetermined, it was also not without precedent. White Americans had historically been of divided mind about their samenesses and differences, acknowledging the inimitabilities of the Japanese and Chinese in their midst, while simultaneously conflating them as Orientals, the yellow peril, and aliens ineligible to citizenship. In hindsight,

The Color of Success: Asian Americans and the Origins of the Model Minority Myth (Princeton University Press, 2014), 242–258. Reprinted by permission.

the consolidation of the two into a single cluster of consummate colored citizens was in a sense a mid-1960s' update of an ingrained American Orientalism that held that all Asians really did look—and act—alike.

Subsequently, watchers tagged Japanese and Chinese Americans as model minorities in the same breath with greater frequency, as when the *Senior Scholastic* attributed their concurrent "reversal of fortunes" to a shared reverence for the family and "near-religious belief[s] in formal education as the best ladder for advancement." Cold War imperatives continued to frame these acclamatory portraits. Speaking before Honolulu's East-West Center in 1966, President Johnson noted that the "promise of Asians at home" boded well for "new surge of promise in Asia," especially Vietnam, to modernize under the tutelage of the United States.

Observers increasingly lumped the two together through their descriptions of a categorical not-blackness (and sometimes not-brownness). In myriad meditations about race in the United States, Japanese and Chinese Americans jointly assumed the position as exemplars of colored mobility. At times the comparison was implied, as when a *Chicago Tribune* reader mused, "There is *another* race that has been subjected to even greater prejudice and discrimination—the Asians." Yet through "quiet dignity," "hard work," and an "order of good citizenship higher than the average white," Asian children stayed in school, were not born out of wedlock, and did not grow up to become criminals or "create slums." More often, the contrast was explicit. Charting the many grievances of America's racial minorities, *Ebony* acknowledged that Orientals faced intermittent barriers in house and job hunting, but concluded that they were "more acceptable to white people" than Native Americans, Mexicans, Puerto Ricans, and blacks. *Pittsburgh Courier* columnist George Schuyler compared the greater economic vitality of the Chinese to his own African American community, provokingly noting, "They talk little, picket nobody, hold no mass meetings, denounce none." In *Beyond the Melting Pot,* one of the era's seminal studies of ethnicity in the United States, sociologist Nathan Glazer accentuated the sluggishness of Puerto Ricans' socioeconomic motility by juxtaposing them with Japanese and Chinese. Puertorriqueños' lack of the "more tightly knit and better integrated systems" as seen in Asian immigrant communities had hobbled their group advancement....

The easy cachet of model minority typecasting rested uncomfortably with many Japanese and Chinese Americans, however. Internal quarrels over such comparisons had brewed for years, reflecting a diversity of opinion about the best way to achieve racial equality. As the 1963 controversy over Imazeki's advice that blacks do some "soul searching" had shown, there was certainly no shortage of individuals who disagreed with the black freedom movement's emphasis on direct action....

But for all those who disapproved of the thrust of 1960s' civil rights activism, countless others felt a kinship with African Americans. Since World War II, numerous Japanese Americans had cultivated ties with blacks in solidarity against racial oppression. Individual community members devoted their energies to such causes as the Congress of Racial Equality and interracial Freedom Rides. Regional organizations including New York's Japanese American Committee for Democracy had made African American civil rights a top priority. On the national scene, JACL had stood at the forefront of this alliance in the postwar period, working with the NAACP on landmark civil rights cases (including *Shelley v. Kramer* [1948] and *Brown v. Board of Education* [1954]) and serving as the lone Asian American founding member of the Leadership Conference on Civil Rights lobbying coalition.

Chinese Americans cultivated fewer bonds to the African American civil rights establishment, turning most of their political attention to China politics, US–China relations, and immigration reform between the 1940s and mid-1960s. Local-level clashes over issues such as the integration of Chinatown's new public housing projects in San Francisco, boycotts of Chinese businesses for their hostile treatment of black customers or failure to hire black employees, and the punishing social costs of black–Chinese relationships in places like Mississippi's Delta region had also impeded sustained cooperation. Still, some championed African Americans' quest for freedom. San Francisco's *Chinese World* occasionally ran editorials supporting black civil rights activists. Journalist Gilbert Woo, a staunch critic of US race relations, steadily alerted readers of the *Chinese Pacific Weekly* to antiblack racism, including discriminatory behaviors perpetrated by the Chinese. "We must sympathize with and support the exceptional black struggle for equality. This is the only way, and we are duty bound to follow it," he insisted, praising Chinese clergy who had recently sided with black protesters. Others joining in such coalition-building efforts included San Francisco's Chinese American Democratic Club, which spearheaded a fund-raising drive for the NAACP in 1963. As club president Harry W. Low urged, "In the past decade, Chinese-Americans have gained many new civil rights. Many of these gains are the result of vigorous efforts on the part of Negro leadership.... The work of all racial minorities for equality continues."

These earlier rumblings erupted into the grassroots political mobilization known as the Asian American movement between the late 1960s and mid-1970s. Inspired by the era's militant struggles against racism and imperialism at home and abroad, thousands of participants nationwide spiritedly questioned existing arrangements of power and authority. They advanced alternative modes of community living through such diverse actions as opposition to the Vietnam War, worker organization, artistic production, and demanding affordable housing for the poor and elderly. Just as important, movement activists reenvisioned their own racialization as a significant facet of this "one struggle, many fronts." Embracing a new, pan-ethnic "Asian American" identity, they consciously rejected the model minority label as an insidious instantiation of the prevailing racist order. Amy Uyematsu expressed this view in her 1969 manifesto, "The Emergence of Yellow Power in America." In this call to arms, Uyematsu argued that Asians in the United States suffered from problems of "self-identity" by assuming the values and attitudes of the white middle class. She criticized Asians for their complicity in perpetuating racial oppression by "allow[ing] white America to hold up the 'successful' Oriental image before other minority groups as the model to emulate. White America justifies the blacks' position by showing that other non-whites—yellow people—have been able to 'adapt' to the system," she charged. The "Myth of Asian American Success," furthermore, harmed not only others but also themselves by glossing over continuing disparities between Asians and whites. Residents of urban "ghetto communities" remained vulnerable to poverty, tuberculosis, and social isolation. The time had come for the rise of "yellow political power" to address injustices "unique" to Asian Americans.

Uyematsu's dictum signaled the Asian American movement's turn away from racial liberalism and its attendant endorsement of US Cold War hegemony as the ideological grounds on which to claim full citizenship. "Today we question whether we want to accept or be accepted by a society whose values are corrupted by greed, who [sic] perpetuates racism, war, and oppression.... We question our 'success' when we see young Asian brothers and sisters getting strung out on drugs, getting busted, fighting each other, and even committing suicide," espoused the Asian American Student Alliance of California State University at Long Beach. Likewise, members of the University of California, Santa Cruz's Third World Political Alliance expressed skepticism about the possibility of unmitigated equality under an assimilationist paradigm: "[We] are allowed to succeed economically, academically, and socially—but only to a certain extent. By an unspoken but real consensus, Asian Americans have not been completely acceptable regardless of how long they have been in this country." Calling attention to Asian America's myriad problems, activists noted that even escape from the traditional inner-city enclaves—the very symbol of assimilation—had not guaranteed dignity and freedom. A feature on Nikkei [Japanese Americans] of Gardena, California, in *Gidra,* the movement's leading publication, drew a portrait of "middle class miseries" plaguing suburban youths, including alienation, an obsession with materialism, and psychological pressures to achieve—the combination of which had led to mounting drug use and suicide.

The movement's repudiation of the model minority and its assimilationist origins necessitated a critical reimagining of the relationship between Asian Americans and other communities of color. Believers deliberately inverted the trope of not-blackness and instead embraced affinities with African Americans, Native Americans, Chicanos, and Puerto Ricans, locating commonalities in their respective histories of exploitation as well as their shared desires for liberation and self-determination. Asian Americans throughout the country were greatly influenced by black thinkers such as Malcolm X and Franz Fanon, and backed an array of causes directly impacting "Third World" populations at home and abroad, ranging from antiprison work and Puerto Rican independence to indigenous sovereignty and especially ending the terrible brutalities in Vietnam. To be sure, cross-racial and transnational identifications were not unheralded. But the political framework within which these linkages were forged was original: Asian Americans made these connections as an integral part of their dual critique of US racism and imperialism in its various guises, including military interventions and anti-Communist nationalism. In connecting the plight of Asian Americans to other racial minorities in the United States and nonwhite peoples everywhere, they exposed the inextricable interdependencies of domestic and foreign structures of power during the era of Cold War liberalism.

Thus Asian American identity was constituted in significant part by the model minority, even if Asian Americans explicitly denounced the model minority's racist logic. While the model minority gave rise to novel modes of racial subordination, it also opened up new possibilities for racial justice by catalyzing the rise of an Asian American political consciousness. By refusing to allow themselves to be used in upholding the distinction between good and bad minorities, those who adopted an Asian American identity articulated a critique of white supremacy and imperial domination—an intent that was the precise opposite of the ideological work of the model minority.

Animated by these imperatives, one of the most enduring legacies of the movement was the creation and first-phase institutionalization of Asian American studies. Students at San Francisco State College struck in November 1968 to demand the rights of all "Third World" peoples to higher education as well as a curriculum that they considered relevant to their communities. Alongside peers of various races, Asian Americans pushed for open admissions, student control of the hiring process, and the implementation of ethnic studies courses. After five contentious and violent months, the students wrested a monumental, if partial, victory when administrators agreed to open the nation's first School of Ethnic Studies. Actions at other campuses soon followed. Demands for an Asian American Studies Center at the University of California, Los Angeles explicated the desire to generate scholarship that more accurately reflected Asian American realities. "Much has been written and said about the 'success' of the 'Orientals.'... But the real experiences of the Asians in this country ... have received no serious attention." By 1973, movement campaigns had resulted in the opening of Asian American studies courses and programs across the nation—no small victory. But although such programs managed to gain an institutional foothold, they were unable to banish completely the model minority from the nation's racial topography....

Model minority discourse of the late twentieth and early twenty-first centuries simultaneously resembles and revises its original, Cold War–era formulations. Once again, contemporary mass media and academicians buttress the gravity of the state's hand in shaping the construction of Asian America. Journalists have maintained their leading role in vivifying the model minority concept in popular thought. Television programs and periodicals have extolled "America's Super Minority" outpacing all others in the classroom and labor force. As with their midcentury progenitors, these updated versions of the nation's "greatest success story" have emphasized the causal role of Asian-Confucian culture, especially reverence for the family, in Asian American achievement. Social scientists, too, have continued to shore up these claims with their findings....

At a time of general unease about the decline of the United States' world stature, economic instability, and widening social inequalities, these anecdotes sustained the nation's mythology as a land of opportunity for all.

☕ FURTHER READING

Aguilar-San Juan, Karin ed. *The State of Asian America: Activism and Resistance in the 1990s* (1994).

Boggs, Grace Lee with Scott Kurashige. *The Next American Revolution: Sustainable Activism for the Twenty-First Century* (2011).

Bow, Leslie, ed. *Asian American Feminisms* (2013).

Chong, Kelly H. "Relevance of Race: Children and the Shifting Engagement with Racial/Ethnic Identity among Second-Generation Interracially Married Asian Americans," *Journal of Asian American Studies,* 16.2 (June 2013): 189–221.

Collier, Malcolm and Dan Gonzales, eds. *At 40, Asian American Studies at San Francisco State University* (2009).

Eng, David, and Alice Hom, eds. *Q & A: Queer in Asian America* (1998).

Espiritu, Yen Le. *Asian American Panethnicity: Bridging Institutions and Identities* (1992).

Fujino, Diane C. *Heartbeat of Struggle: The Revolutionary Life of Yuri Kochiyama* (2005).

Habal, Estella. *San Francisco's International Hotel: Mobilizing the Filipino American Community in the Anti-Eviction Movement* (2007).

Ho, Fred. *Legacy to Liberation: Politics and Culture of Revolutionary Asian/Pacific America* (2000).

Ho, Fred, and Bill V. Mullen, eds. *Afro Asia: Revolutionary Political and Cultural Connections between African Americans and Asian Americans* (2008).

Jun, Helen Heran. *Race for Citizenship: Black Orientalism and Asian Uplift from Pre-Emancipation to Neoliberal America* (2011).

Leong, Russell, ed. *Asian American Sexualities: Dimensions of the Gay and Lesbian Experience* (1996).

Lim-Hing, Shirley, ed. *The Very Inside: An Anthology of Writing by Asian and Pacific Island Lesbian and Bisexual Women* (1994).

Louie, Steve, and Glenn Omatsu, eds. *Asian Americans: The Movement and the Moment* (2001).

Mabalon, Dawn. *Little Manila Is in the Heart: The Making of a Filipina/o American Community in Stockton, CA* (2013).

Maeda, Daryl J. *Chains of Babylon: The Rise of Asian America* (2009).

———. *Rethinking the Asian American Movement* (2011).

Murphy-Shigematsu, Stephen. *When Half Is Whole: Multiethnic Asian American Identities* (2012).

Nemoto, Kumiko. "Intimacy, Desire, and the Construction of Self in Relationships between Asian American Women and White American Men," *Journal of Asian American Studies* 9.1 (2006): 27–54.

Nishime, Leilani. *Undercover Asian Multiracial Asian Americans in Visual Culture* (2014).

Osajima, Keith. "Asian Americans as the Model Minority: An Analysis of Popular Press in the 1960s and 1980s," in *Contemporary Asian America: A Multidisciplinary Reader,* eds. Min Zhous and James V. Gatewood (2000).

Umemoto, Karen. " 'On Strike': San Francisco State College Strike 1968–69: The Role of Asian American Students," *Amerasia Journal* 15.1 (1989): 3–41.

Wei, William. *The Asian American Movement* (1993).

Wu, Judy Tzu-Chun. *Radicals on the Road: Internationalism, Orientalism, and Feminism during the Vietnam Era* (2013).

Young, Cynthia A. *Soul Power: Culture, Radicalism, and the Making of a U.S. Third World Left* (2006).

CHAPTER 12

Post–1965 Immigration and

Asian America

The Immigration and Nationality Act of 1965 dramatically reshaped Asian American communities by allowing streams of new immigrants to enter the United States from countries throughout Asia. Also known as the Hart–Celler Reform Act, this legislation was part of a wider package of civil rights laws in the mid-1960s banning racial discrimination in voting, education, and other areas of public life. The landmark legislation abolished the 1924 national origins system that heavily favored northern Europeans and severely restricted Asian as well as southern and eastern European immigrants. The new immigration act set a quota of 170,000 immigrants from the Eastern Hemisphere, with no more than 20,000 from a single country, and a quota of 120,000 from the Western Hemisphere, without any country limitation. The law also established a preference system for family members of citizens and resident aliens as well as for individuals with educational or job skills needed in the United States.

The new legislation allowed Asian spouses, unmarried minor children, and parents of U.S. citizens to enter as nonquota immigrants without any numerical limits. Naturalization classes quickly filled with Asian immigrants who took the oath of citizenship and then sent for their relatives abroad. Policymakers never anticipated that large numbers of Asians and Latin Americans would use these family reunification provisions to swell the ranks of new immigrants. In the mid-1960s, citizens of Asian ancestry constituted only 0.5 percent of the U.S. population, but by 2010 they grew to 5.6 percent. New immigration fueled the growth of the Asian American population, which expanded from 490,000 in 1940 to 3.5 million in 1980, to 17.3 million in 2010. During the first decade of the twenty-first century, the Asian American population grew faster than any other racial group in the United States, although it remained much smaller than the country's African American or Hispanic populations. The dramatic increase in the number of Asian Americans resulted from immigration patterns that the architects of the 1965 immigration reform never envisioned.

Infusing new life into old ethnic enclaves, this wave of Asian immigrants also established new settlements and changed the ethnic composition of the Asian American population. Before the 1960s, most Asian immigrants were of Chinese, Japanese, or Filipino ancestry, although there were small communities of Korean and Indian immigrants. The arrival of large numbers of immigrants from the Philippines, Korea, China, and India after 1945, along with the influx of Southeast Asian refugees after 1975, made more apparent the remarkable ethnic diversity among Asian Americans. This diversity is matched by differentiation within ethnic groups based on generation, class, gender, sexual orientation, educational backgrounds, language skills, political views, and a multitude of other factors. Even generational status, once a useful category to distinguish the experiences of immigrants and their American-born children, now belies simple generalizations. Chinese immigrants now include politically conservative presidents of multinational corporations, radical gay activists with PhDs, and struggling day laborers. Indian immigrants own successful high tech companies, work as low-paid computer assemblers, and produce leading feminist scholarship. In the twenty-first century, the constant movement of capital, trade, technology, people, and ideas across countries and continents challenges any fixed notions of stable, homogenous ethnic identities.

Despite their differences from the older Asian American immigrants, the new Asian immigrants continued to experience devastating racial conflict. The most powerful example occurred in Los Angeles the week after four police officers were acquitted, on April 29, 1992, for using excessive force in the beating of Rodney King. Angry protesters looted or burned South Central Los Angeles and then went to Koreatown in Central Los Angeles and destroyed approximately 2,300 Korean-owned stores. After Korean radio programs called for volunteers to protect Korean stores that had been abandoned by the police, many armed Korean immigrants rushed to their defense, but in many cases they were too late. A week after the conflict, about 30,000 people joined a Koreatown peace march to clean up the area, denounce police violence, and mourn the death of Eddie Kim, who was mistaken for a looter and shot by Koreans.

DOCUMENTS

Documents 1 to 8 reveal how legislation and political, social, and economic relations between sending countries and the United States shape post-1965 Asian immigration. Document 1 excerpts the Immigration and Nationality Act of 1965, which replaced the national origins quota system with a seven-category system of preferences and sparked a new wave of immigration from Asia.

Documents 2 to 4 recount examples of conflict and cooperation between Asian Americans and other racial groups as new immigrants settled in the United States. In Document 2, Korean Americans commemorate the twentieth anniversary of Sa-I-Gu (four-two-nine or April 29), also known as the Los Angeles riots and Los Angeles uprising, by remembering the devastation to Korean-owned businesses. Document 3 describes how Asian American and Latino American politicians have collaborated to develop training programs to help college students and young professionals become community leaders and strengthen cross-racial alliances. Document 4 presents the Oak Park Tenants Association in Oakland, California, as a model of multiethnic and religious organizing.

Documents 5 to 8 examine Asian immigrant experiences. Document 5 describes how Indian immigrants and their family members own and run about half of all motels in the United States. Using personal networks to become ethnic entrepreneurs, many try to hide their role in the business by employing white staff to interact with customers. They also conceal evidence that they cook and live in the motels. In Document 6, Filipino American and Pulitzer Prize–winning journalist Jose Antonio Vargas testifies before the Senate Judiciary Committee about his life as an undocumented immigrant and urges support for the DREAM Act to provide undocumented immigrants with a path to citizenship through education or military service. Document 7 examines the "brain drain" from Asian countries—caused by the outmigration of highly educated workers—as an asset rather than a liability for developing nations. Menderes Candan and Uwe Unger note that, since the 1990s, increasing numbers of educated professionals from India have invested in their homeland and provided a "brain gain," especially in the information technology industry. The article notes how high immigrant return rates, large remittances, and technology transfers have helped the economies of Korea, the Philippines, China, and Taiwan. Document 8, by a coalition of Asian American and Pacific Islander civil rights and higher education groups, calls for support of affirmative action. Denouncing the model minority myth, the coalition argues that many educationally disadvantaged Filipino, Southeast Asian, and Pacific Islander students could benefit from affirmative action and that all students benefit from diversity in the classroom.

1. The Immigration and Nationality Act Repeals Discriminatory Policies Toward Asian Immigrants, 1965

Be it enacted by the Senate and House of Representatives of the United States of America in Congress assembled, That section 201 of the Immigration and Nationality Act ... be amended to read as follows:

Sec. 201. (a) Exclusive of special immigrants defined in section 101 (a) (27), and of the immediate relatives of United States citizens specified in subsection (b) of this section, the number of aliens who may be issued immigrant visas or who may otherwise acquire the status of an alien lawfully admitted to the United States for permanent residence, or who may, pursuant to section 203 (a) (7) enter conditionally, (i) shall not in any of the first three quarters of any fiscal year exceed a total of 45,000 and (ii) shall not in any fiscal year exceed a total of 170,000.

(b) The "immediate relatives" referred to in subsection (a) of this section will mean the children, spouses, and parents of a citizen of the United States: *Provided,* That in the case of parents, such citizen must be at least twenty-one years of age....

From Immigration and Nationality Act of October 3, 1965, 79 Stat. 911.

Sec. 2. Section 202 of the Immigration and Nationality Act ... is amended to read as follows:

(a) No person shall receive any preference or priority or be discriminated against in the issuance of an immigrant visa because of his race, sex, nationality, place of birth, or place of residence, except as specifically provided in section 101 (a) (27), section 201 (b), and section 203: *Provided,* That the total number of immigrant visas and the number of conditional entries made available to natives of any single foreign state... shall not exceed 20,000 in any fiscal year....

(b) ... For the purposes of this Act the foreign state to which an immigrant is chargeable shall be determined by birth within such foreign state....

Sec. 3. Sec. 203 of the Immigration and Nationality Act ... is amended as follows:
Sec. 203 (a) Aliens who are subject to the numerical limitations ... shall be allotted visas or their conditional entry authorized, as the case may be, as follows:

(1) Visas shall be first made available, in a number not to exceed 20 per centum [one hundred] of the number specified in section 201 (a) (ii), to qualified immigrants who are the unmarried sons or daughters of citizens of the United States.

(2) Visas shall next be made available, in a number not to exceed 20 per centum of the number specified in section 201 (a) (ii), plus visas not required to be classes specified in paragraph (1), to qualified immigrants who are spouses, unmarried sons or unmarried daughters of an alien admitted for permanent residence.

(3) Visas shall next be made available, in a number not to exceed 10 per centum ... to qualified immigrants who are members of the professions, or who because of their exceptional ability in the sciences or arts will substantially benefit prospectively the national economy, cultural interests, or welfare of the United States.

(4) Visas shall next be made available, in a number not to exceed 10 per centum ... to qualified immigrants who are the married sons or married daughters of citizens of the United States.

(5) Visas shall next be made available, in a number not to exceed 24 per centum ... to qualified immigrants who are the brothers or sisters of citizens of the United States.

(6) Visas shall next be made available, in a number not to exceed 10 per centum of the number specified ... to qualified immigrants who are capable of performing specified skilled or unskilled labor, not of a temporary or seasonal nature, for which a shortage of employable and willing persons exists in the United States.

(7) Conditional entries shall next be made available by the Attorney General, pursuant to such regulations as he may prescribe and in a number not to exceed 6 per centum ... to aliens who satisfy an Immigration and Naturalization Service officer at an examination in any non-Communist or non-Communist-dominated country, (A) that (i) because of persecution or fear of persecution on account of race, religion, or political opinion they have fled (I) from any Communist or Communist-dominated country or area, or (II) from any

country within the general area of the Middle East, and (ii) are unable or unwilling to return to such country or area on account of race, religion, or political opinion, and (iii) are not nationals of the countries or areas in which their application for conditional entry is made; or (B) that they are persons uprooted by catastrophic natural calamity as defined by the President who are unable to return to their usual place of abode.

2. Korean Americans Describe the Los Angeles Riots, 1992 (2012)

The events of April 29, 1992, have been referred to as a riot, a rebellion, an uprising, a civil unrest. For many Koreans, it's always been 4.29, following the standard cultural shorthand for the dates of historic tragedies. Yet over the past 20 years, the primary narrative of 4.29 has rarely included Korean American perspectives beyond stereotyped notions of victims or vigilantes. This oral history seeks to rectify that in some small measure, and to give those who didn't witness the traumatic days and nights of fires, chaos and violence a sense of what Korean Americans went through. The events, after all, have been referred to by some as the birth of Korean America, a characterization that isn't far off.

In the period leading up to 4.29, the mainstream media had fed the public a series of stories on the rising tensions in South Central Los Angeles between African American residents and the Korean merchant class that had become a fixture there. Then, in March 1991, Soon Ja Du, a Korean immigrant store-owner, shot and killed Latasha Harlins, a 15-year-old African American customer, following a violent scuffle between the two at Du's South Central liquor store, worsening an already strained situation. Just 13 days earlier, the brutal beating of African American motorist Rodney King by four white Los Angeles Police Department [LAPD] officers vividly demonstrated the iron-fisted tactics under then-Chief Daryl Gates. The social, economic and political structures seemed aligned to oppress, and the city waited uneasily on April 29, 1992, for the verdict in the excessive force case against the police officers who beat King.

(Editor's Note: The titles of subjects in the narrative reflect their age and status in April 1992. Organization names are based on what they were called in 1992. *Quotes indicated by asterisks were translated from Korean.)

April 29, Wednesday

I. RIPE TO EXPLODE

JET LEE

Owner of a liquor store in Compton

In everybody's mind, it was ripe. To be explode. [My customers] were telling me, "Be careful." One of my customers came [the] day before 4.29 and said,

---

Eugene Yi, "LA Riots, in Our Own Words," *KoreAm*, April 29, 2012. Reprinted by permission.

"Don't stay open too late tomorrow. And listen to the radio, what they gonna say about the verdict."

RAPHAEL HONG
UCLA student

Even before the verdicts came out, some younger blacks were coming in [to my parents' toy store in an Inglewood swap meet] and saying, [if the LAPD officers are found not guilty,] "You guys better leave this town or else you guys are going to be in trouble." Everybody [in my family] was already tense and kind of worried, so what they did was close the doors early, and they went home....

II. ACQUITTED

At 3:15 p.m., three of the LAPD officers were acquitted, and one was partially acquitted. Unruly crowds chanted "No justice, no peace!" around Parker Center, LAPD's head-quarters, as well as the courthouse where the verdict was issued, and the intersection of Florence and Normandie, in South Central Los Angeles. Violence erupted. Mobs dragged motorists out of their cars and beat them. Looting began.

JAY LEE★

Owner of a furniture store on Florence and Normandie [Avenue]
[Crowds swarmed his store, and he hid in the attic with his co-workers.]
   They broke glass table tops, carried off ensembles, capped off gunshots. I could see it all from my vantage point.... It was incredible. I told [my wife] to close up [her clothing] shop and go home. "Call the police and tell them we are trapped.".... We hid for three hours while people laughed and stole and rioted. That whole time, I kept thinking the police were coming.

HYUNGWON KANG
Photographer, *Los Angeles Times,* South Bay bureau

I distinctly remember hearing the LAPD police scanner telling all LAPD patrol vehicles to evacuate the intersection of Florence and Normandie. They were no longer engaged in controlling or restoring order. They were ordering their offi-cers to evacuate for their own safety.

JET LEE
Compton merchant

When I heard that the verdict [was] not guilty, I said, "Shit." Excuse my language, that's exactly what I said. I had a kind of fear it might happen like this. I called all my relatives to get the hell out of there. I closed my store down, and on the way home, I heard the news that [at] Normandie and Florence, [an] incident was going on.

HYUNGWON KANG
Photographer

Someone hit my right rear window with a beer bottle. I was on Florence, going eastbound. The intersection was messy with debris rioters threw on the pavement. Shortly afterwards, other people on the sidewalk also started walking towards my car. As I was pulling away from the intersection, there was a call for help on the company radio—[*Times* photographer] Kirk McCoy was stranded, away from his car.

After receiving Kirk's location from [photographer] Bob Chamberlin, I had to re-enter the intersection to get to Kirk.

Looters were all over the road, blocking moving traffic and carrying boxes of liquor from the liquor store at the intersection. My car was again struck with beer bottles, two or three times. One looter pointed a finger at me and started chasing me. I drove on the opposite side of the road, went through the red light and outran the guy....

RAPHAEL HONG
UCLA Student

I'm [in my apartment] watching the news. My parents are watching at [their] home, and we were just communicating over the phone. Helicopters are flying over, and you see the burning buildings [on TV]. They flew by our [swap meet] building, you know, and, oh my God. That's the swap meet. Some guy came, like a year before, and painted all the items that they sell in the swap meet. It says, "Inglewood Swap Meet," and there was a hat, a jacket and toys and all kinds of stuff painted on there. I knew that was our building because of the painted walls. My parents kind of went into shock. They saw the building, and they lost everything. My father wanted to go to the store, and I said, "No way. Don't get out of the house. Stay where you are. Don't even go near L.A.".…

RICHARD CHOI

[Kee Whan Ha] said, "You keep telling people to flee, to go home, but how can we leave Koreatown? We came to this country and we worked like crazy and we made this town, our town. But if we leave, they're going to burn it down. Don't we have to protect our town? Can't you say that on the radio?" And he offered to show us around so we could see what was going on. I couldn't leave because I had to stay on the air, but Jang-hee Lee went out with Ha. And Lee came back and told Ha, "You're right."

KEE WHAN HA

So I went on radio, and I said, "Don't go home. Protect your business. Your business is your life. All your rifles. All your weapons, bring everything out."…

HYUNGWON KANG
Photographer

California Market on 4th and Western was under attack. When I went there, I saw the owner of the shop with his semi-automatic pistol shooting into the air to fend off potential looters who were throwing Molotov cocktails to burn some of the shops. On 6th and Western—that shopping mall was already being torched. This California Market was trying to survive that attack. That's when I realized that Korean Americans were being targeted....

JAMES KANG

They were shooting to kill us. They didn't have the right to shoot to kill, even if we were looters. We weren't on their premises. We were about 30 yards away. If we were any closer, we would have all died ... The gunfire wouldn't stop. There was no place to hide ... It was the most painful feeling ... The hole I got shot in was the size of a silver dollar. I could stick three fingers in it. ... Koreans in [a passing] car and we were making eye contact. Eddie and I were trying to ask for help. But I couldn't talk, make a sound because my mouth was so dry ... They were so close to us, but they just left. I wish I could have gotten down their license plate numbers. Since the time Eddie got shot at, he was alive for another 30 minutes. He was a fighter, he didn't want to die. I know Eddie. You could tell he was fighting for his life ... All I remember is going into the emergency room and seeing all the lights. I was then knocked out.

Eddie Lee became the sole Korean American fatality of the riots.

3. Latinos and Asian Americans Form Political Alliances in San Jose, 2006

One emigrated from Hong Kong, the other from Jalisco. One led an upscale, high-tech South Bay community, the other a working-class town.

But former Cupertino Mayor Michael Chang and current East Palo Alto Mayor Ruben Abrica have much in common when it comes to leadership, including that their election to local government reflected major demographic shifts in their respective suburban communities.

Now the two, both faculty members at De Anza College, are teaching a new leadership training program through the **Asian Pacific American Leadership Institute**, known as APALI, that targets Latinos as well as Asian-Americans.

It is the first known official collaboration between the South Bay's two largest ethnic groups, which make up two-thirds of the valley's population but far fewer of its officials. Chang and Abrica personify the rapid growth and change in both communities as immigrants who—in less than a generation—became elected leaders.

"What's innovative and cutting edge is nurturing Asian-American and Latino leaders together to prepare them for leading very diverse populations," said Chang, 49, who founded APALI in 1997. "It goes to the heart of a multicultural democracy."

The De Anza-based Civic Leadership for Community Empowerment, a 10-week seminar that will start next Jan. 10, is designed to prepare Asian and Latino young professionals and college students for leadership posts in non-profit organizations, appointed boards and commissions, and elected office.

Building bridges

More important, it aims to fortify ties between two groups around issues both care about, such as anti-immigration or English-only movements. It also can

Katherine Corcoran, "Two Cultures, One Goal: Leadership; Latino and Asian-American Officials Join to Promote Political Participation," *San Jose Mercury News*, July 19, 2006. Reprinted by permission.

help build bridges in areas where they might be at odds, including affirmative action and allocation of public school resources.

"In politics there is always conflict," said Abrica, 57, who teaches Chicano studies. "If you establish one-on-one, personal relationships, you can call on each other to help mediate."

The two groups have connected around specific issues in the past, going back to the days when Cesar Chavez worked with Filipino-Americans in organizing farmworkers. The Asian Pacific American Institute for Congressional Studies and the National Association for Elected Latino Officials have arranged joint leadership training.

And there are countless local political links. U.S. Rep. Mike Honda, D-Campbell, is an Asian-American who speaks Spanish and maintains strong ties with the Latino community, while Margaret Abe-Koga, an Asian-American candidate for Mountain View City Council, joined the Latino community group, Mesa de la Comunidad, in that city last year.

"This reflects what's really new in ethnic politics, say, in the last 10 years," said Louis DiSipio, professor of Chicano/Latino studies at University of California-Irvine. "It's a building of the base beyond national origin, the first step, and pan-ethnic, such as Asian, the next step, to now coming up with common voices across ethnic groups."

The new program marks an expansion at APALI, which already offers a youth leadership academy, public service training and a Senior Fellows program for Asian-Americans.

Chang was elected in 1997 as the first Asian-American mayor of Cupertino, a town that has moved from majority white to roughly half Asian during the past 20 years. Abrica is the first Latino mayor of East Palo Alto, which moved from majority black to majority Latino in roughly the same period.

The dynamics of integrating the old and new power structures have been virtually the same in the two cities, even though they differ in income and education levels.

Bones of contention

In Cupertino, white and Asian residents have sparred over issues from Chinese-language signs on businesses to putting an Asian donor's name on a public library. In East Palo Alto, black and Latino residents have split along racial lines over board appointments and affordable-housing slots. Asian and Latino immigrants in both communities have been criticized for not getting involved in their neighborhoods or schools.

"There's a misunderstanding between immigrants and institutions," Abrica said. "Immigrant communities participate, but they're under the radar. They're not recognized."

The challenge for APALI to expand to Latinos was originally put out by advisory board member Hsing Kung, a high-tech entrepreneur and community leader known as a bridge-builder in Silicon Valley. "It makes sense," said James Lai, a Santa Clara University political-science professor. "If you work together, people don't see everything as a zero-sum game: 'If we win, you lose.' It's key to the future of California politics."

Kung's idea "took some time to process," said Chang. But ultimately, said Mae Lee, APALI associate director for leadership training, "When we had the conversation philosophically and in the spirit of what APALI has always done, which is work with underrepresented communities, there was no reason why it didn't make sense."

The program will include speakers, networking, field trips and history and case studies in the two communities. Chang said the program is open to people of any ethnic background who want to learn more about issues in Latino and Asian communities.

At a community meeting last week, Chang invited civic groups, such as Foro Latino and Asian Americans for Community Involvement, to De Anza to introduce the concept and encourage them to enroll candidates.

The commonalities poured forth with little effort.

Tamon Norimoto, who was promoting First Thursdays, a monthly forum for Asian-American concerns, discovered Foro Latino does the same for the Latino community.

The July topic for both groups: immigration.

Norimoto, of the Japanese American Citizens League, and Abrica, a founder of Foro Latino, perked up at the coincidence.

"How do you pronounce your first name?" Abrica asked Norimoto by way of introduction.

"Tah-MONE. Like *jamon* with a 'T,' "Norimoto replied—using the Spanish word for "ham."

4. The California Health Report Talks with Families About Faith-based, Multiethnic Tenant Organizing in Oak Park, 2007

In the past three years, two bullets shattered the front window, a teenager was shot just outside and the downstairs neighbor was mugged. Before that, a woman's lifeless body was unearthed from a trash bin less than a block away.

But that part of East Oakland—where the neighborhoods of Fruitvale and San Antonio meet—is where Dr. Joan Jie-eun Jeung has chosen to live with her husband and their 6-year-old son.

"I just can't imagine living anywhere else," the 39-year-old pediatrician said. "Once I became a mother, I struggled with it.... We know we're putting our son in harm's way and wonder if he'll forgive us.... Some members of our church told us they'd be out of here if they could, and they don't understand why we choose to live here."

Their home is where 25 percent of the population lives below the poverty line and barely 50 percent of the adults graduated from high school. There are

"Christian Activists Show Faith in East Oakland" by Hillary Abramson. Retrieved from http://www.sfgate.com. Also Russell Jeung, "Faith-based, Multiethnic Tenant Organizing: The Oak Park Story," ed. Pierrette Hondagneu-Sotelo, *Religion and Social Justice for Immigrants* (Rutgers, 2007), 59–73. Reprinted by permission.

people who only go outside in daylight. But with more than 40 percent of the residents foreign-born, the community has African American, Latino and Tongan churches, Southeast-Asian American shopkeepers and European Americans.

This community is what Joan (pronounced Jo-ANNE) Jeung and her husband, Russell Jeung, 47, a professor at San Francisco State University, crave.

UCSF Med School Grad

She graduated from UCSF School of Medicine, earned a master's degree in social medicine from UC Berkeley and a bachelor's degree from Harvard. He received his education at Harvard, Stanford and UC Berkeley. But the last thing they want for their son is a sense of entitlement....

The Jeungs are joined by other educated and employed parents who helped establish New Hope Covenant Church. A storefront church, it has activist roots in the neighborhood dating back to the 1980s.

"We're all asking what it means to be a good neighbor," said Joan Jeung, who is Korean American. "If you want to say you care about community, you have to share in the good and the bad."

Good happens for them every Sunday morning, where an average of 45 adults and children come together in a large meeting room at the offices of the Youth Employment Partnership on International Boulevard.

The congregation has included social workers, high school dropouts, Ph.D.s, ex-gangsters, teachers, refugees from Southeast Asia and Latin America, and "refugees from the suburbs" who, as Joan Jeung puts it, "are looking for a more radical and meaningful life."

Unable to find an evangelical Christian service like it, many of them drive there from other neighborhoods.

There is Dan Schmitz, 48, lay pastor of the congregation, who remembers calling his hometown—Burlingame—"Boringame" because "nothing happened there," he said. His father was an engineer at Bechtel Corp. They were Catholics, he said, "who talked about the poor when we went to church but there weren't any poor people around."

Getting Apartments Fixed

There is Carlos Flores, 39, a health educator at nearby La Clinica de la Raza, who grew up in "a somewhat privileged home" in San Jose and graduated from UC Berkeley with a political science degree.

Among others, including two Jeung house roommates who work in public-interest law and a Christian ministry, there is a commitment to this neighborhood that spans 15 years. It started with Schmitz, Russell Jeung and Flores living with Cambodian and Latino families in the Fruitvale Oak Park Apartments, where the landlord ignored raw sewage floods, leaky roofs, infestations of vermin and mold.

With a slew of attorneys, the tenants organized the others to file a lawsuit. In 2000, 45 resident families shared a $1 million settlement. The apartments were rebuilt, and the church transformed the crack house facing the apartments into a preschool.

Schmitz was the first non-refugee resident and only white person. Then came Russell Jeung, who moved into the apartments to study Asian youth gangs for his master's thesis in sociology and helped organize tenants against drug dealers. Joan Jie-eun moved into the neighborhood in 1999 and joined them tutoring, mentoring, cooking, praying and founding New Hope.

At first, Tracy Saephan viewed her neighbors as outsiders. Born in Thailand, she was raised and lived in the East Oakland neighborhood most of her life.

"I was young when I met them but I wondered what they wanted, what their ongoing commitment was," said Saephan, 33. "Long term was five years to me, and I wondered if they were in it for the short term. A lot of us who grew up in the neighborhood were exposed to things to make money, like gangs, prostitution, drugs—easy stuff. For me, it was OK to have sex before marriage, not like what we want now for our children. We were surviving, not knowing what doing 'the right thing' was.

"It didn't take that long to see that this group came in full of mercy for the community," she said. "You could feel their generosity. We started meeting at individuals' homes. Maybe there were 10 or 12 of us. They had the heart to bring us together. In time, there was such a big transformation with the Oak Park Apartments that it was clear they weren't outsiders any more. They wanted to be with us. They were gifts to the neighborhood."

Today, Saephan lives with her husband and three children near Dimond Park in East Oakland's foothills. She sells real estate and her husband runs a company that sweeps parking lots at night. On the church board of directors, she prays with her old neighborhood friends every Sunday.

Accepted as Neighbors

Neighbors who are neither religious nor members of New Hope Covenant Church also accepted the Jeungs and their educated friends, according to Tane Oubkeo. Born in Thailand, the unemployed auto mechanic lived in the neighborhood since he was 5.

"After people experienced the incredible change with Oak Park, they accepted them as neighbors," said Oubkeo, 28. "Before Russell and Joan, you wouldn't see white people walking around and saying 'Hi' to neighbors. Today, it's more of a reality. There's a block party every year, and you can tell that that the founders of New Hope are neighbors, like everyone else."

Before he met his wife and started attending the church, Oubkeo said, he was a teenager involved in "drug dealing, gang banging, robbing, stealing cars." He could have lost his life "maybe five or six times," he said. He witnessed a friend get shot in the head.

These days, Oubkeo lives near Lake Merritt with his wife, Keo Kong, who grew up in the Oak Park Apartments, and their infant son and 5-year-old daughter. They visit her parents often in the neighborhood and attend the church every Sunday.

The Christian activists turn the tables on the stereotype that configures an Ivy League education into a formula for fame and fortune.

5. Pawan Dhingra Describes Indian Motel Owners' Life Behind the Lobby, 2012

Nothing could be more American than road trips and motels. It's also true, though less widely known, that the owners and operators of about half of all motels in the United States are immigrants from India (or their descendants). "Chances are that anyone who has stayed in motels in the last decade has stayed in at least one owned by an Indian American," writes sociologist Pawan Dhingra in his new book "Life Behind the Lobby" out this month from Stanford University Press.

The total number of motel rooms owned by Indian Americans is nearly two million, with property values exceeding $100 billion. The vast majority of these motel owners come from the same Indian state, Gujarat. Even more remarkably, 70 percent of them share the same surname, Patel—an extremely common name in India—though they are not all related.

This dominance of the motel business by Indian Americans has been viewed as a characteristically American success story—the American dream realized. The neoliberal state theorizes entrepreneurs as ideal citizens, as Dhingra points out in the introduction to his book, since they are self-reliant workers who expect little or no help from the government. But the brightly shining rhetoric conceals a less sunny reality, since Indian American motel owners are also viewed as second-class citizens, subject to racial and cultural prejudice that sometimes translates into real inequality. (Indian American owners are concentrated in the bottom half of the industry, in lower- and mid-budget motels.)

"There are two schools of thought about ethnic entrepreneurs," Dhingra says. "Ethnic entrepreneurship is a difficult road, but it does lead to mobility, and it's basically a pathway for a group to uplift itself from difficult conditions. Others argue that ethnic entrepreneurship actually is a subtle form of exploitation—it's the long hours; it's the low wages; it's the need for family resources. Those are the two schools of thought. So where does this population fit in?"

The success of Indian Americans moteliers is, in fact, downright staggering. They came to this country with little knowledge of the motel industry, and yet have come to dominate a quintessentially American business. Yet it's also true that the recession has hit motel owners hard, especially those at the lower end of the industry, who often don't have the financial resources necessary to weather the storm.

Rather than locating them in either mainstream or margin, Dhingra sees them as the "margins in the mainstream," he says. "All that success is real in many ways, and you don't want to take away from what they've done. You don't want to emphasize their problems and take away from their success. The success is real. But they've been successful because they've learned ways to manage the problems they keep encountering, and the way they

Greg Varner, "How a Staple of Americana Became the Indian American Dream," *Colorlines*, April 27, 2012. Reprinted with permission of RaceForward.org, publisher of Colorlines.com.

manage the problems is not necessarily helping to overcome them." Asked for examples of some of the ways Indian American motel owners might purchase short-term convenience at the cost of long-term gain, Dhingra doesn't hesitate.

"For those who can afford to hire staff," he says, "what staff they hire, and for what hours, to do what jobs, is a very strategic decision. This is not universal, but often they will hire whites to be their desk clerks during check-in hours in the afternoon. That way, when someone comes to their motel, the visitor won't know that it's owned by an Indian. This is one of the subtle ways that they diffuse any possible tension. They're not ashamed of being owners, but why draw attention to it? Why create possible problems?"

Dhingra's empathy for the motel owners he has interviewed is obvious in the easy way he begins to speak in their words, whether quoting directly or simply imagining himself in their shoes. "The visitor who comes in may still stay at our hotel if they see us behind the desk," he says, "but you don't want to give them any kind of negative impression, because then they'll start looking for problems. You want to avoid any of that and just have as non-foreign a motel as you can. That strategic decision about who they hire helps them in the business. It also reenforces this notion of whiteness as better than brownness. It reenforces the hierarchy. The success is real, but so are the hierarchies they've got to navigate. Both of these narratives work together."

Many owners live in their motels, especially in the low-budget, independent places, which helps save money on rent but complicates their domestic life.

"They may cook their Indian food at a different time of day than they want to, so that the smell of Indian food doesn't permeate the lobby and make people wonder what's going on," Dhingra says. Again, the awareness that what the customer expects to see may not be in sync with who they are racially and culturally prompts some motel owners to place self-imposed constraints on their identity. Not surprisingly, Indian American motel owners have banded together to form a lobby group, the Asian American Hotel Owners Association (AAHOA), which Dhingra explains has virtually all-Indian membership. To give two examples of its official positions, it is pro-immigration but against increasing the minimum wage.

In "Life Behind the Lobby," Dhingra, who was born in India but grew up in the U.S., tells how Indian Americans came to dominate the motel business. First, an undocumented immigrant from Gujarat leased a residential hotel—organized along the lines of a contemporary youth hostel, with shared bathrooms and so on—in San Francisco in the 1940s. From that small beginning, an empire has grown. While it would be an exaggeration to say it all sprang from a single person, Dhingra explains how this unlikely empire arose, mostly having to do with personal networks and the professional opportunities that did—or did not—present themselves.

"Back in the 1940s, motels were not as common. Around 1946, some Gujaratis came in and this guy was already here in San Francisco, who had sent letters home. Social networks play a huge role. A Gujarati moves to the U.S. and he can choose any business, but will go into motels. Why? Because he knows people in the business who can help him out. The sense of community facilitates his entry into that business. He owns a motel, and he works there with his wife and kids, and then his relatives come over, work with him and live with him. They save a lot of money that way, and will then purchase their own motel. And they'll bring other family members, and then five years later, the same thing happens again."

Another factor, Dhingra explains, is a cultural preference for self-control in the workplace. This may spring, in part, from the experience of generations of farmers in Gujarat, who became accustomed to working for themselves. They like the sense of security in controlling their own fate, and being able to grow as much as they want to grow.

6. Pulitzer Prize Winner and Undocumented Immigrant Jose Antonio Vargas Refuses to Leave the United States, 2012

Thank you Chairman [Patrick] Leahy, Ranking Member [Charles] Grassley, and distinguished members of this Committee.

I come to you as one of our country's 11 million undocumented immigrants, many of us Americans at heart, but without the right papers to show for it. Too often, we're treated as abstractions, faceless and nameless, subjects of debate rather than individuals with families, hopes, fears, and dreams.

I am in America because of the sacrifices of my family. My grandparents legally emigrated from the Philippines to Silicon Valley in the mid 1980s. A few years later, Grandpa Teofilo became a U.S. citizen and legally changed his name to Ted after Ted Danson in "Cheers." Because grandparents cannot petition for their grandkids and because my mother could not come to the United States, grandpa saved up money to get his only grandson, me, a passport and green card to come to America. My mother gave me up to give me a better life.

I arrived in Mountain View, Calif. on August 3, 1993. One of my earliest memories was singing the National Anthem as a 6th grader at Crittenden Middle School, believing the song had somehow something to do with me. I thought the first lines were, "Jose, can you see?"

Four years later, I applied for a driver's permit like any 16 year old. That was when I discovered that the green card that my grandpa gave me was fake.

But I wanted to work. I wanted to contribute to a country that is now my home. At age 17, I decided to be a journalist for a seemingly naive reason: if I am not supposed to be in America because I don't have the right kind of papers, what if my name, my byline, was on the paper? How can they say I don't exist if my name is in newspapers and magazines? I thought I could write my way into America.

As I built a successful career as a journalist, paying Social Security and state and federal taxes along the way, as fear and shame, as denial and pain, enveloped

---

Senate Judiciary Commission Testimony: Jose Antonio Vargas.

me, words became my salvation. I found solace in the words of the Rev. Martin Luther King, quoting St. Augustine: "An unjust law is no law at all."

Ultimately, it took me 12 years to come out as an undocumented American because that is what I am, an American. But I am grateful to have been able to tell the truth. And in the past few years, more undocumented people, particularly young DREAMers, are coming out. Telling the truth about the America we experience.

We dream of a path to citizenship so we can actively participate in our American democracy. We dream of not being separated from our families and our loved ones, regardless of sexual orientation, no matter our skill set. This government has deported more than 1.6 million people, fathers and mothers, sons and daughters, in the past four years.

We dream of contributing to the country we call our home.

In 21st century America, diversity is destiny. That I happen to be gay; that I speak Tagalog, my first language, and want to learn Spanish, that does not threaten my love for this country. How interconnected and integrated we are as Americans makes us stronger.

Sitting behind me today is my Filipino American family, my grandma Leonila, whom I love very much; my Aunt Aida Rivera, who helped raised me; and my Uncle Conrad Salinas, who served, proudly, in the U.S. Navy for 20 years. They're all naturalized American citizens.

I belong in what is called a mixed status family. I am the only one in my extended family of 25 Americans who is undocumented. When you inaccurately call me "illegal," you're not only dehumanizing me, you're offending them. No human being is illegal.

Also here is my Mountain View High School family, my support network of allies who encouraged and protected me since I was a teenager. After I told my high school principal and school superintendent that I was not planning to go to college because I could not apply for financial aid, Pat Hyland and Rich Fischer secured a private scholarship for me. The scholarship was funded by a man named Jim Strand. I am honored that Pat, Rich and Jim are all here today. Across the country, there are countless other Jim Strands, Pat Hylands, and Rich Fischers of all backgrounds who stand alongside their undocumented neighbors. They don't need to see pieces of paper, a passport or a green card, to treat us as human beings.

This is the truth about immigration in our America.

As this Congress decides on fair, humane reform, let us remember that immigration is not merely about borders. "Immigration is in our blood ... part of our founding story," writes Sen. Ted Kennedy, former chairman of this very Committee, in the introduction to President [John F.] Kennedy's book, "A Nation of Immigrants." Immigration is about our future. Immigration is about all of us.

And before I take your questions, I have a few of my own: What do you want to do with me?

What do you want to do with us? How do you define "American"? Thank you.

7. Menderes Candan and Uwe Unger Review Examples of the Brain Drain and the Brain Gain, 2013

Over decades it was a dominating theory in the field of migration research that the emigration of highly qualified employees from developing countries to developed countries is a loss for the economies and societies of the developing countries (so called brain drain). The argumentation was that the emigration of the very best leads to mitigation of innovation and development in country of origin. After the turn of the millennium, the view gained increasing acceptance that emigration of highly qualified from developing countries to developed countries does not only have negative aspects. As soon as migrants establish themselves in the host country, reach high positions in their occupational field, gain competences and accumulate capital, they start to transfer their knowledge and capital to their home countries. Therefore, the initially occurring brain drain turns into a gain (so called brain gain) for the country of origin.

The development of India is an ideal typical example for this phenomenon. India was hit by a large brain drain in the 1970s and '80s. Hundreds of thousands of the highly skilled left the country towards North America and Europe. They were able to establish themselves succesfully in their host countries. In the course of the economic opening of the country at the beginning of the 1990s many members of the Indian diaspora used their know-how, capital, and networks they built up in the countries of residence to invest in India. In doing so, they contribute to the development of the Indian economy. In particular, the development of the IT sector is a perfect example for a development from a brain drain to a brain gain. Indians who once left India for the US have started to build successful companies in the Silicon Valley and established branches of these companies in India. They took advantage of the more favorable production costs (especially labor force) to produce their goods in India, and sold them on the US market. In the meantime, India is leading in the IT sector worldwide. More than half of the IT companies in India were founded by Indians in the USA or, at least, are managed by them. More than two third of their gains are generated in the US market.

The Indian government is aware of this trend, and has already initiated an active policy to stimulate the brain gain of their highly skilled expatriates. The "Ministry of Overseas Indian Affairs" (MOIA) was established in 2004. The MOIA "focuses on developing networks with and amongst Overseas Indians with the intent of building partnership with the Diaspora." Moreover, Indians abroad gained special legal status by the Indian government. One of these legal statuses is the "Non Resident Indian" (NRI). Another one is the status of "People of Indian Origin" (PIO). These two statuses mark quasi dual citizenship. Furthermore, Indians who gained one of these two statuses benefit from many legal

Menderes Candan/Uwe Hunger, "Brain Drain and Brain Gain Debate," *The Brain Drain and Brain Gain: The Recent Debate*, 2013 Network Migration in Europe e.V. www.network-migration.org. Reprinted by permission.

as well as investment appreciations. In addition, there exist different state policies to facilitate investments.

Several sectors followed the example of the IT sector. Doctors, for example, who previously emigrated to the USA and Great Britain, returned to India and built hospitals there. Scientists, who do research in the field of biotechnology, also returned to India to found companies. Every year, many million members of the Indian diaspora transfer billions of US-Dollars as remittances to their country of origin. The annual amount of remittances is constantly rising; for instance from $53.6 billion in the fiscal year of 2009/10 to $55.6 billion in 2010/11, and to $66.1 billion in 2011/12.

This transformation from brain drain to brain gain is not a unique or isolated process in India. Similar trends can be observed in other developing and emerging countries, which formerly suffered from a large emigration of its highly qualified (brain drain), and now are trying to benefit from their offshore population (brain gain). East Asian migration to the United States, for example, which started already in the 19th century, is still increasing and plays an important role in the developing process of these countries. Asian immigrants surpassed even Latin American immigration in 2012. Many of the Asian immigrants come as natural science students and stay as successful members of [the] upper-middle class in the United States. At the same time, they contribute to the development of their home countries over generations: There are high return rates to Korea, large remittances to China and the Phillipines (China is the second and the Phillipines is the fourth largest recipient country of remittances next to India and Mexico), and a wide transfer of technology to Taiwan. This trend seems not to decrease, but rather increase in the future. Collectively, worldwide remittances ($372 billion in 2011), for example, constitute an important proportion of the GDP of many emerging countries and exceed, for example, the amount of the official worldwide development aid ($135 billion in 2011).

8. Asian Americans Support Affirmative Action, 2014

Many Asian American and Pacific Islander (AAPI) Groups Face Low Representation

As noted in the National Commission on Asian American and Pacific Islander Research in Education (CARE) "iCount" report for the White House's Initiative on AAPIs, lack of disaggregated data "conceals the unique challenges faced by AAPIs" and "the aggregation of AAPI sub-groups into a single data category is a civil rights issue for the AAPI community." Specific examples from the iCount report included a case study of UC based on newly available disaggregated data, finding that many groups were below their proportion of the state population in UC Berkeley's applicant pool: **"Low representation among AAPI applicants is a particularly problematic trend for Pacific Islanders (Samoans,**

Asian Americans and Pacific Islanders in California: How Higher Education Diversity Benefits Our Communities, March 2014, 1–5. Reprinted by permission of Asian Americans Advancing Justice.

Guamanians, Tongans, and Native Hawaiians), Southeast Asians (Laotians, Cambodians, Hmong, and Vietnamese), and Filipinos." The report found similar patterns in UCLA's admit pool.

Pacific Islanders, for example, face extensive barriers to opportunity in higher education, and have among the lowest rates of college-going and degree completion nationwide and in California. The chart below illustrates this challenge, and confirms that over an eight year span, Pacific Islanders' admission rates to the UC system were the same as the groups traditionally defined as "underrepresented minorities" (URMs) – i.e., African Americans, Latinos and American Indians combined – and at UC Berkeley, the most selective campus, Pacific Islander admission rates were lower than URM rates.

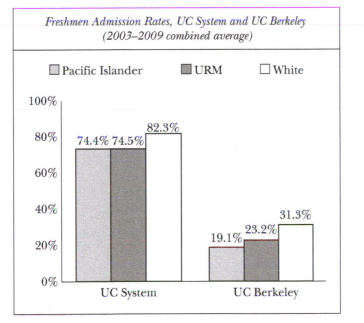

Freshmen Admission Rates, UC System and UC Berkeley (2003–2009 combined average)

FIGURE 12.1

AAPIs and Others Share Educational Benefits

In *Grutter v. Bollinger,* the U.S. Supreme Court recognized that student body diversity "promotes 'cross-racial understanding,' helps to break down racial stereotypes, and 'enables [students] to better understand persons of different races'" and the Court found that these benefits "are substantial." 539 U.S. 306, 330 (2003). An extensive body of social science research corroborates these benefits for students, including AAPI students. For example, students attending institutions that are more engaged with diversity exhibit higher levels of personal change in their knowledge of people of different races or cultures and in their ability to get along with people from different racial or cultural backgrounds.

Large-scale studies analyzing and synthesizing the research literature ("meta-analytic" studies) document the following benefits in higher education:

- Diversity experiences are positively related to cognitive skills development.
- Greater intergroup contact is associated with lower levels of prejudice.
- Cross-group friendships promote positive intergroup attitudes.

Enhanced "pluralistic orientations" and cross-cultural competencies are critical to the success in the global economy.

AAPIs directly benefit from diversity in the classroom and surrounding informal learning environments in college. AAPIs also benefit from diverse learning environments in *indirect* ways. For instance, one important study found that college seniors who interacted more frequently with students of other races exhibited the following patterns, "Black students' contact with Asians was related to improved attitudes toward Hispanics and Whites, and their interactions with Hispanics and Whites were both related to improved attitudes toward Asians." AAPIs' attitudes about others also improve through the same process.

In light of the above evidence, it is not surprising that AAPI college students' support for affirmative action *increases* as they progress from being freshmen to seniors. And racial diversity is particularly important in professional schools settings where the negative impact of Prop 209[1] has been the most dramatic. Several studies show that diversity in the classroom helps AAPIs and others enhance their competencies as future physicians and as future lawyers and community/civic leaders.

Higher Education – An Investment in Our Young People and California's Economic Prosperity

Higher education is a "positive sum game" for our students and our society. Investment in California public higher education pays off not just for students who receive a college education; the State's (and the taxpayers') investment is returned several times over through increased tax revenues and lowered costs for prisons and other programs. Accordingly, AAPIs have a strong interest in ensuring that the overall public higher education system is sound and capable of meeting the needs of California's future economy. While Proposition 30[2] is an important indicator that we have begun to turn a corner, this comes against a backdrop in which California's General Fund spending on prisons increased three times faster than for higher education (UC and Cal State) since the 1990s. Such long-term disinvestment in higher education has troubling enrollment consequences for California students from all backgrounds (including AAPIs).

One concrete example where disinvestment impacts AAPIs is that the UC system is carrying thousands of "unfunded" California resident students who are not supported by the State. A few years ago UC Berkeley significantly scaled

---

[1] A California ballot proposition approved in 1996 that banned state governmental institutions from considering race, sex, or ethnicity, in public employment, public education and public contracting.

[2] A California ballot proposition in 2012 that increased taxes to prevent $6 billion in cuts to California state schools.

back on the number of unfunded students it would enroll, and the number of California resident AAPIs in the freshman class dropped from 1,776 annually in 2006–09 to 1,440 annually in 2010–13 (a 19% decline). To place things in perspective, this drop of 336 AAPI students is more than double the total number of African American and American Indian California resident freshmen enrolling annually at UC Berkeley in recent years. These figures are a reminder of the fact that misplaced attacks on diversity efforts distract us from our more fundamental challenge: As Californians all of us, including AAPIs, must come together to expand and support our excellent universities in order to secure a brighter future for our young people.

ESSAYS

After the 1965 Immigration and Nationality Act provided a clause encouraging the migration of skilled workers to fill labor shortages in the United States, the Philippines became the nation's biggest provider of nurses. In the first essay, Anna Romina Guevarra, a sociologist and interdisciplinary scholar in Asian American Studies at the University of Illinois, Chicago, discusses the transnational support networks and identity of nurses from the Philippines she interviewed in Texas and Arizona. While many nurses celebrated the lifestyle they can afford and their contributions to their families back in the Philippines because of their higher incomes, they also expressed feelings of guilt, loneliness, and disappointment. The second essay, by Edward Taehan Chang, a professor of ethnic studies at the University of California, Riverside, examines the legacy of Sa-I-Gu. His essay looks at structural inequality, entrepreneurship, generational differences, and political lessons learned by Korean Americans during the twenty years that followed America's first multiethnic civil unrest.

Filipina Nurses in Arizona and Texas Look for the American Dream

ANNA ROMINA GUEVARRA

In a 2007 *New York Times Magazine* news article, we meet Rosalie Comodas Villanueva, a Filipina nurse working in Abu Dhabi who has relieved her migrant worker father from being the family's primary breadwinner, a position he had held for almost two decades. Not only does she dutifully remit four hundred dollars a month to her parents; in addition, through her generosity her parents have a home equipped with luxuries atypical of the average Filipino household; a patio, tiled flooring, two kitchens, and flushing toilets. The pages of a new magazine, *Philippine Nurses Monitor*, which professes to serve the Filipino nurse communities in the United States, are filled with information about the many ways

Marketing Dreams, Manufacturing Heroes: The Transnational Labor Brokering of Filipino Workers (Rutgers 2010), 1–21. Reprinted by permission.

that nurses can enjoy the economic fruits of their labor. From taking advantage of the "special no down payment package for OFWs (overseas Filipino workers]" to buying a luxury condo in the Philippines, to receiving tips for leisure and travel from their peers, to learning how to become "nurse entrepreneurs," readers can dream or, perhaps, *fantasize* about the things they can consume or business ventures they can pursue.

Similarly, nurses I interviewed in Texas and Arizona such as Gabriela and Kitty boast the material rewards of working overseas and the pleasures of owning and purchasing commodities of which they can only dream in the Philippines. Being able to own a home or to purchase a car produces celebratory images that reflect the very promises that the state and employment agencies broker to the nurses I interviewed and those that govern their professional consciousness as overseas workers seeking employment in the United States. But these images hide the contradictions and tensions in those promises—the simultaneous gains and losses behind a professional consciousness rooted in chasing the American dream of consumption. America may encapsulate their dream opportunity when it comes to material acquisition, but often, behind these representations is loneliness and estrangement, which this pursuit often veils.

CULTIVATING AMERICANIZED NURSING SUBJECTS

Gabriela and Kitty's presence in the United States defies the kind of economic logic of poverty and any global labor market rationale that labor recruiters proclaim are the driving forces for pursuing overseas employment in the United States. The two women came from middleclass families and did not pursue nursing simply as a mode of economic survival. Rather, nursing was their ticket to work in the United States, a place they perceived would reward them with earnings commensurate to their training and endow them with an elevated social status—an issue I take up later. But this pursuit was made possible by colonial relations between the United States and the Philippines.

Choy's seminal work illustrates how these relations have contributed to the institutionalization of nursing, creating a foundation upon which Filipinos became technically and socially suited to work in U.S. health care settings. The implementation of an Americanized nursing training, the use of English as the language of instruction, and the promotion of an Americanized nursing work culture provided the necessary historical "preconditions" driving the mass migration of Filipinos to the United States beginning in the mid-1960s. Colonial relations between the two countries led to educational and training opportunities, such as the *pensionado* and the Exchange Visitors Program (EVP), that had been a vehicle for Filipino nurses to go to the United States since the 1950s. These programs served as tools for establishing the cultural and intellectual supremacy of U.S. institutions and ultimately were instrumental in shaping familiarity with the Filipino nursing workforce on the part of contemporary foreign employers.

Indeed, an unintended consequence of these colonial relations, as Choy argues, is the mass migration of Filipino nurses to the United States in the second half of the twentieth century. Between 1956 and 1969, following implementation of the EVP, more than eleven thousand Filipino nurses left for the United States; nurses made up more than 50 percent of the total number of exchange visitors from the Philippines. The momentum was maintained by the 1965 Immigration Act, which provided two occupational preference categories reserved for highly skilled migrants, which Filipino nurses were able to use as a means for entering the United States. They also took advantage of the H1-B visas that allowed them to come as temporary workers....

FROM PROVIDING LAVISH RECRUITMENT PACKAGES TO CREATING FILIPINO ENCLAVES

In the recruitment seminars that U.S.-based employers conduct in the Philippines, Filipino nurses are already bombarded with images that suggest that working in the United States will lead to a significant transformation of economic status. They are reminded that this employment opportunity is not only about immigrating to the United States and attaining the rights and privileges afforded to all its permanent residents, but also about partaking in the material rewards of their earnings. The tourist-directed brochures that recruiters distribute and the token Filipino representatives who are paraded as economic success stories and who attest to the glamour of working overseas are supposed to ingrain in the minds of Filipino applicants the reasons why working in the United States is *the* ultimate opportunity.

To further reify this point, recruiters effectively promote an enticing "hiring package" to their applicants. In contrast to earlier waves of foreign nurse recruitment in which H1-B visas were used, in present recruitment efforts many hospitals offer immigrant or green card visas in the form of employment-based visas such as the EB-3, which ultimately carries the promise of U.S. citizenship. Unlike the H1-B visa, the EB-3 allows employers to sponsor a nurse job applicant (and her or his family) for permanent residency (that is, give her or him a green card). Once they are permanent residents, nurses are eligible to apply for U.S. citizenship, after five years of continuous residency in the country. All the nurses I interviewed fit into this pattern, which set them apart from the nurses who had come before them. They had left the Philippines with the express intention of becoming permanent U.S. residents and, ultimately, U.S. citizens....

Nurses I interviewed in Texas and Arizona earned between thirteen and thirty-four dollars an hour. Notwithstanding the cost-of-living indexes in these two places, and the cut that agencies take from nurses' pay, as in the case of some of the nurses in Arizona, their wages seemingly depend on their employers, years of work experience, and the type of specialty care provided (wages of emergency room nurses and cardiac care unit nurses are slightly higher than those of medical oncology nurses). They perceived this salary to be well above anything they could possibly earn in the Philippines and therefore found them sufficiently enticing. According to Pia, a nurse with five years' nursing experience, the 5,000 pesos a month ($116) she would be earning in a provincial hospital in the Philippines could not compare with the $18 an hour ($1,152 a month) offered to her in Texas. Michelle, another nurse in Gray Meadows, recounted that her initial contract offered $13 an hour, an amount that seemed low given that she had been working as a nurse for ten years. However, this rate, upon conversion to Philippine pesos, would allow her, as the eldest daughter, to fulfill her family obligations to put two of her siblings through college. As is clear from this example, employers benefit from the power of the U.S. dollar conversion in the Philippines and the relative competitiveness of U.S. nursing salaries compared with those that Philippine hospitals can offer.

Many Philippine-based agencies that work with U.S. hospitals or staffing registries are able to secure packages (called a surety bond) that include the stipulation that employers pay for the exams required of nurse applicants, airfare and other travel costs for the journey abroad, and all other immigration-related fees. This was the case for one of the employers of nine nurses I interviewed in Gray Meadows. The attractiveness of this employer was based on its ability to shoulder what is typically the costly aspect of a job application to the United States. A typical contract for the nurses employed by this employer included other perks, such as three months' "free" housing in a fully furnished apartment, a relocation bonus of $4,500, a sign-on bonus of $2,000, a $225 gift certificate to purchase hospital uniforms, and a transportation allowance of $4,500. This kind of package has become a source of tension for Filipino nurses in Gray Meadows who work for another employer or who came at a different period, when such perks were not yet offered. While nurses in Arizona did not have the same kind of extensive package, they also received one month of free housing.

Both groups of nurses recounted that upon their arrival in the United States, they were assisted by a representative from their employers who helped to process numerous types of employment-related paperwork, including that needed for their Social Security cards; took them to the bank to open an account; and generally oriented them in affairs of daily living. Above all, however, what was especially helpful for these nurses was the strategic ways in which employers created a sort of mini-Filipino enclave by placing similar workers in the same housing complex. For example, in Texas, I found that one apartment complex was home to all the newly arrived nurses and to a few "old-timers"—those who had been in Gray Meadows for at least two years and who decided to stay in that housing complex. The apartment complex was not only located about two to three miles from the two hospitals where the nurses worked but also situated two blocks from the only Filipino restaurant in town. This restaurant was the heart of this Filipino nurse community. Its owners provided much needed familiar hospitality and its food had become essential for nurses who stopped by before or after their shifts to pick up home-cooked meals that their schedules do not permit them to prepare at home. Similarly, in Arizona, the nurses I interviewed were placed in an apartment complex with a significant concentration of Filipino nurse residents who were working for the same hospital, which was located in close proximity.

This strategy of creating a Filipino nurse mini-enclave is advantageous for employers, who can take credit for fulfilling their promise to nurses—to give them a kind of home away from home where newly arrived nurses can feel that they are in an environment with other nurses who are their peers but at the same time can provide them mentorship and emotional support. This is precisely what has happened in both Texas and Arizona. Filipino nurses themselves have created a support system that at least tries to mitigate the transportation problems that they all face. In both sites, employers provided nurses, in their initial few months, with a financial allowance or a bus card that they could use for public transportation. However, taking public transportation to work became cumbersome for the night shift nurses, who did not feel safe waiting at a bus stop alone, or for those who did not feel comfortable facing the oppressive summer heat. Grocery stores, churches, and shopping centers were not within walking distance from the apartments. Therefore, nurses who owned their cars often reached out to newly arrived nurses either by offering free rides to places to which they were going to already or by establishing official carpooling services for a fee.

Such a community of support is instrumental in relieving the home-sickness that many nurses encounter and in alleviating their fears about a new work environment....

WE ARE BORN TO HAVE THE AMERICAN DREAM

Thanks to transnational corporations, globalized media, and migrant transnational social networks, the images that travel and get imported globally portray the United States as a place of wealth, cosmopolitanism, and limitless opportunities. Another nurse, who will be called HB and who works in Arizona, recounted how as a young child in the Philippines, she perceived her aunts and cousins who worked as nurses in the United States as being able to "buy whatever they wanted" by virtue of the things they brought back on their trips home to the Philippines. The United States is supposed to be *the* place to satisfy one's career and educational aspirations.

But working in the United States is also about having a "voice." Thus Pia, a nurse working in Gray Meadows, observed, "People seem to have more voice here. Whatever they want to say, they can say it. Your rights prevail. In the Philippines, whoever has money, they are the one with rights."...

HEROES TO THEIR FAMILIES

When I met Mabolo in 2004, she had been working in Texas for about four months. During our meeting, she was particularly jovial because of the increasingly real possibility that she would finally be reunited with her husband and four children. She had left them behind because she had not had money then to finance the cost of processing their visas and airfare, a cost that employers typically do not cover. Now, she had saved enough money from the overtime hours she had put in to bring them to the United States, buy a minivan to drive them around in, and even plan to purchase a home before they arrived.... Mabolo's ability to provide her family with these kinds of lifestyle changes redefined her position as her family breadwinner, through her ability to purchase material goods, at the same time that the gratitude that she receives from her children alleviated her sense of guilt and pain that was brought on by familial separation....

Behind the so-called glamorous lifestyles that employment agencies sold the nurses was a sense of loneliness and alienation that gave pause about whether this dream was worth pursuing after all. As Gabriela noted, "You can buy everything you want in America. But it is a lonely place. Although I feel full from the things that I buy, I still feel unhappy…. In the Philippines, while you have very little money, you are happy."…

Many say, *Masarap ang buhay sa Pilipinas* (Life is good in the Philippines) as a way of expressing a sense of pride and longing for a place that they seemingly did not always appreciate as such. They express disdain for the fast-paced world of work that the United States demands and because of which few moments are left for leisure. They are disappointed with how friendships develop and the formal arrangements needed for social gatherings. They all learn very quickly that in the United States, time is like gold and that Americans are obsessed with managing and protecting their time. They also feel socially constrained in workplaces that they think discourage casual and informal conversations on the job and contribute to the social distance they feel from their colleagues.

While there are certainly some nurses who do not wish to return to the Philippines because they have become accustomed to the U.S. lifestyle, most whom I interviewed discussed plans of returning and retiring there. Juxtaposed with their determination to chase the American dream was a fundamental longing to return "home." Many were especially fearful of what they observed was a lack of respect for the elderly, who they saw facing the fate of ending up in a nursing home instead of being under the care of their family….

Contrary to the general perception that agencies promote Filipinos working overseas, many workers are actually committed to returning to the Philippines and see it as their ultimate home. As Justin noted, "Life is good and enjoyable in the Philippines but life is nicer here in America [in terms of material rewards]. These are two different things." This kind of realization and distinction challenges the notion of immigrants as being driven by the desire for material consumption; it paints a richer and more complicated picture of what comes to be defined as "the good life." That is, the promise of the American dream, the good life that nurses imagined they would find in the United States falls short of their expectations, and for many nurses, this unexpectedly propels them back to the Philippines.

CONCLUSION

…Toward the end of our interview, I asked Gabriela to reflect upon her life and career in the United States thus far and offer some "words of wisdom" for nurses who wished to take a piece of this American dream: "Life is good here in terms of the fact that you can do what you want. Just work hard and don't let your emotions take over you. You need to be brave. You come here to get wealthy so don't think of anything else; otherwise, why come here at all? Just work hard. Pray and don't forget why you came here. You will get what you want."

The statement that Gabriela made, imbued with notions of promise and prescription at the same time, bears a striking resemblance to what labor brokers themselves pitch to prospective migrants. But as Gabriela's story has revealed, the cautionary tone behind her statement also unveils the disappointment, estrangement, and loneliness that come with living this dream. The American dream may guarantee economic advancement, but it does not guarantee that Filipino nurses in the United States will live happily ever after.

Confronting Sa-I-Gu:
Twenty Years After the Los Angeles Riots

EDWARD TAEHAN CHANG

Twenty years ago on April 29, Los Angeles erupted and Koreatown cried as it burned. For six-days, the LAPD was missing in action as rioting, looting, burning, and killing devastated the city. The "not guilty" Rodney King verdict ignited anger and frustration felt by South Los Angeles residents who suffered from years of neglect, despair, hopelessness, injustice, and oppression. In the Korean American community, the Los Angeles riot is remembered as Sa-i-gu (April 29 in Korean). Korean Americans suffered disproportionately high economic losses as 2,280 Korean American businesses were looted or burned with $400 million in property damages. Without any political clout and power in the city, Koreatown was unprotected and left to burn since it was not a priority for city politicians and the LAPD. For the Korean American community, Sa-i-gu is known as its most important historical event, a "turning point," "watershed event." or "wake-up call." Sa-i-gu profoundly altered the Korean American discourse, igniting debates and dialogue in search of new directions. The riot served as a catalyst to critically examine what it meant to be Korean American in relation to multicultural politics and race, economics and ideology.

So does race matter in America anymore? On the 20th anniversary of the Los Angeles riots, the answer may depend on whom you ask. We still disagree on how to name what happened on April 29, 1992. Was it a riot? Uprising? Civil unrest or rebellion? A year after the Los Angeles riots in 1993, I along with others tried to organize a symposium to understand what happened and facilitate dialogue between different racial and ethnic groups in Los Angeles. We debated and struggled on how to name Sa-i-gu, and we came up with the term "political-protest-turned-into-riot." Twenty years later, we are still debating how to name the six days of violence that burned Los Angeles in 1992. The argument about how to name the six days of violence symbolizes a still divided city that is "separate and unequal."

Sa-i-gu served as an impetus for fundamental changes in Korean American identity and provided guidance for the future direction of the community. Many observers commented that the "Korean American was born or reborn on April 29, 1992." The Korean American community also began to reevaluate its economic, cultural, and political positions in America. What does it mean to be Korean American in multiethnic and multiracial America?…

According to the U.S. Census (1990), the City of Los Angeles had become truly multiracial and multiethnic: the Latino population constituted 40 percent,

Young Oak Kim Center for Korean American Studies, November 2012, http://yokcenter.ucr.edu. Reprinted by permission.

whites 37 percent, African Americans 13 percent, Asian Americans 9 percent and Native Americans 1 percent....

Indeed, the Los Angeles civil unrest of 1992 was America's first multiethnic civil unrest (Chang 1994). Interestingly, Chinese and Japanese Americans practiced ethnic dis–identification and distancing as they blamed Korean immigrants for causing racial unrest in Los Angeles. Assimilated Chinese and Japanese Americans felt uncomfortable being lumped together with Korean immigrants as Asian Americans. Asian American history is replete with examples of each Asian ethnic group shying away from each other whenever there is racial trouble, in the wishful hope that they are identified as a singular group and not lumped together with other Asian groups.

With the breakdown of legal and residential barriers, middle-class African Americans began to move out of urban ghettos into suburban neighborhoods; this has had a dramatic impact on the demographic composition of South Central Los Angeles which- has traditionally consisted of "black neighborhoods." In the 1980s, the African American population increased only by 13%, but the Latino population increased by 53% and Asian Americans by 108% in South Central Los Angeles. As a result, the Latino community in South Central Los Angeles grew from 6% in the 1970s to roughly 40% in the 1990s. These demographic changes along with the restructuring of the American economy have had a profound impact on racial and ethnic relations in Los Angeles as well as other major metropolitan areas in the form of increasing inter-minority conflicts and white backlash against minority groups....

In particular, the Korean-African-American conflict emerged as one of the most visible and urgent problems of urban America as conflict intensified between the two minority groups during the late 1980s and the early 1990s. Boycotts and protests against Korean immigrant store owners broke out in major cities in the United States throughout the 1980s. The Red Apple boycott (January 18, 1990) in the Flatbush section of Brooklyn, New York pitted Korean immigrants against African Americans as it became a symbol of racial conflict in America. During the early 1990s, the so called "Korean-black conflict" replaced white-black tension as the Red Apple boycott lasted for almost 15 months....

Two distinct characteristics set Korean immigrants apart from other Asian Americans: a church-centered community and entrepreneurship. The church is the most numerous and dominant institution in the Korean American community. Studies have shown that approximately 70 percent of Korean immigrants are regular churchgoers. Korean American churches are the most important social, cultural, and economic institutions that serve the needs of Korean immigrants. Church is a place where recent Korean immigrants can worship God and share their immigrant experiences and cope with language and cultural barriers in a new society.

Since Korean immigrants view small business as an avenue for success in America, Korean immigrants have been actively developing and cultivating a niche in the small business sector. This may explain the reasons why Korean immigrants have the highest self-employment rate in the US. Korean Americans ranked the highest in self-employment in 2007 (12.8%). A combination of factors facilitates high self-employment rates among Korean immigrants. Cultural misunderstanding, language barriers, and unfamiliarity with American society put Korean immigrants at a disadvantage in the U.S. labor market. Korean immigrants also find it difficult to find jobs commensurate with their education level. Korean immigrants come to the US with "ethclass" (ethnic and class) resources because of American immigration policies that encouraged Koreans with capital to immigrate to the United States. Korean immigrants are and were in an advantageous position to enter small businesses by utilizing their ethnic and class resources and networks. In particular, Korean immigrants opened grocery markets, liquor stores, nail salons, garment subcontracting firms, restaurants, and laundry businesses. Furthermore, racial discrimination and structural factors seem to push Korean immigrants as shop owners or "middleman minority" serving largely minority (African American and Latino) clientele. Korean immigrants function as the "middleman minority" as they are heavily concentrated in retail and service industries.

The proliferation of Korean-owned businesses in the African American community during the 1980s exacerbated conflicts between the Korean American and African American communities. Several highly publicized boycotts of Korean-owned businesses by African American residents intensified racial conflict between the two communities during the 1980s and the early 1990s. Cultural misunderstandings and culture clash fueled antagonism between Korean immigrant merchants and African American residents. As a "middleman minority," Korean merchants acted as a buffer between dominant (white) and subordinate (African American and Latino) group conflicts in American society. The middleman minority theory predicts friction between immigrant-seller and poor-minority-buyer relationships in America's inner cities. Volatile relations between Korean American and African American communities in Los Angeles exploded into mass destruction of properties and loss of lives on April 29, 1992....

Sa-I-Gu

Historically, most of the US media has portrayed Asian Americans in general as the "model minority," forcing them into the role of the "middleman minority." This image pits Asian Americans against other minority groups and has fueled resentment particularly toward Korean Americans. By praising Korean immigrant merchants in Los Angeles as a shining example for other minorities to emulate, the press, before Sa-i-gu, implied that African Americans had no one but themselves to blame for their circumstances. Both the "model minority" and the "middleman minority" concepts imply racial stratification, creating a three-tier system with whites on the top, Asians in the middle, and Latinos and blacks at the bottom. As journalist and author Helen Zia noted in *Asian American Dreams* in 2000, Sa-i-gu demonstrated that "... the model minority was taking a beating from blacks, whites, and Latinos who seemed only too glad to deliver their comeuppance." Zia also commented that in Los Angeles, Korean Americans "had taken the hit for all Asian Americans." The mainstream media did nothing to cover the Korean American perspective during and after the riots. Thus, Korean Americans were not only denied the legitimization of political grievances, their grief was entirely unacknowledged. Historical misrepresentations of Asians and Asian Americans had residual effects that continue to this day.

These images have had significant impact on how others see Asian Americans and how Asian Americans see themselves.

Within the Korean American community, Sa-i-gu served as an impetus for a fundamental change in identity, which many observers believe occurred on April 29, 1992. The Korean American community also began to reevaluate its own economic, cultural, and political positions in America. What does it mean to be Korean American in multiethnic and multiracial America? Sa-i-gu also exposed many problems and challenges for the Korean American community: a lack of leadership and political power, generation split, and lack of contact with other communities.

The community did not passively accept riots. Within a matter of days, more than 30,000 Korean Americans in Los Angeles came together for a "Peace March" that is said to be the largest gathering of Asian Americans in all of Asian American history. Also, with an increased awareness of the importance of a Korean American identity was the awareness that the 1.5 and second generations play a critical role in the community. It is the younger generation that will present the community's identity to society at large by getting involved in politics and the media to increase the voice and representation of the community. For second generation Korean Americans, the civil unrest gave them a new sense of belonging and ethnic pride as they participated in relief efforts and peace marches.

Despite suffering and hardship, Korean Americans have learned many valuable lessons from the 1992 Los Angeles riots. Ironically, Sa-i-gu brought visibility to the Korean American identity as they were prominently featured by both ethnic and mainstream media. On May 31, 1994, I published an op-ed piece titled "An Emerging Minority Seeks a Role in a Changing America" in the *Los Angeles Times*. Very few people knew about the plight of Korean immigrants before Sa-i-gu. In the aftermath of Sa-i-gu, many readers were interested in knowing who Korean Americans were. Twenty-years later, I published another op-ed in the *Los Angeles Times*, with the title "A Community Coalesces." The article talks about how the Korean American community is now embraced as an integral part of Los Angeles' diverse mosaic. In particular, Koreatown has emerged from the ashes, resurrected as a vibrant, successful transnational enclave I concluded, "it is proof, one more time, that Los Angeles is anything but black and white." Korean Americans learned that they must politically empower themselves. Korean Americans had no allies in city hall, Sacramento, or Washington D.C. because they solely focused on economic security and betterment in American society. No one cared for the Korean American community, as politicians retreated to their own respective communities. Korean Americans learned the hard way that little would be done for them and they must empower themselves politically. Korean immigrant churches also need to play proactive roles in educating, informing, and transforming the Korean immigrant consciousness. Korean immigrant churches have been static, conservative, and traditional in dealing with community issues. Korean immigrant churches must provide a new leadership and the spirit of community activism to promote peaceful co-existence with different racial and ethnic groups in America. One of the important lessons of Sa-i-gu was to reach out and build a multiethnic and multiracial community in

LA. How can we get along as neighbors, and yet protect our own civil rights and basic needs that may be contradictory to our neighbor's needs and interests? It is a long and painful process, but it must start now. Korean Americans must seek a new role in creating an inclusive, multiracial, and multiethnic America.

Sa-i-gu was not just a wakeup call for Korean Americans alone. It was a wakeup call for Asian Americans and all minorities who are struggling in the economically depressed and crime-ridden inner-city districts. And yet, we still have not learned all the meanings and lessons from Sa-i-gu. The problems and structural conditions that ignited Sa-i-gu still continue in South Los Angeles as well as in impoverished neighborhoods in the United States. Economic disparity between haves and have-nots, poor education, high unemployment rates, police brutality, and racial discrimination were the main causes of Sa-i-gu. Twenty years ago, many observers described Los Angeles as "a keg of dynamite ready to explode" anytime. The Los Angeles civil unrest of 1992 brought major social issues to the surface: racism, class, language, culture, new immigrants, violence, crime, the urban underclass, and ethnic tribalism; but these forces have never been addressed or even discussed not only by the powers that be but by the established minority leadership or new ethnic power elites.

Reflections on Twenty Years Since the LA Riots

Twenty years later, Los Angeles is still divided along racial and ethnic lines and struggling. We have not made any substantial changes and improvements with the structural conditions that caused the LA riots of 1992. Although we are far more accepting of differences and tolerant toward others, it seems that we have a long way to go to improve race relations. We do just enough to get along.

And yet we do not hear much about the so-called "black-Korean conflict" twenty years later. There seem to be several reasons for this change. First, Korean Americans no longer dominate mom-and-pop stores in the South Los Angeles area. During the height of "black-Korean conflict" in the 1980s, the majority of mom-and-pop stores in black communities were owned and operated by Korean immigrants. Recently, however, Southeast Asian refugees. Arab Americans, and Latino businessmen moved into South Los Angeles areas. For example, approximately 30–40% of liquor and grocery markets in South Los Angeles are owned and operated by non-Koreans according to Byung Han Cho of the International Korean Grocers' Association. In particular, middle-eastern business owners are aggressively taking over liquor and grocery stores in South Los Angeles. As a result, Korean immigrant owned stores are no longer singled out or the target of boycotts and racial conflict. The demographic shifts in South Los Angeles have also helped to reduce tensions between Korean immigrant merchants and African American customers. Since 1992, the combination of "black-flight" and the influx of the Latino population in South Los Angeles dramatically altered the landscape of the area. Many blacks relocated to the Inland region of San Bernardino and Riverside counties, and others returned to their roots in the South. More importantly, Latino immigrants moved in and began to compete for scarce resources and services which heightened tensions between the two racial minorities. It appears that tensions between Latino immigrants and black residents of South Los Angeles are more urgent issues than the so-called Korean-black conflict.

Attitude and behavioral changes of both Korean Americans and African Americans may have also eased tension between the two groups. As both Korean immigrant merchants and black residents suffered during and after the Los Angeles riots of 1992, they realized how dependent they are on each other. During the riots, many Korean stores were burned down and African American residents had to walk several more miles to shop and get their basic needs such as milk, diapers, and bread. Korean immigrants also realized that they have to reach out and become part of the community if they wanted to succeed in their businesses. As a result, both Korean immigrant merchants and African American customers became more courteous to one another, and it may have diffused tensions between the two groups.

For Korean Americans, much has changed in the last twenty years. An ethnic minority once virtually invisible in American society – and often mistaken for either Chinese or Japanese Americans – has emerged as an economic and political force in Los Angeles civic life. Korean Americans learned that they had to become politically active and empower themselves. Before Sa-i-gu, Korean Americans had no allies in city hall, Sacramento, or Washington, D.C. Their lack of political clout became apparent as their businesses were abandoned to looters and arsonists during the riots....

Twenty years after Sa-i-gu, Los Angeles still struggles with the issues that led to the devastating riots-economic disparity, poor education, impoverished neighborhoods, high unemployment, police brutality, and racial discrimination. That cannot continue, just as progress in race relations must not be allowed to languish as we continue to grow as a diverse community....

Conclusion

As we commemorate the 20th anniversary of Sa-i-gu, this is an opportune time to launch dialogue among diverse communities, and engage in serious policy formulation on how to address the socio-economic, racial, and political conditions we face today. Some aspects of this work may already be in progress, but now it is time to act for change.

Korean immigrants painfully learned the importance of breaking out of ethnic isolation and reaching out to other communities to forge working and harmonious relations....

Globalization and internationalization also are profoundly influencing younger generations who have grown up with different attitudes, interests, and norms. Hopefully, they will influence racial and ethnic relations in America, making Americans of all kinds more open to diversity and are more willing to embrace people of dissimilar ethnic and racial backgrounds as friends and marriage partners. Young Americans grew up with the Internet and international social networking, so they are more informed and accepting of diversity, pluralism, and multiculturalism. Although America has a long way to go in battling racism, hopefully the future is bright, as our youth no longer see America as simply black and white.

FURTHER READING

Abelman, Nancy, and John Lie. *Blue Dreams: Korean Americans and the Los Angeles Riots* (1995).

Aguilar, Delia, and Ann E. Lacsamana, eds. *Women and Globalization* (2004).

Aoki, Andrew, and Okiyshi Takeda. *Asian American Politics* (2009).

Asian Community Center Archive Group. *Stand Up: An Archive Collection of the Bay Area Asian American Movement 1968–1974* (2009).

Chang, Edward T., and Russell Leong, eds. *Los Angeles: Struggles toward Multiethnic Community* (1994).

Chang, Gordon. *Asian Americans and Politics: Perspectives, Experiences, Prospects* (2001).

Choy, Catherine Ceniza. *Empire of Care: Nursing and Migration in Filipino American History* (2003).

Collet, Christian, and Pei-Te Lien, eds. *Transnational Politics of Asian Americans* (2009).

de Jesus, Melinda L. *Pinay Power: Peminist Critical Theory* (2005).

Dhingra, Pawan. *Managing Multicultural Lives: Asian American Professionals and the Challenge of Multiple Identities* (2007).

Espiritu, Yen Le. *Home Bound: Filipino American Lives across Cultures, Communities, and Countries* (2003).

Kim, Nadia Y. *Imperial Citizens: Koreans and Race from Seoul to LA* (2008).

Lai, James S. *Asian American Political Action: Suburban Transformations* (2011).

Lee, K. W. "The Fire Next Time?: Ten Haunting Questions Cry Out for Answers and Redress," *Amerasia Journal* 38, no. 1 (2012): 85–90.

Leonard, Karen. *Making Ethnic Choices: California's Punjabi-Mexican Americans, 1910–1980* (1991).

Lien, Pei-Te, M. Margaret Conway, and Janelle Wong. *The Politics of Asian Americans: Diversity and Community* (2004).

Liu, Lisong. *Chinese Student Migration and Selective Citizenship: Mobility, Community, and Identity between China and the United States* (2015).

Min, Pyong Gap, and Joe Jeong Ho Han, *Koreans in North America: Their Experiences in the Twenty-First Century* (2013).

Ong, Aihwa. *Flexible Citizenship: The Cultural Logics of Transnationality* (1999).

Pareenas, Rahcel Salazar. *Servants of Globalization: Women, Migration, and Domestic Work* (2001).

Park, Albert L., and David K. Yoo, eds. *Encountering Modernity: Christianity in East Asia and Asian America* (2014).

Takagi, Dana Y. *Retreat from Race: Asian-American Admissions Policies and Racial Politics* (1992).

Vallangca, Caridad Concepcion. *The Second Wave: Pinay & Pinoy, 1945–1960* (1987).

Võ, Linda Trinh, and Rick Bonus, eds. *Contemporary Asian American Communities Intersections and Divergences* (2002).

Wang, L. Ling-chi. "Overrepresentation and Disenfranchisement: Asian Americans in Higher Education," *Amerasia Journal* 33, no. 1 (2007): 77–100.

CHAPTER 13

Refugees and Southeast
Asian Communities

Unlike most immigrants, refugees, who began arriving from Southeast Asia in the mid-1970s, were forced to leave their native countries with little notice or advance planning. Many suffered extreme physical, emotional, and psychological trauma before and during their escape as well as painful memories that haunted them in the United States. Refugees from Vietnam, Cambodia, and Laos fled countries devastated by decades of war. Their accounts vary depending on their political, educational, and cultural backgrounds. For example, many of the 130,000 refugees who fled Vietnam as part of the "first wave" in 1975 were South Vietnamese government and military personnel who were more likely to be urban, Catholic, well-educated English speakers with American contacts. As a result, many of these individuals and their family members were airlifted out of the country by U.S. helicopters and escaped before the fall of Saigon to the Communists in 1975.

Refugees who fled after the Communists assumed power throughout Vietnam, Cambodia, and Laos in 1975 endured the loss of businesses that were nationalized by the government, physical and psychological abuse within Communist "reeducation" camps, and forced migrations to the countryside. Cambodians under the Khmer Rouge suffered from mass executions, starvation, and disease, which killed somewhere between half a million to 3 million people in a country that had a total population of 7 million in early 1975. Hmong hill tribespeople in Laos were targeted for reprisals by the Communist regime for participating in a secret army of 40,000 organized by the U.S. Central Intelligence Agency (CIA) in the 1960s.

A "second wave" of refugees began in 1978 and included "boat people" from Vietnam and land refugees from Cambodia and Laos who had fled to Thailand. This second wave was both ethnically and economically more diverse than the first wave. Approximately 70 percent of the Vietnamese boat people were ethnic Chinese, and the Laotian refugees included lowland Lao and highland Hmong. Second-wave refugees, who disproportionately came from rural areas, were typically Buddhists or animists and spoke little English. Not surprisingly, many of these refugees had greater difficulty finding jobs and adjusting to life in America. Congress passed the 1980 Refugee Act to limit the massive influx of refugees and provide funding for resettlement programs. Setting an annual quota of 50,000 refugees, the act reimbursed state spending on refugees for a period of up to thirty-six months. In 1982, the time limit was reduced to eighteen months, after which refugees became eligible for welfare benefits from the U.S. government.

U.S. officials initially tried to prevent Southeast Asian refugees from congregating in ethnic enclaves once they were settled in the United States because they assumed that scattering them throughout the country would facilitate their assimilation into American society. The officials also resettled nuclear family units without recognizing the importance of extended kinship ties for the refugees. But many Southeast Asian refugees remigrated to form ethnic communities and to reunite extended families. Vietnamese refugees, for example, established Little Saigons in places like Westminster, California, and the Hmong created vibrant communities in Minneapolis, Minnesota, and other areas.

DOCUMENTS

Documents 1 to 3 reflect the diverse backgrounds and experiences of Southeast Asian refugees. In Document 1, Lang Ngan describes being airlifted out of Vietnam in July 1975 as part of the first wave of refugees. Ngan notes that she and her English-speaking siblings have had a much easier time than her parents in adapting to the United States. A ninth-grader when Saigon fell in 1975, Le Tan Si, in contrast to Ngan, left his family and his country as a boat person in 1979. Excerpts from his college essay depicting harrowing encounters with pirates during his escape are included in Document 2. Sen Chul, a Cambodian student, tells an American embassy officer about life under the Khmer Rouge in Document 3. He describes the targeting of ethnic Chinese and students, mass executions, and the intense fear he experienced before he fled to Thailand in 1978. In Document 4, Lieutenant Colonel Wangyee Vang testifies before Congress in 2000 and recounts the bravery and patriotism of Hmong and Lao combat troops who served alongside Americans during the Vietnam War. After U.S. troops withdrew and the Communists took control throughout Indochina, the Hmong and Lao troops were hunted and many were killed. This prompted them to trek through the jungles with their families to find safety in Thailand. Calling on the United States to honor its commitment to these soldiers, Vang urges Congress to help them and their families become U.S. citizens by waiving the five-year residency requirement. He also calls for providing interpreters for their naturalization tests.

Documents 5 and 6 discuss the enduring impact of homeland politics on Southeast Asian American activism. In Document 5, radio host Ira Glass interviews Madison Nguyen about election controversies she faced in 2008 and 2009 after being elected as the first Vietnamese American member of the San Jose city council. A sector of the Vietnamese American community denounced her as a Communist traitor and held mass demonstrations against her because she supported naming an area the Saigon Business District instead of Little Saigon, the traditional name of anti-Communist exile communities. In Document 6, Laotian American Channapha Khamvongsa, executive director of Legacies of War, testifies before Congress in 2010 about how Laos became the most heavily bombed nation in the world during the Vietnam War and how 75 million bombs continue to lurk underground and threaten to maim and kill civilians. He calls on the U.S. government to fund bomb-clearing programs and provide support for the people injured by these bombs in Laos.

Document 7 explores different views of Hmong culture and identity. Rutgers anthropologist and Hmong media expert Louisa Schein interviews Bee Vang, who played the Hmong lead Thao Vang Lor in Clint Eastwood's 2008 film *Gran Torino*. Only sixteen when he acted in the film, Vang explains why he was dismayed at the way Eastwood portrayed Hmong culture and his character's masculinity.

1. Lang Ngan, a First-Wave Refugee, Compares Life in Vietnam and the United States, 1975 (1991)

On April 25th, near the end of the war, my supervisor called me in, and told me that by six o'clock that evening, we had to meet, to get to the airport by nine the next morning. I had worked for the U.S. Embassy in Saigon for seven years. If we had stayed, we would have been persecuted by the new government.

There was no time to talk to friends or relatives because the evacuation was supposed to be secret, and we were not allowed to tell our relatives. We couldn't even take our money out of the bank. We weren't prepared to come to this country. It was a last minute thing. We had to make our decision overnight. We didn't have any time to think about it.

I was allowed to take my family, because I was single. My father, my mother, myself and six brothers and sisters—the nine of us. We were so frightened because we didn't have any friends or relatives in this country to help us. We couldn't sell our property. We literally left with the clothes on our backs. I was twenty-nine when I came to the U.S., one brother was twenty-three, and one was nineteen. The youngest was only eight. The rest were in their teens.

I didn't have the Golden Mountain dream [a Chinese term for America, where making lots of money fast is believed possible]. I knew life wouldn't be easy, especially since we didn't receive a high education in Vietnam. I told my brothers and sisters on the plane coming here that I didn't know whether I could support all of them. If not, then I would have to give them up for adoption. They said they understood but asked that before I left, I give them my address so that when they grew up, they could look for me.

We were transported by military cargo plane. At the time, the evacuation was so sudden the U.S. government didn't have a chance to prepare for our

From Lang Ngan, "The Success Story" from *Asian American Experiences in the United States: Oral Histories of First to Fourth Generation Americans from China, the Philippines, Japan, India, the Pacific Islands, Vietnam, and Cambodia.* © 1991 Joann Faung Jean Lee by permission of McFarland & Company, Inc., Box 611, Jefferson, NC 28640. www.mcfarlandpub.com.

arrival. So we were taken to a military camp in the Philippines for a few days. From there, some of the refugees were sent to Guam. We were sent to Wake Island, and screened for admittance. We left Vietnam April twenty-fifth. We arrived at the camp in Arkansas on May fourth.

At the beginning, there wasn't enough food. There was a shortage because the U.S. government wasn't prepared for us. But really it wasn't bad. It was actually much better than the first asylum camps in Malaysia and Thailand. We felt we were the luckiest. A month later, the government contracted a company to provide food for us, so after that, there was plenty of food. The living situation wasn't bad. The housing was used by soldiers in training, and the facilities were good like staying in dorms. There were bunk beds. The volunteer agencies—refugee resettlement agencies—started sending people to process us. Some of the agencies, such as the one I work for now, are partially funded by the State Department. Currently they provide five hundred twenty-five dollars for the initial resettlement cost. Part of the funding is also provided by public donations, or foundations. These resettlement agencies and the immigration office sent people in to screen us, to see if the refugees have relatives or friends in the country they could go to, and to process them. Because I could speak English, I started helping many of those who couldn't, translating for them. I met the representative from the International Rescue Committee, and started to work as a volunteer for IRC. I ended up in New York because the IRC offered me a job. Southeast Asian refugees were calling the office, and no one could understand what they were saying. I was so happy that I could get a job right away. I asked my boss if he thought that I alone could support a whole family of nine. And he said, "Probably not. Why don't I hire your sister, too?" She was only nineteen at the time, and we've worked for the IRC ever since.

My sister and I left the camp first, and we started work as soon as we got to New York. We started looking for apartments, but at the time, my salary was only one hundred fifty dollars a week, and my sister made one hundred twenty-five dollars. Someone took us to look for an apartment in Flushing, Queens. A two bedroom was two hundred fifty dollars, and a one bedroom was one hundred ninety dollars, and even with a family of nine, we took the one bedroom, because we tried to save as much as possible. Fortunately, the building superintendent was a refugee—from Cuba—and he helped us. He said he wouldn't tell the landlord that there were nine people living there as long as we didn't make any noise, and kept the children quiet. So he helped us get the apartment. He lied to the landlord for us by saying there were only two girls in the apartment—my sister and myself. The superintendent was very helpful. He tried to get some used furniture for us, and used clothes and dishes. He collected them from other tenants and his friends. That is how we started.

Half a month later, we had the rest of our family join us. Even though there was only my sister and I working to support nine, life wasn't bad. We were quite happy. But the only frustration was our parents. They had a lot of difficulty adjusting. They felt isolated, because there were no Cantonese-speaking people in the building, and in the daytime, when all the children were in school, there was nothing for them to do but sit. In the beginning, I wanted to go back to Vietnam, because life was easier there. Here, we had no friends or relatives, and the lifestyle was so different. Even the mailbox was different. Every evening, we opened it and it was full of papers and envelopes. I was afraid to throw away anything in case it was important, so I would read every word—thinking they were letters—not realizing that this was advertising, junk.

As for my siblings, they knew that if I couldn't support them I would give them away. So they were very happy when I didn't have to do that. They felt lucky. So they worked hard. They didn't think about many of the things children think about today—expensive toys, expensive clothes, fixing their hair. We wore whatever people gave us. Today I tell my refugee clients, I wore the same used clothes people gave me until two years ago. I finally threw them out because they were so worn.

The first books we bought were dictionaries. We got three or four of them. We used them a lot. We didn't have any friends or relatives here, but at least we were together as a family. The children studied very hard to catch up in school. We had only one table, and they all had to study together around the same place, and all of them still feel this closeness to this day. We helped each other. I helped the children at that time, but not now. Now they correct my accent.

We had no furniture—just a few chairs and a used sofa that the supervisor gave us, and broken TV. And the rest were mattresses. We had no beds, only mattresses. In the evening, we had to carry all the mattresses to the living room for the males to sleep. All the females slept in the bedroom. And we lived in this condition for two and a half years, until we were able to get a two-bedroom apartment. We waited till we felt financially secure to do this. We had saved some money over the two and a half years, and because I was getting married, I felt that with my husband's income, we could afford to move. My husband and I got a one bedroom apartment and my family moved to a two bedroom place in the same building. We were very happy. We felt that we were one family unit. We were really together, and sharing. There was no privacy, but we all remembered the times we had gone through together, and we were able to work things out with each other without problems.

All my younger sisters and brothers have done very well in school. And the teachers and school counselors have shown them what is the best way for them to go. Actually, we didn't give them that much counselling. They all got it from school. Even though they don't act the same way I did when I was going to school in Vietnam, they still have certain values—such as respect, and obeying teachers, and therefore the teachers liked them, and tried to help them. My sister got a full scholarship to MIT from Bell Labs. I have one brother who got an electrical engineering degree from Columbia, and the other finished at City College. One other brother is going to medical school at New York Med.

I think the problems we had when we first came to this country helped our success. We're not like other people who were born here, and had everything. We went through all those difficulties, so when we have a chance, we grab it. We now own a two family house. My husband and I live in one side, my parents in the other.

2. Le Tan Si Writes a College Essay About His Terrifying Escape by Boat from Vietnam, 1979 (1989)

Around 9:00 P.M. on June 4, 1979, our boat departed in good weather with fifty-eight people on board. Our boat operated safely for the next two days. However, although I had paid for my trip I starved on those days. The trip was full of hardship. Around 2:00 A.M. on June 6, 1979, the overworked engine broke down. Our boat drifted downwind, and so did my life. During this period, I left my life to chance. Early the morning of June 7, the weather changed suddenly. It was raining and the wind was blowing and, because our boat's engine was broken, the boat bobbed up and down with the waves. We were frightened because we had no control over our boat with a dead engine; we prayed to God for help in the heavy rain. Meanwhile, we anchored to make the boat safer. I thought and thought about my life, parents, and friends, and I also wondered if my death was near. Our supply of food and water was gradually decreasing as our boat drifted on the sea, so we starved. We prayed for a savior who could help and rescue us from this hardship.

Around 11:00 A.M. that day, a strange boat came toward our boat. It was a Thai boat in which there were six Thai fishermen. The Thai fishermen tried to help us repair our engine, but they were not able to; however, they took our engine apart. Then they gave us lunch and some cans of water, and they told us that they would help us. By noon, the Thai fishermen towed our boat to Malaysia after they and Vinh, the boat's owner, talked over our situation.

Our boat passed into Thailand's territorial waters. Ten minutes later, the Thai "fishermen" displayed guns, knives, and hooks in order to frighten us. We understood then that the Thai fishermen were pirates. They quickly took our valuables, such as rings, earrings, chains, watches, and bracelets, because they saw another boat coming toward us. Perhaps the pirates were afraid that it might have been a Thai patrol boat, so they left right after they robbed us. However, this other boat was also a fishing boat. They passed by our boat without pity; in fact, they laughed at us, because they perceived that we had been robbed recently. I had not been robbed by the pirates, because I had hidden my gold ring in my mouth, but I was a little scared by the pirates. Almost all of us were flabbergasted at the recent occurrence. We understood that we were faced with Thai pirates and would probably die next time.

"Thai pirates" are words I will never forget for the rest of my life. I don't like to remember why. In fact, they were simple fishermen but they availed themselves of the opportunity of becoming pirates. More than one thousand Vietnamese were killed or committed suicide when confronted by such robbers. From the Vietnamese newspaper I learned that pirates captured over one hundred Vietnamese girls and women and took them to a deserted island to rape them. Some of those females killed themselves. Others contracted venereal disease. The pirates raped the Vietnamese girls and women on our boats, and killed the people who struggled with them....

The pirates, the same we had encountered that morning, jumped aboard. I was the first person who dove into the ocean when I heard someone call "jump," and then others followed. I was in the water a few minutes with fear, because I realized that if I stayed long in the ocean I might be a shark's prey, so my people and I swam back to our boat. Then the pirates checked everyone elaborately and robbed some more of our valuables. Next, the pirates ordered us to get in the front of our boat, where almost all the people fainted from gasoline vapors. The owner of our boat told us that someone had emptied out the gas tank because he wanted to be supported with that tank in the sea.

Those real situations made me think about death, which seemed to lessen my own energy. Besides, I thought that if I were to have an easy death I would have to pass out. Pass out ... the phrase haunted my mind continually until I heard someone laughing. The laughter became fainter and fainter in my ears, and I lost consciousness.

The day after, I woke up and I was very happy that I had not died that night. The pirates left us an hour after they had robbed us. Then I went back to the cabin and found my ring, which I had thrown into the engine room. So I was not robbed the second time either. After that, I had my property in the corner of our boat. I felt starved again, so I thought in my starved mind that the pirates came to us, because we had some food and water.

Around 10:30 A.M. on June 9, other pirates came to rob us, and they gave us some food and water. They left us after they took a gold ring from us, but they refused to help us by towing our boat to land or to Malaysia. We despaired and could not do anything with our boat, so everyone prayed again to God to help us. A few hours later it rained, so we had some rainwater by using a parachute to catch it. The rain stopped around 3:00 P.M., but we had no control over our boat. We would sail by the parachute, and our boat would drift to our country or Cambodia in one or two weeks, but we would probably die of starvation before then while our boat floated on the sea. No one had a choice. Everyone's life was left to chance. Fortunately, a Thai boat came toward us after we sailed about ten minutes. They were saviors. They let us have a night on their boat, gave us some soup and water, and tried to repair our engine. Before I slept, I checked my ring for security, and I saw some Thai fishermen check our property. I was silent. On June 10, the Thai fishermen drew our boat to Malaysia. When we spotted the Malaysian islands, they left us after they gave us some food and water. Then we thanked God and our saviors from the bottom of our hearts before we joyfully sailed our boat to Malaysia.

We arrived at the shore about 5:00 P.M. on June 11, and our engine was broken again. We then stopped at the Malaysian seashore and spent a night there. During our time on the island, we exchanged gasoline for some food, packs of cigarettes, and water. Next day, June 12, a Malaysian patrol boat came toward us and towed us toward them. The captain promised us that they would take us to the Malaysian refugee camp on the next day; we were pleased with that news....

About 10:00 A.M. on June 13, the patrol boat's captain refused to guide our boats to their refugee camp, because their government had stopped accepting refugees. There were about thirty thousand Vietnamese refugees in the refugee camp, so the camp was full. Then the captain ordered his patrol boat to tow our boats to Singapore. That news disappointed us and struck us with consternation.... However, they towed us for only about thirty hours; then they left us after they told us to navigate our boats to some islands. We again resigned ourselves to our fate. I thought about death again because our engine was broken....

Finally, our boat came to the unknown islands about 9:00 P.M. on June 14. I saw that there were many Vietnamese people on those islands, and then I learned that I had arrived in Indonesia. I really had survived, because I was a legal refugee in the Indonesian refugee camp when I landed on those islands.

I had a miraculous escape, but my mind was still haunted by death. I did not lose my golden ring, which helped me buy some food in the refugee camp. In January 1980, approval was given for me to migrate to the United States. I lived in the KuKu and Galang refugee camps [in Indonesia] for fourteen months under the support of the United Nations. On August 20, 1980, I set foot in Seattle. I then really had freedom and a new life in this country.

3. Sen Chul Tells an American Embassy Officer of Life and Death Under the Khmer Rouge in Cambodia, 1978

Interview with Cambodian Refugee in Surin, Thailand, Conducted by American Embassy Officer in June 1978

Account of Sen Chul★

Sen Chul, 27, came from Koukman village, Ampil District, Oddar Meanchey Province. He studied eleven years and attended college at Samrong one year, where he received a diploma. He was in Samrong when the Khmer Rouge took over and subsequently returned home to Koukmon. After the takeover, the Khmer Rouge held mass meetings in which everyone was told to identify himself. Chul admitted that he was a student. Chul arrived in Thailand in February 1978.

Conditions of living in Democratic Kampuchea.—"Life was better in Koukmon than in other places. In the mobile youth group in which I worked, we had enough to eat. We had plenty of rice but no fish or meat. In the village, where my family lived, and I lived with my wife after we got married, food was also adequate but limited to rice. The crop was better this year than last year when we had a drought.

"Account of Sen Chul," Interview with Cambodian Refugee in Surin, Thailand, Conducted by American Embassy officer in June 1978. From Indochina Hearing, August 21, 1978. Committee on Foreign Relations, Subcommittee on East Asian and Pacific Affairs.

★(Refugee agreed to use of his name in public document.)

"We were issued one set of clothes when we could no longer mend the ones we had been wearing. For those who worked hard, the clothes wore out in about four months. To get a new set, you had to present concrete evidence that your present ones were worn out. This was easy since they were usually rags. We got one scarf and a set of black pajamas.

"We worked from 0400 to 1100, 1300 to 1700 and 1900 to 2200 each day since 1975.

"I was with a mobile youth until 1976 when I got married. After that I moved to the village and worked as a farmer. Once or twice a year we had a 'mating period.' For two days, while also working, young men and young women were allowed to talk with each other. Except during the mating period, young men and women were not allowed to talk with each other, day or night, except for talk about developing the country. If the Khmer Rouge knew that you had violated this 'ethics code' you would both be executed immediately. I knew of about twenty young men and women caught flirting, who were executed. No romantic chit-chat is allowed. After the two day mating period, you report to the authorities that you have found a suitable partner. Aside from the mating period, you cannot tell a girl that you like her. You must go to the village chief and tell him. If you tell her directly, you will be killed. In either case, if the chief agrees, you must wait until the mass marriages are held about every six months at the same time as the mating season.

Girls have no right to refuse. Even if the man is crippled, had one hand, or is ugly, the girl must accept. She is summoned and told that she must marry. If she refuses, she will be executed. In some cases, she and her family are told that they must be 'relocated' far away. In 1976 about fifteen families of girls who refused to marry were relocated. But, in fact, the Khmer Rouge escorts returned the next day with all their clothes and distributed them to others. Everyone thought that the families were executed. Being 'relocated' frequently means being executed."

Executions.—"The Khmer Rouge have executed all the former soldiers and government officials they can identify. They also forcibly relocated the families of former soldiers. I knew of about fifty families of former soldiers who were sent to the northern district, but everyone thinks they were also executed.

"In 1978, the Khmer Rouge started executing former students, former members of village defense forces, or former militiamen. They started with the leaders and with those who studied to higher grades. In January and February, about twenty students, who had studied five years or more and had then been assigned to the mobile youth, and about thirty former militiamen were executed. I know of thirteen young men, some of whom were my friends, who were killed. The Khmer Rouge tied their hands behind them and took them to the forest. The next day I saw 13 fresh mounds. No one knew of any reason why they would have been killed except that they were former students.

"The worst crime is criticizing the way people are being treated and administered. If you do so, the Khmer Rouge say, 'you are a bad element' and 'do not support Angka'. If they want to kill anyone, the Khmer Rouge merely say, 'you are supporting the enemy' or 'you are a spy.' These are only pretexts. These charges are made either before you are executed or afterward. Before killing students, there were usually no meeting. The Khmer Rouge would just round up ten or so and take them away.

"In Koukman now there are only one fourth as many men as women. There are many, many widows. In 1975 there were 2500 people in my village. There are only 1500 now. More than 250 were killed; others fled to Thailand. Others were assigned to the mobile youth groups.

"There were not many Chinese in my village, only three families. They were all killed in 1978. Friends from other villages told me the same thing, that many Chinese families were executed in January 1978. The Khmer Rouge said, 'the Chinese used to exploit the Cambodian people.'

"I had two cousins killed in 1978. They were Chhum Bu, about 50, and Sin Sok, about 45. After they were executed, their families were taken away to be 'relocated.' We believe that all eleven members of their families were also executed. There were about 60 families 'relocated' since 1975."

Human, civil and political rights.—"There are no rights or freedoms in Cambodia. The Khmer Rouge have clamped down on every facet of life. The central government's policy is to exterminate all the old people to have a new generation of Cambodians who have never known a good life. Their policy can be compared to burning a field of grass so that new grass can replace the old. They are succeeding very well because they are killing everybody."

4. Lao Veterans of America President Colonel Wangyee Vang Requests Naturalization Rights, 2000

Mr. Chairman, I want to extend my deepest gratitude to you and the distinguished members of the Immigration Subcommittee for holding this crucial hearing on H.R. 371, The Hmong Veterans' Naturalization Act of 1997. For many years, the Hmong people have enjoyed the staunch and tireless support of Congressman Bill McCollum, Congressman Henry Hyde, Congressman Steve Chabot, Congresswoman Zoe Lofgren and many other members of the Judiciary Committee in the struggle against genocide and human rights violations in communist Laos. We are, indebted to Congressman Bruce Vento for his leadership role in introducing this important legislation that, if enacted, will help Hmong veterans who faithfully served in the U.S. Secret Army in Laos finally become U.S. citizens.

Because of a number of key individuals, many Hmong veterans and their refugee families are fortunate to enjoy freedom in the United States of America and to attend this historic occasion before the U.S. Congress. I would like to mention Major General Vang Pao, former commander of the U.S. Secret Army in Laos; Theodore G. Shackley, former Central Intelligence Agency (CIA) Station Chief in Laos and South Vietnam; Mr. Philip Smith, former Legislative Assistant for U.S. Congressman Don Ritter and Washington Director for

Hmong Veterans' Naturalization Act of 1997; and Canadian Border Boat Landing Permit Requirements: Hearing on H.R. 371 Before the Subcommittee on Immigration and Claims, 105th Cong. (June 26, 1997) (Washington, D.C.: Government Printing Office, 1997).

the Lao Veterans of America; Brigadier General Paul Carroll, USAF–Ret.; Major General Ronald Markarian, USA–Ret; Colonel James Arthur, USAF–Ret.; Jack Matthews, former CIA officer in Laos; Dr. Jane Hamilton-Merritt, distinguished journalist and scholar; and, other dedicated individuals.

Mr. Chairman, the Lao Veterans of America, Inc. (LVA), like the American Legion and the Veterans of Foreign Wars (VFW), represents veterans who served the United States honorably. It is the largest veterans organization of its kind in the United States and includes tens of thousands of Hmong and Lao veterans and their families who played a critical role in the U.S. covert war in Laos and Vietnam. It is a non-profit corporation—with chapters organized throughout the United States in states such as Alabama, California, Florida, Georgia, Hawaii, Iowa, Illinois, Kansas, Louisiana, Massachusetts, Minnesota, Nebraska, North Carolina, Oklahoma, Ohio, Pennsylvania, Rhode Island, South Carolina, Washington and Wisconsin. The LVA membership include significant numbers of women who served in combat, and combat support roles.

The LVA and its work have been honored by Members of Congress as well as current and former U.S. military and intelligence officials. Members of the LVA have been presented the Vietnam Veterans National Medal as well as other military honors. The LVA has received bipartisan support on Capitol Hill for its efforts. It has been singled out with Congressional awards and citations as well as being honored in Congressional Record statements. In recent years, the Hmong and Lao veterans—and their leadership—have also been cited in Congressional hearing testimony by former CIA Director William Colby and by Dr. Jane Hamilton-Merritt.

Mr. Chairman and Honorable Committee Members, just last month, on May 14–15, after over two decades of silence since the end of the Vietnam War, the Hmong and Lao veterans who served in the U.S. Secret Army were honored for the first time nationally at the Vietnam War Memorial and Arlington National Cemetery. The national news media recorded this historic occasion—"The Lao Veterans of America National Recognition Day." I would urge the Chairman and Members of this committee who did not have the opportunity to attend these national recognition and memorial services to review the public record about these events. Then, please join us in visiting Arlington National Cemetery. The monument that the Department of Defense and Arlington National Cemetery authorized reads: "Dedicated to the U.S. Secret Army, Laos 1961–1973. In memory of the Hmong and Lao combat veterans and their American advisors who served freedom's cause in Southeast Asia. Their patriotic valor and loyalty in the defense of liberty and democracy will never be forgotten. You will never be forgotten (In Lao and Hmong), Lao Veterans of America, May 15, 1997."

Mr. Chairman and Honorable Committee Members, I would urge you to carefully examine the newly declassified information regarding the heroic sacrifices that Hmong special units made on behalf of U.S. national security interests.

Secret, classified studies conducted by the defense policy think-tank RAND [Research And Development], for the Department of Defenses' (DOD) Advanced Research Projects Agency [(ARPA) *since renamed DARPA*] have recently been declassified. *Organizing and Managing Unconventional War in Laos, 1962–1970,* published in 1972, outlines the special case history of the Hmong tribal people. This and other RAND/DOD/ARPA studies reveal the critical role the Hmong played in support of U.S. clandestine and military activities in Laos—and how this force was specially created by the United States government. The unique role played by the Hmong in the U.S. Secret Army is important and relative to the legislation before the Subcommittee today.

Hmong of all ages—men, women and children fought and died alongside U.S. clandestine and military personnel in units recruited, organized, trained, funded, and paid by the United States CIA, U.S. Air Force and others agencies.

It is estimated that during the United State's involvement in the Vietnam conflict, 35,000 to 40,000 Hmong veterans and their families were killed in combat; 50,000 to 58,000 were wounded; and 2,500 to 3,000 were missing. When the United States withdrew from Southeast Asia, genocide followed the Hmong—thousands of Hmong were murdered by the Communists or fled to neighboring Thailand.

Edgar Buell, for U.S. AID [Agency for International Development]/CIA official working with the U.S. Secret Army in Laos during the war years, said on *60 Minutes,* on March 4, 1979: "Everyone of them that died (Hmong), that was an American back home that didn't die, or one that was injured that wasn't injured. Somebody in nearly every Hmong family was either fighting or died from fighting.... They became refugees because we (United State Government) ... encouraged them to fight for us. I promised them myself: 'Have no fear, we will take care of you.'"

About April 1975, the United States withdrew its troops from Indochina. From May 12–14, 1975, the CIA evacuated about 2,500 Hmong officers and their families from the secret base at Long Cheng in Laos (Headquarters of Major General Vang Pao—the combined base for the Hmong, CIA, Air America, and U.S. Air Force "Ravens") to the U.S. air base Namphong, Khonekene, Thailand. The rest of the Special Guerrilla Units (SGUs) and other special units who were left behind began to walk to the Mekong River and crossed to Thailand. Thousands of these soldiers and their families were killed by the Communists forces. During the Communist forces or died of starvation as they fled toward the security and freedom on the other shore of the Mekong river. Thousands drowned in the river before reaching the Thai border. Even today, despite official denials at senior levels of the Pathet Lao government, the Communist regime in Laos continues to persecute and discriminate against the Hmong because of their role in the U.S. Secret Army.

Currently, the majority of these former soldiers and their refugee family members who are now in America cannot become U.S. citizens, because they lack sufficient English language skills to pass the naturalization test. The intense and protracted clandestine war in Laos and the exodus of the Hmong and Lao veterans into squalid refugees camps, or internment in reeducation camps, did not permit the veterans the opportunity to go to school. Once in America, they have led a difficult life—often in poverty-stricken inner-city conditions, raising large families, not permitting them sufficient opportunity to formally study English. Cultural barriers and the fact that a written Hmong language was not used in much of Laos until late in its history have compounded the problems of literacy for the Hmong and taking the U.S. citizenship test in English.

Mr. Chairman and Honorable Committee members, the Hmong soldiers did not come to America as economic migrants; they came to America as political refugees because they were veterans of the U.S. Special Guerrilla Units and other special units in the United States' Secret Army in Laos. The United States has a special obligation to them.

Some 20,000 Hmong veterans—most elderly and aging—will likely achieve citizenship if you act positively on this legislation. On behalf of the Hmong and Lao veterans, I ask that this be done so that America can honorably close this chapter in its history and honor the commitments and pledges it made to care for the Hmong people—and not forsake them.

Thank you.

5. San Jose City Council Member Madison Nguyen Fights a Recall and Charges That She's a Communist, 2009

Ira Glass

This is Councilwoman Madison Nguyen. The San Jose politician at the center of all this controversy. She says that although a vocal portion of her Vietnamese constituents definitely preferred Little Saigon, Vietnamese-Americans only make up a third of her district. Non-Vietnamese people and businesses in the district wanted other names. And she thought it would be better to avoid a name that was so political. So she chose what she thought was a compromise.

Madison Nguyen

And so I thought, OK, well both names have the name Saigon in it, and this is a business district designation. Why don't we just called it Saigon Business District and hopefully that will make everyone happy.

Ira Glass

I want to play you a recording from this six and a half hour City Council meeting about this. And it's many people standing up, saying that they don't want this name. And here's one man and—there's a point in the tape where he says if Madison wins, what he means is if you get your way and the community is not called Little Saigon. Here let me play this for you.

[AUDIO PLAYBACK]

–Before 1975, I was Ranger Commander in Vietnam. I was in jail nine year. Tonight I come here to request only one vote from you for Little Saigon.

"Turncoat", *This American Life*, May 22, 2009. Retrieved from http://www.thisamericanlife.org. Used with permission.

I strongly support you from the beginning. But if Madison win, we stay away from her, because she's pro-Communist. Thank you.

[END AUDIO PLAYBACK]

What's your reaction to that kind of thing?

Madison Nguyen

It was torture to have all these people, who are pretty much at the age of my parents or grandparents, coming up and looking you, staring you in the face, in your eyes and said we no longer trust you. You're not one of us. We regret that we ever supported you. To hear that over, and over, and over, and over again. I mean it's painful.

Ira Glass

Then there's the fact that she was being called a Communist, widely.

Madison Nguyen

The first time I heard it, I was very hurt. I felt that—I came here as a boat child back in the late 1970s. I escaped Communism in Vietnam and I came here. We pretty much risked our lives to come to this great country. And to have this particular group of people in the Vietnamese community label me as a Communist sympathizer, I thought was really beyond absurd.

Ira Glass

Madison is convinced that if she had been a non-Vietnamese City Councilperson suggesting the exact same name, Saigon Business District, it never would have gone this far. No protest. Nobody would have been labeled a Communist.

People felt betrayed, she says, because she was one of them. They expected her to do what they wanted. And they couldn't believe it when she didn't. To them, she was a turncoat. What strikes deeper than that?

Act One. Code Red.

My Thuan Tran

If you listen to Vietnamese radio during that time period, a lot of people would come out and say they believe she was a Communist.

Ira Glass

Again, reporter My Thuan Tran.

My Thuan Tran

I just felt that it was a really interesting case because it kind of showed the challenges of being a Vietnamese-American politician. That you kind of had to navigate among all these lingering emotions from this war that had ended 34 years ago.

Ira Glass

Yeah, you wrote, "The rules of politics are different for a Vietnamese-American politician. Even business owners, reporters, and pop singers carefully tiptoe around inferences and innuendo that can cast a person as being soft on Communism. A misstep can launch vocal protests and accusations. Reputations can be tarnished. People must bow to the pressure."

My Thuan Tran

Right. I think it's a surprise for many people who are kind of unfamiliar with the Vietnamese-American community how much this name-calling and suspicion still resonates. I think some people feel like it looks like out of the McCarthy era when they view the Vietnamese-American community.

Ira Glass

There are tons of examples of this kind of red-baiting. The first Vietnamese Superintendent of Schools in the Westminster School District in Orange County was removed a week after she was appointed, she says, because an activist lobbied school board members, saying she was a Communist. In Saint Paul, Minnesota, when a Catholic bishop visited from Vietnam, he asked that [he] not be photograph with anything political. So his Vietnamese-American host in Minnesota, a man named Tuan Pham, took down the flag of the old country of South Vietnam which was in many exile communities. Tuan Pham was vilified as a pro-Communist because of that.

Protests at his store were so intense that customers stopped coming. His business went bankrupt. Tuan Pham not only battled the Communists as a soldier during the war, but was held in one of their prison camps for two years.

My Thuan Tran

There's another interesting example I wanted to bring up. There was a Vietnamese-American pop singer named Tommy Ngo. And in one of the posters for a concert, he's wearing a belt with the word L-O-V-E on it. And the O has a star in it. And the word "LOVE" is in red and the star is white, but on the poster it kind of looked like the star was yellow. And a yellow star on a red background is actually the symbol of the official Vietnamese flag, which is known as the Communist flag. So, even that concert was protested against, and Tommy Ngo was protested against. And a lot of people didn't end up going to the concert.

Even one of the contributors to our radio show, Thanh Tan, who is a reporter from Boise Public Television, has watched as her dad, who runs a Vietnamese community organization in Olympia, Washington, has been red-baited. It's particularly galling to her, she says, because she spent her childhood resenting how much time her dad spent at anti-Communist demonstrations.

Thanh Tan

It's just really upsetting to hear these accusations against somebody who—his idea of fun with the family was to take us to a protest in Seattle, and to wave around the old nationalist flag, the yellow flag with the three stripes.

Ira Glass

You mean an anti-Communist protest?

Thanh Tan

Yeah. Like, I grew up on that. I have pictures of me when I was like, six years old, holding a sign that says Ho Chi Minh is a criminal.

Ira Glass

Thanh's dad has now won a defamation against the activists who called him a Communist sympathizer. The Thurston County Court awarded him and his organization $310,000. But Thanh says that the stress of all this has hurt her parents' marriage and her dad's health. And somehow her family doesn't feel a sense of victory after all this.

Thanh Tan

You know, I don't just because like right after the trial, like within a week, I saw a television, like a Vietnamese television report where the defendants were interviewed. And the main guy, he said that my dad—he said something along the lines of Communists don't wear their badge on their chest. And to me that just said going through this whole trial, three week trial was not enough to prove to him that my dad apparently is not a Communist. And that really was pretty upsetting.

I mean my mother, she calls me, and she just said Thanh, what do we do? Like, what we do? Like, the Vietnamese media is still reporting that your dad could be a Communist. Like, I don't know what to do.

Ira Glass

I understand that there's a Vietnamese phrase for red-baiting that's used here in the States.

Thanh Tan

Mm-hmm. It's called "chup mu."

Ira Glass

And what does it mean literally?

Thanh Tan

It literally means to put the Communist hat on someone.

Ira Glass

The City Councilwoman in San Jose, Madison Nguyen, faced a recall election and she won. Mainly, she's just tired of the red-baiting. At the height of all the protests she wondered, is this why we came to this country? So we could fight over who's a Communist?

Madison Nguyen

Even now, which is really sad, but I'll share with you anyways. My in-laws, they're still living in Vietnam right now, and I was recently married. And my father-in-law had a stroke about two months ago. And so, I wanted to have the opportunity to go back. But I can't, because I know that if I go back now, imagine what's going to happen when I come back here to San Jose.

Ira Glass

You can't say you're visiting a relative?

Madison Nguyen

Yeah, good luck.

Ira Glass

Why? What will they say?

Madison Nguyen

I mean, I really—and when I tell people, I tell my friends that, they're like, there's no way you can go because if you go, the first thing that's going to happen when you come back is that, oh look! She's going back there. She's probably trying to connect with the Vietnamese government, or get in some kind of relationship.

And so it's just—and so, here I am thinking like, am I ready to put up another fight?

Ira Glass

She says she doesn't want to put her supporters through all that again. So she's careful. But she wants to be in politics, she says. With so many people ready to see her as a traitor. And that's just how it's got to be.

6. Channapha Khamvongsa Calls on Congress to Fund the Removal of Unexploded Bombs in Laos, 2010

Statement of Channapha Khamvongsa
Executive Director
Legacies of War

Committee on House Foreign Affairs
Subcommittee on Asia, The Pacific, and The Global Environment

April 22, 2010

Thank you Chairman [Eni] Faleomavaega, Subcommittee Members, ladies and gentlemen. First of all, I would like to extend my sincere thanks to Chairman Faleomavaega, the Subcommittee and its wonderful staff for organizing this historic hearing entitled "Legacies of War: Unexploded Ordnances in Laos."

From what I understand, this is the first U.S. House of Representatives hearing on the scourge of unexploded ordnance (UXO) in Laos, a legacy of the U.S. bombing of Laos during the Vietnam War. Tragically, more than four decades after the end of the bombing, more than 300 Lao people, one third of them children, continue to be killed or injured by UXO every year.

Just this year, on February 19, 2010, eight children from Champassak Province came upon a cluster bomb in the rice paddies near their home. Like many bombs this deadly weapon resembled a toy, and the children tossed it around in play. The bomb exploded; two children survived, one was severely injured, and five were killed. They lived in an area not identified as having been bombed; there had been no UXO risk education in their village and the children suffered for it. Beyond this terrible human toll, UXO continues to hamper economic development in one of the poorest countries in the world.

Today is also significant because exactly 39 years ago this week the U.S. Senate held an historic hearing on the status of refugees in Laos. This hearing, chaired by the late Senator Edward M. Kennedy on April 21 and 22, 1971, helped expose the U.S. secret bombing of Laos. The bombing had begun in 1964 and had displaced hundreds of thousands of civilians within Laos but had never been disclosed to Congress or the American public....

The 1971 hearing and a peace treaty between the U.S. and North Vietnam finally brought a halt to the bombings in Laos in 1973. This was the same year I was born in Vientiane, the capital of Laos. When I was six years old, my family left Laos due to the country's political instability. We spent a year in a Thai refugee camp and eventually resettled in Virginia. Many of the 400,000 Lao refugees who now reside in the U.S. have similar stories. We were fortunate to resettle in America, but were sad to leave behind family members and friends who we feared we might never see again.

Statement of Channapha Khamvongsa, "Unexploded Ordnances in Lao," April 22, 2010, Committee on House Foreign Affairs, Subcommittee on Asia, The Pacific, and The Global Environment, Committee on Foreign Affairs Serial No. 111–117, http://congressional.proquest.com:80/congressional/docview/t05.d06.2011-h381-28?accountid=14523

Much has changed since then. Over the past ten years, improved relations between the Lao and U.S. governments have allowed me to travel back to Laos numerous times. Like thousands of other tourists who visit Laos every year, I feel a deep affection for the people, culture and land that I barely remember from my childhood.

Reconnecting with my Lao heritage included discovering the dark history and lingering effects of what is often referred to as the Secret War in Laos. This discovery led me to establish Legacies of War ("Legacies"), where I currently serve as executive director. Legacies is the only U.S.-based organization dedicated to raising awareness about the current devastation that has resulted from the Vietnam War-era bombing in Laos. Our mission is to advocate for the clearance of unexploded bombs and provide space for healing the wounds of war. Since our founding in 2004, we have worked with LaoAmericans, bombing survivors, veterans, artists, non-governmental organizations and others to establish a credible voice for reconciliation and justice.

The 1971 Senate hearing began to expose the bombings in Laos, but it would be decades before declassified U.S. military data revealed the true extent of the bombing and the ongoing devastation from UXO in Laos.

Background

We now know that Laos is the most heavily bombed country per capita in history. U.S. Vietnam War-era bombings from 1964 to 1973 left nearly half of Laos contaminated with vast quantities of unexploded ordnance. At least 25,000 people have been killed or injured by UXO in Laos since the bombing ceased.... I would like to share with you some other disturbing facts about the U.S. bombing of Laos and its tragic aftermath;

—260 million cluster bombs were dropped on Laos during the Vietnam War' ... (210 million more bombs than were dropped on Iraq in 1991, 1998 and 2006 combined)...

An estimated 75 million cluster bombs did not detonate, scattering throughout Lao villages, rice fields, schoolyards, pastureland and forests....

During the bombing, the equivalent of a planeload of bombs was dropped every eight minutes, 24-hours a day for nine years.

—About one-third of the land in Laos is littered with UXO.

The Clean Up So Far

For more than 20 years after the war ended, Lao villagers struggled to survive among vast quantities of unexploded ordnance without any organized technical assistance or clearance program. The relationship between Laos and the U.S. was strained, and there were no humanitarian demining programs operational in the Lao NGO [Non-governmental organization] sector. In the 1970s and early 1980s, about 1,000 casualties from UXO occurred every year. This number declined slowly, and has remained at about 300 casualties per year through the 1990s and 2000s....

The humanitarian demining program in Laos began in 1994 under the auspices of the Lao National Committee for Social and Veterans Affairs, as a result of an initiative from the U.S.-based Mennonite Central Committee with technical support and training provided by the UK-based Mines Advisory Group. Each of these organizations has provided testimony to the Subcommittee today.

In the 15 years since the demining program began, it has grown, employing Lao nationals in nine Lao provinces. Undoubtedly, thousands of lives have been saved and injuries avoided as a result of this work. Yet fewer than 500,000 of the estimated 75 million unexploded bomblets remaining at the end of the war have been destroyed, and less than 1% of the contaminated land has been cleared....

Initially, I was surprised by the small percentage of land that has been cleared. Then, during a trip to Laos in 2008 as part of a Legacies of War delegation, I observed a clearance team working in the field. I witnessed the slow, dangerous, tedious process of surveying, detecting and detonating UXO. Over the last four decades, many of the cluster bomblets have become deeply embedded in the earth-waiting for an unsuspecting farmer to place a shovel in the earth or the Monsoon rains to uncover them. It often takes several visits to one village to detect and clear all the bomblets. I was humbled by the men and women we met during our visit to Laos, who risk their lives daily to make the land safe for others.

Clear Problem, Effective Solution

Formal UXO clearance work in Laos is now done under the auspices of the Lao government's National Regulatory Authority (NRA), with several dozen partner organizations and international donors that support the UXO clearance, victim assistance and risk education.

The UXO clearance sector has built up a well-trained and experienced work force. Through new, more effective equipment and careful planning, clearance teams have dramatically improved their efficiency. An official of the State Department's Office of Weapons Removal and Abatement (WRA) has called the National Regulatory Authority UXO program in Laos "one of the best programs in the world – the gold standard."

The NRA's newly completed strategic plan, entitled Safe Path Forward.-2010–2020, offers clear, achievable goals:

1. Reduce the number of UXO casualties from 300 to less than 75 per year
2. Ensure that the medical and rehabilitation needs of all UXO Survivors are met in line with treaty obligations
3. Release priority land and clear UXO in accordance with National Standards and treaty obligations
4. Ensure effective leadership, coordination and implementation of the national program
5. Establish sustainable national capacity fully integrated into the regular set-up of the Government
6. Meet international treaty obligations

In addition to its domestic leadership, Laos was one of the first nations to sign and ratify the Convention on Cluster Munitions, an international agreement signed by 106 countries to ban the production, transfer, and sale of cluster munitions and to destroy current stockpiles.... In addition, participating countries must clear cluster munitions from the land and provide victim assistance. The agreement emphasizes the need for increased international financial support to Laos.

The Convention enters into force in August of this year, and Laos will host the First Meeting of the State Parties in Vientiane in November to discuss implementation of the agreement. Laos' leadership in gaining international approval of the Convention and hosting the First Meeting of the State Parties signals its shift from mere victim of cluster munitions to key voice for their eradication.

Funding Requirements

According to the NRA, during each of the past three years, a total of $12 to $14 million was spent for clearance goals.... Funding for clearance comes from international donors, including the U.S., but the NRA estimates that the UXO sector will need at least double that amount per year to meet its ten-year goals. As it always has been, the problem for UXO clearance in Laos is the absence of a consistent, long-term funding commitment that matches the scale of the problem. In order to buy equipment and train and maintain adequate staffing, clearance organizations working in the field must have assurances of a continued, reliable stream of funding.

Consistent, increased international support for clearance would dramatically reduce the impact of UXO in Laos. With this kind of consistent support, the casualty rate would fall from hundreds a year to dozens or less, and the highest priority clearance projects would all be accomplished.

We recommend a U.S. commitment of $7 million to support UXO clearance in Laos in FYI [fiscal year 1] 1, a measured increase from this year's allocation of $5 million. Thereafter, we recommend an annual U.S. commitment of $10 million over the next 10 years to strengthen and secure the UXO sector's capacity and bring its already effective programs to scale. This ten-year $100 million commitment to UXO removal in Laos would total less than what the U.S. spent in one week bombing Laos....

I have focused primarily on UXO clearance in this statement, but I also want to note the related need for victim assistance. Close to 40% of UXO accidents result in death, leaving many families without the primary breadwinner or caregiver. For the 60% who survive, their lives will never be the same. Almost 14,000 injuries have resulted in the loss of one limb, while close to 3,000 victims have lost two limbs.

Many gave been blinded. In Laos, the vast majority of the population is dependent on subsistence farming. UXO accidents leave many farmers unable to work in their fields. There is a serious need for better emergency health care after accidents occur as well as longer term needs for prosthetics, physical rehabilitation and vocational retraining....

According to the NRA, only $2.5 million a year currently goes towards victim assistance needs in Laos. Agency staff estimates that at least $5 million a year will be required to adequately help victims and their families....

Current U.S. Funding Support

The U.S. spent $17 million a day (today's dollars) for nine years bombing Laos. However, the U.S. has provided on average only $2.7 million per year for clearance in Laos over the past 15 years. Put another way, the U.S. spent more in three days dropping bombs on Laos ($51 million in today's dollars) than they have spent in the last 15 years ($40 million) cleaning them up.

In Fiscal Year 2010, Congress designated $5 million specifically for UXO clearance in Laos, the largest amount allocated in any given year to date....

We applaud this specific allocation. It represented a tremendous step forward – or so we thought. Unfortunately, despite a specific Congressional mandate for $5 million for bomb removal in Laos this year and in subsequent years, the Department of State is only requesting $1.9 million for next year (FYI 1)....

Conclusion

It has been nearly 40 years since the secret U.S. bombing campaign in Laos was finally revealed to Congress and the American public. Yet, all these years later, massive quantities of UXO remain a dangerous threat to the daily lives of the people in Laos.

This is Mol, a five-year-old Lao girl from Thajok Village in Xieng Khouang Province. Unlike hundreds of Lao children who have been killed or injured by cluster bombs each year, Mol is still alive and healthy. But she lives and plays among these deadly weapons every day. She has never known a bomb-free backyard. We must do what we can to protect children like Mol and clear the land so that when she walks to school, her family plows their fields, or her neighbor forages for bamboo in the forest, everyone returns home safely at the end of the day. We should want this for Mol and the generations that will follow her.

The problem of UXO in Laos has been allowed to persist far too long. Too many innocent lives have been lost. Too many farmers and children have been left disabled, their lives forever changed. But it is not too late to stop this senseless suffering. This is one of those rare tractable problems with a clear and effective solution. The U.S. has a responsibility to clean up the unexploded bombs it left behind in Laos and to provide support for those who have been harmed since the end of the war. It would require only a relatively modest increase in U.S. funding to dramatically improve clearance activities and victim assistance in Laos.

If we had the cure for a disease, would we let people continue to suffer and die from it? Clearing cluster bombs in Laos and supporting those injured by them is an act of humanity and decency. It is the right thing to do.

The State Department must make a sustained commitment to solving this problem. We recommend an allocation of at least $7 million next year followed a subsequent increase to $10 million per year over the next 10 years. With this kind of consistent support, the casualty rate would fall from hundreds a year to dozens or less, and the highest priority clearance projects would all be accomplished.

Thank you Chairman Faleomavaega and Subcommittee Members for the opportunity to offer our statement today. We appreciate the attention you have brought to this important issue.

7. *Gran Torino*'s Hmong Lead Bee Vang Comments on Film, Race, and Masculinity, 2010

LS (Louisa Schein): *So what went through your head when you started to hear about Gran Torino?*

BV (Bee Vang): I never thought I would try out. I heard about the story and the "sides"—the excerpts from the script that were used for auditions—and I was just really repulsed by what I read. I tried to make sense of the characters and their lines. But there were things I couldn't figure out about the relations between Walt and the Hmong characters. For instance, at some point Thao tells Walt "Go ahead. I don't care if you insult me or say racist things, because you know what? I'll take it." I didn't understand why a character like Thao would say that. Why wouldn't he object to being insulted? What does "taking it" even mean? What was intended by the screenwriter or was this just careless writing?

LS: *The story, as we know, takes place in Detroit and centers on a white man who is probably dying and doesn't have much time left. His Asian neighbors are a backdrop to his search for redemption from acts in the Korean war—*

BV: Of course, those Asians are nothing but FOBs [fresh off the boat] or youth on the streets killing each other...

LS: *Right. So Walt has to teach them the "right" way to behave, and to save the good ones from the bad. In the process, he valiantly takes the fall. Talk about your impressions of the plot, the script itself.*

BV: The thing is, the story can't take place without those Hmong characters, especially mine. But in the end, it's Walt that gets glorified. We fade out in favor of his heroism. I felt negated by the script and by extension in my assuming the role. It's almost like a non-role. Strange for a lead...

LS: *What about the script's portrayal of Thao's masculinity?*

BV: Well first off, the girlfriend part is totally crazy....Walt and the gangsters and the grandma—all of them have nothing but insults about Thao's manliness—or lack thereof. He doesn't cut it in any way and he's not super-hot. So why is it that the gorgeous girl decides to pick him over all the other guys?

"Hmong Lead Bee Vang on Film, Race, and Masculinity: Conversations with Louisa Schein," *Hmong Studies Journal* 11 (Spring 2010): 2–10. Reprinted by permission of the author and the *Hmong Studies Journal*.

LS: *It sends an incoherent message, doesn't it?*

BV: That the dumb, passive, quiet, loner guy can still get the best girl. It pained me that Thao let his masculinity suffer so badly over the course of the story....

LS: *So you were uneasy about the lines and character descriptions. Why did you audition and ultimately take the part?*

BV: Friends kept pushing me to try out. I didn't take it seriously. Didn't think I'd get the part. But when I was called back for another round of auditioning, I realized I wanted to be part of the hype, because this would become a great cultural event of our time, especially for Hmong. Most importantly, my intentions were, as I continued to audition and do my best, to try to improve on the script and the ways Hmong were portrayed. I wanted to create a character that people could love. I decided to commit to developing the role of Thao, making him more complex and credible. I imagined a guy who would chafe at his subordination more. So even when he had to obey, he did it with more attitude.

LS: *Did you feel you succeeded in creating this character?*

BV: I added a lot of intonation and gestures to try to give Thao some dignity. For instance, when my sister is offering me to work for Walt, I raised my voice to a shout to indicate I hated the idea of slaving for Walt. That outburst wasn't in the script. But most of the script was not very open to interpretation and it was premised on his not having any dignity. He needs to be clueless and have no self-respect in order for the white elder man to achieve his savior role. He has to hang his head and absorb abuse. So it makes me wonder how a character like Thao could bring any change to Walt....

LS: *Were you able to draw on parts of yourself or your experience for this role?*

BV: Well that was the idea, from what I could tell. The production process didn't include rehearsals or coaching. Eastwood didn't want us to consult with him. He just wanted us to be ourselves. The plan was for us to be so-called "natural actors," just stepping out of our lives and into the frames. This way the production could move efficiently. So we didn't get the scripts until a week before the shooting started and had no prep time to get into the psychology of the character.

LS: *What did this mean in terms of your process, then?*

BV: The roadblock for me was that I couldn't identify with Thao as the demeaned boy that he was. All the while, hearing that my performance was to be as a so-called "natural," I found myself resisting the character more and more. So I had to draw instead on my best acting skills to counter my feelings about Eastwood's lack of direction. I had to put aside my doubts about the character, and create a contradictory guy who was sometimes just submissive and sometimes struggled to stand up for himself. I wanted him to have depth and complexity. I had to make that up myself … to the extent that it was possible within the script.…

LS: *Say more about the role itself.*

BV: But then I think that maybe it's not about the quality of my acting. It's the fact of the character being unsympathetic because of his weakness. It's an odd thing, as a first time actor, to have to step into a role that's disparaged by the script and humiliated by the other characters. Playing him well is like making a deal with the devil. To the extent that I did a good job, I reinforced that image of effeminate Asian guys who are wimps, geeks and can't advocate for themselves.

LS: *Does Thao become a man in your opinion? Does he get stronger?*

BV: I worked on that. It wasn't easy because the scenes were shot completely out of sequence so it was hard to get a sense of the continuity and the progression. I tried to show Thao's change through the physicality of my performances. I hung my head less and less. In the barbershop scene, I made my voice get a bit raspier and more like Eastwood's as they tried to "man me up." I threw in some sassy gestures. By the time I was getting the job at the construction site, I added more of a swagger to my walk. Things like that.

LS: *So did this mean he was achieving manhood?*

BV: I'm pretty iffy about that. For instance, at the end of the barbershop scene, the humor comes from the fact that Thao doesn't know what he's saying. He supposedly tries to talk like the older white men, but stupidly comes up with a line that makes him out to be an object of male gang-rape or something. What the barber and Walt laugh at him for is that he doesn't even know what he's saying. This relies on a kind of a dumb refugee image. The line he says—'boy does my ass hurt from all the guys at my construction job'—is just nonsensical to him. Only the white guys get the homophobic joke. So, Thao really doesn't grow in this scene; for some reason, the scene ends and segues to the construction site scene. Only there does Thao put what he learned to use, which I find is strange.

This kind of scene could have been done so much better. The script would have been so much tighter if Thao had understood what he was saying and come up with a line that showed that part of his becoming a man was being able to craft his speech to show it. How does that laughable line indicate he's ready to go get a construction job?

LS: *Did you feel like you were playing Hmong in Gran Torino? At what points in the story, if any, did you feel you drew on your Hmong identity to play the role?*

BV: I know there were a lot of Hmong references and scenes in the film, but I didn't feel it in my character. What I felt was being called on to perform the pan-Asian stereotype of the submissive, kow-towing geek with no girlfriend. Plus there's no real reason for us to be Hmong in the script. We could be any minority. And not only that, but Walt is always confusing us with Koreans and other Asians. Even with the enemies he fought in Korea. So Hmong culture, Hmong identity didn't end up seeming so relevant.

LS: *How do you feel about what audiences reflect back to you regarding the film?*

BV: Y'know a middle-aged white guy was telling me the thing he loved most about *Gran* Torino was the interactions between Walt and the Hmong people—that the film "rings true" to him in some kind of way. A lot of people say this. Well—"rings true" for who? Maybe to people who live in a world where whites are the only heroes. Or to those who take the film as a documentary about Hmong culture. Even other Asians do this a lot. And then they tell me how much they learned about my culture. Meanwhile, what a lot of us Hmong feel is that the film is distorting and *un*-true. I guess watching *Gran Torino* is really subjective. People get all sorts of different things out of it.

LS: *You've said a lot about the Asian masculinities portrayed in mainstream media. Talk about your own background, how you were brought up, what kind of male role models you had…*

BV: When I was young, my Dad was a very important figure in my life. I was expected to follow him around to funerals and weddings and other rituals and help him with whatever he was doing. Through him and my other male relatives, I was learning to be strong and respectable, to shake hands and be good with words, I saw how to be polite, especially to elders—even to ancestors. It was very important to be able to speak well, including in front of groups, and not make an ass of yourself.

LS: *Would you describe these things as part of masculinity?*

BV: Yes, an alternative masculinity you could say…. Y'know helping is a big part of it. There are different takes on helping. Remember the scene in *Gran Torino* where the old white lady neighbor spills her groceries? Thao helps her pick them up, which is nice and Walt is impressed. *But* Thao is contrasted with two other Hmong guys who pass by her and don't help and even make humping motions behind her back. This kind of shameless macho seems more white to me and it makes Thao's helping seem more effeminate. In Walt's eyes, Thao's helping makes him a good kid, but also makes him less masculine. That's the turning point, where Walt decides to make an effort to man him up. To me, it's also where Walt starts imposing his version of white masculinity on Thao. He sees that Thao has the impulse to be respectful and help. But it's not just anyone he helps—it's a senior white lady. At this point Walt *also* sees that Thao can subordinate himself to a white person by picking up her groceries. So he decides that Thao could bend over to take Walt's instruction too...

LS: *Say more about what's white about that masculinity.*

BV: In my own upbringing, helping—especially helping elders—just didn't feel this way at all. It didn't have any association with femininity.... My Dad is a shaman. His sons are supposed to assist him in ceremonies and it's an honor to do that. I felt that a lot growing up. We would carry his stuff and set up for him. We would bow at the right times and we would support him to make sure he was safe when he was in trance. We would sacrifice chickens for him while he communicated with the spirits. I loved doing all that. I will miss it.

LS: *What about helping in relation to women and girls?*

BV: Well, one thing is that men who are courting or married are supposed to convey their caring by helping women with their work. It's not about becoming emasculated and doing women's work. It's about showing consideration and respect ... about being thoughtful and helpful with whatever her burden is.... Instead of showing himself off in terms of the individual qualities he's supposed to be proud of in himself, it's about a man showing how he can subordinate all this to the relationship. Guys who do this well are *more* desirable to women, not *less* masculine.

LS: *Say more about what your home life was like.*

BV: Growing up I had five brothers and only one sister. So we five boys had to pitch in to make things work around the house. In *Gran Torino* there's all those lines about "women's work" when Thao does the dishes or does gardening. I don't know: Sometimes when we'd have a lot of people in the house for a ceremony or something, I'd be the one washing the vegetables—and it was no big deal. The work just needs to get done. My Dad would pitch in too.

LS: *So there was no stigma—it didn't make you seem effeminate or gay to do that stuff?*

BV: Well maybe for some people who choose to see these differences. But that's so retro. I love deliberately crossing gender lines and messing with social boundaries. And I actually like cleaning house and washing dishes. It doesn't feel scary femme to me.... Also it really annoys me that it would be associated with homosexuality. What does housework have to do with sexual partners anyway? Asians have enough to deal with being framed as homosexual in the American racial scene. If it's so hard for the mainstream to see us as straight, the last thing we need to do [is] call *each other* gay for irrelevant reasons. Also where does that leave Asians who actually want to be comfortable in gay identities? There's no space for them to own their sexuality....

LS: *Yes of course.*

BV: The thing is, it makes all of us guys who are in school feel invisible. Maybe those *other* Asian Americans are supposed to value education and be super-achievers, but that one little line defines Hmong boys as the opposite. It's like Hmong will always be nothing more than peasants and footsoldiers. In America we'll turn into manual laborers and gangsters. It's like our past determines us forever. I mean, jeez, my parents had basically no education, and that hasn't stopped *us*.

LS: *What do you think of the fact that Sue is the one who says this line?*

BV: It compounds the problem. A lot of Americans—even Hmong—say that she is describing a "truth" of Hmong refugee social life. It makes me so angry! The fact that a Hmong girl says it makes it seem like it's not racist to say such a thing. But those lines were put in her mouth by a non-Hmong writer who invented her. I wish audiences were not so passive and could remind themselves more often about the authorship here...

LS: *What's next for you?*

BV: I have a lot of ideas. I'm on my way to college at Brown in Rhode Island. I'm going to study filmmaking and pursue my acting. And I'm also going to study Chinese and see where it all takes me. Whatever I do, I want to keep social justice work in the mix.

LS: *What are your social justice issues?*

BV: In terms of my own activism, I've been working on Hmong and Asian visibility stuff. I've done a lot of public speaking on *Gran Torino,* and I try to increase awareness of some of the racial issues in the film ... and in the production too. I'd like to get more audiences to see that films can't help being about race if there are immigrants and minorities in the mix. They can never be simply universal human stories about heroes who get redeemed or whatever.

LS: *Other issues you try to make visible?*

BV: Well, there's also the issue of class and mobility for minorities. I feel like the racial barriers to economic improvement that exist in the US are not acknowledged enough. You can see this in *Gran Torino* too—in the scenes where Walt implies that all Thao has to do to be good enough for a job is to become manly like a white guy. If you look at the lines in the barbershop scene though, it's all premised on his being ethnically different and not getting the jokes. By the end of the scene, he's still the clueless immigrant kid. The film acknowledges that he's not just like them in terms of his job prospects, but then it denies that difference by having him go and get a job successfully....

LS: *Say more about the future you envision for Hmong filmmaking.*

BV: Since *Gran Torino* there are lots more Hmong Americans in their twenties and thirties making their own amateur films. And also applying to film programs. Some of these people are getting their works into film festivals and distributing in Asia. This is promising because we have a lot of stories to tell. And they'll be Hmong stories, but not just *the* Hmong story. We need great scripts, complex, relatable characters, and high production values. Controlling the images of Hmong people *in* the films is just the first step. Our films also need to be high quality and show the level of art we are capable of. For me, I'm looking for substance, deep ideas and amazing performances...

ESSAYS

These two essays analyze how Southeast Asian communities have been sources of support and conflict for refugees. In the first essay, a team of Asian American scholars critiques model minority depictions of the Vietnamese American community's return to New Orleans and rapid rebuilding after Hurricane Katrina. The scholars analyze the role of religious leaders and familiarity with government assistance programs and note how the community joined with African Americans to shut down the creation of a landfill and develop a cooperative rebuilding program. The second essay, by Chia Youyee Vang, a University of Wisconsin, Milwaukee, historian, discusses how Hmong New Year celebrations have evolved in Minnesota from small potluck dinners to major extravaganzas held in convention centers. As the celebrations have grown to include dances from Bollywood and China, nontraditional clothing, beauty pageants, and even hip-hop performances, organizers have increasingly disagreed about the "authenticity," commercialism, and political implications of these celebrations.

A Critique of Model Minority Portrayals of Vietnamese Americans in New Orleans After Hurricane Katrina

KAREN J. LEONG, CHRISTOPHER A. AIRRIESS, WEI LI, ANGELA CHIA-CHEN CHEN, AND VERNA M. KEITH

As the floodwaters have receded from New Orleans and rebuilding has begun, new stories of race relations have emerged and new histories are being written. One is the history of a predominantly Catholic Vietnamese American community located in eastern New Orleans. Before Hurricane Katrina, Vietnamese

---

"Resilient History and the Rebuilding of a Community: The Vietnamese American Community in New Orleans East," Karen J. Leong, Christopher A. Airriess, Wei Li, Angela Chia-Chen Chen, and Verna M. Keith, *Journal of American History* 94 (December 2007): 770–79.

Americans constituted less than 1.5 percent of the city's population. Since Katrina, the small Vietnamese American community in eastern New Orleans has received significant press coverage due to its members' high rate of return and the rapid rebuilding of their community. This essay will explore how shared refugee experiences, the leadership role of the Catholic Church, and the historically specific circumstances of Vietnamese immigrant settlement in eastern New Orleans contributed to this community's mobilization and empowerment. Some might attribute the community's ability to recover so quickly to a strong work ethic and an innate identity—both features of the myth of Asian Americans as "model minorities." That myth is a 1950s and 1960s construction that has since been deployed to justify racist assumptions about African Americans, Hispanics, and American Indians. It also obscures historical processes. This essay argues that the eastern New Orleans Vietnamese American community's response to Katrina is clearly rooted in its particular history and collective memory. As the experience of the Vietnamese American community in Village de L'Est demonstrates, history and memory are more than analytical artifacts—they are political resources....

This particular Vietnamese American community, a legacy from the refugee resettlement beginning in the 1970s, is located in a residential suburb known as Village de L'Est in easternmost New Orleans. In the aftermath of the Vietnam War, the United States government relied on nongovernment and faith-based organizations to help relocate refugees from Vietnam in the United States across 821 zip codes. The Associated Catholic Charities of New Orleans, for example, relocated Vietnamese in New Orleans and found federally subsidized, low-income housing for 1,000 refugees in 1975 at the Versailles Arms Apartments. Chain migration—in which initial immigrants attract further migration of friends and family from the same place of origin—resulted in 2,000 more Vietnamese moving into the neighborhood near the apartments from their initial settlement locations. The Vietnamese population grew to nearly 5,000 by 1990.

The influx of Vietnamese refugees and the white flight that began in the 1980s significantly changed the complexion of the neighborhood. By 1990 the neighborhood's population was almost equally divided between African Americans and Vietnamese Americans.

Due to Katrina, the dynamics of eastern New Orleans have been altered yet again. By spring 2007 over 90 percent of the Vietnamese American residents but fewer than 50 percent of the African Americans had returned to Village de L'Est. For African American renters the unavailability of affordable rental housing has constituted a barrier to return; three apartment complexes had housed nearly 40 percent of the African American population in the neighborhood. During the first year of recovery, the Vietnamese American survivors' early and high rate of return heightened their visibility and political leverage. By early December 2005, two months after Mayor C. Ray Nagin declared New Orleans safe for return, church leaders estimated that about six hundred individuals had returned and had begun cleaning and repairing Vietnamese American-owned homes in the neighborhood. The visible turnout of residents forced the city to provide dumpsters, and a petition signed by residents who stated their commitment to return to the neighborhood persuaded the utility company to restore power in mid–October 2005.

To survive after Katrina, residents in this eastern New Orleans community had to establish themselves as active stakeholders both in their community and in the city. Fears that the city would not support efforts to rebuild its eastern part seemed confirmed in February 2006 when the mayor authorized the opening of a hurricane debris landfill less than two miles from Village de L'Est. Already faced with the burden of rebuilding their lives, residents had to organize quickly and collaboratively to oppose the landfill. Protest against the Chef Menteur landfill united Vietnamese Americans, African Americans, environmentalists, other social justice advocates, and elected officials in the multiethnic Coalition for a Strong New Orleans East, which brought such pressure to bear on the city that the mayor chose not to renew the landfill contract in August 2006. The coalition's political success, coupled with the relatively rapid repopulation of the isolated suburb with little city government assistance, became a highly popular Katrina story for national media outlets including the *New York Times*, CNN, and NBC *Nightly News*.

National media coverage of the "Vietnamese Versailles community" generally presented a narrative that fit the stereotypical Asian American model-minority myth: in less than three generations the New Orleans Vietnamese refugees had seemingly mastered the political system and overcome Katrina through the self-sufficiency and hard work associated with Asian Americans in general. One New Orleans blogger observed in February 2006, "The story of this community is being touted across the city and region as an example of the power of 'anchoring' in the redevelopment of New Orleans neighborhoods." Media reports emphasized individual choice and community cohesion without noting the lack of rental units, racial discrimination, or differences in environmental impact that prevented others from returning. Participants in online discussion boards drew comparisons between the Vietnamese American community and "the African American community in New Orleans," even if media reports did not. One online participant stated, "These vietnamese folks are self-starters the *last* thing they want is more governmental interference. NOLA's blacks, on the other hand, would rather sit around and wait for the government to save them." The *New Orleans Louisiana Weekly*, a local African American newspaper, in January 2006 hailed "The Miracle of Versailles: New Orleans Vietnamese Community Rebuilds" and ultimately concluded, "Perhaps the most important key to their success is that the Vietnamese community refused to place its salvation into the hands of the government. They simply came home." Such emphasis on self-sufficiency ignores the voices of some members of the Vietnamese American community who have stated—echoing some African American community members—that federal government assistance is critical to rebuilding. Indeed, in separate interviews held in early 2006, Vietnamese American and African American residents of New Orleans East agreed that their community had received inadequate assistance in rebuilding from the state and city.

This immigrant story is not simply one of resolve and initiative nor of the faith and community emphasized in media reports, but of a cultural hybridity and historically specific transformation that preceded migration. A historical perspective on the Village de L'Est Vietnamese American community's faith and cohesion demonstrates how collective history and memory, in addition to the spatial concentration of this small Vietnamese American community, contributed to the ability to rebuild so quickly after Hurricane Katrina. Father The Vien Nguyen, the pastor of Mary Queen of Vietnam Church, explained that the central role of the church in the community was not a postmigration phenomenon; it grew out of a pattern of church leadership that had developed in Vietnam over several hundred years. Catholicism, a foreign faith, was introduced into certain villages and transformed over time into a form of local leadership, subsequently motivating villagers to flee their homeland for fear of religious and political persecution. Spanish and Portuguese colonizers brought Catholicism to Vietnam in the sixteenth century. Vietnamese suspicion of foreign influences resulted in the persecution of Catholic Vietnamese in the early nineteenth century, and the persecution resulted in increased French intervention. After French colonial rule was established in the late nineteenth century, Vietnamese Catholics were free to worship. Initially, when Ho Chi Minh's resistance army overthrew Japanese forces in 1945, the Catholics strongly supported his government, which benefited from nationalist sentiment that united the Vietnamese populace. That unity, however, soon unraveled after the formation of the second Ho Chi Minh government following national elections in 1946, as divisions increased between the Communists (Viet Minh) and noncommunists. This split fully manifested itself with the third Ho Chi Minh government, formed in November 1946, in which Communists dominated an overwhelming majority of the offices. By the 1950s Vietnamese Catholic leaders increasingly and openly condemned the Communist government of Ho Chi Minh.

The 1954 Geneva agreements split the country into two—with Communists governing the north and the noncommunists the south. Many Vietnamese Catholics had moved north, and now, under Clause 14d of the agreements, had a limited period—the time the troops took to assemble in their respective locations—to move to the opposite zone if they so chose. As a result, some nine hundred thousand refugees, mostly Catholics, fled from their villages in the Red River delta diocese of Bui Chu to the south. In rural areas the priest was often the only source of leadership and assistance for a community. After the siege of Saigon in 1975, many Vietnamese in South Vietnam attempted to flee, and some of those who succeeded found shelter in refugee camps lining the South China Sea coast and processing centers in Guam or the Philippines. Of those who arrived in the United States, research suggests that at Camp Pendleton [Virginia] half the refugees (55 percent) were Roman Catholic and that at Fort Indiantown Gap [Pennsylvania] 40 percent were. The majority of refugees who left the camps were sponsored by families or groups. The U.S. Catholic Conference accounted for 35 percent of the group sponsorships.

After visiting the refugee camps, Archbishop Philip M. Hannan of New Orleans invited priests he met there to establish resettlement communities in New Orleans. He asked the Associated Catholic Charities of New Orleans to assist in finding Section 8 housing for the refugees. Vietnamese refugees in Village de L'Est originated from villages in the vicinity of Vung Tau city or the nearby village of Phuc Tinh, both located in the Ba Ria–Vung Tau province some 120 kilometers southeast of

Saigon. In 1985 the community founded its own ethnic parish, centered on Mary Queen of Vietnam Church. The religious faith, church leadership, and social organization that informed the migration decisions of these Vietnamese refugees and immigrants have contributed to a strong community identity.

The concentrated settlement pattern of Vietnamese Americans in Village de L'Est, 75 percent of whom are Catholic, facilitated the implementation of the leadership structure and village-based community in the New Orleans neighborhood. The primary adaptation among the immigrant community has been that "the involvement of laypeople in meeting the needs of the community has increased since migration to the United States." As he did in Vietnam, the priest serves as the primary leader not only of religious life but also of the parish community. He is supported by a council that makes parish decisions, with each member representing a specific zone within the parish (in Village de L'Est, there are seven designated zones). Each zone, in turn, is divided into street units called "hamlets," with their own representatives and saints. The celebration of feast and saints' days facilitates community building among neighbors. The representatives have increasingly brought the political and social concerns of their constituents to the attention of the council. The council has responded by organizing committees to take care of specific community needs, including raising funds for burial expenses or assisting newcomers.

The preexisting leadership structure was one of the most important community resources in the rebuilding process, allowing the church to keep track of its members' locations in Katrina's diaspora. Community members largely relied on their own social networks to evacuate with family and friends and to locate temporary housing in shelters or in other Vietnamese communities throughout the nation. The church choir, for example, caravaned as a group out of New Orleans days before the hurricane. The parish priests cared for the remaining elderly and those unable to evacuate on their own until they were all able to evacuate the flooded neighborhood. The community's limited size allowed Father Nguyen to visit parish members scattered throughout various states and set up a recovery network. He recalled, "My people were scattered in Austin, San Antonio, Dallas, Houston, and Arkansas.… My people were in California, Georgia, Florida, Washington, Minnesota, Michigan, and the Carolinas. They even went so far as New Hampshire and Connecticut." The pastor asked available council and hamlet representatives to meet in Houston to plan for the return to the parish as soon as permission was granted for people to reenter New Orleans. According to Nguyen, on October 5, the first day people could return to the city to begin the cleanup, more than three hundred parish members did so. It must be noted that the pastor has been a prominent source of information about the community. His role in narrating the Vietnamese community's collective dispersal and return to New Orleans serves to define both a cohesive faith identity for the Catholic Vietnamese Americans and a broader refugee identity of survival and sociocultural adjustment that includes all Vietnamese American residents regardless of religion.

The Vietnamese American community in New Orleans East possesses social and cultural capital that is based on its members' lived experience and historical memory. Because migration occurred within the past three generations and under the conditions of war, the community has sustained the strong social networks that operated during the refugee and migration experience as well as confidence in the efficacy of those networks. Members of the community exhibit a sense of strength derived from their experiences as war refugees or as recent immigrants. When asked about the difference between leaving Vietnam and evacuating from New Orleans, one person who had just arrived in the United States in 2004 and had not yet returned to New Orleans from Houston by March 2006 noted that the former was much more dangerous: "It is harder leaving from your culture. Hurricane is nothing. In the hurricane, you have your family with you all the time." Observing that "our life is not as hard as it was before," this individual, like many others in the community, perceived the evacuation and rebuilding of New Orleans as less difficult than complete relocation from one's place of origin. That memory, along with the experience of adjusting to the United States, is shared by Catholic and Buddhist Vietnamese Americans and further contributes to a collective community identity.

In addition to the role of religious faith in shaping immigrant life and ethnic community, the particular timing of Katrina also afforded the Vietnamese American community certain resources. Local activists had been working within the community to develop homeowner associations in response to concerns about community safety and had been attending city council meetings to articulate those concerns. National networks that had originated with the first waves of Vietnamese refugees arriving in the United States, such as Boat People SOS, also offered their assistance to evacuees as they negotiated the bureaucracy of Federal Emergency Management Agency (FEMA) claims, insurance claims, and food stamps. Although those networks did not limit their assistance to Southeast Asian Americans, they built on their knowledge of those communities, familiarity in guiding recent immigrants through paper work, and ability to speak in various Asian languages, and they operated mainly in locations with high concentrations of Southeast Asian evacuees. In other words, having as refugees developed a community with limited (but not insignificant) federal and local government assistance, community members can draw on their relatively recent experience in rebuilding yet again.

Over the two years since Katrina made landfall, the community has gained confidence as it successfully leverages its newly found political power. Neighborhood Catholic and Protestant churches have worked together since the hurricane to forge multiracial cooperation in the rebuilding of the community. The *Oakland Tribune* reported that Mary Queen of Vietnam provided volunteers to assist the primarily African American churches in the neighborhood with their cleanup. In May 2006 the Vietnamese American and African American Village de L'Est community joined with representatives of the Southern Poverty Law Center, a civil rights organization, to demand the closing of the Chef Menteur landfill. All those efforts appear to be creating a new, more extended form of community. One African American focus group participant recalled that "those Vietnamese spent like 20 hours came to our church, clean our church and prepare for us" and that the priest had visited the service to talk about the Vietnamese American community. Another observed of the Vietnamese American community, "These people can teach us different things, they can teach us things ... like I'm saying ... they'll all become the real community." When asked if the possibility for Vietnamese Americans and African

Americans to work together had increased, focus group participants agreed that Katrina "brought us closer." The most recent New Orleans rebuilding plan proposed by Mayor Nagin and Dr. Ed Blakely, director of the city's Office of Recovery Management, in April 2007 listed the area among the top seventeen neighborhoods that will receive further assistance as a result of the recognized high return and rebuilding rates. Local Vietnamese American leaders consider making the list a collective victory in deciding the fate of the community.

The newly forged history of working together to survive sudden change and uncertainty provides a shared hope for this neighborhood, and even for the city. Cynthia Willard-Lewis, an African American member of the city council who represents the neighborhood (and in April 2006 hired a Vietnamese American to work in her office), suggested that the cooperation and rebuilding exhibited by the Vietnamese American community "can be a model for other communities. They are fighting to stay united and connected." This community unity is already being mobilized to face a new challenge. In late August 2007, two weeks of deadly shootings and robberies suggested that Village de L'Est is now a target for violence, perhaps as a result of the publicity surrounding the community's success in rebuilding. Willard-Lewis, Father Nguyen, and other community leaders have responded by working to increase police response time and protection for residents.

Historians are well aware that historical memory can be, and has been, mobilized in dangerous ways. Yet the experience of this Vietnamese community in eastern New Orleans in the aftermath of the catastrophe of Hurricane Katrina is a powerful reminder that memories and knowledge of the past can also function as a significant source of community resilience and transformation.

Continuity and the Reinvention of Hmong New Year Celebrations

CHIA YOUYEE VANG

In the late 1970s, when few Hmong families lived in Minnesota, the New Year celebration was a small event but one with great significance for its participants. As part of the first family to arrive in Minnesota in December 1975, Dang Her remembers yearning for opportunities to connect with other people from his ethnic group. He explains the driving force behind the initial diasporic New Year celebrations: "We missed our friends and families so much that when we learned about other Hmong families in Minnesota, we immediately tried to contact them. The New Year celebration was quite different from what you see today. Each family contributed some food. It was a potluck. We were all just happy to be with other Hmong families."...

The continued flow of Hmong refugees throughout the last quarter of the twentieth century permitted the celebrations to increase in size, scope, and frequency.

Although New Year celebrations were celebrated during slightly different times in Laos, a shared country of origin inspired Hmong and ethnic Lao refugees in Minnesota to create interethnic solidarity by co-hosting a celebration. Tong Vang, a former board president of Lao Family Community of Minnesota Inc., recalls, "When we first got here, we actually started an organization with the Lao refugees because we [all came] from the same country.... We had one New Year celebration together, then when we started the Hmong Association, we began to have our own celebrations. It was small. We did wear our traditional clothes and ate great Hmong food." The Lao New Year is celebrated in April, so perhaps the time difference influenced the decision to no longer collaborate. A closer examination, however, suggests that ethnicity and religion may have further divided the two ethnic groups. Although some of the early refugees from both ethnic groups had converted to Christianity in Laos, many Hmong practiced ancestral worship, which differed greatly from most Lao following Buddhist traditions. One can further speculate that because the growth of the Hmong population in Minnesota surpassed that of the Lao, Hmong community leaders no longer needed to collaborate since their population was large enough to allow them to hold events specifically for their own ethnic group.

The process by which the Hmong in Minnesota expanded their celebrations would reflect their population increase in the state. As the demand for activities beyond tossing ball and singing folk songs increased, organizers developed additional ways to attract attendees of all ages. Music and dance competitions provided an avenue for musicians and artists to exhibit their skills. Beauty pageants permitted young Hmong women to display their beauty and talents. Vendors set up booths in the hope of making a profit. Ly Vang, a Hmong American woman and community leader who had been involved with New Year event planning since the late 1970s, reminisces about the evolution of diasporic New Year celebrations: "In 1977, we gathered a lot because we were all still dealing with loss of our own family support. I think 1978 was the bigger New Year celebration. I think there were about twenty-five families. Then we started to move to churches in St. Paul, then International Institute [of Minnesota]. The first big New Year was 1983, and 1984 we had the first beauty pageant."

When the population was very small, families would gather at individual homes. As the number of people grew, so did the spaces from private homes to church banquet rooms to community centers to hold the celebrations. The events eventually moved to large convention centers. In 1980 with the largest arrival of Hmong refugees to the United States, the critical mass enabled Hmong Minnesotans to expand their New Year celebrations to the civic center, as a staff member for the *Association of Hmong* newsletter reveals: "It has been many long days plan for the Hmong New Year 1980–81. Many Hmong and their leaders in the Twin Cities did not have enough time to sleep and enjoy their families as usual. They put a lot of effort to make the New Year possible for the Hmong people to chase away bad luck and ugly thoughts that they have in mind and heart during the past twelve months, and to welcome the New Year with new hope, new spirit, best luck and good opportunities for the incoming year.... Over 6,000 (six thousand) Hmong were gathering at the St. Paul Civic Center to cheer each other as a traditional celebration."

The passage shows that at the outset, the event was as much a community-building effort as it was a means for cultural preservation. The event is envisioned as a display of Hmong unity where attendees come and "cheer each other": "To share their happiness, Mr. Ly Teng, the President of the Lao Family Community in Minnesota, and the Hmong also invited the Honor of Mrs. and Mr. [George] Latimer, the Mayor of the City of Saint Paul and many other high rank officers from various departments in the State of Minnesota as well as many Americans in the area along with General Vang Pao, the International Chairperson of the Lao Family Community Inc. from California and many other fellow Hmong from other neighboring states of Minnesota to share the happiness together. To open the New Year Celebration, Mr. Ly Teng briefly expressed that the Hmong New Year cannot be celebrated on the exact date of the traditional calendar because we have to wait for the weekend and the availability of spaces to get together for a long time." This practice of inviting elected and appointed officials and General Vang Pao to deliver speeches has continued to the present. The distance from which the New Year celebrations drew their participants over the years has increased significantly with the change in Hmong American economic status. In the early years, most attendees were residents of the state or from neighboring Midwestern locations. Today, it is common to see participants from all parts of the United States and from other countries of resettlement. Occasionally, some Hmong from Laos attend if they visit family members in the state.

An ongoing question about New Year celebrations is whether transformations occurred only in the United States or were there changes prior to migration out of Laos. Many in the general immigrant population assign blame partially to American society for the lack of understanding and the devaluing of Hmong traditions. However, a closer historical analysis reveals that changes in New Year traditions, in large part, stem from the relocation of displaced Hmong during the war years and from Hmong exposure to Lao cultural practices. Ly Vang shares her observation, "I saw the changes. Back then [in Laos], we do a lot of things based on traditions. In rural areas, your frame of reference is very narrow. So, you have bullfights, folk songs, qee. [an instrument made from six bamboo pipes attached to a wooden wind chamber]. No dance. Those are the traditions they learned from agricultural way of life. Not much room for incorporation of others. After 1970, changes began to emerge. In Long Cheng, the urban settlement allowed for beauty pageants to be added. I think there were two or three pageants that were held. In that historical moment, we began to add dance performances to the New Year. But, they did classical Lao dance." Ly Vang's statement reveals that the New Year as celebrated in isolated village contexts before the Vietnam War era changed when Hmong became exposed to other forms of entertainment. As time progressed and new additions became common practices, people then began to appropriate them as Hmong traditions.

The practice of borrowing from other cultures seems to have been an integral part of Hmong history as the Hmong migrated from one area to another. The process of becoming a refugee and the displacing effects of refugee camps further facilitated the transformation of old and the invention of new traditions. Critiquing the claim that the "traditional" dance commonly used to entertain

Americans was a Hmong tradition, former Hmong artist and entertainer Yia Lee comments, "I was one of the first Hmong to learn *laavong* [classical Lao dance]. There is no Hmong *laavong*. But, there was dancing prior to migration. What we call Hmong traditional dance is in fact not Hmong. We learned from the Lao. I don't mind the use of all kinds of popular art at the Hmong New Year. It's natural. I know this. All these new art forms are fine. What troubles me a lot is that artists don't know how to compose their own music. They would write the lyrics and then use other peoples' tunes. This is sad." Yia Lee, known for taking risks in art and entertainment, elaborates, "In Laos when we first started to sing modern songs, I was criticized. In the refugee camp, people laughed at our Western-style music." Ly Vang agrees that modern Hmong music and dance expanded in the refugee camps. Amidst the significant boredom of camp life emerged new cultural expressions. The refugee state of confinement, loss, and uncertainty ironically energized camp inhabitants to create new meanings for themselves through art.

Shong Yang, who is a prominent businessman and former chairman of the Hmong American New Year (HANY) in Minneapolis, believes that differences in New Year celebration practices between the United States and Laos are due to rules and regulations in American society that prevent certain religious rituals from occurring in public spaces: "[In Laos, there] were no contests, either beauty pageants or music. Part of this has to do with the fact that few people were educated. In this country, one of the activities missing is the bullfights because we can't do that here. We still *lwm qaib* [conduct chicken ceremony], ball toss, sing folk songs. We have added new activities that are available to us because of technology, such as music and beauty pageants like other people. Additionally, we have added sports competitions at the Minneapolis New Year. All of these activities are new."

Hmong Americanization has come to signify increasing American cultural and economic influence. Technology, education, and capital all seem to contradict tradition. Many Hmong Americans contend that New Year celebrations have become too commercialized. They negatively view charging money because it takes away the fun elements of New Year celebrations that are free for all and because they believe that the event organizers tend to be more concerned with making money than with preserving culture. Other community members require higher-quality performances and activities because they pay a fee to enter. Many call for greater accountability by New Year organizers in addition to using proceeds to better the community.

There appear to be two competing perspectives about performances at New Year celebrations. One is that the current performances have abandoned Hmong culture and its traditions, attributed both to the borrowing of other cultures' arts and to the lack of interest in traditional activities. The other perspective is that a balance needs to be kept between culture and entertainment. In the former, a lack of control over the content and types of performances frequently places organizers in uncomfortable positions. As Ly Vang explains, "You can't really turn performers away but you don't have a way to determine the content of their performances. It's sometimes frustrating because we have a lot of political leaders who attend and some things may not be appropriate, but we don't know how to control that." Here, inappropriateness refers to the poor-quality performances of both genders and to young women dressing in provocative clothing. Often, the performances would be more appropriate in a nightclub scene than in a cultural event with a diverse audience of small children, elderly grandparents, and distinguished guests from the larger community. Shong Yang cautions against the incorporation of other cultural forms: "In terms of traditions, I want to see young people maintain as much Hmong cultural practices as possible. If they are going to sing, sing in Hmong. I can't control what people prefer to use as examples of their skills, but I hope that they do not replace Hmong culture." His suggestion privileges Hmong language as the true Hmong culture. It seems that, to him, artistic style is less important than the need to ensure that Hmong language is used in the performances.

With respect to the perspective of balancing culture and entertainment, many interviewees are open to change. Chou Vang believes that the performance of dances borrowed from Bollywood and China is inevitable: "How can you stop the kids? They live here. They grow up here. That's what they like. Soon after we all die, they will not know much anymore. You can't stop them from doing whatever they like." As one of the women who had received an education in Laos and was active in organizing diasporic New Year celebrations during her early years in the United States, Chou argues that the younger generation will become less interested and knowledgeable about Hmong traditions. She indicates that they should create something that is meaningful to them. Daobay Ly, former chair of the St. Paul New Year committee, adds, "That's part of encouraging the youth to be expressive in whatever they like.... What is amazing is that some youth are appreciating Hmong culture and traditions, except that they have different ways of expressing them. While we do have young people who just don't want anything to do with the 'old ways,' there are others who amaze the elders by learning folksongs and being confident enough to perform in front of thousands." Daobay Ly is a member of the one-and-a-half generation Hmong Americans. He has observed a difference in how young people are perceived by their peers and by the immigrant generation. Although some youth regard their peers who embrace Hmong traditions as old-fashioned, the young people who follow tradition are highly regarded by the older generation, who see such an act as evidence of their Hmongness.

What can one expect to experience at the large New Year celebrations? It is common to see Hmong American women wear costumes from their Hmong coethnics throughout Asia alongside those wearing prom dresses, business suits, and torn blue jeans. The ethnic costumes include coins dangling from all sides of the body, silver necklaces, turbans, and high heels. Women and girls wrapped in shawls walk through the parking lot in cold weather, because their heavy costumes prevent them from wearing winter coats. The dress of men and boys varies from jeans to casual shirts with slacks to business suits. Those who wear Hmong costumes, however, usually do so with a Western-style shirt worn underneath a vest covered all over with coins. After standing in line to purchase tickets, attendees are expected to pass through the security station. Then, they may proceed toward the auditorium. Entrepreneurial elderly women spread their important, dried herbal medicines, jewelry, and handicrafts throughout the hallway. The new arrivals are soon consumed by the smell of homemade sausages, compounded with those of papaya salad and fried chicken. Vendors sell items ranging from amateur videos, clothing, music albums, and toys to photography booths with the latest technology to ensure that attendees are able to preserve memories of having attended the celebration. Although attendees are overwhelmingly Hmong Americans, non-Hmong people are present at these celebrations. Often, they are individuals who work with and/or are friends with Hmong individuals. Occasionally, one will encounter others who attend out of curiosity.

In the main auditorium, elected and appointed officials focus on "cultural performances" by youth of all ages. Performers enter and exit the stage. Young women dressed in provocative outfits performing to music by such American artists as Janet Jackson and Madonna can be immediately followed by another group of females, dressed in sweat pants and dancing to Korean hip-hop music. When the group finishes its performance, another troupe, dressed in Asian Indian clothes, dances to a Bollywood tune. The next group, dressed in beautiful Lao clothes, performs a classical Lao dance. The evening may end with a Chinese dance performance, which has become a vibrant component of diasporic New Year celebrations.

Politics and Economics

Critics of diasporic New Year celebrations often question the authenticity of the various elements now referred to as Hmong tradition. Determining celebration components' authenticity is further complicated because of the commercialization and political activities embedded in diasporic celebrations. Regarding larger community politics, candidates seeking office in the urban districts, both St. Paul and Minneapolis, and in state and federal offices often attend Hmong New Year events. Some have booths and distribute literature, while others attend either to deliver speeches or to be recognized for their status as politicians, regardless of their rank within government entities.

The presence of non-Hmong individuals suggests that race plays a contradictory role in this semipublic context. Because the event is attended predominantly by Hmong Americans, non-Hmong, in particular those of European descent, sometimes regardless of their socioeconomic status, are honored by organizers. They are treated as distinguished guests, while Hmong Americans of similar or higher status are not honored in the same manner. Organizers seem to go out of their way to display Hmong culture in honoring these non-Hmong individuals. From the outset, New Year celebrations were used as a forum to acknowledge Hmong Americans' alliance with Americans during the Vietnam War, as evidenced by the frequent appearance of men dressed in military uniforms. One political candidate and/or elected official after another has publicly thanked the Hmong people for their contributions to America before they even set foot in the United States. While elected and appointed officials from the larger community consistently praise the Hmong American community publicly during their speeches at New Year celebrations, these praises are heard only by those who physically attend—almost all of whom are Hmong Americans. Although these politically inspired words of thanks may serve to gain Hmong support, they do not, in fact, bolster mainstream public sentiment toward Hmong people because these sentiments are rarely heard by the

American public. Mainstream-media coverage of the celebrations almost always zooms in on the exotic elements of Hmong culture and its traditions, in particular the colorful clothing worn by women.

In addition to the contradictions above, organizers are frequently questioned about their business practices and accountability. A perception of organizers receiving personal financial kickbacks has plagued those involved in celebration planning, despite the fact that many others profit from the existence of these events. Organizers do charge an entrance fee, but they suggest that the fees help to pay for costs associated with holding the event....

Gender Inequality

Community politics and controversies over both the process and outcome of New Year celebrations have become more evident as the size of the events has increased. The first sign of dissatisfaction came from the leaders within the Women's Association of Hmong and Lao (WAHL), which was established in 1979 to support Hmong women and give them voice. Discussing the ways in which she and other progressive Hmong women leaders tried to influence New Year celebration practices, Gaoly Yang, a former WAHL executive director, states, "From the very beginning, Lao Family was pretty open. We partnered. Our board members helped to volunteer, and the organization benefited from participation. But, all along, we had an issue. Again, it's about radical feminist thoughts. We just didn't agree with the pageant. They said it was just entertainment. We've always known that Hmong men have abused Hmong women, and this is something that we would be perpetuating by supporting the celebrations." Early New Year celebration planning attempted to operate in a democratic fashion. The celebration chair position rotated annually among the half-dozen sponsoring organizations. The disagreements intensified one year in the mid-1980s, when WAHL chaired and attempted to reorder the celebration program. In addition to contradicting the religious order, WAHL's leaders also opened the door to Christian groups to sing songs. Gaoly Yang further explains the contentious situation, "When we chaired, we did let everything happen. Because we changed the order of events, they didn't like that. They wanted to have the New Year rituals before anything else. They said you have to *lwm taws qaib* (chicken-sacrifice ritual) before you celebrate the New Year. We actually celebrated the New Year before we had the rituals. In retrospect, I think we probably overdid it. We crossed the line because it was religion. We probably should have stayed out of it altogether." Still, these missteps were not central to WAHL ceasing its cosponsorship of the St. Paul celebrations. The primary reason for this action was in protest to the Miss Hmong Minnesota pageant, which WAHL members believed to be demeaning of Hmong women and girls....

Prior to their emigration, Hmong in Long Cheng had held a couple of beauty pageants (*xaiv ntxhais nkauj ntsuab*), thereby familiarizing local Hmong with this concept. In fact, only young women from wealthy families were able to participate in those earlier pageants, thereby rendering the event a marker of social class. Although beauty pageants were not completely new diasporic cultural inventions, progressive Hmong women criticized the objectification of women....

In addition to this portrayal of Hmong women, Ly Vang recalls women's designated peripheral role in organizing diasporic New Year celebrations during the earlier years in America: "When we first got involved in 1983, I think we got kicked out a lot. We were denied a lot. The men didn't think we had the capability, the vision, and strength to put everything in place for the New Year. Women volunteered a lot, and when they see the value of women, then we got invited to participate. When they saw that women had a lot of skills, and their participation benefited the community, they then let us join. If was not open. It was tight. It took a lot of time for those men to realize our contributions." She remembers negotiating with Lao Family's board president: "We said that if Lao Family was not open for the whole community to enjoy the New Year, then we would have one in Minneapolis, too." As the negotiations proceeded, those involved decided that they did not want the community to be divided and that it was important for everyone to work together. It was agreed upon that as a community event, the New Year planning process would become more inclusive.

☾ FURTHER READING

Aguilar-San Juan, Karin. *Little Saigons: Staying Vietnamese in America* (2009).

Chan, Sucheng. *Survivors: Cambodian Refugees in the United States* (2006).

———. *The Vietnamese American 1.5 Generation: Stories of War, Revolution, Flight and New Beginnings* (2006).

Chea, Jolie. "Refugee Acts: Articulating Silences through Critical Remembering and Re-Membering," *Amerasia Journal* 35, no. 1 (2009): 20–43.

Collet, Christian, and Hiroko Furuya, "Enclave, Place, or Nation? Defining Little Saigon in the Midst of Incorporation, Transnationalism, and Long Distance Activism," *Amerasia Journal* 36, no. 3 (2010): 1–27.

Conquergood, Dwight. *I Am a Shaman: A Hmong Life Story with Ethnographic Commentary* (1989).

Dang, Thuy Vo, Linda Trinh Vo, and Tram Le. *Vietnamese in Orange County* (2015).

Duong, Lan P. *Treacherous Subjects: Gender, Culture, and Trans-Vietnamese Feminism* (2012).

Espiritu, Yen Le. *Body Counts: The Vietnam War and Militarized Refuge(es)* (2014).

Her, Vincent K., and Mary Louise Buley-Meissner, *Hmong and American: From Refugees to Citizens* (2012).

Khmer Girls in Action. "Khmer Girls in Action," *Amerasia Journal* 35, no. 1 (2009): 188–193.

Le, Long. "Exploring the Function of the Anti-Communist Ideology in the Vietnamese American Diasporic Community," *Journal of Southeast Asian American Education and Advancement* 6 (2011): 1–25.

Lee, Gary Yia. "Diaspora and the Predicament of Origins: Interrogating Hmong Postcolonial History and Identity," *Hmong Studies Journal* 8 (2007): 1–25.

Lipman, Jana K. "The Face Is the Road Map: Vietnamese Amerasians in U.S. Political and Popular Culture, 1980–1988," *Journal of Asian American Studies* (February 2011): 33–68.

Moua, Mai Neng. *Bamboo among the Oaks: Contemporary Writing by Hmong Americans* (2002).

Nguyen, Linh. "Recalling the Refugee: Culture Clash and Melancholic Racial Formation in *Daughter from Danang*," *Amerasia Journal* 39, no. 3 (2013): 103–121.

Nguyen, Nathalie Huynh Chau. *Memory Is Another Country: Women of the Vietnamese Diaspora* (2009).

Nguyen, Viet Thanh. "Refugee Memories and Asian American Critique," *Positions: East Asia Cultures Critique* 20, no. 3 (Summer 2012): 911–942.

Schlund-Vials, Cathy J. *War, Genocide, and Justice: Cambodian American Memory Work* (2012).

Shah, Bindi. *Laotian Daughters: Working toward Community, Belonging, and Environmental Justice* (2011).

Shimizu, Celine Parreñas. *Straightjacket Sexualities: Unbinding Asian American Manhoods in the Movies* (2012).

Tang, Eric. "A Gulf Unites Us: The Vietnamese Americans of Black New Orleans East," *American Quarterly* 63, no. 1 (2011): 117–149.

Valverde, Kieu-Linh Caroline. *Transnationalizing Viet Nam: Community, Culture, and Politics in the Diaspora* (2012).

Vang, Chia Youyee. *Hmong America: Reconstructing Community in Diaspora* (2010).

Vo, Nghia M. *The Viet Kieu in America: Personal Accounts of Postwar Immigrants from Vietnam* (2009).

CHAPTER 14

Memory Politics, Redress Campaigns, and International Relations

In the 1980s and 1990s, Asian American activists launched various campaigns to redress historical injustices. Popular images of Asian Americans as a model minority incited angry demonstrations in the 1960s and 1970s but also gave more conservative Asian American leaders political clout among the white American majority. The division between Japanese American progressive and more conservative factions mobilized different parts of the community in the struggle to redress the World War II mass incarceration. Japanese American protesters criticized ethnic leaders for cooperating with the government during the war and called on former internees to break decades of silence about the deep wounds left by internment. A group of Japanese American activists filed a $27 billion class action lawsuit against the U.S. government for the internment. Another group sought to vacate the wartime convictions of a handful of Japanese Americans who had challenged the mass removal and internment orders. Initially hesitant to "rock the boat," more conservative Japanese American leaders played critical roles in lobbying Congress to pass legislation, first, to investigate the causes of mass removal and internment and, second, to implement the commission's recommendations to provide an apology, individual compensation payments of $20,000, and a public education fund in the Civil Liberties Act of 1988.

A total of 2,264 Japanese Latin Americans who had been held in U.S. "enemy alien" camps were left out of the Civil Liberties Act because they were not permanent residents or citizens of the United States. Initially held as hostages to exchange for U.S. civilians held captive by the Imperial Japanese, these internees had to fight U.S. orders to deport them to Japan at the end of the war. While Japanese Latin Americans have testified before Congress to secure reparations, they have yet to obtain commission hearings to examine their claims.

Other groups fought to make the United States fulfill wartime promises to reward military service. During World War II, the U.S. government promised Filipino soldiers naturalization rights and full veterans' benefits but allowed only a small number of them to become U.S. citizens before the Rescission Act halted this process in 1946. More recently, activists have fought to make the U.S. government keep its wartime promise. In 2009, President Barack Obama signed the American Recovery and Reinvestment Act, providing a one-time, lump-sum payment to Filipino veterans who were members of the Commonwealth Army, scouts, or guerilla fighters before July 1, 1946. Veterans who were U.S. citizens were paid $15,000, while noncitizens were paid $9,000.

Hmong American and Lao American veterans of the Vietnam War supported the activism by Filipino war veterans because they too felt inadequately compensated for fighting alongside U.S. troops during the "secret war" in Laos from 1961 to 1975. As a result of Hmong and Lao activism, President Clinton in 2000 signed the Hmong Veteran's Naturalization Act, facilitating their naturalization by waiving the English language requirement and providing special consideration for the civics requirement. Hmong veterans' spouses and spouses of veterans killed in Laos, Thailand, or Vietnam also became eligible for U.S. citizenship.

In more recent years, Asian Americans have joined with activists in Asia to pursue redress claims as a result of atrocities committed during World War II. For example, Asian American support has grown for Korean women who suffered as sexual slaves, euphemistically known as "comfort women," for the Japanese military during World War II. Throughout the 1990s, the redress effort for these women focused on legal claims filed in Japanese and U.S. courts that ultimately were dismissed and on criticism of the Japanese government's creation of the Asian Women's Fund, a private foundation, in 1994. Some of the former sex slaves refused to accept the fund's private "charity" of approximately $20,000 because it was not official government compensation. The struggle continued and intensified as women's rights and human rights activists in Japan, Korea, China, and the United States focused on passing government resolutions, building memorials, and revising history textbooks to publicize the women's wartime suffering to the international community. In 2015 an agreement between Japan and South Korea made Japan's culpability more explicit through its direct apology and payment of $8.3 million to the few surviving victims.

The U.S. Congress apologized to the Native Hawaiian people in 1993 for the military's role in overthrowing indigenous rule and acknowledged that Native Hawaiians never gave up claims for sovereignty. This action revitalized sovereignty claims by Native Hawaiian activists who have refused to subsume Pacific Islanders as part of the Asian American community and who argue that Asian Americans have also colonized and oppressed Native Hawaiians. In 1959, the people of Hawai'i voted to become a U.S. state. Activists attacked the election because it failed to include the option of becoming an independent nation. Some campaigned for a UN hearing on Hawaiian decolonization, while others pushed for federal funds for Native Hawaiian health, education, and housing.

Activists in Guam have also criticized the history of U.S. colonial rule. In 1951 the United States signed a peace treaty with Japan that barred Guamanians from directly seeking redress for war crimes Japanese soldiers committed during World War II. Seventy years after the war ended, activists continue to lobby the U.S. Congress to resolve these war claims. Other Guamanians have attempted to expose the history of the U.S. discrimination of the indigenous Chamorro population. Some groups have campaigned for the U.S. territory to become a commonwealth or a state. Other activists have fought for complete separation from the United States and the removal of U.S. military bases.

⊕ DOCUMENTS

These documents demonstrate the diverse campaigns for redress by Asian Americans and Pacific Islanders. Many Japanese American former internees found it too painful to remember or discuss their wartime experiences until 1981 when a government commission held twenty days of hearings throughout the country. The commission's report, excerpted in Document 1, proclaimed that the internment was unjustified and caused tremendous suffering. Document 2 provides excerpts from the 1984 decision by District Court Judge Marilyn Hall Patel that vacated the wartime conviction of Fred Korematsu for violating mass removal orders on the grounds that the Justice Department had deliberately concealed FBI, military intelligence, and Federal Communications Commission evidence from the Supreme Court.

In Document 3, Haunani-Kay Trask, a Native Hawaiian activist and professor of Hawaiian studies at the University of Hawai'i, Manoa, criticizes Asian American scholars and activists for framing the struggle for Hawaiian sovereignty as a domestic civil rights issue rather than as an international human rights issue. Denouncing "Asian settler" scholarship for assuming the authority to speak for and about Native Hawaiians, Trask calls for an acknowledgment of the role of Asian Americans in the oppression of Native Hawaiians.

Documents 4 to 7 address grievances beyond Japanese American redress that stemmed from mistreatment during World War II. In Document 4, Franco Arcebal urges Congress to pass the Filipino Equity Act to make up for the U.S. government's failure to adhere to its promise to treat Filipinos as American veterans. A guerilla intelligence officer, Arcebal was tortured, sentenced to death, escaped, and helped liberate the Philippines from Japanese occupation. In Document 5, Yong Soo Lee, a former Korean sex slave of the Japanese military, urges Congress to pressure Japan to formally and unequivocally apologize for coercing young women into sexual slavery. She describes being beaten and repeatedly raped for three years and enduring this trauma in silence and shame for decades later. Lee asks Congress to pass House Resolution 121, presented in Document 6. Introduced by Representative Michael Honda, the resolution calls on Japan to formally and unequivocally apologize for coercing young women into sexual slavery. Honda, a third-generation Japanese American and former internee, spearheaded the campaign because he viewed the suffering of military sexual slaves as a crime against humanity. Document 7 excerpts the 2009 testimony of Japanese Peruvian internee Libia Yamamoto, who requests that Congress create a commission to investigate why she and her family were kidnapped and imprisoned without trial during World War II. Yamamoto was seven years old when she and her family left everything they had in Peru and took only what they could carry to join her father at the Crystal City camp in Texas. After confiscating their passports and other forms of identification, the U.S. government branded them all "illegal aliens" and tried to deport them to Japan after the war.

Documents 8 and 9 reflect the impact of activism on self-determination campaigns in Guam and Hawai'i. Document 8 excerpts public statements by

Hope Alvarez Cristobal, a Chamorro and former senator in Guam, in which she asks a UN Special Committee to recognize that the United States has a history of violating Chamorro sovereignty and should make amends by recognizing Guamanian independence. Criticizing plans to rebase U.S. marines from Japan to Guam, Alvarez denounces the impact on population growth, local infrastructure, and the environment. Document 9 reprints Kana'iolowalu Act 195, a 2011 Hawaiian state law that supports the development of a reorganized Native Hawaiian governing entity. Kana'iolowalu is the Hawaiian name for the Native Hawaiian Roll Commission that, on July 10, 2015, certified a list of more than 95,000 qualified Native Hawaiians to participate in future nation-building campaigns.

1. A Government Commission Proclaims Internment a "Grave Injustice," 1982

The exclusion, removal and detention inflicted tremendous human cost. There was the obvious cost of homes and businesses sold or abandoned under circumstances of great distress, as well as injury to careers and professional advancement. But, most important, there was the loss of liberty and the personal stigma of suspected disloyalty for thousands of people who knew themselves to be devoted to their country's cause and to its ideals but whose repeated protestations of loyalty were discounted—only to be demonstrated beyond any doubt by the record of Nisei soldiers, who returned from the battlefields of Europe as the most decorated and distinguished combat unit of World War II, and by the thousands of other Nisei who served against the enemy in the Pacific, mostly in military intelligence. The wounds of the exclusion and detention have healed in some respects, but the scars of that experience remain, painfully real in the minds of those who lived through the suffering and deprivation of the camps....

The Effect of the Exclusion and Detention

The history of the relocation camps and the assembly centers that preceded them is one of suffering and deprivation visited on people against whom no charges were, or could have been, brought. The Commission hearing record is full of poignant, searing testimony that recounts the economic and personal losses and injury caused by the exclusion and the deprivations of detention. No summary can do this testimony justice....

The promulgation of Executive Order 9066 was not justified by military necessity, and the decisions which followed from it—detention, ending detention and ending exclusion—were not driven by analysis of military conditions.

From Commission on Wartime Relocation and Internment of Civilians, *Personal Justice Denied: Report of the Commission on Wartime Relocation and Internment of Civilians* (Washington, D.C.: U.S. Government Printing Office, December 1982), 3, 10–11, 18.

The broad historical causes which shaped these decisions were race prejudice, war hysteria and a failure of political leadership. Widespread ignorance of Japanese Americans contributed to a policy conceived in haste and executed in an atmosphere of fear and anger at Japan. A grave injustice was done to American citizens and resident aliens of Japanese ancestry who, without individual review or any probative evidence against them, were excluded, removed and detained by the United States during World War II.

2. A District Court Acknowledges Government Misconduct Before the Supreme Court During World War II, 1984

[19] The substance of the statements contained in the documents and the fact the statements were made demonstrate that the government knowingly withheld information from the courts when they were considering the critical question of military necessity in this case. A series of correspondence regarding what information should be included in the government's brief before the Supreme Court culminated in two different versions of a footnote that was to be used to specify the factual data upon which the government relied for its military necessity justification. The first version read as follows:

> The Final Report of General DeWitt (which is dated June 5, 1943, but which was not made public until January 1944) is relied on in this brief for statistics and other details concerning the actual evacuation and the events that took place subsequent thereto. *The recital of the circumstances justifying the evacuation as a matter of military necessity, however, is in several respects*, particularly with reference to the use of illegal radio transmitters and to shore-to-ship signalling by persons of Japanese ancestry, *in conflict with information in the possession of the Department of Justice. In view of the contrariety of the reports on this matter we do not ask the Court to take judicial notice of the recital of those facts contained in the Report.*
>
> Petitioner's Exhibit AA, Memorandum of John L. Burling to Assistant Attorney General Herbert Wechsler, September 11, 1944 (emphasis added).

The footnote that appeared in the final version of the brief merely read as follows:

> The Final Report of General DeWitt (which is dated June 5, 1943, but which was not made public until January 1944), hereinafter cited as Final report, is relied on this brief for statistics and other details concerning the actual evacuation and the events that took place subsequent thereto *We have specifically recited in this brief the facts relating to the*

From *Korematsu v. United States*, United States District Court, Northern District of California, 1984 584 F. Supp. 1406; reprinted in *American Justice: Japanese American Evacuation and Redress Cases*, ed. Nobuya Tsuchida (Minneapolis: University of Minnesota, Asian/Pacific American Learning Resource Center, 1988), 129–131.

justification for the evacuation, of which we ask the Court to take judicial notice, and we rely upon the Final Report only to the extent that it relates to such facts.

Brief for the United States, *Korematsu v. United States*, October Term, 1944, No. 22, at 11.

The final version made no mention of the contradictory reports. The record is replete with protestations of various Justice Department officials that the government had the obligation to advise the courts of the contrary facts and opinions. Petitioner's Exhibit A-FF. In fact, several Department of Justice officials pointed out to their superiors and others the "willful historical inaccuracies and intentional falsehoods" contained in the DeWitt Report....

... Omitted from the reports presented to the courts was information possessed by the Federal Communications Commission, the Department of Navy, and the Justice Department which directly contradicted General DeWitt's statements. Thus, the court had before it a selective record.

Whether a fuller, more accurate record would have prompted a different decision cannot be determined. Nor need it be determined. Where relevant evidence has been withheld, it is ample justification for the government's concurrence that the conviction should be set aside. It is sufficient to satisfy the court's independent inquiry and justify the relief sought by petitioner.

3. Hawaiian Sovereignty Leader Haunani-Kay Trask Criticizes Asian "Settler" Privilege and Collaboration with Colonialism, 2000

After nearly two thousand years of self-governance, we were colonized by Euro-American capitalists and missionaries in the eighteenth and nineteenth centuries. In 1893, the United States invaded our nation, overthrew our government, and secured an all-white planter oligarchy in place of our reigning *ali'i*, Queen Lili'uokalani. By resolution of the American Congress and against great Native opposition, Hawai'i was annexed in 1898. Dispossession of our government, our territory, and our legal citizenship made of us a colonized Native people.

Today, modern Hawai'i, like its colonial parent the United States, is a settler society. Our Native people and territories have been overrun by non-Natives, including Asians. Calling themselves "local," the children of Asian settlers greatly outnumber us. They claim Hawai'i as their own, denying indigenous history, their long collaboration in our continued dispossession, and the benefits therefrom.

Part of this denial is the substitution of the term "local" for "immigrant," which is, itself, a particularly celebrated American gloss for "settler." As on the continent, so in our island home. Settlers and their children recast the American tale of nationhood: Hawai'i, like the continent, is naturalized as but another tell-ing illustration of the uniqueness of America's "nation of immigrants." The ide-ology weaves a story of success: poor Japanese, Chinese, and Filipino settlers supplied the labor for wealthy, white sugar planters during the long period of the Territory (1900–1959). Exploitative plantation conditions thus underpin a master narrative of hard work and the endlessly celebrated triumph over anti-Asian racism. Settler children, ever industrious and deserving, obtain technical and liberal educations, thereby learning the political system through which they agitate for full voting rights as American citizens. Politically, the vehicle for Asian ascendancy is statehood. As a majority of voters at mid-century, the Japanese and other Asians moved into the middle class and eventually into seats of power in the legislature and the governor's house.

For our Native people, Asian success proves to be but the latest elaboration of foreign hegemony. The history of our colonization becomes a twice-told tale, first of discovery and settlement by European and American businessmen and missionaries, then of the plantation Japanese, Chinese, and eventually Filipino rise to dominance in the islands. Some Hawaiians, the best educated and articu-late, benefit from the triumph of the Democratic Party over the *haole* Republi-can Party. But as a people, Hawaiians remain a politically subordinated group suffering all the legacies of conquest: landlessness, disastrous health, diaspora, institutionalization in the military and prisons, poor educational attainment, and confinement to the service sector of employment.

While Asians, particularly the Japanese, come to dominate post-Statehood, Democratic Party politics, new racial tensions arise. The attainment of full Amer-ican citizenship actually heightens prejudice against Natives. Because the ideol-ogy of the United States as a mosaic of races is reproduced in Hawai'i through the celebration of the fact that no single "immigrant group" constitutes a numer-ical majority, the post-statehood euphoria stigmatizes Hawaiians as a failed indig-enous people whose conditions, including out-migration, actually worsen after statehood. Hawaiians are characterized as strangely unsuited, whether because of culture or genetics, to the game of assimilation....

Against this kind of disparaging colonial ideology, Hawaiians have been asserting their claims as indigenous people to land, economic power and political sovereignty for at least the last twenty years. Hawaiian communities are seriously engaged in all manner of historical, cultural, and political educa-tion. *Hālau hula* (dance academies), language classes, and varied resistance organizations link cultural practice to the struggle for self-determination. In this way, cultural groups have become conduits for reconnection to the *lāhui*, or nation. Political education occurs as the groups participate in sover-eignty marches, rallies, and political lobbying. The substance of the "nation" is made obvious when thousands of Hawaiians gather to protest the theft of their sovereignty. The power of such public rituals to de-colonize the mind can be seen in the rise of a new national identification among Hawaiians. After the 1993 sovereignty protests at the Palace of our chiefs, Hawaiians, especially the youth, began to discard national identity as Americans and reclaim indigenous identification as Natives....

On the international stage, the vehicle which has represented Hawaiians most effectively is Ka Lāhui Hawai'i [a native sovereignty organization]....

... [T]he goals of Ka Lāhui Hawai'i are simple: final resolution of the historic claims of the Hawaiian people relating to the overthrow, State and Federal misuse of Native trust lands (totaling some two million acres) and resources, and violations of human and civil rights. Resolution of claims will be followed by self-determination for Hawaiians; Federal recognition of Ka Lāhui Hawai'i as the Hawaiian Nation; restoration of traditional lands, natural resources, and energy resources to the Ka Lāhui National Land Trust....

Asians and *haole* have been thrown into a cauldron of defensive actions by our nationalist struggle. Either they must justify their continued benefit from Hawaiian subjugation, thus serving as support for that subjugation, or they must repudiate American hegemony and work with the Hawaiian nationalist movement. In plain language, serious and thoughtful individuals, whether *haole* or Asian, must choose to support a form of Hawaiian self-determination created by Hawaiians.

4. Filipino Veteran Franco Arcebal Calls on Congress to Restore the Citizenship He Was Promised During World War II, 2007

Mr. Arcebal. Honorable Chairman and Members of the House Committee on Veterans' Affairs, good morning, and Happy Valentine's Day.

Thank you for including me in this panel today. My name is Franco Arcebal, a Filipino World War II veteran, and the Vice President of Membership of the American Coalition for Filipino Veterans, Incorporated.

Our nonprofit, nonpartisan advocacy organization has more than 4,000 individual members in the United States. I am now 83 years old and a retired sales executive. I reside in Los Angeles.

Thank you for holding this early hearing on the equity bill, House Resolution 760 for Filipino World War II veterans. Never in the history of our long quest for recognition has this hearing been scheduled within 2 weeks after it was introduced. We owe this to the Honorable Bob Filner, our undaunted and tireless champion.

May we have an applause for him. [Applause.] The Chairman. You are all out of order. [Laughter.]

Mr. Arcebal. With twelve of my comrades for this allegiance, when we chained ourselves in front of the White House in July 1997—that is almost 10 years ago—sadly, we were unable to convince the Clinton Administration to support our bill.

I am honored to present the appeal of my comrades today. Like all of us, we have personal stories to tell about the war, and I want to give you a brief one.

Equity for Filipino Veterans: 'Hearing Before the Committee on Veterans' Affairs, U.S. House of Representatives, One Hundred Tenth Congress, first session, February 15, 2007, Volume 4, Serial No. 110–3, 1–2.

During the second World War, I was a guerrilla intelligence officer. I was caught and severely tortured by the Japanese soldier as a spy. I was sentenced by decapitation. Lucky for me, during the rainstorm at night, I was able to escape and fought again in the liberation of the Philippines against General Yamashita for seven continuous months in north Luzon until he surrendered in September 1945.

In 1997, I became a new U.S. permanent resident. At that time, I had a painful dental problem. I sought treatment at the Los Angeles VA clinic. I was terribly shocked when I was told my service in the U.S. Army forces was by law deemed not active service for the purposes of VA benefits.

I concluded that the United States whom I served loyally and risked my life did me injustice. I felt discriminated against. The denial of my benefit was a result of the "Rescission Act" of February 18, 1946, 60 years today this month. This law was enacted over the objection of President Truman.

Before this law, Filipino veterans were recognized as American veterans and entitled to all benefits. And today I expect many credible witnesses to present testimonies in favor of our bill. And I join this Colonel because it is my duty to speak on behalf of my comrades who are now elderly, disabled, and poor.

Over the past decades, our coalition mission was to restore full U.S. Government recognition and win equitable VA benefits. We believe that by passing the "Filipino Equity Act" or the realistic bill of our sponsors, we can finally overcome the discriminatory effects of the "Rescission Act."

We estimate that about 4,000 Filipino veterans in the United States and about 10,000 in the Philippines may benefit if this bill is approved.

Mr. Chairman, there are three requests I would like to make today from this Committee. First, pass an authorizing language of the equity bill, House Resolution 760, with a strong bipartisan support from this Committee.

Second, obtain an estimated budget of no less than $18 million from the Appropriations Committee with the support of President Bush and the support of our VA Secretary Nicholson that would provide an equitable VA benefit monthly in the amount of $200 per month for us low-income veterans.

Third, and this is very crucial to us, create a task force of representatives of the House Veterans' Affairs Committee, representative of the Secretary of the Veterans' Administration, a representative of the Philippine government, Philippine Embassy, and the leaders of key groups.

This task force should determine within 45 days the accurate number of living World War II Filipino veterans in the United States and in the Philippines, assess their economic and health needs, actual needs, and recommend a realistic budget. We must solve this national travesty now.

Let me close by quoting President Truman on February 20, 1946, when he objected to the "Rescission Act." And he said, I quote, "I consider it a moral obligation of the United States to look after the welfare of the Filipino veterans."

Thank you.

5. Yong Soo Lee Testifies Before Congress About Being a Military Sexual Slave of the Japanese During World War II, 2007

I remember crawling towards the bathroom, throwing up as I went along, when I was grabbed by a man and dragged into a cabin. I tried to shake him off, biting his arm. I did my best to get away. But he slapped me and threw me into the cabin with such force that I couldn't fight him off. In this way I was raped. It was my first sexual experience. I was so frightened that what actually happened didn't sink in at the time. I vaguely thought that this man had forced me into the room just to do this.

People kept shouting that we would all die since the ship had been torn to pieces. We were told to put life-jackets on and to stay calm. We thought we were going to drown. Dying seemed better than going on like this. But the ship somehow managed to keep going. Later I found out that I was not the only one who had been raped. Punsun and the others had also suffered that same fate. From then on, we were often raped on the ship. I wept constantly, until my eyes became swollen. I was frightened about everything. I think that I was too young to hold a grudge against my aggressors, though looking back I feel angry and full of the desire for revenge. At that time I was so scared I didn't even dare look any man squarely in the face. One day I opened the window of our cabin and tried to jump into the water. It would have been better to end my life then and there, I thought. But the water, blue-green and white with waves, scared me so much that I lost the courage to throw myself out.

Eventually we arrived in Taiwan. When we disembarked I couldn't walk properly as my abdomen hurt so much. My glands had swollen up in my groin, and blood had coagulated around my vagina. I could walk only with great difficulty, since I was so swollen that I couldn't keep my two legs straight.

The man who had accompanied us from Taegu turned out to be the proprietor of the comfort station we were taken to. We called him Oyaji. I was the youngest amongst us. Punsun was a year older than me and the others were 18, 19 and 20. The proprietor told me to go into a certain room, but I refused. He dragged me by my hair to another room. There I was tortured with electric shocks. He was very cruel. He pulled out the telephone cord and tied my wrists and ankles with it. Then, shouting 'honoyaro!' he twirled the telephone receiver. Lights flashed before my eyes, and my body shook all over. I couldn't stand it and begged him to stop. I said I would do anything he asked. But he turned the receiver once more. I blacked out. When I came round my body was wet; I think that he had probably poured water on me.

Life in the Comfort Station

The comfort station was a two-storey Japanese-style building with 20 rooms. There were already many women there when we arrived. About ten, all of

House of Representatives, Subcommittee on Asia, the Pacific, and the Global Environment, Committee on Foreign Affairs, 110th Congress, Feb. 15, 2007, 19–23.

whom looked much older than us, wore kimonos. There was a Japanese woman, the proprietor's wife. We changed into dresses given to us by the other women. The proprietor told us to call them 'nesang,' 'big sister' and to do whatever they told us to. We began to take turns to wash their clothes and cook for them. The food was again not enough. We ate gruel made with millet or rice. I was terrified of being beaten; I was always scared. I was never beaten by soldiers, but I was frequently beaten by the proprietor. I was so frightened that I couldn't harbor any thoughts of running away. After having crossed an ocean and not knowing where I was, how could I think of escape?

The rooms were very small. Each was big enough for two people to lie down in. At the entrance of each hung a blanket in place of a door. The walls and floor were laid with wooden boards, and there was nothing else. We were each given a military blanket and had to sleep on the bare planks. One day, a man came in and asked my name. I was still frightened and just sat in a corner shaking my head without answering. So he said he would give me a name, and began to call me Tosiko. After that day I was always called Tosiko in the station.

We mainly had to serve a commando unit. They were not in the slightest way sympathetic towards us. They wore uniforms, but I had no idea whether they were from the army, navy or air force. I served four or five men a day. They finished their business quickly and left. Hardly any stayed overnight. I had to use old clothes, washed thoroughly, during my period. Even then I had to serve men. I was never paid for these services.

There were frequent air raids, and on some days we had to be evacuated several times. Whenever there was a raid, we were forced to hide ourselves in mountain undergrowth or in a cave. If the bombing ceased, the men would set up make-shift tents anywhere, on dry fields or in paddies, and they would make us serve them. Even if the tents were blown down by the wind, the men didn't pay any attention but finished what they were doing to us. Those men were worse than dogs or pigs. They never wore condoms. I don't remember ever having a medical examination.

One day, while we were in an underground shelter, the comfort station collapsed in a bombing attack. Our shelter was buried under the rubble. We dug through the soil, trying to get out. After a while we saw light through a small hole. I was incredibly relieved to be able to look out and shouted 'At last I can see outside!' Then I smelt smoke, and blood gushed out of my nose and mouth. I lost consciousness. The proprietor's wife and mistress both died. As the house had collapsed, we were moved into a bomb shelter at the foot of a hill, and there we again had to serve the men. After a while, the proprietor got hold of some material and built a rough and ready house. It didn't take him long. We continued to serve the men. In the end I was infected with venereal disease and the proprietor gave me the injection of the serum known as No. 606, which was used before penicillin became widely available. The fluid had a reddish tint. The disease stayed with me for a long time because I had to continue to serve men before I was clear. So I had to have constant injections. There was no hospital or clinic in the vicinity. Medical care—such as it was—was haphazard.

Apart from going to the bomb shelters we weren't allowed out at all. We were warned that if we tried to venture beyond the confines of the station we would be killed, and I was sufficiently scared not to try anything. The men we served in the unit were all young; they seemed to be 19 or 20 years old, not much older than we girls were.

One evening, a soldier came to me and said he would be in combat later that same evening and that this battle would mark the end of his early life. I asked him what his commando unit was. He explained that one or two men would fly an airplane to attack an enemy ship or base. They would be suicide pilots. He gave me his photo and the toiletries he had been using. He had come to me twice before and said he had got venereal disease from me. He said he would take the disease to his grave as my present to him. Then he taught me a song:

> I take off with courage, leaving Sinzhu behind,
> Over the golden and silver clouds.
> There is no one to see me off:
> Only Tosiko grieves for me.

Until then I had known we were somewhere in Taiwan, but because we were kept in such close confinement and isolation, I had no idea of exactly where. From his song I learned we were in Sinzhu.

When we were evacuated to avoid the bombing we stole sugar cane. We were that hungry. But if we were caught we were beaten. We were not allowed to speak in Korean. Again, if we were caught doing so, we were beaten.

The War Ends

One day, one of the older girls who normally hardly spoke a word to us announced that she, too, was Korean. She told me, in Korean, that the war was over. We hugged each other and wept with joy. She held my hand tightly and told me I must return to Korea. We could hear people shouting and running about. This confirmed to us that the war was really over. By the time we had calmed down, the proprietor and the other women who had been at the station before us were nowhere to be found. We walked to a refugee camp by the pier. It looked like a warehouse. We were given balls of boiled rice which had dead insects mixed in. We waited for a ship. I was scared even then that someone might drag me away, so I sat, shaking with fear, in a corner wrapped in a blanket. I kept crying so much that my small eyes got even smaller.

We finally got a ship. When it arrived in Pusan, the barley was green. As we disembarked, someone sprayed us with DDT and gave us each 300 won. There were four of us: Punsun, two other girls, and myself. We said farewell and went our separate ways. I got a train to Taegu. I kept weeping and tried to hide myself from other passengers in fear that someone might take me away again. I found my house, just as run down and poor as before. My mother asked if I was a ghost or a real person and fainted.

After my return, I couldn't dare think about getting married. How could I dream of marriage? Until recently I had suffered from venereal disease. My parents and brothers did not know what I had been through; I could not tell them. My father was upset merely because his only daughter wouldn't get married. Both my parents resented the fact that they weren't able to see me hitched before they died. I worked in a drinking house which also sold fishballs, and I ran a small shop on the beach in Ulsan. For some time I ran a small market stall selling string. Then I worked as a saleswoman for an insurance company. I gave up when I began to get too old.

Return My Youth to Me!

In 1992, encouraged by the existence of the Korean Council for the Women Drafted for Military Sexual Slavery by Japan, I told my story. It poured out from me and I felt so relieved, but I was also faced with the question, How many more years can I live?

I am grateful that the Korean Council is trying to help us. These days I hum a song, Katusa, putting my own words to the tune: 'I am so miserable; return my youth to me; apologize.... You dragged us off against our own will. You trod on us. Apologize ... This lament, can you hear it, my mother and father? My own people will avenge my sorrows.'

I visited my parents' graves the other day. I said to them: 'Mother, I know you won't come back to life however much I may wish for it. My own people will avenge me. Please close your eyes and go to paradise.'

Mr. Chairman, members of the subcommittee, thank you again for this opportunity to appear before you and tell my story. I am happy to answer any questions you might have.

6. House Resolution 121 Urges Japan to Apologize for Coercing "Comfort Women" into Sexual Slavery During World War II, 2007

In the House of Representatives, U.S.,

July 30, 2007.

Whereas the Government of Japan, during its colonial and wartime occupation of Asia and the Pacific Islands from the 1930s through the duration of World War II, officially commissioned the acquisition of young women for the sole purpose of sexual servitude to its Imperial Armed Forces, who became known to the world as *ianfu* or "comfort women";

Whereas the "comfort women" system of forced military prostitution by the Government of Japan, considered unprecedented in its cruelty and magnitude, included gang rape, forced abortions, humiliation, and sexual violence resulting

House of Representatives, Subcommittee on Asia, the Pacific, and the Global Environment, Committee on Foreign Affairs, 110th Congress, July 30, 2007.

in mutilation, death, or eventual suicide in one of the largest cases of human trafficking in the 20th century;

Whereas some new textbooks used in Japanese schools seek to downplay the "comfort women" tragedy and other Japanese war crimes during World War II;

Whereas Japanese public and private officials have recently expressed a desire to dilute or rescind the 1993 statement by Chief Cabinet Secretary Yohei Kono on the "comfort women," which expressed the Government's sincere apologies and remorse for their ordeal;

Whereas the Government of Japan did sign the 1921 International Convention for the Suppression of the Traffic in Women and Children and supported the 2000 United Nations Security Council Resolution 1325 on Women, Peace, and Security which recognized the unique impact on women of armed conflict;

Whereas the House of Representatives commends Japan's efforts to promote human security, human rights, democratic values, and rule of law, as well as for being a supporter of Security Council Resolution 1325;

Whereas the United States-Japan alliance is the cornerstone of United States security interests in Asia and the Pacific and is fundamental to regional stability and prosperity;

Whereas, despite the changes in the post-cold war strategic landscape, the United States-Japan alliance continues to be based on shared vital interests and values in the Asia-Pacific region, including the preservation and promotion of political and economic freedoms, support for human rights and democratic institutions, and the securing of prosperity for the people of both countries and the international community;

Whereas the House of Representatives commends those Japanese officials and private citizens whose hard work and compassion resulted in the establishment in 1995 of Japan's private Asian Women's Fund;

Whereas the Asian Women's Fund has raised $5,700,000 to extend "atonement" from the Japanese people to the comfort women; and

Whereas the mandate of the Asian Women's Fund, a government-initiated and largely government-funded private foundation whose purpose was the carrying out of programs and projects with the aim of atonement for the maltreatment and suffering of the "comfort women," came to an end on March 31, 2007, and the Fund has been disbanded as of that date: Now, therefore, be it

Resolved, That it is the sense of the House of Representatives that the Government of Japan—

   (1) should formally acknowledge, apologize, and accept historical responsibility in a clear and unequivocal manner for its Imperial Armed Forces' coercion of young women into sexual slavery, known to the world as "comfort women," during its colonial and wartime occupation of Asia and the Pacific Islands from the 1930s through the duration of World War II;

   (2) would help to resolve recurring questions about the sincerity and status of prior statements if the Prime Minister of Japan were to make such an apology as a public statement in his official capacity;

(3) should clearly and publicly refute any claims that the sexual enslavement and trafficking of the "comfort women" for the Japanese Imperial Armed Forces never occurred; and

(4) should educate current and future generations about this horrible crime while following the recommendations of the international community with respect to the "comfort women."

7. Japanese Latin American Libia Yamamoto Remembers Being Held as a Hostage During World War II, 2009

Finally, after an entire month of excruciating mental anguish during which we heard no news of him, we received a letter from my father. The timing was perfect; it came on my sister's birthday: February 13th. He wrote telling us that he was OK and in Panama. For my sister, he enclosed some pressed flowers as a present to her. He apologized for not being there for her or having a gift for her on her birthday but hoped that those pressed flowers would do. That was the best present my sister and the entire family could have had on that day. We were just so happy to hear that he was alive and that he was OK. It was only later on that we found out that he and the others were working digging ditches in a military army camp; many of them were terrified at the idea that they were digging their own graves.

Fortunately, they were not, and my father and the others were taken to Department of Justice camps in Texas. There, their passports and paperwork were confiscated. It is in these camps that my father found out that they were going to be shipped to Japan in a prisoner exchange program. This news terrified my father and the others, and they began protesting because they knew that being sent to Japan would certainly mean separation from their families.

A 'compromise' was reached and the so-called 'solution to this problem' was to reunite these men with their families in Department of Justice camps. I think the U.S. government did not mind this solution because, in effect, it provided more persons for the hostage exchange program with Japan. In most cases after the initial separation of fathers from their families, they were reunited in Crystal City camp. However, there were some families who were never able to reunite. My heart goes out to those who had family members just disappear, never seeing their father, or mother, sister, or brother or other close relatives.

In this respect, I was one of the 'lucky ones.' Somehow, my father was able to communicate to my mother instructions on how to get rid of the inventory from the store, and as I recall she went to work, fast and furious....

We left Peru from the Port of Callao [Peru] in July of 1943, bringing only what we could carry. Boarding the ships in Callao was horrifying because there were soldiers on those ships pointing their big guns at us. We had never seen guns that close to us, and even worse, pointed at us as if we were horrible people.

"Libia Yamamoto Testimony," March 19, 2009, Hearing on: The Treatment of Latin Americans of Japanese Descent, European Americans, and Jewish Refugees During World War II, 2–7.

The entire trip last 21 days, and we were not allowed to leave our cabins, which were unbearably small and cramped. We were not allowed on deck, so we could not see what was going on outside. Many folks got seasick in the cabins, which made the situation even worse. I especially remember the ship going through a very strong storm, which made almost everybody sick.

When we got to New Orleans, we were finally allowed off the ship. There, officials inspected all the belongings that everybody had brought. My mother had to take my sister to the bathroom, so she told me to look after all our luggage. While my mother was gone, I saw the inspectors go through people's luggage, taking things and throwing them in the water. The water was full off boxes, memories, and people's valuables. I was frightened at what they were doing. As for myself, I only had one object that was important to me. It was the doll my father had brought me while I was sick at three-years-old. Back in Peru, my mother had told my siblings and me that we could only bring one thing that was ours to the U.S. There was nothing for me to think about. This was the only possession that mattered to me because it represented the love of my father and everything he meant to me. I silently pleaded: "Take anything, just not my doll." My mother was still in the bathroom when the inspectors reached me. To this day, I am not certain as to why, but the inspectors did not throw the doll away, in fact they did not do a very thorough search. Maybe they felt sorry for me, a seven-year old girl guarding her family's luggage with fear in her eyes.

When we finally reached Texas, we expected to see my father, but didn't. We were told that we would see him in one week. I remember when I did see him for the first time and being so happy and hugging him. He had lost a lot of weight. He said he was fine, but he didn't look fine. Even so, we were just so glad to see him. Reuniting with him after such a long time felt so good that the guard towers with the machine guns pointed at us didn't seem that bad. Still, in all our relief, I remember it was made very clear to all of us not to get too close to the fence because we would get shot.

I think that life in the camps was a lot tougher for my parents than it was for us children. Our parents made it so that the children could have as normal a life as possible in the camp. Most of all, being reunited with my father seemed to be enough to help my family get through this difficult time.

At the end of the war, we faced even more trying times. The U.S. government told us to leave the country in which we had been imprisoned against our will. They told us we were "illegal aliens." But how could we be "illegal aliens" when they were the ones who brought us here and confiscated our passports? It was all very frustrating and infuriating. It was like we had no rights; we were treated like we were not even human beings, and they could do with us as they pleased. We could not go back to Peru, as the Peruvian government refused to take back the Japanese folks it had sent to the U.S. There was no choice but to go to Japan. My sister and her family went to Japan first, and we knew things were not bright due to the devastation the war had caused. My sister wrote to us that her family had to pull out weeds from the ground just to feed themselves and little Sumiko, her five-month-old baby, died from malnutrition.

When it was our family's turn to leave, my father became very ill, and our deportation to Japan had to be cancelled. But by this time, the government said that if we could find our own sponsors to stay in the U.S., we could stay. Fortunately, we had relatives in Berkeley who sponsored us. However, we had to pool together our own travel money. My father used what little money he had been fortunate to earn doing underpaid work in the camps. We left camp in 1947. By this time, I had reached twelve-years-old.

Once in Berkeley, we couldn't find a place to stay. But my relatives talked to their church and the church allowed us to use two rooms in the church's basement as bedrooms. We lived there for eleven months. Because my parents didn't speak English, they both had to take whatever job was available to them. For my parents, this whole transition was very, very difficult. They found themselves doing the kind of work that they were not used to doing. In Peru, they had been the ones hiring domestic workers, and now they were doing that work themselves. This made my parents think more and more about everything they had lost in Peru. Not just the financial success, but the prestige and status they held in the community as well.

The transition was very tough for me as well. Because my parents were always working, I had to do all the heavy housework and take care of my younger siblings. So, at the age of twelve, I had to do the family laundry by hand, with a dashboard. My hands weren't very big, and it took a lot of effort and time for me to do it. I also had to change the dirty water I used to wash the laundry, and this was way too much weight for my 12-year-old body.

At school, learning English proved a harrowing task. I vividly remember kids making fun of my imperfect pronunciation, asking me to repeat a word over and over again just because they were amused by the way I said it. I felt like an outsider and was completely mortified.

But we all got through it by working hard. My father always told me that no matter what I did, I should always do my best. He'd say, "Nobody can say anything if you do your very best." This life lesson carried me through adulthood. No matter what I did I always tried to do my best.

As difficult as things were for them during this time, my parents would prepare care packages to send to our relatives in Japan who were less fortunate. My parents always sent them coffee, tea, candy – all kinds of things.

The fall from what our lives had been in Peru to what they became in Berkeley seemed precipitous. We became very poor and struggled all the way through. As a family with five children, it was very rough for all of us. Father was never able to get back what he had accomplished in Peru. He and mother would be stuck doing manual labor until their retirement....

I just wonder when reflecting upon all of this ... was it really necessary to turn our lives upside down? For ten years, after being forcibly removed from our home country and taken to the United States, we lived as a people without a state, labeled as "illegal aliens." We had been living a good life in Peru, a country that was not involved in the war. So to remove us from our country, where I was born, to bring us to a strange land and force us to live in a concentration camp... I don't know if it was absolutely necessary. We didn't commit any crime, and they would never charge us with anything. We had no trial.

All we are asking for here today is a much needed investigation into our experience and the experiences of so many other Latin Americans of Japanese descent who were also kidnapped from their homes in twelve other Latin American countries. I come here today to ask that you consider this bill that would only bring justice to those who were affected by shedding light on these WWII violations that remain with so many of us today and with this nation.

8. Hope Alvarez Cristobal Argues for Guamanian Self-Determination and Decolonization, 2010

What we find unacceptable, Mr. Chairman, is that the administering power's WWII adversary, Guam's brutal occupier of WWII, Japan, is now complicit in Guam's modern day colonization and militarization through its joint Bi-lateral Agreement with the U.S. With respect to Guam, the Special Committee's work was not only stymied; rather, it has been made to fail in its mission to make colonialism a fact of the past—in not having developed a programme of work for the decolonization of the NSGT [Non-Self-Governing Territory] of Guam in view of the US's active, massive militarization plans. Included is the failure in dispatching a UN visiting mission at the time Guam was actively negotiating its political status over two decades ago; and today, with US plans for our militarization.

For 21st century Guam, it is déjà vu old-style colonialism again. This time it is not 17th C. Spain but the US administering Power utilizing its military forces in a kind of "*reduccion*" process of "subduing, converting and gathering the natives through the establishment of missions and stationing of soldiers to protect those missions." The exploitation of our colonial status as a people, U.S. militarization, assimilationist immigration policies, the rising tide of cultural genocide, environmental degradation and contamination, the dispossession of our lands, etc., are direct violations of our rights as NSG people....

Clearly, the US continues to behave contrary to its concrete UN obligations as the administering Power over Guam. There is no mistaking that US dominance and subordination of Guam is a consequence of US military power dynamics over the Asia-Pacific region. And, without the United Nations assertion of its moral authority and oversight of its non self-governing territory of Guam, our home island and our people will continue to be treated as inferior having no sovereignty or agency in relation to US foreign policy and security interests. Gone unchallenged, the possibility of a free, decolonized and self-governing Guam will be sealed and buried under by our own administering Power.

At his opening statement of the House Armed Services Committee hearing on March 25, 2010, Congressman Ike Skelton spoke about the rebasing of U.S. Marines from Japan to Guam as "one of the largest movements of military assets in decades"—estimated to cost over ten billion dollars. He further stated that the

Hope Alvarez Cristobal, "The Question of Guam," Statement of the Guahan Coalition for Peace and Justice and the Chamorro Studies Association, Before the United Nations Special Committee on the Situation with Regard to the Implementation of the Granting of Independence to Colonial Countries and Peoples (C-24), 2010 Pacific Regional Seminar, May 18–20, 2010, 3–8. Reprinted by permission.

changes being planned as part of that move will not only affect U.S. bilateral relationship with Japan; they will shape U.S. strategic posture throughout the critical Asia-Pacific region for 50 years or more. Congressman Skelton stated that the US "must be proactively engaged in the Asia-Pacific region on multiple fronts," and that U.S. actions may well influence the choices and actions of others." For Guam, our exclusion from the decision made about the massive militarization of our island home through US military expansion and restructuring of its bases and military operations is unconscionable. Moreover, we have had no choice and no options offered vis-à-vis our colonial status or US actions having political implications on our colonial status....

On The Human Environment

Mr. Chairman, the U.S. military's militarization plans bodes great harm for the people and our island home environment. These plans include the construction of facilities and structure to support the full spectrum of warfare training for some 8,600 marines (and their dependants) being relocated from Okinawa to Guam; the construction of a deep-draft wharf in Guam's only harbor to provide for nuclear-powered aircraft carriers, destroying over 287,000 sqm (71 acres) of healthy and endangered coral reef; the construction of an Army Missile Defense Task Force modeled on the Marshall Islands-based Ronald Reagan Ballistic Missile Defense Test Site, for the practice by US military personnel of intercepting intercontinental ballistic missiles; the forcible land-grabbing of an additional 2,200 acres of indigenous Chamorro land; the desecration of Pagat, one of Guam's oldest ancient villages dating back to 2,000 B.C.; the dangerous over-tapping of Guam's water system to include the drilling of 22 additional wells; and the denial of the most fundamental human right of the Chamorro people of Guam to self-determination.

The militarization plan calls for an alarming 80,000 new residents within the next five years. These new residents include the 8,600 Marines and 1,000 Army troops with 9,000 of their dependents and large numbers of construction workers that will add to our current 180,000 residents. This is obviously not about demographics alone as we see US hegemony flourish and cultural genocide work for the administering power. As non-US citizens after WWII, we were over 95% of the population. As United States citizens 50 years later, our population is reduced to 42% (2000 Census). Five years ago, we comprised some 35% of our home population. But with the new US plan, the Chamorro population can be expected to drop to around 24%! This is perhaps the most plausible reason why all information impacting our people's lives were kept secret until the official release of the draft environmental impact study last November 20, 2009....

The selective and exclusive sharing of information on the military's plans prevented our full participation and served to silence our voices in this critical process. The community scrambled to respond to the 11,000-page report within the rigid schedule. The "record speed" of a two-year environmental impact study for such unprecedented militarization of a non self-governing territory was obviously suspect. We were not told about the 80,000 people or that the

US had planned to go outside their existing footprint. At the public outreach meetings, hundreds spoke resoundingly against the military's plans. At the close of the public comment window, the military received over 10,000 comments from various indigenous Chamorro groups, community members and stakeholders and other external stakeholders.

The fear of being overwhelmed by the construction of a new US Marine base has permeated the community. In reference to the local government's costs grossly underfunded in the plan, Lt. Governor Michael Cruz, M.D. who himself is a Colonel in the Army National Guard, stated "Our nation knows how to find us when it comes to war and fighting for war, but when it comes to war preparations—which is what the military buildup essentially is—nobody seems to know where Guam is." Government officials put the total direct and indirect costs of coping with the military buildup at about $3 billion, including $1.7 billion to improve roads and $100 million to expand the already overburdened public hospital.

Three days after the DEIS [Draft Environmental Impact System] was released, the Pacific Daily News conducted a straw poll asking, "Do you support the Guam buildup?" Of 773 respondents, 55% stated "No" and 45% stated "Yes." Since then, the community has been flooded with all kinds of promilitary community relations activities. We have also seen a steady stream of federal officials and Japanese officials visit our island.

Last January 22, the 30th Guam Legislature adopted a resolution expressing the "strong and abiding opposition of the Guam Legislature and the People of Guam to any use of eminent domain [condemnation] for the purpose of obtaining Guam lands for either the currently planned military buildup or other U.S. Federal Government purposes, or both." Copies were transmitted to the President of the United States, the Speaker of the House of Representatives of the United States, the President Pro-Tem of the U.S. Senate, to UN Secretary General, Ban Ki-moon, and other officials....

Of grave concern is the fact that Chamorro self-determination and decolonization was not even addressed by the military in the DEIS and the fact that decisions have been made in the context of a huge power imbalance in which the US has the ultimate decision-making power with the social, cultural and political implications to the Chamorro community being grossly understated. It is no secret that the US and its military representatives are fully cognizant of the irreversible and significant consequences that their decision will have on its colonial people. Broad concerns relating to local infrastructure, environmental, labor and workforce, socioeconomic and health and human services are being discussed among government and military officials. But the difference is: The US has completely ignored the negative implications to its colonial people's human, political and legal right to self-determination. Just as select private businesses collectively predict positive gain by Guam's militarization, the Chamorro people alone have historically and will predictably bear the unequal proportion of the burden.

On the last day of the public comment period, the federal Environmental Protection Agency issued the lowest possible rating of the DEIS of "environmentally unsatisfactory" and providing "inadequate information." In its strongly worded six-page letter, the US EPA stated that "The impacts are of sufficient magnitude that ... action should not proceed as proposed and improved analyses are necessary to ensure the information in the EIS is adequate to fully inform decision makers." Specifically, the EPA stated that the military's plan would lead to:

a. A shortfall in Guam's water supply, resulting in low water pressure that would expose people to water borne diseases from sewage.

b. Increased sewage flows to wastewater plants already failing to comply with the Clean Water Act regulations.

c. More raw sewage spills that would contaminate the water supply and the ocean.

d. "Unacceptable impacts" to the 287,000 sqm (71 acres) of a high quality coral reef.

But even with this indictment of its draft EIS, the military continues with its military expansion and restructuring plans today....

Obstacles/Opportunities/Recommendations

The Question of Guam shall remain a question of Chamorro self-determination and decolonization for Guam. As a process of decolonization, the exercise of Chamorro self-determination must necessarily occur outside the influences of the administering Power and with the cooperation of the United Nations.

We make the following recommendations to this seminar:

1. That the inalienable right of the Chamorro people of Guam to self-determination in conformity with all relevant UN documents be given utmost priority by the Special Committee on Decolonization in view of the administering power's massive militarization planned from 2010 to 2014.

2. That a *customized* process of decolonization for the Chamorro people of Guam be immediately adopted in view of the severe irreversible impacts on Guam by the US administering power.

3. That an investigation be conducted as to the compliance of the administering power with its treaty obligations under the Charter of the United Nations to promote the economic and social development and to preserve the cultural identity of the Territories as related earlier in this text.

4. That a study be conducted on the implications of US militarization plans on Guam's decolonization and that UN funding be allocated immediately.

5. That the UN denounce the militarization of the non-self-governing territory of Guam without the consent of the people of Guam due to irreparable harm to the inalienable human rights of the Chamorro people and interests of the people of Guam.

6. That a work programme be adopted by the Special Committee to carry out its objectives for the decolonization of Guam.

Closing

Thank you, Mr. Chairman and delegations for the opportunity to make this presentation. My people's journey towards decolonization is at a very critical juncture. We can only rely on the United Nations to assure that the US live up to its obligations under the United Nations Charter and to its promise of self-determination and decolonization for the people of Guam.

9. Hawaiian State Law, Act 195, Creates a Commission to Enroll Native Hawaiians to Organize a Sovereign Government, 2011

KANA'IOLOWALU Act 195

SECTION 1. The legislature finds that the State has never explicitly acknowledged that Native Hawaiians are the only indigenous, aboriginal, maoli [native] population of Hawai'i.

Native Hawaiians are the indigenous, native people of the Hawaiian archipelago and are a distinctly native community. From its inception, the State has had a special political and legal relationship with the Native Hawaiian people and has continually enacted legislation for the betterment of their condition.

In section 5(f) of the Admission Act of 1959, Congress created what is commonly known as the ceded lands trust. The ceded lands trust, consisting of lands, including submerged lands, natural resources, and the proceeds from the disposition or use of those lands—purportedly ceded to the United States by the Republic of Hawai'i—is for five purposes, one of which remains the betterment of the conditions of native Hawaiians.

At the 1978 Constitutional Convention, the delegates proposed a constitutional amendment to establish the office of Hawaiian affairs. The amendment was ratified by the voters on November 7, 1978, and codified as article XII, sections 5 and 6 of the Hawai'i State Constitution, and in chapter 10, Hawai'i Revised Statutes.

The State's designation of the office of Hawaiian affairs as a trust vehicle to act on behalf of Native Hawaiians until a Native Hawaiian governing entity could be reestablished reaffirmed the State's obligations to the Native Hawaiian people.

Delegates to the 1978 Constitutional Convention further proposed to amend the Hawai'i State Constitution to affirm protection of all "rights, customarily and traditionally exercised for subsistence, cultural and religious purposes and possessed by ahupua'a [traditional land division in Hawai'i] tenants who are descendants of native Hawaiians who inhabited the Hawaiian Islands prior to 1778..." Moreover, state law also specifically protects Hawaiians' ability to practice their traditional and customary rights. The federal and state courts have continuously recognized the right of the Native Hawaiian people to engage in customary and traditional practices on public lands.

In 1993, the United States formally apologized to Native Hawaiians for the United States' role in the overthrow of the Hawaiian Kingdom through Public

Senate Bill No. 1520, State of Hawaii, Senate, 26th Legislature, 2011, http://www.capitol.hawaii.gov/session2011/Bills/SB1520_CD1_.HTM

Law 103-150 (107 Stat. 1510), commonly known as the "Apology Resolution." The Apology Resolution acknowledges that the illegal overthrow of the Hawaiian Kingdom occurred with the active participation of agents and citizens of the United States and further acknowledges that the Native Hawaiian people never directly relinquished to the United States their claims to their inherent sovereignty as a people over their national lands, either through a Treaty of Annexation or through a plebiscite or referendum. The Apology Resolution expresses the commitment of Congress and the President to acknowledge the ramifications of the overthrow of the Hawaiian Kingdom and to support reconciliation efforts between the United States and Native Hawaiians. Pursuant to the Apology Resolution, the United States Departments of Justice and the Interior conducted reconciliation hearings with the Native Hawaiian people in 1999 and issued a joint report entitled, "From Mauka to Makai: The River of Justice Must Flow Freely," which identified promoting the reorganization of a Native Hawaiian government as a priority recommendation for continuing the process of reconciliation. To further this process of reconciliation, Congress created the Office of Native Hawaiian Relations within the Department of the Interior, to consult with Native Hawaiians on the reconciliation process.

In December 2010, the Departments of Justice and the Interior reaffirmed the federal support for the Native Hawaiian Government Reorganization Act of 2010. This reaffirmation recognized that Native Hawaiians are the only one of the nation's three major indigenous peoples who currently lack a formal government-to-government relationship with the United States.

The United States became a charter member of the United Nations in 1945. The United States submitted Hawai'i as a territory of the United States to be listed as a non-self-governing territory entitled to self-government under Article 73, Charter of the United Nations, via United Nations General Assembly Resolution 66 (1946), although it was later de-listed at the time of statehood. Also in December 2010, the United States endorsed the United Nations Declaration on the Rights of Indigenous Peoples, which acknowledged, among other things:

ARTICLE 3 — Indigenous peoples have the right to self-determination. By virtue of that right they freely determine their political status and freely pursue their economic, social and cultural development.

The United States' endorsement of the United Nations Declaration on the Rights of Indigenous Peoples included recognition of its support not only for the Native Hawaiian Government Reorganization Act of 2010 but also many additional laws for Native Hawaiians such as the National Historic Preservation Act, the Native Hawaiian Education Act, the Native American Housing Assistance and Self-Determination Act, and the Native American Graves Protection and Repatriation Act.

Native Hawaiians have continued to maintain their separate identity as a single, distinctly native political community through cultural, social, and political institutions and have continued to maintain their rights to self-determination, self-governance, and economic self-sufficiency.

The State has supported the reorganization of a Native Hawaiian governing entity. It has supported the Sovereignty Advisory Council, the Hawaiian

Sovereignty Advisory Commission, the Hawaiian Sovereignty Elections Council, and Native Hawaiian Vote, and the convening of the Aha Hawai'i 'Oiwi (the Native Hawaiian Convention). The legislature has adopted various resolutions during its regular sessions throughout the 1990s and 2000s. The Governor has testified before Congress regarding the State's support for Native Hawaiians as the indigenous people of Hawai'i with the right to self-government. Recognizing the likelihood of a reorganized Native Hawaiian governing entity, the State has also provided for the transfer of the management and control of the island of Kahoolawe and its waters to the sovereign Native Hawaiian entity upon its recognition by the United States and the State of Hawai'i.

The purpose of this Act is to recognize Native Hawaiians as the only indigenous, aboriginal, maoli population of Hawai'i. It is also the State's desire to support the continuing development of a reorganized Native Hawaiian governing entity and, ultimately, the federal recognition of Native Hawaiians.

The legislature urges the office of Hawaiian affairs to continue to support the self-determination process by Native Hawaiians in the formation of their chosen governmental entity.

SECTION 2. The Hawai'i Revised Statutes is amended by adding a new chapter to be appropriately designated and to read as follows:

CHAPTER NATIVE Hawaiian RECOGNITION

Statement of Recognition. The Native Hawaiian people are hereby recognized as the only indigenous, aboriginal, maoli people of Hawai'i.

Purpose. The purpose of this chapter is to provide for and to implement the recognition of the Native Hawaiian people by means and methods that will facilitate their self-governance, including the establishment of, or the amendment to, programs, entities, and other matters pursuant to law that relate, or affect ownership, possession, or use of lands by the Native Hawaiian people, and by further promoting their culture, heritage, entitlements, health, education, and welfare.

Native Hawaiian Roll Commission. (a) There is established a five-member Native Hawaiian roll commission within the office of Hawaiian affairs for administrative purposes only. The Native Hawaiian roll commission shall be responsible for:

(1) Preparing and maintaining a roll of qualified Native Hawaiians; and

(2) Certifying that the individuals on the roll of qualified Native Hawaiians meet the definition of qualified Native Hawaiians. For purposes of establishing the roll, a "qualified Native Hawaiian" means an individual who the commission determines has satisfied the following criteria and who makes a written statement certifying that the individual:

(A) Is:

(i) An individual who is a descendant of the aboriginal peoples who, prior to 1778, occupied and exercised sovereignty in the Hawaiian islands, the area that now constitutes the State of Hawai'i; or

(ii) An individual who is one of the indigenous, native people of Hawai'i and who was eligible in 1921 for the programs authorized by the Hawaiian Homes Commission Act, 1920, or a direct lineal descendant of that individual;

(B) Has maintained a significant cultural, social, or civic connection to the Native Hawaiian community and wishes to participate in the organization of the Native Hawaiian governing entity; and

(C) Is eighteen years of age or older.

(b) No later than one hundred eighty days after the effective date of this chapter, the governor shall appoint the members of the Native Hawaiian roll commission from nominations submitted by qualified Native Hawaiians and qualified Native Hawaiian membership organizations. For the purposes of this subsection, a qualified Native Hawaiian membership organization includes an organization that, on the effective date of this Act, has been in existence for at least ten years, and whose purpose has been and is the betterment of the conditions of the Native Hawaiian people.

In selecting the five members from nominations submitted by qualified Native Hawaiians and qualified Native Hawaiian membership organizations, the governor shall appoint the members as follows:

1) One member shall reside in the county of Hawai'i;
2) One member shall reside in the city and county of Honolulu;
3) One member shall reside in the county of Kauai;
4) One member shall reside in the county of Maui; and
5) One member shall serve at-large.

(c) A vacancy on the commission shall not affect the powers of the commission and shall be filled in the same manner as the original appointment.

(d) Members of the commission shall serve without compensation but shall be allowed travel expenses, including per diem in lieu of subsistence while away from their homes or regular places of business in the performance of services for the commission.

(e) The commission, without regard to chapter 76, may appoint and terminate an executive director and other additional personnel as are necessary to enable the commission to perform the duties of the commission.

(f) The commission may fix the compensation of the executive director and other commission personnel.

(g) The commission may procure temporary and intermittent services.

Notice of qualified Native Hawaiian roll. (a) The commission shall publish notice of the certification of the qualified Native Hawaiian roll, update the roll as necessary, and publish notice of the updated roll of qualified Native Hawaiians. (b) The publication of the initial and updated rolls shall serve as the basis for the eligibility of qualified Native Hawaiians whose names are listed on the rolls to participate in the organization of the Native Hawaiian governing entity.

Native Hawaiian convention. The publication of the roll of qualified Native Hawaiians, as provided in section 4, is intended to facilitate the process under which qualified Native Hawaiians may independently commence the organization of a convention of qualified Native Hawaiians, established for the purpose of organizing themselves.

Dissolution of the Native Hawaiian roll commission. The governor shall dissolve the Native Hawaiian roll commission upon being informed by the Native Hawaiian roll commission that it has published notice of any updated roll of qualified Native Hawaiians, as provided in section -4, and thereby completed its work.

No diminishment of rights or privileges. Nothing contained in this chapter shall diminish, alter, or amend any existing rights or privileges enjoyed by the Native Hawaiian people that are not inconsistent with this chapter.

Reaffirmation of delegation of federal authority; governmental authority and power; negotiations. (a) The delegation by the United States of authority to the State of Hawai'i to address the conditions of the indigenous, native people of Hawai'i contained in the Act entitled "An Act to Provide for the Admission of the State of Hawai'i into the Union", approved March 18, 1959 (Public Law 86-3), is reaffirmed. (b) Consistent with the policies of the State of Hawai'i, the members of the qualified Native Hawaiian roll, and their descendants, shall be acknowledged by the State of Hawai'i as the indigenous, aboriginal, maoli population of Hawai'i.

Disclaimer. Nothing in this chapter is intended to serve as a settlement of any claims against the State of Hawai'i, or affect the rights of the Native Hawaiian people under state, federal, or international law."

SECTION 3. The Hawaiian Homes Commission Act, 1920, shall be amended, subject to approval by the United States Congress, if necessary, to accomplish the purposes set forth in this Act in a manner that is expeditious, timely, and consistent with the current needs and requirements of the Native Hawaiian people and the current beneficiaries of the Hawaiian Homes Commission Act, 1920.

SECTION 4. Funding for the Native Hawaiian roll commission shall be provided by the office of Hawaiian affairs.

SECTION 5. The Native Hawaiian roll commission, in cooperation with the office of Hawaiian affairs, shall report to the governor and the legislature no later than twenty days prior to the convening of the regular session of 2012, on the status of the preparation of a roll of qualified Native Hawaiians, expenditures related to the responsibilities of the Native Hawaiian roll commission, and any concerns or recommendations as deemed appropriate by the Native Hawaiian roll commission.

SECTION 6. If any provision of this Act, or the application thereof to any person or circumstance is held invalid, the invalidity does not affect other provisions or applications of the Act, which can be given effect without the invalid provision or application, and to this end the provisions of this Act are severable.

SECTION 7. This Act does not affect rights and duties that matured, penalties that were incurred, and proceedings that were begun before its effective date.

SECTION 8. This Act shall take effect upon its approval.

◉ ESSAYS

The following two essays examine redress campaigns by activists documenting the history of women forced into serving as sexual slaves of the Japanese military during the Asia-Pacific War and by activists reclaiming Hawaiian land and resources. The first essay, by Tessa Morris-Suzuki, an Australian National University historian, criticizes Japanese politicians who dismiss proof of the Japanese military's role in recruiting, transporting, and organizing sexual slavery. Morris-Suzuki notes that this credible evidence includes testimony by surviving military sexual slaves, military records, soldiers' diaries, and the testimony of Japanese veterans. The second essay is written by Melody Kapilialoha MacKenzie, Susan K. Serrano, and Koalani Laura Kaulukukui. MacKenzie is a law professor at the University of Hawai'i, Manoa; Serrano is the Director of Research and Scholarship at the Center for Excellence in Native Hawaiian Law at the University of Hawai'i, Manoa; and Kaulukukui is a lawyer with the Office of Hawaiian Affairs. Their essay celebrates the efforts of Native Hawaiians to protect and restore Kaho'olawe, an island subjected to a half-century of bombing by the U.S. Navy. The authors present this campaign as a model for Native Hawaiian restorative environmental justice that also strives for sovereignty, economic self-sufficiency, and cultural renewal.

History, Responsibility, and Japan's Military Sexual Slaves During the Asia-Pacific War

TESSA MORRIS-SUZUKI

Contesting the Kōno Statement

On 4 August 1993, Japan's Chief Cabinet Secretary Kōno Yōhei issued an official declaration on the issue of the so-called 'comfort women'—women recruited to work in a large network of brothels operated by the Japanese military during the Asia-Pacific War, where many suffered terrible sexual and other physical and mental abuse, and many died. The declaration, based on a study conducted by the Japanese government, read in part as follows:

> Comfort stations were operated in response to the request of the military authorities of the day... The Government study has revealed that in many cases [the comfort women] were recruited against their own will,

Tessa Morris-Suzuki, "Addressing Japan's 'Comfort Women' Issue From an Academic Standpoint," *The Asia-Pacific Journal* 12, Issue 9, no. 1, March 2, 2014. Reprinted by permission.

through coaxing, coercion, etc., and that, at times, administrative/military personnel directly took part in the recruitments. They lived in misery at comfort stations under a coercive atmosphere.

The Kōno Declaration went on to express the government's 'sincere apologies and remorse' to the women concerned, and to say:

We shall face squarely the historical facts as described above instead of evading them, and take them to heart as lessons of history. We hereby reiterated our firm determination never to repeat the same mistake by forever engraving such issues in our memories through the study and teaching of history.

Kōno's statement resulted not only from demands for an apology from countries like Korea, where many 'comfort women' had been recruited, but also from the work of many grassroots groups within Japan, who had worked tirelessly to seek recompense for the victims. The study carried out by the Japanese government involved the collection of official documents showing army involvement in the control and running of the 'comfort station' system. Testimony was also collected from sixteen former 'comfort women' in Korea, but not from victims of the system in more than a dozen other Asian countries.

Ever since 1993, the Kōno Declaration has been a target of the Japanese political right, who insist that it dishonored Japan's dignity. In 2007, during the first Abe administration, the cabinet issued a 'decision' (kakugi kettei) which partially retracted the Kōno Declaration, denying that Japanese military or government officials had been personally involved in forcible recruitment of 'comfort women'.

On 20 February this year, Restoration Party politician Yamada Hiroshi launched a fierce and emotional attack on the Kōno Declaration in the Japanese Diet. Yamada's ammunition for this attack included a statement by Ishihara Nobuo, who had been Deputy Cabinet Secretary at the time when the Kōno Declaration was issued. Ishihara (as he has done several times in public) argued that Japan had bowed to pressure from South Korea in devising the wording of the Declaration and in its use of the testimony of the sixteen comfort women. By agreement with the women, the content of their testimony has never been made public. Ishihara and Yamada imply that the women's testimony of forced recruitment was false, and demand that this testimony should be made public and 're-investigated' by the government.

Suga Yoshihide, Chief Cabinet Secretary in the present Abe government, responded by announcing that the government now intends to reexamine the testimony and evidence gathered in 1993. According to Japanese newspaper reports, Prime Minister Abe went on to applaud Yamada for his intervention, stating that 'thanks to your questions, public support for a possible reexamination of the comfort women statements is high'.

The official stance of the Japanese government on the issue is that during the first Abe government, a cabinet decision was made regarding this issue. Based on this, the Abe government believes it is ideal for more discussions to be had in the future in regard to this issue from an academic stand point as historians and intellectuals are currently conducting research on various issues surrounding comfort women.

There are, of course, many aspects of the 'comfort women's' history that need more academic research. Surprisingly little is known, for example, about the stories of the many Japanese women recruited to work in the military's sexual empire. A serious plan by the Japanese government to promote research on the history of the 'comfort women' issue, and to communicate that history to the public (as promised by the Kōno Declaration), would be welcomed.

Genuine historical research should begin with a careful, responsible and open-minded review of the existing academic literature and other relevant documentation such as memoirs by Japanese officials and soldiers, and accounts by 'comfort women'. It would involve a willingness to look at the evidence as a whole, and draw balanced conclusions from that evidence, even if those conclusions turn out to be politically inconvenient. This is not a simple process. Many military and government documents were deliberately destroyed at the end of the war. Much evidence on the 'comfort women' issue is oral testimony, which does need to be used with care, as human memories are fallible and stories may sometimes be altered in the telling. Official documents too need to be read with care, since they may be designed to conceal as much as to reveal the truth.

In spite of these difficulties, a very large amount of information on the 'comfort women' has already been collected by Japanese and international academic researchers, UN enquiries, the Japanese government, NGO [Non-Governmental Organization] groups, including evidence collected for a number of court cases. This information unequivocally documents the existence of a vast network of 'comfort stations' throughout the empire and including the front lines of battle. The system was a complex one. Some 'comfort stations' were operated directly by the military; others by civilians for military use. Some were temporary and local, created by troops on the ground rather than by command from on high. Many thousands of women were recruited in various ways, sometimes by members of the military but often by brokers, who commonly used deceptive promises of work in factories or restaurants to lure women into 'comfort stations'. Once there, some women were physically imprisoned, but even those who were allowed out could rarely escape, as most had been transported to places hundreds or thousands of miles from their homes, frequently on Japanese navy ships, and had no means of return.

The attack on the Kōno Declaration focuses on the claim that there are no official documents showing the direct engagement of the Japanese military in the forcible drafting and transportation of 'comfort women'. This is sometimes expanded into a claim that there is no evidence of forcible recruitment at all. But in fact there is very credible testimony from numerous women that they were directly and violently abducted by Japanese soldiers. Among them is Jan Ruff-O'Herne, a Dutch citizen, who was forcibly taken by the military to a 'comfort station' in Indonesia, and who, at age 91, courageously continues to speak out on behalf of the former 'former comfort women'. Responding to the latest Japanese government statement, Mrs. Ruff-O'Herne says, 'it's just hideous to not acknowledge it, there are so many witnesses who have spoken out about this' (*The Age* newspaper, 25 February 2014).

Testimony of direct forcible abduction by Japanese military or police has also come from victims and other witnesses in many countries including China, the Philippines and Taiwan, Vietnam and Indonesia.

There is also abundant credible testimony of recruitment by brokers who worked closely with Japanese military or police using deception to lure women to 'comfort stations'; and even where women were recruited by third parties, this in no way diminishes the responsibility of the Japanese military on whose behalf the brokers were working. Japanese military records, soldiers' diaries and recorded recollections by veterans unmistakably record the close involvement of the military in the recruitment, transport and organization of women. Just one of numerous examples of such evidence is an Imperial Japanese Navy document recording the 'collection of native women' for a 'comfort station' in Balikpapan, Indonesia, carried out under the 'management' of the chief accounts officer of a local Japanese naval unit. The chief accounts officer in question (the document notes) was Nakasone Yasuhiro, who went on to serve as prime minister of Japan from 1982 to 1987, and is now a Liberal Democratic Party elder statesman. This document was presented and discussed in the Japanese Diet by an opposition parliamentarian in May 2013, but has been ignored in the recent debate.

Will the Japanese government's planned study examine all this evidence and produce a balanced conclusion? Or has the conclusion already been determined before the research is even begun? Will the 'discussions from an academic view point' follow genuinely scholarly practices, or will they be an exercise in that pseudo-scholarship which (as Hannah Arendt put it) 'destroys its object'? Will they aim to create memory and understanding of this history, or to un-make memory by selecting and sewing together a few disconnected fragments into a veil that distorts and conceals the past?

The Road Forward

A second prong in the attack on the Kōno Declaration is the claim that all countries have had equivalents of the 'comfort women' system in wartime: an argument made, for example, by the new Director General of NHK [Nippon Hōsō Kyōkai or Japan Broadcasting Corporation] Momii Katsuto who, specifically citing France and Germany, stated that similar systems 'existed everywhere in Europe' during the war.

Of course Japan is far from being the only country whose military has been guilty of sexual violence in war. Momii is incorrect to suggest that military-run networks of brothels existed throughout wartime Europe; but they have existed in places outside the Japanese empire. In colonial India, for example, British rulers authorized a system of brothels in military cantonments between the 1850s and the 1880s. Troops from many counties have been responsible for sexual violence against women in occupied territories—including in occupied Japan itself, where a short-lived system of government-authorized brothels specifically for the use of the allied occupying forces existed between 1945 and 1946, and where events like the Kokura riot of July 1950 resulted in the reported rape of dozens of women by US troops. The system of military 'comfort stations' created in the Japanese empire was not unprecedented in nature; but it was unprecedented in scale, and the misery it caused continues to afflict its victims and their families to this day.

The Japanese government must confront its nation's past with honesty if it is to regain the trust of invaded and colonized nations such as China and Korea who now number among its major trade partners. And if it is to stand among those nations seeking to prevent sexual violence in the contemporary world. Other countries like Britain and the US can help this process by facing up to their own dark histories, while committing themselves to new ways to prevent sexual violence in contemporary war zones and within their military forces. We should also remember, celebrate and seek to empower the work of Japanese citizens groups like the Violence Against Women in War Network (VAWW-NET Japan) which have worked for so long to seek justice for the 'comfort women'. The history of the 'comfort women' is not (as some commentators in both countries wish to portray it) an issue of 'Japanese-versus-Koreans'. It is an issue of human rights and human dignity whose implications extend throughout East Asia and beyond.

Native Hawaiians Reclaim Their Land and Fight for Environmental Justice

MELODY KAPILIALOHA MACKENZIE, SUSAN K. SERRANO, AND KOALANI LAURA KAULUKUKUI

Hānau ka ʻāina, hānau ke aliʻi, hānau ke kanaka. Born was the land, born were the chiefs, born were the common people. Mary Kawena Pukui, *Ōlelo Noʻeau, Hawaiian Proverbs & Poetical Sayings* 56 (1983). So begins an ancient proverb that describes the inseparable spiritual—and genealogical—connection between Native Hawaiians and their land and environment. For Native Hawaiians, the land, or *ʻāina*, is not a mere physical reality. Instead, it is an integral component of Native Hawaiian social, cultural, and spiritual life. Like many indigenous peoples, Native Hawaiians see an interdependent, reciprocal relationship between the gods, the land, and the people.

In stark contrast to the Western notion of privately held property, Hawaiians did not conceive of land as exclusive and alienable, but instead communal and shared. The land, like a cherished relative, cared for the Native Hawaiian people and, in

Melody Kapilialoha MacKenzie, Susan K. Serrano, and Koalani Laura Kaulukukui, "Environmental Justice for Indigenous Hawaiians: Reclaiming Land and Resources." *Natural Resources & Environment,* 21.3 (Winter 2007): 37–42, 79. Reprinted by permission of the American Bar Association.

return, the people cared for the land. The principle of *mālama ʻāina* (to take care of the land) is therefore directly linked to conserving and protecting not only the land and its resources but also humankind and the spiritual world as well.

Western colonialism throughout the eighteenth and nineteenth centuries dramatically altered Hawaiians' relationship to the land. Hawaiian lands were divided, confiscated, sold away; Native Hawaiian cultural practices were barred and ways of life denigrated. In 1893, the independent and sovereign Hawaiian nation was illegally overthrown with direct U.S. military support. Large sugar plantations diverted water from Hawaiian communities. More Hawaiians were separated from the land, thereby severing cultural and spiritual connections.

Hawaiians in their homeland still bear the worst socioeconomic indicators of all of Hawaiʻi's people—the highest rates of illness, prison incarceration, and homelessness, and the lowest rates of higher education and family income.

But Native Hawaiians are again reclaiming their land. In partnership with conservation nonprofits and governmental bodies, Native Hawaiians are regaining control over the management of their land, environment, and cultural resources ... and perhaps most well known, is the return of Kahoʻolawe island to the protection and stewardship of the Native Hawaiian people after the ravages of deforestation, massive erosion, and nearly fifty years of U.S. military live-fire bombing....

For Hawaiians, restorative environmental justice is in large part about doing justice through reclamation and restoration of land and culture. A new environmental justice framework thus expands the focus beyond discrimination and ill health to integrate community history, political identity, and socioeconomic and cultural needs in defining environmental problems and fashioning remedies.

These Hawaiian land reclamations are therefore types of restorative justice; not only are they attempts to preserve the fragile ecosystems of Hawaiʻi, they are efforts to restore to Native Hawaiians a measure of "sovereignty, economic self-sufficiency, and cultural restoration—an expansive, group-resonant type of environmental justice."...

Kahoʻolawe

The island of Kahoʻolawe is the smallest of the eight main islands in the Hawaiian archipelago. Centuries ago, ancient Hawaiians dedicated the island to Kanaloa, the god of the ocean, ocean currents, and navigation. Kahoʻolawe was viewed as the physical embodiment of Kanaloa, and the god's *mana*, or spiritual power, was held within the island's soil. Also known as Kukulu Kaʻiwi O Ka ʻĀina, or "the bone of the land standing upright," and Kohemālamalama O Kanaloa, "the shining womb of Kanaloa," the island has been a center of religious, cultural, historical, and political importance to Native Hawaiians....

For hundreds of years the island was fruitful and supported Native Hawaiian communities that were skilled in astronomy, navigation, fishing, and adz [axlike tool] making....

During the 1800s, Western colonialism dramatically reduced the island's population. Although no sale of any part of the island was made, in 1858 a lease of the entire island was granted for sheep ranching, marking the beginning of years of ranching operations. Throughout the ranching period, the uncontrolled grazing of cattle, sheep, and goats contributed to the massive erosion and environmental degradation of the island....

In 1898, Kaho'olawe, which was Hawaiian government land, was "ceded" to the United States upon annexation of Hawai'i....

Through a lease with the Kaho'olawe Ranch Company, the U.S. military began its use of Kaho'olawe as a practice target for aerial bombs in the 1920s. During World War II, the U.S. government took control of the island, banned all civilian access, and closed traditionally used fishing areas. In a 1953 executive order, President Eisenhower set the island aside for massive target practice by navy bombers. The navy conducted ship-to-shore bombardment of the island and submarine commanders tested torpedoes by firing them at Kaho'olawe's shoreline cliffs. The bombing of Kaho'olawe (including surface-to-air missiles and underwater and surface high-explosive detonations) continued unabated for nearly half a century, causing massive damage to hundreds of cultural sites and fragile environmental resources.

When Hawai'i became a state in 1959, the Admissions Act stated that lands set aside pursuant to any act of Congress, executive order, or proclamation of the president were to remain the property of the United States if needed for continued use. Thus, military control of the island was guaranteed for the unascertainable future.

By the 1970s, Native Hawaiians and nearby island residents could no longer accept the reverberations of bombs, the restricted fishing around the island, and the desecration of sacred lands. In 1971, Maui Mayor Elmer Cravalho and the nonprofit environmental organization Life of the Land brought suit against the Department of Defense under the newly enacted National Environmental Policy Act of 1969 (NEPA). In *Cravalho v. Laird*, Civ. No. 71-3391 (1972), the plaintiffs requested a halt to live-fire training and contended that NEPA required the navy to prepare an environmental impact statement (EIS) to document the effects of military use of the island. The navy responded that it planned to keep the island indefinitely, and if it were denied use of Kaho'olawe, it would be forced to cut back use of Pearl Harbor, thus depriving the state of a major source of income. The court did not order a halt to the bombing, but the navy was ordered to produce an EIS and the case was dismissed.

During the 1970s, a group of young Native Hawaiians founded the Protect Kaho'olawe 'Ohana (family), an organization dedicated to stopping the bombing and reclaiming Kaho'olawe for the Native Hawaiian people. An integral part of a growing political and cultural resurgence among Native Hawaiians, the group began a campaign to raise awareness about the destruction of their sacred land. In January of 1976, nine people landed on the island in an act of peaceful civil disobedience. Although the Coast Guard quickly escorted the protestors off the island and cited several for trespass, the 'Ohana continued its landings on the island. In conjunction with their continued landings, the 'Ohana filed a federal lawsuit against the Department of Defense, *Aluli v. Brown*, 437 F. Supp. 602, 604 (1977), to enjoin the navy from further bombing.

In early 1977, 'Ohana leaders George Helm and Kimo Mitchell returned to the island to search for two others who had remained on the island. In trying to paddle-surf back to Maui seven miles away, Helm and Mitchell were lost at sea. Their death marked a critical point in the 'Ohana's struggle to halt the bombings and reclaim Kaho'olawe.

While the *Aluli* appeal was pending in May of 1979, the 'Ohana and the navy began settlement negotiations. In October 1980, the parties entered into a Consent Decree. In it, the navy did not promise to cease live-fire training, but it did agree to use inert ordnance "to the maximum extent possible," prevent ordnance from landing in the surrounding waters and document and remove any that did, and clear ordnance from approximately 10,000 acres designated by the 'Ohana. The cleared areas were to be reserved for "religious, cultural, scientific, and educational purposes." The navy also promised to take measures to protect historic sites, which specifically included adz quarries and burial sites. Finally, the navy agreed to give the 'Ohana limited access to the island to implement its environmental and cultural restoration plan.

In March of 1981, the entire island was listed on the National Register for Historical Places and designated the Kaho'olawe Archaeological District. In 1990, nearly fifty years after the bombing began, President Bush halted the bombing of Kaho'olawe. The United States transferred title to Kaho'olawe to the state in May of 1994 and established a joint venture among the federal and state governments and the 'Ohana to oversee restoration of the island. The navy was given ten years and allocated $400 million to remove unexploded ordnance and to complete environmental restoration of the island.

The transfer and eventual control of the island was placed under the responsibility of the Kaho'olawe Island Reserve Commission (KIRC), part of DLNR [Department of Land and Natural Resources]. KIRC, now headed by Native Hawaiian Sol Kaho'ohalahala, has authority over all actions occurring on the island, including proper treatment of any burial sites discovered there and entering into stewardship agreements with Hawaiian organizations. KIRC works in partnership with the 'Ohana, which is the official steward of the island.

Four exclusive and perpetual purposes and uses of the island were made part of Hawai'i State law: the preservation and practice of customary and traditional Native Hawaiian rights for cultural, spiritual, and subsistence purposes; the preservation of the island's archaeological, historical, and environmental resources; rehabilitation, revegetation, habitat restoration, and preservation; and education. Chapter 6K also guarantees that when a sovereign Native Hawaiian entity is established and recognized by the United States, the state will transfer management and control of Kaho'olawe to that entity.

The navy declared the island's cleanup complete in April of 2004. Even with the removal of 10 million pounds of metal, the cleanup fell far short of the promised 100 percent surface clearance and 30 percent subsurface clearance. About 70 percent of the island had been surface cleared, and about 9 percent was cleared to a subsurface level of four feet. Places on the island will likely never be cleared of ordnance....

Despite the incomplete navy cleanup, KIRC and the 'Ohana carried on their restoration plans, including planting over 100,000 native species on the island. The current focus of restoration is to prevent further erosion and to build up soil and ground cover to enable reforestation. Once ground cover shrubs and grasses are restored, trees will be planted to further hold in soil and moisture, and eventually to help bring rain back to the island.

The 'Ohana has focused on restoring many important cultural sites, such as the Hale O Papa *heiau*. Between February and October each year, volunteers access the island through the 'Ohana to help in restoration efforts. In November through January, cultural practitioners access the island for the annual *Makahiki*, a traditional Hawaiian celebration of the harvest and time of personal, spiritual, and cultural renewal.

Hawaiians have long recognized Kaho'olawe as a *wahi pana* (a legendary place) and *pu'uhonua* (a place of refuge), and today it is being protected and restored as a result of Native Hawaiian efforts. Native Hawaiians are participating directly in the preservation and protection of Kaho'olawe's archaeological, historical, and environmental resources and are engaged in rehabilitation and rehabitation of the island. As KIRC director Sol Kaho'ohalahala recognized, "Aloha 'Āina [(love for the land)] and the navy's bombing target range on the island of Kaho'olawe were in direct conflict. The movement to stop the bombing of Kaho'olawe was significant and symbolic of the struggle that we faced as a people disenfranchised in their own island home."...

Native Hawaiians are doing justice by reclaiming and restoring Hawaiian land and culture. Although these land reclamations are attempts to preserve Hawai'i's natural environment, they are also hard-fought efforts to restore to Native Hawaiians a measure of self-determination, cultural restoration, and economic self-sufficiency. This expansive view of restorative "environmental justice" goes beyond rectifying the discriminatory siting of toxic facilities. The framework embraces the complexity of the Native Hawaiian experience by integrating cultural values, history, socioeconomic power, and group needs and goals in defining environmental problems and fashioning meaningful remedies.

☾ FURTHER READING

Connell, Thomas. *America's Japanese Hostages: The World War II Plan for a Japanese Free Latin America* (2002).

Daniels, Roger, Sandra C. Taylor, and Harry H.L. Kitano, eds. *Japanese Americans: From Relocation to Redress* (1986).

Fogerty, Naomi. "Remembering the Forgotten Internment: Attempts at Redress for Japanese Latin American Internees of World War II," *Documents to the People* 38.4 (Winter 2010), 17–20.

Fujikane, Candace, and Jonathan Y. Okamura, eds. *Asian Settler Colonialism: From Governance to the Habits of Everyday Life in Hawai'i* (2008).

Goodyear-Kaopua, Noelani, and Ikaika Hussey. *A Nation Rising: Hawaiian Movements for Life, Land, and Sovereignty* (2014).

Hohri, William Minoru. *Repairing America: An Account of the Movement for Japanese American Redress* (1988).

Irons, Peter. *Justice at War: The Story of the Japanese American Internment Cases* (1983).

Kauanui, J. Kehaulani. *Hawaiian Blood: Colonialism and the Politics of Sovereignty and Indigeneity* (2008).

Maki, Mitchell T., Harry H. L. Kitano, and Berthold, S. Megan. *Achieving the Impossible Dream: How Japanese American Obtained Redress* (1999).

Murray, Alice Yang. *Historical Memories of the Japanese American Internment and the Struggle for Redress* (2008).

Nakano, Satoshi. "Nation, Nationalism, and Citizenship in the Filipino World War II Veterans Equity Movement, 1945–1999," *Hitotsubashi Journal of Social Studies* 32, no. 2 (December 2000): 33–53.

Okamura, Jonathan Y., and Mary Yu Danico, "Challenging Inequalities: Nations, Races, and Communities," *Journal of Asian American Studies* 13, no. 3 (October 2010): 261–281.

Raimundo, Antonio. "The Filipino Veterans Equity Movement: A Case Study in Reparations Theory," *California Law Review* 98, no. 2 (2010): 575–623.

Rocamora, Rick, and Bob Filner. *Filipino World War II Soldiers: America's Second-Class Veterans* (2008).

Sai, David Keanu. *Ua Mau Ke Ea Sovereignty Endures: An Overview of the Political and Legal History of the Hawaiian Islands* (2011).

Saito, Natsu Taylor. "Justice Held Hostage: U.S. Disregard for International Law in the World War II Internment of Japanese Peruvians—A Case Study," *Boston College Third World Law Journal* 19, no. 1 (1998): 275–348.

Saranillio, Dean Itsuji. "Colliding Histories: Hawai'i Statehood at the Intersection of Asian 'Ineligible to Citizenship' and Hawaiians 'Unfit for Self-Government,'" *Journal of Asian American Studies* (2010): 283–309.

Shigematsu, Setsu, and Keith L. Camacho, eds. *Militarized Currents: Toward a Decolonized Future in Asia and the Pacific* (2010).

Shimabukuro, Robert Sadamu. *Born in Seattle: The Campaign for Japanese American Redress* (2001).

Soh, C. Sarah. *The Comfort Women: Sexual Violence and Postcolonial Memory in Korea and Japan* (2009).

Takezawa, Yasuko. *Breaking the Silence: The Redress Movement in Seattle* (1995).

Trask, Haunani-Kay. *From a Native Daughter: Colonialism and Sovereignty in Hawai'i* (1993).

Vang, Ma. "The Refugee Soldier: A Critique of Recognition and Citizenship in the Hmong Veterans' Naturalization Act of 1997," *Positions: East Asia Cultures Critique* 20, no. 3 (Summer 2012): 685–712.

Yamamoto, Eric. *Interracial Justice: Conflict and Reconciliation in Post-Civil Rights America* (1999).

Yamamoto, Eric K., et al. *Race, Rights and Reparation: Law and the Japanese American Internment* (2001).

CHAPTER 15

Asian Americans and
National Security

Being viewed as perpetual foreigners led Asian Americans to worry about being scapegoated as spies and terrorists before and after 9/11. In 1999, Wen Ho Lee, a Taiwanese-born scientist at Los Alamos National Laboratory, was accused but never convicted of stealing nuclear weapons secrets for China. As the media publicized claims that Chinese Americans were more prone to espionage because of their ethnic ties, Asian Americans began to declare that Wen Ho Lee was a victim of ethnic profiling. Lee later won $1.6 million in a civil suit against the government and five media organizations for leaking his name to the press before any charges had been filed. President Bill Clinton publicly stated he was "troubled" by the way Lee's case was handled, and Federal Judge James Parker apologized to Lee for the way he was mistreated while being held in solitary confinement.

After the terrorist attacks on September 11, 2001, Asian Americans provided diverse views of how the U.S. government should respond to new terrorist threats and balance national security needs with the protection of civil liberties. Some played prominent roles in the Bush administration and shaped the development of security policies. As assistant attorney general, Vietnamese American Viet Dinh oversaw the drafting and implementation of the Patriot Act, the nation's major overhaul of antiterrorist measures approved in the wake of the 9/11 attacks. Korean American law professor John Yoo co-authored a memo on torture in 2002 while serving in the Justice Department's Office of Legal Counsel. Yoo argued in this memo that the Geneva Conventions did not protect individuals the government deemed members of the terrorist group Al Qaeda or the Taliban. Other Asian Americans protested the torture and abuse of "enemy combatants." Filipino American General Antonio Taguba investigated and then denounced the abuse of prisoners at the U.S.-controlled Abu Ghraib prison in Iraq after the 2004 publication of photographs showing soldiers taunting naked Iraqi prisoners who were forced to assume sexually degrading poses.

Other Asian Americans worried about the heated political and popular media rhetoric against suspected terrorist groups in the United States and the secrecy surrounding U.S. interrogations and detentions of people accused of supporting enemies of the United States.

Chinese American James Yee, a Muslim U.S. Army chaplain, was unfairly arrested, interrogated, and detained on charges of spying after counseling Muslim detainees captured in Afghanistan and Pakistan and held at Guantanamo Bay. The army then dropped all criminal charges but accused Yee of committing adultery and possessing pornography on his government computer. Activism by Muslim and Chinese American groups helped Yee garner nationwide support as the victim of an unfounded smear campaign. Some groups, such as Justice for New Americans, linked Yee with Wen Ho Lee, asserting that both were victims of anti-Asian racism. Like Lee, Yee was eventually exonerated and his reprimand was expunged from his army record.

Mistaken for Arab Americans because of their turbans and beards, Sikh Americans became targets of civil rights violations and hate crimes. Right after the 9/11 attacks on the World Trade Center, the media played up photographs of the arrest of Sher Singh, a turbaned and bearded Sikh American commuter in Providence, Rhode Island, as a possible terror suspect, and then neglected to note that he was cleared of any wrongdoing. On September 15, 2001, Frank Silva Roque shot and killed Balbir Singh Sodhi, a Sikh American gas station owner in Mesa, Arizona, because Roque thought Sodhi was an Arab Muslim. In addition, South Asian Americans protested the post-9/11 raids of Pakistani immigrant communities in New York that resulted in the detention of nearly 2,000 individuals and the charge that 200 of those individuals held in Paterson, New Jersey, suffered physical abuse during their imprisonment. The activists publicized the mistreatment of Pakistani detainees, who were often held on nothing more than minor visa or immigration violations. Other Asian American protesters criticized the war in Afghanistan and Iraq, became peace activists, and called for an end to the U.S. war on terror.

🌐 DOCUMENTS

Documents 1 to 5 examine Asian American individuals and groups that have been victimized by antiterroism policies. In Document 1, Korean American lawyer Angela E. Oh condemns the U.S. prosecution of Wen Ho Lee as an example of racial profiling, selective prosecution, and the demonization of China as the "great twenty-first century threat" to the United States. In Document 2, a report by the Office of the Inspector General documents the verbal and physical abuse of Pakistani American detainees held at the Metropolitan Detention Center in Brooklyn after 9/11. In Document 3, an online message circulated among Asian American activists in 2003, Filipino Americans in Hawai'i explain why they support Native Hawaiian protests of U.S. military expansion in Hawai'i and the Philippines and demands for the U.S. military to clean up toxic contamination in both sites. The Filipino American activists also call for an end to human rights violations in the southern Philippines and the return of military-controlled land to Hawaiians. Document 4 recounts James Yee's ordeal as a suspected spy after he counseled Muslim detainees in a Guantanamo Bay prison. In Document 5, Lillian Nakano, a third-generation Japanese American, draws parallels between the war hysteria and racist scapegoating that caused Japanese American internment and post-9/11 antiterrorism policies targeting Americans who are Muslims or of Arab or Middle Eastern descent.

Documents 6 to 8 explore criticisms of U.S. interrogation tactics, detention centers, and military policies in Afghanistan and Iraq. Document 6 provides excerpts of an antiwar speech given by Japanese American Lieutenant Ehren Watada, the first U.S. commissioned officer to refuse deployment to Iraq and to publicly denounce the war as immoral and unlawful. Speaking before the Veterans for Peace National Convention in 2006, Watada urges soldiers to stop the unjust war by refusing to fight and calls on the public to express their support for these protesting soldiers. Document 7 is Filipino American Major General Antonio Taguba's indictment of the George W. Bush administration for committing war crimes that violated the Geneva Conventions, the UN Convention against Torture, and the Uniform Code of Military Justice. Taguba's charges appeared in his preface to a 2008 report by Physicians for Human Rights documenting the suffering of men tortured in U.S. detention facilities in Iraq, Afghanistan, and Guantanamo Bay. In Document 8, Judge Amy Berman Jackson rules in 2015 that Iknoor Singh, a Hofstra University student, cannot be barred from enrolling in the Army's Reserve Officer Training Corps program for refusing to shave his beard, cut his hair, or remove his turban because of his Sikh religious beliefs.

1. Lawyer Angela E. Oh Describes the Significance of the Government Prosecution of Los Alamos Scientist Wen Ho Lee, 2000

Compared to the thousands of other criminal cases filed by the federal government each year, nothing is unique about Dr. Lee's dilemma except its political, social, and media aspects. As news of the case continues to be reported, we Asian Americans are feeling a familiar uneasiness about the events unfolding. The fact that this case has emerged in the midst of a Presidential campaign in which many Chinese Americans have "opted out" because of the fund-raising experiences of 1996 has added complexity to the political landscape for Asian Americans.

Unfortunately, the case may have reinforced the feelings of antipathy and alienation toward politicians and politics when it should inspire greater involvement in the political process, particularly since it so clearly demonstrates that America's foreign relations policies have a direct impact on Asian American citizens. Whether Wen Ho Lee is innocent or not is a question to be answered by a judge or jury. Whether Wen Ho Lee's case will mark a significant loss of political ground for Asian Americans, however, is a question that must be answered by Asian Americans.

For many of us following the case, the political symbolism of this prosecution is enormous. At a time when China should be viewed as a major potential partner in formulating new foreign policy initiatives, in establishing innovative new business opportunities, and in introducing expansive cultural and intellectual exchange programs, America has begun to set its sights on China as its next candidate for national enmity. China is being cast as "the great 21st century threat" against America, and many foresee turmoil for Asian Americans. The Los Alamos investigation raises reasonable anxiety about the peace and security of our nation. However, without diminishing the importance of national security concerns, Asian Americans know too well the consequences of silence in the face of mounting fears and questioned loyalty....

The case of Wen Ho Lee and a current climate of China-bashing have also had a major impact on Asian American society, and they are deservedly receiving our political attention. In terms of community organizing, the intergenerational and cross-ethnic support for Dr. Lee has been impressive. Dr. Lee is, like tens of thousands of others, a naturalized citizen, and his ethnic heritage has played a significant role in decisions to investigate, interrogate, and incarcerate. Not only has his case spurred interest among Chinese Americans, but it has created pan-Asian coalitions among individuals and organizations with no prior history of mutual support to monitor the case. The results have been extraordinary. Defense committees and new alliances have formed in all parts of the nation. Detailed analysis of the information gathered has brought attention to problems such as racial profiling, employment discrimination, abuse of authority, and selective prosecution. Moreover, this case has helped to clarify for many lay persons the role of anti-discrimination agencies such as the U.S. Commission on Civil Rights, and the operation of the American criminal justice system....

Now, members of the scientific community are seeking new alliances with broader Asian American political, civic, and legal organizations that understand the political and social landscape that has emerged.

The Wen Ho Lee case is already a significant story in Asian American history.

2. The Office of the Inspector General Describes Abuse Against September 11 Immigrant Detainees, 2003

VI. Allegations of Physical and Verbal Abuse

Based on our interviews of 19 September 11 detainees and our investigation of allegations of abuse raised by several detainees, we believe the evidence indicates a pattern of physical and verbal abuse against some September 11 detainees held at the MDC [Metropolitan Detention Center] by some correctional officers, particularly during the first months after the terrorist attacks. Although the allegations have been declined for criminal prosecution, the OIG [Office of the Inspector General] is continuing to investigate these matters administratively...

A. OIG Site Visit In connection with this review of the treatment of September 11 detainees, our inspection team interviewed 19 detainees who were being held at the MDC when we visited the facility in May 2002. All 19

Excerpt from the US Department of Justice, Office of the Inspector General, "The September 11 Detainees: A Review of the Treatment of Aliens Held on Immigration Charges in Connection with the Investigation of the September 11 Attacks," April 2003, pp. 157–164.

detainees complained of some form of abuse. Twelve complained about physical abuse and 10 complained about verbal abuse. The complaints of physical abuse ranged from painfully tight handcuffs to allegations they were slammed against the wall by MDC staff. The detainees told us that the physical abuse usually occurred upon their arrival at the MDC, while being moved to and from their cells, or when the hand-held surveillance camera was turned off.

Ten of the 19 detainees we interviewed during our inspection visit alleged they had been subjected to verbal abuse by MDC staff, consisting of slurs and threats. According to detainees, the verbal abuse included taunts such as "Bin Laden Junior" or threats such as "you're going to die here," "you're never going to get out of here," and "you will be here for 20-25 years like the Cuban people." They said most of the verbal abuse occurred during intake and during movement to and from the detainees' cells.

Our inspection team interviewed 12 correctional officers about the detainees' allegations of physical abuse. All 12 officers denied witnessing or committing any acts of abuse. Further, they denied knowledge of any rumors about allegations of abuse. The correctional officers we interviewed also denied they verbally abused the detainees and denied making these specific comments to the detainees.

B. OIG Investigation of Abuse   On October 30, 2001, the OIG reviewed a newspaper article in which a September 11 detainee alleged he was physically abused when he arrived at the MDC on October 4, 2001. Based on the allegations in the article, the OIG's Investigations Division initiated an investigation into the matter. When we interviewed the detainee, he complained that MDC officers repeatedly slammed him against walls while twisting his arm behind his back. He also alleged officers dragged him by his handcuffed arms and frequently stepped on the chain between his ankle cuffs. The detainee stated his ankles and wrists were injured as a result of the officers' abuse. He also identified three other September 11 detainees who allegedly had been abused by MDC staff members.

We interviewed these three other September 11 detainees. They stated that when they arrived at the MDC, they were forcefully pulled out of the vehicle and slammed against walls. One detainee further alleged that his handcuffs were painfully tight around his wrists and that MDC officers repeatedly stepped on the chain between his ankle cuffs. Another detainee alleged officers dragged him by his handcuffs and twisted his wrist every time they moved him. All three detainees alleged that officers verbally abused them with racial slurs and threats like "you will feel pain" and "someone thinks you have something to do with the World Trade Center so don't expect to be treated well."

During our investigation of these complaints, we received similar allegations from other September 11 detainees. On February 11, 2002, four September 11 detainees held at the MDC (including one of the detainees we interviewed previously) told MDC officers that certain MDC officers were physically and verbally abusing them. Those complaints were provided to us.

In interviews with our investigators, these detainees alleged that when they arrived at the MDC in September and October 2001, MDC officers forcefully pulled them from the car, slammed them into walls, dragged them by their arms, stepped on the chain between their ankle cuffs, verbally abused them, and twisted their arms, hands, wrists, and fingers. One of the detainees alleged that when he was being taken to the MDC's medical department following a 4-day hunger strike, an officer bent his finger back until it touched his wrist. Another detainee alleged that when he arrived at the MDC, officers repeatedly twisted his arm, which was in a cast, and finger, which was healing from a recent operation. He also alleged that when he was transferred to another cell in December 2001, officers slammed him into a wall and twisted his wrist. One detainee claimed his chin was cut open and he had to receive stitches because officers slammed him against a wall.

During our investigation, the OIG asked the detainees individually to identify the officers who had committed the abuse through photographic line-ups. The detainees identified many of the same officers as the perpetrators, and the OIG focused its investigation on eight officers. The OIG interviewed seven of these officers. Six of them denied physically or verbally abusing any of the detainees or witnessing any other officer abuse the detainees. Five remembered at least one of the detainees and some of them remembered a few of the detainees. Two officers described two detainees as disruptive and uncooperative. One of the officers explained that the high-security procedures in place during the weeks following the September 11 attacks required four officers to physically control inmates during all escorts; face them toward the wall while waiting for doors, elevators, or the application and removal of leg restraints; and place them against the wall if they became aggressive during these escorts.

The seventh officer interviewed by the OIG told us that he witnessed officers "slam" inmates against walls and stated this was a common practice before the MDC began videotaping the detainees. He said he did not believe these actions were warranted. He said he told MDC officers to "ease up" and not to be so aggressive when escorting detainees. He also said he witnessed a supervising officer slam detainees against walls, but when he spoke with the officer about this practice the officer told him it was all part of being in jail and not to worry about it. The seventh officer signed a sworn affidavit to this effect. In a subsequent interview with the OIG, this officer recharacterized the action as "placing" the detainees against the wall, and said he did not want to use the word "slam." He denied that the officers acted in an abusive or inappropriate manner.

The OIG reviewed the detainees' medical records. The medical records do not indicate that most of the detainees received medical treatment for the injuries they asserted they received from officers. Two of the detainees' medical records indicate they were treated for injuries that they later claimed were caused by officers, but the medical records did not indicate that they alleged their injuries were caused by officers at the time they were treated. One detainee's records do not mention the cause of the injury and the other detainee's records state the detainee said he was injured when he fell. In his interview with the OIG, the detainee alleged his chin was badly cut when detention officers slammed him against the wall. He said that nobody ever asked him how his injury occurred. The other five detainees did not seek treatment for their alleged injuries.

Based on the scarcity of medical records documenting injuries and the lack of evidence of serious injuries to most of the detainees, the U.S. Attorney's Office for the Eastern District of New York and the Civil Rights Division declined criminal prosecution in this case. All of the detainees, with the exception of one, now have been removed from the United States. Nevertheless, the OIG is continuing its investigation of these allegations as an administrative matter. Because this case is ongoing, we are not describing in detail all the evidence in the case about the detainees' allegations. However, we believe there is evidence supporting the detainees' claims of abuse, including the fact that similar – although not identical – allegations of abuse have been raised by other detainees, which we describe in the next section.

3. Filipinos Stand in Solidarity with Native Hawaiians in Opposing United States Military Expansion in Hawaii and the Philippines, 2003

As Filipino co-habitants of Oahu, we strongly oppose the US military's proposal to expand its training sites to include Waikane, Kualoa, Hakipuu, and Kaaawa, or any other sites in the Hawaiian archipelago. We demand that the US military take full responsibility for the human displacement and environmental damage caused by its usage of Hawaiian lands. We fully support the Kamaka family's struggle to hold the US military accountable for its failure to properly clean up their land. We join with Kanaka Maoli groups in calling for a return of control of all land in use by the US military to its rightful ancestral stewards and descendants.

We oppose the use of Hawaiian lands for US military training for the following reasons: The current military expansion in Windward Oahu is, at least in part, aimed at an escalation of US military operations in the Philippines.

We oppose continued US military intervention in our ancestral homeland because: Joint US-Philippine military operations are unconstitutional, violate Philippine sovereignty, and are strongly opposed by Philippine citizens. The Philippine Constitution expressly prohibits foreign troops from engaging in combat against Philippine citizens on Philippine soil. Top Philippine elected officials oppose Balikatan ["shoulder-to-shoulder" training exercise] '03-1 and have raised concerns about its violation of the terms of the Mutual Defense Treaty and the Visiting Forces Agreement. On March 1, 2003, more than 40,000 Filipinos representing churches, schools, NGOs, and civil society groups rallied for

"Filipinos Stand in Solidarity with Native Hawaiians in Opposing United States Military Expansion in Hawaii and the Philippines, March 2003," Contributed by Grace Alvaro Caligtan, Darlene Rodrigues, Melisa S.L. Casumbal, Catherine Betts, Grace Duenas, Gigi Miranda, Cindy Ramirez, Sonya Zabala, Tamara Freedman, Maile Labasan. Used with permission.

peace in Manila, while thousands more participated in peace rallies elsewhere in the country.

Joint US-Philippine military operations such as Balikatan '02-1 and '03-1 have not achieved their purported goal of ridding the Philippines of Abu Sayyaf ["bearer-of-the-sword" militant group]. Instead, they have provoked such strong opposition that groups such as the CPP/NPA (Communist Party of the Philippines/New People's Army) and the MILF (Moro Islamic Liberation Front) have actually experienced resurgence and increase in popular support. Joint US-Philippine military operations have destabilized the fragile and ongoing process of peace talks between these opposition groups and the Philippine government. Joint US-Philippine military operations have resulted in the deaths and casualties of innocent Philippine civilians in Zamboanga and Basilan. KARAPATAN, a Philippine human rights organization, has documented several cases of farmers and fishermen, even a child, being killed as they are evacuating their homes or because their fishing boat was accidentally bombed. Further, on July 25, 2002, an American soldier shot Moro civilian Buyong-Buyong Isnijal in his own home in Tuburan, Basilan.

Joint US-Philippine military operations have resulted in the escalation of human rights violations in the southern Philippines. These human rights violations, according to KARAPATAN, include illegal searches of Moro homes, and increases in disappearances and 'salvagings' (murders) of members of legitimate, peaceful organizations opposing the remilitarization of the southern Philippines.

Joint US-Philippine military operations have resulted in the forced relocation of tens of thousands of civilians, including Muslims and indigenous peoples, to ill-equipped evacuation centers in the southern Philippines.

The conflict between legitimate Muslim opposition groups (excluding the Abu Sayaff, which is a tiny band of fringe elements with little to no popular support) and the Philippine government has a complex, decades-long history that cannot be resolved by US military intervention. The only lasting and peaceful resolution to this historic and civil, not international, conflict will come from peace talks, not US military presence.

As Filipino co-habitants of Hawaii, we stand in solidarity with Native Hawaiian families and organizations in opposition to militarization of their land because: The colonization of the Philippines and Hawaii are intimately tied together. Since the illegal annexation of Hawaii in 1898, native Hawaiians and other indigenous peoples and nations have shouldered the brunt of military build-up in Pacific. We see this current expansion into the Windward ahupuaas as a part of [a] long genealogy of a continued dispossession of Native Hawaiians from their land. We see the military's failure to clean the Kamaka family land as assault on Native Hawaiian traditional values, livelihood, health and well-being.

We are familiar with the legacy of environmental pollution [the] US military presence creates from our own history with US bases in the Philippines. Groups like FACES [Filipino/American Coalition for Environmental Solutions], a coalition of American- and Philippine-based Filipinos working to clean up former US bases in the Philippines, have extensively documented the contamination of former base sites with toxic solvents, pesticides, asbestos, heavy metals, unexploded ordnance and other hazardous substances. Serious groundwater and soil contamination in over 46 sites on Clark and Subic [air bases] is documented in reports by the US General Accounting Office (GAO), World Health Organization, Independent US and Philippine experts, two US-based environmental firms, and the Department of Defense's internal reports. US failure to meet its environmental safety standards is also documented by the GAO. Yet, US officials refuse to even acknowledge the problem.

As descendants of Filipino migrant labor to Hawaii and the US continent, our health and well-being are also affected by the adverse environmental impact the US military presence has in Hawaii. The US military is the largest single polluter in the island chain. It controls nearly 200,000 acres of land and nearly 25% of the land on Oahu. And it has only been through public pressure and close scrutiny that the US government has recently begun cleaning up its deadly toxic waste in sacred places such as Kahoolowe.

The military's slow action and refusal to be accountable to Native Hawaiians and cohabiting communities further imperil future generations. True security derives from stewardship of the aina [earth], economic equity, and an honoring of all peoples.

We call for a speedy clean-up of polluted lands and military accountability to all communities in Hawaii. We call on other communities to stand up against the US military's acts of violence, amoralism, and disregard for Native peoples and others who live here. The continuation of the peoples and the places of the earth committed to renewal and sustainability is imperative.

4. Former Guantanamo Chaplain James Yee Is Exonerated After Being Imprisoned as a Terrorist, 2004

James Yee is an American of Chinese descent who graduated from West Point in 1990. Shortly afterwards he converted to Islam from Christianity. Yee wanted to become a Muslim Army chaplain, but that required a doctorate in divinity studies. So in 1993 he went on reserve status to complete the programs necessary to become a military chaplain. Yee moved to Damascus and studied under Syria's grand mucti (supreme religious leader). While there he learned Arabic and married a Syrian woman.

Yee returned to the U.S. in 1999 after completing his Islamic studies, and obtained the certification necessary to become a military chaplain. Yee then returned to active Army duty and was assigned as a Muslim chaplain at Fort Lewis, Washington.

After the events of September 11, 2001, Yee, an Army Captain, spent much of his time explaining Islam to both the public and military personnel.

In November 2002 Yee was assigned as the chaplain for the Muslims detained at the Guantanamo Bay, Cuba military prison – also known as Camp Delta. He soon began clashing with his superiors over what he considered mistreatment of the Muslim prisoners. Among his complaints was the prisoners were in an atmosphere of "unrelieved tension and boredom." Yee's complaining successfully resulted in "recordings of the ritual calls to prayer broadcast through

---

Hans Sherrer, "Muslim Army Chaplain Falsely Imprisoned as Terrorist," *Justice: Denied* magazine, Issue 25, page 12. Reprinted by permission.

the" prison, and ensuring the prisoner's "food was prepared according to Islamic dietary guidelines."

The military's response to Yee's concerns about prisoner treatment was a form of 'shoot the messenger' – it began investigating him. Yee's every move was watched. On September 10, 2003 he flew from Guantanamo Bay to the Jacksonville, Florida naval air station. Customs Service agents inspecting his luggage allegedly found diagrams of cells at the Guantanamo Bay prison, and the names of detainees and their interrogators. Yee was arrested on the spot "for suspicion of espionage and aiding captured Taliban and al-Qaida fighters." Newspaper headlines and news broadcasts across the country trumpeted Yee's arrest for espionage and aiding international terrorists. Those are capital offenses – so at the time of his arrest Yee was potentially facing charges that could result in his execution. Yee was immediately transported to the maximum-security Naval brig (prison) in Charleston, South Carolina and put in solitary confinement. The private lawyer hired to defend Yee, Eugene Fidell of Seattle, said, "It's shocking an officer is in a maximum-security prison."

On October 10th Yee was charged with two counts of failing to obey a lawful order: "taking classified information home," and "wrongly transporting classified information." Those are relatively minor charges that could result in a maximum of a year in prison and a bad conduct discharge.

After the Army's intensive six week investigation of Yee following his arrest, four more charges were filed against him on November 24, 2003: making a false official statement; failure to obey an order or regulation; adultery; and conduct unbecoming an officer. After the last of the six charges against him were filed, Yee was released from maximum security, after spending 76 days in solitary confinement.

The six charges were relatively minor infractions compared with the alleged espionage and treasonous aiding of the enemy that precipitated his arrest. Kevin Barry, a retired Coast Guard captain and military judge commented, "All this suggests they really don't have much on him. It indicates the Army has decided to lowball this."

Muslims and Chinese-American's across the country rallied in support of Yee. His treatment as an Army officer imprisoned in a solitary confinement was compared with the mistreatment of Wen Ho Lee after his false arrest for allegedly passing US nuclear secrets to China. Samia El-Moslimany of the Seattle chapter of Council on American-Islamic Relations said at a November 2003 rally in support of Yee, "Captain Yee has already been tried and convicted in the media before there were even charges brought against him. He was basically branded as a spy and traitor to his country. We think this is happening because he's a Muslim and Chinese-American." Yee's wife, Huda Suboh spoke through a translator, "the only news in the paper about my husband is coming from the government. James wants me to tell you all that he is innocent. He is going to fight the charges with all his energy." A spokesman for Justice for New Americans said, "there is no evidence that Yee ever gave anything to a foreign government."

On March 20, 2004, the case against Yee that had begun with allegations he had committed capital offenses, including "spying, mutiny, sedition and aiding the enemy," completely collapsed: the Army dropped all six charges against him. Yee's lawyer, Eugene Fidell said, "Captain Yee has won."

Yee was assigned to Fort Lewis, and on April 5th he returned to his home in Olympia (near Fort Lewis) and was reunited with his wife and four year-old daughter. The 36 year-old Yee told people gathered at Seattle-Tacoma International Airport, "It's a great day to be back in Washington state, and to be back with my family." Somewhat ironically, he said of his ordeals impact on his daughter, "Every time she sees me on TV or in the news, she says, 'Everybody loves my daddy.'"

However in a classic example of the 'sore losers syndrome,' after dropping the criminal charges, the Army decided to publicly smear Yee by administratively charging and finding him guilty of adultery and having adult images stored in his computer. Yee appealed the finding, and in mid-April, General James T. Hill, commander of the U.S. Southern Command ruled in Yee's favor. Yee's lawyer Eugene Fidell, said Yee's clearing of all criminal and administrative charges was a "bittersweet victory. It wouldn't have killed them to admit a mistake. The Army has to be big enough to admit a mistake. In that regard, today was disappointing."

After Yee's exoneration, two members of the Senate Armed Services Committee, Senators Carl Levin (D-MI) and Edward Kennedy (D-MA), request in an April 23rd letter to Secretary of Defense Donald Rumsfeld that he initiate an official investigation of Captain Yee's treatment. The two senators wrote, "The manner in which Chaplain Yee was detained and prosecuted raises serious questions about the fair and effective administration of military justice. We urge you to give this issue your immediate attention." In a June 4th letter to Secretary Rumsfeld, four members of Congress joined in calling for an official investigation into Yee's treatment.

At a June 25th event to raise money to help pay his legal fees, James Yee said, I'm not here tonight to talk about my case, but to thank those who stand in support of civil liberties." At the same event, Wayne Lum observed that "James Yee would not have been targeted if it were not for this heightened hysteria against Muslims. This case was calculated. It was a coldly calculated targeting of an innocent person."

On August 2nd James Yee released a letter of resignation from the Army effective in January 2005. He wrote, "In 2003, I was unfairly accused of grave offenses under the Uniform Code of Military Justice and unjustifiably placed in solitary confinement for 76 days. Those unfounded allegations – which were leaked to the media – irreparably injured my personal and professional reputation and destroyed my prospects for a career in the United States Army."

The irony of the Army's systematic destruction of James Yee's career is that two days before his arrest, his commander at Guantanamo Bay gave him the highest possible performance rating. It is also ironic that seven months after Yee's arrest that was precipitated by his whistleblowing about prisoner mistreatment at Guantanamo Bay, news reports informed the entire world of the U.S. military's mistreatment of prisoners there and in Iraq. As this is written in August 2004, new revelations of prisoner mistreatment at the Guantanamo Bay prison continue to be reported.

5. Lillian Nakano Compares Racial Profiling of Japanese Americans in 1942 and Muslim Americans During the War on Terror, 2005

Feb. 19, 1942, was a day that changed the lives of Japanese Americans forever. I was a teenager growing up in Hawaii when President Franklin D. Roosevelt signed Executive Order 9066, which set into motion the removal and incarceration of more than 110,000 people of Japanese ancestry in inland concentration camps.

After Japan attacked Pearl Harbor, a tense atmosphere of suspicion and hysteria engulfed the West Coast and Hawaii. Decades of anti-Japanese and anti-Asian legislation and racism had already laid the foundation for the events that soon took place. We were rounded up without due process even though we had nothing to do with the attack. Our family was shipped to California, then to Arkansas and finally to Wyoming, where we spent the duration of the war.

Upon our release from the camps, Japanese Americans began to pick up the pieces of wrecked lives, in the face of continuing racism and hostility. For years, we suppressed our anger, bitterness and shame about the unfair treatment we got.

Today, many in the Japanese American community will attend the annual Day of Remembrance events in Los Angeles, San Francisco and other cities, with the goal of teaching new generations the lessons from that painful time. Some of my fellow Americans are now being targeted because they are Muslim, Arab or Middle Eastern. When the attacks of Sept. 11 happened, I mourned for the innocent lives that were lost. But I also began to identify and sympathize with the innocent Muslim Americans who immediately became victims of the same kind of stereotyping and scapegoating we faced 63 years ago. They too have become targets of suspicion, hate crimes, vandalism and violence, all in the name of patriotism and national security.

Feb. 19 is a day I do not wish upon anyone else. Now, the lessons are not just about events in a distant past, but events as they are occurring on a daily basis.

Let's not forget the infamous words of Gen. John DeWitt—who was in charge of West Coast defenses—in 1943, "A Jap is a Jap." Or Secretary of War Henry Stimson, who said, "Their racial characteristics are such that we cannot understand or even trust the citizen Japanese." How painfully familiar it seemed to see Muslim and Arab Americans suspected and ostracized as potential terrorists solely on the basis of ethnicity and religion.

In the 1970s and '80s, inspired by the civil rights struggle, the Japanese American community fought a 10-year-long campaign and won redress and an apology from the U.S. government in 1988. This was to be the official government acknowledgment that the internment was morally and legally wrong, and we were given hope that such an event would not be repeated.

Lillian Nakano, "1942-Style Bigotry Targets Muslims in the U.S. Today," *Los Angeles Times*, February 19, 2005, http://articles.latimes.com. Reprinted by permission of the author.

Yet today there are renewed attacks on civil liberties in the name of the "war on terrorism." Legislation such as the Patriot Act and the government's willingness to arrest and charge innocent people contribute to an atmosphere that could lead to future internment camps.

Some ideologues on the right seek to rewrite history in order to justify government policy and racial profiling. One example is Michelle Malkin's 2004 book, *In Defense of Internment: The Case for 'Racial Profiling' in World War II and the War on Terror,* which not only rehashes the untruths that Japanese Americans have heard for years but also asserts: "The most damaging legacy of this apologia and compensation package [redress won by Japanese Americans] has been its impact on national security efforts. The ethnic grievance industry and civil liberties Chicken Littles wield the reparations law like a bludgeon over the War on Terror debate."

There is no justification for racism or denial of civil liberties—not in 1942 and not in 2005.

6. Lt. Ehren Watada Vows to Stop an Illegal and Unjust War, 2006

Today, I speak with you about a radical idea. It is one born from the very concept of the American soldier (or service member). It became instrumental in ending the Vietnam War – but it has been long since forgotten. The idea is this: that to stop an illegal and unjust war, the soldiers can choose to stop fighting it.

Now it is not an easy task for the soldier. For he or she must be aware that they are being used for ill-gain. They must hold themselves responsible for individual action. They must remember duty to the Constitution and the people supersedes the ideologies of their leadership. The soldier must be willing to face ostracism by their peers, worry over the survival of their families, and of course the loss of personal freedom. They must know that resisting an authoritarian government at home is equally important to fighting a foreign aggressor on the battlefield. Finally, those wearing the uniform must know beyond any shadow of a doubt that by refusing immoral and illegal orders they will be supported by the people not with mere words but by action.

The American soldier must rise above the socialization that tells them authority should always be obeyed without question. Rank should be respected but never blindly followed. Awareness of the history of atrocities and destruction committed in the name of America – either through direct military intervention or by proxy war – is crucial. They must realize that this is a war not out of self-defense but by choice, for profit and imperialistic domination. WMD [weapons of mass destruction], ties to Al Qaeda, and ties to 9/11 never existed and never will. The soldier must know that our narrowly and questionably elected officials intentionally manipulated the evidence presented to Congress, the public, and

---

the world to make the case for war. They must know that neither Congress nor this administration has the authority to violate the prohibition against pre-emptive war – an American law that still stands today. This same administration uses us for rampant violations of time-tested laws banning torture and degradation of prisoners of war. Though the American soldier wants to do right, the illegitimacy of the occupation itself, the policies of this administration, and rules of engagement of desperate field commanders will ultimately force them to be party to war crimes. They must know some of these facts, if not all, in order to act.

Mark Twain once remarked, "Each man must for himself alone decide what is right and what is wrong, which course is patriotic and which isn't. You cannot shirk this and be a man. To decide against your conviction is to be an unqualified and inexcusable traitor, both to yourself and to your country …" By this, each and every American soldier, marine, airman, and sailor is responsible for their choices and their actions. The freedom to choose is only one that we can deny ourselves.

The oath we take swears allegiance not to one man but to a document of principles and laws designed to protect the people. Enlisting in the military does not relinquish one's right to seek the truth – neither does it excuse one from rational thought nor the ability to distinguish between right and wrong. "I was only following orders" is never an excuse.

The Nuremburg Trials showed America and the world that citizenry as well as soldiers have the unrelinquishable obligation to refuse complicity in war crimes perpetrated by their government. Widespread torture and inhumane treatment of detainees is a war crime. A war of aggression born through an unofficial policy of prevention is a crime against the peace. An occupation violating the very essence of international humanitarian law and sovereignty is a crime against humanity. These crimes are funded by our tax dollars. Should citizens choose to remain silent through self-imposed ignorance or choice, it makes them as culpable as the soldier in these crimes….

I tell this to you because you must know that to stop this war, for the soldiers to stop fighting it, they must have the unconditional support of the people. I have seen this support with my own eyes. For me it was a leap of faith. For other soldiers, they do not have that luxury. They must know it and you must show it to them. Convince them that no matter how long they sit in prison, no matter how long this country takes to right itself, their families will have a roof over their heads, food in their stomachs, opportunities and education. This is a daunting task. It requires the sacrifice of all of us. Why must Canadians feed and house our fellow Americans who have chosen to do the right thing? We should be the ones taking care of our own. Are we that powerless—are we that unwilling to risk something for those who can truly end this war? How do you support the troops but not the war? By supporting those who can truly stop it; let them know that resistance to participate in an illegal war is not futile and not without a future.

I have broken no law but the code of silence and unquestioning loyalty. If I am guilty of any crime, it is that I learned too much and cared too deeply for the meaningless loss of my fellow soldiers and my fellow human beings. If I am to be punished it should be for following the rule of law over the immoral orders of one man. If I am to be punished it should be for not acting sooner. Martin

Luther King Jr. once said, "History will have to record that the greatest tragedy of this period … was not the strident clamor of the bad people, but the appalling silence of the good people."

Now, I'm not a hero. I am a leader of men who said enough is enough. Those who called for war prior to the invasion compared diplomacy with Saddam to the compromises made with Hitler. I say, we compromise now by allowing a government that uses war as the first option instead of the last to act with impunity. Many have said this about the World Trade Towers, "Never Again." I agree. Never again will we allow those who threaten our way of life to reign free – be they terrorists or elected officials. The time to fight back is now - the time to stand up and be counted is today.

I'll end with one more Martin Luther King Jr. quote:

> "One who breaks an unjust law that conscience tells him is unjust, and who willingly accepts the penalty of imprisonment in order to arouse the conscience of the community over its injustice, is in reality expressing the highest respect for law."

Thank you and bless you all.

7. Major General Antonio Taguba Indicts Bush Administration War Crimes, 2008

This report tells the largely untold human story of what happened to detainees in our custody when the Commander-in-Chief and those under him authorized a systematic regime of torture. This story is not only written in words: It is scrawled for the rest of these individuals' lives on their bodies and minds. Our national honor is stained by the indignity and inhumane treatment these men received from their captors.

The profiles of these eleven former detainees, none of whom were ever charged with a crime or told why they were detained, are tragic and brutal rebuttals to those who claim that torture is ever justified. Through the experiences of these men in Iraq, Afghanistan, and Guantanamo Bay, we can see the full scope of the damage this illegal and unsound policy has inflicted—both on America's institutions and our nation's founding values, which the military, intelligence services, and our justice system are duty-bound to defend.

In order for these individuals to suffer the wanton cruelty to which they were subjected, a government policy was promulgated to the field whereby the Geneva Conventions and the Uniform Code of Military Justice were disregarded. The UN Convention Against Torture was indiscriminately ignored. And the healing professions, including physicians and psychologists, became complicit in the willful infliction of harm against those the Hippocratic Oath demands they protect.

Preface to *Broken Laws, Broken Lives: Medical Evidence of Torture by US Personnel and Its Impact*, Physicians for Human Rights, 2008, viii, http://phr.org/broken-laws-broken-lives. Reprinted by permission.

After years of disclosures by government investigations, media accounts, and reports from human rights organizations, there is no longer any doubt as to whether the current administration has committed war crimes. The only question that remains to be answered is whether those who ordered the use of torture will be held to account. The former detainees in this report, each of whom is fighting a lonely and difficult battle to rebuild his life, require reparations for what they endured, comprehensive psycho–social and medical assistance, and even an official apology from our government.

But most of all, these men deserve justice as required under the tenets of international law and the United States Constitution.

And so do the American people.

8. Judge Amy Berman Jackson Rules That the Army's ROTC Program Must Accommodate Iknoor Singh's Religious Beliefs, 2015

MEMORANDUM OPINION

Plaintiff Iknoor Singh is a rising junior at Hofstra University and an observant Sikh. In accordance with his religion, plaintiff does not cut his hair or beard, and he wears a turban. He has endeavored to enroll in the Reserve Officers' Training Corps ("ROTC") program run by the United States Army at his university, but his religious practices do not conform to Army uniform and grooming standards. Plaintiff sought a religious accommodation that would enable him to enroll in ROTC with his articles of faith intact, but the Army denied the request. Plaintiff contends that the Army's refusal to accommodate his religious exercise violates the Religious Freedom Restoration Act ("RFRA"), and he brought this lawsuit against John McHugh, in his official capacity as Secretary of the United States Army; Lieutenant General James C. McConville, in his official capacity as Deputy Chief of Staff, G-1, United States Army; Brigadier General Peggy C. Combs, in her official capacity as Commanding General, United States Army Cadet Command; and Lieutenant Colonel Daniel L. Cederman, in his official capacity as Commander of the ROTC program at Hofstra University.

In their motion for summary judgment, defendants remind the Court of the doctrine that cautions judges to afford substantial deference to the judgment of military commanders and to decline to interpose their own views in matters involving the composition and training of military officers. In opposing defendants' motion and advancing his own, plaintiff points out that like all government agencies, the Armed Services are governed by the congressional determination – enshrined in RFRA – to tip the scale in favor of individual religious rights. He notes that even the military must be able to demonstrate that a policy that imposes a substantial burden upon an individual's ability to practice

---

Iknoor Singh v John McHugh, et. al. Civil Action No. 14-1906 (ABJ), US District Court for the District of Columbia, June 12, 2015.

his religion furthers a compelling government interest, and is the least restrictive alternative available for furthering that interest. In other words, while the Court must accord the military a great deal of respect, particularly in its identification of the compelling interests involved, the defendants still bear the burden to come forward with sufficient evidence to satisfy the strict scrutiny inquiry: does the specific application of Army policy to this plaintiff further the asserted compelling interest and do so in the least restrictive manner?

The Court finds that defendants have failed to show that the application of the Army's regulations to this plaintiff and the denial of the particular religious accommodation he seeks further a compelling government interest by the least restrictive means. Therefore, and for the additional reasons set forth below, defendants' dispositive motions will be denied and judgment will be entered in favor of the plaintiff. The Court accords substantial deference to the Army's judgments concerning the essential role that uniformity plays in military training and effectiveness. But given the tens of thousands of exceptions the Army has already made to its grooming and uniform policies, its successful accommodation of observant Sikhs in the past, and the fact that, at this time, plaintiff is seeking only to enroll in the ROTC program, the Army's refusal to permit him to do so while adhering to his faith cannot survive the strict scrutiny that RFRA demands. This decision is limited to the narrow issue presently before the Court – plaintiff's ability to enroll in ROTC with his turban, unshorn hair, and beard – and it does not address plaintiff's eventual receipt of a contract or an Army commission....

The Decision at Issue in This Case:

The Denial of Plaintiff's Request for a Religious Accommodation   Plaintiff "has long dreamed of serving his country," and he has explained that he wishes to enroll as a cadet in the Hofstra ROTC program so that he may compete for a contract. Plaintiff has participated in ROTC classes at Hofstra as an unenrolled student since his freshman year. In April 2013, plaintiff requested a religious accommodation so that he could fully enroll in ROTC, and complete all of the training necessary to compete for a contract, while maintaining his unshorn hair, beard, and turban. The Enrollment Officer of the Hofstra ROTC program denied plaintiff's request for an accommodation, stating that "[t]he Army whenever possible, makes all attempts to accommodate religious practices and belief but not when it has an adverse impact on readiness, unit cohesion, standards, health, safety or discipline."

After the initial denial, plaintiff continued to seek an accommodation. In June 2013, the organization UNITED SIKHS sent a letter on plaintiff's behalf to the ROTC Department Chair at the time, Lieutenant Colonel ("LTC") David Daniel, urging him to approve a religious exemption for the plaintiff. LTC Daniel denied the request on August 16, 2013, stating that "the contracting of Cadets into the ROTC program who cannot comply with the wear and appearance and personal grooming standards of Army Regulation (AR) 670-1 is not permitted under AR 145-1," and that neither he nor U.S. Army Cadet

Command had the authority to permit an exception to this policy. LTC Daniel further stated that it was "not legally permissible under AR 145-1 to grant religious exceptions to allow a Sikh Cadet to enroll in the ROTC program while maintaining his religious articles."...

After plaintiff filed this lawsuit, the Army decided to process his accommodation request. On December 19, 2014, plaintiff received a letter from LTG McConville denying the religious accommodation on substantive grounds.

LTG McConville's letter stated that, after balancing "the facts of [plaintiff's] individual case" against considerations of "military necessity," the Army was denying the accommodation request on several grounds. McConville explained that "Army ROTC is the primary means of generating the officer leaders of the Army," and so "it is important that Cadets are inculcated into the Army and its values, training methods, and traditions in a way that is reflective of what their future [S]oldiers will expect of them." Citing his "over thirty years of experience as a leader and commander of [S]oldiers," he determined that "[p]ermitting an obvious deviation from these standards in an officer training program" by granting plaintiff's requested accommodation "would, in the eyes of the [S]oldiers whom Cadets are being trained to lead, damage the esteem and credibility of ROTC and the officer corps in general...."

B. Defendants have not demonstrated that denying an accommodation to plaintiff furthers the government's compelling interests.   Defendants assert that "[t]he Army's decision to deny Plaintiff's request for a grooming accommodation while in an officer training program furthers compelling interests in maintaining a credible officer corps and an effective fighting force that is capable of meeting the Nation's defensive needs."... According to LTG McConville, "[u]niformity is a primary way the Army builds an effective fighting force" because "[i]t allows a strong team identity to be forged, distinguishes service members from the civilian population, reinforces notions of selfless service, and provides a routine that instills discipline in Soldiers and leaders, while connecting the Army to its past in a visible way." Defendants assert that "[t]he interest in maintaining an effective Army by developing a disciplined, well trained, credible, cohesively bonded, and reliable corps of officers in ROTC is undeniably compelling."

There can be no doubt that military readiness and the unit cohesion and discipline of the Army officer corps constitute highly compelling government interests....

But the Religious Freedom Restoration Act of 1993 (RFRA) "requires the Government to demonstrate that the compelling interest test is satisfied through application of the challenged law 'to the person'—the particular claimant whose sincere exercise of religion is being substantially burdened." Thus, the Court must determine whether defendants have proven that the decision to deny *this plaintiff* a religious accommodation that would enable him to enroll in ROTC actually furthers the compelling interests defendants have identified....

In this case, there is ample undisputed evidence that soldiers in all corners of the Army are permitted to maintain beards and to wear religious headgear while in uniform, as well as to deviate from the grooming standards in other ways. And the Army has allowed several Sikhs to serve – albeit, in different circumstances than plaintiff – with accommodations for their turbans, beards, and unshorn hair. So defendants cannot simply invoke general principles here – they must make the necessary heightened showing to justify the specific refusal to grant an exception to plaintiff.

The Court finds that defendants have not overcome this hurdle.

1. LTG McConville's Decision   LTG McConville's decision to deny an accommodation to plaintiff rested on his conclusion that permitting "an obvious deviation" from the uniform and grooming regulations in an officer training program would undermine:

- "Unit cohesion and morale," because it would "undermine the common Army identity we are attempting to develop in ROTC, and adversely impact efforts to develop cohesive teams,"

- "Good order and discipline," because "the even handed enforcement of grooming standards instills the self-discipline necessary for the military member to perform effectively"; "[g]ranting [plaintiff] an exception in a military officer training program would undercut this fundamental component of [the] program, and dramatically change the nature of how we train officers for the future needs of the Army"; and "[i]f officer training does not reflect Army training, the credibility of the officer corps will be called into question,"

- "Individual and unit readiness," because "allowing [plaintiff] to continue in officer training without any emphasis on uniformity would leave [him] generally unprepared to lead Soldiers, viewed as an outsider by [his] peers, and trained in a manner that is wholly inconsistent with how we develop strong military officers," thereby weakening "good order, discipline, the credibility of the officer corps, cohesion, and morale," as well as military readiness in general, and

- Plaintiff's "health and safety," based on an Army study that shows that "facial hair significantly degrades the protection factor of all approved protective masks," and because compliance with Army grooming standards is "[o]ne of the most important mechanisms for managing risk" because it facilitates "the ability to assess a Soldier's competency and attention to detail,"

McConville acknowledged that the Army had granted religious accommodations to Sikh soldiers in the past, but he differentiated those individuals because the exceptions were granted "based on the military necessity factors that existed at the time," and the soldiers were "selected to serve in positions requiring unique skills or professional credentials to meet the Army's operational needs." McConville also offered his view that issuing temporary medical exceptions to grooming standards did not undercut the Army's ability to enforce grooming and appearance policies in general because those exceptions are "subject to approval by military commanders" and often limited in duration, and still they require the recipient to "trim his beard as close to his face as possible."

Notwithstanding the undeniable importance of uniformity to military discipline, unit cohesion, and safety in general, these justifications for the Army's decision do not withstand strict scrutiny.

2. The Army has permitted numerous exceptions to its grooming and uniform policies. Defendants' contention that denying plaintiff a religious accommodation furthers the stated compelling interests is undermined by the fact that the Army routinely grants soldiers exceptions to its grooming and uniform regulations.

First, since 2007, the Army has permitted more than 100,000 service members to grow beards for medical reasons; it has authorized at least 49,690 permanent "shaving profiles," and at least 57,616 temporary ones. These soldiers with beards include not only enlisted men but officers bound to ensure that the men who serve under them are clean-shaven....

It is undisputed that there are differences between the religious accommodation plaintiff seeks for his beard and the shaving profiles the Army has granted. But defendants have not carried their burden to show that permitting plaintiff's unshorn beard would undermine the Army's compelling interests any more than the medical beard accommodations the Army has provided, especially considering that the Army permits soldiers to grow beards longer than a quarter of an inch "if medically necessary." And although some shaving profiles are classified as temporary, tens of thousands of them are "permanent," and defendants have offered no evidence that any soldier has been separated on that basis.

Moreover, while soldiers who are granted shaving profiles may be required to shave by their commanders, the Army's own rules provide that this authority "should not [b]e used to require that a Soldier be clean shaven for maneuvers and other tactical simulations," but should be invoked only "when there is an actual need to wear the protective mask in a real tactical operation." Therefore, the fact that other shaving exceptions may be revocable does not support the outright denial of the accommodation sought here: as an ROTC enrollee, or even as a contracted cadet, plaintiff would never encounter the "real tactical operation" that would permit a commander to require a soldier with a medically-necessary beard to shave.

For the same reason, the concern about plaintiff's health and safety is misplaced, at least for the duration of his participation in ROTC.

Finally, the Court notes that defendants have not claimed or shown that even one of the more than 100,000 soldiers who have been permitted to grow a beard since 2007—including many who have served in deployed environments—has been ordered to shave it for any reason.

In sum, it is difficult to see how accommodating plaintiff's religious exercise would do greater damage to the Army's compelling interests in uniformity, discipline, credibility, unit cohesion, and training than the tens of thousands of medical shaving profiles the Army has already granted....

("[T]he Department has provided no legitimate explanation as to why the presence of officers who wear beards for medical reasons does not have [the same] effect [as] the presence of officers who wear beards for religious reason would.... We are at a loss to understand why religious exemptions threaten important city interests but medical exemptions do not."). Defendants have not claimed or shown that any of the soldiers and officers who have served with beards have been less disciplined, less credible, less socially integrated, or less well-trained than their clean-shaven colleagues. In addition, to the extent that the Army has also asserted an interest in diversity, that interest would plainly be furthered by permitting plaintiff's enrollment in ROTC.

Medically-based shaving profiles are not the only large-scale exception the Army makes to its grooming policies. In March of 2014, the Army tightened its policies related to tattoos, but it grandfathered in nearly 200,000 soldiers with non-conforming tattoos—including officers who will be bound to enforce the policy in the future. The tattoos cover a wide range of personal expression, and they include religious iconography, symbols of cultural or ethnic heritage, images from popular culture, and more. The fact that the Army is able to tolerate so many idiosyncratic deviations from its grooming regulations further undermines LTG McConville's assertion that "the even handed enforcement of grooming standards" is critical to "instill[] the self-discipline necessary for the military member to perform effectively."

Neither LTG McConville's decision nor defendants' pleadings say much about plaintiff's request to maintain his turban and unshorn hair. LTG McConville's letter states that "[h]air and clothing are a very visible way that individuals express their identity," and that "[b]y eliminating the social distinctions that different civilian attire implies, uniforms emphasize the professional equality of all military people." But it is undisputed that the Army's own regulations permit soldiers to wear yarmulkes and other religious headgear, and defendants do not contend that a turban would necessarily fail to satisfy the religious headgear rules. Moreover, although Army regulations require male soldiers to keep the hair on their heads cut short, defendants do not—and cannot—contend that plaintiff's unshorn hair, when tucked into a turban in accordance with religious precepts, would "fall over the ears or eyebrows, or touch the collar," or present an appearance that is anything other than "neat and conservative." In view of the vast number of exceptions to the grooming and uniform standards that the Army has granted, the Court finds that defendants have not shown that denying this plaintiff a religious accommodation would make him less credible, disciplined, or ready than the other officers and soldiers who similarly do not meet all of the requirements of uniformity.

Finally, defendants have not carried their burden to show that "the compelling interest test is satisfied through application of the challenged law 'to the person.'" LTG McConville's decision emphasizes the general importance of uniformity in cultivating and reflecting Army discipline. McConville explains that "[u]niformity is a key component of the learning process" for ROTC cadets because it is "a readily available means of instilling the practice of inspection and compliance that not only sharpens Soldiers, but also leaders." He insists that "[u]niformity helps to inhibit personal desires and impulses that may be anti-thetical to mission accomplishment," noting that "[t]he obligations Soldiers undertake, risking life and well-being for the greater good, require[] dedication, selfless service, and discipline." And he notes that compliance with Army groom-ing standards facilitates "the ability to assess a Soldier's competency and attention to detail."

But the accommodation this plaintiff seeks does not stem from any lack of self-control, dedication, or attention to detail. To the contrary: plaintiff seeks an accommodation because he faithfully adheres to the strict dictates of his religion. So even if, in some cases, a soldier's failure to follow the Army's standards might signal a rebellious streak or reflect a lack of impulse control or discipline, LTG McConville's decision fails to grapple with the fact that any deviation from the rules on plaintiff's part flows from a very different source. And therefore, the decision lacks the individual assessment that is fundamental under RFRA.

3. The Army has granted religious accommodations to other Sikh soldiers. Defendants' contention that denying this plaintiff an accommoda-tion advances the Army's compelling interests is further undermined by the undisputed fact that at least four Sikh men who served in the Army with tre-mendous success received similar accommodations. Corp. Simran Preet Singh Lamba enlisted in 2009, served as a medic, received a promotion to Corporal, and currently serves in the U.S. Army Individual Ready Reserve. Maj. Kamal-jeet Singh Kalsi is an Army doctor who served in Afghanistan, received a pro-motion to Major, and is currently serving in the Army Active Reserves. Capt. Tejdeep Singh Rattan is an active duty Army dentist who served in Afghani-stan. Gopal Singh Khalsa enlisted in the Army as a private in 1976, served in Military Intelligence, served overseas, received numerous promotions, and eventually retired as a Colonel in 2009. Each of these soldiers received an accommodation that permitted him to serve while maintaining unshorn hair, an unshorn beard, and a turban. And, notwithstanding the deviation from the uniformity that is undeniably a core aspect of military life, each of them has earned commendations and outstanding reviews:

- Corp. Lamba's superiors described him as "easily one of the most impressive Soldiers in the company," "an exceptional Soldier [who] possess[es] all the attributes ... required to be an outstanding Army Officer," and "a tremen-dous Soldier, an invaluable member of [the] team, and [someone who had] an amazing impact on his peers and supervisors." In addition, one of his Drill Sergeants noted that "[d]espite any spoken or unspoken stereotypes surrounding his enlistment in the United States Army, SPC Lamba displayed ... intelligence, courage, and inner strength; enabling him to push forward with his training in a manner that would make seasoned Soldiers proud to have him on their team." Lamba also received an Army Com-mendation Medal in acknowledgment of his "exceptionally meritorious service," his "selfless service and dedication to duty," and the fact that "his actions [were in] keeping with the finest traditions of military service."

- Maj. Kalsi's superiors described his performance as "[t]ruly exceptional," stating that he "can be expected to excel in positions of leadership," and that "[h]e possesses absolutely unlimited potential as a leader, military officer, and physician." Kalsi was awarded a Bronze Star for his service in Afghanistan.

- Capt. Rattan's superiors believe that his "potential is unlimited as an Army Dental Officer and leader," and have described his performance as "exemplary," "tireless," "in keeping with the highest traditions of the … United States Army," "outstanding," and "extraordinary." In addition, Rattan's commander stated that he had "done everything within his power to keep within the [grooming and uniform] regulation" and had "[gone] leaps and bounds beyond what others have had to do." The commander further noted that "[t]he only struggle is that when some people get a first look, they are going to stereotype him," but "[t]hat is the good thing about having Rattan out there, to show that this is a proud individual, he knows what he is doing, and he is doing a phenomenal job." Capt. Rattan has received numerous awards, including a NATO Medal and the Army Commendation Medal for his service.

- During more than three decades of Army service, Col. (Ret.) Khalsa received an enormous volume of praise and numerous promotions. In training in 1977, he was selected from among 600 peers as the Outstanding Soldier of the Cycle; in Officer Candidate School, he was named the Distinguished Leadership Graduate, and was later inducted into the school's hall of fame; in 1998, after being promoted to Lieutenant Colonel, Khalsa was appointed Battalion Commander for the Reserves' 368th Military Intelligence Battalion, a position in which he commanded 700 soldiers, including commissioned officers, warrant officers, and enlisted soldiers; he was repeatedly rated "Best Qualified" for promotion; in 2003, he was promoted to full Colonel and became the Deputy Chief of Staff, G7 for Training for the 63rd Regional Readiness Command, a position that charged him with coordinating and resourcing all individual, unit, and professional development training for all U.S. Army Reserve units in Arizona, California, and Nevada; and he delayed his retirement at the Army's request to accept an appointment as Course Director for the Army's Company Team Leader Development Course. Khalsa was praised for being "a total soldier who demonstrates mental and physical readiness and sets the highest example for his troops to follow," as having "unlimited potential," as "our best battalion commander, bar none," for being "held in the highest esteem by his superiors and subordinates alike," "a highly disciplined officer," "capable of commanding any brigade," and the "[b]est of the best."

Defendants point to undisputed facts that distinguish each of these soldiers from the plaintiff. They note that Maj. Kalsi, Capt. Rattan, and Corp. Lamba each "joined the military in response to specialized programs that actively sought the unique skills these individuals possessed during a time of growing conflict," and all three served in medical roles in the Special Branches, which "focus on professional technical skills and less on the leadership of large teams of soldiers." Plaintiff, by contrast, wishes to become a Military Intelligence officer in the Basic Branches of the Army.

Faced with the fact that Col. (Ret.) Khalsa served in Military Intelligence in the Basic Branches and had a long and distinguished career as an Army officer, defendants note that he was "commissioned and grandfathered under the prior regulatory system" that permitted religious accommodations for Sikhs. Also, according to defendants, "[t]he needs of the Army now are also far different than when other exceptions were granted."

Finally, defendants argue that "[t]he relative professional success" of Corp. Lamba, Maj. Kalsi, Capt. Rattan, and Col. (Ret.) Khalsa "validates the Army's decision-making process and its decision to grant accommodations in appropriate circumstances."

But despite the differences between plaintiff and Corp. Lamba, Maj. Kalsi, Capt. Rattan, and Col. (Ret.) Khalsa, the undisputed evidence in the record indicates that each of these men served—or are serving—with their articles of faith intact without any of the negative consequences that defendants predict would flow from granting a similar exception in this case. The praise heaped on each man's service—including, in particular, for their discipline and leadership—stands in stark contrast to LTG McConville's conclusion that permitting plaintiff to maintain his articles of faith would undermine the quality of his training, unit cohesion and morale, military readiness, and the credibility of the officer corps.

Furthermore, the Army's own research stands in stark contradiction to LTG McConville's opinion. The Army conducted an internal examination of the effect of Corp. Lamba's religious accommodation on his service, and the study concluded that "the Soldier's religious accommodations did not have a significant impact on unit morale, cohesion, good order, and discipline," and that it "had no significant impact on his own, or any other Soldier's, health and safety." The defendants point to no contrary empirical evidence.

Thus, instead of "validat[ing] the Army's decision-making process," the exemplary service records of the four Sikh soldiers with religious accommodations serve to highlight the flaws in the Army's analysis in this case. Those soldiers had the chance to prove themselves, and that is all plaintiff is seeking here. Defendants have no way of knowing whether plaintiff, too, might be qualified to serve because they have not yet even allowed him to enroll in ROTC.

In conclusion, defendants failed to come forward with any evidence to diminish the force of the evidence produced by plaintiff, as is their burden, and they seem to suggest that LTG McConville's say-so is sufficient to justify the decision here. Notwithstanding his thirty-four years of experience in the Army, and his superior judgment about military matters, adopting his conclusion without more would entail abdicating the role that RFRA requires the Court to play. Defendants have failed to sustain the heavy burden that applies when a governmental entity refuses to grant an exception to a policy already riddled with exceptions, and they have failed to satisfy their burden of demonstrating that the compelling government interests they cite are furthered by the unwavering application of Army policies to this plaintiff in this particular context. Under these circumstances, and in light of the evidence presented here, the Court finds that it would require "a degree of deference that is tantamount to unquestioning acceptance," to credit defendants' assertion that denying a religious accommodation to plaintiff while he enrolls in ROTC advances the Army's asserted compelling interests as applied to him.

C. Defendants have not shown that denying an accommodation to plaintiff is the least restrictive means of furthering their interests.

While the Court accords defendants a high level of deference in their identification of compelling military interests, it finds that it is well within its purview to hold that the Army's refusal to grant this plaintiff a religious accommodation is not the least restrictive means of advancing those interests....

Defendants contend that "there is no less restrictive means to promote and maintain teamwork, motivation, discipline, esprit de corps and image, within the context of an officer development program," than to deny a religious accommodation to plaintiff. Plaintiff's individual readiness, they argue, would be irretrievably undermined by allowing him "to continue in officer training without any emphasis on uniformity," because he would be "trained in a manner that is wholly inconsistent with how we develop strong military officers." Moreover, defendants point out that plaintiff, if qualified, would not receive a commission until 2017, and that "[t]he Army cannot decide now that it will simply find Plaintiff a branch within the organization ... where his accommodation may have some potentially lesser impact on the military necessity factors." Finally, according to defendants, "[t]he fact remains Plaintiff would subject himself, his fellow soldiers, and his unit to greater risk by virtue of his wearing a beard in an environment with chemical or biological weapons."

But the Court has already found that defendants have failed to show that if plaintiff's religious exercise were to be accommodated, his individual readiness will be diminished any more than the readiness of the tens of thousands of soldiers and officers who have received grooming and uniform accommodations for other reasons. Nor have defendants demonstrated that plaintiff's training would be devoid of *"any* emphasis on uniformity" by virtue of his accommodation, (emphasis added), or that these concerns could not be advanced some other way. For example, the Army's letter granting an accommodation to Corp. Lamba stated that it was "[then-]SPC Lamba's responsibility to ensure his beard is well maintained and presents a neat and orderly appearance."

Furthermore, although the Court does not doubt that the Army cannot anticipate at this time what its needs will be in 2017, that only serves to underscore the fact that a temporary accommodation is a less restrictive means here. As plaintiff points out, a temporary accommodation "would be especially workable" because it would give the Army "ample opportunity to determine whether [plaintiff's] articles of faith *actually* interfere with his performance," and would permit defendants to "observe Mr. Singh in action with his accommodation as he competes with his peers for an ROTC contract." It would also permit defendants to troubleshoot any issues that might arise, including with respect to gas masks, as appropriate.

Finally, the undisputed evidence shows that, in 2010, the Army granted Corp. Lamba a temporary accommodation that was virtually identical to the one sought by plaintiff here for the purpose of Lamba's "attendance at basic military training and military occupational school." Lamba's temporary accommodation included the proviso that the accommodation could not "be guaranteed at all times" and might "be revoked due to changed conditions," which no doubt served to protect many of the interests that defendants have asserted in this case. Defendants have not shown that the less restrictive alternative of a temporary accommodation with similar conditions would be insufficient to protect the Army's interests here.

In sum, defendants have not carried the "'exceptionally demanding'" burden to "'sho[w] that [the Army] lacks other means of achieving its desired goal without imposing a substantial burden on [plaintiff's] exercise of religion.'" The relief plaintiff seeks—an accommodation that would permit him to enroll in ROTC with his articles of faith intact—would not require the Army to guarantee him a commission, or even a contract, and it stops far short of the permanent relief the Army has granted to tens of thousands of soldiers for medical and religious reasons, Moreover, because providing plaintiff with a temporary religious accommodation for the purpose of enrolling in ROTC, which could be revocable if necessary, is an available less restrictive means, the Army must employ that alternative.

Conclusion

For the foregoing reasons, the Court will deny defendants' motion to dismiss and for summary judgment, and it will grant plaintiff's cross-motion for summary judgment....

And it is...

ORDERED that defendants are permanently and immediately enjoined from conditioning plaintiff's enrollment in ROTC and his ability to compete for a contract on plaintiff's compliance with the Army uniform and grooming regulations that would require him to abandon his turban and beard, and to cut his hair, in violation of his sincerely held religious beliefs.

SO ORDERED.

/s/ Amy Berman Jackson
AMY BERMAN JACKSON
United States District Judge
DATE: June 12, 2015

☀ ESSAYS

The first essay, by journalist John H. Richardson, discusses the controversy surrounding John Yoo, a Korean American law professor at the University of California, Berkeley, who drafted legal memos in 2002, as deputy assistant attorney general in the George W. Bush administration, on the use of "enhanced interrogation techniques" of detainees. While Yoo's defenders argue these techniques are a necessary application of executive authority to effectively fight a new kind of war on terror, his critics charge that Yoo condones torture that violates the Geneva Conventions. The second essay, by Jaideep Singh, a professor of ethnic studies at California State University, East Bay, examines how media depictions of turbaned and bearded men after 9/11 unleashed a wave of violence against the half million Sikh Americans living in the United States. After personally experiencing attacks linking him with suspected terrorists, Singh states that he was not surprised when he learned that Wade Michael Page, a U.S. Army veteran and white supremacist, fatally shot six people and wounded four others at a Sikh temple in Oak Creek, Wisconsin, in 2012.

"Enhanced Interrogation" and the Definition of Torture During the War on Terror

JOHN H. RICHARDSON

HE IS THE YOUNG JUSTICE DEPARTMENT LAWYER—thirty-four at the time—who wrote the Bush administration's first decisions on prisoner detention, interrogation, habeas corpus, military commissions, and the Geneva Conventions. He is the man who defined torture as pain equivalent to "death or organ failure," who said that the president could crush the testicles of a child to make his father talk, who picked the lock on Pandora's box and unleashed the demons of Abu Ghraib. He's been accused of war crimes and compared to the Nazi lawyers who justified Hitler. Many good Americans would like to see him fired, shamed, even imprisoned....

Jose Padilla's lawyers certainly think so. "We are talking about the torture of an American citizen in an American prison by American officials," one of them told me, indignation rising fresh in his voice. Padilla is the former Chicago gang member who was arrested in O'Hare Airport in May 2002 as he returned from terrorist training camps in the Middle East with plans-or so the government believed—to explode a "dirty" nuclear bomb in the United States. After he was convicted on more general terrorism-conspiracy charges, his lawyers took the extraordinary step of filing a lawsuit against the junior-level lawyer they saw as the first link in the chain. "Defendant Yoo prepared the Torture Memos," they said, referring to several Justice Department opinions, including a memo that was sighed on August 1, 2002, and withdrawn in shame two years later. "He knew the Torture Memos would be transmitted to senior government officials, including officials at the White House and Department of Defense, and would be relied upon by military and intelligence officers in formulating and implementing programs of confinement and interrogation for suspected 'enemy combatants.'" Yoo also wrote the memo that put the "enemy combatant" label on Padilla. As a result, the lawsuit claims, Padilla was held

"Is This Man a Monster?" by John Richardson from *Esquire*, 149, no. 6 (June 2008): 126–152. Reprinted by permission of *Esquire* Magazine.

without charges for three years and eight months, completely alone under twenty-four-hour camera surveillance, with his windows blacked out and no clock or radio or TV to help him mark time. Sometimes the lights were left on for days, sometimes he was left in the dark for days, sometimes the cell was extremely hot, sometimes extremely cold. His sleep was constantly interrupted and he was threatened with death and given disorienting drugs and shackled and forced into stress positions for hours at a time. Whenever he was moved, he wore a blindfold and noise-canceling headphones to reinforce his isolation and helplessness. After a few years of this intentional effort to break his will and destroy his mind, Padilla was given to "involuntary twitching and self-inflicted scratch wounds" and his jailers often observed him weeping in his cell, so broken and passive that he had become "like a piece of furniture."

Padilla's claims have not been proven. Some of them, like the accusations of death threats and use of drugs, go beyond even Yoo's liberal interpretation of interrogation laws. But they remind us of what we have done and what we will continue to do. Consider the fight over Michael Mukasey's nomination for attorney general, when Mukasey refused to call waterboarding torture. He said he didn't want to put the CIA officers who made these judgments in the heat of battle "in personal legal jeopardy." It seemed so ridiculous, right out of 1984. The Khmer Rouge used waterboarding. We prosecuted Japanese generals for doing it. But Mukasey was confirmed anyway, and four months later President Bush vetoed a law that banned waterboarding. Consider also that courts and Congress have endorsed many of Yoo's opinions, including the use of military commissions and the extended detention without criminal charges of "enemy combatants" who are American citizens....

From his office, he has a million-dollar view of San Francisco and the Golden Gate Bridge. There are law books everywhere. His screen saver is a picture of his wife. His iPhone screen saver is a picture of his wife too, which helps take the edge off all the hate calls. On the floor, there's a shopping bag from a local hippie institution called Amoeba Music. On the wall, a framed goodbye card from the Department of Justice. "Thank you for your excellent service to America," John Ashcroft wrote. "We are stronger and safer because of you."

He turns out to have lots of unexpected quirks. He's pro-choice. He thinks flag burning is a legitimate form of free speech. He thinks the government is "wasting a lot of resources" in the war on drugs. He thinks the phrase "war on terror" is misleading political rhetoric. He's cowriting an article that makes a conservative case for gay marriage. "Our argument is, the state should just stay out of these things, because it doesn't hurt anybody." And he's definitely alarmed by the more theocratic Republicans. "When Mike Huckabee says he wants to amend the Constitution so that it's consistent with God's law, that scares the bejesus out of me."...

"It's the level of anger that really shocks me," he says.

"I'm surprised that you're surprised," I say.

The anger is often directed at him. Protesters in Guantánamo orange have disrupted his class and dogged him in public forums. I talked to another Berkeley law professor who refuses to attend faculty meetings with him. "Until he atones," he said, "I don't want to be in the same room with him." But Yoo shrugs it all off. He likes living among liberals, he says. "Liberals from the sixties do a great job of creating all the comforts of life—gourmet food, specialty jams, the best environmentally conscious waters."...

At Steve's Korean B.B.Q., Yoo talks about his parents. They were teenagers during the Korean War, a serious pair who both became doctors and moved to the U. S. out of gratitude and a love of democracy. "They saw the United States as saving their country, and I agree with them," he says. "It did save their country. And then it let people in. It was extraordinarily generous. I wouldn't be here if it wasn't for the generosity of the United States."

He grew up in the elite Main Line area of Philadelphia and went to a prep school where he wore a suit and tie and learned Greek and Latin. He seems to have been a natural-born conservative, attracted even as a teenager to Ronald Reagan's message of anticommunism, low taxes, and small government, values that resonated with the immigrant dream of personal freedom. But he was never angry or righteous about it. "He was completely open and tolerant of everyone," says Gordon Getter, a prep-school classmate. "He had a genuine sense of humor," says Thomas Schwartz, one of his professors at Harvard. "He would argue and people would get mad at him, but he never seemed to take it personally."

He was also exceptionally brilliant, Schwartz says. "These were extraordinary students, and John was a star among them."

As an undergraduate in the history department, Yoo developed a deep interest in presidential power. His senior thesis was about Eisenhower's plan to share nuclear weapons with the other members of NATO. The example of Truman in Korea was never far from his mind—with North Korean troops sweeping south, Truman rushed U. S. troops to war without pausing for a congressional debate and tried to seize the steel companies to guarantee arms production.

But when Yoo arrived at Yale Law School, everyone seemed to agree that Congress was the dominant policymaker and should approve every war. It was the standard liberal position in the wake of Vietnam, but Yoo saw Vietnam through the lens of Korea, imagining how life would have been for his parents under the savage dictatorship of Kim Il Sung. His preference for Truman's lonely fortitude only deepened when he became a clerk for Laurence Silberman, one of the leading champions of the "unitary executive" theory of expansive presidential powers. In free moments around the courthouse, Silberman painted Congress as a flock of tiny men with tiny ropes intent on binding the president down-annoying in peace but dangerous in war.

Over the next few years, Yoo alternated between stints as a professor at Berkeley and jobs in Washington, first with Justice Clarence Thomas and next with Senator Orrin Hatch. Though he disagreed with them on basic issues like abortion and the attempt to remove Clinton from office, he was drawn to their lonely integrity. Hatch was "one of the few guys in the Senate who really would go to the mat on principle," he says. He also picked up another crucial lesson during the Whitewater investigation, when Senate committee members would demand documents and President Clinton refused to provide them, each side insisting that the Constitution supported its position. "But they worked out deals," Yoo says. "The system is almost designed for them to come into conflict, and they work out a deal. So that had a big effect on me."

Back at Berkeley, he started putting it all into a book. As the first chapters hit the legal journals, he became a star on the lecture circuit, a young hotshot with a provocative theory. His basic idea was that the Constitution has tons of rules on how to pass legislation but almost nothing on war. So the president takes action and Congress fights back, an improvisation with one partner leading, and that is the way it was meant to be—the real reason Truman didn't ask Congress for an authorization before going into Korea, the reason Clinton continued to bomb the Serbs in defiance of the War Powers Act, the reason Bush has resisted every attempt by Congress to restrict his war policies.

Yoo's analysis hinges on the Declare War Clause. Most scholars—most people—believe it was intended to give Congress power to decide whether to go to war and that the founders saw this as an essential bulwark against tyranny. Yoo makes a case that it was really meant as a formal recognition of wars already under way, and the founders intended the real bulwark against tyranny to be Congress's power of the purse. "Several times every year, Congress has a chance to vote on funding the Iraq war," he keeps telling me. "It's an amazing power—if 51 percent of them refuse to vote for it, the war is over."

Abraham Lincoln is Yoo's best argument. Congress had already passed a statute laying out an explicit legal procedure for freeing slaves, but Lincoln ignored the law and freed the slaves under his "unilateral executive authority in wartime as commander in chief to take measures necessary to win a war," as Yoo puts it. Lincoln used the same grounds to suspend habeas corpus, a right the Constitution explicitly grants to Congress. If you really believe that Yoo is all wrong and the unitary-executive theory completely false, you kind of have to say Lincoln behaved like a tyrant.

Jonathan Freiman, Jose Padilla's attorney, bristles when I run Yoo's arguments down for him. "The Supreme Court has said every time it's been asked since 9/11, a state of war is not a blank check. The Constitution applies."

But Congress and the Supreme Court also accepted the military commissions and the enemy-combatant designation and even the indefinite detention of an American citizen named Yaser Hamdi, Yoo would say.

Freiman concedes the point. But Hamdi was arrested in a foreign country in the zone of combat, he says. "That's a pretty small category, a battlefield in a foreign country. It's not a category that encompasses Padilla."

But that's exactly the problem. Padilla was arrested a few months after his associates killed three thousand people in New York City. So where is this battlefield?

It's a dangerous question, Freiman says. "The argument that the entire United States has become a battlefield by virtue of those heinous attacks on 9/11 is just an argument to make the Constitution completely optional, an argument to extend presidential power to the level of monarchy—to every inch of life in this country."

For the next two hours, he pounds Yoo from every possible angle: They already had Padilla under arrest and could have held him under charges like conspiracy or levying war. But they wanted to interrogate him and they wanted to use harsh methods, so they just made up their own rules. This was the natural result of rejecting the Geneva Conventions instead of treating Al Qaeda members as ordinary war criminals. "Before 9/11, you're either a criminal or a soldier. What the government said was, We want a third category where the black shade is drawn, where there are no protections whatsoever, where there is no law."

Freiman is particularly passionate when he rips into the torture memo itself. Did I know that the Justice Department was now investigating how it ever came to be written? Did I know that the man who took over Yoo's department withdrew it, calling it "deeply flawed, sloppily reasoned, overbroad, and incautious in asserting extraordinary constitutional authorities on behalf of the president?" What Yoo should have done was look at the Eighth Amendment, which forbids cruel and unusual punishment. He should have considered international treaties against torture and cruelty and Civil rights along with a host of domestic laws and statutes. But Yoo wasn't acting as an honest lawyer, he says. As the Padilla lawsuit states, he was "a key member of a small, secretive group of executive officials who exerted tremendous influence over antiterrorism policy and who were known as the 'War Council.'" So he bent the law to justify a course of action he was already determined to take.

Freiman is especially scornful about the "necessity argument," as legal philosophers call it—the idea that the president can take extraordinary actions in an emergency to protect the nation, that the information in Padilla's head was worth cracking it open. "That's the argument that every despotic regime in every corner of the globe has been making for sixty years," he says. "Necessity, national security. The Nazis invoked necessity too. The question is, How do you deal with those threats? Are you bound by human rights, or are you not?"

This is why Freiman filed Padilla's lawsuit against Yoo. To redraw that line, he says, to recover our sense of justice and decency, to salvage the idealism that once shone so bright, America must pass judgment on John Yoo.

So let's go back to that moment in the heat of battle. The way Yoo tells the story, he was sitting at his desk at the Justice Department when the first plane hit the World Trade Center. He had only been working there two months, hired to answer the White House's questions on foreign-policy laws at a time when the biggest legal issue before him was a treaty about polar bears. When the order came to evacuate Washington and people began heading out into the streets, someone from the attorney general's office told him to stick around.

Soon the questions came:

Is this a war?
Do we need to declare war?
Can we scramble planes?
And again: Is this a war?

There was no obvious precedent. Yoo considered the level of violence and the source, thousands of civilians killed in coordinated attacks by a foreign enemy intent on crippling our government. He considered the Civil War, when people asked if it was a war or a rebellion and if Southerners should be treated as traitors or members of a foreign nation. He considered our history of warfare against nonstate groups like Indians and pirates.

He considered the level of military response that might be likely, because a military response itself would imply a state of war. He may have considered his friend Barbara Olson, dead on one of the planes. He found himself returning to this thought:

If a nation had done it, would we have any doubt it was a war?

So yes, it was a war. That's the decision he made while the buildings were still burning.

He stayed till two or three in the morning and when he left Justice and crossed the Fourteenth Street Bridge, the Pentagon was still burning. He saw the flames reaching up so high they lit the sky. But he didn't sleep because his phone kept ringing, each call another variation on the theme: Can we use force? What standards would guide the use of force? Is this a war?

Everyone reviewed his war memo. Ashcroft signed off. And Congress passed the Authorization to Use Military Force with only one opposing vote. If this was the first mistake in the war on terror, as many now believe, it was a mistake the nation made together.

The decision on military commissions came next and seemed like a no-brainer, Yoo says. We had always used military commissions in wartime because they were less cumbersome and many civilian laws (like stalking and assault) made no sense in a war context. It also seemed like a good idea to keep the prison camps distant from U.S. soil, both for safety and to insulate them from those same domestic laws.

The Geneva Conventions issue came up in December 2001. In retrospect it may seem obvious that any departure from Geneva was a policy mistake, the first step down the slippery slope, but Yoo points out that President Reagan explicitly refused to extend Geneva rights to terrorists in 1987. There were also technical problems, such as Geneva requirements that POWs be held in barracks instead of prisons, which didn't seem a practical approach to enemies who didn't wear uniforms and deliberately killed civilians, war criminals by definition. The Taliban was a tougher issue because Afghanistan had something closer to regular-army units and had signed the Geneva Conventions, but Yoo argued that Afghanistan was a failed state, so its signature didn't mean anything—which even he admits was pushing it. The point was, they weren't massing orderly brigades to attack the United States. They gave safe haven to terrorists. With Colin Powell pushing back, Bush finally decided to deny Geneva rights to Al Qaeda but to extend them to the Taliban—a necessary improvisation, Yoo says, a recognition that something new had entered the world.

The interrogation question came up only briefly, Yoo insists. In one meeting he attended in the White House Situation Room, someone worried that under Geneva, "we would only be able to ask Osama bin Laden loud questions, and nothing more." But this was all just an academic exercise until late March 2002, when the CIA captured Al Qaeda's chief of operations, a man named Abu

Zubaydah. They approached Yoo and said they had solid reasons to believe that Zubaydah knew the names of hundreds of terrorists and the details of attack plans that could include nuclear weapons. On top of that, Zubaydah was an expert in interrogation and how to resist interrogation. If it wasn't exactly the famous "ticking bomb" scenario come to life, where you are certain there is a bomb and certain your captive knows where it is, it was close enough. Yoo insists that nobody ever proposed crossing the line into outright torture and that he personally considers torture repugnant and unjustified under any conditions. But they did believe that this was a strange new kind of war, where the front lines were inside the heads of men like Padilla and Abu Zubaydah. So, what about things like isolation, prolonged interrogation, forced exercise, and limited sleep? Where was the line, exactly?

"How long did it take to come up with an answer?"

"I don't remember."

"Weeks? Months?"

"Probably weeks."

The Eighth Amendment did not apply, Yoo decided. It forbade cruel and unusual punishment, but punishment came only after a criminal conviction. His critics savage him for not considering American laws against coerced confessions and police brutality, but Yoo points out that the memo only applies to noncitizens "outside the United States." They say he should have considered our treaty obligations under the United Nations Convention Against Torture, which also forbids "cruel, inhuman, or degrading treatment," but Yoo believed that treaties were only binding when Congress passed statutes translating them into domestic law, a position recently affirmed by the Supreme Court. That meant the binding law was the antitorture statute Congress passed in 1994 in the wake of the convention, a statute that forbade "severe" physical pain and "prolonged mental harm." So these were the critical questions:

How do you define "severe pain"? How do you define "prolonged mental harm"?

Some say this is where he should have balked. "Torture violates the very premise of the legal system itself, that there is something irreducible and inviolable about every person," says Yoo's fellow Berkeley law professor Robert H. Cole. "You can't write a memo about it the way you would write about snowmobiling in Yosemite." At the very least, they say, Yoo should have warned of the moral danger the question posed to the essence of America.

Yoo says he shared those concerns. He says he thought he was writing a memo for exceptional cases, for the highly trained specialists of the CIA. "I never thought it would be a good idea for the Army to do it, to put it in the hands of eighteen-year-old kids. But it would be inappropriate if I had that worry and it changed the way I interpreted the law."

So he buckled down to one of the world's most thankless jobs, defining the limits of acceptable pain. He knew it would be easy to draw a vague standard that sounded good and then give the CIA a meaningful wink. But that wouldn't be fair to the officers in the field.

He wanted to draw a clear line.

The problem was, the Justice Department had never prosecuted anyone under the anti-torture statute, so there were no judicial opinions to guide him. Dictionaries defined severe as "extreme" and "hard to endure." Yoo studied all the international precedents he could find, including the judgment of the European Court of Human Rights in Ireland v. the United Kingdom, which found that the use of hoods, continuous loud noise, sleep deprivation, reduced diet, and a stress position called "wall-standing" were all cruel and degrading but not torture.

So where was the line?

He got the crucial phrasing about organ failure and death from a U.S. law concerning health care.

I can't let this pass. "John, you're a very engaging guy. I like you. I can't picture you writing that phrase, 'organ failure or death.'"

"It's the phrase Congress used," he says.

"But health care and interrogation are wildly different subjects."

"That's a fair criticism. But it's still the closest you can get to any definition of that phrase at all."

"But this isn't legal theory anymore. It's going to have a body count."

"It's a difficult issue, I admit. It's the use of violence. It's unpleasant. I don't disagree with that."

"You could have drawn the line in a different place."

"I really tried to distinguish between law and policy," he insists. Despite Yoo's shocking language defining severe pain as "equivalent to" organ failure or death, he points out that the memo clearly defines as torture mock executions, threats of imminent death, and beatings. He also says it's unfair for people to confuse the war crimes of Abu Ghraib with the aggressive interrogations he authorized. His memo also includes a long list of examples of acts that various courts have found to be torture, page after page of severe beatings and electric shocks and even one case where guards shackled a man to a bed, placed a towel over his face, and poured water down his nose-a nearly exact description of waterboarding, "which people ignore because they focus on that one sentence," Yoo says. "So if you read the whole opinion, I don't think of it as a license to do anything you want to."

It's true, the list is there, the cautionary intent clear. I've never seen it mentioned by any of his critics. But so is Yoo's pet theory about the president's unlimited war powers in an emergency, the passage that would, at least in theory, justify crushing testicles: "Congress may no more regulate the President's ability to detain and interrogate enemy combatants than it may regulate his ability to direct troop movements in the field." This is the section that drives people crazy. When the new head of the Justice Department's Office of Legal Counsel officially withdrew the memo, he singled it out for its "unusual lack of care and sobriety," its "cursory and one-sided legal arguments." No matter what Lincoln or Truman did, they say, Yoo never should have tried to make presidential law-breaking legal. But Yoo insists that suicide terrorism in the age of nuclear weapons is precisely the kind of situation he anticipated in his law-school theory, the reason the founders left the president's war powers vague.

"But at the same time," I say, "you know that by writing that opinion, by using those words, you're opening the gates."

"I agree," he answers. "The language is not pleasing, it's not politically savvy—I didn't see that as my job."

"And you didn't have any moral qualms?"

He looks me right in the eye. "I think there are some moral questions. But the other side of the moral question is the lives you might save. I have a hard time believing any responsible American president would have said, 'No, absolutely not, do not ask him any more questions, give him a lawyer.' I don't think Al Gore would have said that."

But those harsh interrogation techniques migrated straight to Iraq. What about that?

"That was definitely not permitted under the decision-making level I was at," Yoo says. "It was clearly not. The Geneva Conventions fully applied in Iraq."

And the memo he wrote that was made public this spring, which justified harsh interrogation techniques for military interrogators?

That worried him, he says. But it only applied to interrogators of Al Qaeda prisoners in Guantánamo, and Yoo says that he expressed his concerns to officials "at high levels of the Department of Justice, the White House, and the Department of Defense."

Is it possible that partisan loyalty blinded him to the dangers of putting all that power into the hands of a president so reckless and extreme, the worst combination of cowboy machismo with this radical theory of executive power?

"I can see why people have that view, but I just don't think this is the product of people who have this radical worldview."

"But Cheney was primed. He said we would have to go to the dark side."

Yoo doesn't say anything for a moment, then answers in his usual measured tone. "In World War II, we interned people, tens of thousands of citizens. We tried citizens who were enemy spies under military commissions which had no procedures at all. We let the Air Force kill hundreds of thousands of civilians in firebombing runs in Europe. We dropped a nuclear weapon on Japan. Water boarding we think is torture, but it happened to three people. The scale of magnitude is different."

"But if the war goes on forever, we've created a torture state."

"We've done it three times," he repeats.

"The White House launched an elective war against a country based on false premises."

"They made a mistake."

"But your theory puts the power in the hands of a person who then can invade the wrong country."

"Who can make a mistake. The Constitution can't protect against bad decisions," he insists. "What the framers were really worried about was not that the president would make a mistake, but that the president would become a dictator, and I really don't think Bush has become that."

And looking back? Does he still think it was the right decision?

"I still think I would have done the same—with Abu Zubaydah. But I didn't want the military to use these methods. My advice was not taken on that."

Yoo left the Justice Department in May of 2003, just after Mission Accomplished, three months before Major General Geoffrey Miller was sent to Iraq to "Gitmoize" Abu Ghraib.

So what is severe pain? We asked John Yoo, and he drew the line for us, and now he is tainted in our eyes, rendered unclean by his contact with the unspeakable. The broken figure of Jose Padilla and the horrors of Abu Ghraib will loom behind him forever. "I got a call from the *L.A. Times* asking me if he was a war criminal," says his old Harvard professor sadly. "All my friends see him in that light." But if you read the thousands of essays and books and blogs that rage against him, you will find very few that give a satisfactory answer to the question Yoo was asked. How would you define severe pain? If thousands of lives are at stake and time is of the essence? Would you allow sleep manipulation? Heat and cold? Isolation? Hunger? I asked Jose Padilla's lawyer three times. Where would you draw the line, Mr. Freiman? He dodged it twice. The third time he said outright, "I'm not going to draw that line for you. But I'll tell you where I would have looked—I would have first looked at the Constitution to see what was permissible, then I would have looked at the Geneva Conventions...."

So we still don't have an answer to the question. Some people take comfort in the argument that torture never works. Others say that only an imminent threat to the existence of the nation would justify it. Some say that torture should always be against the law as long as we remember that some laws are meant to be broken, a camp that includes John McCain and Judge Richard Posner in his recent book, *Not a Suicide Pact: The Constitution in a Time of National Emergency*: "In national emergencies most soldiers and other security personnel are willing to do what the situation demands and leave their legal liabilities to be sorted out later. They live for such emergencies, and are selected for courage."

Was that Yoo's real mistake? Saying it out loud?

I ask him the question nobody in the Bush administration wants to answer. "Is waterboarding torture?"

He doesn't hesitate. "It's on the line. It doesn't cause long-term or permanent pain, but it does cause intense pain. It seems to meet the requirements of the statute in some ways—but not all.

So it seems to me that in very limited circumstances, you can use it."

Is what was done to Jose Padilla morally wrong?

"I really cannot talk about that, however much I would like to, because of the litigation brought by Padilla against me," Yoo says. "But perhaps I can say that the memos only applied to captured Al Qaeda and Taliban leaders held outside the United States. They would not apply to an American citizen or permanent resident alien held anywhere in the world, or to anyone held within the United States."

He has other regrets. "I could have tried to press harder on what the Army should have done," he says. But he won't back down on the rest. He'd write the torture memos the same today, he told me. Alone among Bush administration officials, he does not run from what he has done. He writes editorials and participates in as many as forty public forums a year. In Los Angeles, I even saw him debate a professor of queer theory, an absurd spectacle. "No man is above the law," she said, wanting it to be simple. "This is a question of tragic choices," he answered, insisting it is not.

Not that anyone is listening. Yoo has become the focus of national anger about every excess in the war on terrorism, and minds are made up. But dismissing him as a monster just means that we don't have to think about why he did what he did. Grant him his good intentions, entertain the possibility that he did it to save lives, recognize the honor in his refusal to hide, and his story becomes a cautionary tale about the incremental steps that can lead a nation to disaster.

Memory, Invisibility, and the Oak Creek *Gurdwara* Massacre: A Sikh American Perspective of the Post-Racial United States

JAIDEEP SINGH

On 9/11, I was in my second week teaching at Oberlin College, while living in a rural suburb of Cleveland. Within an hour's drive of my apartment, a *gurdwara* [a Sikh place of worship] was fire-bombed (fortunately, very incompetently) and a man drove his vehicle into a *masjid* (Muslim house of worship) at high speed. But sadly, this local drama paled in comparison to the terror that was gripping Sikh, Muslim, Arab, and South Asian communities throughout the nation. For weeks and months after 9/11, many immigrant communities lived under a virtual state of siege, as entire neighborhoods feared leaving their homes. After 9/11, the Pakistanis who dominated a neighborhood in Brooklyn disappeared permanently within a matter of weeks.

The spring following the terrorist attacks, I was in New York City to give lectures detailing the ground-level impact of racial and religious bigotry in contemporary society, with an emphasis on the Sikh American experience after 9/11. I had given a talk at Princeton on my first day of the trip, and was enjoying a shopping trip with a friend in lower Manhattan, prior to the following day's talk at Columbia. Just across the street from the wreckage of the World Trade Center, as I checked my voicemail, I was asked malevolently by a massive Euro-American construction worker in a bright orange vest walking in the other direction on a packed sidewalk: 'Planning your next move, buddy?'.

I was back on the east coast during the tenth anniversary of the 9/11 attacks, beginning the fieldwork for my study of the Sikh American response to the moment of 9/11. In Boston and New York City, I interviewed a half dozen Sikh Americans who emerged as community activists in the days following 9/11.

Jaideep Singh, "Memory, Invisibility, and the Oak Creek Gurdwara Massacre: A Sikh American Perspective of the 'Post-Racial' U.S.," *Sikh Formations: Religion, Culture, Theory* 9, no. 2 (2013): 215–225. Reprinted by permission of Taylor & Francis Ltd, http://www.tandfonline.com.

The one consistent theme that emerged from that series of painful-to-conduct interviews, among geographically dispersed and occupationally diverse activists, was that things really have not changed all that much in the intervening decade. They insisted that, for a Sikh man with a beard and turban in the USA, life was very much like walking around with a target on your body.

They spoke of insults hurled on subways trains, confrontations in bars, on the street, and in restaurants. Most distressingly, they told of a general uneasiness that accompanied them in various public settings. There remained in their lives—a decade after the terrorist attacks of 9/11—a constant, usually low-intensity, level of public violence. Such violence is especially insidious because it engenders a constant paranoia and hyper-vigilance about one's surroundings when alone in public, significantly enhancing one's level of personal stress. To observant, visibly identifiable Sikh Americans, the notion that we live in a 'post-racial' world would be farcical, if it did not impinge so painfully on our daily lives.

With a long history of violence accompanying my personal and community history in this country, I have to admit that the massacre in Oak Creek was not shocking, nor even surprising. As someone who studies and writes about race and racial violence, the long list of attacks on Sikh bodies and sites of worship is so long, so ongoing, that it is almost numbing. Just the attacks on Sikh Americans since 9/11 in my home of northern California puts in sharp perspective what it means to be a Sikh in this country, at this time.

Balbir Singh Sodhi and the Erasure of the Sikh American Experience

Particularly horrifying for Sikh Americans was the 15 September 2001 murder of Balbir Singh Sodhi, in Mesa, Arizona. The first person to die from domestic terrorism after 9/11, Mr Sodhi was a Sikh American gas station owner who was killed on his business property by a vigilante racist. But Mr Sodhi's murder, a hateful act of racist vengeance, was largely lost in the broader narrative of our national tragedy, much like that of the Sikh American community itself. While we can debate the reasons for this, his murder made little long-term national impact, except in Sikh and progressive South Asian American communities.

Mr Sodhi's marginalization is evidenced by the scarcity of his name in public discourse around discussions of such topics as contemporary hate crimes, religious intolerance, or the grass roots impact of the nation's increasingly vicious political discourse demonizing immigrants, racialized minorities, and the followers of Islam. Despite the direct linkage of his murder to 9/11, and the fact that he was killed because of the way he looked, news reports about his death rarely presented the public with a photo of Mr Sodhi. The impact of that omission by the news media in this country is now evident.

Balbir Singh Sodhi has never become a symbol of contemporary hate violence in this country, and neither have Sikh Americans. Mr Sodhi is a nonentity to the vast majority of Americans—forgotten like so many true American heroes of color who emerged in the wake of the national trauma of 9/11. The dearth of visually impactful depictions of Mr Sodhi after his murder reinforced the pervasive western media trope that still represents bearded, tur-baned men as religious fundamentalists, misogynists, movie villains, foreigners who seek to harm the country, and terrorists. These vicious stereotypes contrast sharply with the reality of Mr Sodhi being a model immigrant, who came to the USA not only for economic opportunity but to find religious freedom unavailable in his homeland. The immigrant business–owner had just emptied his wallet to donate to the victims of 9/11 at a local store, before returning to his business and being gunned down by a man claiming: 'I'm a patriot ... I'm a damn American all the way'.

As a matter of fact, Mr Sodhi is so obscure that in April 2011, both houses of Arizona's legislature passed a bill that would have removed Mr Sodhi's name from the state's 9/11 memorial, to sell it for scrap metal. A voracious protest led by the Sikh American Legal Defense and Education Fund flooded Arizona Governor Jan Brewer's office with 7500 letters in less than three days, forcing her to meet with the Sodhi family and veto the bill. However, Mr Sodhi was not an anonymous casualty of 9/11 to Sikh Americans. He represented so much more to us—our vulnerability, our visibility, our version of the American Dream, and how paralyzingly fragile that dream actually is for so many of us. In Balbir Singh Sodhi's American experience, many Sikh Americans saw their American dream becoming a nightmare.

When we look back and assess the larger impact of the historic, grassroots, political mobilizations by Sikh Americans after 9/11 and then Oak Creek, this inci-dent is instructive. It is not only Mr Sodhi, and what his murder represented to Sikhs and many other brown Americans, that is missing from our national remem-brance of that tragic, fearful time. Almost entirely absent from the public history of that seminal period in our collective national history is the overlooked fact that, in the immediate aftermath of 9/11, brown Americans endured the greatest epidemic of hate crimes in this nation's modern history. But this is never part of the story we remember when the nation looks back on 9/11. In those retrospectives of our sup-posed 'collective past', the victims of tragedy are usually white.

For one Sikh American, the national hate crime epidemic began just moments after the twin towers fell. Walking to work, a young Sikh American man was yelled at, cursed, and chased by several men—who somehow identified him as responsible for the attack that had just occurred. The screaming, cursing group forced the young Sikh American to flee in terror, ducking into a subway station to hide, where—in fear for his life—he removed his turban. Yards away, another Sikh American, this one a young physician, helped save the lives of his fellow Americans by setting up and manning the first triage station at ground zero. This brave doctor risked his health near the base of the collapsed buildings to save others, while simultaneously risking attack from misguided bigots.

Case Study: Muslim Americans at the Intersection of Racial and Religious Bigotry

... The wave of hate crimes affecting Sikh Americans was exacerbated by the irresponsibility of the US media. Within minutes of the first plane hitting the

World Trade Center, images of Osama bin Laden proliferated on television, despite the fact that no possible connection could be shown at the time or for quite some time afterwards. Later in the day, a press conference from Afghanistan showed a Taliban leader denying any involvement in the attacks. Both bin Laden and the leaders of the Taliban wear turbans, keep long beards, and have swarthy complexions—the prototypical image of a terrorist in the western media.

The salience, weight, and lasting power of those first images broadcast by the media subsequently had a devastating effect on the lives of the nation's half million Sikh Americans. This fact became all the more poignant and ironic, as it became evident that not one of the hijackers and their suspected accomplices wore a turban. Nonetheless, the violent hatred against Sikh Americans did not abate in any appreciable way for months.

Sikh Americans continued to receive verbal and gestured threats, were spat upon, had garbage thrown at them, had their homes and property violated, were run off the road and tailgated, were shot at with guns, stabbed with knives, and suffered numerous cases of arson, firebombings, beatings, and murder. It was not until weeks later that scattered reports began to appear in the media, after the hard work and outreach of Sikh American community activists, that the vast majority of people wearing turbans in the USA were actually Sikhs. Mainstream media sources were predictably late in picking up this vital and readily available information, but it did little to displace the image of a terrorist already firmly implanted in the American psyche by the media, and the State through its arbitrary scrutiny of 'apparently Muslim' individuals.

The failures of the media are well encapsulated in a comparison of the stories of two Sikh Americans: Sher Singh and Mr Sodhi. Despite the national significance of Mr Sodhi's murder, almost none of the national television reports or print media articles about his death included a photo of him. This fact was made even more appalling by the fact Mr Sodhi was killed because of his appearance. His face was never shown and he was never truly humanized, thus preventing most Americans from actually imagining him as a person, tragically murdered because of the way he looked. In fact, the murder was treated as a minor story by the media—certainly far less newsworthy than if Mr Sodhi had been a white man murdered for similar hateful reasons.

The lone image of a Sikh American the national media did project throughout the country was that of Sher Singh, a Sikh American commuter who was removed from a train by authorities in Providence, Rhode Island, because he looked 'suspicious'. Rumors that a possible terrorist had been arrested spread rapidly, and national media outlets swiftly reported the story. In doing so, they failed in their journalistic duty to investigate the nature of the incident before reporting it as a possible terrorism-related arrest. The verity that the bearded, turban-wearing man could be an innocent victim of racist hysteria never occurred to the members of the media reporting the incident, as the assumption of innocence seems to have been dwarfed in import by the exterior of the Sikh American man.

Almost immediately, video clips of a young man with a green turban and a long, flowing beard being led away in handcuffs inundated the nation's airwaves, doing incalculable damage to the nation's perceptions of visibly observant Sikh

Americans. CNN, Fox, the Associated Press, and others carried video and still photos of Sher Singh being arrested. They, however, gave *far* less attention to the subsequent, critical information that he was released and charged only with a misdemeanor for carrying a *kirpan*—a small, ceremonial sword that is a Sikh religious article of faith. That charge was later dropped because of the obvious religious nature of the *kirpan*. Nonetheless, Sher Singh's image flooded the airwaves and internet over the next several days, long after it had been established that he had nothing to do with the terrorist attacks.

Media misrepresentations of Sher Singh's arrest added further animus to the prejudice already being engendered against bearded and turbaned individuals by media outlets' concurrent bombardment of images of bin Laden and the Taliban. The images on television neatly fit the stereotype of a terrorist the western media had fabricated. By showing Sher Singh being led away in handcuffs, and mentioning that the train was stopped because of the presence of 'suspicious' individuals, the media managed to firmly associate Sher Singh—and those who looked like him—with the terrorist attacks. The bias evident in this repellent episode is blatant racial and religious profiling. Still, the media never apologized, nor did it seek to correct the misleading and dangerous impressions they had created by repeatedly showing images of Sher Singh in close juxtaposition with those of bin Laden and the Taliban.

In fact, the media missed the real story, that of illegal profiling by police in arresting an innocent American, who was singled out for arbitrary scrutiny, harassment, and detention by the state because of his racial and religious uniforms. Further substantiating the bias informing the entire episode, it is unimaginable that a story about a man arrested on a minor weapons charge could have risen to the level of national prominence it assumed if the accused had not been wearing a turban and beard. Yet, this seminal issue has—not surprisingly—been ignored.

While the President, religious leaders, and members of the media reiterated the fact that Muslim, Arab, and Sikh Americans are part of the national mosaic, the rhetoric did not match reality. Since 9/11 non-Christian Asian Americans have repeatedly been singled out because of their religious affiliation as well as their race, demonstrating that they still are not part of the 'mainstream'. Almost without exception, media stories dealing with the post-attack hate crime epidemic were tokenistic in their positioning. Unlike other stories which detailed 'The American Experience', these stories were reported as outside the purview of the mainstream of society. The direct implication was that those in these stories were not part of that mainstream, but were marginal figures in society. Their problems were 'minority' issues, not issues for all Americans to ponder.

'Post-Racial' Life in Sikh America

So has anything changed in the wake of the Oak Creek Massacre, an armed invasion of a sacred site that has no real parallel in post-World War II US history? Less than a month after the Oak Creek Massacre, the small Indiana town of Garrett was the site of a chillingly representative illustration of the social climate which today confronts Sikh Americans—and others viewed as 'apparently Muslim'—in much of the USA. About 250 miles from the site of the massacre, the sitting mayor of Garrett, Tonya Hoeffel, committed an act of vandalism fed by and exhibiting open religio-racial hostility, and undergirded by a sense of entrenched privilege and superiority.

In the wake of the nearby *gurdwara* massacre, Kulwinder Singh Nagra placed pamphlets about his faith on the counter of his convenience store, hoping to diminish the vast ignorance about Sikhs where he lived: 'I just wanted to let people know who I am.... After 9/11, there was a lot of misunderstanding'.

On August 28, Mayor Tonya Hoeffel was caught on surveillance video entering Mr Nagra's business, purchasing a soft drink, then walking away from the counter where the pamphlets were placed. She then returned to the counter, 'grabbed the small stack of pamphlets, took them outside and threw them into a trash bin'. When Mr Nagra confronted her about what she had done, he received the following response: 'She said, "It's against my beliefs." ... She said, "This is against Christianity".'

Obviously receiving wise counsel in the interim, Ms Hoeffel later claimed that 'she disposed of the pamphlets because of a lack of personal interest, not as a statement about the religion'. Her rapidly changing, obviously disingenuous account of the incident eventually evolved into the equally implausible: 'I just grabbed what was there. I just decided I didn't want it.'

She has since apologized to Mr Nagra, meeting with him and his business partners, along with a member of the city council. For his part, Mr Nagra explained, 'the Sikh religion teaches forgiveness and the issue was resolved for him when Hoeffel apologized'.

Despite the apparently amicable resolution of the matter, it demands further interrogation because of what it reveals about the state of our nation. This jarring event mirrors the recent personal experiences of the overwhelming majority of the nation's Sikh Americans as well as members of many other non-white, non-Christian communities. Throughout the nation, many—probably most—have experienced some level of hate crime in the past several years or know someone who has suffered such an assault. Without a doubt, in the years since 9/11, hate violence has become completely normalized in the experiences of Sikh Americans and others who are 'apparently Muslim'.

The low-level hate crime by the mayor of Garrett, Indiana, not only illuminates the level and constancy of the acerbic hatred Sikh Americans continue to confront on a daily basis, but it sets a very dangerous precedent. Simran Jeet Singh and Savneet Singh write:

> We must demand more from our elected officials and hold them accountable for their actions ... because our elected officials maintain enormous influence.... We also hold them to a higher standard. It is unacceptable for any of our political representatives to act with intolerance and bigotry.... This divisive rhetoric will continue to fragment this nation until we take ownership and begin calling out our elected officials to stop dividing and start uniting.

... The attempt to remove Balbir Singh Sodhi from the 9/11 memorial represented an effort by the State to obliterate his memory, simultaneously brushing aside his family's and the national Sikh American's community's aching remembrance of his racist murder. It was a symbolic erasure of Sikh American pain, presence, and our sense of belonging within the national fabric that is all too common, even in the wake of Oak Creek. This is nothing new in our recurrent national efforts to forget our sordid, blood-drenched history of white supremacy, as the long-suppressed histories of African and Asian Americans, American Indians, and Chicano/Latinos illustrate in graphic detail. After all, we live in a time when the same state of Arizona can ban the teaching of truth (history) under the guise of preventing 'resentment toward a race or class of people'....

In fact, we are running from the truth as a society once again. As alluded to above, political leaders in Arizona have attacked the teaching of historical truth by passing laws attacking Ethnic Studies programs. Our cowardly, destructive retreat from our past is now matched by an equally disturbing, similarly politicized, distortion of the science curriculum within our schools. These trends bode ill for our nation's economic future in an increasingly complex and interdependent world economy.

As the iconic historian Howard Zinn explained:

> History is important. If you don't know history it is as if you were born yesterday. And if you were born yesterday, anybody up there in a position of power can tell you anything, and you have no way of checking up on it.

A historically illiterate people has little hope of ending the centuries of bigotry toward racialized, religious minorities that has characterized our past and coarsened the fabric of our present. If we stop running from the truth, it may just save us.

☾ FURTHER READING

Das Gupta, Monisha. *Unruly Immigrants: Rights, Activism, and Transnational South Asian Politics in the United States* (2006).

Dinh, Viet. *The USA Patriot Act: Preserving Life and Liberty* (2008).

Fluri, Jennifer. "Feminist-Nation Building in Afghanistan: An Examination of the Revolutionary Association of the Women of Afghanistan," *Feminist Review* 89 (2008): 34–54.

Itagaki, Kohshi. *The Trials of War: Lt. Ehren Watada and the Asian American Movement* (2010).

Karam, Nicoletta. *The 9/11 Backlash: A Decade of U.S. Hate Crimes Targeting the Innocent* (2012).

Lee, Wen Ho with Helen Zia. *My Country Versus Me: The First-Hand Account by the Los Alamos Scientist Who Was Falsely Accused of Being a Spy* (2001).

Leong, Russell C., and Don T. Nakanishi, eds. *Asian Americans on War and Peace* (2002).

Malkin, Michelle. *In Defense of Internment: The Case for Racial Profiling in World War II and the War on Terror* (2004).

Mishra, Sangay. "Rights at Risk: South Asians in the Post-9/11 United States," *AAPI Nexus* 9, nos. 1–2 (Fall 2011): 21–28.

Nguyen, Tram. *We Are All Suspects Now: Untold Stories from Immigrant Communities after 9/11* (2005).

Ono, Kent, and Vincent Pham. *Asian Americans and the Media* (2008).

Puar, Jasbir K. "'The Turban Is Not a Hat': Queer Diaspora and Practices of Profiling," *Sikh Formations* 4, no. 1 (June 008): 47–91.

Ramakrishnan, S. Karthick, and Irene Bloemraad, eds. *Civic Hopes and Political Realities: Immigrants, Community Organizations, and Political Engagement* (2008).

Reuter, Dean, and John Yoo. *Confronting Terror: 9/11 and the Future of American National Security* (2011).

Saito, Natsu Taylor. *From Chinese Exclusion to Guantanamo Bay: Plenary Power and the Prerogative State* (2007).

Shah, Nayan. *Stranger Intimacy: Contesting Race, Sexuality, and the Law in the North American West* (2012).

Shani, Giorgio. *Sikh Nationalism and Identity in a Global Age* (2007).

Shankar, Lavina Dhingra, and Rajini Srikanth, eds. *A Part Yet Apart: South Asians in Asian America* (1998): 69–78.

Shukla, Sandhya. *India Abroad: Diasporic Cultures of Postwar America and England* (2003).

Sikkink, Kathryn. *The Justice Cascade: How Human Rights Prosecutions Are Changing World Politics* (2011).

Taguba, Antonio. *The Taguba Report on Treatment of Abu Ghraib Prisoners* (2004).

Varela, María do Mar Castro, and Nikita Dhawan. *Hegemony and Heteronormativity* (2011).

Women of South Asian Descent Collective. *Our Feet Walk the Sky: Women of the South Asian Diaspora* (1993).

Yee, James. *For God and Country: Faith and Patriotism under Fire* (2005).

Yoo, John. *Point of Attack: Preventive War, International Law, and Global Welfare* (2014).

CPSIA information can be obtained
at www.ICGtesting.com
Printed in the USA
FFHW022259031019
55373506-61114FF